The Shakespeare Head Brontë

EDITED BY THOMAS JAMES WISE, HON. M.A. OXON
HONORARY FELLOW OF WORCESTER COLLEGE
AND JOHN ALEXANDER SYMINGTON
BROTHERTON LIBRARIAN

THE BRONTËS: THEIR LIVES, FRIEND-
SHIPS & CORRESPONDENCE

VOLUME THE THIRD

1849 - 1852

VOLUME THE FOURTH

1852 - 1928

Mrs Gaskell
from the portrait by George Richmond, R.A.

Emery Walker. Ph. sc.

THE BRONTËS

THEIR LIVES, FRIENDSHIPS AND CORRESPONDENCE

VOLUME III

Chapters XXI-XXVII   1849-1852

VOLUME IV

Chapters XXVIII-XXXVI 1852-1928

BASIL BLACKWELL • OXFORD
THE SHAKESPEARE HEAD PRESS

First edition 1933
Printed at the Shakespeare Head Press
and Published for the Press
by Basil Blackwell • Oxford

· Reprinted in two volumes 1980 by
Basil Blackwell Publisher Limited
5, Alfred Street, Oxford, England 0X1 4HB

British Library Cataloguing in Publication Data

The Brontës: their lives, friendships and correspondence.
     1. Novelists, English—19th century—correspondence.
     2. Brontë family.   I. Wise, Thomas James.   II.
Symington, John Alex.
823'.8 09   PR4168.A44
ISBN 0-631-12431-4

Manufactured in the United States of America

THE BRONTËS: THEIR LIVES, FRIEND-
SHIPS & CORRESPONDENCE

VOLUME THE THIRD

1849 - 1852

THIS EDITION OF THE WORKS AND LIVES
OF THE BRONTËS IS DEDICATED TO
SIR JAMES AND LADY ROBERTS
OF FAIRLIGHT HALL AND
OF STRATHALLAN CASTLE SCOTLAND
BY WHOSE GENEROSITY
THE BRONTË PARSONAGE AT HAWORTH
HAS BEEN ESTABLISHED AS
ONE OF OUR NATIONAL
LITERARY SHRINES

THE ILLUSTRATIONS

FACSIMILES

CONTENTS OF VOLUME III

A BRONTË CHRONOLOGY

VOLUME III. 1849–1852.

Shirley published   October 26, 1849

Charlotte in London—First meeting with Thackeray and Harriet Martineau   November–December, 1849

Charlotte's first visit to Sir J. Kay-Shuttleworth at Gawthorpe Hall, Lancashire   March, 1850

Visit to London, sits for Portrait to Richmond, meets G. H. Lewes and Miss Kavanagh   June, 1850

Visit to Edinburgh with George Smith   July, 1850

Visit to Sir James Kay-Shuttleworth at Windermere, and first meeting with Mrs Gaskell   August, 1850

Edits her sisters' works   September–November, 1850

Visit to Harriet Martineau at Ambleside   December, 1850

Charlotte's third proposal of Marriage (James Taylor of Messrs Smith, Elder & Co.)   April, 1851

Visit to London for Thackeray's Lectures and the Great Exhibition   May–June, 1851

Visit to Mrs. Gaskell at Manchester   June 27–30, 1851

Charlotte's illness   December, 1851–February, 1852

The Writing of *Villette* commenced   November, 1851

Visit to Filey   June, 1852

Visit to Anne's Grave at Scarborough   June, 1852

CHAPTER XXI

'SHIRLEY'

CHARLOTTE BRONTË began writing her third novel, *Shirley*, shortly after the publication of *Jane Eyre*, but her work was sadly interrupted during the unhappy period from October 1848 to June 1849. 'Down into the very midst of her writing,' says Mrs Gaskell, 'came the bolts of death. She had nearly finished the second volume of her tale when Branwell died —after him Emily—after her Anne; the pen, laid down when there were three sisters living and loving, was taken up when one alone remained. Well might she call the first chapter that she wrote after this "The Valley of the Shadow of Death." '[1]

On February 4th, 1849, Charlotte sent Mr Williams the first volume of the manuscript of *Shirley* for his criticism, but it was not until the following June that she was able to make any material progress with the work.

As one of our great modern authors has written, 'Tisn't Life that matters, it's the courage you bring to it'; and certainly Charlotte Brontë was not lacking in fortitude. After the death of Anne she went from Scarborough to Filey and then on to Easton near Bridlington, to stay with Mr and Mrs Hudson, whom she had first visited with Ellen Nussey in September, 1839. Mrs Hudson said that whilst Charlotte was staying with them at the farm she was writing continually. She had evidently taken the manuscript of *Shirley* with her to Scarborough, hoping that Anne would get better, and that during her convalescence she herself might have the additional satisfaction of getting on with her new work, which her publishers were impatient to receive.

The writing of *Shirley* must have proved a very onerous task. It was completed during a period of acute distress and mental

---

[1]*The Life of Charlotte Brontë*, by Mrs Gaskell, Haworth edition, p. 415. Mrs Gaskell's statement is not quite correct. The letters show that Charlotte was occasionally employed in writing *Shirley* during Anne's illness.

suffering, and yet Charlotte laboured at it most conscientiously and diligently. She was very anxious that it should not fall below the standard of *Jane Eyre*, and she carefully studied the reviews of that work in the hopes of profiting by their criticism.

The book was finished by the end of August, 1849, and published on October 26th, 1849 in three volumes by Messrs Smith, Elder & Co. The scene of the story of *Shirley* is set in the heart of the woollen manufacturing district of the West Riding of Yorkshire, and all the chief characters in the book are drawn from life —so well drawn that the prototypes who were still alive when the book was published were easily able to recognise themselves.[1] The character of Shirley herself is Charlotte's representation of her sister Emily, as she might have been 'had she been placed in health and prosperity.' This alone should claim for the book a special interest. The three curates also were drawn from men of Charlotte's personal acquaintance, who have sometimes been mentioned in her letters to her friend Ellen Nussey.[2] We follow the story of Mr Donne, Mr Malone, and Mr Sweeting with a desire to know something of their later career. Mr Donne, or Joseph Brett Grant, was the master of the Haworth Grammar School at the time. He became curate and afterwards vicar of Oxenhope, where he died greatly esteemed more than a quarter of a century later. Peter Augustus Malone, who was James William Smith in real life, was for two years curate to Mr Brontë at Haworth. He had graduated at Trinity College, Dublin, and after a two years' curacy at Haworth he became curate of the neighbouring parish of Keighley. In 1847, his family having suffered frightfully from the Irish famine, he determined to try and build up a home for them on the American continent, and sailed for Canada. The last that was heard of him was from Minnesota, where he was cutting down trees for lumbermen; and he probably perished on his way to the goldfields of California.

David Sweeting, the third curate, was the Rev. James Chesterton Bradley (who had been educated at Queen's College, Oxford), from the neighbouring parish of Oakworth, to which he

[1] See *The Persons and Places of the Brontë Novels—Shirley*. By Herbert E. Wroot. *Brontë Society Transactions*, Vol. III.   [2] See letters July—September, 1844. Vol. II p. 7 *et sq.*

had been curate since 1843. He went in 1847 to All Saints', Paddington; in 1856 he went to Corfe Castle, Dorset, and in 1863 he became rector of Sutton-under-Brayles, Warwickshire, a living which he held until 1904, when he retired. Mr Bradley always found great pleasure in recalling the fact that he was the prototype of Mr Sweeting in *Shirley*, although he declared that the meetings of the curates at each other's lodgings were exclusively for a series of two-hours' readings of the Greek fathers, and not for the drunken orgies described in *Shirley*.

Under the title *A Well-known Character in Fiction*, the true story of Mr Peter Malone in *Shirley*, is told by his nephew, Robert Keating Smith, in *The Tatler*, April 2, 1902. Mr R. K. Smith writes with enthusiasm of his uncle, and his article in *The Tatler* brought him a letter from Mr Bradley. It is only fair to the memory of the curates that this letter should be published.

SUTTON RECTORY, BRAYLES, BANBURY,
ENGLAND, May 3rd, 1902.

REV. ROBERT KEATING SMITH.

DEAR SIR,—A short paper of yours in 'The Tatler' of April 2nd brought before me my old friend James W. Smith. He and I were fellow-curates in Yorkshire, he curate of Haworth, and I of the hill part of Keighley which joined on to Haworth. Of course I saw a great deal of him, and we were great friends. He and I with another of the name of Grant were the three curates in Charlotte Bronte's 'Shirley.' I need not say how indignant I have often been at the way in which she speaks of him in the novel. He was a thorough gentleman in every sense of the word, and there was not the slightest ground for the insinuation she makes against him. But my chief object in writing is to ask if you can tell me anything more about him than what you have written in the periodical. I, the 'Davy Sweeting' of the novel, was obliged to resign the incumbency of Oakworth from ill-health not very long before he left, and during my illness I had a letter from him (lost now, I grieve to say), and then I heard that he had gone abroad, and the rumour was spread that he had been wrecked on the coast of Canada. It was after this, I believe, that the novel came out. We used to read together, walk together, and as often

as we could, about once a week, meet either at his or my lodgings. Please excuse me for thus intruding on you, but I was
anxious to give my testimony against the false and cruel way in
which Charlotte Brontë has held him up in her book. — Believe
me, yours very truly,

(Signed) JAMES C. BRADLEY.

A fourth curate is introduced in the concluding chapter of the
novel; this is Mr Macarthey, who succeeded Mr Malone in the
curacy of Briarfield. The original of this character was the Rev.
A. B. Nicholls, who afterwards became Charlotte Brontë's husband. He thoroughly enjoyed reading *Shirley*, and to quote Charlotte's words 'he triumphed in his own character.'[1] Possibly the
flattering portrait that Charlotte drew of Mr Nicholls as Mr
Macarthey was the first step towards their subsequent engagement and marriage.

452 (358). To W. S. WILLIAMS.

July 3rd, 1849.

MY DEAR SIR, — You do right to address me on subjects which
compel me, in order to give a coherent answer, to quit for a
moment my habitual train of thought. The mention of your
healthy living daughters reminds me of the world where other
people live — where I lived once. Theirs are cheerful images —
as you present them: I have no wish to shut them out.

From all you say of Ellen — the eldest — I am inclined to respect her much; I like practical sense which works to the good of
others; I esteem a dutiful daughter who makes her parents
happy.

Fanny's character I would take on second-hand from nobody
— least of all from her kind father whose estimate of human
nature, in general, inclines rather to what ought to be than to
what *is*. Of Fanny I would judge for myself — and that not hastily
nor on first impressions.

I am glad to learn that Louisa has a chance of a presentation to
Queen's College. I hope she will succeed. Do not — my dear Sir
— be indifferent — be earnest about it. Come what may after-

[1] See the letter to Ellen Nussey dated January 28, 1850. See also Chapter XXIX.

wards, an education secured is an advantage gained—a priceless advantage. Come what may it is a step towards independency—and one great curse of a single female life is its dependency. It does credit both to Louisa's heart and head that she herself wishes to get this presentation: encourage her in the wish. Your daughters—no more than your sons—should be a burden on your hands: your daughters—as much as your sons—should aim at making their way honourably through life. Do not wish to keep them at home. Believe me—teachers may be hard-worked, ill-paid and despised—but the girl who stays at home doing nothing is worse off than the hardest-wrought and worst-paid drudge of a school. Whenever I have seen, not merely in humble, but in affluent homes—families of daughters sitting waiting to be married, I have pitied them from my heart. It is doubtless well—very well—if Fate decrees them a happy marriage—but if otherwise—give their existence some object—their time some occupation—or the peevishness of disappointment and the listlessness of idleness will infallibly degrade their nature.

Should Louisa eventually go out as a governess—do not be uneasy respecting her lot. The sketch you give of her character, leads me to think she has a better chance of happiness than one in a hundred of her sisterhood. Of pleasing exterior (that is always an advantage—children like it), good sense, obliging disposition, cheerful, healthy, possessing a good average capacity, but no prominent master talent to make her miserable, by its cravings for exercise, by its mutiny under restraint—Louisa thus endowed will find the post of governess comparatively easy. If she be like her mother—as you say she is—if consequently she is fond of children and possesses tact for managing them—their care is her natural vocation: she ought to be a governess.

Your sketch of Braxborne, as it is and as it was, is sadly pleasing. I remember your first picture of it in a letter written a year ago—only a year ago. I was in this room—where I now am when I received it: I was not alone then. In those days your letters often served as a text for comment—a theme for talk: now—I read them—return them to their covers and put them away. Johnson—I think—makes mournful mention somewhere of the pleasure that accrues when we are 'solitary, and cannot impart it.' Thoughts—under such circumstances—cannot grow to words, impulses fail to ripen to actions.

Lonely as I am—how should I be if Providence had never given me courage to adopt a career—perseverance to plead through two long, weary years with publishers till they admitted me? How should I be with youth past—sisters lost—a resident in a moorland parish where there is not a single educated family? In that case I should have no world at all: the raven, weary of surveying the deluge and without an ark to return to, would be my type. As it is, something like a hope and motive sustains me still. I wish all your daughters—I wish every woman in England had also a hope and motive: Alas there are many old maids who have neither.—Believe me, Yours sincerely,

C. BRONTË.

453 (359). *To* ELLEN NUSSEY.

July 4th, 1849.

DEAR ELLEN,—As far as I can understand your brother John's proposal it seems to me very grasping—if it is so—you do right to resist it. Still you must consider well lest unreflecting opposition should do incalculable mischief—As you say your own actual present interest in the matter is small, and none can read the future—none can say because I am younger than this man or woman I shall live longer than he.

Your brother of course does not mean to say that in case you should marry and have children of your own, you should not be at liberty to will anything you might have to them. Should this never happen—certainly his family are the nearest to you all:— to them—whether bound to do so or not—you would naturally leave your property. It might under such circumstances be unwise to make a great sacrifice of present comfort and security for the sake of future possible contingencies. As to the principle of the matter—it is not a thing of which you are called upon to make a religion; it is sometimes more meritorious to yield our own rights than to cling to them too tenaciously—if yielding will add greatly to the comfort of others. But there may be sides of the question known to you, of which I am ignorant.

I get on as well as I can. Home is not the home it used to be, that you may well conceive—but so far—I get on.

I cannot boast of vast benefits derived from change of air yet; but unfortunately I brought back the seeds of a cold with me from that dismal Easton—and I have not got rid of it yet. Still I think I look better than I did before I went. How are you? You have never told me.

Mr Williams has written to me twice since my return —chiefly on the subject of his third daughter who wishes to be a governess —and has some chance of a presentation to Queen's College, an establishment connected with the Governess Institution —this will secure her four years of Instruction —he says Mr Smith is kindly using his influence to obtain votes —but there are so many candidates he is not sanguine of success.

I had a long letter from Mary Taylor, interesting but sad — because it contained many allusions to those who are in this world no more. She mentioned you and seemed impressed with an idea of the lamentable nature of your unoccupied life. —she spoke of her own health as being excellent.

Give my love to your mother and sisters, and believe me. — Yours &c.,

C. B.

I am sorry to hear so sad an account of poor Mrs Atkinson. Consumption —I understand —has been reaping a whole harvest of victims in this neighbourhood.

454 (360). *To* ELLEN NUSSEY.

HAWORTH, July 14th, '49.

DEAR ELLEN, —I owe you a letter and had better pay the debt —if it be only for the sake of placing you on the debtor side.

You did very right to go and consult Wm Carr about your brother's proposal —I believe in such cases it is always best to consult a clever lawyer at once. As he explains it —unconditional compliance is of course out of the question —but be sure and save yourself for a quiet opposition when it comes to your turn —and by no means put yourself in the front of the battle —You are not called upon to do so —because your actual stake in the matter is not large. Let your sisters agree to what they will —they will never have children and the proposal is neither so injurious nor so unfair to them as to you —for it must not be forgotten — that your brother John while grasping at future prospects — offers to relinquish a present claim in your sisters' favour —he will make them more comfortable now —if they will promise to benefit him hereafter —the arrangement is worldly but not inequitable—Over you, however, it appears to me—he has no right and ought not to attempt to drag you into the transaction. Guard your own interests Nell—but don't appear in the light of instigator to your sisters' movements.

Your account of Mrs Burnley's party and the Taylors interested me of course. Alas for John! The metamorphosis though deplorable, is just what was to be expected from his mode of life.

I do not much like giving you an account of myself—I like better to go out of myself and talk of something more cheerful. My cold—wherever I got it—whether at Easton or elsewhere—is not vanished yet—it began in my head—then I had a sore throat and then a sore chest—with a cough but only a trifling cough which I still have at times. The pains between my shoulders likewise annoyed me much—Say nothing about it—for I confess I am too much disposed to be nervous—This nervousness is a horrid phantom—I dare communicate no ailment to papa—his anxiety harasses me inexpressibly.

My life is what I expected it to be—sometimes when I wake in the morning—and know that Solitude, Remembrance and Longing are to be almost my sole companions all day through— that at night I shall go to bed with them, that they will long keep me sleepless—that next morning I shall wake to them again— Sometimes—Nell—I have a heavy heart of it.

But crushed I am not—yet: nor robbed of elasticity nor of hope—nor quite of endeavour—Still I have some strength to fight the battle of life. I am aware and can acknowledge I have many comforts—many mercies—still I can *get on*.

But I do hope and pray—that never may you or any one I love, be placed as I am. To sit in a lonely room—the clock ticking loud through a still house—and to have open before the mind's eye the record of the last year with its shocks, sufferings, losses —is a trial.

I write to you freely because I believe you will hear me with moderation—that you will not take alarm or think me in any way worse off than I am.

Give my love to your Mother and sisters and believe me— Yours sincerely,

C. B.

I hope Mercy is better. How is poor Mrs Atkinson?

455 (362). *To* W. S. WILLIAMS.

MY DEAR SIR,—I must rouse myself to write a line to you, lest a more protracted silence should seem strange.

Truly glad was I to hear of your daughter's success—I trust its results may conduce to the permanent advantage both of herself and her parents.

Of still more importance than your children's education is your wife's health, and therefore it is still more gratifying to learn that your anxiety on that account is likely to be alleviated. For her own sake, no less than for that of others, it is to be hoped that she is now secured from a recurrence of her painful and dangerous attacks.

It was pleasing too to hear of good qualities being developed in the daughters by the mother's danger. May your girls always so act as to justify their father's kind estimate of their characters —May they never do what might disappoint or grieve him.

Your suggestion relative to myself is a good one in some respects, but there are two persons whom it would not suit— and not the least incommoded of these would be the young person whom I might request to come and bury herself in the hills of Haworth—to take a church and stony churchyard for her prospect—the dead silence of a village parsonage—in which the tick of the clock is heard all day long—for her atmosphere—and a grave, silent spinster for her companion, I should not like to see youth thus immured. The hush and gloom of our house would be more oppressive to a buoyant than to a subdued spirit. The fact is, my work is my best companion—hereafter I look for no great earthly comfort except what congenial occupation can give—For society—long seclusion has in a great measure unfitted me—I doubt whether I should enjoy it if I might have it. Sometimes I think I should, and I thirst for it—but at other times I doubt my capability of pleasing or deriving pleasure. The prisoner in solitary confinement—the toad in the block of marble—all in time shape themselves to their lot. —

Yours sincerely,

C. BRONTË.

July 26th, '49.

456 (361). *To* ELLEN NUSSEY.

HAWORTH, July 27th, —49.

DEAR ELLEN,—I enclose a 5£ note which I hope you will receive safely—First I request you to deduct therefrom 10*s*. and to take the same as commission-money and to please and satisfy me: this is a sine qua non.

With the remaining £4 10*s*.—I will thank you to buy a patent shower-bath and such a boa and cuffs as you can get for the money—As to the colour of the fur I can only say I prefer grey or dark furs to the yellow and tawny kinds.

I am glad to hear Ann is going to be married soon—I dare not give advice about her dress—it is above me—you will settle all that as right as a trivet—I doubt not—When you marry—I will give you your choice of two costumes. Silver-grey and white—or dove-colour and pale pink: but for Ann I should say some shade of violet would be preferable. Not that I understand the code of laws in these matters—in the least.

I am truly glad to hear that Rosy Ringrose is better—I have often thought of her but did not like to ask after her lest I should hear bad news—her symptoms seemed to me threatening. I shall not soon forget her face—so pretty—modest—*sensitive*—*that* was the peculiar charm in my eyes—pretty faces—modest faces I see sometimes—*sensitive* faces seldom indeed. It was odd—in Amelia's face—I could not discover that trace of feeling—had I found it—it would for me have given something better than beauty to her otherwise homely features—wanting it—had I not known how very amiable she is—I should hardly have judged of her so favourably as she deserves—you must let me know soon whether the cash reaches you safely.—Yrs truly,   C. B.

Louisa Williams has obtained her presentation—Poor Mary Swaine!

457 (363). *To* ELLEN NUSSEY.

August 3rd, '49.

DEAR ELLEN,—I have received the furs safely, I like the sables very much, and shall keep them, and 'to save them' shall keep the squirrel, as you prudently suggested. I hope it is not too much like using the steel poker to save the brass one. I return

Mary Gorham's letter, it is another page from the volume of life, and at the bottom is written 'Finis,' mournful word. Macaulay's History was only *lent* to myself; all the books I have from London I accept only as a loan, except in peculiar cases, where it is the author's wish I should possess his work.

Do you think in a few weeks it will be possible for you to come to see me? I am only waiting to get my labour off my hands to permit myself the pleasure of asking you.

I am sadly afraid Ann's marriage will come in the way. At our house you can read as much as you please.

I have been much better, very free from oppression or irritation of the chest, during the last fortnight or ten days. Love to all.—Good-bye, dear Nell,

C. B.

458 (364). *To* W. S. WILLIAMS.

August 16th, 1849.

MY DEAR SIR,—Since I last wrote to you I have been getting on with my book as well as I can, and I think I may now venture to say that in a few weeks I hope to have the pleasure of placing the MS. in the hands of Mr Smith.

The 'North British Review' duly reached me. I read attentively all it says about 'E. Wyndham,' 'Jane Eyre,' and 'F. Hervey.' Much of the article is clever, and yet there are remarks which—for me—rob it of importance.

To value praise or stand in awe of blame we must respect the source whence the praise and blame proceed, and I do not respect an inconsistent critic. He says, 'if "Jane Eyre" be the production of a woman, she must be a woman unsexed.'

In that case the book is an unredeemed error and should be unreservedly condemned. 'Jane Eyre' is a woman's autobiography, by a woman it is professedly written. If it is written as no woman would write, condemn it with spirit and decision—say it is bad, but do not eulogise and then detract. I am reminded of the 'Economist.' The literary critic of that paper praised the book if written by a man, and pronounced it 'odious' if the work of a woman.

To such critics I would say, 'To you I am neither man nor woman—I come before you as an author only. It is the sole standard by which you have a right to judge me—the sole ground on which I accept your judgment.'

There is a weak comment, having no pretence either to justice or discrimination, on the works of Ellis and Acton Bell. The critic did not know that those writers had passed from time and life. I have read no review since either of my sisters died which I could have wished *them* to read—none even which did not render the thought of their departure more tolerable to me. To hear myself praised beyond them was cruel, to hear qualities ascribed to them so strangely the reverse of their real characteristics was scarce supportable. It is sad even now; but they are so remote from earth, so safe from its turmoils, I can bear it better.

But on one point do I now feel vulnerable; I should grieve to see my father's peace of mind perturbed on my account; for which reason I keep my author's existence as much as possible out of his way. I have always given him a carefully diluted and modified account of the success of 'Jane Eyre'—just what would please without startling him. The book is not mentioned between us once a month. The 'Quarterly' I kept to myself—it would have worried papa. To that same 'Quarterly' I must speak in the introduction to my present work—just one little word. You once, I remember, said that the review was written by a lady—Miss Rigby. Are you sure of this?

Give no hint of my intention of discoursing a little with the 'Quarterly.' It would look too important to speak of it beforehand. All plans are best conceived and executed without noise. —Believe me, yours sincerely,

C. B.

459 (365). *To* W. S. WILLIAMS.

MY DEAR SIR,—I can only write very briefly at present, first to thank you for your interesting letter and the graphic description it contains of the neighbourhood where you have been staying —and then to decide about the title of the book.

If I remember rightly my Cornhill critics object to 'Hollow's Mill' nor do I find it appropriate. It might rather be called 'Fieldhead'—though I think 'Shirley' would perhaps be the best title: 'Shirley' I fancy, has turned out the most prominent and peculiar character in the work.

Cornhill may decide between 'Fieldhead' and 'Shirley.' Believe me, Yours sincerely,

C. BRONTË.

Augst 21st, '49.

460 (366). *To* ELLEN NUSSEY.

August 23rd, 1849.

DEAR ELLEN,—Papa has not been well at all lately. He has had another attack of bronchitis. I felt very uneasy about him for some days, more wretched indeed than I care to tell you. After what has happened, one trembles at any appearance of sickness; and when anything ails papa, I feel too keenly that he is the *last*, the *only* near and dear relation I have in the world. Yesterday and to-day he has seemed much better, for which I am truly thankful.

For myself I should be pretty well, but for a continually recurring feeling of slight cold, slight hoarseness in the throat and chest, of which—do what I will—I cannot quite get rid. Has *your* cough entirely left you? I wish the atmosphere would return to a salubrious condition, for I really think it is not healthy. English cholera has been very prevalent here. I *do* wish to see you.

From what you say of Mr Clapham, I think I should like him very much. Ann wants shaking to be put out about his appearance. What does it matter whether her husband dines in a dress-coat or a market-coat, provided there be worth, and honesty, and a clean shirt underneath?

I should like to make Ann a small present. Give me a hint what would be acceptable.

I suppose you have not yet heard anything more of poor Mr Gorham. Does Rosy Ringrose continue to improve? How are Mrs Atkinson and Mrs Charles Carr? I am glad to hear that Miss Heald continues tolerable, but, as you say, it really seems wonderful. I hope Mercy will derive benefit from her excursion. Good-bye for the present. Write to me again soon.

C. B.

With what remains after paying for the furs you must buy something for yourself to make your bride's-maid gear.

461 (367). *To* W. S. WILLIAMS.

Augst 24th, '49.

MY DEAR SIR,—I think the best title for the book would be 'Shirley' without any explanation or addition—the simpler and briefer, the better.

If Mr Taylor calls here on his return to Town, he might take charge of the MS.; I would rather entrust it to him than send it by the ordinary conveyance. Did I see Mr Taylor when I was in London? I cannot remember him.

I would with pleasure offer him the homely hospitalities of the Parsonage for a few days, if I could at the same time offer him the company of a brother or if my Father were young enough and strong enough to walk with him on the moors and shew him the neighbourhood, or if the peculiar retirement of papa's habits were not such as to render it irksome to him to give much of his society to a stranger even in the house: without being in the least misanthropical or sour-natured—papa habitually prefers solitude to society, and Custom is a tyrant whose fetters it would now be impossible for him to break. Were it not for difficulties of this sort, I believe I should ere this have asked you to come down to Yorkshire. Papa—I know, would receive any friend of Mr Smith's with perfect kindness and good will, but I likewise know that, unless greatly put out of his way—he could not give a guest much of his company, and that, consequently, his entertainment would be but dull.

You will see the force of these considerations, and understand why I only ask Mr Taylor to come for a day instead of requesting the pleasure of his company for a longer period; you will believe me also, and so will he, when I say I shall be most happy to see him. He will find Haworth a strange uncivilized little place such as—I daresay—he never saw before. It is twenty miles distant from Leeds; he will have to come by rail to Keighley (there are trains every two hours I believe) he must remember that at a station called Shipley the carriages are changed—otherwise they will take him on to Skipton or Colne, or I know not where; when he reaches Keighley, he will yet have four miles to travel—a conveyance may be hired at the Devonshire Arms; there is no coach or other regular communication.

I should like to hear from him before he comes and to know on what day to expect him that I may have the MS. ready—if it is not quite finished I might send the concluding chapter or two by post.

I advise you to send this letter to Mr Taylor—it will save you the trouble of much explanation—and will serve to apprise him of what lies before him; he can then weigh well with himself whether it would suit him to take so much trouble for so slight an end.—Believe me, my dear Sir, Yours sincerely,

C. Brontë.

462 (368). *To* W. S. WILLIAMS.

August 29th, 1849.

DEAR SIR,—The book is now finished (thank God) and ready for Mr Taylor, but I have not yet heard from him. I thought I should be able to tell whether it was equal to 'Jane Eyre' or not, but I find I cannot—it may be better, it may be worse. I shall be curious to hear your opinion, my own is of no value. I send the Preface or 'Word to the "Quarterly"' for your perusal.

Whatever now becomes of the work, the occupation of writing it has been a boon to me. It took me out of dark and desolate reality into an unreal but happier region. The worst of it is, my eyes are grown somewhat weak and my head somewhat weary and prone to ache with close work. You can write nothing of value unless you give yourself wholly to the theme, and when you so give yourself you lose appetite and sleep—it cannot be helped.

At what time does Mr Smith intend to bring the book out? It is his now. I hand it and all the trouble and care and anxiety over to him—a good riddance, only I wish he fairly had it.—Yours sincerely,

C. BRONTË.

463 (369). *To* W. S. WILLIAMS.

August 31st, 1849.

MY DEAR SIR,—I cannot change my preface. I can shed no tears before the public, nor utter any groan in the public ear. The deep, real tragedy of our domestic experience is yet terribly fresh in my mind and memory. It is not a time to be talked about to the indifferent; it is not a topic for allusion to in print.

No righteous indignation can I lavish on the 'Quarterly.' I can condescend but to touch it with the lightest satire. Believe me, my dear sir, 'C. Brontë' must not here appear; what she feels or has felt is not the question—it is 'Currer Bell' who was insulted —he must reply. Let Mr Smith fearlessly print the preface I have sent—let him depend upon me this once; even if I prove a broken reed, his fall cannot be dangerous: a preface is a short distance, it is not three volumes.

I have always felt certain that it is a deplorable error in an author to assume the tragic tone in addressing the public about his own wrongs or griefs. What does the public care about him as an individual? His wrongs are its sport; his griefs would be a bore. What we deeply feel is our own — we must keep it to ourselves. Ellis and Acton Bell were, for me, Emily and Anne; my sisters — to me intimately near, tenderly dear — to the public they were nothing — worse than nothing — beings speculated upon, misunderstood, misrepresented. If I live, the hour may come when the spirit will move me to speak of them, but it is not come yet. — I am, my dear sir, yours sincerely,

C. Brontë.

464. *To* George Smith.

August 31st, 1849.

My dear Sir, — I do not know whether you share Mr Williams's disapprobation of the preface I sent, but, if you do, ask him to show you the note wherein I contumaciously persist in urging it upon you. I really cannot condescend to be serious with the 'Quarterly': it is too silly for solemnity.

Mr Taylor has just written; he says he shall be at Haworth on Saturday, the 8th September, so I shall wait with what patience I may. I am perhaps unduly anxious to know that the manuscript is safely deposited at 65 Cornhill, and to hear the opinions of my critics there. Those opinions are by no means the less valuable because I cannot always reconcile them to my own convictions. 'In the multitude of counsellors there is safety.'

It is my intention to pack with the MS. some of the books you have been so kind as to lend me — if the charge of so large a parcel will not be too burdensome for Mr Taylor. Such works as I have not yet perused I shall take the liberty of retaining a little longer.

Permit me to thank you for the kind interest you express in my welfare; I am not ill, but only somewhat overwrought and unnerved. — Believe me, Yours sincerely,

C. Brontë.

465 (370). *To* JAMES TAYLOR, *Cornhill.*

September 3rd, 1849.

MY DEAR SIR,—It will be convenient to my father and myself to secure your visit on Saturday the 8th inst.

The MS. is now complete, and ready for you.

Trusting that you have enjoyed your holiday and derived from your excursion both pleasure and profit,—I am, dear sir, yours sincerely,

C. BRONTË.

466 (371). *To* W. S. WILLIAMS.[1]

[September 10th, 1849].

DEAR SIR,—Your advice is very good, and yet I cannot follow it: I *cannot* alter now. It sounds absurd, but so it is.

The circumstances of Shirley's being nervous on such a matter may appear incongruous because I fear it is not well managed; otherwise it is perfectly natural. In such minds, such odd points, such queer unexpected inconsistent weaknesses *are* found —perhaps there never was an ardent poetic temperament, however healthy, quite without them; but they never communicate them unless forced, they have a suspicion that the terror is absurd, and keep it hidden. Still the thing is badly managed, and I bend my head and expect in resignation what, *here*, I know I deserve—the lash of criticism. I shall wince when it falls, but not scream.

You are right about Goethe, you are very right—he is clear, deep, but very cold. I acknowledge him great, but cannot feel him genial.

You mention the literary coteries. To speak the truth, I recoil from them, though I long to see some of the truly great literary characters. However, this is not to be yet—I cannot sacrifice my incognito. And let me be content with seclusion—it has its advantages. In general, indeed, I am tranquil, it is only now and then that a struggle disturbs me—that I wish for a wider world than Haworth. When it is past, Reason tells me how unfit I am for anything very different.—Yours sincerely, C. BRONTË.

[1]The original of this letter is bound up in a volume of the first edition of *Shirley*, and is now in the Bonnell Collection, Brontë Parsonage Museum, Haworth.

467 (372). *To* ELLEN NUSSEY.

DEAR ELLEN,—My piece of work is at last finished and despatched to its destination—you must now tell me when there is
a chance of your being able to come here—I fear it will now be
difficult to arrange as it is so near the marriage-day—Note well
—it would spoil all my pleasure if you put yourself or any one
else to inconvenience to come to Haworth—but when it is *convenient* I shall be truly glad to see you.

I thought the patterns you sent charming and all quite appropriate—the dove colour is—as they say—'a sweet thing.' Your
suggestion of the card-case is quite judicious—but the worst of
it is I cannot act on it—unless I chanced to be in Leeds or elsewhere where such things are to be got—However she will not
want it just yet—and don't let her buy one.

Is Mercy come home? Have you heard anything more about
Joe Taylor?

Papa—I am thankful to say is still better—though not strong
—he is often troubled with a sensation of nausea—My cold is
very much less troublesome—I am sometimes quite free from it
—a few days since I had a severe bilious attack—the consequence
of sitting too closely to my writing—but it is gone now—it is
the first from which I have suffered since my return from the seaside; I had them every month before.

I hope you are pretty well and also your Mother and Sisters.—
    Yours sincerely,
                                        C. B.
Sept. 10th, '49.

468 (373). *To* ELLEN NUSSEY.

[September 13th, 1849].

DEAR ELLEN,—If duty and the well-being of others require
that you should stay at home I cannot permit myself to complain
—still I am very *very* sorry that circumstances will not permit us
to meet just now—I would without hesitation come to Brookroyd if papa were stronger—but uncertain as are both his health
and spirits—I could not possibly prevail on myself to leave him
now. Let us hope that when we do see each other our meeting
will be all the more pleasurable for being delayed.

Tell Mercy to keep up her spirits—I believe the general effect of the sea is to make people feel somewhat queer for the first fortnight or so after their return home—If you remember Miss Lockwood made that remark and I found it true in my own case.

Dear Nell—you certainly have a heavy burden laid on your shoulders— . . .[1] —but such burdens, if well borne, benefit the character—only we must take the *greatest, closest, most watchful* care—not to grow proud of our strength in case we should be enabled to bear up under the trial—that pride, indeed, would be a sign of radical weakness—the strength—if strength we have— is certainly never in our own selves—it is given us. Let me know when you go to Leeds—I will then commission you about the card-case—would £1 buy a nice one? I should like it to be a really nice one.

Amelia Ringrose wrote me a very kind note—which—shameful to say—I have not answered. She will form a bad opinion of me, and I deserve it. I was glad to hear that Rosy was better. I should be tempted to make a pet of that Rosy—to spoil her— and I daresay—like poor Martha Taylor—she might soon be spoiled. Engaging as I think her—I ascribe to her no great or profound qualities.

Write to me when you can find a corner of time—Remember me to your Mother.—Yours,

C. B.

Be as forbearing with Mercy as you can: I daresay there mixes in her feelings just now some little sense of bitterness that *she* too is not going to be married—it is a pity if such is the case, but for one with her habits of thought it is natural.

Poor Mr Gorham lingers long—it is said a tedious illness prepares the survivors for the last scene: perhaps it may—but it is a painful preparation.

469 (374). *To* W. S. WILLIAMS.

September 13th, 1849.

MY DEAR SIR,—I want to know your opinion of the subject of this proof-sheet. Mr Taylor censured it; he considers as defective all that portion which relates to Shirley's nervousness—the bite of a dog, etc. How did it strike you on reading it?

---

[1] Here two lines in the original letter have been scored out by Miss Nussey.

I ask this though I well know it cannot now be altered. I can work indefatigably at the correction of a work before it leaves my hands, but when once I have looked on it as completed and submitted to the inspection of others, it becomes next to impossible to alter or amend. With the heavy suspicion on my mind that all may not be right, I yet feel forced to put up with the inevitably wrong.

Reading has, of late, been my great solace and recreation. I have read J. C. Hare's 'Guesses at Truth,'[1] a book containing things that in depth and far-sought wisdom sometimes recall the 'Thoughts' of Pascal, only it is as the light of the moon recalls that of the sun.

I have read with pleasure a little book on 'English Social Life'[2] by the wife of Archbishop Whately. Good and intelligent women write well on such subjects. This lady speaks of governesses. I was struck by the contrast offered in her manner of treating the topic to that of Miss Rigby in the 'Quarterly.' How much finer the feeling—how much truer the feeling—how much more delicate the mind here revealed!

I have read 'David Copperfield'; it seems to me very good—admirable in some parts. You said it had affinity to 'Jane Eyre.' It has, now and then—only what an advantage has Dickens in his varied knowledge of men and things! I am beginning to read Eckermann's 'Goethe'[3]—it promises to be a most interesting work. Honest, simple, single-minded Eckermann! Great, powerful, giant-souled, but also profoundly egotistical, old Johann Wolfgang von Goethe! He *was* a mighty egotist—I see he was: he thought no more of swallowing up poor Eckermann's existence in his own than the whale thought of swallowing Jonah.

The worst of reading graphic accounts of such men, of seeing graphic pictures of the scenes, the society, in which they moved, is that it excites a too tormenting longing to look on the reality. But does such reality now exist? Amidst all the troubled waters of European society does such a vast, strong, selfish, old Leviathan now roll ponderous! I suppose not.—Believe me, yours sincerely,

C. BRONTË.

---

[1] *Guesses at Truth*, by Julius and Augustus Hare. Published anonymously in 1827.
[2] *English Life, Social and Domestic, in the 19th Century*. By Mrs Whateley, 1847.

[3] This was probably John Oxenford's translation of Eckermann's *Conversations with Goethe*, made in 1849.

470 (375). *To* W. S. WILLIAMS.

September 15th, 1849.
MY DEAR SIR,—You observed that the French of 'Shirley' might be cavilled at. There is a long paragraph written in the French language in that chapter entitled 'Le cheval dompté.' I forget the number. I fear it will have a pretentious air. If you deem it advisable and will return the chapter, I will efface and substitute something else in English.—Yours sincerely,
CHARLOTTE BRONTË.

471 (376). *To* W. S. WILLIAMS.

MY DEAR SIR,—Your letter gave me great pleasure. An author who has shewn his book to none, held no consultation about plan, subject, characters or incidents, asked and had no opinion from one living being, but fabricated it darkly in the silent workshop of his own brain—such an author awaits with a singular feeling the report of the first impression produced by his creation in a quarter where he places confidence, and truly glad he is when that report proves favourable.

Do you think this book will tend to strengthen the idea that *Currer Bell* is a woman—or will it favour a contrary opinion?

I return the Proof-sheets—Will they print all the French phrases in Italics? I hope not; it makes them look somehow obtrusively conspicuous—

I have no time to add more lest I should be too late for the post.—Yours sincerely,
C. BRONTË.
Sept. 17th, '49.

472 (476). *To* ELLEN NUSSEY.

[September, 1849].
DEAR NELL,—Being too lazy to send for a Post Office Order, I have sent the accompanying coin in a little box—tell me whether it reaches you safely—Should it be too late to get the card-case—get something else, anything you think will please, and offer it with my kind love.

I am glad to hear Mr Clapham so fully meets your approbation, and hope he will continue to do so.

Instead of sending a card for the 15th, I think I shall write a little note.

Poor Mercy! I pity her, and yet I am angry with her. What a wretched misfortune to be deficient in sense and self-government!

Miss Wooler's idea amazed me—it is perfectly groundless—I am unconscious of the slightest change—my regard for her is altogether unaltered. I wish she may mention it to me herself.

I shall certainly not come till you get your 'stirs' in some measure over. Good-bye, dear Nell.

C. B.

473 (377). *To* JAMES TAYLOR, *Cornhill.*

September 20th, 1849.

MY DEAR SIR,—It is time I answered the note which I received from you last Thursday; I should have replied to it before had I not been kept more than usually engaged by the presence of a clergyman in the house, and the indisposition of one of our servants.

As you may conjecture, it cheered and pleased me much to learn that the opinion of my friends in Cornhill was favourable to 'Shirley'—that, on the whole, it was considered no falling off from 'Jane Eyre.' I am trying, however, not to encourage too sanguine an expectation of a favourable reception by the public: the seeds of prejudice have been sown, and I suppose the produce will have to be reaped—but we shall see.

I read with pleasure 'Friends in Council,'[1] and with very great pleasure 'The Thoughts and Opinions of a Statesman.'[2] It is the record of what may with truth be termed a beautiful mind—serene, harmonious, elevated, and pure; it bespeaks, too, a heart full of kindness and sympathy. I like it much.

Papa has been pretty well during the past week. He begs to join me in kind remembrances to yourself.—Believe me, my dear sir, yours very sincerely,

C. BRONTË.

[1] *Friends in Council: a Series of Readings and Discourses thereon.* By Sir Arthur Helps, 1847–1859.

[2] *Thoughts and Opinions of a Statesman* (Small Books on Great Subjects), 1845.

474 (378). *To* W. S. WILLIAMS.

September 21st, 1849.

MY DEAR SIR, — I am obliged to you for preserving my secret, being at least as anxious as ever (*more* anxious I cannot well be) to keep quiet. You asked me in one of your letters lately whether I thought I should escape identification in Yorkshire. I am so little known that I think I shall. Besides, the book is far less founded on the Real than perhaps appears. It would be difficult to explain to you how little actual experience I have had of life, how few persons I have known, and how very few have known me.

As an instance how the characters have been managed take that of Mr Helstone.[1] If this character had an original it was in the person of a clergyman who died some years since at the advanced age of eighty. I never saw him except once — at the consecration of a church — when I was a child of ten years old. I was then struck with his appearance and stern, martial air. At a subsequent period I heard him talked about in the neighbourhood where he had resided: some mentioned him with enthusiasm, others with detestation. I listened to various anecdotes, balanced evidence against evidence, and drew an inference. The original of Mr Hall[2] I have seen; he knows me slightly; but he would as soon think I had closely observed him or taken him for a character — he would as soon, indeed, suspect me of writing a book — a novel — as he would his dog Prince. Margaret Hall called 'Jane Eyre' a 'wicked book,' on the authority of the 'Quarterly'; an expression which, coming from her, I will here confess, struck somewhat deep. It opened my eyes to the harm the 'Quarterly' had done. Margaret would not have called it 'wicked' if she had not been told so.

No matter — whether known or unknown — misjudged or the contrary — I am resolved not to write otherwise. I shall bend as my powers tend. The two human beings who understood me, and whom I understood, are gone. I have some that love me yet, and whom I love without expecting, or having a right to expect,

---

[1] The original of the character of the Rev. Matthewson Helstone in *Shirley* was the Rev. Hammond Roberson of Liversedge. See Vol. I. p. 99.

[2] The character of the Rev. Cyril Hall, Vicar of Nunnely, was based on the Rev. William Margetson Heald, who was for many years Vicar of Birstall. See his letter to Ellen Nussey, January 8th, 1850.

that they shall perfectly understand me. I am satisfied; but I must have my own way in the matter of writing. The loss of what we possess nearest and dearest to us in this world produces an effect upon the character: we search out what we have yet left that can support, and, when found, we cling to it with a hold of new-strung tenacity. The faculty of imagination lifted me when I was sinking, three months ago; its active exercise has kept my head above water since; its results cheer me now, for I feel they have enabled me to give pleasure to others. I am thankful to God, who gave me the faculty; and it is for me a part of my religion to defend this gift and to profit by its possession. — Yours sincerely,

CHARLOTTE BRONTË.

475 (379). *To* ELLEN NUSSEY.

September 24th, 1849.

DEAR ELLEN, — You have to fight your way through labour and difficulty it appears, but I am truly glad now you did not come to Haworth. As matters have turned out, you would have found only discomfort and gloom. Both Tabby and Martha are at this moment ill in bed. Martha's illness has been most serious; she was seized with inflammation ten days ago. Tabby's lame leg has broken out; she cannot stand or walk. I have one of Martha's sisters, and her mother comes up sometimes. There was one day last week when I fairly broke down for ten minutes, and sat down and cried like a fool. Martha's illness was at its height, a cry from Tabby had called me into the kitchen and I had found her laid on the floor, her head under the kitchen grate; she had fallen from her chair in attempting to rise. Papa had just been declaring that Martha was in imminent danger. I was myself depressed with headache and sickness. That day I hardly knew what to do, or where to turn. Thank God, Martha is now con-valescent; Tabby, I trust, will be better soon. Papa is pretty well. I have the satisfaction of knowing that my publishers are delight-ed with what I sent them. This supports me, but life is a battle. May we *all* be enabled to fight it well. — Yours faithfully,

C. B.

476 (380). *To* ELLEN NUSSEY.

Septb. 28th, '49.

DEAR ELLEN,—Martha is now almost well and Tabby much better. A huge Monster-package from 'Nelson, Leeds,' came yesterday. You want chastising roundly and soundly. Such are the thanks you get for all your trouble. I am sorry I could not send the cash for the card-case when I intended. I am obliged to wait a while.

I congratulate both you and Ann[1] on the business being well over—May the married pair be happy and never regret their union.

Mr Allbutt I see, by the paper, is married at last—and poor Rebecca Taylor is dead. Mr Gorham too, it seems, has done with this life and its sorrows; doubtless likewise he has changed its joys for a better and more perfect portion.

Whenever you come to Haworth you shall certainly have a thorough drenching in your own shower-bath. I have not yet unpacked the wretch.—Yours as you deserve,

C. B.

477 (381). *To* W. S. WILLIAMS.

September 29th, 1849.

DEAR SIR,—I have made the alteration; but I have made it to please Cornhill, not the public nor the critics.

I am sorry to say Newby does know my real name. I wish he did not, but that cannot be helped. Meantime, though I earnestly wish to preserve my incognito, I live under no slavish fear of discovery. I am ashamed of nothing I have written—not a line.

The envelope containing the first proof and your letter had been received open at the General Post Office and resealed there. Perhaps it was accident, but I think it better to inform you of the circumstance.—Yours sincerely,

C. BRONTË.

[1] Ann Nussey (1796–1878) was married to Mr Clapham on September 26th, 1849.

478 (382). *To* W. S. WILLIAMS.

October 1st, 1849.

MY DEAR SIR,—I am chagrined about the envelope being opened: I see it is the work of prying curiosity, and now it would be useless to make a stir—what mischief is to be apprehended is already done. It was not done at Haworth. I know the people of the post-office there, and am sure they would not venture on such a step; besides, the Haworth people have long since set me down as bookish and quiet, and trouble themselves no farther about me. But the gossiping inquisitiveness of small towns is rife at Keighley; there they are sadly puzzled to guess why I never visit, encourage no overtures to acquaintance, and always stay at home. Those packets passing backwards and forwards by the post have doubtless aggravated their curiosity. Well, I am sorry, but I shall try to wait patiently and not vex myself too much, come what will.

I am glad you like the English substitute for the French *devoir*.

The parcel of books came on Saturday. I write to Mr Taylor by this post to acknowledge its receipt. His opinion of 'Shirley' seems in a great measure to coincide with yours, only he expresses it rather differently to you, owing to the difference in your casts of mind. Are you not different on some points?—Yours sincerely,

C. BRONTË.

As intimated in her letter to Mr Williams, Charlotte wrote to Mr Taylor, acknowledging the safe receipt of the books from Cornhill, and expressing her appreciation of his kindness in sending them. Unfortunately only a portion of this letter has been preserved.

479. *To* JAMES TAYLOR.

October 1st, 1849.

. . . What, I sometimes ask, could I do without them? I have recourse to them as to friends; they shorten and cheer many a hour that would be too long and too desolate otherwise; even

when my tired sight will not permit me to continue reading, it is
pleasant to see them on the shelf or on the table. I am still very
rich, for my stock is far from exhausted. Some other friends have
sent me books lately. The perusal of Harriet Martineau's 'Eastern Life'[1] has afforded me great pleasure; and I have found a
deep and interesting subject of study in Newman's work on the
'Soul.'[2] Have you read this work? It is daring—it may be mistaken—but it is pure and elevated. Froude's 'Nemesis of Faith'[3]
I did not like; I thought it morbid; yet in its pages, too, are found
sprinklings of truth.

480 (383). *To* GEORGE SMITH.

October 4th, 1849.

MY DEAR SIR,—I must not *thank* you for, but acknowledge the
receipt of, your letter. The business is certainly very bad; worse
than I thought, and much worse than my father has any idea of.
In fact, the little railway property I possessed, according to
original prices, formed already a small competency for me, with
my views and habits. Now scarcely any portion of it can, with
security, be calculated upon. I must open this view of the case to
my father by degrees; and, meanwhile, wait patiently till I see
how affairs are likely to turn. . . . However the matter may terminate, I ought perhaps to be rather thankful than dissatisfied.
When I look at my own case, and compare it with that of
thousands besides, I scarcely see room for a murmur. Many,
very many, are by the late strange railway system deprived
almost of their daily bread. Such, then, as have only lost provision laid up for the future should take care how they complain.
The thought that 'Shirley' has given pleasure at Cornhill yields
me much quiet comfort. No doubt, however, you are, as I am,
prepared for critical severity; but I have good hopes that the
vessel is sufficiently sound of construction to weather a gale or
two, and to make a prosperous voyage for you in the end.

C. BRONTË.

[1]Harriet Martineau's *Eastern Life* was
published in 1848, after a visit to Egypt and
Palestine.
[2]Francis William Newman (1805–1897),
brother of Cardinal Newman, published in

1849 *The Soul: her Sorrows and her Aspirations: an Essay towards the Natural History of
the Soul as the Basis of Theology.*
[3]James Anthony Froude (1818–1894)
published *The Nemesis of Faith* in 1849.

481 (404). *To* ELLEN NUSSEY.

[October 20th, 1849].

DEAR ELLEN,—As Papa happens to be pretty well just now—and as Martha is likewise quite recovered—I think I really should like to come to you for a few days.

Could you without inconvenience meet me at Leeds on Tuesday morning—about 12 o'clock? I ask this because I find I really must go to Mr Atkinson the dentist and ask him if he can do anything for my teeth—and I thought I might as well get the pleasant errand over on my way to Brookroyd—I have some other trifling matters to look after likewise but I should have wished to consult you about them beforehand, and if you think I had better go from Brookroyd to Leeds—or if it would inconvenience you to meet me there—say so—and I will come by Bradford.

If you write by return of post—I shall get your note on Monday morning and shall know how to arrange.

Give my kind regards to all and believe me—Yours sincerely,

C. B.

482. *To* GEORGE SMITH.

BROOKROYD, October 24th, 1849.

MY DEAR SIR,—Your note enclosing the banker's receipt, reached me safely. I should have acknowledged it before had I not been from home.

I am glad 'Shirley'[1] is so near the day of publication, as I now and then feel anxious to know its doom and learn what sort of reception it will get. In another month some of the critics will have pronounced their fiat, and the public also will have evinced their mood towards it. Meanwhile patience.—Yours sincerely,

C. BRONTË.

---

[1] Published on Oct. 26th, 1849.

483 (384). *To* W. S. WILLIAMS.

November 1st, 1849.

MY DEAR SIR,—I reached home yesterday, and found your letter and one from Mr Lewes, and one from the Peace Congress Committee, awaiting my arrival. The last document it is now too late to answer, for it was an invitation to Currer Bell to appear on the platform at their meeting at Exeter Hall last Tuesday! A wonderful figure Mr Currer Bell would have cut under such circumstances! Should the 'Peace Congress' chance to read 'Shirley' they will wash their hands of its author.

I am glad to hear that Mr Thackeray is better, but I did not know he had been seriously ill, I thought it was only a literary indisposition. You must tell me what he thinks of 'Shirley' if he gives you any opinion on the subject.

I am also glad to hear that Mr Smith is pleased with the commercial prospects of the work. I try not to be anxious about its literary fate; and if I cannot be quite stoical, I think I am still tolerably resigned.

Mr Lewes does not like the opening chapter, wherein he resembles you.

I have permitted myself the treat of spending the last week with my friend Ellen. Her residence is in a far more populous and stirring neighbourhood than this. Whenever I go there I am unavoidably forced into society—clerical society chiefly.

During my late visit I have too often had reason, sometimes in a pleasant, sometimes in a painful form, to fear that I no longer walk invisible. 'Jane Eyre,' it appears, has been read all over the district—a fact of which I never dreamt—a circumstance of which the possibility never occurred to me. I met sometimes with new deference, with augmented kindness: old schoolfellows and old teachers, too, greeted me with generous warmth. And again, ecclesiastical brows lowered thunder on me. When I confronted one or two large-made priests, I longed for the battle to come on. I wish they would speak out plainly. You must not understand that my schoolfellows and teachers were of the Clergy Daughters' School—in fact, I was never there but for one little year as a very little girl. I am certain I have long been forgotten; though for myself, I remember all and everything clearly: early impressions are ineffaceable.

I have just received the 'Daily News.' Let me speak the truth —when I read it my heart sickened over it. It is not a good review, it is unutterably false. If 'Shirley' strikes all readers as it has struck that one, but—I shall not say what follows.

On the whole I am glad a decidedly bad notice has come first —a notice whose inexpressible ignorance first stuns and then stirs me. Are there no such men as the Helstones and Yorkes?

Yes, there are.

Is the first chapter disgusting or vulgar?

It is not, it is real.

As for the praise of such a critic, I find it silly and nauseous, and I scorn it.

Were my sisters now alive they and I would laugh over this notice; but they sleep, they will wake no more for me, and I am a fool to be so moved by what is not worth a sigh.—Believe me, yours sincerely,

C. B.

You must spare me if I seem hasty, I fear I really am not so firm as I used to be, nor so patient. Whenever any shock comes, I feel that almost all supports have been withdrawn.

484 (385). *To* Ellen Nussey.

November 1st, '49.

Dear Ellen,—I reached home safely about 3 o'clock. You too would have fine weather for your journey, to-day it is wet and foggy, so it is well I did not stay.

I found papa very well, Tabby better, and Martha quite fat and strong, for which state of things I was most thankful. Some letters were awaiting my arrival; I enclose one for your perusal, which may perhaps amuse you. Send it back. All the house with one voice inquired after you. Also many questions were asked about the Bride. Be sure when you write to tell me how Amelia Ringrose is. In haste.—Yours,

C. B.

I send two letters, one from the Peace Congress to Currer Bell! The other from Williams.

485 (386). *To* G. H. LEWES.

November 1st, 1849.

MY DEAR SIR,—It is about a year and a half since you wrote to me; but it seems a longer period, because since then it has been my lot to pass some black milestones in the journey of life. Since then there have been intervals when I have ceased to care about literature and critics and fame; when I have lost sight of whatever was prominent in my thoughts at the first publication of 'Jane Eyre'; but now I want these things to come back vividly, if possible: consequently it was a pleasure to receive your note. I wish you did not think me a woman. I wish all reviewers believed 'Currer Bell' to be a man; they would be more just to him. You will, I know, keep measuring me by some standard of what you deem becoming to my sex; where I am not what you consider graceful you will condemn me. All mouths will be open against that first chapter, and that first chapter is as true as the Bible, nor is it exceptionable. Come what will, I cannot, when I write, think always of myself and of what is elegant and charming in femininity; it is not on those terms, or with such ideas, I ever took pen in hand: and if it is only on such terms my writing will be tolerated, I shall pass away from the public and trouble it no more. Out of obscurity I came, to obscurity I can easily return. Standing afar off, I now watch to see what will become of 'Shirley.' My expectations are very low, and my anticipations somewhat sad and bitter; still, I earnestly conjure you to say honestly what you think; flattery would be worse than vain; there is no consolation in flattery. As for condemnation, I cannot, on reflection, see why I should much fear it; there is no one but myself to suffer therefrom, and both happiness and suffering in this life soon pass away. Wishing you all success in your Scottish expedition,—I am, dear sir, yours sincerely,

C. BELL.

486. *To* AMELIA RINGROSE.

Nov. 5th, '49.

DEAR AMELIA,—You say you do not expect an answer to your letter: I am not however quite such a heathen as not at least to acknowledge my sense of the kind feeling by which that letter was prompted; besides, I found it interesting and must thank you for the amusement its perusal afforded me.

I had observed and regretted your depression of spirits, and Ellen had intimated to me the cause to which it was attributable. Under the circumstances it is but too natural that you should feel as you do; I can therefore only express my sincere sympathy with your sadness, and equally sincere wish that time may alleviate its sting.

Ellen has a heavy burden laid on her and an intricate task placed before her in the management of minds not easily managed—of minds too weak to walk alone, and too little tractable to yield willingly to guidance. May Providence help her well through!

All you say about Joe Taylor amused me. Mrs Nussey's remark is not without sagacity, as you will probably discover— Observe when you go to Hunsworth.

Since you did not expect any letter from me you will not be surprised that I write a short one.—Yours sincerely,

C. BRONTË.

487 (387). *To* ELLEN NUSSEY.

HAWORTH, Novr 5th, '49.

DEAR ELLEN,—I am afraid by Amelia's account you were sadly fagged with your Leeds expedition; she says you looked very pale and weary—and then all this settling of accounts—and explanation to your Mother and Mercy will be fatiguing work— tell me when you write again if all is satisfactorily arranged.

I shall be interested in hearing your account of the visit to Hunsworth—it is not at all impossible that Amelia Ringrose may be singled out by Joe Taylor as an object of special attention. Take notice.

The Station people in our part of the world have a strange notion of the proper plan of discharging their duties—my parcel of copies from London has been lying at Bradford nearly a week—when I sent for it they made answer 'there was none'— and it is only just now I have got it. I will (D.V.) send you two copies on Thursday—one for yourself—and one for Mary Gorham—I shall order the parcel to be left at the Commerical Inn.

Hoping to hear from you soon again I am dear Nell,—Yours faithfully,   C. BRONTË.

My chest has felt much better since I came home. I think change of air or weather occasioned greater irritation than usual while I was at Brookroyd. I think of you and Amelia often: sometimes I *do* wish I was near enough to step in and spend the evening with you.

488 (388). *To* W. S. WILLIAMS.

November 5th, 1849.

MY DEAR SIR,—I did not receive the parcel of copies till Saturday evening. Everything sent by Bradford is long in reaching me. It is, I think, better to direct: Keighley. I was very much pleased with the appearance and getting up of the book; it looks well.

I have got the 'Examiner' and your letter. You are very good not to be angry with me, for I wrote in indignation and grief. The critic of the 'Daily News' struck me as to the last degree incompetent, ignorant, flippant. A thrill of mutiny went all through me when I read his small effusion. To be judged by such a one revolted me. I ought, however, to have controlled myself, and I did not. I am willing to be judged by the 'Examiner'—I like the 'Examiner.' Fonblanque[1] has power, he has discernment —I bend to his censorship, I am grateful for his praise; his blame deserves consideration; when he approves, I permit myself a moderate emotion of pride. Am I wrong in supposing that critique to be written by Mr Fonblanque? But whether it is by him or Forster, I am thankful.

In reading the critiques of the other papers—when I get them —I will try to follow your advice and preserve my equanimity. But I cannot be sure of doing this, for I had good resolutions and intentions before, and, you see, I failed.

You ask me if I am related to Nelson. No, I never heard that I was. The rumour must have originated in our name resembling his title. I wonder who that former schoolfellow of mine was that told Mr Lewes, or how she had been enabled to identify Currer Bell with C. Brontë. She could not have been a Cowan Bridge girl, none of them can possibly remember me. They

---

[1] Albany William Fonblanque (1793–1872) edited the *Examiner* from 1830–47, when he became statistical Secretary to the Board of Trade. He was succeeded in the Editorship of the *Examiner* by John Forster (1812–1876) who held the position from 1847–55.

might remember my eldest sister, Maria; her prematurely-
developed and remarkable intellect, as well as the mildness,
wisdom, and fortitude of her character, *might* have left an
indelible impression on some observant mind amongst her
companions. My second sister, Elizabeth, too, may perhaps be
remembered, but I cannot conceive that I left a trace behind me.
My career was a very quiet one. I was plodding and industrious,
perhaps I was very grave, for I suffered to see my sisters perish-
ing, but I think I was remarkable for nothing. —Believe, my
dear sir, yours sincerely,

C. BRONTË.

489 (389). *To* JAMES TAYLOR, *Cornhill.*

November 6th, 1849.

MY DEAR SIR, —I am afraid Mr Williams told you I was sadly
'put out' about the 'Daily News,' and I believe it is to that circumstance I owe your letters. But I have now made good resolutions, which were tried this morning by another notice in the
same style in the 'Observer.' The praise of such critics mortifies
more than their blame; an author who becomes the object of it
cannot help momentarily wishing he had never written. And to
speak of the press being still ignorant of my being a woman!
Why can they not be content to take Currer Bell for a man?

I imagined, mistakenly it now appears, that 'Shirley' bore
fewer traces of a female hand than 'Jane Eyre'; that I have misjudged disappoints me a little, though I cannot exactly see where
the error lies. You keep to your point about the curates. Since
you think me to blame, you do right to tell me so. I rather fancy I
shall be left in a minority of one on that subject.

I was indeed very much interested in the books you sent.
Eckermann's 'Conversations with Goethe,' 'Guesses at Truth,'
'Friends in Council,' and the little work on English social life
pleased me particularly, and the last not least. We sometimes
take a partiality to books as to characters, not on account of any
brilliant intellect or striking peculiarity they boast, but for the
sake of something good, delicate, and genuine. I thought that
small book the production of a lady, and an amiable, sensible
woman, and I like it.

You must not think of selecting any more works for me, yet,
my stock is still far from exhausted.

I accept your offer respecting the 'Athenæum'; it is a paper I should like much to see, providing you can send it without trouble. It shall be punctually returned.

Papa's health has, I am thankful to say, been very satisfactory of late. The other day he walked to Keighley and back, and was very little fatigued. I am myself pretty well.

With thanks for your kind letter and good wishes, —Believe me, yours sincerely,

C. BRONTË.

490 (390). *To* W. S. WILLIAMS.

Novr 15th, '49.

MY DEAR SIR, —I have received since I wrote last 'the Globe,' 'Standard of Freedom,' 'Britannia,' 'Economist' and 'Weekly Chronicle.'

How is 'Shirley' getting on—and what is now the general feeling respecting the work?

As far as I can judge from the tone of the Newspapers it seems that those who were most charmed with 'Jane Eyre' are the least pleased with 'Shirley'; they are disappointed at not finding the same excitement, interest, stimulus, while those who spoke disparagingly of 'Jane Eyre'—like 'Shirley' a little better than her predecessor. I suppose its dryer matter suits their dryer minds. But I feel that the fiat for which I wait does not depend on Newspapers—except indeed such newspapers as the 'Examiner'—the monthlies and Quarterlies will pronounce it—I suppose. Mere novel-readers, it is evident, think 'Shirley' something of a failure: Still the majority of the notice has on the whole been favourable: that in the 'Standard of Freedom' was very kindly expressed—and coming from a dissenter—William Howitt[1]—I wonder thereat.

Are you satisfied at Cornhill, or the contrary? I have read part of the 'Caxtons'[2] and when I have finished—will tell you what I think of it—meantime I should very much like to hear your opinion—perhaps I shall keep mine till I see you—whenever that may be. I am trying by degrees to inure myself to the thought

[1]William Howitt (1792–1879), husband of Mary Howitt (see letter dated April 2nd, 1849), wrote innumerable works, of which *Visits to Remarkable Places* (1838–41), and *Homes and Haunts of the Poets* (1847), are best remembered.

[2]*The Caxtons*, a novel by Edward George Bulwer-Lytton, First Baron Lytton, 1849, originally published in *Blackwood's Magazine*.

of some day stepping over to Keighley, taking the train to Leeds —thence to London—and once more venturing to set foot in the strange, busy whirl of the Strand and Cornhill. I want to talk to you a little and to hear by word of mouth how matters are progressing—Whenever I come I must come quietly and but for a short time—I should be unhappy to leave Papa longer than a fortnight.—Believe me, Yours sincerely,

C. BRONTË.

491. *To* AMELIA RINGROSE.

[November 16th, 1849].

DEAR AMELIA,—I write a single line to thank you for your truly interesting letter—it really described your visit so well that I seemed to enjoy it with you—the '*bonny little room*' was before me and all its occupants—Take notice—you will see more of Mr Joe.

Of course I shall be glad to hear from you again—I have the profit of this correspondence all on my side—You give me a pound—I repay you with a farthing—it suits me exactly.— Yours sincerely,

C. BRONTË.

I am sorry to hear so indifferent an account of Ellen—tell me whether she looks better when you again write.

492 (391). *To* ELLEN NUSSEY.

November 16th, 1849.

DEAR ELLEN,—Amelia's letter gave me a full and true account of your visit to Hunsworth. It was really very interesting and very well written. All the little details so nicely put in, making such a graphic whole. I can gather from it that she was an object of special attention. Joe Taylor has written to me to ask an opinion of Miss Ringrose. Perhaps you had better not tell her this. It might embarrass her painfully when he sees her again, and he is certain to call. I gave him a faithful opinion. I said she was what I called truly amiable, actively useful, genuinely good-natured, sufficiently sensible, neither unobservant nor without discrimination, but not highly intellectual, brilliant or profound. I did not, of course, say whether I thought she would suit him or not. I did not treat the subject as if I suspected he had any thoughts of her. I simply answered his question without the slightest comment.

You are not to suppose any of the characters in 'Shirley' intended as literal portraits. It would not suit the rules of art, nor my own feelings, to write in that style. We only suffer reality to *suggest*, never to *dictate*. The heroines are abstractions, and the heroes also. Qualities I have seen, loved, and admired, are here and there put in as decorative gems, to be preserved in that setting. Since you say you could recognise the originals of all except the heroines, pray whom did you suppose the two Moores to represent? I send you a couple of reviews; the one in the 'Examiner' is written by Albany Fonblanque, who is called the most brilliant political writer of the day, a man whose dictum is much thought of in London. The other, in the 'Standard of Freedom,' is written by William Howitt, a Quaker! You must take care of the papers, bring them with you when you come to Haworth. I have some thoughts of getting my London trip over before you come, and then I shall have something to tell you. Amelia gives only a poor account of you. Take care of yourself. I have the dressmaker with me just now. I don't know how I shall like her. Her manners, etc., are not to my taste. Whether she is 'a good hand' I don't yet know. I should be pretty well, if it were not for headaches and indigestion. My chest has been better lately. Good-bye for the present. — Yours faithfully,

C. B.

493. *To* George Smith.

November 19th, 1849.

My dear Sir, — I am sorry that you should have had the trouble of writing to me at a time when business claims all your thoughts, and doubly sorry am I for the cause of this unwonted excess of occupation; it is to be hoped Mr Taylor's health and strength will soon be restored to him, both for your sake and his own.

I thank you for your kind invitation; at first I thought I should be under the necessity of declining it, having received a prior invitation some months ago from a family lately come to reside in London, whose acquaintance I formed in Brussels.[1] But these friends only know me as Miss Brontë, and they are of the class,

[1]The Wheelwrights.

perfectly worthy but in no sort remarkable, to whom I should feel it quite superfluous to introduce Currer Bell; I know they would not understand the author. Under these circumstances my movements would have been very much restrained, and in fact this consideration formed a difficulty in the way of my coming to London at all. I think, however, I might conscientiously spend part of the time with my other friends. Finding me a guest at the house of a publisher, and knowing my tastes, they may and probably will suspect me of literary pursuits, but I care not for that; it would bring none of the *éclat* and bustle which an open declaration of authorship would certainly entail.

As the present does not seem to be a very favourable time for my visit, I will defer it awhile.

With acknowledgments to your Mother and Sisters as well as to yourself, —I am, my dear Sir, Yours sincerely,

C. Brontë.

494 (392). *To* W. S. Williams.

November 19th, 1849.

My dear Sir,—I am very sorry to hear that Mr Taylor's illness has proved so much more serious than was anticipated, but I do hope he is now better. That he should be quite well cannot be as yet expected, for I believe rheumatic fever is a complaint slow to leave the system it has invaded.

Now that I have almost formed the resolution of coming to London, the thought begins to present itself to me under a pleasant aspect. At first it was sad; it recalled the last time I went and with whom, and to whom I came home, and in what dear companionship I again and again narrated all that had been seen, heard, and uttered in that visit. Emily would never go into any sort of society herself, and whenever I went I could on my return communicate to her a pleasure that suited her, by giving the distinct faithful impression of each scene I had witnessed. When pressed to go, she would sometimes say, 'What is the use? Charlotte will bring it all home to me.' And indeed I delighted to please her thus. My occupation is gone now.

I shall come to be lectured. I perceive you are ready with animadversion; you are not at all well satisfied on some points, so I will open my ears to hear, nor will I close my heart against conviction; but I forewarn you, I have my own doctrines, not acquired, but innate, some that I fear cannot be rooted up without tearing away all the soil from which they spring, and leaving only unproductive rock for new seed.

I have read the 'Caxtons,' I have looked at 'Fanny Hervey,'[1] I think I will not write what I think of either—should I see you I will speak it.

Take a hundred, take a thousand of such works and weigh them in the balance against a page of Thackeray. I hope Mr Thackeray is recovered.

The 'Sun,' the 'Morning Herald,' and the 'Critic' came this morning. None of them express disappointment from 'Shirley,' or on the whole compare her disadvantageously with 'Jane.' It strikes me that those worthies—the 'Athenæum,' 'Spectator,' 'Economist,' made haste to be first with their notices that they might give the tone; if so, their manœuvre has not yet quite succeeded.

The 'Critic,' our old friend, is a friend still. Why does the pulse of pain beat in every pleasure? Ellis and Acton Bell are referred to, and where are they? I will not repine. Faith whispers they are not in those graves to which imagination turns—the feeling, thinking, the inspired natures are beyond earth, in a region more glorious. I believe them blessed. I think, I *will* think, my loss has been *their* gain. Does it weary you that I refer to them? If so, forgive me.—Yours sincerely,

C. Brontë.

Before closing this I glanced over the letter enclosed under your cover. Did you read it? It is from a lady, not quite an old maid, but nearly one, she says; no signature or date; a queer but good-natured production, it made me half cry, half laugh. I am sure 'Shirley' has been exciting enough for her, and too exciting. I cannot well reply to the letter since it bears no address, and I am glad—I should not know what to say. She is not sure whether I am a gentleman or not, but I fancy she thinks so. Have you any idea who she is? If I were a gentleman and like my heroes, she suspects she should fall in love with me. She had better not. It would be a pity to cause such a waste of sensibility. You and Mr Smith would not let me announce myself as a single gentleman of mature age in my preface, but if you had permitted it, a great many elderly spinsters would have been pleased.

---

[1] *Fanny Hervey; or, the Mother's Choice*, by Mrs Stirling, 2 vols. 1849.

495 (393). *To* W. S. WILLIAMS.

[November 20th, 1849].

MY DEAR SIR, —You said that if I wished for any copies of 'Shirley' to be sent to individuals I was to name the parties. I have thought of one person to whom I should much like a copy to be offered—Harriet Martineau. For her character—as revealed in her works—I have a lively admiration—a deep esteem. Will you enclose with the volumes the accompanying note.

The letter you forwarded this morning was from Mrs Gaskell —authoress of 'Mary Barton.' She said I was not to answer it, but I cannot help doing so. Her note brought the tears to my eyes: she is a good—she is a great woman—proud am I that I can touch a chord of sympathy in souls so noble. In Mrs Gaskell's nature it mournfully pleases me to fancy a remote affinity to my sister Emily—In Miss Martineau's mind I have always felt the same—though there are wide differences—Both these ladies are above me—certainly far my superiors in attainment and experience—I think I could look up to them if I knew them.

The parcel of newspapers is not yet arrived—it will come some time I suppose—but these delays weary.—I am, my dear Sir, Yours sincerely,

C. BRONTË.

496 (394). *To* W. S. WILLIAMS.

November 22nd, 1849.

MY DEAR SIR, —If it is discouraging to an author to see his work mouthed over by the entirely ignorant and incompetent, it is equally reviving to hear what you have written discussed and analysed by a critic who is master of his subject—by one whose heart feels, whose power grasps the matter he undertakes to handle. Such refreshment Eugène Forçade has given me. Were I to see that man, my impulse would be to say, 'Monsieur, you know me, I shall deem it an honour to know you.'

I do not find that Forçade detects any coarseness in the work —it is for the smaller critics to find that out. The master in the art—the subtle-thoughted, keen-eyed, quick-feeling Frenchman, knows the true nature of the ingredients which went to the composition of the creation he analyses—he knows the true nature of things, and he gives them their right name.

Yours of yesterday has just reached me. Let me, in the first place, express my sincere sympathy with your anxiety on Mrs Williams's account. I know how sad it is when pain and suffering attack those we love, when that mournful guest sickness comes and takes a place in the household circle. That the shadow may soon leave your home is my earnest hope.

Thank you for Sir J. Herschel's[1] note. I am happy to hear Mr Taylor is convalescent. It may, perhaps, be some weeks yet before his hand is well, but that his general health is in the way of re-establishment is a matter of thankfulness.

One of the letters you sent to-day addressed 'Currer Bell' has almost startled me. The writer first describes his family, and then proceeds to give a particular account of himself in colours the most candid, if not, to my ideas, the most attractive. He runs on in a strain of wild enthusiasm about 'Shirley,' and concludes by announcing a fixed, deliberate resolution to institute a search after Currer Bell, and sooner or later to find him out. There is power in the letter—talent; it is at times eloquently expressed. The writer somewhat boastfully intimates that he is acknowledged the possessor of high intellectual attainments, but, if I mistake not, he betrays a temper to be shunned, habits to be mistrusted. While laying claim to the character of being affectionate, warmhearted, and adhesive, there is but a single member of his own family of whom he speaks with kindness. He confesses himself indolent and wilful, but asserts that he is studious and, to some influences, docile. This letter would have struck me no more than the others rather like it have done, but for its rash power, and the disagreeable resolves it announces to seek and find Currer Bell. It almost makes me like a wizard who has raised a spirit he may find it difficult to lay. But I shall not think about it. This sort of fervour often foams itself away in words.

Trusting that the serenity of your home is by this time restored with your wife's health,—I am, yours sincerely,

C. BRONTË.

<hr>

[1] Sir John Frederick William Herschel (1792–1871) the famous astronomer.

497 (395). *To* ELLEN NUSSEY.

[Nov. 22nd, 1849].

DEAR ELLEN,—Amelia—in her last note—mentioned something to me unintelligible about a parcel containing 'Sidney Wine' which I was to receive from Bradford, I waited a day or two before I wrote to see whether it would come, but as no such enigmatical parcel makes its appearance—I shall wait no longer.

'Shirley' works her way. The reviews shower in fast—I send you a couple more by this post—you may take care of them and bring them with the others. The best critique which has yet appeared is in the 'Revue des deux Mondes'; a sort of European, Cosmopolitan periodical whose headquarters are at Paris. Comparatively few reviewers—even in their praise—evince a just comprehension of the author's meaning—Eugène Forçade— the reviewer in question—follows Currer Bell through every winding, discerns every point, discriminates every shade— proves himself master of the subject and lord of the aim. With that man I would shake hands if I saw him. I would say 'you know me, Monsieur—I shall deem it an honour to know you.'

I could not say so much to the mass of London critics. Perhaps I could not say so much to 500 men and women in all the millions of Great Britain. That matters little. My own Conscience I satisfy first—and, having done that—if I further content and delight a Forçade, a Fonblanque and a Thackeraye [sic]—my ambition has had its ration—it is fed—it lies down for the present satisfied—this work done—my faculties have wrought a day's task and earned a day's wages.

I am no teacher—to look on me in that light is to mistake me —to teach is not my vocation—what *I am*, it is useless to say— those whom it concerns feel and find it out. To all others I wish only to be an obscure, steady-going, private character.

To you, dear Nell, I wish to be a sincere friend—give me your faithful regard—I willingly dispense with admiration.

Offer my thanks to Amelia for her kind note—say that such is my encroaching disposition—I must have another from her before she gets an answer from me. My regards to your Mother, Mercy and the Claphams.

C. B.

Have you yet heard from Mary Gorham?

I have just recd yours—all you say about J[oe] T[aylor] and A[melia] agrees with my anticipations—They are scarcely suited—but A. is pliable—it is just a case in which none but those immediately concerned should meddle.

498 (396). *To* Ellen Nussey.

Novb. 26th, '49.

Dear Ellen,—I return Mr V[incent]'s precious note; in my judgment you are quite dispensed from answering it—unless you feel so inclined—there is indeed nothing to answer save the very slight question about Mr and Mrs Clapham—for which he is not entitled to expect you should be at the trouble of taking pen and ink.

It is like you to pronounce the reviews not good enough—and belongs to the same part of your character which will not permit you to bestow unqualified approbation on any dress, decoration &c. belonging to you. Know that the reviews are superb—and were I dissatisfied with them, I should be a conceited ape. Nothing higher is ever said—from *perfectly disinterested motives* of any living author. Wealthy writers who give dinners—and Authors of rank—who have toadies in their train, may command a fulsome strain of flattery—but a mite of praise bestowed on an unknown, obscure author is worth raptures thus *bought*.

If all be well I go to London this week—Wednesday—I think—The dress-maker has done my small matters—pretty well—but I wish you could have looked over them and given a dictum—I insisted on the dresses been [sic] made quite plainly.

The box will come sometime doubtless—but is not come yet—if it is a present from J[oe] T[aylor] explain to him when you see him why he has not been thanked.—Yours in some haste,

C. B.

499. *To* Amelia Ringrose.

[November, 1849].

Dear Amelia,—You ought to publish a treatise called the 'art of Domestic Letter-writing,' of that art you certainly are Mistress—for you beat everything for putting one in possession of the actual place, circumstances, persons which you describe.

In reading your little notes, I am at Brookroyd, I am with
Ellen — I see her sewing, reading, writing, trying on her dresses,
finding fault with them — (that of course — fastidious person as
she is — I never yet knew her express full satisfaction with a gar-
ment) I see her cooking — and you kindly helping her with all.

The secret of the charm you put into these notes lies full as
much in the heart as the head — you know what interests your
correspondent — you think nothing too much trouble to please.
Be thankful for such a disposition — it is a blessing — greater than
more shewy gifts — it is a talent — to be as carefully turned to
account as the highest intellect, the greatest wealth — the rarest
worldly advantages.

My note — as before — is but an acknowledgment of yours —
not an equivalent. I am truly glad you are permitted to stay a
little longer with Ellen — as, if all be well — I am myself going
from home for a week or two. — Yours sincerely,

C. BRONTË.

After the publication of *Shirley*, as we have seen from Charlotte's letter to Mr Williams of November 20th, Mrs Gaskell
communicated with *Currer Bell* through the medium of her publishers, but as yet the true identity of the author was quite unknown, and it was a point of much conjecture and controversy
amongst the literary circles of the day. In a letter to her friend
Miss Eliza Fox, Mrs Gaskell writes on November 26th, 1849:

'. . . Have you read Southey's memoir? but of course you
have, happy creature — and do you know Dr Epps — I think you
do — ask him to tell you who wrote "Jane Eyre" and "Shirley,"
— . . . *Do* tell me who wrote "Jane Eyre." . . .'

A little later, Mrs Gaskell writes:

'Currer Bell (aha! what will you give me for a secret?) She's a
she — that I will tell you — who has sent me "Shirley." '

Charlotte's next letter shows that Harriet Martineau had followed Mrs Gaskell's example.

500 (397). *To* W. S. WILLIAMS.

November 24th, 1849.

DEAR SIR,—I inclose two notes for postage. The note you sent yesterday was from Harriet Martineau; its contents were more than gratifying. I ought to be thankful, and I trust I am for such testimonies of sympathy from the first order of minds. When Mrs Gaskell tells me she shall keep my works as a treasure for her daughters, and when Harriet Martineau testifies affectionate approbation, I feel the sting taken from the strictures of another class of critics. My resolution of seclusion withholds me from communicating further with these ladies at present, but I now know how they are inclined to me—I know how my writings have affected their wise and pure minds. The knowledge is present support and, perhaps, may be future armour.

I trust Mrs Williams's health and, consequently, your spirits are by this time quite restored. If all be well, perhaps I shall see you next week.[1]—Yours sincerely,

C. BRONTË.

[1]Charlotte Brontë went to London on Thursday, Nov. 29th, 1849.

CHAPTER XXII
LITERARY RECOGNITION

IF no great pecuniary reward[1] was destined to attach to Charlotte Brontë's efforts as an author, she received in fullest measure the recognition of her great contemporaries in literature, and particularly of Thackeray.

Thackeray himself has drawn a touching picture of Charlotte Brontë as he first saw her:

I saw her first just as I rose out of an illness from which I had never thought to recover. I remember the trembling little frame, the little hand, the great honest eyes. An impetuous honesty seemed to me to characterise the woman. . . . New to the London world, she entered it with an independent, indomitable spirit of her own; and judged of contemporaries, and especially spied out arrogance or affectation, with extraordinary keenness of vision.

In 1848, Thackeray sent Miss Brontë a copy of *Vanity Fair*, and in 1852, he sent her a copy of *Esmond*, with the inscription: 'Miss Brontë, with W. M. Thackeray's grateful regards, October 28, 1852.'

The second edition of *Jane Eyre* was dedicated to Thackeray as possessed of 'an intellect profounder and more unique than his contemporaries have recognised,' and as 'the first social regenerator of the day.' And when Currer Bell was dead, it was Thackeray who wrote by far the most eloquent tribute to her memory.[2] When a copy of Laurence's portrait of Thackeray was sent to Haworth by Mr George Smith, Charlotte Brontë stood in front of it and, half playfully, half seriously, shook her fist, apostrophising its original as 'Thou Titan!'

[1]Charlotte Brontë received £1,500 in all for the copyright of her three novels, *Jane Eyre*, *Shirley*, and *Villette*.

[2]*Emma*. The Fragment of a Story by Charlotte Brontë. With an Introduction entitled *The Last Sketch* by W. M. Thackeray. *The Cornhill Magazine*, Vol. I, 1860.

With all this hero-worship, it may be imagined that no favourable criticism gave her more unqualified pleasure than that which came from her 'master,' as she was not indisposed to consider one who was only seven years her senior, and whose best books were practically contemporaneous with her own. People had indeed suggested that *Jane Eyre* might have been written by Thackeray under a pseudonym; others had implied, knowing that there was 'something about a woman' in Thackeray's life that it was written by a mistress of the great novelist. Indeed, the *Quarterly* had half hinted as much. Currer Bell, knowing nothing of the gossip of London, had dedicated her book in single-minded enthusiasm. Her distress was keen when it was revealed to her that the wife of Mr Thackeray, like the wife of Rochester in *Jane Eyre*, was of unsound mind. Thackeray writes to Mr Brookfield,[1] in October 1848, as follows:

'Old Dilke of the *Athenæum* vows that Procter and his wife, between them, wrote *Jane Eyre*; and when I protest ignorance, says, "Pooh! you know who wrote it—you are the deepest rogue in England, etc." I wonder whether it can be true? It is just possible. And then what a singular circumstance is the + fire of the two dedications' [*Jane Eyre* to Thackeray, *Vanity Fair* to Barry Cornwall].

It cannot be said that Charlotte Brontë and Thackeray gained by personal contact. 'With him I was painfully stupid,' she says. It was the case of Heine and Goethe over again. Heine in the presence of the king of German literature could talk only of the plums in his garden. Charlotte Brontë in the presence of her hero Thackeray could not express herself with the vigour and intelligence which belonged to her correspondence with Mr Williams. Miss Brontë, again, was hypercritical of the smaller vanities of men, and, as has been pointed out, she emphasised in *Villette* a trivial piece of not unpleasant egotism on Thackeray's part after a lecture—his asking her if she had liked it. This question, which nine men out of ten would be prone to ask of a woman friend, was 'over-eagerness' and '*naïveté*' in her eyes.

---

[1] *A Collection of Letters to W. M. Thackeray*, 1847–1855 (Smith and Elder).

Thackeray, on his side, found conversation difficult, if we may judge by a reminiscence by his daughter Lady Ritchie:

One of the most notable persons who ever came into our bow-windowed drawing-room in Young Street is a guest never to be forgotten by me—a tiny, delicate, little person, whose small hand nevertheless grasped a mighty lever which set all the literary world of that day vibrating. I can still see the scene quite plainly—the hot summer evening, the open windows, the carriage driving to the door as we all sat silent and expectant; my father, who rarely waited, waiting with us; our governess and my sister and I all in a row, and prepared for the great event. We saw the carriage stop, and out of it sprang the active, well-knit figure of Mr George Smith, who was bringing Miss Brontë to see our father. My father, who had been walking up and down the room, goes out into the hall to meet his guests, and then, after a moment's delay, the door opens wide, and the two gentlemen come in, leading a tiny, delicate, serious, little lady, pale, with fair straight hair, and steady eyes. She may be a little over thirty; she is dressed in a little *barège* dress, with a pattern of faint green moss. She enters in mittens, in silence, in seriousness; our hearts are beating with wild excitement. This, then, is the authoress, the unknown power whose books have set all London talking, reading, speculating; some people even say our father wrote the books—the wonderful books. To say that we little girls had been given *Jane Eyre* to read scarcely represents the facts of the case; to say that we had taken it without leave, read bits here and read bits there, been carried away by an undreamed-of and hitherto unimagined whirlwind into things, times, places, all utterly absorbing, and at the same time absolutely unintelligible to us, would more accurately describe our state of mind on that summer's evening as we look at Jane Eyre—the great Jane Eyre —the tiny little lady. The moment is so breathless that dinner comes as a relief to the solemnity of the occasion, and we all smile as my father stoops to offer his arm; for, though genius she may be, Miss Brontë can barely reach his elbow. My own personal impressions are that she is somewhat grave and stern, especially to forward little girls who wish to chatter. Mr George Smith has since told me how she afterwards remarked upon my father's wonderful forbearance and gentleness with our uncalled-for incursions into the conversation. She sat gazing at him with kindling eyes of interest, lighting up with a sort of illumination every now and then as she answered him. I can see her bending forward over the table, not eating, but listening to what he said as he carved the dish before him.

I think it must have been on this very occasion that my father invited some of his friends in the evening to meet Miss Brontë — for everybody was interested and anxious to see her. Mrs Crowe,[1] the reciter of ghost-stories, was there. Mrs Brookfield, Mrs Carlyle, Mr Carlyle himself was present, so I am told, railing at the appearance of cockneys upon Scotch mountain sides; there were also too many Americans for his taste, 'but the Americans were as gods compared to the cockneys,' says the philosopher. Besides the Carlyles, there were Mrs Elliott and Miss Perry, Mrs Procter[2] and her daughter, most of my father's habitual friends and companions. In the recent life of Lord Houghton I was amused to see a note quoted in which Lord Houghton also was convened. Would that he had been present — perhaps the party would have gone off better. It was a gloomy and a silent evening. Every one waited for the brilliant conversation which never began at all. Miss Brontë retired to the sofa in the study and murmured a low word now and then to our kind governess, Miss Truelock. The room looked very dark, the lamp began to smoke a little, the conversation grew dimmer and more dim, the ladies sat round still expectant, my father was too much perturbed by the gloom and the silence to be able to cope with it at all. Mrs Brookfield, who was in the doorway by the study, near the corner in which Miss Brontë was sitting, leant forward with a little commonplace, since brilliance was not to be the order of the evening. 'Do you like London, Miss Brontë?' she said; another silence, a pause, then Miss Brontë answers, 'Yes and No,' very gravely. Mrs Brookfield has herself reported the conversation. My sister and I were much too young to be bored in those days; alarmed, impressed we might be, but not yet bored. A party was a party, a lioness was a lioness; and — shall I confess it? — at that time an extra dish of biscuits was enough to mark the evening. We felt all the importance of the occasion: tea spread in the dining-room, ladies in the drawing-room. We roamed about inconveniently, no doubt, and excitedly, and in one of my incursions crossing the hall, after Miss Brontë had left, I was surprised

---

[1]Catherine Crowe (1800?–1876) novelist and writer on the supernatural. Author of *Susan Hopley* (1841), *Lilly Dawson* (1847), *The Night Side of Nature* (1848), and other works.

[2]Mrs Procter, wife of Bryan Waller Procter (Barry Cornwall), and mother of Adelaide Anne Procter, the poetess.

to see my father opening the front door with his hat on. He put his fingers to his lips, walked out into the darkness, and shut the door quietly behind him. When I went back to the drawing-room again, the ladies asked me where he was. I vaguely answered that I thought he was coming back. I was puzzled at the time, nor was it all made clear to me till long years afterwards, when one day Mrs Procter asked me if I knew what had happened once when my father had invited a party to meet Jane Eyre at his house. It was one of the dullest evenings she had ever spent in her life, she said. And then with a good deal of humour she described the situation—the ladies who had all come expecting so much delightful conversation, and the gloom and the constraint, and how, finally, overwhelmed by the situation, my father had quietly left the room, left the house, and gone off to his club. The ladies waited, wondered, and finally departed also; and as we were going up to bed with our candles after everybody was gone, I remember two pretty Miss L——s, in shiny silk dresses, arriving, full of expectation. . . . We still said we thought our father would soon be back, but the Miss L——s declined to wait upon the chance, laughed, and drove away again almost immediately.[1]

Other interesting references to Charlotte Brontë's meetings with Thackeray are contained in *Mrs Brookfield and Her Circle*, by Charles and Frances Brookfield:

It was towards the end of November (1849), and when Mr Thackeray was fairly well restored to health again, that he gave a dinner to Miss Brontë, then in London practically for the first time. Mrs Brookfield says, speaking of that lady and that visit:

There was just then a fashion for wearing a plait of hair across the head, and Miss Brontë, a timid little woman with a firm mouth, did not possess a large enough quantity of hair to enable her to form a plait, so therefore wore a very obvious crown of brown silk. Mr Thackeray on his way down to dinner addressed her as Currer Bell. She tossed her head and said 'she believed there were books being published by a person named Currer Bell . . . but the person he was talking to was Miss Brontë—and she saw no connection between the two.'

[1] *Chapters from Some Memories*, by Anne Thackeray Ritchie.

Charlotte Brontë was present at some of the lectures[1] and while they were still going on Thackeray most amiably arranged a party for her. As the first he had made for her ... was not a great success, he now, in order to get together what he thought would be an interesting entertainment, invited several lady authors to meet her, as well as one or two of his especial intimates. Mrs Elliott and Miss Perry were amongst these, and of this event Miss Perry says to Mrs Brookfield, in a letter in which she speaks back upon those times:—'there was no one present but those advanced ladies, about six or seven of them, and by accident, Carlyle, who had not been asked, as Thackeray said in his invitation to Jane (Mrs Elliott) and me, "and there will not be a Jack amongst us." I remember every detail of it, such a comedy it turned out. I have somewhere dear Thackeray's amusing list of the names he asked and their works.'

The probable reason of the failure of the first party was perhaps Miss Brontë's own inability to fall in with the easy *badinage* of the well-bred people with whom she found herself surrounded.

Alert minded and keen brained herself, she was accustomed only to the narrow literalness of her own circle, and could scarcely have understood the rapid give and take, or the easy conversational grace of these new friends. Also she may hardly have appreciated the charming conciseness with which they told their stories; for the members of this set were the first to break away from the pedantic ponderousness usual with all the great talkers, even those of their own time; and Miss Brontë, a square peg in a round hole, was doubtless, too, dismayed at anecdotes that gained in elegance as they lost in accuracy.

Charlotte Brontë stayed with but two friends in London, with her publisher, Mr George Smith, and his mother, and at 29 Phillimore Gardens, Kensington, with Dr Wheelwright, and his daughter Lætitia, who had been Charlotte's great friend in Brussels.

Miss Wheelwright and her sisters well remembered certain episodes in connection with these London visits. They recalled Charlotte's anxiety and trepidation at the prospect of meeting Thackeray, her simple, dainty dress, her shy demeanour, and her

[1]Thackeray's lectures on *The English Humorists of the Eighteenth Century*. See letters dated May 29th, 1851, *et seq.*

absolutely unspoiled character. They said it was in the *Illustrated London News*, about the time of the publication of *Shirley*, that they first learnt that Currer Bell and Charlotte Brontë were one. They would, however, have known that *Shirley* was by a Brussels pupil, they declared, from the absolute resemblance of Hortense Moore to one of their governesses—Mlle Haussé.

George Smith, in his reminiscences of Charlotte Brontë published in the Cornhill Magazine[1], gives the following description of her appearance:

She was very small, and had a quaint old-fashioned look. Her head seemed too large for her body. She had fine eyes, but her face was marred by the shape of the mouth and by the complexion. There was but little feminine charm about her; and of this fact she herself was uneasily and perpetually conscious. It may seem strange that the possession of genius did not lift her above the weakness of an excessive anxiety about her personal appearance. But I believe that she would have given all her genius and her fame to have been beautiful. Perhaps few women ever existed more anxious to be pretty than she, or more angrily conscious of the circumstance that she was *not* pretty.

What Charlotte Brontë thought of her publisher may be gathered from her frank acknowledgment that he was the original of Dr John in *Villette*, as his mother was the original of Mrs Bretton—perhaps the two most entirely charming characters in Charlotte Brontë's novels. Mrs Smith and her son lived, at the beginning of the friendship, at Westbourne Place, but afterwards removed to Gloucester Terrace, and Charlotte stayed with them at both houses. It was from the former that her next letter was addressed.

501 (398). *To* ELLEN NUSSEY.

WESTBOURNE PLACE, BISHOP'S ROAD,
LONDON, [December 4th, 1849].

DEAR ELLEN,—I have just remembered that as you do not know my address, you cannot write to me till you get it; it is as above.

[1] *Charlotte Brontë*, by George M. Smith. *The Cornhill Magazine*, No. 54 December, 1900.

I came to this big Babylon last Thursday, and have been in what seems to me a sort of whirl ever since, for changes, scenes, and stimulus which would be a trifle to others, are much to me. I found when I mentioned to Mr Smith my plan of going to Dr Wheelwright's it would not do at all—he would have been seriously hurt; he made his mother write to me, and thus I was persuaded to make my principal stay at his house. So far I have found no reason to regret this decision. Mrs Smith received me at first like one who had received the strictest orders to be scrupulously attentive. I had fires in my bedroom evening and morning, two wax candles, etc. and Mrs Smith and her daughters seemed to look upon me with a mixture of respect and alarm. But all this is changed—that is to say, the attention and politeness continue as great as ever, but the alarm and estrangement are quite gone. She treats me as if she liked me, and I begin to like her much; kindness is a potent heartwinner. I had not judged too favourably of her son on a first impression; he pleases me much. I like him better even as a son and brother than as a man of business. Mr Williams, too, is really most gentlemanly and well-informed. His weak points he certainly has, but these are not seen in society. Mr Taylor—the little man—has again shown his parts; of him I have not yet come to a clear decision; abilities he has, for he rules the firm (which Dr Wheelwright told me the other day, is considerably the largest publishing concern in London) he keeps 40 young men under strict control of his iron will. His young superior likes him, which, to speak truth is more than I do at present; in fact, I suspect he is of the Helstone order of men—rigid, despotic, and self-willed. He tries to be very kind and even to express sympathy sometimes, but he does not manage it. He has a determined, dreadful nose in the middle of his face which when poked into my countenance cuts into my soul like iron. Still he is horribly intelligent, quick, searching, sagacious, and with a memory of relentless tenacity. To turn to Williams after him, or to Smith himself, is to turn from granite to easy down or warm fur. I have seen Thackeray.

No more at present from yours, etc.,

C. BRONTË.

How is Amelia getting on? What more of J. Taylor? Give my love to her.

502 (510). *To* The Rev. P. Brontë.

Dec. 4th, 1849.

Dear Papa,—I must write another line to you to tell you how I am getting on. I have seen a great many things since I left home about which I hope to talk to you at future tea-times at home. I have been to the theatre and seen Macready in 'Macbeth,' I have seen the pictures in the National Gallery. I have seen a beautiful exhibition of Turner's paintings, and yesterday I saw Mr Thackeray. He dined here with some other gentlemen. He is a very tall man—above six feet high, with a peculiar face—not handsome, very ugly indeed, generally somewhat stern and satirical in expression, but capable also of a kind look. He was not told who I was, he was not introduced to me, but I soon saw him looking at me through his spectacles; and when we all rose to go down to dinner he just stepped quietly up and said, 'Shake hands'; so I shook hands. He spoke very few words to me, but when he went away he shook hands again in a very kind way. It is better, I should think, to have him for a friend than an enemy, for he is a most formidable-looking personage. I listened to him as he conversed with the other gentlemen. All he says is most simple, but often cynical, harsh, and contradictory. I get on quietly. Most people know me, I think, but they are far too well bred to show that they know me, so that there is none of that bustle or that sense of publicity I dislike.

I hope you continue pretty well; be sure to take care of yourself. The weather here is exceedingly changeful, and often damp and misty, so that it is necessary to guard against taking cold. I do not mean to stay in London above a week longer, but I shall write again two or three days before I return. You need not give yourself the trouble of answering this letter unless you have something particular to say. Remember me to Tabby and Martha.—I remain, dear papa, your affectionate daughter,

C. Brontë.

503. CATHERINE WINKWORTH *to* ELIZA PATERSON.

16 GREAT ORMOND STREET,
5th Dec. 1849.

. . . So you like 'Shirley' better than 'Jane Eyre'; so do I, in some points. In power and in descriptions of scenery, there is nothing in 'Shirley' which seems to me to come up to some parts of 'Jane Eyre,' but then there is nothing also in 'Shirley' like the disagreeable parts of 'Jane Eyre.' The book is infinitely more original and full of character than the ordinary run of novels—it belongs quite to a higher class—but it is also infinitely below such as 'Mary Barton'[1] and 'Deerbrook.'[2] Caroline and Mr Helstone are thoroughly good characters. Shirley and Mrs Pryor are good ideas, but badly worked out—the rest seem to me all exaggerated—Oh, Hortense Moore should be excepted, she is good, too. The conversations seem to me astonishingly poor; here and there comes an eloquent speech, as in Shirley's conversation with Mr Yorke, but the stiffness and dryness of the whole book, its utter want of brilliancy of wit or humour, and the unhappy tone of all the meditations make it altogether painful. That is not, however, so much to be wondered at, when one knows that the author is herself threatened with consumption at this time, and has lost her two sisters, Ellis and Acton Bell, by it. Their real name is Brontë. . . .[3]

504 (399). *To* ELLEN NUSSEY.

LONDON, [December 9th, 1849].

DEAR ELLEN,—I was very glad to get the two notes from Brookroyd, yours and Amelia's. I am only going to pen a very hasty reply now, as there are several people in the room and I cannot write in company. You seem to suppose I must be very happy, dear Nell, and I see you have twenty romantic notions in your head about me. These last you may dismiss at once. As to being happy, I am under scenes and circumstances of excitement; but I suffer acute pain sometimes, mental pain, I mean. At

[1] By Mrs E. C. Gaskell.
[2] By Harriet Martineau.
[3] *Memorials of Two Sisters, Susanna and Catherine Winkworth*, Edited by Margaret

J. Shaen, 1908. Charlotte Brontë afterwards met the Misses Winkworth at the home of Mrs Gaskell.

the moment Mr Thackeray presented himself, I was thoroughly faint from inanition, having eaten nothing since a very slight breakfast, and it was then *seven* o'clock in the evening. Excitement and exhaustion together made savage work of me that evening. What he thought of me I cannot tell. This evening I am going to meet Miss Martineau. She has written to me most kindly. She knows me only as Currer Bell. I am going alone in the carriage; how I shall get on I do not know. If Mrs Smith were not kind, I should sometimes be miserable, but she treats me almost affectionately, her attentions never flag.

I have seen many things. I hope some day to tell you what. Yesterday I went over the New Houses of Parliament with Mr Williams. An attack of rheumatic fever has kept poor Mr Taylor out of the way since I wrote last. I am sorry for his sake. It grows quite dark. I must stop. I shall not stay in London a day longer than I first intended. On those points I form my resolutions and will not be shaken.

The thundering 'Times' has attacked me savagely.—Yours sincerely,

C. BRONTË.

Sunday.—Love to Amelia, and thanks. I can hardly tell what to say about her and J. T. I do not like to think about it; I shudder sometimes.

One of the most interesting of Charlotte's new friends was Harriet Martineau. Before leaving Haworth she had asked that a copy of her book be sent to Harriet Martineau with the following note enclosed:

'Currer Bell offers a copy of *Shirley* to Miss Martineau's acceptance, in acknowledgment of the pleasure and profit she-[*sic*] he has derived from her works. When C. B. first read *Deerbrook* he tasted a new and keen pleasure, and experienced a genuine benefit. In his mind *Deerbrook* ranks with the writings that have really done him good, added to his stock of ideas and rectified his views of life.'[1]

Miss Martineau replied, addressing her letter to 'Currer Bell, Esq.,' but beginning it 'Dear Madam.' On December 8th she received a letter signed 'Currer Bell,' saying that the writer was in town and desired to see her. Miss Martineau has left an amusing

---

[1] Harriet Martineau's *Autobiography*, vol. ii.

account of the interview, the arrival of a male visitor six feet high, whom some of her friends believed to be the new author, and finally the appearance of 'Miss Brontë,' whom the footman announced as 'Miss Brogden.' 'I thought her the smallest creature I had ever seen, except at a fair,' was Miss Martineau's first impression.

Mrs Gaskell describes this meeting in a letter to a friend.

505. MRS GASKELL *to* ANN SHAEN.[1]
December 21st, 1849.

. . . Have you heard that Harriet Martineau has sworn an eternal friendship with the authoress of 'Shirley,' if not I'll tell you. She sent 'Shirley' to Harriet Martineau. H. M. acknowledged it in a note directed to Currer Bell Esq.—but inside written to a *lady*. Then came an answer requesting a personal interview. This was towards or about last Saturday week, and the time appointed was 6 o'clock on Sunday Eveng and the place appointed was at Mr Richard Martineau's (married a Miss Needham) in Hyde Park Square, so Mr and Mrs R. Martineau and Harriet M. sat with early tea before them, awaiting six o'clock, and their mysterious visitor, when lo! and behold, as the clock struck in walked a little, very little, bright haired sprite, looking not above 15, very unsophisticated, neat and tidy. She sat down and had tea with them, her name being still unknown; she said to H. M. 'What did you really think of "Jane Eyre"?' H. M. 'I thought it a first rate book.' Whereupon the little sprite went red all over with pleasure. After tea Mr and Mrs R. M. withdrew, and left sprite to a 2 hours tête à tête with H. M. to whom she revealed her name and the history of her life. Her father a Yorkshire clergyman who has never slept out of his house for 26 years;[2] she has lived a most retired life;—her first visit to London, never been in society and many other particulars which H. M. is not at liberty to divulge any more than her name, which she keeps a profound secret; but Thackeray does *not*. H. M. is charmed with her; she is full of life and power &c. &c. and H. M. hopes to be of great use to her. There! that's all I know, but I think it's a pretty good deal! . . .

[1]Ann Shaen, sister of William Shaen (1822–1887) who married Emily Winkworth, sister of Susanna and Catherine Winkworth, on September 2nd, 1851. Their home was at Crix, near Chelmsford.

[2]Not correct. He visited Brussels and returned home through France in Feby., 1842, and spent several weeks in Manchester in Aug. and Sept., 1846.

506. *To* MRS SMITH, 4, *Westbourne Place.*

December 17th, 1849.

MY DEAR MRS SMITH,—I am once again at home, where I arrived safely on Saturday afternoon, and, I am thankful to say, found papa quite well.

It was a fortunate chance that obliged me to stay at Derby, for by the time I had travelled so far weariness quite overpowered me; I was glad to go to bed as soon as I reached the inn; an unbroken sleep refreshed me against the next day, and I performed the rest of the journey with comparative ease. Tell Miss Smith that her little boots are a perfect treasure of comfort; they kept my feet quite warm the whole way.

It made me rather sad to leave you; regretful partings are the inevitable penalty of pleasant visits. I believe I made no special acknowledgement of your kindness when I took leave, but I thought you very kind. I am glad to have had the opportunity of knowing you, and, whether I ever see you again or not, I must always recall with grateful pleasure the fortnight I spent under your roof.

Write a line to me when you have time, to tell me how you and your daughters are; remember me to them all (including good, quiet, studious little Bell); accept for them and yourself the assurance of my true regard, and believe me, my dear Madam, — Yours sincerely,

CHARLOTTE BRONTË.

I enclose a note for Mr Smith; he must have a word to himself.

507. *To* GEORGE SMITH.

December 17th, 1849.

MY DEAR SIR,—I should not feel content if I omitted writing to you as well as to your mother, for I must tell you as well as her how much the pleasure of my late visit was enhanced by her most considerate attention and goodness. As to yourself, what can I say? Nothing. And it is as well; words are not at all needed. Very easy is it to discover that with you to gratify others is to gratify yourself; to serve others is to afford yourself a pleasure. I suppose you will experience your share of ingratitude and encroachment, but do not let them alter you. Happily, they are the less likely to do this because you are half a Scotchman, and therefore must have inherited a fair share of prudence to qualify your generosity, and of caution to protect your benevolence. Currer Bell bids you farewell for the present.

C. B.

508 (400). *To* LÆTITIA WHEELWRIGHT.

HAWORTH, KEIGHLEY, December 17th, 1849.

MY DEAR LÆTITIA,—I have just time to save the post by writing a brief note. I reached home safely on Saturday afternoon, and, I am thankful to say, found papa quite well.

The evening after I left you passed better than I expected. Thanks to my substantial lunch and cheering cup of coffee, I was able to wait the eight o'clock dinner with complete resignation, and to endure its length quite courageously, nor was I too much exhausted to converse; and of this I was glad, for otherwise I know my kind host and hostess would have been much disappointed. There were only seven gentlemen at dinner besides Mr Smith, but of these, five were critics—a formidable band, including the literary Rhadamanthi of the 'Times,' the 'Athenæum,' the 'Examiner,' the 'Spectator,' and the 'Atlas': men more dreaded in the world of letters than you can conceive. I did not know how much their presence and conversation had excited me till they were gone, and then reaction commenced. When I had retired for the night I wished to sleep; the effort to do so was vain—I could not close my eyes. Night passed, morning came, and I rose without having known a moment's slumber. So utterly worn out was I when I got to Derby, that I was obliged to stay there all night.

The post is going. Give my affectionate love to your mamma, Emily, Fanny, and Sarah Anne. Remember me respectfully to your papa, and—Believe me, dear Lætitia, yours faithfully,

C. BRONTË.

509 (402). *To* ELLEN NUSSEY.

HAWORTH, December 18th, 1849.

DEAR ELLEN,—Here I am at Haworth once more. I feel as if I had come out of an exciting whirl. Not that the hurry or stimulus would have seemed much to one accustomed to society and change, but to me they were very marked. My strength and spirits too often proved quite insufficient for the demand on their exertions. I used to bear up as well and as long as I possibly could, for, whenever I flagged, I could see Mr Smith became disturbed; he always thought that something had been said or done to annoy me, which never once happened, for I met with perfect good-breeding even from antagonists, men who had done their best or worst to write me down. I explained to him, over and over again, that my occasional silence was only failure of the power to talk, never of the will, but still he always seemed to fear there was another cause underneath.

Mrs Smith is rather stern, but she has sense and discrimination; she watched me very narrowly when surrounded by gentlemen, she never took her eye from me. I liked the surveillance, both when it kept guard over me amongst many, or only with her cherished one. She soon, I am convinced, saw in what light I received all, Thackeray included. Her 'George' is a very fine specimen of a young English man-of-business; so I regard him, and I am proud to be one of his props.

Thackeray is a Titan of mind. His presence and powers impress me deeply in an intellectual sense; I do not see him or know him as a man. All the others are subordinate to these. I have esteem for some, and, I trust, courtesy for all. I do not, of course, know what they thought of me, but I believe most of them expected me to come out in a more marked, eccentric, striking light. I believe they desired more to admire and more to blame. I felt sufficiently at my ease with all except Thackeray; and with him I was painfully stupid.

Now, dear Nell, when can you come to Haworth? Settle and let me know as soon as you can. Give my best love to all. I enclose a word for Amelia. Have things come to any crisis in that quarter? I cannot help thinking of the lion mated with the lamb, the leopard with the kid. It does not content me. The first year or two may be well enough. I do not like to look forward any farther. Let nothing prevent you from coming.—Yours,   C. B.

510 (401). *To* W. S. WILLIAMS.

December 19th, 1849.

MY DEAR SIR,—I am again at home; and after the first sensations consequent on returning to a place more dumb and vacant than it once was, I am beginning to feel settled. I think the contrast with London does not make Haworth more desolate; on the contrary, I have gleaned ideas, images, pleasant feelings, such as may perhaps cheer many a long winter evening.

You ask my opinion of your daughters. I wish I could give you one worth acceptance. A single evening's acquaintance does not suffice with me to form an *opinion*, it only leaves on my mind an *impression*. They impressed me, then, as pleasing in manners and appearance: Ellen's is a character to which I could soon attach myself, and Fanny and Louisa have each their separate advantages. I can, however, read more in a face like Mrs Williams's than in the smooth young features of her daughters — time, trial, and exertion write a distinct hand, more legible than smile or dimple. I was told you had once some thoughts of bringing out Fanny as a professional singer, and it was added Fanny did not like the project. I thought to myself, if she does not like it, it can never be successfully executed. It seems to me that to achieve triumph in a career so arduous, the artist's own bent to the course must be inborn, decided, resistless. There should be no urging, no goading; native genius and vigorous will should lend their wings to the aspirant — nothing less can lift her to real fame, and who would rise feebly only to fall ignobly? An inferior artist, I am sure, you would not wish your daughter to be, and if she is to stand in the foremost rank, only her own courage and resolve can place her there; so, at least, the case appears to me. Fanny probably looks on publicity as degrading, and I believe that for a woman it is degrading if it is not glorious. If I could not be a Lind, I would not be a singer.

Brief as my visit to London was, it must for me be memorable. I sometimes fancied myself in a dream — I could scarcely credit the reality of what passed. For instance, when I walked into the room and put my hand into Miss Martineau's, the action of saluting her and the fact of her presence seemed visionary. Again, when Mr Thackeray was announced, and I saw him enter, looked up at his tall figure, heard his voice, the whole incident was truly dream-like, I was only certain it was true because I became miserably destitute of self-possession. *Amour propre* suffers terribly under such circumstances: woe to him that thinks of himself in the presence of intellectual greatness! Had I not been obliged to speak, I could have managed well, but it behoved me to answer when addressed, and the effort was torture—I spoke stupidly.

As to the band of critics, I cannot say they overawed me much; I enjoyed the spectacle of them greatly. The two contrasts, Forster and Chorley, have each a certain edifying carriage and conversation good to contemplate. I by no means dislike Mr Forster—quite the contrary, but the distance from his loud swagger to Thackeray's simple port is as the distance from Shakespeare's writing to Macready's acting.

Mr Chorley tantalised me. He is a peculiar specimen—one whom you could set yourself to examine, uncertain whether, when you had probed all the small recesses of his character, the result would be utter contempt and aversion, or whether for the sake of latent good you would forgive obvious evil. One could well pardon his unpleasant features, his strange voice, even his very foppery and grimace, if one found these disadvantages connected with living talent and any spark of genuine goodness. If there is nothing more than acquirement, smartness, and the affectation of philanthropy, Chorley is a fine creature.

Remember me kindly to your wife and daughters, and—Believe me, yours sincerely,

C. BRONTË.

511 (403). *To* ELLEN NUSSEY.

December 22nd, 1849.

DEAR ELLEN,—I should have answered yours yesterday, had I not received by the same post a missive from Joseph Taylor announcing that he was coming to dinner that blessed day, and shortly after he made his appearance. This errand was to persuade me to go to Birmingham to spend Christmas at Hay Hall with the Dixons. Of course I could not go. He stayed till about 6 o'clock—he talked a good deal. . . . I don't think it will make the least difference with him. He had written to me a few days before, explaining the degree and sort of interest he took in Amelia; I will show you the letter when you come.

Let nothing prevent you from coming on Thursday. There is a train leaves Bradford at a quarter past twelve and arrives at Keighley about thirty-four minutes past, perhaps you had better come by that. I will send a gig to meet you if possible; if I cannot get one you must hire a conveyance at the Devonshire Arms — don't walk. Joe Taylor says he will come here again while you are with me, after he has been to Tranby and knows his doom.

C. B.

512 (405). *To* W. S. WILLIAMS.

Jany 3rd, 1850.

MY DEAR SIR, — I have to acknowledge the receipt of the 'Morning Chronicle' with a good review — and of the 'Church of England Quarterly' and the 'Westminster' with bad ones: I have also to thank you for your letter which would have been answered sooner had I been alone, but just now I am enjoying the treat of my friend Ellen's society and she makes me indolent and negligent — I am too busy talking to her all day to do anything else. You allude to the subject of female friendship and express wonder at the infrequency of sincere attachments amongst women — As to married women, I can well understand that they should be absorbed in their husbands and children — but single women often like each other much and derive great solace from their mutual regard. Friendship however is a plant which cannot be forced — true friendship is no gourd springing in a night and withering in a day. When I first saw Ellen I did not care for her — we were schoolfellows — in the course of time we learnt each others faults and good points — we were contrasts — still we suited — affection was first a germ, then a sapling — then a strong tree: now — no new friend, however lofty or profound in intellect — not even Miss Martineau herself could be to me what Ellen is, yet she is no more than a conscientious, observant, calm, well-bred Yorkshire girl. She is without romance — if she attempts to read poetry — or poetic prose aloud — I am irritated and deprive her of her book — if she talks of it I stop my ears — but she is good — she is true — she is faithful and I love her.

Since I came home Miss Martineau has written me a long and truly kind letter — she invites me to visit her at Ambleside — I like the idea, whether I can realize it or not — it is pleasant to have in prospect.

You ask me to write to Mrs Williams; I would rather she wrote to me first, and let her send any kind of letter she likes, without studying mood or manner. — Yours sincerely,

C. BRONTË.

Meanwhile the interest which *Shirley* was exciting in Currer Bell's home circle was not confined to the curates. Here is a letter which Canon Heald, the prototype of 'Cyril Hall', wrote at this time:

513 (406). *To* ELLEN NUSSEY.

BIRSTALL, NEAR LEEDS,
January 8th, 1850.

DEAR ELLEN, — Fame says you are on a visit with the renowned Currer Bell, the 'great unknown' of the present day. The celebrated 'Shirley' has just found its way hither. And as one always reads a book with more interest when one has a correct insight into the writer's designs, I write to ask a favour, which I ought not to be regarded as presumptuous in saying that I think I have a species of claim to ask, on the ground of a sort of 'poetical justice.' The interpretation of this enigma is, that the story goes that either I or my father, I do not exactly know which, are part of 'Currer Bell's' stock-in-trade, under the title of Mr Hall, in that Mr Hall is represented as black, bilious, and of dismal aspect, stooping a trifle, and indulging a little now and then in the indigenous dialect. This seems to sit very well on your humble servant — other traits do better for my good father than myself. However, though I had no idea that I should be made a means to amuse the public, Currer Bell is perfectly welcome to what she can make of so unpromising a subject. But I think *I have a fair claim in return to be let into the secret of the company I have got into.* Some of them are good enough to tell, and need no Œdipus to solve the riddle. I can tabulate, for instance, the Yorke family for the Taylors, Mr Moore — Mr Cartwright, and Mr Helstone is clearly meant for Mr Roberson, though the authoress has evidently got her idea of his character through an unfavourable medium, and does not understand the full value of one of the most admirable characters I ever knew or expect to know. Mary thinks she descries Cecilia Crowther and Miss Johnstone (afterwards Mrs Westerman) in two old maids.

Now pray get us a full light on all other names and localities that are adumbrated in this said 'Shirley.' When some of the prominent characters will be recognised by every one who knows our quarters, there can be no harm in letting one know who may be intended by the rest. And, if necessary, I will bear Currer Bell harmless, and not let the world know that I have my intelligence from headquarters. As I said before, I repeat now, that as I or mine are part of the stock-in-trade, I think I have an equitable claim to this intelligence, by way of my dividend. Mary and Harriet wish also to get at this information; and the latter at all events seems to have her own peculiar claim, as fame says she is 'in the book' too. One had need 'walk . . . warily in these dangerous days,' when, as Burns (is it not he?) says —

'A chield's among you taking notes,
And faith he'll prent it.' —

Yours sincerely,
W. M. HEALD.

Mary and Harriet unite with me in the best wishes of the season to you and C—— B——. Pray give my best respects to Mr Brontë also, who may have some slight remembrance of me as a child. I just remember him when at Hartshead.

514. *To* MRS SMITH, 4, *Westbourne Place.*

4 WESTBOURNE PLACE,
Jany 9th, '50.

MY DEAR MRS SMITH, — Since you are kind enough to answer my letter, you shall occasionally hear from me, but not too often; you shall not be 'bored' (as Mr Thackeray would say) with too frequent a call for replies.

Speaking of Mr Thackeray, you ask me what I think of his Christmas Book. I think it is like himself, and all he says and writes; harsh and kindly, wayward and wise, benignant and bitter; its pages are over-shadowed with cynicism, and yet they sparkle with feeling. As to his abuse of Rowena and of women in general — I will tell you my dear Madam what I think he deserves — first to be arrested, to be kept in prison for a month, then to be tried by a jury of twelve matrons, and subsequently to undergo any punishment they might think proper to inflict; and I trust they would not spare him; for the scene of Rowena's death-bed

Vol. III f

alone he merits the extremest penalty — the poor woman is made
with her last breath to prove that a narrow rankling jealousy
was a sentiment more rooted in her heart than either conjugal or
maternal love. It is too bad. For that scene his mother ought to
chastise him.

You suggest the election of Mr Chorley as our champion; no,
no, my dear Madam — we will not have Mr Chorley — I doubt
whether he would be true to us; I will tell you who would better
espouse and defend our cause; the very man who attacks us; in
Mr Thackeray's nature is a good angel and a bad, and I would
match the one against the other.

Will you ask Mr Smith whether the 2 vols. of 'Violet'[1] reached
him safely; I returned them by post as I remembered he said they
were borrowed.

Give my kind regards to all your family circle, tell little Bell to
be sure and not wear out her eyes with too much reading, or she
will repent it when she is grown a woman. Believe me, my dear
Mrs Smith — Yours sincerely,   C. Brontë.

You demand a bulletin respecting the 'little socks.'[2] I am
sorry I cannot issue a more favourable one; they continue much
the same. Should they ever be finished you shall certainly have
them as a memento of 'Currer Bell.'

515 (407). *To* W. S. Williams.

January 10th, 1850.

My dear Sir, — Mrs Ellis has made 'her morning call.' I rather
relished her chat about 'Shirley' and 'Jane Eyre.' She praises
reluctantly and blames too often affectedly. But whenever a
reviewer betrays that he has been thoroughly influenced and
stirred by the work he criticises, it is easy to forgive the rest —
hate and personality excepted.

I have received and perused the 'Edinburgh Review' — it is
very brutal and savage. I am not angry with Lewes, but I wish in
future he would let me alone, and not write again what makes
me feel so cold and sick as I am feeling just now.

Thackeray's Christmas Book at once grieved and pleased me,
as most of his writings do. I have come to the conclusion that

---

[1] *Violet, or The Danseuse* (Anon.) 1836.   [2] The reference is to a pair of baby's socks
which Charlotte was knitting.

whenever he writes, Mephistopheles stands on his right hand and Raphael on his left; the great doubter and sneerer usually guides the pen, the Angel, noble and gentle, interlines letters of light here and there. Alas! Thackeray, I wish your strong wings would lift you oftener above the smoke of cities into the pure region nearer heaven!

Good-bye for the present. — Yours sincerely,

C. BRONTË.

516 (408). *To* G. H. LEWES.

[January, 1850].

I can be on my guard against my enemies, but God deliver me from my friends!

CURRER BELL.

517. *To* GEORGE SMITH.

January 15th, 1850.

MY DEAR SIR, — I have received the 'Morning Chronicle.' I like Mr Thackeray's letter. As you say, it is manly; it breathes rectitude and independence; now and then the satirist puts in a word, but, on the whole, its tone is as earnest as its style is simple. It needs a comparison between Mr Thackeray and all the whining small fry of quill-drivers to take the full measure of his stature; it needs such a comparison as his own words suggest to discover what a giant he is (morally I mean, not physically), and with what advantage and command he towers above the Leigh Hunts, the Levers, the Jerrolds.

I have likewise got Mr Doyle's book in its beautiful lapis-lazuli cover. All comment on the circumstances of your sending a second copy after the first had been lost would, I feel, be quite unavailing. I leave the correction of such proceeding to the 'man of business' within you: on the 'close-fisted' Head of the Establishment in Cornhill devolves the duty of reprimanding Mr G——e S——th; they may settle accounts between themselves, while Currer Bell looks on and wonders, but keeps out of the *mêlée*.

On reflection I think it would be wiser to abstain from adding any more prefatory remarks to the cheap edition of 'Jane Eyre,' for it does not appear that I am very happy in such matters; I lack Mr Thackeray's nice quiet tact and finished ease. I am glad to hear that the bonnets suited, and regret exceedingly that it is not in my power to give any assurance of the substantial existence of Miss Helstone. You must be satisfied if that young person has furnished your mind with a pleasant idea; she is a native of Dreamland, and as such can have neither voice nor presence except for the fancy, neither being nor dwelling except in thought.

N.B.—That last sentence is not to be read by the 'man of business'; it sounds much too bookish.—Believe me, Yours sincerely,

C. BRONTË.

518 (409). *To* G. H. LEWES.

January 19th, 1850.

MY DEAR SIR,—I will tell you why I was so hurt by that review in the 'Edinburgh'—not because its criticism was keen or its blame sometimes severe; not because its praise was stinted (for, indeed, I think you give me quite as much praise as I deserve), but because after I had said earnestly that I wished critics would judge me as an *author*, not as a woman, you so roughly—I even thought so cruelly—handled the question of sex. I dare say you meant no harm, and perhaps you will not now be able to understand why I was so grieved at what you will probably deem such a trifle; but grieved I was, and indignant too.

There was a passage or two which you did quite wrong to write.

However, I will not bear malice against you for it; I know what your nature is: it is not a bad or unkind one, though you would often jar terribly on some feelings with whose recoil and quiver you could not possibly sympathise. I imagine you are both enthusiastic and implacable, as you are at once sagacious and careless; you know much and discover much, but you are in such a hurry to tell it all you never give yourself time to think how your reckless eloquence may affect others; and, what is more, if you knew how it did affect them, you would not much care.

However, I shake hands with you: you have excellent points; you can be generous. I still feel angry, and think I do well to be angry; but it is the anger one experiences for rough play rather than for foul play.—I am yours, with a certain respect, and more chagrin,

CURRER BELL.

519 (410). *To* ELLEN NUSSEY.

[Jan. 19th, 1850].

DEAR NELL, — You had a weary long time to wait at Bradford and a most crushing ride home — and then the necessity of entertaining company when you ought to have rested was rather too bad. I am glad to hear Amelia does not *fret*; I trust her spirit will keep her up through the tedious period of suspense she will probably have to endure. How it will end God knows, but I *think* they will be married — I *think* from the first J. T. has deliberately intended this shall be the finale — I feel sure the visit to Tranby rather confirmed than shook this resolution.

I feel angry with myself every day that I have not yet written to Amelia — but in truth I hardly know what to say — however I shall pluck up courage as soon as possible.

All you tell me about the notoriety of 'Shirley' in Dewsbury &c. is almost as good as an emetic to me — I should really 'go off at side' if I thought too much about it. Mr Nicholls having finished 'Jane Eyre' is now crying out for the 'other book' — he is to have it next week — much good may it do him.

I answered Sir J. K. Shuttleworth's[1] note yesterday — thanking and declining as neatly as I knew how —

Since you left I have had no letters from London — I think if Lewes had any thoughts of answering my missive he would have done it at once for he generally bolts his replies by return of post.

Dear Nell — it is lonesome without you — Write again soon — Good-bye.

Love to all at Brookroyd.

C. B.

520. *To* AMELIA RINGROSE.

[January 25th, 1850].

DEAR AMELIA, — Much as I hold letter writing in aversion, I must write you a little note however brief, for my conscience will no longer let me rest till I have done so. I trust the coughs

[1] Sir James Kay-Shuttleworth (1804–1877), a doctor of medicine, who was made a baronet in 1849 on resigning the secretaryship of the Committee of the Council on Education. He assumed the name of Shuttleworth in 1842 on his marriage to Janet, the only child and heiress of Robert Shuttleworth of Gawthorpe Hall, Burnley. It was during her visit to Sir James Kay-Shuttleworth in August, 1850, that Charlotte Brontë first met Mrs Gaskell.

and colds which disquieted your household are by this time nearly removed and that especially yourself and Rosy are pretty well. Does Rosy still continue to take cod-liver-oil and does it still agree with her?

I have to thank you for a pretty pair of cuffs—which I shall keep as a sort of company decoration. E. Nussey said something about your intending to work me a cushion like the one I saw at Brookroyd—The intention is like yourself because it is kind, but allow me to prohibit it—I see not the slightest earthly cause to justify your imposing such a task on yourself on *my* account.

E. Nussey stayed with me just three weeks—but the time seemed to pass like one week. I found her presence a comfort and her absence is now a loss; still I get on; there are desolate moments with which I contend as well as I can—they pass—I seek employment and so manage pretty well. I have no lack of books—that is one great blessing.

I should like to know how *you* are—how your *spirits* are— You must not let them droop. Be courageous as well as patient. However events may turn out, hold fast to the faith that all is for the best.

Remember me to your sister Rosy and believe me, dear Amelia, yours sincerely,

C. BRONTË.

521 (411). *To* ELLEN NUSSEY.

January 25th, 1850.

DEAR ELLEN,—Your indisposition was, I have no doubt, in a great measure owing to the change in the weather from frost to thaw. I had one sick-headachy day; but, for me, only a slight attack. You must be careful of cold. I have just written to Amelia a brief note thanking her for the cuffs, etc. It was a burning shame I did not write sooner. Herewith are enclosed three letters for your perusal, the first from Mary Taylor, which you are to read immediately—so the order runs—and not to send it to Mrs Burnley. There is also one from Lewes and one from Sir J. K. Shuttleworth, both which peruse and return. I have also, since you went, had a remarkable epistle from Thackeray, long, interesting, characteristic, but it unfortunately concludes with the strict injunction, *show this letter to no one*, adding that if he thought his letters were seen by others, he should either cease to write or write only what was conventional; but for this circumstance I should have sent it with the others. I answered it at length. Whether my reply will give satisfaction or displeasure remains yet to be ascertained. Thackeray's feelings are not such as can be gauged by ordinary calculation: variable weather is what I should ever expect from that quarter, yet in correspondence as in verbal intercourse, this would torment me. — Yours faithfully,

C. B.

522 (413). *To* Ellen Nussey.

January 28th, 1850.

Dear Ellen, — I cannot but be concerned to hear of your mother's illness; write again soon, if it be but a line, to tell me how she gets on. This shadow will, I trust and believe, be but a passing one, but it is a foretaste and warning of what *must come* one day. Let it prepare your mind, dear Ellen, for that great trial which, if you live, it *must* in the course of a few years be your lot to undergo. That cutting asunder of the ties of nature is the pain we most dread and which we are most certain to experience. Perhaps you will have seen Joe Taylor ere this. I had a brief note from him, dated Hull: he had seen Mr Ringrose, whom he found 'inimical though not avowedly so, desirous to refuse but wanting a pretext.' 'Such a reception,' he says, 'would, six weeks ago, have made him give it up.' He does not mention whether he saw Amelia. He will go on. Lewes' letter made me laugh, I cannot respect him more for it. Sir J. K. Shuttleworth's letter did not make me laugh. He has written again since. I have received to-day a note from Miss Alexander, Lupset Cottage, Wakefield, daughter, she says, of Dr Alexander. Do you know anything of her? Mary Taylor seems in good health and spirits and in the way of doing well. I shall feel anxious to hear again soon.

C. B.

P.S. — Mr Nicholls has finished reading 'Shirley,' he is delighted with it. John Brown's wife seriously thought he had gone wrong in the head as she heard him giving vent to roars of laughter as he sat alone, clapping his hands and stamping on the floor. He would read all the scenes about the curates aloud to papa, he triumphed in his own character. What Mr Grant will say is another thing. No matter.

523 (414). *To* ELLEN NUSSEY.

Thursday, January 31st, 1850.

DEAR ELLEN,—I wonder how your poor mother is this morning, and how you are too; I wonder also whether you have yet heard from your brothers, and whether the news of their mother's serious illness has penetrated the crust of worldliness with which their hearts are too completely overgrown, and wakened something like the sensation of natural affection. You must let me have a line as soon as you can to tell me how matters progress.

As to Joe Taylor—I really dare not write what I think of him, or what I feel respecting him. I grow more and more convinced that his state of mind approximates to that which was so appallingly exhibited in poor Branwell during the last few years of his life, and if such be the case, she who marries him will join hands with misery—and, as you say, *hopeless* misery. The note I had from him dated Hull just breathed the spirit which you describe as pervading his conversation with you; it was short, but imbued with selfishness and with a sort of unmanly absence of true value for the woman whose hand he seeks. Should he continue in this frame of mind, he cannot be worthy of Amelia. I could infuse no word of sympathy into my answer—I involuntarily made it sharp and stern. With what I said he cannot be pleased, nor will it encourage him to come here; and indeed the thought of his coming would be a nightmare to me. What power Joe Taylor still possesses to interest and influence is an *unreal* power; I greatly fear it all depends on *skilful acting*.

I had just written so far when I received a letter from him (J. T.). I enclose it. Is this acting, or what is it? Does he give me the rug to pay off some imaginary debt? I wish him well, but both gifts and loans and letters and visits from that quarter have all now something about them from which one shrinks. All seems done on system—nothing from feeling. Write by return of post if you can, dear Nell. Good-bye.

C. B.

524 (416). *To* ELLEN NUSSEY.

February 4th, 1850.

DEAR ELLEN,—I am truly glad to hear of the happy change in your mother's state, I hope nothing will occur to give it a check. The relief when a hope of recovery succeeds to the dread of danger must be sweet indeed. I remember it was what I intensely longed for, but what it was not seen good I should enjoy.

Thank you for the scrap of information respecting Sir J. K. Shuttleworth. Mr Morgan has finished reading 'Jane Eyre,' and writes not in blame, but in the highest strains of eulogy! He says it thoroughly fascinated and enchained him, etc., etc., etc.

Martha came in yesterday, puffing and blowing, and much excited. 'I've heard sich news,' she began. 'What about?' 'Please ma'am, you've been and written two books, the grandest books that ever was seen. My father has heard it at Halifax, and Mr George Taylor and Mr Greenwood, and Mr Merrall at Bradford; and they are going to have a meeting at the Mechanics' Institute, and to settle about ordering them.' 'Hold your tongue Martha, and be off.' I fell into a cold sweat. 'Jane Eyre' will be read by John Brown, by Mrs Taylor, and Betty. God help, keep, and deliver me! Good-bye.

C. B.

525 (417). *To* ELLEN NUSSEY.

[February 5th, 1850].

DEAR ELLEN,—I return Amelia's letter. The business is a most unpleasant one to be concerned in; it seems to me *now* altogether unworthy, in its beginning, progress, and probable ending. Amelia is the only pure thing about it; she stands between her coarse father and cold unloving suitor like innocence between a pair of world-hardened knaves. The comparison seems rather hard to be applied to Joseph Taylor, but as I see him now he merits it. If Joseph Taylor has no means of keeping a wife—if he does not possess a sixpence he is sure of, how can he think of marrying a woman from whom he cannot expect she should work to keep herself. Joe Taylor's want of candour, the twice falsified account he gave of the matter, tells painfully and deeply against his cause. It shows a glimpse of his hidden motives such as I refrain from describing in words. It gives a strangely heartless calculation to the whole proceeding — a cast of which he was conscious, but which, knowing how we should judge it, he carefully and jealously veiled from us. After all, he is perhaps only like the majority of men. Certainly those men who lead a gay life in their youth, and arrive at middle age with feelings blunted and passions exhausted, who have but one aim in marriage, the selfish advancement of their interest, and to think that such men take as wives, as second selves, women young, modest, sincere, pure in heart and life, with feeling all fresh, and emotions all unworn, and bind such virtue and vitality to their own withered existence, such sincerity to their own hollowness, such disinterestedness to their own haggard avarice, — to think this — troubles the soul to its inmost depths. Nature and Justice forbid the banns of such wedlock. I write under excitement. Amelia's letter seems to have lifted so fraudulent a veil, and to show both father and suitor lurking behind in shadow so dark, acting from motives so poor and low, so conscious of each other's littleness, and consequently so destitute of mutual respect! these things incense me, but I shall cool down.

I am glad your mother continues better. Good-bye.

C. Brontë.

One good thing can still be said: he was candid to Mr Ringrose. He explained his circumstances truthfully. The germs of all good are not extirpated.

526 (419). *To* Margaret Wooler.

Haworth, Feby 14th, '50.

My dear Miss Wooler, — You told me, I remember, when I saw you last, that your sight had been injured by inflammation consequent on cold, and I am truly sorry to hear it is not yet well. Intimate as I am myself with the privations attached to enfeebled vision, it is a calamity with which I specially sympathize; I trust and believe however that the affection in your case will not be permanent; it is not like organic change such as takes place in cataract &c. Should you not consult some skilful occulist?

As to 'Jane Eyre' and 'Shirley,' the books are taking their chance in the world, getting abused here, praised there, knocked about everywhere. Currer Bell does not break his heart about the opinion of a discriminating public; if his friends object to the works he is sorry—but he could change nothing; what is written, is written, and in his conscience he is very quiet.

I am sorry the Clergy do not like the doctrine of Universal Salvation; I think it a great pity for their sakes, but surely they are not so unreasonable as to expect me to deny or suppress what I believe the truth!

Some of the clergy will not like 'Shirley'; I confess the work has one prevailing fault—that of too tenderly and partially veiling the errors of 'the Curates.' Had Currer Bell written all he has seen and knows concerning those worthies—a singular work would have been the result.

I need not thank you for the sincerity and frankness with which you have spoken to me about 'Jane Eyre.' Of course, knowing you as I do, I was certain that whenever you did speak, you would speak sincerely. You seem to think that I had feared some loss in your esteem owing to my being the reputed Author of this book—such a fear—one so unjust to both you and myself, never crossed my mind. When I was in London—a woman whose celebrity is not wider than her moral standard is elevated —and in each point she has no living superior—said to me '*I have ever observed that it is to the coarse-minded alone—"Jane Eyre" is coarse.*' This remark tallied with what I had myself noticed; I felt its truth; And, feeling it, be assured my dear Miss Wooler—I was at ease on the secret opinion of *your* heart—you may and do object to certain phrases, exclamations &c. phrases and exclamations however, which, viewing them from an artistic point of view, my judgment ratifies as consistent and characteristic—but I have not hitherto fancied that you have withdrawn from me your esteem.

I own when I hear of any one making an exaggerated outcry against 'Jane Eyre' immediately in my own mind I come to no very complimentary conclusion respecting the natural quality of that persons tastes and propensities.

Certain of the Clergy have thought proper to be bitter against the work—some of them good men in their way—but men in whom the animal obviously predominates over the intellectual —I smile inwardly when I hear of their disapprobation.

Ellen Nussey—it seems—told you that I spent a fortnight in London last Decbr; they wished me very much to stay a month, alleging that I should in that time be able to secure a complete

circle of acquaintance—but I found a fortnight of such excitement quite enough: the whole day was usually devoted to sight-
seeing—and often the evening was spent in society—it was
more than I could bear for any length of time—On one occasion
I met a party of my critics—seven of them—some of them had
been very bitter foes in print but they were prodigiously civil
face to face; these gentlemen seemed infinitely grander, more
pompous, dashing, shewy than the few authors I saw; Mr Thackeray, for instance, is a man of very quiet, simple demeanour; he is
however looked upon with some awe and even distrust. His
conversation is very peculiar—too perverse to be pleasant—It
was proposed to me to see Charles Dickens, Lady Morgan,
Mesdames Trollope, Gore and some others—but I was aware
these introductions would bring a degree of notoriety I was not
disposed to encounter; I declined therefore with thanks.

Nothing charmed me more during my stay in Town than the
pictures I saw—one or two private collections of Turner's best
water-colour drawings were indeed a treat: his later oil-paint-
ings are strange things—things that baffle description—

I twice saw Macready act—once in 'Macbeth' and once in
'Othello'—I astounded a dinner-party by honestly saying I did
not like him. It is the fashion to rave about his splendid acting—
anything more false and artificial—less genuinely impressive
than his whole style I could scarcely have imagined—The fact is
the stage-system altogether is hollow nonsense—they act farces
well enough—the actors comprehend their parts and do them
justice—they comprehend nothing about tragedy or Shakespere
and it is a failure. I said so—and by so saying produced a blank
silence—a mute consternation. I was, indeed, obliged to dissent
on many occasions and to offend by dissenting—It seems now
very much the custom to admire a certain wordy, intricate,
obscure style of poetry—such as Elizabeth Barrett Browning
writes—Some pieces were referred to about which Currer Bell
was expected to be very rapturous—and failing in this—he disappointed.

London people strike a provincial as being very much taken
up with little matters about which no one out of particular town-
circles cares much—they talk too of persons—literary men and
women whose names are scarcely heard in the country—and in
whom you cannot get up an interest—I think I should scarcely
like to live in London—and were I obliged to live there, I should

certainly go little into company —especially I should eschew the literary coteries —

You told me —my dear Miss Wooler—to write a long letter —I have obeyed you.

Believe me now —Yours affectionately and respectfully,

C. BRONTË.

527 (418). *To* ELLEN NUSSEY.

February 16th, 1850.

DEAR NELL,—I believe I should have written to you before, but I don't know what heaviness of spirit has beset me of late, made my faculties dull, made rest weariness, and occupation burdensome. Now and then the silence of the house, the solitude of the room has pressed on me with a weight I found it difficult to bear, and recollection has not failed to be as alert, poignant, obtrusive as other feelings were languid. I attribute this state of things partly to the weather. Quicksilver invariably falls low in storms and high winds, and I have ere this been warned of approaching disturbance in the atmosphere by a sense of bodily weakness and deep, heavy mental sadness, such as some would call *presentiment*, —presentiment it is, but not at all supernatural.

The Haworth people have been making great fools of themselves about 'Shirley.' They take it in an enthusiastic light. When they got the volumes at the Mechanics' Institute, all the members wanted them. They cast lots for the whole three, and whoever got a volume was only allowed to keep it two days, and was to be fined a shilling per diem for longer detention. It would be mere nonsense and vanity to tell you what they say.

I have had no letters from London for a long time, and am very much ashamed of myself to find, now when that stimulus is withdrawn, how dependent on it I had become. I cannot help feeling something of the excitement of expectation till the post hour comes, and when, day after day, it brings nothing, I get low. This is a stupid, disgraceful, unmeaning state of things. I feel bitterly enraged at my own dependence and folly; but it is so bad for the mind to be quite alone, and to have none with whom to talk over little crosses and disappointments, and laugh them away. If I could write, I dare say I should be better, but I cannot write a line. However (D. V.), I shall contend against the idiocy.

I had a rather foolish letter from Miss Wooler the other day.

Some things in it nettled me, especially an unnecessarily earnest assurance that, in spite of all I had gone and done in the writing line, I still retained a place in her esteem. My answer took strong and high ground at once. I said I had been troubled by no doubts on the subject; that I neither did myself nor her the injustice to suppose there was anything in what I had written to incur the just forfeiture of esteem. I was aware, I intimated, that some persons thought proper to take exceptions at 'Jane Eyre,' and that for their own sakes I was sorry, as I invariably found them individuals in whom the animal largely predominated over the intellectual, persons by nature coarse, by inclination sensual, whatever they might be by education and principle.

A few days since, a little incident happened which curiously touched me. Papa put into my hands a little packet of letters and papers, telling me that they were mamma's, and that I might read them. I did read them, in a frame of mind I cannot describe. The papers were yellow with time, all having been written before I was born; it was strange now to peruse, for the first time, the records of a mind whence my own sprang; and most strange, and at once sad and sweet, to find that mind of a truly fine, pure, and elevated order. They were written to papa before they were married. There is a rectitude, a refinement, a constancy, a modesty, a sense, a gentleness about them indescribable. I wish she had lived, and that I had known her.

Yesterday, just after dinner, I heard a loud bustling voice in the kitchen demanding to see Mr Brontë, somebody was shown into the parlour; shortly after wine was rung for. 'Who is it, Martha?' I asked. 'Some mak of a tradesman,' said she, 'he's not a gentleman, I'm sure.' The personage stayed about an hour, talking in a loud vulgar key all the time. At tea-time I asked papa who it was. 'Why,' said he, 'no other than the Rev. ——,[1] vicar of Bierley!' Papa had invited him to take some refreshment, but the creature had ordered his dinner at the Black Bull, and was quite urgent with papa to go down there and join him, offering by way of inducement a bottle, or if papa liked, 'two or three bottles of the best wine Haworth could afford!' He said he was come with a Mr C——, I think, from Bradford, just to look at the place, and reckoned to be in raptures with the wild scenery! He warmly pressed papa to come and see him at ——, and to bring his daughter with him!!! Does he know anything about the

[1] The Rev. John Barber became incumbent of Bierley, Yorks. in 1839.

books, do you think? he made no allusion to them. I did not see him, not so much as the tail of his coat. Martha said he looked no more like a parson than she did. Papa described him as rather shabby-looking, but said he was wondrous cordial and friendly. Papa, in his usual fashion, put him through a regular catechism of questions; what his living was worth, etc., etc. In answer to inquiries respecting his age he affirmed himself to be thirty-seven—is not this a lie? He must be more. Papa asked him if he were married. He said no, he had no thoughts of being married, he did not like the trouble of a wife; he described himself as 'living in style, and keeping a very hospitable house.'

Dear Nell, I have written you a long letter; write me a long one in answer.

C. B.

Does your mother continue better? How are you, yourself? Do you get the papers regularly? I have just got a note from Amelia Ringrose enclosing a little ear-cap. I hope she won't trouble herself to make me these small presents often. She writes in good spirits but says nothing about Joe Taylor, indeed she has never named him to me, nor I to her.

528 (415). *To* W. S. WILLIAMS.

Feby 22nd, 1850.

MY DEAR SIR,—I have despatched to-day a parcel containing the Caxtons—Macaulay's Essays, Humboldt's letters and such other of the books as I have read, packed with a picturesque irregularity well-calculated to excite the envy and admiration of your skilful functionary in Cornhill; by the by he ought to be careful of the few pins stuck in here and there as he may find them useful at a future day in case of having more bonnets to pack for the East Indies. Whenever you send me a new supply of books may I request that you will have the goodness to include one or two of Miss Austen's—I am often asked whether I have read them, and I excite amazement by replying in the negative— I have read none except 'Pride and Prejudice.' Miss Martineau mentioned 'Persuasion' as the best.

Thank you for your account of the 'First Performance'; it was cheering and pleasant to read it for in your animated description I seemed to realize the scene; your criticism also enables me to form some idea of the play. Lewes is a strange being; I always regret that I did not see him when in London; he seems to me clever, sharp and coarse; I used to think him sagacious, but I believe now he is no more than shrewd—for I have observed once or twice that he brings forward as grand discoveries of his own, information he has casually received from others—true sagacity disdains little tricks of this sort—but, though Lewes has many smart and some deserving points about him, he has nothing truly great—and nothing truly great, I should think, will he ever produce. Yet he merits just such successes as the one you describe—triumphs public, brief and noisy—Notoriety suits Lewes—Fame—were it possible that he could achieve her— would be a thing uncongenial to him; he could not wait for the solemn blast of her trumpet—sounding long, and slowly waxing louder.

I always like your way of mentioning Mr Smith, because my own opinion of him concurs with yours, and it is as pleasant to have a favourable impression of character confirmed, as it is painful to see it dispelled: I am sure he possesses a fine nature, and I trust the selfishness of the world, and the hard habits of business, though they may and must modify his disposition, will never quite spoil it.

Can you give me any information respecting Sheridan Knowles?[1] A few lines received from him lately and a present of his 'George Lovel' induce me to ask the question—of course I am aware that he is a dramatic writer of eminence, but do you know anything about him as a man?

I believe both 'Shirley' and 'Jane Eyre' are being a good deal read in the North just now—but I only hear fitful rumours from time to time—I ask nothing—and my life of anchorite seclusion shuts out all bearers of tidings. One or two curiosity-hunters have made their way to Haworth Parsonage—but our rude hills and rugged neighbourhood will I doubt not form a sufficient barrier to the frequent repetition of such visits.—Believe me, Yours sincerely,

C. BRONTË.

[1] James Sheridan Knowles (1784–1862) dramatist and novelist, produced many plays, including *Caius Gracchus* (1815), *William Tell* (1825), *The Hunchback* (1832), and *The Love-Chase* (1837). His novel *George Lovell* was published in 1847.

529 (420). *To* ELLEN NUSSEY.

March 5th, 1850.

DEAR ELLEN,—I scribble you a line in haste to tell you of my proceedings. Various folks are beginning to come boring to Haworth, on the wise errand of seeing the scenery described in 'Jane Eyre' and 'Shirley'; amongst others, Sir J. K. Shuttleworth and Lady Shuttleworth have persisted in coming; they were here on Friday. The baronet looks in vigorous health, he scarcely appears more than thirty-five, but he says he is forty-four; Lady Shuttleworth is rather handsome and still young. They were both quite unpretending, etc. When here they again urged me to visit them. Papa took their side at once, would not hear of my refusing; I must go, —this left me without plea or defence. I con-sented to go for three days, they wanted me to return with them in the carriage, but I pleaded off till to-morrow. I wish it was well over.

If all be well I shall be able to write more about them when I come back. Sir James is very courtly, fine-looking; I wish he may be as sincere as he is polished. He shows his white teeth with too frequent a smile; but I will not prejudge him.—In haste, yours faithfully,

C. B.

530. *To* JOHN STORES SMITH.

March 6th, 1850.

DEAR SIR,—I have to thank you very sincerely for your kind note and the volumes accompanying it. Through the kindness of my Publishers, I had already enjoyed the opportunity of read-ing 'Mirabeau,'[1] but it is an additional pleasure to possess the work as a gift from the author.

I am happy to learn that my writings have afforded you some agreeable moments, and if my gratification is a little chastened by the fear that you ascribe to me a merit beyond my deserts, perhaps it is better so; the unmixed cup is rarely salutary.

With every good wish for your success in the honourable but difficult career of literature, —I am, my dear Sir, Yours sincerely,

CURRER BELL.

[1] See letter dated June 22nd, 1848. Vol. II, pp. 224-225

531 (421). *To* W. S. WILLIAMS.

March 16th, '50.

MY DEAR SIR,—I found your letter with several others await-ing me on my return home from a brief stay in Lancashire: the mourning border alarmed me much; I feared that dread visitant before whose coming every household trembles had invaded your hearth and taken from you, perhaps a child, perhaps some-thing dearer still. The loss you have actually sustained is painful, but so much *less* painful than what I had anticipated that to read your letter was to be greatly relieved. Still I know what Mrs Williams will feel. We can have but one father, but one mother, and when either is gone, we have lost what can never be replaced. Offer her, under this affliction, my sincere sympathy. I can well imagine the cloud these sad tidings would cast over your young cheerful family; poor little Dick's exclamation and burst of grief are most naïve and natural—he felt the sorrow of a child; a keen, but, happily, a transient pang. Time will I trust ere long restore your own and your wife's serenity and your children's cheerful-ness.

I mentioned—I think—that we had had one or two visitors at Haworth lately—amongst them were Sir James Kaye Shuttle-worth and his Lady—before departing they exacted a promise that I would visit them at Gawthorpe Hall their residence on the borders of East Lancashire. I went reluctantly for it is always a difficult and painful thing to me to meet the advances of people whose kindness I am in no position to repay. Sir James is a man of polished manners with clear intellect and highly cultivated mind. On the whole I got on very well with him; his health is just now somewhat broken by his severe official labours, and the quiet drives to old ruins and old halls situated amongst older hills and woods, the dialogues (perhaps I should rather say monologues for I listened far more than I talked) by the fireside in his antique oak-panelled drawing-room, while they suited him, did not too much oppress and exhaust me—the house too is very much to my taste—near three centuries old, grey, stately and picturesque; on the whole—now that the visit is over, I do not regret having paid it. The worst of it is that there is now some menace hanging over my head of an invitation to go to them in London during the season—this, which would doubt-less be a great enjoyment to some people, is a perfect terror to me. I should highly prize the advantages to be gained in an extended range of observation—but I tremble at the thought of the price I must necessarily pay in mental distress and physical wear and tear. But you shall have no more of my confessions—to you they will appear folly.

Will you have the kindness to apologize to Mr Taylor for my apparent want of punctuality in returning the 'Athenaeum' this week—by the by, I was happy to see in a recent number a . . .[1]

[C. Brontë.]

532 (422). *To* George Smith.

March 16th, 1850.

My dear Sir,—I return Mr H——'s note, after reading it carefully. I tried very hard to understand all he says about art; but, to speak truth, my efforts were crowned with incomplete success. There is a certain jargon in use amongst critics on this point through which it is physically and morally impossible to me to see daylight. One thing, however, I see plainly enough, and that is Mr Currer Bell needs improvement, and ought to strive after it; and this (D.V.) he honestly intends to do—taking his time, however, and following as his guides Nature and Truth. If these lead to what the critics call art, it is all very well; but if not, that grand desideratum has no chance of being run after or caught. The puzzle is, that while the people of the South object to my delineation of Northern life and manners, the people of Yorkshire and Lancashire approve. They say it is precisely the contrast of rough nature with highly artificial cultivation which forms one of their main characteristics. Such, or something very similar, has been the observation made to me lately, whilst I have been from home, by members of some of the ancient East Lancashire families, whose mansions lie on the hilly borderland between the two counties. The question arises, whether do the London critics, or the old Northern squires, understand the matter best?

Any promise you require respecting the books shall be willingly given, provided only I am allowed the Jesuit's principle of a mental reservation, giving licence to forget and promise whenever oblivion shall appear expedient. The last two or three numbers of 'Pendennis' will not, I dare say, be generally thought

[1]This letter is incomplete.

sufficiently exciting, yet I like them. Though the story lingers (for me), the interest does not flag. Here and there we feel that the pen has been guided by a tired hand, that the mind of the writer has been somewhat chafed and depressed by his recent illness, or by some other cause; but Thackeray still proves himself greater when he is weary than other writers are when they are fresh. The public, of course, will have no compassion for his fatigue, and make no allowance for the ebb of inspiration; but some true-hearted readers here and there, while grieving that such a man should be obliged to write when he is not in the mood, will wonder that, under such circumstances, he should write so well. The parcel of books will come, I doubt not, at such time as it shall suit the good pleasure of the railway officials to send it on—or rather to yield it up to the repeated and humble solicitations of Haworth carriers—till when I wait in all reasonable patience and resignation, looking with docility to that model of active self-helpfulness 'Punch' friendly offers the 'Women of England' in his 'Unprotected Female.'[1]

C. BRONTË.

533. *To* AMELIA RINGROSE.

HAWORTH, March 16th, '50.

MY DEAR AMELIA,—I have been away from home staying a few days in Lancashire, and my letters were not sent after me, that is the reason yours remained till now unanswered. You are right in saying I am interested in you; certainly I am; I have meditated many an hour on this matter which concerns you. Often I have felt puzzled; I am puzzled now, but I repeat, however it terminates, the event will undoubtedly be ordered for the best. 'Truth, sincerity and Affection' are indeed requisites not to be dispensed with—wherever and whenever you shall find these united with *Sense* and *Principle* and *Industry*—there you need not fear to marry whether there be riches in addition or not—but till you are quite convinced you have found them, watch and wait. I think it would be very dreadful to take the most important—the most irrevocable step in life under the influence of illusive impressions—and when it was too late to retreat to find all was a mistake.

---

[1]In *Punch*, from November 3, 1849, to April 20, 1850, there appeared twenty　'Scenes from the Life of an Unprotected Female,' in dialogue and stage directions.

It would be superfluous, dear Amelia, to offer you advice, your own opinions and resolutions, as expressed in your letter, seem to me all that can be wished; be firm to them. What Ellen has said, has been said in the spirit of truest friendship, and as such you have evidently received it.

I am glad to hear that both you and Rosy are better; health and strength must indeed be much needed by you now when you have a mother to nurse through what is too probably her last illness; I hope strength will be given to you both for whatever you may be called upon to endure in this life of trials.

The cushion is come at last; I think it extremely beautiful — quite splendid — I do not see how it could be better — Thank you for it and also for the pretty and comfortable little ear-cap you sent me some time since.

As I have an accumulation of letters to answer you will excuse me for abridging this, and believe me, — Yours faithfully,

C. BRONTË.

Let me have the bill as soon as you can; I shall always be glad to hear from you; you know I think your letters interesting. Remember me kindly to your sister.

534. *To* THORNTON HUNT.[1]

March 16th, 1850.

MY DEAR SIR, — Your note would have been answered sooner had not my absence from home prevented its reaching me till to-day.

While thanking you for the kind terms in which you offer me a place in your band, I must, for the present, decline enlisting. To similar proposals from other quarters I have already found it necessary to return a negative reply, and in this case it would be superfluous to add any expression of regret, for I am sure that amongst names so eminent as those you have secured, that of Currer Bell will never be missed.

Wishing you every success in the work undertaken, —I am, my dear Sir, Yours sincerely,

CURRER BELL.

[1]Thornton Leigh Hunt (1810–1873), journalist, eldest son of James Henry Leigh Hunt. He was director of the political department of the *Constitutional* and later editor first of the *North Cheshire Reformer* and then of the *Glasgow Argus*. In 1850, he helped G. H. Lewes to establish the *Leader*. He published *The Foster-Brother*, an historical romance, in 1845, and edited Leigh Hunt's *Autobiography* in 1850.

535. To MISS ALEXANDER, *Lupset Cottage, Wakefield.*

March 18th, 1850.

MY DEAR MADAM, —I received your first note as well as your second, and if I did not answer it, my silence arose, not from in-difference to the kind feeling it expressed, but simply from the fact that a reply would have been an acknowledgment of what I still thought it possible to conceal. It seems however that silence has on all sides been interpreted into assent and I now confess nothing in saying that I am happy if my works have given you pleasure. As to the little book of rhymes, it has no other title than 'Poems by Currer, Ellis and Acton Bell' published by Smith Elder & Co., 65 Cornhill. Let me warn you that it is scarcely worth your while to send for it. It is a collection of short fugitive pieces; my own share are chiefly juvenile productions written several years ago, before taste was chastened or judgment ma-tured—accordingly they now appear to me very crude. But I have no right to forestall your opinion by anticipatory criticism. —Believe me, dear Madam, Yours sincerely,

C. BELL.[1]

536 (423). To ELLEN NUSSEY.

HAWORTH, March 19th, 1850.

DEAR ELLEN, —I have got home again, and now that the visit is over, I am, as usual, glad I have been: not that I could have endured to prolong it—a few days at once in an utterly strange place, amongst utterly strange faces, is quite enough for me.

When the train stopped at Burnley—I found Sir James wait-ing for me—a drive of about 3 miles brought us to the gates of Gawthorpe and after passing up a somewhat desolate avenue—there towered the Hall, grey, antique, castellated and stately before me. It is 250 years old and within as without is a model of old English architecture—The arms and the strange crest of the Shuttleworths are carved on the oak-panelling of each room. They are not a parvenue family but date from the days of Richard

[1]This letter was given to Lady Catherine Milnes Gaskell by Dr Alexander, January 20th, 1894. It was written a few months after the publication of *Shirley*, when the authorship of the novels was first discover-ed. It is now bound in a copy of the first edition of *Shirley* in the Brotherton Library.

the 3rd. This part of Lancashire seems rather remarkable for its houses of ancient race—the Townleys—another family who live near—go back to the Conquest.

The people however were of still more interest to me than the house—Lady Shuttleworth is a little woman 32 years old with a pretty, smooth, lively face. Of pretension to aristocratic airs, she may be entirely acquitted—of frankness, good-humour and activity she has enough—truth obliges me to add that as it seemed to me—grace, dignity, fine feeling were not in the inventory of her qualities. These last are precisely what her husband possesses—in manner he can be gracious and dignified—his tastes and feelings are capable of elevation: frank he is not, but on the contrary—politic—he calls himself a man of the world and knows the world's ways; courtly and affable in some points of view—he is strict and rigorous in others. In him high mental cultivation is combined with an extended range of observation, and thoroughly practical views and habits. His nerves are naturally acutely sensitive, and the present very critical state of his health—has exaggerated sensitiveness into irritability. His lady is of a temperament precisely suited to nurse him and wait on him—if her sensations were more delicate and acute she would not do half so well. They get on perfectly together. The children —there are four of them—are all fine children in their way— They have a young German lady as governess—a quiet, well-instructed, interesting girl whom I took to at once—and, in my heart, liked better than anything else in the house. She also instinctively took to me. She is very well treated for a governess —but wore the usual pale, despondent look of her class—She told me she was home-sick—and she looked so.

I have received the parcel containing the cushion and all the etceteras—for which I thank you very much. I suppose I must begin with the group of flowers—I don't know how I shall manage it—but I shall try. You need not to mind about keeping a feather-bed for me. I have a good number of letters to answer —from Smith—from Williams, from Thornton Hunt—Lætitia Wheelwright, Harriet Dyson—and that Miss Alexander who has written again though I did not answer her first letter—(more shame to me) so I must bid you good-bye for the present—write to me soon—The brief absence from home—though in some respects trying and painful in itself—has I think given a better tone to my spirits—All through the month of Feby—I had a

crushing time of it—I could not escape from or rise above certain most mournful recollections—the last days—the sufferings
—the remembered words—most sorrowful to me—of those
who—Faith assures me—are now happy. At evening—and bedtime such thoughts would haunt me—bringing a weary heart-
ache.—Good-bye dear Ellen, Yours faithfully,

C. B.

537 (424). *To* W. S. WILLIAMS.

March 19th, 1850.

MY DEAR SIR,—The books came yesterday evening just as I
was wishing for them very much. There is much interest for me
in opening the Cornhill parcel. I wish there was not pain too—
but so it is. As I untie the cords and take out the volumes, I am
reminded of those who once on similar occasions looked on
eagerly; I miss familiar voices commenting mirthfully and pleasantly; the room seems very still, very empty; but yet there is
consolation in remembering that papa will take pleasure in some
of the books. Happiness quite unshared can scarcely be called
happiness—it has no taste.

I wonder how you can choose so well; on no account would I
forestall the choice. I am sure any selection I might make for
myself would be less satisfactory than the selection others so
kindly and judiciously make for me; besides, if I knew all that
was coming it would be comparatively flat. I would much rather
not know.

Amongst the especially welcome works are 'Southey's Life,'[1]
the 'Women of France,'[2] Hazlitt's 'Essays,' Emerson's 'Representative Men'; but it seems invidious to particularise when all
are good. . . . I took up a second small book, Scott's 'Suggestions
on Female Education'[3]; that, too, I read, and with unalloyed
pleasure. It is very good; justly thought, and clearly and felicitously expressed. The girls of this generation have great advantages; it seems to me that they receive much encouragement in
the acquisition of knowledge and the cultivation of their minds;
in these days women may be thoughtful and well read, without

[1] *The Life and Correspondence of the late Robert Southey*, in six volumes, edited by his son the Rev. Charles Cuthbert Southey, 1849-50.

[2] *Woman in France during the Eighteenth Century*. By Julia Kavanagh, 1850.

[3] *Suggestions on Female Education*, by Alexander John Scott (1805-1866), the first Principal of Owens College, 1849.

being universally stigmatised as 'Blues' and 'Pedants.' Men begin to approve and aid, instead of ridiculing or checking them in their efforts to be wise. I must say that, for my own part, whenever I have been so happy as to share the conversation of a really intellectual man, my feeling has been, not that the little I knew was accounted a superfluity and impertinence, but that I did not know enough to satisfy just expectation. I have always to explain, 'In me you must not look for great attainments: what seems to you the result of reading and study is chiefly spontaneous and intuitive.' . . . Against the teaching of some (even clever) men, one instinctively revolts. They may possess attainments, they may boast varied knowledge of life and of the world; but if of the finer perceptions, of the more delicate phases of feeling, they may be destitute and incapable, of what avail is the rest? Believe me, while hints well worth consideration may come from unpretending sources, from minds not highly cultured, but naturally fine and delicate, from hearts kindly, feeling, and unenvious, learned dictums delivered with pomp and sound may be perfectly empty, stupid, and contemptible. No man ever yet 'by aid of Greek climbed Parnassus,' or taught others to climb it. . . .

I enclose for your perusal a scrap of paper which came into my hands without the knowledge of the writer. He is a poor working man of this village—a thoughtful, reading, feeling being, whose mind is too keen for his frame, and wears it out. I have not spoken to him above thrice in my life, for he is a Dissenter, and has rarely come in my way. The document is a sort of record of his feelings, after the perusal of 'Jane Eyre'; it is artless and earnest, genuine and generous. You must return it to me, for I value it more than testimonies from higher sources. He said: 'Miss Brontë, if she knew he had written it, would scorn him'; but, indeed, Miss Brontë does not scorn him; she only grieves that a mind of which this is the emanation should be kept crushed by the leaden hand of poverty—by the trials of uncertain health and the claims of a large family.

As to the 'Times,' as you say, the acrimony of its critique has proved, in some measure, its own antidote; to have been more effective it should have been juster. I think it has had little weight up here in the North: it may be that annoying remarks, if made, are not suffered to reach my ear; but certainly, while I heard little condemnatory of 'Shirley,' more than once have I been deeply moved by manifestations of even enthusiastic approbation. I

deem it unwise to dwell much on these matters; but for once I
must permit myself to remark, that the generous pride many of
the Yorkshire people have taken in the matter has been such as
to awake and claim my gratitude, especially since it has afforded
a source of reviving pleasure to my father in his old age. The
very curates, poor fellows! show no resentment: each character-
istically finds solace for his own wounds in crowing over his
brethren. Mr Donne was, at first, a little disturbed; for a week or
two he was in disquietude, but he is now soothed down; only
yesterday I had the pleasure of making him a comfortable cup of
tea, and seeing him sip it with revived complacency. It is a
curious fact that, since he read 'Shirley,' he has come to the house
oftener than ever, and been remarkably meek, and assiduous to
please. Some people's natures are veritable enigmas: I quite expected to have had one good scene at least with him; but as yet
nothing of the sort has occurred.

I hope Mrs Williams continues well, and that she is beginning
to regain composure after the shock of her recent bereavement.
She has indeed sustained a loss for which there is no substitute.
But rich as she still is in objects for her best affections, I trust the
void will not be long or severely felt. She must think, not of
what she has lost, but of what she possesses. With eight fine
children, how can she ever be poor or solitary!—Believe me,
dear sir, yours sincerely,   C. BRONTË.

538 (425). *To* ELLEN NUSSEY.

March 30th, 1850.

DEAR ELLEN,—You must not wait for me to come to Brookroyd before you go to Tranby—I have no intention of leaving
home at present—especially as it may be necessary (though this
is quite uncertain) that I should go to London for a week or two
in the course of the Spring, and if I *do*, I should like to see you
after my return, since then I should have more to tell you.

I had a letter from Amelia yesterday—very kindly and sensibly
written—She speaks of J. T. and seems to wish to get from me
a distinct opinion of his character &c. this, however, I cannot
give her, for were there no other objection—I have as yet no
distinct opinion, though I may have many *strong impressions*, for
my own use. Have you seen or heard anything of him lately?

I enclose a slip of newspaper for your amusement—me it both

amused and touched—for it alludes to some who are in this world no longer. It is an extract from an American Paper—and is written by an emigrant from Haworth—you will find it a curious mixture of truth and inaccuracy, return it when you write again. I also send you for perusal an opinion of 'Jane Eyre' written by a *working man* in this village; rather I should say a record of the feelings the book excited in the poor fellow's mind; it was not written for my inspection nor does the writer now know that his little document has by intricate ways—come into my possession—and I have forced those who gave it, to promise that they will never inform him of this circumstance. He is a modest, thoughtful, feeling, reading being—to whom I have spoken perhaps about three times in the course of my life —his delicate health renders him incapable of hard or close labour, he and his family are often under the pressure of want. He feared that if 'Miss Brontë saw what he had written she would laugh it to scorn,' but Miss Brontë considers it one of the highest, because one of the most truthful and artless tributes her work has yet received, you must return this likewise; I do you great honour in showing it to you.

Give my love to all at Brookroyd and believe me—Yours faithfully,

C. B.

539. *To* AMELIA RINGROSE.

March 31st, 1850.

DEAR AMELIA,—Experience has taught me to enter fully into all you say respecting your poor Mamma's last illness and death. It is indeed difficult under such circumstances for near relatives to realize the actual parting of soul from body. The longer we have watched the gradual attenuation of the thread of life, the more its final severance seems to take us by surprise. And then too, most truly do you describe the oblivion of faults which suc-ceeds to Death. No sooner are the eyes grown dim, no sooner is the pulse stilled than we forget what anxiety, what anguish, what shame the frailties and vices of that poor unconscious mould of clay once caused us; yearning love and bitter pity are the only sentiments the heart admits, but with these, for a time, it is sorely oppressed. Sometimes, in thinking over this, I have said to myself: If man can so forgive his fellow, how much more shall God pardon his creature?

The bustle with which you are now surrounded is painful in one sense, but—in another—I hope it will be profitable. We should never shrink with cowardice from the contemplation of Death, but after a near view, an actual contact with that King of terrors it is not good to be left unoccupied and solitary to brood over his awful lineaments. Often when I am alone, I try with all my might to look beyond the grave, to follow my dear sisters and my poor brother to that better world where—I trust—they are all now happy, but still, dear Amelia, I cannot help recalling all the details of the weeks of sickness, of the mortal conflict, of the last difficult agony, there are moments when I know not whither to turn or what to do, so sharp, so dark and distressing are these remembrances, so afflicted am I that beings so loved should have had to pass out of Time into Eternity—by a track so rough and painful. I ought not to write this, but you have a kind heart and will forgive me. Mention not a word of it to Ellen; it is a relief to write it down, but it would be great pain to talk it over.

I read with interest all you say about J. T. and I earnestly hope you may be led so to act as will be for your own best happiness. Whatever you may choose to say to me in confidence, I shall of course consider sacred. I believe you are too sensible to look much to the advice of any third party; yours is a position where reliance on God and yourself can alone be available. Be cautious but not timid, watchful but not suspicious. More I—for my part —cannot say—for this good reason—it is not given to man or woman to read the heart of others: they can but conjecture—they can but infer—and whether the conjecture or inference be just God only knows. Even after an acquaintance of years—of a whole life—we may still be uncertain about the bearings of a character—we find in human nature such anomalies, such con- tradictions, such enigmas. The carefully formed opinion of to- day may be at once over-turned by the opposing evidence of to-morrow.

Remember me very kindly to Rosey: I do not like to hear of her being thin and having a cough; she should be very, very careful of herself—does she still take the cod-liver-oil?

When you write again put another violet into the letter—I like the scent of the sweet violet better than any other perfume. You have not yet sent my bill—I am never easy while in debt. — Believe me, dear Amelia, Yours sincerely,

C. BRONTË.

540 (426). *To* ELLEN NUSSEY.

April 3rd, 1850.

DEAR ELLEN, — I certainly do think that you are generally too venturesome in risking exposure to all weathers — there are sudden changes from hot to cold and *vice versâ*—there are fogs, cold penetrating winds during which all people of constitutions not robust are better in the house than out of doors; regular exercise is an excellent thing, but in very cold or damp and stormy weather, you cannot always with prudence enjoy it. I do not wish you to coddle yourself, but trust you will be careful, ... maladies are sooner caught than cured. In your position it is your positive duty to run no risks; if anything happened to you what would be your mother's condition? Do not write again till you can do it without fatigue, but, as soon as you feel able, indite me a *particular*, detailed account of your state, speak the *exact* truth and give me no deceiving gloss. — Yours,

C. B.

541 (427). *To* W. S. WILLIAMS.

April 3rd, 1850.

MY DEAR SIR, — I have received the 'Dublin Review,' and your letter enclosing the Indian Notices. I hope these reviews will do good; they are all favourable, and one of them (the 'Dublin') is very able. I have read no critique so discriminating since that in the 'Revue des deux Mondes.' It offers a curious contrast to Lewes's in the 'Edinburgh,' where forced praise, given by jerks, and obviously without real and cordial liking, and censure, crude, conceited, and ignorant, were mixed in random lumps — forming a very loose and inconsistent whole.

Are you aware whether there are any grounds for that conjecture in the 'Bengal Hurkaru,' that the critique in the 'Times' was from the pen of Mr Thackeray? I should much like to know this. If such were the case (and I feel as if it were by no means impossible), the circumstance would open a most curious and novel glimpse of a very peculiar disposition. Do you think it likely to be true?

The account you give of Mrs Williams's health is not cheering, but I should think her indisposition is partly owing to the variable weather; at least, if you have had the same keen frost and cold east winds in London, from which we have lately suffered in Yorkshire. I trust the milder temperature we are now enjoying may quickly confirm her convalescence. With kind regards to Mrs Williams, —Believe me, my dear sir, yours sincerely,

C. BRONTË.

542. *To* CHARLOTTE BRONTË.

WELLINGTON, April 5th, 1850.

DEAR CHARLOTTE, —About a week since I received your last melancholy letter with the account of Anne's death and your utter indifference to every thing, even to the success of your last book. Though you do not say this it is pretty plain to be seen from the style of your letter. It seems to me hard indeed that you who would succeed better than anyone in making friends and keeping them should be condemned to solitude from your poverty. To no one would money bring more happiness, for no one would use it better than you would. —For me with my headlong self-indulgent habits I am perhaps better without it, but I am convinced it would give you great and noble pleasures. Look out then for success in writing. You ought to care as much for that as you do for going to Heaven. Though the advantages of being employed appear to you now the best part of the business you will soon please God have other enjoyments from your success. Railway shares will rise, your books will sell and you will acquire influence and power—and then most certainly you will find something to use it in, which will interest you and make you exert yourself.

What you say of Joe agrees with the melancholy account of him both in his own letters and other people's. I cannot give advice or propose a remedy. All seems to depend on himself and he—like all other people with his disease, is so powerless! His passion for marrying seems just to have come because it is the only thing serious enough to excite him —if that were done what would there be left? Your endeavour to persuade him to repose and quiet is certainly the best that could be made—may you succeed as you deserve! You will certainly do yourself good, tho it will be to both sides a melancholy meeting.

My own concerns have advanced rapidly. As much in this last

6 months as in the 4 years before. Ellen has come out with just the same wish to earn her living as I have and just the same objection to sedentary employment. We both enter heart and soul into the project of keeping a shop and actually hope to make £300 or £400 a year by it. John and Joe have helped her and me both with gifts and loans so that we begin with as large a capital as probably any in Wellington. We hope to have together fm £600 to £800. Our first step was to take some land (a st. corner) and build a house 28ft by 26. This is just in the heart of the town (*as laid out*) nevertheless until our house was built you could not see a st. at all, and the usual cart-road goes just thro the middle of it. Since we leased our bit 3 more people have taken the rest and one man has built a house and got into it.

It is just now blowing a cold south easter. I am sitting upstairs in a room with 2 windows looking to the east; by a glowing fire. In one room behind are 6 pieces paper hangings to be hung tomorrow; it is our best room. In the other some crockery to be sold—when the house is finished. Our back room downstairs is top full of groceries, to be sold when the house is finished but alas in each of the other 2 rooms is a carpenter's bench and there are 6 doorways wanting doors. Our new house delights us with its roomy comfort and now let me tell you what roomy comfort is. First understand it is made of boards overlapping, nailed to upright posts—our uprights are 2½ inches by 3. and the level piece at the bottom is of blue gum a very hard heavy lasting wood fm Hobart town. Inside the house is lined with boards—but without overlapping. In the shop and kitchen these boards are planed and grooved together, in our bedroom they will be stretched with calico and papered and for the present the other 3 rooms will be unfinished. [Diagrams]. The rooms upstairs are only 2ft high at the eaves. The best is 19ft by 12. We think it handsome. —Now for what we are to do. First remember we have by far the best house on our acre and the best but one in our 2 streets. The shop will be *among* the first in the town and the situation too. I can scarcely tell you how I have learnt something of most of the people whom I shall have to buy of. Waring has dealt with them and I have lived in the same small town with them these 4 or 5 years. I know too the extent to which Waring sells on credit and how glad any of these people would be to sell for money. Of most things too I know pretty well the prices I can get for them and what I ought to give. Waring gives us his opinion too and many things we can get fm him and know the prices at home too. Is this interesting? Well if it isn't here's some gossip. We have got a mechanic's institute and as it is the only place of (respectable) amusement in the town we encourage it with all our hearts —i.e. encourage everything abt it but the objects it was instituted for. One of these not-objects is dancing. So we are going to open the new Hall with a dance by and bye, one half the member's sulking at it and the other half just carrying their point by dint of cunning. My share of the business is to find young ladies for these young gentlemen—of course the dancers are all young and I hope to get 6 or 7 who will be glad to avail themselves of the bachelors tickets. I cannot tell you with what zeal I labour to spite the 'uneasy virtues' that are always saying something against 'promiscuous dancing'—what a phrase. With many of them the objection is not to the character of the company but to their station. Of course *we* think our character much above our station. I don't approve of being so slighted. Besides we have and can have a pretty even number of ladies and gentlemen which is not easy to get any where else. So we crow over them and *won't* have them—as we don't want them. I have got into all this heap of social trickery since Ellen came, never having troubled my head before abt the comparative numbers of young ladies and young gentlemen. To Ellen it is quite new to be of such importance by the mere fact of her femininity. She tho^t. she was coming wofully down in the world when she came out and finds herself better received than ever she was in her life before. And the class are not *in education* inferior though they are in money. They are decent well to do people. 1 grocer 1 draper 2 parsons 2 clerks 2 lawyers and 3 or four nondescripts. All these but one have families to 'take tea with' and there are a lot more single men to flirt with.

For the last 3 months we have been out every Sunday sketching. We seldom succeed in making the slightest resemblance to the thing we sit down to but it is wonderfully interesting. Next year we hope to send a lot home. Mrs Taylor has got another little girl. Miss Knox, the third sister is going to follow Mrs Cowper's example and marry a rich old man of disgraceful character. She is just abt 17 and her intended (Capt. Rhodes) has just put her to school. Waring has a good trade and fair health so has Mrs Taylor and the children—the health, not the trade. My cattle are nearly all in existence yet and instead of gaining I shall lose by them in consequence of keeping them so long. Meat sells for 5d. a lb. and I shall not get 3d. I should be ill off, but that Joe and John have given me the money which at first they lent me. With the increase I shall probably escape loss. With all this my novel stands still — it might have done so if I had had nothing to do, for it is not want of time but want of freedom of mind that makes me unable to direct my attention to it. Meantime it grows in my head, for I never give up the idea. I have written abt a volume I suppose. Read this letter to Ellen and ask her what was the impending event of importance to her which she promised to tell me of when she 'was more sure abt it.'

There has been a man talking of cholera in England till he has made me melancholy — His 'brother's wife's father' died of it at Bradford.

MARY TAYLOR.

543. *To* AMELIA RINGROSE.

HAWORTH, April 6th, '50.

DEAR AMELIA, — I enclose a Post-Office Order for £1 10s. being the amount of your bill. Consider it as accompanied by my sincere thanks for the trouble which remains unpaid.

The violets came safely — instead of putting them in water I dried them hoping they would retain their scent and intending to preserve them in a muslin bag. The experiment however failed, in drying; the fragrance vanished.

I am sorry to say that Ellen has been very ill — I heard from her to-day; she is now better and regaining her appetite. I hope she will be careful and have done my best in the way of lecturing her on this point.

For myself (I suppose I must not forget this time to answer your reiterated question) Spring is a season which never agrees with me very well and during which I always grow thin, but so far I have more reason for thankfulness than complaint; I have only, as yet, had slight colds and my headaches are less frequent than formerly.

You ask what I meant by the recommendation to be cautious but not timid, watchful but not suspicious; I had no hidden meaning, dear Amelia; I simply wished you to keep your mind clear of any feeling that might warp your judgment, and give it a bias detrimental to your interest. You intimate that you would like some advice on a certain subject. If I with certainty knew anything which I thought *you* should know —be assured no consideration should induce me to withold it from you—as it is, advice from me would be mere foolish interference; the longer I consider the matter the more thoroughly am I convinced that you and J. T. will be best left to manage your own matters — neither match-maker nor match-marrer ought to step between you. May God bless you and guide you to a right decision. Give my kind love to Rosey, and believe me, —Yours sincerely,

C. BRONTË.

544 (428). *To* W. S. WILLIAMS.

April 12th, 1850.

My DEAR SIR, —I own I was glad to receive your assurance that the Calcutta paper's surmise was unfounded.[1] It is said that when we *wish* a thing to be true, we are prone to believe it true, but I think (judging from myself) we adopt with a still prompter credulity the rumour which shocks.

It is very kind in Dr Forbes to give me his book; I hope Mr Smith will have the goodness to convey my thanks for the present. You can keep it to send with the next parcel, or perhaps I may be in London myself before May is over; that invitation I mentioned in a previous letter is still urged upon me, and well as I know what penance its acceptance would entail in some points, I also know the advantage it would bring in others. My conscience tells me it would be the act of a moral poltroon to let the fear of suffering stand in the way of improvement. But suffer— I shall. No matter.

The perusal of Southey's Life has lately afforded me much pleasure; the autobiography with which it commences is deeply interesting and the letters which follow are scarcely less so, disclosing as they do a character most estimable in its integrity and a nature most amiable in its benevolence, as well as a mind admirable in its talent. Some people assert that Genius is inconsistent with domestic happiness, and yet Southey was happy at home and made his home happy; he not only loved his wife and children *though* he was a poet, but he loved them the better *because* he was a poet. He seems to have been without taint of

---

[1]That Thackeray had written the *Times* review of *Shirley*.

worldliness; London, with its pomp and vanities, learned coteries with their dry pedantry rather scared than attracted him; he found his prime glory in his genius, and his chief felicity in home-affections. I like Southey.

I have likewise read one of Miss Austen's works 'Emma' — read it with interest and with just the degree of admiration which Miss Austen herself would have thought sensible and suitable — anything like warmth or enthusiasm; anything energetic, poignant, heartfelt, is utterly out of place in commending these works: all such demonstration the authoress would have met with a well-bred sneer, would have calmly scorned as outré and extravagant. She does her business of delineating the surface of the lives of genteel English people curiously well; there is a Chinese fidelity, a miniature delicacy in the painting: she ruffles her reader by nothing vehement, disturbs him by nothing profound: the Passions are perfectly unknown to her; she rejects even a speaking acquaintance with that stormy Sisterhood; even to the Feelings she vouchsafes no more than an occasional graceful but distant recognition; too frequent converse with them would ruffle the smooth elegance of her progress. Her business is not half so much with the human heart as with the human eyes, mouth, hands and feet; what sees keenly, speaks aptly, moves flexibly, it suits her to study, but what throbs fast and full, though hidden, what the blood rushes through, what is the unseen seat of Life and the sentient target of death — *this* Miss Austen ignores; she no more, with her mind's eye, beholds the heart of her race than each man, with bodily vision sees the heart in his heaving breast. Jane Austen was a complete and most sensible lady, but a very incomplete, and rather insensible (*not senseless*) woman, if this is heresy — I cannot help it. If I said it to some people (Lewes for instance) they would directly accuse me of advocating exaggerated heroics, but I am not afraid of your falling into any such vulgar error. — Believe me, Yours sincerely,   C. BRONTË.

545 (429). *To* ELLEN NUSSEY.

April 12th, 1850.

DEAR ELLEN, — I cannot find your last letter to refer to and therefore this will be no answer to it — you must write again by return of post if possible, and let me know how you are progressing. What you said in your last confirmed my opinion that your late attack had been coming on for a long time. Your wish for a cold water bath is, I should think, the result of fever; almost every one has complained lately of tendency to low fever. I have felt it in frequent thirst and infrequent appetite. Papa, too, and Martha, have complained. I fear this damp weather will scarcely suit you, but write and say all. Of late I have had many letters to answer — and some very bewildering ones — from people who want opinions about their books, who seek acquaintance and who flatter to get it — people who utterly mistake all about me. They are most difficult to answer, put off, and appease without offending, for such characters are excessively touchy and when affronted turn malignant. Their books are too often deplorable. Sir J. K. Shuttleworth and family are in London. I enclose the last note received from him. You are to read and comment. This was his theme when I was at Gawthorpe. I then gave notice that I would not be lionised; that is why he talks of 'small parties.' I shall probably go. I know what the effect and what the pain will be, how wretched I shall often feel, how thin and haggard I shall get; but he who shuns suffering will never win victory. If I mean to improve, I must strive and endure. The visit, if made, will, however, be *short*, as short as I can possibly make it. Would to God it were well over! I have one safeguard. Sir James has been a physician, and looks at me with a physician's eye: he saw at once that I could not stand much fatigue, nor bear the presence of many strangers. I believe he could partly understand how soon my stock of animal spirits was brought to a low ebb; but none — not the most skilful physician — can get at more than the outside of these things; the heart knows its own bitterness and the frame its own poverty, and the mind its own struggles. Papa is eager and restless for me to go; the idea of a refusal quite hurt him. Once more, would it were well over! — Yours, dear Nell,

C. B.

Amelia still writes to me. I sometimes find it difficult to answer her letters, but am always touched by their amiability. Tom Dixon wrote a note to say they would be here on Saturday week.

546 (430). *To* ELLEN NUSSEY.

Monday morn^g [April 15th, '50].

MY DEAR ELLEN,—It shall be my endeavour to come to see you on Thursday of this week—Of course I cannot be very easy till I have seen you, but it is quite useless to dilate on any impression your condition makes on me. I most earnestly wish you could have Mr Teale instead of Mr Carr—in Mr Carr one really cannot feel much confidence—and as to trifling with serious illness, the thought makes one sick—

God bless and protect you.   C. BRONTË.

I think you said the Birstall Omnibus started from the George about 4 o'clock p.m. Do not be discouraged if you happen to feel worse to-day—the weather is terribly unfavourable—an east-wind giving everybody cold. I cannot tell whether your complaint in any respect resembles Anne's—but I trust and hope there is in your case this great difference viz. that no vital organ, such as the lungs, is already by its inherent unsoundness predisposed to malady—I wonder what 'strong medicine' Mr Carr intends to give you—I abhor and distrust their 'strong medicines.' He is not dealing with a horse or an elephant.

In case of any decided change for the better in your state—a single line will relieve me from some anxiety—dear Nell—if prayers will do any good—I shall remember you.

547. *To* GEORGE SMITH.

April 18th, 1850.

MY DEAR SIR,—As you say, the dividend business had better be deferred till I come to London; I shall then have an opportunity of emulating 'Mrs Martha Struggles'[1] by going to the Bank for myself.

You must be kind enough to thank your mother and sisters for their friendly remembrances. Probably I shall look forward to seeing them with at least as much pleasure as they will anticipate seeing me. I have but a vague idea of the chances for observing society my intended visit may afford, but my imagination is very much inclined to repose on the few persons I already know, as a sort of oasis in the wilderness. Introduction to strangers is only a trial; it is the meeting with friends that gives pleasure.

[1] *Punch's* 'Unprotected Female'. See note p. 84 above.

On no account should you have dreamed that I was coming to town; I confess with shame that I have so much superstition in my nature as makes me reluctant to hear of the fulfilment of my dream, however pleasant; if the good dreams come true, so may the bad ones, and we have more of the latter than of the former.

That there are certain organisations liable to anticipating impressions in the form of dream or presentiment I half believe, but that you, a man of business, have any right to be one of these I wholly deny. 'No prophet can come out of Nazareth' (i.e. Cornhill).—Yours sincerely,

C. BRONTË.

548 (431). *To* ELLEN NUSSEY.

April 24th, 1850. Wednesday.

DEAR ELLEN,—I arrived home safely about half-past seven on Monday evening, and I am sorry to say I found papa far from well, with a bad cold; to-day, however, he is much better. I hope, with care, he will soon be much as usual. Joe Taylor came yesterday punctually at 2 o'clock. At first he was in an odious humour, behaving just as you described him that evening at Brookroyd. He had not been in the house 10 minutes before he began abusing 'old Ringrose,' in this strain he ran on—'he would not be kept waiting, it was humbug, he would give it up,' etc. I was beginning to feel much disgusted and to wonder how the time would pass till six o'clock. Papa being in bed, I had my visitor utterly to myself. Soon after dinner he took a turn, began gradually to calm, soften, talk rather affectionately of Miss Ringrose, and less bitterly of her father; to these topics he stuck almost the whole time, waxing more and more amiable towards the close. He had not a word to say that was new, his visit was, as I told you, a caprice. When he left at six, he announced that he should come again soon, and if he does come, he will talk the same things over again. I shall listen, mind my sewing, and be as patient as I possibly can. The visit did not exhaust me, I never once got excited, and talked very little. In talking of Miss Ringrose, his aim and pleasure seemed to be to reason himself into illusion and something like love, he repeated over and over again that she looked 'very nice' last time he saw her, and commended her conduct to the servants and to all round her. He said, in short, what was true and right, but he said it so often I was some-times at a loss for responses. No need to comment on the affair.

How are you, and what are the results of the tooth extraction? Give my love to all at Brookroyd, tell Mercy that I was much concerned at not bidding her good-bye. Tell Mrs Clapham that I made the pigeons into a pie and that they were excellent. Papa found them quite a treat and he had no appetite for meat. I send the 'Examiner' and 'Courier.' — Yours faithfully,

C. B.

549 (432). *To* W. S. WILLIAMS.

April 25th, 1850.

MY DEAR SIR, — I cannot let the Post go without thanking Mr Smith through you for the kind reply to Greenwood's applica-tion,[1] and, I am sure, both you and he would feel true pleasure could you see the delight and hope with which these liberal terms have inspired a good and intelligent though poor man. He thinks he now sees a prospect of getting his livelihood by a method which will suit him better than his wool-combing work has hitherto done, exercising more of his faculties and sparing his health. He will do his best, I am sure, to extend the sale of the cheap edition of 'Jane Eyre,' and whatever twinges I may still feel at the thought of that work being in the possession of all the worthy folk of Haworth and Keighley — such scruples are more than counterbalanced by the attendant good — I mean — by the assistance it will give a man who deserves assistance. I wish he could permanently establish a little bookselling business in Ha-worth; it would benefit the place as well as himself.

Thank you for the 'Leader' which I read with pleasure — the notice of Newman's work in a late number was very good.

Believe me, my dear Sir, in haste, Yours sincerely,

C. BRONTË.

[1] That he should be assisted in adding bookselling to the little stationery store which helped him to a livelihood. The in-scription on his tomb in Haworth church-yard runs: 'In loving memory of John Greenwood of Haworth, who died March 25, 1863, aged 56 years.' He gave Mrs Gaskell a brief reminiscence of the Brontë sisters buying writing-paper from him.

550 (433). *To* CHARLOTTE BRONTË.

WELLINGTON, NEW ZEALAND,
[April 25th, 1850].

DEAR CHARLOTTE,—I have set up shop! I am delighted with it as a whole—that is it is as pleasant, or as little disagreeable as you can expect an employment to be that you earn your living by. The best of it is that your labour has some return and you are not forced to work on hopelessly without result. Du reste—it is very odd—I keep looking at myself with one eye while I'm using the other and I sometimes find myself in very queer positions. Yesterday, I went along the shore past two wharves and several warehouses on a st. where I had never been before during all the 5 years I have been in Wellington. I opened the door of a long place filled with packages with a passage up the middle and a row of high windows on one side. At the far end of the room a man was writing at a desk beneath a window. I walked all the length of the room very slowly, for what I had come for had completely gone out of my head. Fortunately the man never heard me until I had recollected it. Then he got up and I asked him for some stone blue, saltpetre, tea, pickles, salt &c. He was very civil; I bought some things and asked for a note of them. He went to his desk again and I looked at some newspapers lying near. On the top was a circular from Smith and Elder, containing notices of the most important new works. The first and longest was given to 'Shirley' a book I had seen mentioned in the 'Manchester Examiner' as written by Currer Bell. I blushed all over; the man got up, folding the note. I pulled it out of his hand and set off to the door—looking odder than ever for a partner had come in and was watching. The clerk said something about sending them and I said something too, I hope it was not very silly—I took my departure.

I have seen some extracts from 'Shirley' in which you talk of women working. And this first duty, this great necessity you seem to think that some women may indulge in—if they give up marriage and don't make themselves too disagreeable to the other sex. You are a coward and a traitor. A woman who works is by that alone better than one who does not and a woman who does not happen to be rich and who *still* earns no money and does not wish to do so, is guilty of a great fault—almost a crime —a dereliction of duty which leads rapidly and almost certainly to all manner of degradation. It is very wrong of you to *plead* for toleration for workers on the ground of their being in peculiar circumstances and few in number or singular in disposition. Work or degradation is the lot of all except the very small number born to wealth.

For the last month I have really had a good excuse for not writing any more book. I have worked hard at something else. We have been moving, cleaning, shopkeeping until I was really tired every night—a wonder for me. It does me good, and I had much rather be tired than ennuyée. Have you seen Joe? or heard anything of John? There is a change gradually come over them in the last five years that I am only half acquainted with. Joe's gloom and John's wandering both shew wretched health, and Joe's cure seems to me very fantastic. By the eagerness with which he seeks to be married he evidently hopes more from the change than it will bring. It is certainly better to be married but to look forward to such great things is just insuring disappointment. Their business gives no subject for such depression and perhaps if they were poorer they would have more to care for. We all here thrive wonderfully. Waring and his babies, Ellen and myself. Ellen is worst—that is least well—she was seriously ill on the passage out. Henry is in Sydney. I think he will learn Waring's trade and settle in Auckland. John and Joe have promised to help him. Ellen is with me or I with her, I cannot tell how our shop will turn out but I am as sanguine as ever. Meantime we certainly amuse ourselves better than if we had nothing to do. We *like* it? that's the truth—By the Cornelia we are going to send our sketches and fern leaves. You must look at them and it will need all your eyes to understand them for they are a mass of confusion. They are all within 2 miles of Wellington and some of them rather like; Ellen's sketch of me especially. During the last 6 months I have seen more 'society' than in all the last 4 years. Ellen is half the reason of my being invited and my improved circumstances besides. There is no one worth mentioning particularly, the women are all ignorant and narrow and the men selfish. They are of a decent honest kind and some intelligent and able. Mrs Taylor's parson (Woodward) is the only *literary* man we know and he seems to have fair sense. This was the clerk I bought the stone blue of. We have just got a mechanic's Institute and weekly lectures delivered there. It is amusing to see people trying to find out whether or not it is fashionable and proper to patronise it. Somehow it seems it is. I think I have told you all this before, which shows I have got to the end of my news. Your next letter to me ought to bring me good news; more cheerful than the last. You will somehow get drawn out of your hole and find interests among your fellow creatures. Do you know that living among people with whom you have not the slightest interest in common is just like living alone, or worse. Ellen Nussey is the only one you can talk to, that I know of at least.

Give my love to her, and to Miss Wooler if you have the opportunity. I am writing this on just such a night as you will likely read it, rain and storm — coming winter and a glowing fire — Ours is on the ground, wood, no fender or irons — no matter we are very comfortable.

PAG.[1]

551. *To* AMELIA RINGROSE.

[April 28th, 1850].

DEAR AMELIA, — I found Ellen looking very poorly but still not at all worse than I had anticipated; she improved in looks, strength and appetite during the few days I stayed and indeed was so much recovered as to be able to accompany me as far as Leeds and there undergo the completion of the dentist-operation. I consider however that this step was rather premature and the one letter I have received from her since my return shewed that she had felt it in some degree though not more than was to be expected — I feel anxious to hear from her again.

It pleases me greatly to see that you write in tolerable spirits; keep up your serenity and sustain your patience as well as you possibly can, hoping and trusting that all will end well. I think you are right in saying little on the subject you refer to.

You and Rosy must indeed feel comfort in one another but when I read the expression of your mutual affection, a warning voice seems to whisper 'rejoice with trembling.' You may, and I trust will, long be spared to one another — but we know that it

[1]Mary Taylor.

may be otherwise—however, beyond and above the fear of separation, we acknowledge the hope of eternal re-union. With love to Rosy and yourself—believe me,—Yours faithfully,

C. BRONTË.

Sunday evening.

552 (434). *To* ELLEN NUSSEY.

[April 29th, 1850].

DEAR ELLEN,—I return Miss Wooler's little note which it gave me melancholy pleasure to read; it is, as you say, very like her—thoroughly characteristic both of some of her faults and of much of her excellence. By this time I suppose you are at Bradford—has the change of air done you any good? We have had but a poor week of it at Haworth; Papa continues far from well —he is often very sickly in the morning, a symptom which I have remarked before in his aggravated attacks of bronchitis— unless he should get much better—I shall never think of leaving him to go to London. Martha has suffered from tic-douloureux with sickness and fever just like you—she is however much better at present—I have a bad cold and stubborn sore throat— in short every body but old Tabby is out of sorts. When Joe Taylor was here, he complained of a sudden head-ache, and the night after he was gone—I had something similar—very bad— lasting about three hours—he seemed to bring a lot of illness with him into the house.

I have just got another letter from Amelia—she is a good and kind girl—but when she is married she must take care to be more sparing of her love to her spouse than she is of epistles to her friends.

The wind is in the east—I fear it will not suit you—send me a bulletin quickly.—Yours truly,

C. B.

I have received the plait—it is very nice and I shall keep it— but I will thank you also to get me 3 yds of brown satin ribbon— I will pay for both.

I have just discovered that I don't know your address in Bradford, so I shall direct at random.

553 (435). *To* W. S. Williams.

May 6th, 1850.

My dear Sir,—I have received the copy of 'Jane Eyre.'[1] To me the printing and paper seem very tolerable. Will not the public in general be of the same opinion? And are you not making yourselves causelessly uneasy on the subject?

I imagine few will discover the defects of typography unless they are pointed out. There are, no doubt, technical faults and perfections in the art of printing to which printers and publishers ascribe a greater importance than the majority of readers.

I will mention Mr Smith's proposal respecting the cheap publications to Greenwood. I believe him to be a man on whom encouragement is not likely to be thrown away, and who, if fortune should not prove quite adverse, will contrive to effect something by dint of intelligence and perseverance.

I am sorry to say my father has been far from well lately—the cold weather has tried him severely; and, till I see him better, my intended journey to town must be deferred. With sincere regards to yourself and other Cornhill friends,—I am, my dear sir, yours faithfully,

C. Brontë.

554 (436). *To* Ellen Nussey.

May 11th, 1850.

Dear Ellen,—I trust papa is now really better, but he has been very unwell since I wrote last—without appetite, feeble, and sickly. I felt for some days great anxiety about him, it is impossible to disguise from myself that these repeated attacks of bronchitis are a serious matter. There is something that appears very strange, that shocks, in the rapid advance of Miss Walker's illness. Consumption seems to be more rapid as well as more general in its ravages than formerly.

The Miss Wooler and M —— business is characteristic of each. I can well conceive the annoyance ——'s vagaries must cause. I fear I should be almost driven beside myself; certainly few things are more annoying than the wilfulness of a weak person. So long as they are tractable their deficiencies can be

[1] The cheap one-volume reprint.

borne with, but when they reject counsel and blunder into difficulties of their own making, one does not know how to manage.
Last Friday was the day appointed for me to go to Lancashire,
but I did not think papa well enough to be left, and accordingly
begged Sir James and Lady Shuttleworth to return to London
without me. It was arranged that we were to stay at several of
their friends' and relatives' houses on the way; a week or more
would have been taken up in the journey. I cannot say that I
regret having missed this ordeal; I would as lief have walked
among red-hot ploughshares; but I do regret one great treat,
which I shall now miss. Next Wednesday is the anniversary
dinner of the Royal Literary Fund Society, held in Freemasons'
Hall. Octavian Blewitt, the secretary, offered me a ticket for the
Ladies' Gallery. I should have seen all the great literati and
artists gathered in the hall below, and heard them speak. Thackeray and Dickens are always present among the rest. This cannot now be. I don't think all London can afford another sight to
me so interesting.[1]

With regards to all at Brookroyd,—I am, dear Nell, yours
faithfully,

C. B.

555 (437). *To* W. S. Williams.

May 20th, 1850.

My dear Sir,—I am thankful to say that papa is now so much
better—so nearly indeed restored to his usual state of health,
that I trust to be at liberty to come to town next[2] Thursday. I look
forward to the visit with mixed feelings, desiring it on some
accounts, dreading it on others.

Illness has of late been, and still is, very general here; from
what you say such seems also to have been the case in the South;
I am glad, however, to learn that the invalids in your own family
are convalescent.

Probably you can give me no information respecting the
writer of the letter forwarded by you. There was something
about it which took it out of the usual category of the letters I

[1]At Royal Literary Fund dinners it was
the custom to admit ladies to the Gallery
when the dinner was over, so that they
might listen to the speeches. Ladies were
first invited to the banquet on the occasion
when Mr. J. M. Barrie took the chair in
1905.

[2]Charlotte Brontë went to London on
Thursday, May 30th, 1850.

receive—genuine, earnest, unaffected; it deserved an answer, and should have had one, had the address been given.—Hoping to see you soon, I am, dear sir, yours sincerely,

C. BRONTË.

556 (438). *To* ELLEN NUSSEY.

May 21st, 1850.

DEAR ELLEN,—My visit is again postponed. Sir James, I am sorry to say, is most seriously ill, two physicians are in attendance twice a day, and company and conversation, even with his own relatives, are prohibited as too exciting. Notwithstanding this, he has written two notes to me himself, claiming a promise that I will wait till he is better, and not allow any one else 'to introduce me,' as he says, 'into the Oceanic life of London.' Sincerely sorry as I was for him, I could not help smiling at this sentence. But I shall willingly promise. I know something of him, and like part at least of what I do know. I do not feel in the least tempted to change him for another. His sufferings are very great; I trust and hope God will be pleased to spare his mind. I have just got a note informing me that he is something better; but, of course, he will vary. Lady Shuttleworth is much, much to be pitied too; his nights, it seems, are most distressing.

Poor Mrs Gorham and Mary! The cloud which has come over them seems to linger. Good-bye, dear Nell. Write soon to

C. B.

557. *To* JOHN DRIVER.

HAWORTH, May 22nd, '50.

MY DEAR SIR,—I know not whether it is absolutely necessary, but I think it better to write a single line to inform you that my journey to Town is again postponed—and as this second delay is owing to the severe illness of Sir J. K. Shuttleworth—it is—of course, quite uncertain when I shall be able to go.

My Father, I am thankful to say—remains much better—he unites with me in kind regards to yourself and Mrs Driver.—Believe me, my dear Sir, Yours very sincerely,

C. BRONTË.

558 (439). *To* JAMES TAYLOR.

May 22nd, 1850.

MY DEAR SIR,—I had thought to bring the 'Leader' and the 'Athenæum' myself this time, and not to have to send them by post, but it turns out otherwise; my journey to London is again postponed, and this time indefinitely. Sir James Kay-Shuttleworth's state of health is the cause—a cause, I fear, not likely to be soon removed. . . . Once more, then, I settle myself down in the quietude of Haworth Parsonage, with books for my household companions and an occasional letter for a visitor; a mute society, but neither quarrelsome, nor vulgarising, nor unimproving.

One of the pleasures I had promised myself consisted in asking you several questions about the 'Leader,' which is really, in its way, an interesting paper. I wanted, amongst other things, to ask you the real names of some of the contributors, and also what Lewes writes besides his 'Apprenticeship of Life.' I always think the article headed 'Literature' is his. Some of the communications in the 'Open Council' department are odd productions; but it seems to me very fair and right to admit them. Is not the system of the paper altogether a novel one? I do not remember seeing anything precisely like it before.

I have just received yours of this morning; thank you for the enclosed note. The longings for liberty and leisure, which May sunshine wakens in you, stir my sympathy. I am afraid Cornhill is little better than a prison for its inmates on warm spring or summer days. It is a pity to think of you all toiling at your desks in such genial weather as this. For my part, I am free to walk on the moors; but when I go out there alone everything reminds me of the times when others were with me, and then the moors seem a wilderness, featureless, solitary, saddening. My sister Emily had a particular love for them, and there is not a knoll of heather, not a branch of fern, not a young bilberry leaf, not a fluttering lark or linnet, but reminds me of her. The distant prospects were Anne's delight, and when I look round she is in the blue tints, the pale mists, the waves and shadows of the horizon. In the hill-country silence their poetry comes by lines and stanzas into my mind: once I loved it; now I dare not read it, and am driven often to wish I could taste one draught of oblivion, and forget much that, while mind remains, I never shall forget. Many people seem to recall their departed relatives with a sort of melancholy complacency, but I think these have not watched them through lingering sickness, nor witnessed their last moments: it is these reminiscences that stand by your bedside at night, and rise at your pillow in the morning. At the end of all, however, exists the Great Hope. Eternal Life is theirs now.

C. BRONTË.

559 (440). *To* A YOUNG MAN.[1]

May 23rd, 1850.

DEAR SIR,—Apologies are indeed unnecessary for a 'reality of feeling, for a genuine, unaffected impulse of the spirit,' such as prompted you to write the letter which I now briefly acknowledge.

Certainly it is 'something to me' that what I write should be acceptable to the feeling heart and refined intellect; undoubtedly it is much to me that my creations (such as they are) should find harbourage, appreciation, indulgence at any friendly hand, or from any generous mind. You are very welcome to take Jane, Caroline, and Shirley for your sisters, and I trust they will often speak to their adopted brother when he is solitary, and soothe him when he is sad. If they cannot make themselves at home in a thoughtful, sympathetic mind, and diffuse through its twilight a cheering domestic glow, it is their fault; they are not, in that case, so amiable, so benignant, not so *real* as they ought to be. If they *can*, and can find household altars in human hearts, they will fulfil the best design of their creation in therein maintaining a genial flame, which shall warm but not scorch, light but not dazzle.

What does it matter that part of your pleasure in such beings has its source in the poetry of your own youth rather than any magic of theirs? What that perhaps, ten years hence, you may smile to remember your present recollections, and view under another light both 'Currer Bell' and his writings? To me this consideration does not detract from the value of what you now feel. Youth has its romance, and maturity its wisdom, as morning

---

[1]Reprinted from Mrs Gaskell's *Life*, and there described as to a young man at Cambridge who had expressed admiration for her books.

and spring have their freshness, noon and summer their power, night and winter their repose. Each attribute is good in its own season. Your letter gave me pleasure, and I thank you for it.

CURRER BELL.

560. *To* MRS SMITH.

May 25th, 1850.

MY DEAR MRS SMITH, — You shall hear exactly how I am situated. Yesterday's post brought me a note from Sir J. K. Shuttleworth, intimating that he is something better, reminding me that my visit is only postponed, and requesting an assurance to the effect that I will keep myself disengaged, adding these words: 'Promise me that your first venture in this oceanic life shall be with me.' As the note betrayed much of that nervous anxiety inseparable from his state of health, I hastened to give him this promise; this, you will perceive, ties me down for the present.

I consider it, however, very doubtful whether he will be well enough to render my visit advisable; and even should I go, still my conviction is that a brief stay will seem to me the best. In that case, after a few days with my 'fashionable friends,' as you call them, I believe I should be excessively disposed, and probably profoundly thankful, to subside into any quiet corner of your drawing-room where I might find a chair of suitable height.

I am sorry you have changed your residence,[1] as I shall now again lose my way in going up and down stairs, and stand in great tribulation, contemplating several doors and not knowing which to open.

I regret that my answer to your kind note must be so inconclusive; the lapse of a fortnight or three weeks will probably facilitate a decision. In the meantime, with kindest regards to your family circle, — Believe me, my dear Mrs. Smith, Yours sincerely,

C. BRONTË.

Any peculant Post-office clerk who shall mistake the contents of this letter for a bank-note will find himself in the wrong box. You see they are finished.[2]

---

[1] The Smiths had removed from Westbourne Place to 76 Gloucester Terrace.

[2] The baby's socks that Miss Brontë had knitted.

561 (441). *To* Ellen Nussey.

May 27th, 1850.

Dear Ellen,—Papa has continued to improve since I last wrote; he preached twice yesterday, and as he is extremely anxious I should get over my London visit, I intend if all be well to go at the close of this week.

I return the Pen and Ink portrait. I cannot say it encourages me to have my own taken. In three things it happens to hit the truth: in making you fond of giving, disposed rather to spend than save, and in representing you as conscientious and affection-ate. Most of the other points offer so complete and violent an opposition to the truth as to prove the whole thing quackery.

As this is Whit-Monday I am busy. Good-bye, dear Nell.— Yours faithfully,

C. B.

CHAPTER XXIII

LONDON, EDINBURGH AND THE LAKES

CHARLOTTE BRONTË may be counted among those who have felt the glamour of London. Her praise of it is well known to all who collect the verdict of distinguished writers on that great city. Her visits to it were many, but it was the fifth visit in the summer of 1850 that probably secured to her the greatest personal pleasure. She spent the opening of her fortnight's visit with Mrs Smith, now removed to Gloucester Terrace, Hyde Park, and she closed it with her friend Lætitia Wheelwright at Phillimore Gardens. It was on this occasion that she first saw her hero, the Duke of Wellington; she had a conversation with Thackeray, whom she appears to have 'lectured'; and she met George Henry Lewes, with whom she had corresponded with so much vigour.

562 (442). *To* ELLEN NUSSEY.

76 GLOUCESTER TERRACE, HYDE PARK GARDENS,
LONDON, June 3rd, 1850.

DEAR ELLEN,—I came to London last Thursday. I am staying at Mrs Smith's, who has changed her residence as the address will show. A good deal of writing backwards and forwards, persuasion, etc., took place before this step was resolved on, but at last I explained to Sir James that I had some little matters of business to transact, and that I should stay quietly at my publishers. He has called twice, and Lady Shuttleworth once; each of them alone. He is in a fearfully nervous state. To my great horror he talks of my going with them to Hampton Court, Windsor, etc. God knows how I shall get on. I perfectly dread it.

Here I feel very comfortable, Mrs Smith treats me with a serene equable kindness which just suits me. Her son is as before genial and kindly. I have seen very few persons, and am not likely to see many, as the agreement was that I was to be very quiet. We have been to the Exhibition of the Royal Academy, to the Opera, and the Zoological Gardens. The weather is splendid. I shall not stay longer than a fortnight in London. The feverishness and exhaustion beset me somewhat, but not quite so badly as before, as indeed I have not yet been so much tried. I hope you will write soon and tell me how you are getting on. Give my regards to all. — Yours faithfully,

C. B.

563 (443). *To* LÆTITIA WHEELWRIGHT.

76 GLOUCESTER TERRACE,
HYDE PARK GARDENS, June 3rd, '50.

DEAR LÆTITIA, —I came to London last Thursday and shall stay perhaps a fortnight. To-morrow I expect to go out of town for a few days — but next week, if all be well, I hope to have the pleasure of calling on you. If you write to me meanwhile, address as above, and I shall find the letter on my return.

Give my sincere regards to your papa, mamma, and all round the circle — Emily, Fanny, Sarah-Anne, and, last not least — take a good share of them to your regal self. —I am, yours sincerely,

C. BRONTË.

564 (444). *To* the REV. P. BRONTË.

76 GLOUCESTER TERRACE,
HYDE PARK GARDENS, June 4th, 1850.

DEAR PAPA, —I was very glad to get your letter this morning, and still more glad to learn that your health continues in some degree to improve. I fear you will feel the present weather somewhat debilitating, at least if it is as warm in Yorkshire as in London. I cannot help grudging these fine days on account of the roofing of the house. It is a great pity the workmen were not prepared to begin a week ago.

Since I wrote I have been to the Opera; to the Exhibition of the Royal Academy, where there were some fine paintings, especially a large one by Landseer of the Duke of Wellington on the field of Waterloo, and a grand, wonderful picture of Martin's from Campbell's poem of the 'Last Man,' showing the red sun fading out of the sky, and all the soil of the foreground made up of bones and skulls. The secretary of the Zoological Society also sent me an honorary ticket of admission to their gardens, which

I wish you could see. There are animals from all parts of the world enclosed in great cages in the open air amongst trees and shrubs—lions, tigers, leopards, elephants, numberless monkeys, camels, five or six camelopards, a young hippopotamus with an Egyptian for its keeper; birds of all kind—eagles, ostriches, a pair of great condors from the Andes, strange ducks and water-fowl which seem very happy and comfortable, and build their nests among the reeds and edges of the lakes where they are kept. Some of the American birds make inexpressible noises.

There are also all sorts of living snakes and lizards in cages, some great Ceylon toads not much smaller than Flossy, some large foreign rats nearly as large and fierce as little bull-dogs. The most ferocious and deadly-looking things in the place were these rats, a laughing hyena (which every now and then uttered a hideous peal of laughter such as a score of maniacs might produce) and a cobra di capello snake. I think this snake was the worst of all: it had the eyes and face of a fiend, and darted out its barbed tongue sharply and incessantly.

I am glad to hear that Tabby and Martha are pretty well. Remember me to them, and—Believe me, dear papa, your affectionate daughter,

C. BRONTË.

I hope you don't care for the notice in 'Sharpe's Magazine'; it does not disturb me in the least. Mr Smith says it is of no consequence whatever in a literary sense. Sharpe, the proprietor, was an apprentice of Mr Smith's father.

565 (445). *To* ELLEN NUSSEY.

June 12th, '50.

DEAR ELLEN,—Since I wrote to you last, I have not had many moments to myself except such as it was *absolutely* necessary to give to rest. On the whole, however, I have thus far got on very well, suffering much less from exhaustion than I did last time—

Of course I cannot in a letter give you a regular chronicle of how my time has been spent—I can only just notify what I deem three of the chief incidents—A sight of the Duke of Wellington at the Chapel Royal—(he is a real grand old man) a visit to the House of Commons (which I hope to describe to you some day when I see you) and—last not least—an interview with Mr Thackeray. He made a morning-call and sat above two hours—

Mr Smith only was in the room the whole time. He described it afterwards as a queer scene; and I suppose it was. The giant sat before me—I was moved to speak to him of some of his short-comings (literary of course) one by one the faults came into my mind and one by one I brought them out and sought some ex-planation or defence—He did defend himself like a great Turk and heathen—that is to say, the excuses were often worse than the crime itself. The matter ended in decent amity—if all be well I am to dine at his house this evening.

I have seen Lewes too—he is a man with both weaknesses and sins; but unless I err greatly the foundation of his nature is not bad—and were he almost a fiend in character—I could not feel otherwise to him than half sadly, half tenderly—a queer word the last—but I use it because the aspect of Lewes' face almost moves me to tears—it is so wonderfully like Emily—her eyes, her fea-tures—the very nose, the somewhat prominent mouth, the fore-head—even at moments the expression: whatever Lewes does or says I believe I cannot hate him.[1]

Another likeness I have seen too that touched me sorrow-fully. Do you remember my speaking of a Miss Kavanagh—a young authoress who supported her mother by her writings? Hearing from Mr Williams that she had a longing to see me I called on her yesterday—I found a little, almost dwarfish figure to which even *I* had to look down—not deformed—that is—not hunchbacked but long-armed and with a large head and (at first sight) a strange face. She met me half-frankly, half tremb-lingly; we sat down together and when I had talked with her five minutes that face was no longer strange but mournfully familiar —it was Martha Taylor in every lineament—I shall try to find a moment to see her again. She lives in a poor but clean and neat little lodging—her mother seems a somewhat weak-minded woman who can be no companion to her—her father has quite deserted his wife and child—and this poor little feeble, intelli-gent, cordial thing wastes her brain to gain a living. She is twenty-five years old.

I have seen considerably more of the Williams' family but would rather communicate my impressions in conversation than by writing—Mr Williams—his three daughters and his son were here at a ball Mrs Smith gave last Friday—the ease and

[1] Lewes described Charlotte Brontë as 'a little, plain, provincial, sickly-looking old maid.' (*Life of George Eliot*, by J. W. Cross).

William Smith Williams Esq.
after a photograph by his son Richard Smith Williams

Emery Walker Ph sc.

grace, the natural gentility of the manners of all five were re-markable—their dress—their appearance were a decoration to the rooms—as Mrs Smith afterwards remarked—I called at their house yesterday—and I can hardly tell why I came away much pained—others do not see—or at least do not mention—what I seem to see in that family—whether I am partly mistaken I do not know. Mrs Williams has been here too—her conversation is most fluent and intelligent—her manners perfectly good—of her character—in a moral point of view—I can have now no doubts—and yet I confess there is a something about all except-ing the father himself and the eldest daughter—from which I feel inclined to shrink.

I do not intend to stay here at the furthest more than a week longer—but at the end of that time I cannot go home for the house at Haworth is just now unroofed—repairs were become necessary—if I get any cash (of which I see no signs) I should like to go for a week or two to the sea-side—in which case I wonder whether it would be possible for you to join me—but this point will require deliberation.

Meantime with regards to all believe me—Yours faithfully,

C. B.

Write directly.

566 (446). *To* MARTHA BROWN.

LONDON, June 12th, '50.

DEAR MARTHA,—I have not forgotten my promise of writing to you, though a multitude and variety of engagements have hitherto prevented me from fulfilling it.

It appears, from a letter I received from papa this morning, that you are now all in the hustle of unroofing; and I look with anxiety at a somewhat cloudy sky, hoping and trusting that it will not rain till all is covered in.

You and Martha Redman are to take care not to break your backs with attempting to lift and carry heavy weights; also you are not foolishly to run into draughts, go out without caps and bonnets, or otherwise take measures to make yourselves ill. I was rather curious to know how you have managed about a sleeping-place for yourself and Tabby.

You must not expect that I should give you any particular

description of London, as that would take up a great deal of time, and I have only a few minutes to spare. I shall merely say that it is a Babylon of a place, and just now particularly gay and noisy, as this is what is called the height of the London Season, and all the fine people are in Town. I saw a good many Lords and Ladies at the Opera a few nights since, and, except for their elegant dresses, do not think them either much better or much worse than other people.

In answer to this you may, when you have time, write me a few lines, in which you may say how Papa is; how you and Tabby are, how the house is getting on, and how John Greenwood prospers.

With kind regards to Tabby, and Martha Redman, I am, dear Martha, your sincere friend,

C. BRONTË.

567. *To* JAMES HOGG, ESQ.[1]

LONDON, June 13th, '50.

DEAR SIR,—I regret much that absence from home has prevented my receiving and, consequently, answering your letter earlier, and am the more concerned because my answer must be couched in the form of a refusal.

While I decline to sanction the publication of any portrait of myself for the present—permit me at the same time to express my sense of the considerate and gentlemanly form in which your application is made, and believe me—Yours sincerely,

C. BRONTË.

568 (447). *To* ELLEN NUSSEY.

76 GLOUCESTER TERRACE,
HYDE PARK GARDENS, June 21st, 1850.

DEAR ELLEN,—I am leaving London, if all be well, on Tuesday, and shall be very glad to come to you for a few days, if that arrangement still remains convenient to you. I intend to start at 9 o'clock a.m. by the express train which arrives in Leeds 35 m. past two. I should then be at Batley about 4 in the afternoon.

---

[1]James Hogg (1806–1888), Edinburgh publisher; edited the *Weekly Instructor or* *Titan*, 1845–59; published De Quincey's and Gilfillan's works, and *London Society*.

Would that suit? My London visit has much surpassed my expectations this time; I have suffered less and enjoyed more than before; rather a trying termination yet remains to me. Mrs Smith's youngest son is at school in Scotland, and George, her eldest, is going to fetch him home for the vacation; the other evening he announced his intention of taking one of his sisters with him, and proposed that Miss Brontë should go down to Edinburgh and join them there, and see that city and its suburbs. I concluded he was joking, laughed and declined: however, it seems he was in earnest. The thing appearing to me perfectly out of the question, I still refused. Mrs Smith did not favour it; you may easily fancy how she helped me to sustain my opposition, but her worthy son only waxed more determined. His mother is master of the house, but he is master of his mother. This morning she came and entreated me to go. 'George wished it so much'; he had begged her to use her influence, etc., etc. Now I believe that George and I understand each other very well, and respect each other very sincerely. We both know the wide breach time has made between us; we do not embarrass each other, or very rarely, my six or eight years of seniority, to say nothing of lack of all pretension to beauty, etc., are a perfect safeguard. I should not in the least fear to go with him to China. I like to see him pleased, I greatly *dis*like to ruffle and disappoint him, so he shall have his mind, and, if all be well, I mean to join him in Edinburgh after I shall have spent a few days with you. With his buoyant animal spirits and youthful vigour he will make severe demands on my muscles and nerves, but I dare say I shall get through somehow, and then perhaps come back to rest a few days with you before I go home. With kind regards to all at Brookroyd, your guests included,—I am, dear Ellen, yours faithfully,   C. Brontë.

Write by return of post.

569. *To* George Smith.

Brookroyd, June 27th, 1850.

My dear Sir,—It is written that I should not meet you at Tarbet, and at this perversity of the Fates I should be much more concerned than I am if I did not feel very certain that the loss in the matter will be chiefly my own. Of your three plans the last is the only one found practicable; Edinburgh is the true

Philippi, and there I hope (D.V.) to see you again next Wednesday.

I left Sarah much better, but I think your mother had decided against her going to Scotland, thinking the journey too long.

Before I left London I had the opportunity of bidding Mr Thackeray good-bye without going to his house for the purpose, and of this I was very glad.

My call on Mrs and Miss —— proved ineffectual, as the two ladies were gone out of town for the day, a circumstance keenly to be regretted, as I thus lose the pleasure of communicating a few words of 'latest intelligence' where they would be so acceptable.

With kind regards to your sister, and hopes that she has thus far borne her journey well, —I am, Yours sincerely,

C. BRONTË.

570. *To* MRS SMITH, 76, *Gloucester Terrace.*

BROOKROYD, BIRSTALL, LEEDS,
June 28th, 1850.

MY DEAR MRS SMITH,—I arrived here safely about four o'clock on Tuesday afternoon, having performed the journey with less inconvenience from headache, &c., than I ever remember to have experienced before; nor was I ill the next day.

It is now settled that I may go to Edinburgh, but not to Tarbet, and I have written to Mr Smith to that effect—I only hope he will not be at all disappointed—and indeed, as he is now in the full excitement of his tour, the change of plan will probably appear of no consequence.

I could fill a page or two with acknowledgements of your kindness to me while in London, but I don't think you would care to hear much on the subject; I will only say then that I never remember to have enjoyed myself more in the same length of time. With love to Sarah and Bell, believe me, my dear Mrs Smith. . . . Yours sincerely,

C. BRONTË.

571 (448). *To* ELLEN NUSSEY.

July 5th, 1850.

DEAR ELLEN,—We shall leave Edinburgh to-morrow morning at a quarter to ten, arrive in York at 40 m. past three. From York I think there is no train to Leeds till about 6.30. If so, I shall not reach Leeds till 8 o'clock; too late for the train to Batley. If it is really too late I shall take a cab at Leeds, for I would rather do that than stay at an Inn all night. I got to Edinburgh very safely; it is a glorious city. I wish you were with us and could see all we saw yesterday. London seems a dreary place compared to it. Mr Smith was a little bit angry at first about my not having come. Unless plans are again changed we shall travel all together as far as York. We are just going out, so good-bye, dear Nell. Kind regards to all.—Yours faithfully,

C. B.

572 (449). *To* ELLEN NUSSEY.

Monday. HAWORTH,
[July 15th, 1850].

DEAR NELL,—I got home very well—and full glad was I that no insuperable obstacle had deferred my return one single day longer. Just at the foot of Bridgehouse hill I met John Greenwood—staff in hand, he fortunately saw me in the cab—stopped and informed me he was setting off to Brookroyd by Mr Brontë's orders to see how I was—for that he had been quite miserable ever since he got Miss Nussey's letter—I found on my arrival that papa had worked himself up to a sad pitch of nervous excitement and alarm—in which Martha and Tabby were but too obviously joining him—I can't deny but I was annoyed; there really being small cause for it all.

I hope you got to Hull well and that you are now no worse for your journey and the botheration preceding it.

The house looks very clean and—I think—is not damp—there is however still a great deal to do in the way of settling and arranging—enough to keep me disagreeably busy for some time to come.

I was truly thankful to find papa pretty well—but I fear he is just beginning to shew symptoms of a cold: my cold continues better.

I have recently found that Papa's great discomposure had its origin in two sources—the vague fear of my being somehow about to be married to somebody—having 'received some overtures' as he expressed himself—as well as in apprehension of illness—I have distinctly cleared away the first cause of uneasiness.

An article in a Newspaper I found awaiting me on my arrival amused me—it was a paper published while I was in London—I enclose it to give you a laugh—it professes to be written by an Author jealous of Authoresses—I do not know who he is—but he must be one of those I met—I saw Geraldine Jewsbury[1] and Mrs Crowe as I think I told you—the 'ugly men' giving themselves 'Rochester airs' is no bad hit—some of those alluded to will not like it.

Give my love to Amelia and repeat to her my thanks for her kind invitation and my regret that I could not accept it. Yours faithfully,

C. BRONTË.

Martha has just told me John Greenwood's opinion of 'Miss Ellen Nussey'—'a nice mild, sweet-tempered looking lady' 'the best body he saw at yon' spot—he didn't make mich 'count o' t' others.' Yet on the whole it seems he was greatly pleased with his little excursion.

Write immediately.

573 (451). *To* ELLEN NUSSEY.

July 18th, 1850.

DEAR ELLEN,—You must cheer up, for your letter proves to me that you are low-spirited. As for me, what I said is to be taken in this sense—that, under the circumstances, it would be presumption in me to calculate on a long life. A truth obvious enough. For the rest, we are all in the hands of Him who apportions his gifts—health or sickness—length or brevity of days as is best for the receiver; to him, who has work to do, time will be given in which to do it, for him to whom no task is assigned, the season of rest will come earlier: as to the suffering preceding our last sleep—the sickness, decay, the struggle of spirit and flesh — it *must* come sooner or later to all. If, in one point of view, it is

---

[1]Geraldine Endsor Jewsbury (1812–1880) novelist, friend of the Carlyles, Helen Faucit and William Edward Forster; published *Zoë*, 1845, *The Half-Sisters*, 1848, *Marian Withers*, 1851, *Right or Wrong*, 1859, and juvenile fiction.

sad to have few ties in the world, in another point of view it is soothing; women who have husbands and children must look forward to death with more pain—more fear than those who have none. To dismiss the subject I wish (without cant, and not in any hackney sense) that both you and I could always say in this matter—the will of God be done.

I am beginning to get settled at home—but the solitude seems heavy as yet—it is a great change, but in looking forward—I try to hope for the best. So little faith have I in the power of any temporary excitement to do real good—that I put off day by day writing to London to tell them I am come home—and till then it was agreed I should not hear from them. It is painful to be dependent on the small stimulus letters give—I sometimes think I will renounce it altogether, close all correspondence on some quiet pretext, and cease to look forward at post-time for any letters but yours.

I send the French newspaper to-day—the 'Examiner' went on Tuesday. Give my love to Amelia—and believe me—Yours faithfully,

C. BRONTË.

574 (450). *To* W. S. WILLIAMS.

July 20th, 1850.

MY DEAR SIR,—I would not write to you immediately on my arrival at home, because each return to this old house brings with it a phase of feeling which it is better to pass through quietly before beginning to indite letters.

The six weeks of change and enjoyment are past but they are not lost; Memory took a sketch of each as it went by and especially, a distinct daguerrotype of the two days I spent in Scotland. Those were two very pleasant days. I always liked Scotland as an idea, but now, as a reality, I like it far better; it furnished me with some hours as happy almost as any I ever spent. Do not fear however that I am going to bore you with descriptions; you will, before now, have received a pithy and pleasant report of all things, to which any addition of mine would be superfluous.

My present endeavours are directed towards recalling my thoughts, cropping their wings, drilling them into correct discipline and forcing them to settle to some useful work: they are idle and keep taking the train down to London or making a foray over the Border, especially are they prone to perpetrate that last excursion—and who indeed that has once seen Edinburgh, with its couchant crag-lion, but must see it again in dreams waking or sleeping? My dear Sir, do not think I blaspheme when I tell you that your Great London as compared to Dun-Edin 'mine own romantic town' is as prose compared to poetry, or as a great rumbling, rambling, heavy Epic—compared to a lyric, brief, bright, clear and vital as a flash of lightning. You have nothing like Scott's Monument, or, if you had that and all the glories of architecture assembled together, you have nothing like Arthur's Seat, and above all you have not the Scotch National Character—and it is that grand character after all which gives the land its true charm, its true greatness.

In dread of becoming enthusiastic I close my letter, prolonging it only to beg that you will give my kind remembrances to Mrs Williams and your family, and to request that when you write you will tell me how my travelling companions got home and how they now are.—I am yours sincerely,

C. BRONTË.

575. *To* JOHN STORES SMITH.

HAWORTH, July 25th, 1850.

MY DEAR SIR,—I have not yet read the whole of the work you have kindly sent me, but I have read enough of it to feel impatient to offer my sincere congratulations on the marked—the important progress made by the author since the publication of his 'Mirabeau.' I find 'Social Aspects' deeply interesting, as all must find it who accord the book an attentive perusal. It seems to me that the views here expressed have a peculiar rectitude, that the thoughts are full of sound sense, and that these views are advocated, and these thoughts advanced with an earnestness that deserves, and, I trust, will command general attention.

In writing this book you have cast good seed into the ground; that you may see it ripen and gather the produce a hundredfold, is the sincere wish of—Yours very truly,

C. BRONTË.

P.S.—You mention Mrs Gaskell and Miss Jewsbury. I regard as an honour any expression of interest from these ladies. The latter I had once the pleasure of meeting in London.

It was during this visit to London in June, 1850, that Charlotte Brontë sat for her portrait to Richmond. It is the only portrait extant of her with any degree of accuracy or any certainty of pedigree. This crayon drawing was the gift of Mr George Smith to her father. It hung during her lifetime in the parlour at Haworth, but after her death was taken by her husband, Mr Arthur Bell Nicholls, to his home at Banagher, Ireland. It was twice brought to London for short periods during the next fifty years, and bequeathed by Mr Nicholls in his will to the National Portrait Gallery, where it found a permanent home in the year 1907.

576. *To* GEORGE SMITH.

July 27th, 1850.

MY DEAR SIR,—Papa will write and thank you himself for the portrait when it arrives. As for me, you know, a standing interdict seals my lips.

You thought inaccurately about the copy of the picture as far as my feelings are concerned, and yet you judged rightly on the whole; for it is my intention that the original drawing shall one day return to your hands. As the production of a true artist it will always have a certain worth, independently of subject.

I owe you two debts: I did not pay for my cards, nor for the power of attorney. Let me request you to be at once good and just, and tell me to what these little items amounted.

Were you still in Glencoe, or even in Edinburgh, I might write you a longer and more discursive letter, but, mindful of the 'fitness of things' and of the effect of locality, reverent too of the claims of business, I will detain your attention no longer.

Tell your sister Eliza I am truly glad to hear that she has derived so much benefit from her excursion; remember me very kindly to her, your mother, and the rest of your circle. —And believe me, Sincerely yours,

C. BRONTË.

577 (452). *To* LÆTITIA WHEELWRIGHT.

HAWORTH, July 30th, 1850.

MY DEAR LÆTITIA,—I promised to write to you when I should have returned home. Returned home I am, but you may conceive that many, many matters solicit attention and demand arrangement in a house which has lately been turned topsy-turvy in the operation of unroofing. Drawers and cupboards must wait a moment, however, while I fulfil my promise, though it is imperatively necessary that this fulfilment should be achieved with brevity.

My stay in Scotland was short, and what I saw was chiefly comprised in Edinburgh and the neighbourhood, in Abbotsford and Melrose, for I was obliged to relinquish my first intention of going from Glasgow to Oban and thence through a portion of the Highlands. But though the time was brief, and the view of objects limited, I found such a charm of situation, association, and circumstances that I think the enjoyment experienced in that little space equalled in degree and excelled in kind all which London yielded during a month's sojourn. Edinburgh compared to London is like a vivid page of history compared to a huge dull treatise on political economy; and as to Melrose and Abbotsford, the very names possess music and magic.

I am thankful to say that on my return home I found papa pretty well. Full often had I thought of him when I was far away; and deeply sad as it is on many accounts to come back to this old house, yet I was glad to be with him once more.

You were proposing, I remember, to go into the country; I trust you are there now and enjoying this fine day in some scene where the air will not be tainted, nor the sunshine dimmed, by London smoke. If your papa, mamma, or any of your sisters are within reach, give them my kindest remembrances—if not, save such remembrances till you see them.—Believe me, my dear Lætitia, yours hurriedly but faithfully,

C. BRONTË.

578 (454). *To* ELLEN NUSSEY.

Augst 1st, 1850.

MY DEAR ELLEN, — I have certainly felt the late wet weather a good deal and been somewhat bothered with frequently returning colds and so has Papa — about him I have been far from happy — every cold seems to make and leave him so weak — it is easy to say this world is only a scene of probation but it is a hard thing to feel.

Your friends the Ringroses seem to be happy just now, and long may they continue to be so! Give C. Brontë's sincere love to Rosy, and tell her she hopes Mr John Dugdale will make her a good husband: if he does not — woe be to him!

I wish a similar wish for Amelia — and there I do really think there will be a kind of happiness — that proposition about remaining at Hunsworth sounds like beginning life sensibly — with no shewy dash — I like it.

Are you comfortable amongst all these turtle-doves? I could not maintain your present position at Tranby for a day — I should feel 'de trop' as the French say, that is, in the way: but you are different to me.

My portrait is come from London — and the Duke of Wellington's and kind letters enough — Papa thinks the portrait looks older than I do — he says the features are far from flattered, but acknowledges that the expression is wonderfully good and lifelike.

I left the book called 'Social Aspects' at Brookroyd; accept it from me. I may well give it you, for the author has kindly sent me another copy.

Write to me again soon and believe me dear Ellen — Yours faithfully,

C. B.

You ask for some promise — Who that does not know the future can make promises? Not I.

579 (453). *To* GEORGE SMITH.

HAWORTH, August 1st, 1850.

MY DEAR SIR, — The little box for me came at the same time as the large one for papa. When you first told me that you had had the Duke's picture framed, and had given it to me, I felt half provoked with you for performing such a work of supereroga-tion, but now, when I see it again, I cannot but acknowledge that, in so doing, you were felicitously inspired. It is his very image, and, as papa said when he saw it, scarcely in the least like the ordinary portraits; not only the expression, but even the form of the head is different, and of a far nobler character. I esteem it a treasure. The lady who left the parcel for me was, it seems, Mrs Gore.[1] The parcel contained one of her works, 'The Hamiltons,' and a very civil and friendly note, in which I find myself ad-dressed as 'Dear Jane.' Papa seems much pleased with the por-trait, as do the few other persons who have seen it, with one notable exception, viz. our old servant, who tenaciously main-tains that it is not like — that it is too old-looking — but, as she, with equal tenacity, asserts that the Duke of Wellington's pic-ture is a portrait of 'the Master' (meaning papa), I am afraid not much weight is to be ascribed to her opinion; doubtless she confuses her recollections of me as I was in childhood with present impressions. Requesting always to be very kindly remem-bered to your mother and sisters, I am yours very thanklessly (according to desire),

C. BRONTË.

580. *To* GEORGE SMITH.

HAWORTH, near KEIGHLEY,
August 2nd, 1850.

MY DEAR SIR, — The two portraits have, at length, safely arrived, and have been as safely hung up, in the best light and most favourable position. Without flattery the artist, in the portrait of my daughter, has fully proved that the fame which he has acquired has been fairly earned. Without ostentatious dis-play, with admirable tact and delicacy, he has produced a correct

[1]Catherine Grace Frances Moody, Mrs Gore (1799–1861), wrote about seventy books, *The Hamiltons, or the New Era* (1834) being her sixteenth.

likeness, and succeeded in a graphic representation of mind as well as matter, and with only black and white has given prominence and seeming life, and speech, and motion. I may be partial, and perhaps somewhat enthusiastic, in this case, but in looking on the picture, which improves upon acquaintance, as all real works of art do, I fancy I see strong indications of the genius of the author of 'Shirley' and 'Jane Eyre.'

The portrait of the Duke of Wellington of all which I have seen comes the nearest to my preconceived idea of that great man, to whom Europe, and the other portions of the civilised world, in the most dangerous crisis of their affairs, entrusted their cause, and in whom, under Providence, they did not trust in vain. It now remains for me only to thank you, which I do most sincerely. For the sake of the giver as well as the gift I will lay the portraits up for life amongst my most highly valued treasures, and have only to regret that some are missing who, with better taste and skill than I have, would have fully partaken of my joy. —I beg leave to remain, with much respect, My dear Sir, Yours faithfully,

P. BRONTË.

Please to give my kindest and most respectful regards to Mr Williams, whom I have often heard of but never seen, and to Mr Taylor, whom I had the pleasure of seeing when he ventured into this wild region.

581. *To* GEORGE SMITH.

August 5th, 1850.

MY DEAR SIR,—You are rather formidable in your last note, and yet your menace has for me little terror. The charge is drawn from your two barrels by this fact: I do not thank you in ignorance, nor in puerile misconception, nor on hollow grounds. Do not fear that I suppose the benefit to be all on my side. Rest assured I regard these matters from a less unpractical point of view than you perhaps imagine. Though women are not taught the minutiæ and the mysteries of business, yet in the course of observation they manage to gather up some general idea of the leading principles on which it is conducted, and, if you reflect, it would betray a redundancy of vanity, as well as a lack of common sense, in any individual who should imagine that, in carrying out those principles, an exception has been made in her favour.

Apart, however, from considerations of business there are others such as cannot indeed be entered in a ledger, nor calculated by rules of arithmetic, but of which, nevertheless, we all keep a record, and to which, according to our cast of mind, and also our cast of circumstances, we ascribe a greater or less value. The manner of doing a kind, or, if you will, merely a just action, the degree of pleasure that manner imparts, the amount of happiness derived from a given source — these things cannot indeed be handled, paid away and bartered for material possessions, as many can, but they colour our thoughts and leaven our feelings, just as the sunshine of a warm day or the impressions of delight left by fine scenery might do. We may owe as deep a debt for golden moments as can ever be incurred for golden coin.

This will be read in Cornhill, and will not sound practical, but yet it *is* practical; I believe it to be a sober theory enough.

I enclose a post-office order for 1£ 11*s*. 6*d*., and beg to subscribe myself yours &c. (is not this an unobjectionable form?),

C. BRONTË.

P.S. — The peculating post-office clerk, evidently holding a publisher's principles respecting the value of poetry, has not paid Wordsworth's book the compliment of detaining it; it arrived safely and promptly.

May I tell you how your mourning reveries respecting Glencoe and Loch Katrine will probably end? The thought has just come into my head and must be written down. Some day — you will be *even later than usual* in making your appearance at breakfast — your anxious mother, on going up to make enquiries, will find you deep in undeniable inspiration, on the point of completing the 12th canto of 'The Highlands: a Grand Descriptive, Romantic, and Sentimental POEM, by George Smith, Esq.'

582 (455). *To* ELLEN NUSSEY.

Augt 7th, '50.

MY DEAR ELLEN, — I am truly sorry that I allowed the words to which you refer — to escape my lips, since their effect on you has been unpleasant — but try — dear Ellen — to chase every shadow of anxiety from your mind — and — unless the restraint be very disagreeable to you—permit me to add an earnest request that you will broach the subject to me no more—It is the undisguised and most harassing anxiety of others that has fixed in my mind thoughts and expectations which must canker wherever they take root—against which every effort either of religion or philosophy must at times totally fail—and subjugation to which is a cruel and terrible fate—the fate indeed of him whose life was passed under a sword suspended by a horse-hair. I have had to entreat Papa's consideration on this point—indeed I have had to *command* it—my nervous system is soon wrought on—I should wish to keep it in rational strength and coolness—but to do so I must determinedly resist the kindly meant, but too irksome expression of an apprehension for the realization or defeat of which I have no possible power to be responsible. At present I am pretty well—Thank God! Papa—I trust—is no worse, but he complains of weakness.

Amelia tells me you are looking well which I am truly glad to hear and glad also to learn that you get on pleasantly with the turtle-doves, and even—it seems—have your share of billing and cooing—I own I should be better pleased if the latter were something substantial and serious and likely to lead to permanent happiness. I am glad to hear a good account of J. T.—let us hope for the best. Take care of yourself. —Good-bye—dear Nell—

C. BRONTË.

583 (457). *To* CHARLOTTE BRONTË.

WELLINGTON, N.Z.
[August, 1850].

MY DEAR MISS BRONTË,—I shall tell you everything I can think of, since you said in one of your letters to Pag that you wished me to write to you. I have been here a year. It seems a much shorter time, and yet I have thought more and done more than I ever did in my life before. When we arrived, Henry and I were in such a hurry to leave the ship that we didn't wait to be fetched, but got into the first boat that came alongside. When we landed we inquired where Waring lived, but hadn't walked far before we met him. I had never seen him before, but he guessed we were the cousins he expected, so caught us and took us along with him. Mary soon joined us, and we went home together. At first I thought Mary was not the least altered, but when I had seen her for about a week I thought she looked rather older. The first night Mary and I sat up till 2 A.M. talking. Next day we went to tea to the Knoxes, Waring's new relations; you have no doubt heard of them. The Doctor is an idle fool and his wife not very much better; he might earn his living if he would, but he won't. In a few days we began to talk about doing something; it seemed the only thing for Henry to do was to buy sheep and go and keep them in the country. He went to look at Rangitike, a large district bought of the natives, it is somewhere on the West Coast between here and Taranaki; he came back and said it was too wet for sheep, but he thought he would have to go there. In November he went to Sydney to buy the sheep, but he found freights too high there, so he settled to wait a bit; and he is waiting yet, that is, he hasn't come back, and we haven't heard a word of or from him for five months. He must have gone into the bush, but if he has he ought to have told us. I wish he'd come back. Mary and I settled we would do something together, and we talked for a fortnight before we decided whether we would have a school or shop; it ended in favour of the shop. Waring thought we had better be quiet, and I believe he still thinks we are doing it for amusement; but he never refuses to help us. He is teaching us book-keeping, and he buys things for us now and then. Mary gets as fierce as a dragon and goes to all the wholesale stores and looks at things, gets patterns, samples, etc., and asks prices, and then comes home, and we talk it over; and then she goes again and buys what we want. She says the people are always civil to her. Our keeping shop astonishes everybody here; I believe they think we do it for fun. Some think we shall make nothing of it, or that we shall get tired; and all laugh at us. Before I left home I used to be afraid of being laughed at, but now it has very little effect upon me.

Mary and I are settled together now: I can't do without Mary and she couldn't get on by herself. I built the house we live in, and we made the plan ourselves, so it suits us. We take it in turns to serve in the shop, and keep the accounts, and do the housework —I mean, Mary takes the shop for a week and I the kitchen, and then we change. I think we shall do very well if no more severe earthquakes come, and if we can prevent fire. When a wooden house takes fire it doesn't stop; and we have got an oil cask about as high as I am, that would help it. If some sparks go

out at the chimney-top the shingles are in danger. The last earthquake but one about a fortnight ago threw down two medicine
bottles that were standing on the table and made other things
jingle, but did no damage. If we have nothing worse than that I
don't care, but I don't want the chimney to come down—it
would cost £10 to build it up again. Mary is making me stop
because it is nearly 9 P.M. and we are going to Waring's to supper. Good-bye.—Yours truly,

ELLEN TAYLOR.

584 (456). *To* CHARLOTTE BRONTË.

WELLINGTON, August 13th, 1850.

DEAR CHARLOTTE,—After waiting about six months we have
just got 'Shirley.' It was landed from the *Constantinople* on Monday afternoon, just in the thick of our preparations for a 'small
party' for the next day. We stopped spreading red blankets over
everything (New Zealand way of arranging a room) and opened
the box and read all the letters. Soyer's 'Housewife'[1] and 'Shirley'
were there all right, but Miss Martineau's book was not. In its
place was a silly child's tale called 'Edward Orland.' This was
Joe's fault, no doubt, for I see in one of your letters you suspect
him of it. On Tuesday we stayed up dancing till three or four
o'clock, what for I can't imagine. However, it was a piece of
business done. On Wednesday I began 'Shirley' and continued
in a curious confusion of mind till now, principally at the handsome foreigner who was nursed in our house when I was a little
girl. By the way, you've put him in the servant's bedroom. You
make us all talk much as I think we should have done if we'd
ventured to speak at all. What a little lump of perfection you've
made me! There is a strange feeling in reading it of hearing us all
talking. I have not seen the matted hall and painted parlour windows so plain these five years. But my father is not like. He hates
well enough and perhaps loves too, but he is not honest enough.
It was from my father I learnt not to marry for money nor to
tolerate any one who did, and he never would advise any one to
do so, or fail to speak with contempt of those who did. 'Shirley'
is much more interesting than 'Jane Eyre,' who never interests

---

[1]Alexis Soyer (d. 1858) a Frenchman by
birth, author of *Culinary Relaxations* (1845),
Charitable Cookery (1847), *Gastronomic*
Regenerator (1847), *The Modern Housewife*
(1849), and other works.

you at all until she has something to suffer. All through this last novel there is so much more life and stir that it leaves you far more to remember than the other. Did you go to London about this too! What for? I see by a letter of yours to Mr Dixon that you *have* been. I wanted to contradict some of your opinions, now I can't. As to when I'm coming home, you may well ask. I have wished for fifteen years to begin to earn my own living; last April I began to try—it is too soon to say yet with what success. I am woefully ignorant, terribly wanting in tact, and obstinately lazy, and almost too old to mend. Luckily there is no other dance for me, so I must work. Ellen takes to it kindly, it gratifies a deep ardent *wish* of hers as of mine, and she is habitually industrious. For *her*, ten years younger, our shop will be a blessing. She may possibly secure an independence, and skill to keep it and use it, before the prime of life is past. As to my writings, you may as well ask the Fates about that too. I can give you no information. I write a page now and then. I never forget or get strange to what I have written. When I read it over it looks very interesting.

MARY TAYLOR.

585 (458). *To* ELLEN NUSSEY.

WELLINGTON, August 15th, 1850.

DEAR ELLEN,—Last Monday we stopped working to open a box and read letters. Your pretty thing, what ever is the name of it? came almost the first, and fine amusement it was to open it. What veritable old maids you and Charlotte must be grown if you really use such a thing. Ellen and I pulled out all the things, one after another, and disputed for them. The staylace was particularly amusing! I have not seen such a thing this five years. But the best was the garters. I have had almost a daily lecture from Ellen because my stockings wrinkled owing to my having been reduced to two bits of tape for the last six months, and being too stingy to buy any more and too idle to knit them. Ellen says you might have known.

Your letter is the most cheerful I have had from you. I suppose 'Charlotte' was or had been with you; or was going to be. It contained more news, too, than any I have received by this ship. Ann's marriage does not seem to have made you more uncomfortable—perhaps the reverse. Was this the news you hinted at in your last but which you would not tell me? I had guessed it was your own marriage that was going to be! I had imagined, too, that Miss Gorham must be the daughter of the Rev. Mr Gorham who is having such a quarrel with the Bishop of Exeter,[1] which of course I highly approve of, though I don't know what it's all about. I wish you or Charlotte would give me some particulars of her last London visit. The account of the first one was most interesting.

Ellen is roasting her toes and discussing how little she'll be content with. It seems to be about £200 a year, though it is doubtful if this will do. It is blowing cold and rain and hail—just to make a fire comfortable. She (Ellen) chatters like a pie, and the theme is how much we must have before we go home again. We think it possible to buy and send goods out here after four or five years' experience in shop-keeping.

You and Charlotte ought to be on the other side the table to hear all the nonsense. For the last month or two Ellen has been very well and I too. Before that time she was often very poorly and I had repeatedly tic douloureux in the face. We were frightened, shy, and anxious. Neither the shyness nor the anxiety are at an end, as we very well know, but we know what we have to contend with and can never feel so thick a mist round us as there was when we first began. I wish I could give you some account of the amount of our success, but the time is as yet too short to pronounce. The gist of the matter is that John and Joe have lent me £100 and given me £300. Ellen's means are rather less.

Besides nonsense we talk over other things that I never could talk about before she came. Some of them had got to look so strange I used to think sometimes I had dreamt them. Charlotte's books were of this kind. Politics were another thing where I had all the interest to myself, and a number of opinions of my own I had got so used to keep to myself that at last I thought one side of my head filled with crazy stuff.

Is it that your brothers won't give you money that prevents you coming out? You should *plague* them till they are glad to be

[1]George Cornelius Gorham (1787–1857) divine and antiquary, vicar of St Just in Penwith, Cornwall, 1846, and of Brampford Speke, Devonshire, 1847–57. He was refused institution in 1847 on account of his Calvinistic views on baptismal regeneration, by Henry Phillpotts, Bishop of Exeter, who was supported by the Court of Arches. Gorham appealed to the judicial committee of the Privy Council, who granted him institution in 1850. Gorham published his account of the case in *The Great Gorham Case: a History in Five Books* (1850), and other works. Mary Taylor was mistaken in thinking he was the father of Ellen's friend, Mary Gorham.

rid of you. But I fancy you write more hopefully than you did before. And yet you seem almost turned out of doors by the new arrangement. In fact, there is only your mother that really belongs to you in it.

Joe's admiration of Miss Ringrose is amusing—if it is so. Is she German? or half-German? Have you seen or heard of Halle's chamber concerts? His father was my music master and a genius. His mother is living with him. I have some notion that you are near them, though I believe in point of fact you are as far off as I am. There was a girl of 14 to 20 whom I should much like to hear of.

For some reason—or rather for no reason—I think my hopes this afternoon are peculiarly vivid about coming home again. All the news by last vessel has been good and reacting—the letters have brought it all vividly before me. Keep yourself well and happy, you and Charlotte, till I come, and above all don't turn sulky. We shall meet again yet.

You have both suffered, Charlotte especially. I am older in that way too, but there is sweet in the orange yet, at least I think so.

Mary Taylor.

586 (455 *in part*). *To* Ellen Nussey.

Augst 16th, 1850.

Dear Ellen,—I was indeed strangely astonished by what you say about Mrs Atkinson it struck me like some miracle. To think that the poor wasted being you and I saw about five weeks ago, was then within a month of becoming a mother seems truly incredible. And that the doctors should not have known amazes me too—What do they now say to their own stupid ignorance? Can it be that she will yet recover? That—indeed—is too much to hope—but I cannot help fancying or wishing that she may be partially restored and live some time longer—it would seem hard that a new charm should be given to life at the moment when she is snatched from it. I wonder what poor Mr Atkinson thinks or feels in the matter—they can scarcely expect to rear a child born under such circumstances—in short it seems to me rather an accumulation of grief than otherwise.

Poor Amelia cannot be very comfortable at home with her father in such a mood—her letter to you is very affectionate—it puzzles me to know how all this affection will find repose in J. T.

unless he is something very different to what a hundred things would lead one to augur—feelings like hers must at last encounter disappointment—the day will come when the feigned (if feigned it be) response to her tenderness will cease to be made—and she must just put up with a chilly silence. I fancy—however—this is the fate of most feeling women—and when they find there is no remedy for the inevitable—they submit to circumstances—and take resignation as a substitute for content. Amelia will do this; but not yet—nor for two or three years will it be required of her. You will see her happy for that time—nor *after that time* will she admit herself to be otherwise than happy—indeed if children come—the mother will well support the wife: the bridal interest lost—maternal interest will replace it.

I am going on Monday (D.V.) a journey—whereof the prospect cheers me not at all—to Windermere in Westmoreland to spend a few days with Sir J. K. Shuttleworth who has taken a house there for the Autumn and Winter—I consented to go with reluctance—chiefly to please Papa whom a refusal on my part would much have annoyed—but I dislike to leave him—I trust he is not worse—but his complaint is still weakness—weakness—It is not right to anticipate evil, and to be always looking forward with an apprehensive spirit—but I think grief is a two-edged sword—it cuts both ways—the memory of one loss is the anticipation of another. Take moderate exercise and be careful—dear Nell and believe me—Yours sincerely,

C. Brontë.

The English Lakes have many happy literary associations, and among the long list of names which that delightful district recalls one must never neglect to include that of Charlotte Brontë. She paid two visits there in this year, 1850, the first to Sir James Kay-Shuttleworth, the second to Harriet Martineau.

587 (460). *To* The Rev. P. Brontë.

The Briery, Windermere,
August 19th, 1850.

Dear Papa,—I reached this place yesterday evening at eight o'clock, after a safe though rather tedious journey. I had to change carriages three times and to wait an hour and a half at Lancaster. Sir James came to meet me at the station; both he and

Lady Shuttleworth gave me a very kind reception. This place is exquisitely beautiful, though the weather is cloudy, misty, and stormy; but the sun bursts out occasionally and shows the hills and the lake. Mrs Gaskell is coming here this evening, and one or two other people. Miss Martineau, I am sorry to say, I shall not see, as she is already gone from home for the autumn.

Be kind enough to write by return of post and tell me how you are getting on and how you are. Give my kind regards to Tabby and Martha, and—Believe me, dear papa, your affectionate daughter,

C. BRONTË.

This was Miss Brontë's first meeting with her future biographer. It is interesting to record Mrs Gaskell's impression as conveyed to her friends at the time.

588 (461). MRS GASKELL *to* CATHERINE WINKWORTH.

PLYMOUTH GROVE, Sunday Evng.
[August 25th, 1850].

MY DEAREST KATIE,—If I don't write now I shall never. A fortnight ago I was in despair because I had so much to say to you I thought I should never get through it, and now, as you may suppose, I shall find I have more to do. Only I'll let you know I'm alive. And that on Thursday last I was as near as possible drinking tea with the Tennysons—and that I have been spending the week in the same house with Miss Brontë. Now is not this enough material for one letter, let alone my home events? Oh, how I wish you were here. I have so much to say I don't know where to begin. Wm is in Birmingham preaching to-day. He stays over to-morrow. The two Greens[1] are here; and Fanny Holland expected any day. That's all *here* I think. Last Monday came a note from Lady Kay-Shuttleworth asking Wm and me to go to see them at a house called Briery Close they have taken just above Low-wood; and meeting Miss Brontë who was going to stay with them for 3 or 4 days. Wm hesitated, but his Birmingham sermons kept him at home and I went on Tuesday afternoon. Dark when I got to Windermere station; a drive along the level road to Low-wood, then a regular clamber up a steep lane; then a stoppage at a pretty house, and then a pretty drawing-

---

[1]Annie and Ellen Green, friends of Mrs Gaskell's daughters.

Plymouth Grove.
Sunday Eveng.

[My dearest Katie,
If I don't write now
I shall never. A fortnight ago I was in
Wales, because I had so much to say
to you I thought I had never get through it.
and now, as you may suppose, I shall
find I have more to do. Only I'll let you
know I'm alive. And that on Thursday
last I was as near as possible drinking
the white tea Surreyfous — and that I have
been spending the week in the same
house with Miss Brontë, — now is not this
enough material for one letter, let alone
the home worth, — a fortnight ago. Either
bit of material? Oh dear I wish you
were here. I have so much to say, I don't
know where to begin. Wm is in training
them preaching today. He stays out tonn.
too. The two friends are here; and Fanny
Holland expected any day. That's all the
friends.

room much like the South End one, in which were Sir James and Lady K.-S., and a little lady in black silk gown, whom I could not see at first for the dazzle in the room; she came up and shook hands with me at once—I went up to unbonnet, etc., came down to tea. The little lady worked away and hardly spoke, but I had time for a good look at her. She is (as she calls herself) *undeveloped*; thin and more than half a head shorter than I, soft brown hair, not so dark as mine; eyes (very good and expressive, looking straight and open at you) of the same colour, a reddish face; large mouth and many teeth gone; altogether *plain*; the forehead square, broad, and *rather* overhanging. She has a very sweet voice, rather hesitates in choosing her expressions, but when chosen they seem without an effort, *admirable* and *just* befitting the occasion. There is nothing overstrained but perfectly simple. Well, of course we went to bed; and of course we got up again (I had the most lovely view from my bedroom over Windermere on to Esthwaite, Langdale, etc.) Lady K.-S. was ill, so I made breakfast all the time I staid, and an old jolly Mr Moseley, Inspector of Schools, came to breakfast, who abused our Mr Newman soundly for having tried to acquire various branches of knowledge which 'savoured of vanity and was a temptation of the D.'—'literal.' After breakfast we 4 went on the Lake; and Miss B. and I agreed in thinking Mr Moseley a good goose; in liking Mr Newman's 'Soul,' in liking 'Modern Painters,' and the idea of the Seven Lamps; and she told me about Father Newman's lectures in a very quiet, concise, graphic way. After dinner we went a drive to Coniston to call on the Tennysons, who are staying at Mr Marshall's Hut Lodge—Sir James on the box, Miss B. and I inside, very cozy; but alas it began to rain, so we had to turn back without our call being paid, which grieved me sorely and made me cross. I'm not going to worry you with as particular an account of every day; simply to tell you bits about Miss Brontë. She is more like Miss Fox[1] in character and ways than anyone, if you can fancy Miss Fox to have gone through suffering enough to have taken out every spark of merriment and shy and silent from the habit of extreme intense solitude. Such a life as Miss B.'s I never heard of before. Lady K.-S. described her home to me as in a village of a few grey stone

---

[1] The common friend with whom Mrs Gaskell constantly corresponded. She was the daughter of Mr W. J. Fox, a well-known Unitarian divine, writer and politician, who for many years, represented Oldham in Parliament.

houses perched up on the north side of a bleak moor—looking
over sweeps of bleak moors. There is a court of turf and a stone
wall. (No flowers or shrubs will grow there) a straight walk, and
you come to the parsonage door with a window on each side
of it. The parsonage has never had a touch of paint or an article
of new furniture for 30 years; never since Miss B.'s mother died.
She was a 'pretty young creature' brought from Penzance in
Cornwall by the Irish Curate, who got his moorland living. Her
friends disowned her at her marriage. She had 6 children as fast
as could be; and what with that and the climate, and the strange
half-mad husband she had chosen, she died at the end of 9 years.
An old woman at Burnley who nursed her at last, says she used
to lie crying in bed, and saying 'Oh God, my poor children—oh
God my poor children!' continually. Mr Brontë vented his anger
against *things* not persons; for instance, once in one of his wife's
confinements something went wrong, so he got a saw and went
and sawed up all the chairs in her bedroom, never answering her
remonstrances or minding her tears. Another time he was vexed
and took the hearth rug and tied it in a tight bundle and set it on
fire in the grate, and sat before it with a leg on each hob, heaping
on more coals till it was burnt, no one else being able to endure
in the room because of the stifling smoke. All this Lady K.-S.
told me. The sitting-room at the Parsonage looks into the
Church-yard, filled with graves. Mr B. has never taken a meal
with his children since his wife's death unless he invites them to
tea—*never* to dinner. And he has only once left home since to
come to Manchester to be operated upon by Mr Wilson for
cataract; at which time they lodged in Boundary St. Well! these
5 daughters and one son grew older—their father never taught
the girls anything—only the servant taught them to read and
write. But I suppose they laid their heads together, for at 12
Charlotte (this one) presented a request to the father that they
might go to school; so they were sent to Cowan Bridge (the
place where the Daughters of the Clergy were before they were
removed to Casterton). There the two elder died in that fever.
Miss B. says the pain she suffered from hunger was not to be told,
and her two younger sisters laid the foundation of the consumption of which they are now dead. They all came home ill.
But the poverty of home was very great ('at 19 I should have
been thankful for an allowance of 1d a week. I asked my father,
but he said what did women want with money?'). So at 19 she

advertised and got a teacher's place in a school—(where she did not say, only said it was preferable to the governess' place she got afterwards) but she saved up enough to pay for her journey to a school in Brussels. She had never been out of Yorkshire before; and was so frightened when she got to London—she took a cab, it was night, and drove down to the Tower Stairs and went to the Ostend Packet and they refused to take her in; but at last they did. She was in this school at Brussels two years without a holiday except one week with one of her Belgian schoolfellows. Then she came home and her sisters were ill, and her father going blind—so she thought she ought to stay at home. She tried to teach herself drawing and to be an artist but she could not—and yet her own health independently of the home calls upon her would not allow of her going out again as a governess. She had always wished to write and believed that she could; at 16 she had sent some of her poems to Southey, and had 'kind, stringent' answers from him. So she and her sisters tried. They kept their initials and took names that would do either for a man or a woman. They used to read to each other when they had written so much—their father never knew a word about it. He had never heard of 'Jane Eyre' when, 3 months after its publication, she promised her sisters one day at dinner she would tell him before tea. So she marched into his study with a copy wrapped up and the reviews. She said (I think I can remember the exact words): 'Papa, I've been writing a book.' 'Have you, my dear?' and he went on reading. 'But, Papa, I want you to look at it.' 'I can't be troubled to read MS.' 'But it is printed.' 'I hope you have not been involving yourself in any such silly expense.' 'I think I shall gain money by it. May I read you some reviews?' So she read them; and then she asked him if he would read the book. He said she might leave it, and he would see. But he sent them an invitation to tea that night, and towards the end of tea he said, 'Children, Charlotte has been writing a book—and I think it is a better one than I expected.' He never spoke about it again till about a month ago and they never dared to tell him of the books her sisters wrote. Just in the success of 'Jane Eyre' her sisters died of rapid consumption *unattended by any* doctor, why I don't know. But she says she will have none and that her death will be quite lonely; having no friend or relation in the world to nurse her, and her father dreading a sick room above all places. There seems little doubt she herself is already tainted with consumption.

12.

lonely; having no friend or relation
in the world to nurse her. & her father
dreading a sick room above all
places. There seems little doubt she
herself is already tainted with consumption. Now I shan't write
any more till you write again,
& tell me how to get a letter
to Annie — Shaw kind of happen to
be used to — & how you & Emma
are. & a quantity more I want
to know. how & F. Emma. Emily
is At rix? King Con & Selina A. [?]
to Annesley Danyi's W. Y. ...
Yours very affec.

Aug 25th 1850.

E Gaskell

Now I shan't write any more till you write again and tell me how to get a letter to Annie Shaen, kind of paper to be used, etc., and how you and Emma are and a quantity more I want to know. Love to dear Emma. Emily is at Crix. Kind love to Selina. I went to Arnolds — met some Bunsens,[1] and was to have met Tennyson — Davys's, Mr Prestons. — Yours very affectionately,

Aug. 25th, 1850.   E. C. GASKELL.

589. MRS GASKELL to TOTTIE FOX.

Tuesday, Aug. 1850.

... Wm is at Birmingham; he was preaching there last Sunday; and is staying for some days. It is funny how we *never* go from home together. He is so anxious about the children; he says he is never easy if we are both away; it takes away all his pleasure, so first he went to Edinburgh scientific association, and prowled about Scotland, then last week quite unexpectedly Lady Kay-Shuttleworth wanted us to come and meet Miss Brontë, and William could not go — and then the people he is with at Birmingham wanted us to go; and he said he shd not be happy if I went; so we are like Adam and Eve in the weather glass. I wish, my dear, you were here. It would be a charming beguiling of my sofa imprisonment. I am very happy nevertheless making flannel petticoats and reading 'Modern Painters.' Miss Brontë *is* a nice person. Like you, Tottie, without your merriment; poor thing, she can hardly smile she has led such a hard, cruel (if one may dare to say so) life. She is quiet, sensible, unaffected, with high, noble aims. Lady K.-S. was confined to one room, so she and I had much of our day to ourselves, with the exception of some lectures on art, and 'bringing ourselves down to a lower level,' and 'the beauty of expediency,' from that eminently practical man, Sir James, who has never indulged in the exercise of any talent which could not bring him a tangible and speedy return. However, he was very kind, and really took trouble in giving us, Miss Brontë especially, good advice, which she received with calm resignation. She is sterling and true; and if she is a little bitter she checks herself, and speaks kindly and hopefully of things and people directly; the wonder to me is how she

[1]Christian Charles Josias, Chevalier de Bunsen (1791–1860), German diplomatist and scholar, was Prussian Ambassador in London from 1842–1854. It was his son and daughter whom Mrs Gaskell met on this occasion.

can have kept heart and power alive in her life of desolation. I made her give me an account of the 'Editorial party,' . . . Do you know I was as near as possible seeing Tennyson. He and Mrs are staying at Coniston, and Sir James, Miss B. and I were on the Lake there, when we heard it; and Sir James knows him; and said he would go and call; and then looked up at the sky and thought it was going to rain, so he didn't. I held my peace and bit my lips. All the world at the Lakes was full of the 'Prelude,' have you read it? Miss Brontë has promised that Mr Smith (& Elder) shall lend it to me. . . .

590 (*part of* 461). MRS GASKELL *to a* FRIEND.

[August, 1850].

. . . We were only three days together, the greater part of which was spent in driving about, in order to show Miss Brontë the Westmoreland scenery, as she had never been there before. We were both included in an invitation to drink tea quietly at Fox How; and then I saw how severely her nerves were taxed by the effort of going amongst strangers. We knew beforehand that the number of the party would not exceed twelve; but she suffered the whole day from an acute headache brought on by apprehension of the evening.

Briery Close was situated high above Low-wood, and of course commanded an extensive view and wide horizon. I was struck by Miss Brontë's careful examination of the shape of the clouds and the signs of the heavens, in which she read, as from a book, what the coming weather would be. I told her that I saw she must have a view equal in extent at her own home. She said that I was right, but that the character of the prospect from Haworth was very different; that I had no idea what a companion the sky became to any one living in solitude—more than any inanimate object on earth—more than the moors themselves.

591 (462). *To* ELLEN NUSSEY.

HAWORTH, Augst 26th, 1850.

DEAR ELLEN,—You said I should stay longer than a week in Westmoreland—you ought by this time to know me better—is it my habit to keep dawdling on at a place long after the time I first fixed on departing?

I have got home and I am thankful to say Papa seems—to say the least—no worse than when I left him—yet I wish he were stronger. My visit passed off very well—now that it is over I am glad I went—The scenery is of course grand; could I have wandered about amongst those hills *alone*—I could have drank in all their beauty—even in a carriage—with company, it was very well. Sir James was all the while as kind and friendly as he could be—he is in much better health—Lady Shuttleworth never got out—being confined to the house with a cold—but fortunately there was Mrs Gaskell (the authoress of 'Mary Barton') who came to the Briery the day after me—I was truly glad of her companionship. She is a woman of the most genuine talent—of cheerful, pleasing and cordial manners and—I believe—of a kind and good heart. Miss Martineau was from home—she always leaves her house at Ambleside during the Lake Season to avoid the constant influx of visitors to which she would otherwise be subject.

I went out to spend the evening once at Fox-House[1] the residence of Dr Arnold's widow—there was a considerable party, amongst the rest the son and daughter of the Chevalier Bunsen, the Prussian Ambassador, to whom Lord Brougham lately behaved with such outrageous impertinence in the House of Lords—as you may happen to have seen in the papers.

My previous opinions both of Sir James and Lady Shuttleworth are confirmed—I honour his intellect—with his heart—I believe I shall never have sympathy—He behaves to me with marked kindness—Mrs Gaskell said she believes he had for me a sincere and strong friendship—I am grateful for this—yet I scarcely desire a continuation of the interest he professes in me—were he to forget me—I could not feel regret—In observing his behaviour to others—I find that when once offended his forgiveness is not to be again purchased except perhaps by servile submission. The substratum of his character is hard as flint. To authors as a class (the imaginative portion of them) he has a natural antipathy. Their virtues give him no pleasure—their faults are wormwood and gall in his soul: he perpetually threatens a visit to Haworth—may this be averted!

Tell me, when you write, how poor Mrs Atkinson is getting on—I have thought of her often—Remember me to your Mother and believe me—Always yours faithfully,

C. BRONTË.

[1]Fox-How.

I forgot to tell you that about a week before I went to West-moreland there came an invitation to Harden Grange — Busfeild Ferrand's place[1] — which of course I declined. Two or three days after — a large party made their appearance here, consisting of Mrs Ferrand and sundry other ladies and two gentlemen, one tall, stately, black-haired and whiskered, who turned out to be Lord John Manners, the other not so distinguished-looking, shy and a little queer, who was Mr Smythe, the son of Lord Strangford. I found Mrs Ferrand a true lady in manners and appearance. She is the sister or daughter, I forget which, of Lord Blantyre, very gentle and unassuming, not so pretty as Lady Shuttleworth, but I like her better. Lord John Manners brought in his hand two brace of grouse for papa, which was a well-timed present; a day or two before, papa had been wishing for some. —

Yours faithfully,

C. BRONTË.

592 (463). *To* MRS GASKELL.

August 27th, 1850.

. . . Papa and I have just had tea; he is sitting quietly in his room, and I in mine; 'storms of rain' are sweeping over the garden and churchyard: as to the moors, they are hidden in thick fog. Though alone I am not unhappy; I have a thousand things to be thankful for, and, amongst the rest, that this morning I received a letter from you, and that this evening I have the privilege of answering it.

I do not know the 'Life of Sydney Taylor';[2] whenever I have the opportunity I will get it. The little French book you mention shall also take its place on the list of books to be procured as soon as possible. It treats a subject interesting to all women — perhaps more especially to single women, though, indeed, mo-thers like you study it for the sake of their daughters. The 'West-minster Review' is not a periodical I see regularly, but some time since I got hold of a number — for last January, I think — in which there was an article entitled 'Woman's Mission' (the

[1]Mr Ferrand was a considerable land-owner, whose 'place,' Harden Grange, is four miles from Haworth. He died in 1889. His wife was the second daughter of the eleventh Lord Blantyre. Mrs Ferrand died in 1896.

[2]*Selections from the Writings of J. Sydney Taylor, with a Brief Sketch of his Life.* London, 1843. John Sydney Taylor (1795–1841) was a London journalist of Irish origin.

phrase is hackneyed), containing a great deal that seemed to me just and sensible. Men begin to regard the position of woman in another light than they used to do; and a few men, whose sympathies are fine and whose sense of justice is strong, think and speak of it with a candour that commands my admiration. They say, however — and, to an extent, truly — that the amelioration of our condition depends on ourselves. Certainly there are evils which our own efforts will best reach; but as certainly there are other evils — deep-rooted in the foundations of the social system — which no efforts of ours can touch; of which we cannot complain; of which it is advisable not too often to think.

I have read Tennyson's 'In Memoriam,'[1] or rather part of it; I closed the book when I had got about half-way. It is beautiful; it is mournful; it is monotonous. Many of the feelings expressed bear, in their utterance, the stamp of truth; yet, if Arthur Hallam had been somewhat nearer Alfred Tennyson — his brother instead of his friend — I should have distrusted this rhymed, and measured, and printed monument of grief. What change the lapse of years may work I do not know; but it seems to me that bitter sorrow, while recent, does not flow out in verse.

I promised to send you Wordsworth's 'Prelude,'[2] and, accordingly, despatch it by this post; the other little volume shall follow in a day or two. I shall be glad to hear from you whenever you have time to write to me, *but you are never on any account to do this except when inclination prompts and leisure permits*. I should never thank you for a letter which you had felt it a task to write. . . .

C. BRONTË.

593. *To* MRS C. F. G. GORE.

Aug. 27th, 1850.

. . . The book had for me its own peculiar value as a work often heard of and long wished for: I have now read it; it has given me much pleasure because I found in its pages, not the echo of another mind — the pale reflection of a reflection. I knew nothing of the circles you describe before I read 'The Hamiltons,' but I feel I do know something of them now.

C. BRONTË.

[1] Tennyson's *In Memoriam* was published in 1850.
[2] *The Prelude; or, Growth of a Poet's Mind: an Autobiographical Poem*, by William Wordsworth, was published, after his death in 1850, by Edward Moxon, Dover Street, London.

From the following letter it appears that Catherine Wink-worth had sent on to her sister, Mrs Gaskell's long letter of August 25th describing her meeting with Charlotte Brontë.

594. EMILY WINKWORTH *to* CATHERINE WINKWORTH.

CRIX, August 30th, 1850.

. . . Thanks for Mrs Gaskell's. Poor Miss Brontë, I cannot get the look of the grey, square, cold, dead-coloured house out of my head. One feels as if one ought to go to her at once, and do some-thing for her. She has friends though now, surely? I wonder whether she has any unmarried ones; people who could go and look after her a little if she were ill. Oh dear, if the single sisters in this world were but banded together a little, so that they could help each other out as well as other people, and know how important they were, and what a quantity of work lies ready for them! One feels that her life at least *almost* makes one like her books, though one does not want there to be any more Miss Brontës. . . .

595 (465). *To* ELLEN NUSSEY.

HAWORTH, Septr 2nd, '50.

DEAR ELLEN,—Poor Mrs Atkinson it seems is gone; I saw her death in the papers; it is another lesson on the nature of life, on its strange brevity and, in many instances, apparent futility. I should think her child—conceived and fostered in the arms of death; born on the very brink of its mother's grave—cannot live—and I trust it will not; it could only be reared to die; the seeds of disease must be thickly sown in its constitution. I wonder if Mrs A. suffered much at last—or if she died peacefully.

Joe Taylor came here on Saturday but Tom Dixon who was to have accompanied him—was prevented from executing his intention. I regretted his absence, for I by no means coveted the long tête-à-tête with J. T. However it passed off pretty well—he is satisfied now with his own prospects which makes him—on the surface satisfied with other things—he spoke of A. with content and approbation—He looks forward to marriage as a sort of harbour where he is to lay up his now somewhat battered vessel in quiet moorings—He has seen all he wants to see of life —now he is prepared to settle. I listened to all with equanimity and cheerfulness—not assumed but real, for papa is now some-what better—his appetite and spirits are improved—and that eases my mind of cankering anxiety. My own health too—is I think really benefited by the late changes of air and scene—I fancy, at any rate, that I feel stronger. Still I mused—in my own way—on J. T.'s character—its depth and scope I believe are ascertained.

I saw the governess at Sir J. K. S.'s; she looked a little better and more cheerful—she was almost as pleased to see me as if we had been related—and when I bid her good bye, expressed an earnest hope that I would soon come again. The children seem fond of her—and on the whole obedient—two great alleviations of the inevitable evil of her position.

Cheer up—dear Nell—and try not to stagnate—or when you cannot help it—and when your heart is constricted and oppress-ed—remember what life is and must be to all—some moments of sunshine alternating with many overclouded, and often temp-estuous darkness—Humanity cannot escape its fate which is to drink a mixed cup—Let us believe that the gall and the vinegar are salutary.

I return A[melia]'s letter. She has written to me.—Yours faithfully,

C. BRONTË.

CHAPTER XXIV
CHARLOTTE ON HER SISTERS' WORKS

IN September, 1850, a highly appreciative article[1] on Currer Bell appeared in the *Palladium*. The article, as Charlotte afterwards discovered, was written by Sydney Dobell, who, in spite of the disclaimers printed in the later editions of *Jane Eyre* and *The Tenant of Wildfell Hall*, still maintained that Currer, Ellis and Acton Bell were in reality one and the same person. Charlotte was greatly encouraged by Mr Dobell's article, and particularly grateful for his brilliant appreciation of *Wuthering Heights*. In order to clear up the mystery of the authorship of the novels, Mr Williams suggested that a new edition of *Wuthering Heights* and *Agnes Grey* should be published, to which Charlotte should contribute a short biographical notice of her sisters, explaining the origin and authorship of the books written by Currer, Ellis and Acton Bell. This she agreed to do, and also to select a few poems from her sisters' remaining MSS. to be inserted in the volume. She further decided to write a separate preface to *Wuthering Heights*, and to modify the original punctuation and the spelling of the dialect. Charlotte considered the editing of her sisters' works in the light of a duty which must be performed, and she very conscientiously threw her heart and soul into the task. Throughout the next three months practically the whole of her time was devoted to this work.

596 (466). *To* JAMES TAYLOR.

September 5th, 1850.

MY DEAR SIR,—The reappearance of the 'Athenæum' is very acceptable, not merely for its own sake—though I esteem the opportunity of its perusal a privilege—but because it comes from Cornhill and, as a weekly token of the remembrance of friends, cheers and gives pleasure. I only fear that its regular

[1]Reprinted in *The Brontë Society Transactions*, Part XXVIII.

transmission may become a task to you; in that case, discontinue it at once.

I did indeed enjoy my trip to Scotland, and yet I saw little of the face of the country, nothing of its grander or finer scenic features; but Edinburgh, Melrose, Abbotsford, these three in themselves sufficed to stir feelings of such deep interest and admiration that, neither at the time did I regret, nor have I since regretted, the want of wider space to diffuse the sense of enjoyment. There was room and variety enough to be very happy, and 'enough', the proverb says, 'is as good as a feast.' The Queen was right indeed to climb Arthur Seat with her husband and children; I shall not soon forget how I felt, when, having reached its summit, we all sat down and looked over the city, towards the sea and Leith, and the Pentland Hills. No doubt you are proud of being a native of Scotland, proud of your country, her capital, her children, and her literature. You cannot be blamed.

The article in the 'Palladium' is one of those notices over which an author rejoices with trembling. He rejoices to find his work finely, fully, fervently appreciated, and trembles under the responsibility such appreciation seems to devolve upon him. I am counselled to wait and watch. D.V., I will do so. Yet it is harder work to wait with the hands bound and the observant and reflective faculties at their silent unseen work, than to labour mechanically.

I need not say how I felt the remarks on 'Wuthering Heights'; they woke the saddest yet most grateful feelings; they are true, they are discriminating; they are full of late justice—but it is very late—alas! in one sense too late. Of this, however, and of the pang of regret for a light prematurely extinguished, it is not wise to speak much. Whoever the author of this article may be, I remain his debtor.

Yet, you see, even here, 'Shirley' is disparaged in comparison with 'Jane Eyre,' and yet I took great pains with 'Shirley.' I did not hurry; I tried to do my best, and my own impression was that it was not inferior to the former work; indeed I had bestowed on it more time, thought, and anxiety: but great part of it was written under the shadow of impending calamity, and the last volume I cannot deny was composed in the eager, restless endeavour to combat mental sufferings that were scarcely tolerable.

You sent the tragedy of 'Galileo Galilei,' by Samuel Brown,[1] in one of the Cornhill parcels; it contained, I remember, passages of very great beauty. Whenever you send any more books (but that must not be till I return what I now have) I should be glad if you would include amongst them the Life of Dr Arnold. Do you know also the Life of Sydney Taylor? I am not familiar even with the name, but it has been recommended to me as a work meriting perusal. Of course, when I name any book, it is always understood that it should be quite convenient to send it.

With thanks for your kind letter, —I am, my dear sir, yours very sincerely,

C. BRONTË.

597 (467). *To* W. S. WILLIAMS.

Sept 5th, 1850.

MY DEAR SIR, —I trust your suggestion for Miss Kavanagh's benefit will have all success. It seems to me truly felicitous and excellent, and, I doubt not, she will think so too. The last class of female character will be difficult to manage: there will be nice points in it—yet, well managed, both an attractive and instructive book might result therefrom. One thing may be depended upon in the execution of this plan—Miss Kavanagh will commit no error, either of taste, judgment, or principle; and even when she deals with the feelings, I would rather follow the calm course of her quiet pen than the flourishes of a more redundant one, where there is not strength to restrain as well as ardour to impel.

I fear I seemed to you to speak coolly of the beauty of the Lake scenery. The truth is, it was, as scenery, exquisite—far beyond anything I saw in Scotland; but it did not give me half so much pleasure, because I saw it under less congenial auspices. Mr Smith and Sir J. K. Shuttleworth are two different people with whom to travel. I need say nothing of the former—you know him. The latter offers me his friendship, and I do my best to be grateful for the gift; but his is a nature with which it is difficult to assimilate—and where there is no assimilation, how can there be real regard? Nine parts out of ten in him are utilitarian—the tenth is artistic. This tithe of his nature seems to me at war with

---

[1]Samuel Brown (1817–1856) was a cousin of Dr John Brown, author of *Rab and his Friends*. He was a chemist and wrote *Lectures on the Atomic Theory and Essays Scientific and Literary*. His tragedy *Galileo Galilei* was published in 1850.

all the rest—it is just enough to incline him restlessly towards the artist class, and far too little to make him one of them. The consequent inability to *do* things which he *admires*, embitters him I think—it makes him doubt perfections and dwell on faults. Then his notice or presence scarcely tend to set one at ease or make one happy: he is worldly and formal. But I must stop—have I already said too much? I think not, for you will feel it is said in confidence and will not repeat it.

The article in the 'Palladium' is indeed such as to atone for a hundred unfavourable or imbecile reviews. I have expressed what I think of it to Mr Taylor, who kindly wrote me a letter on the subject. I thank you also for the newspaper notices, and for some you sent me a few weeks ago.

I should much like to carry out your suggestion respecting a reprint of 'Wuthering Heights' and 'Agnes Grey' in 1 vol. with a prefatory and explanatory notice of the authors; but the question occurs—would Newby claim it? I could not bear to commit it to any other hands than those of Mr Smith. 'Wildfell Hall' it hardly appears to me desirable to preserve. The choice of subject in that work is a mistake: it was too little consonant with the character, tastes, and ideas of the gentle, retiring, in-experienced writer. She wrote it under a strange, conscientious, half-ascetic notion of accomplishing a painful penance and a severe duty. Blameless in deed and almost in thought, there was from her very childhood a tinge of religious melancholy in her mind. This I ever suspected, and I have found amongst her papers mournful proofs that such was the case. As to additional compositions, I think there would be none, as I would not offer a line to the publication of which my sisters themselves would have objected.

I must conclude or I shall be too late for the post.—Believe me, yours sincerely,

C. BRONTË.

598 (468). *To* W. S. WILLIAMS.

September 13th, 1850.

MY DEAR SIR,—Mr Newby undertook first to print 350 copies of 'Wuthering Heights,' but he afterwards declared he had only printed 250. I doubt whether he could be induced to return the £50 without a good deal of trouble—much more than I should

feel justified in delegating to Mr Smith. For my part, the conclusion I drew from the whole of Mr Newby's conduct to my
sisters was that he is a man with whom it is desirable to have
little to do. I think he must be needy as well as tricky—and if he
is, one would not distress him, even for one's rights.

If Mr Smith thinks proper to reprint 'Wuthering Heights' and
'Agnes Grey,' I would prepare a preface comprising a brief and
simple notice of the authors, such as might set at rest all erroneous conjectures respecting their identity—and adding a few
poetical remains of each.

In case this arrangement is approved, you will kindly let me
know, and I will commence the task (a sad, but, I believe, a
necessary one), and send it when finished.—I am, my dear sir,
  yours sincerely,
                                             C. BRONTË.

599 (469). *To* ELLEN NUSSEY.

September 14th, 1850.

DEAR ELLEN,—I found after sealing my last note to you that
I had forgotten after all to enclose Amelia's letter; however, it
appears it does not signify. While I think of it I must refer to an
act of petty larceny committed by me when I was last in Brookroyd. Do you remember lending me a parasol which I should
have left with you when we parted at Leeds. I unconsciously
carried it away in my hand. You shall have it when you next
come to Haworth.

I wish, dear Ellen, you would tell me what is the 'twaddle
about my marrying, etc.,' which you hear. If I knew the details
I should have a better chance of guessing the quarter from which
such gossip comes; as it is, I am quite at a loss. Whom am I to
marry? I think I have scarcely seen a single man with whom such
a union would be possible since I left London. Doubtless there
are men whom if I chose to encourage I might marry, but no
matrimonial lot is even remotely offered me which seems to me
truly desirable: and even if that were the case, there would be
many obstacles; the least allusion to such a thing is most offensive to papa.

An article entitled 'Currer Bell' has lately appeared in the
'Palladium,' a new periodical published in Edinburgh. It is an
eloquent production and one of such warm sympathy and high

appreciation as I had never expected to see, it makes mistakes about authorship, etc., but these I hope one day to set right. Mr Taylor (the little man) first informed me of this article—I was somewhat surprised to receive his letter—having concluded nine months ago that there would be no more correspondence from that quarter. I enclose you a note from him received subsequently—in answer to my acknowledgment—read it and tell me exactly how it impresses you regarding the writer's character, etc.

This little newspaper[1] disappeared for some weeks and I thought it was gone to the tomb of the Capulets—however it has reappeared with an explanation that he had feared its regular transmission might rather annoy than gratify—I told him this was a mistake—that I was well enough pleased to receive it— but hoped he would not make a task of sending it. For the rest I cannot consider myself placed under any personal obligation by accepting this newspaper—for it belongs to the establishment of Smith & Elder. This little Taylor is deficient neither in spirit nor sense.

The report about my having published again is, of course, an arrant lie.

Give my kind regards to all and believe me yours faithfully,

C. BRONTË.

Papa continues in an invalid state—still subject to bronchitis and often complaining of weakness—I have wished him to consult Mr Teale or to try change of air—but his objection to both these alternatives is insuperable—I think I am pretty well. Write soon.

600. *To* GEORGE SMITH.

September 18th, 1850.

MY DEAR SIR,—Feeling sure that any application of mine to Mr Newby would merely result in some evasive reply, I have adopted your second suggestion and written the statement enclosed. I felt more than reluctant to give you any trouble about the matter, but your note presents the case in a manner which seems to do away with much of its intricacy and difficulty; in your hands, therefore, I leave it.

---

[1]*The Athenæum*, which Mr Taylor had sent as a method of literary courtship.

If you *should* extract any money from Mr Newby (of which I am not sanguine), I shall regard it in the light of a providential windfall and dispose of part of it—at least—accordingly; one half of whatever you may realise must be retained in your possession to add to any sum you may decide on giving Miss Kavanagh for her next work. This, however, is a presumptuous enumeration of chickens ere the eggs are hatched.

Mr Thackeray did very right to bring his Christmas book[1] to you; I hope it will be a good one, better (that is, juster and more amiable) than 'Rebecca and Rowena;' if otherwise I can only wish that whenever he goes to the Elysian Fields (long may it be ere then!) he may be immediately caught by his own Rowena (not Sir Walter Scott's) and compelled by her into a conjugal union. That would be '*poetical justice*,' I think.

Mr Ruskin's fairy tale[2] will no doubt offer a delicate contrast to the Christmas book—something like a flower and a branch of oak. Mrs Gaskell, it seems, has likewise written a Christmas book.[3] I wonder by whom it is to be published; I half expected from some things that were said when I saw her that you would have had the first offer of her next work.

You should be very thankful that books cannot 'talk to each other as well as to their reader.' Conceive the state of your warehouse if such were the case. The confusion of tongues at Babel, or a congregation of Irvingites[4] in full exercise of their miraculous gift, would offer but a feeble type of it. Terrible, too, would be the quarrelling. Yourself and Mr Taylor and Mr Williams would all have to go in several times in the day to part or silence the disputants. Dr Knox alone, with his 'Race: a Fragment'[5] (a book which I read with combined interest, amusement, and edification), would deliver the voice of a Stentor if any other book ventured to call in question his favourite dogmas.

Still I like the notion of a mystic whispering amongst the lettered leaves, and perhaps at night, when London is asleep and

[1] *The Kickleburys on the Rhine: A New Picture-Book drawn and written by Mr M. A. Titmarsh* [W. M. Thackeray], published December 21st, 1850.

[2] *The King of the Golden River.* By John Ruskin. Smith, Elder & Co., 1851.

[3] *The Moorland Cottage.* By Mrs E. C. Gaskell, 1850.

[4] Followers of Edward Irving (1792–1834), founder of the Catholic Apostolic Church. Irving became a very successful preacher in London. He lectured on spiritual gifts, particularly miraculous healing, prophecy and the gift of tongues.

[5] *The Races of Men.* By Robert Knox, M.D. 1850. Robert Knox (1791–1862), was a distinguished anatomical teacher and ethnologist. He was a Fellow of the Royal College of Surgeons, Edinburgh, but became unpopular for procuring his subjects for dissection from the resurrectionists.

Cornhill desert, when all your clerks and men are away, and the warehouse is shut up, such a whispering may be heard—by those who have ears to hear.

I find, on referring again to Mr Newby's letter to my sister, he says that the sale of 250 copies of 'Wuthering Heights' would 'leave a *surplus* of 100*l*. to be divided.'—Yours sincerely,

C. BRONTË.

Poor Mr Newby! One is very sorry for him after all. I hope your conscience fined you in the sum of five shillings for that pun on the Nubian Desert.

C. B.

601. *To* GEORGE SMITH.

[September, 18th, 1850].

MY DEAR SIR,—'Wuthering Heights' and 'Agnes Grey' were published by Mr Newby on the condition that my sisters should share the risk. Accordingly they advanced £50. Mr Newby engaging to repay it as soon as the work should have sold a sufficient number of copies to defray expenses; and Mr Newby mentions in his letter to my sister on the subject that 'the sale of 250 copies would leave a *surplus* of 100*l*. to be divided.' No portion of the sum advanced has yet been returned, and, as it appears that the work is now entirely out of print, I should feel greatly obliged if you would call upon Mr Newby and enquire whether it be convenient to him to refund the amount received.

For 'The Tenant of Wildfall Hall' my sister Anne was to receive 25*l*. on the day of publication, a second 25*l*. on the sale reaching 250 copies, 50*l*. more on its extending to 400 copies, and another 50*l*. on 500 being sold.

Two instalments of 25*l*. each were paid to my sister. I should be glad if you could learn how many copies of the work have been sold on the whole, and whether any further sum is now due.—Yours sincerely,

C. BRONTË.

602. *To* ELLEN HUDSON, *Manchester*.

Sept. 18th, 1850.

DEAR MADAM,—I know not whether the accompanying little piece will be found suitable to your Album; if not you can destroy it as it is not worth returning. With best wishes for the success of your efforts — I am — dear Madam, Yours sincerely,

CURRER BELL.[1]

603 (470). *To* W. S. WILLIAMS.

Septr 20th, 1850.

MY DEAR SIR, — I herewith send you a very roughly written copy of what I have to say about my Sisters. When you have read it, you can better judge whether the word 'Notice' or 'Memoir' is the most appropriate. I think the former. Memoir seems to me to express a more circumstantial and different sort of account. My aim is to give a just idea of their identity, not to write any narrative of their simple, uneventful lives. I depend on you for faithfully pointing out whatever may strike you as faulty. I could not write it in the conventional form — *that* I found impossible.

It gives me real pleasure to hear of your son's success. I trust he may persevere and go on improving and give his parents increasing cause for satisfaction and honest pride.

I am truly pleased too to learn that Miss Kavanagh has managed so well with Mr Colburn.[2] Her position seems to me one deserving of all sympathy. I often think of her. Will her novel soon be published? Somehow, I expect it to be interesting.

I certainly did hope that Mrs Gaskell would offer her next work to Smith & Elder. She and I had some conversation about publishers — a comparison of our literary experiences was made; she seemed much struck with the difference between hers and mine — though I did not enter into details or tell her all. Unless I greatly mistake — she and you and Mr Smith would get on well together — but one does not know what causes there may be to prevent her from doing as she would wish in such a case. I think Mr Smith will not object to my occasionally sending her any of the Cornhill books that she may like to see. I have already taken the liberty of lending her Wordsworth's 'Prelude' — as she was saying how much she wished to have the opportunity of reading it.

I do not tack remembrances to Mrs Williams and your

[1] This letter is accompanied by a copy of the poem 'Sweet Sybil,' by Charles Gavan Duffy, written in Charlotte Brontë's autograph.

[2] Henry Colburn, the London Publisher.

daughters and Miss Kavanagh to all my letters—because that
makes an empty form of what should be a sincere wish, but I
trust this mark of courtesy and regard, though rarely expressed,
is always understood.—Believe me, Yours sincerely,

                                                    C. BRONTË.

604 (464). *To* MRS GASKELL.

HAWORTH, Septbr 26th, 1850.

MY DEAR MRS GASKELL,—On no account must you give
yourself the trouble of sending the 'Prelude' to Smith & Elder
—nor, indeed, need you return it to me at present; keep it in
pledge till I come and redeem it—though when that will be, I
cannot say. My Father is not well—yet better than he has been;
he has taken scarcely any Duty for some weeks past; I should not
like to leave him now.

I told Mr Smith that I had sent you the 'Prelude,' and his
answer was that he should be very happy if any of the books he
lends me, could be made available for your entertainment also.
I expect another batch by and by; when they come, I will tell you
their titles and you shall make a choice.

The little book of Rhymes[1] was sent by way of fulfilling a
rashly made promise; and the promise was made to prevent you
from throwing away four shillings in an injudicious purchase: I
do not like my own share of the work, nor care that it should be
read. Ellis Bell's poems I think good and vigorous, and Acton's
have the merit of truth and simplicity. Mine are chiefly juvenile
productions; the restless effervescence of a mind that would not
be still. In those days, the sea too often 'wrought and was tem-
pestuous,' and weed, sand, shingle—all turned up in the tumult.
This image is much too magnificent for the subject, but you will
pardon it.

I wonder what it was I said that suited you; in vain have I
puzzled my memory to make out what it could be.

You were well neither in mind nor body when you wrote last:
I trust you are better now. Rumour says we are to expect from
you a Christmas Book—but Rumour so often errs, I scarce dare
trust her assertions—especially when they are pleasant.

[1] *Poems* by Currer, Ellis and Acton Bell.

Thank you for your flowers; when put in water they revived and looked quite fresh and very beautiful. I kept them for more than a week; the bit of heliotrope I especially prized for its incomparable perfume.

For the present, good bye, my dear Mrs Gaskell. When you have time, write one line to say how you are. If the report about the Christmas Book is not true—make it true. I am hungry for a genuine bit of refreshment—but you must mind not to pierce one with too keen-edged emotion. There are parts of 'Mary Barton' I shall never dare to read a second time. Is that unconscionable Mr Chapman[1] satisfied yet—now that 'Mary Barton' has reached a fourth edition?—Believe me, Yours sincerely,

C. BRONTË.

605 (471). To MARGARET WOOLER.

HAWORTH, September 27th, 1850.

MY DEAR MISS WOOLER,—When I tell you that I have already been to the Lakes this season, and that it is scarcely more than a month since I returned, you will understand that it is no longer within my power to accept your kind invitation.

I wish I could have gone to you: I wish your invitation had come first; to speak the truth, it would have suited me better than the one by which I profited; it would have been pleasant—soothing—in many ways beneficial, to have spent two weeks with you in your cottage-lodgings—but these reflections are vain; I have already had my excursion, and there is an end of it. Sir James Kay Shuttleworth is residing near Windermere at a house called 'The Briery' and it was there I was staying for a little time in August. He very kindly showed me the scenery—*as it can be seen from a carriage*—and I discerned that the 'Lake-Country' is a glorious region—of which I had only seen the similitude in dreams—waking or sleeping—but—my dear Miss Wooler—I only half enjoyed it—because I was only half at my ease. Decidedly, I find it does not agree with me to prosecute the search of the picturesque in a carriage. A waggon, a spring-cart, even a post-chaise might do—but the carriage upsets everything. I longed to slip out unseen, and to run away by myself in amongst the hills and dales. Erratic and vagrant instincts tormented me,

---

[1] Mr Chapman of Messrs Chapman & Hall, Mrs Gaskell's publishers.

and these I was obliged to control, or rather, suppress—for fear
of growing in any degree enthusiastic, and thus drawing attention to the 'lioness,' the authoress—the she-artist. Sir James is a
man of ability—even of intellect—but not a man in whose presence one willingly unbends.

You say you suspect I have formed a large circle of acquaintance by this time. No: I cannot say that I have. I doubt whether I
possess either the wish or the power to do so. A few friends I
should like to have—and these few I should like to know well—
if such knowledge brought proportionate regard—I could not
help concentrating my feelings—Dissipation—I think, appears
synonymous with dilution. However, I have as yet scarcely been
tried. During the month I spent in London in the Spring—I
kept very quiet—having the fear of 'lionizing' before my eyes:
I only went out once to dinner, and was once present at an
evening party—and the only visits I have paid have been to Sir
J. K. S's and my publishers. From this system, I should not like
to depart; as far as I can see, indiscriminate visiting tends only to
a waste of time and a vulgarizing of character. Besides—it would
be wrong to leave Papa often; he is now in his 75th year, the
infirmities of age begin to creep upon him; during the Summer
he has been much harassed by chronic bronchitis, but I am
thankful to say he is now somewhat better. I think my own
health has derived benefit from change and exercise.

You ask after the inmates of Brookroyd. I believe they are all
pretty well. When I saw Ellen Nussey about two months ago,
she looked remarkably well. I sometimes hear through her small
fragments of gossip which amuse me. Somebody in Dewsbury
professes to have authority for saying that 'When Miss Brontë
was in London she neglected to attend divine service on the
Sabbath—and in the week, spent her time in going about to
balls, theatres, and operas.' On the other hand, the London
quidnuncs make my seclusion a matter of wonder, and devise
twenty romantic fictions to account for it. Formerly I used to
listen to Report with interest and a certain credulity; I am now
grown deaf and sceptical—experience has taught me how absolutely devoid of foundations her stories may be.

You will probably have heard that Mr Joe Taylor is on the
eve of marriage with Miss Ringrose. Strangely incongruous
would that union have seemed a year since—yet—widely different as are their characters, natures &c. I trust there is a rational

prospect of the marriage proving a happy one. She is of a pliant and thoroughly amiable character and will in all things try to suit him.

With the sincere hope that your own health is better—and kind remembrances to all old friends whenever you see them or write to them—(and whether or not their feeling to me has ceased to be friendly, which I fear is the case in some instances), —I am, my dear Miss Wooler, always yours, affectionately and respectfully,

C. BRONTË.

606. *To* W. S. WILLIAMS.

September 29th, 1850.

MY DEAR SIR,—It is my intention to write a few lines of re-mark on 'Wuthering Heights,' which, however, I propose to place apart as a brief preface before the tale. I am likewise com-pelling myself to read it over, for the first time of opening the book since my sister's death. Its power fills me with renewed admiration; but yet I am oppressed: the reader is scarcely ever permitted a taste of unalloyed pleasure; every beam of sunshine is poured down through black bars of threatening cloud; every page is surcharged with a sort of moral electricity; and the writer was unconscious of all this—nothing could make her conscious of it.

And this makes me reflect; perhaps I am too incapable of perceiving the faults and peculiarities of my own style.

I should wish to revise the proofs, if it be not too great an inconvenience to send them. It seems to me advisable to modify the orthography of the old servant Joseph's speeches; for though as it stands it exactly renders the Yorkshire dialect to a Yorkshire ear, yet I am sure Southerns must find it unintelligible; and thus one of the most graphic characters in the book is lost on them.

I grieve to say that I possess no portrait of either of my sisters. —Yours sincerely,

C. BRONTË.

607 (475). *To* ELLEN NUSSEY.

September, 1850.

DEAR ELLEN, — There is nothing wrong, and I write you a line as you desire, merely to say that I *am* busy just now — Mr Smith wishes to reprint some of Emily's and Anne's works — with a few little additions from the papers they have left — and I have been closely engaged in revising, transcribing — preparing a Preface — Notice, &c. As the time for doing this is limited I am obliged to be industrious — I found the task at first exquisitely painful and depressing — but regarding it in the light of *a sacred duty* — I went on — and now can bear it better — It is work however that I cannot do in the evening — for if I did, I should have no sleep at night.

Papa, I am most thankful to say, is in improved health — and so — I think — am I; I trust you are the same.

I have just received a kind letter from Miss Martineau — she has got back to Ambleside and had heard there of my visit to the Lakes — she expresses her regret &c. at not being at home.

You will be better able to judge about Amelia when you see her — I received the cards — Mr and Mrs Joseph Taylor — it seemed strange — I fancy they will be happier when they get home to Hunsworth than wandering about. — Good-bye —

Yours faithfully,

C. BRONTË.

608 (472). *To* W. S. WILLIAMS.

October 2nd, 1850.

MY DEAR SIR, — I have to thank you for the care and kindness with which you have assisted me throughout in correcting these 'Remains.'

Whether — when they are published — they will appear to others as they do to me — I cannot tell — I hope not — and indeed I suppose what to me is bitter pain will only be soft pathos to the general reader.

Miss Martineau has several times lately asked me to go and see her — and though this is a dreary season for travelling northward — I think if Papa continues pretty well I shall go in a week or two. I feel to my deep sorrow — to my humiliation — that it is not in my power to bear the canker of constant solitude—I had calculated that when shut out from every enjoyment—from every stimulus but what could be derived from intellectual exertion—my mind would rouse itself perforce—It is not so: even intellect—even imagination—will not dispense with the ray of domestic cheerfulness—with the gentle spur of family discussion—Late in the evenings and all through the nights—I fall into a condition of mind which turns entirely to the Past—to memory, and memory is both sad and relentless. This will never do and will produce no good—I tell you this that you may check false anticipations.

You cannot help me—and must not trouble yourself in any shape to sympathize with me. It is my cup—I must drink it as others drink theirs—Yours sincerely,

C. B.

609 (474). A FRIEND *to* MRS GASKELL.[1]

October 3rd, 1850.

Though the weather was drizzly we resolved to make our long-planned excursion to Haworth; so we packed ourselves into the buffalo skin, and that into the gig, and set off about eleven. The rain ceased, and the day was just suited to the scenery—wild and chill—with great masses of cloud glooming over the moors, and here and there a ray of sunshine covertly stealing through, and resting with a dim magical light upon some high bleak village; or darting down into some deep glen, lighting up the tall chimney, or glistening on the windows and wet roof of the mill which lies couching in the bottom. The country got wilder and wilder as we approached Haworth; for the last four miles we were ascending a huge moor, at the very top of which lies the dreary, black-looking village of Haworth. The village street itself is one of the steepest hills I have ever seen, and the stones are so horribly jolting that I should have got out and walked with W——, if possible, but, having once begun the ascent, to stop was out of the question. At the top was the inn where we put up, close by the church; and the clergyman's house, we were told, was at the top of the churchyard. So through that we went—a dreary, dreary place, literally *paved* with

[1] Describing a visit to Haworth in 1850. See Mrs Gaskell's *Life*, Haworth ed: pp.485-7.

rain-blackened tombstones, and all on the slope; for at Haworth there is on the highest height a higher still, and Mr Brontë's house stands considerably above the church. There was the house before us, a small oblong stone house, with not a tree to screen it from the cutting wind; but how we were to get at it from the churchyard we could not see! There was an old man in the churchyard, brooding like a ghoul over the graves, with a sort of grim hilarity on his face. I thought he looked hardly human; however, he was human enough to tell us the way, and presently we found ourselves in the little bare parlour. Presently the door opened, and in came a superannuated mastiff, followed by an old gentleman very like Miss Brontë, who shook hands with us, and then went to call his daughter. A long interval, during which we coaxed the old dog, and looked at a picture of Miss Brontë, by Richmond, the solitary ornament of the room, looking strangely out of place on the bare walls, and at the books on the little shelves, most of them evidently the gift of the authors since Miss Brontë's celebrity. Presently she came in, and welcomed us very kindly, and took me upstairs to take off my bonnet, and herself brought me water and towels. The uncarpeted stone stairs and floors, the old drawers propped on wood, were all scrupulously clean and neat. When we went into the parlour again we began talking very comfortably, when the door opened and Mr Brontë looked in; seeing his daughter there, I suppose he thought it was all right, and he retreated to his study on the opposite side of the passage, presently emerging again to bring W—— a country newspaper. This was his last appearance till we went. Miss Brontë spoke with the greatest warmth of Miss Martineau, and of the good she had gained from her. Well! we talked about various things—the character of the people, about her solitude, etc.—till she left the room to help about dinner, I suppose, for she did not return for an age. The old dog had vanished; a fat curly-haired dog honoured us with his company for some time, but finally manifested a wish to get out, so we were left alone. At last she returned, followed by the maid and dinner, which made us all more comfortable; and we had some very pleasant conversation, in the midst of which time passed quicker than we supposed, for at last W—— found that it was half-past three, and we had fourteen or fifteen miles before us. So we hurried off, having obtained from her a promise to pay us a visit in the spring; and the old gentleman having issued once more from his study to say good-bye, we returned to the inn, and made the best of our way homewards.

Miss Brontë put me so in mind of her own 'Jane Eyre.' She looked smaller than ever, and moved about so quietly, and noiselessly, just like a little bird, as Rochester called her, barring that all birds are joyous, and that joy can never have entered that house since it was first built; and yet, perhaps, when that old man married, and took home his bride, and children's voices and feet were heard about the house, even that desolate crowded graveyard and biting blast could not quench cheerfulness and hope. Now there is something touching in the sight of that little creature entombed in such a place, and moving about herself like a spirit, especially when you think that the slight still frame encloses a force of strong fiery life, which nothing has been able to freeze or extinguish.

610. *To* Ellen Nussey.

[Oct. 14th, 1850].

DEAR ELLEN, — I return A.'s letter. She seems quite happy and fully satisfied of her husband's affection. Is this the usual way of spending the honeymoon? — to me it seems as if they overdo it — that travelling — and tugging and fagging about and getting drenched and mudded, by no means harmonizes with my notions of happiness — besides — the two meals a day &c. would do one up — it all reminds me too sharply of the few days I spent with Joe in London nearly 10 years since[1] — when I was many a time fit to drop with the fever and faintness resulting from long fasting and excessive fatigue — However, no doubt, a bride can bear such things better than others. I smiled to myself at some passages — she has wondrous faith in her husband's intellectual powers and acquirements: Joe's illusion will soon be over — but Amelia's will not — and therein she is happier than he —

What will be the proper thing for me to do when they come home — by way of acknowledging the cards sent me? I suppose I must send my card — didn't you say so?

John Taylor will probably discover that he too wants a wife when he gets to Ropely — the opposite hill will form a conveni-

---

[1]In Feb. 1842 when on her way to Brussels with her sister Emily and her father, Mary and Joe Taylor accompanied them.

ent prospect—but I will say no more—you know I disapprove jesting and teasing on these matters. Idle words sometimes do unintentional harm.

I have had a letter from Mary lately—she is well, happy and prosperous—her shop thriving—herself content—I am glad of this.—Good-bye, dear Nell—God bless you!

C. BRONTË.

Papa continues *much better*.

Soon after the publication in the *Palladium* of the article on 'Currer Bell,' Miss Brontë had written to Miss Martineau.

611. *To* HARRIET MARTINEAU.

[October (?), 1850].

DEAR MISS MARTINEAU,—Do not give yourself the trouble of sending 'The Palladium,' as I have already seen that number containing the notice of 'Currer Bell,' and, while admiring with my whole soul the eloquence and fire of the composition, have mutely and somewhat grimly wondered what grounds have yet been given, by the author reviewed, for the lofty expectations here set forth in language the most shining and glowing. Did Mr Dobell possess Prince Ali's ivory tube, and could he, with its aid, see Currer Bell sometimes mending a stocking or making a pie in the kitchen of an old Parsonage House in the obscurest of Yorkshire villages, I am afraid the young poet would 'fold his silver wings' over his offended eyes, and desire to recall his fervid words.[1] Yet I am glad to learn by whom that article was written, for one passage in it touched a deep chord; I mean where allusion is made to my sister Emily's work, 'Wuthering Heights'; the justice there rendered comes indeed late, the wreath awarded drops on a grave, but no matter—I am grateful. . . .

Regarding my occupations, I have no good account to give.

[1] Writing to his friend, Dr Samuel Brown, on November 22nd, 1850, Sydney Dobell says: 'Of larger calibre and "metal more tried in the fire" is Currer Bell. You would have been charmed with a letter of hers, which her friend Miss Martineau sent me the other day. A noble letter, simple and strong; but tender all over with amenities that showed like ripple on a wave. I was amused with her playful suspicion that "if Mr Dobell could see her sometimes darning a stocking, or making a pie, in the kitchen of an old Parsonage House in the obscurest of Yorkshire villages," he might recall his sentence. A fig for Mr D.'s discernment if he did not confirm it—with costs.'

... Mr Dobell tells me to wait—and wait I will;—were I dependent on my exertions for my daily bread, I think I would rather hire myself out again as a governess than write against the grain or out of the mood. I am not like you, who have no bad days. I have bad days, bad weeks, aye! bad months.—Yours sincerely,

C. Brontë.

612 (477). *To* W. S. Williams.

Octb. 16th, 1850.

My dear Sir,—On the whole it is perhaps as well that the last paragraph of the Preface should be omitted, for I believe it was not expressed with the best grace in the world.

You must not however, apologize for your suggestion, it was kindly meant, and, believe me—kindly taken: it was not *you* I misunderstood—not for a moment—I never misunderstand you —I was thinking of the Critics and the Public, who are always crying for a moral like the Pharisees for a Sign. Does this assurance quite satisfy you?

I forgot to say that I had already heard—first from Miss Martineau—and subsequently through an intimate friend of Sydney Yendys (whose real name is Mr Dobell) that it was to the author of 'The Roman' we are indebted for that eloquent article in the 'Palladium.' I am glad you are going to send his poem for I much wished to see it.

May I trouble you to look at a sentence in the Preface which I have erased—because on reading it over—I was not quite sure about the scientific correctness of the expressions used—Metal, I know, will burn in vivid, coloured flame, exposed to galvanic action—but whether it is consumed I am not sure—Perhaps you or Mr Taylor can tell me whether there is any blunder in the term employed—if not—it might stand.—I am—Yours very sincerely,

C. Brontë.

During the last visit to London, as mentioned in her letter of June 12th, 1850, Charlotte had made the acquaintance of Mr G. H. Lewes, who wrote:

Some months after [the appearance of the review of *Shirley* in the *Edinburgh*] Currer Bell came to London, and I was invited to

meet her at your house. You may remember she asked you not to
point me out to her, but allow her to discover me if she could.
She *did* recognise me almost as soon as I came into the room.
You tried me in the same way; I was less sagacious. However I
sat by her side a great part of the evening, and was greatly interested by her conversation. On parting we shook hands, and she
said, 'We are friends now, are we not?' 'Were we not always,
then?' I asked. 'No! not always,' she said, significantly; and that
was the only allusion she made to the offending article. I lent
her some of Balzac's and George Sand's novels to take with her
into the country; and the following letter was written when they
were returned:

613 (473). *To* G. H. LEWES.

Octb. 17th, 1850.

MY DEAR SIR,—I am sure you will have thought me very dila-
tory in returning the books you so kindly lent me. The fact is,
having some other books to send—I retained yours—to include
them in the same parcel.

Accept my thanks for some hours of pleasant reading. Balzac
was for me quite a new author, and in making his acquaintance,
through the medium of 'Modeste Mignon' and 'Illusions Per-
dues'—you cannot doubt I have felt some interest.[1]

At first I thought he was going to be painfully minute, and
fearfully tedious; one grew impatient of his long parade of detail, his slow revelation of unimportant circumstances, as he
assembled his personages on the stage; but by-and-by, I seemed
to enter into the mystery of his craft and to discover with delight
where his force lay: is it not in the analysis of motive, and in a
subtle perception of the most obscure and secret workings of the
mind? Still—admire Balzac as we may—I think we do not like
him. We rather feel towards him as towards an ungenial acquaintance who is for ever holding up, in strong light, our
defects, and who rarely draws forth our better qualities.

Truly—I like George Sand better. Fantastic, fanatical, unpractical enthusiast as she often is—far from truthful as are
many of her views of Life—misled as she is apt to be by her feelings—George Sand has a better nature than M. de Balzac—her

[1]Compare with the letter to George Smith, dated Feb. 7th, 1853, where she states that she has not read the works of Balzac.

brain is larger—her heart warmer than his. The 'Lettres d'un Voyageur' are full of the writer's self, and I never felt so strongly as in the perusal of this work—that most of her very faults spring from the excess of her good qualities; it is this excess which has often hurried her into difficulty, which has prepared for her enduring regret. But—I believe—her mind is of that order which disastrous experience teaches without weakening or too much disheartening, and in that case—the longer she lives the better she will grow. A hopeful point in all her writings is the scarcity of false French sentiment—I wish I could say its absence—but the weed flourishes here and there in the 'Lettres.'

Remember me kindly to Mrs Lewes, and believe me—my Dear Sir, yours very sincerely,

C. BRONTË.

614 (475). *To* ELLEN NUSSEY.

HAWORTH, Octb. 23rd, 1850.

DEAR ELLEN,—Poor George! One cannot help pitying him— I trust the painful impression made on his mind will never be obliterated and that he will forget what crossed it.

It strikes me as rather unfortunate that Mercy should so frequently be the person who goes to see him, though perfectly well-meaning and affectionate, I should greatly doubt whether her proceedings would be altogether so judicious as might be wished. She might with excellent intentions communicate things that had better never be spoken of, or she might treat them in a way that would do harm—however I dare say there is no help for it.

I trust you are well—dear Ellen—I am very decent indeed in bodily health and am both angry and surprised at myself for not being better in spirits—for not growing accustomed or at least resigned to the solitude and isolation of my lot—But my late occupation left a result for some days and indeed still, very painful. The reading over of papers, the renewal of remembrances brought back the pang of bereavement and occasioned a depression of spirits well nigh intolerable—for one or two nights I scarcely knew how to get on till morning—and when morning came I was still haunted with a sense of sickening distress—I tell you these things—because it is absolutely necessary to me to have some relief—You will forgive me—and not to trouble yourself—or imagine that I am one whit worse than I say—it is quite a mental ailment—and I believe and hope is better now—I think so because I can speak about it which I never can when grief is at its worst. I thought to find occupation and interest in writing when alone at home—but hitherto my efforts have been very vain—the deficiency of every stimulus is so complete.

You will recommend me I daresay to go from home—but that does no good—even could I again leave Papa with an easy mind (thank God! he is still better) I cannot describe what a time of it I had after my return from London—Scotland &c. there was a reaction that sunk me to the earth—the deadly silence, solitude, desolation were awful—the craving for companionship—the hopelessness of relief—were what I should dread to feel again.

Dear Nell—when I think of you—it is with a compassion and tenderness that scarcely cheer me—mentally, I feel you also are too lonely and too little occupied. It seems our doom for the present at least—May God in his mercy help us to bear it! Yours faithfully,

C. BRONTË.

615. *To* W. S. WILLIAMS.

Octr 25th, 1850.

MY DEAR SIR,—The box of books came last night and—as usual—I have only gratefully to admire the selection made: Jeffrey's Essays, Dr Arnold's Life, the Roman, Alton Locke—these were all wished-for and welcome.

You say I keep no books: pardon me—I am ashamed of my own rapaciousness: I have kept Macaulay's History and Wordsworth's 'Prelude' and Taylor's 'Philip Van Artevelde,' I soothe my conscience by saying that the two last—being poetry—do not count—This is a convenient doctrine for me; I meditate acting upon it with reference to the 'Roman,' so I trust that nobody in Cornhill will dispute its validity or affirm that 'poetry' has a value except for the trunkmakers.

I have already had Macaulay's Essays—Sydney Smith's lectures on Moral Philosophy, and Knox on Race. Pickering's work on the same subject I have not seen—nor all the vols of Leigh Hunt's Autobiography. However—I am now abundantly supplied for a long time to come. I liked Hazlitt's essays much.

The Autumn—as you say—has been very fine—I and Solitude and Memory have often profited by its sunshine on the
Moors.

I had felt some disappointment at the non-arrival of the proof-
sheets of 'Wuthering Heights'—a feverish impatience to complete the revision is apt to beset me—the work of looking over
papers &c. could not be gone through with impunity or with
unaltered spirits—associations too tender—regrets too bitter
sprang out of it—

Meantime—the Cornhill books now as heretofore, are my
best medicine—affording a solace which could not be yielded by
the very same books procured from a common library.

Already I have read the greatest part of the 'Roman'—passages in it possess a kindling virtue such as true poetry alone can
boast—there are images of genuine grandeur—there are lines
that at once stamp themselves on the memory—can it be true
that a new planet has risen on the heaven whence all stars seemed
fast fading? I believe it is—for this Sydney or Dobell speaks
with a voice of his own, unborrowed—unwicked. You hear
Tennyson indeed sometimes—and Byron sometimes in some
passages of the 'Roman'—but then again you hear a new note—
nowhere clearer than in a certain brief lyric—sung in a meeting
of minstrels—a sort of dirge over a dead brother—*that* not only
charmed the ear and brain—it smote the heart. Not all the
tinkling cymbals—not all the word-twisters—not all the Brownings or Barrett Brownings or Lytton Bulwer's in the world can
do as much.—Yours sincerely,   C. BRONTË.

616. *To* GEORGE SMITH.

October 31st., 1850.

MY DEAR SIR,—It is pleasing to find that already a species of
preparation is commencing in your mind, and, I doubt not, in
the minds of others in Cornhill, &c., towards a due reception of
that 'Coming Man' the great Cardinal Archbishop Wiseman.[1]
After his arrival London will not be what it was, nor will this

---

[1]Nicholas Patrick Stephen Wiseman
(1802–1865) was born at Seville. He became Vicar-Apostolic of the London district in 1849, and in 1850 was created Archbishop and Cardinal of Westminster. His
works include *Horae Syriacae*; *Letters on the
Catholic Church*; *Fabiola, or the Church of the
Catacombs*; and *Recollections of the Last Four
Popes*. For Charlotte Brontë's impression
of him, see her letter dated June 17th, 1851.

day and generation be either *what* or *where* they were. A new Joshua—a greater even than Joshua—will command the sun—not merely to stand still, but to go back six centuries.

I could have fancied something—if not in your letter yet in the clever scribe it enclosed—savouring of the 'Middle Ages.' Yielding to the impulse of fancy, I cannot help anticipating the time when 65 Cornhill shall be honoured by the daily domiciliary visit of 'a friar of orders grey,' and when that small back room (I do not know what its present mundane use and denomination may be), lit by a skylight, shall be fitted up as an oratory, with a saint in a niche, two candles always burning, a *prie-dieu*, and a handsomely bound Missal; also a confessional chair—very comfortable—for the priest, and a square of carpet, or better the bare boards, for the penitent.

Here, every morning, when you, Mr Taylor, and Mr Williams come in to business, you will, instead of at once repairing to your desks in heathenish sort, enter, tell your beads (each of you will wear a godly rosary and crucifix), sign yourselves with holy water (of which there will always be a small vase properly replenished), and—once a month at least—you will duly make confession and receive absolution. The ease this will give to your now never-disburthened heretic consciences words can but feebly express.

So gratifying is this picture that I feel reluctant to look on any other; Imagination, however, obstinately persists in showing the reverse. What if your organs of Firmness should withstand 'Holy Obedience'? What if your causative and investigatory faculties should question the infallibility of Rome? What if that presumptuous self-reliance, that audacious championship of Reason and Common Sense which ought to have been crushed out of you all in your cradles, or at least during your school days, and which, perhaps, on the contrary, were encouraged and developed, what if these things should induce you madly to oppose the returning supremacy and advancing victory of the Holy Catholic Church?

The answer is afflicting, but must be given; indeed, you give it yourself when you allude to 'the preparations in Smithfield.' The chances are that some First Sunday in Advent (1880) you find yourselves duly robed in the yellow 'San Benito,' walking in the procession of as fine an 'auto da fe' as ever made Christendom exult.

The two post-office orders came safely. I showed papa the 'Paper Lantern';[1] he was greatly amused with it, and would like to see the whole when it is completed to show the curates, whose case it will fit with much nicety.

What you say about the present dulness and dreariness of London, and the sort of longing for fresh air and freedom your words rather imply than express, contain for me the germs of a wholesome sermon—a sermon which I shall often preach to myself on these long autumn evenings and longer winter evenings that approach. To quote an old Puritan tract, 'there is a crook in every lot.'

Be sure not to give yourself much trouble about Mr Newby; I have not the least expectation that you will be able to get anything from him; he has an evasive, shuffling plan of meeting, or rather eluding, such demands, against which it is fatiguing to contend. If you think payment would be really inconvenient, do not urge it. I must now, however, dissuade you from calling on him. As to that information which is to earn 'a statue in Paternoster Row,' I hope Mr Wyatt[2] will have nothing to do with the said statue, and also that it will not be equestrian. As to the costume, doubtless felicitous ideas will be suggested on that head by the novelties which, report says, are likely to be introduced at the Great Exhibition.

Forgive all the nonsense of this letter, there is such a pleasure and relief either in writing or talking a little nonsense sometimes to anybody who is sensible enough to understand and good-natured enough to pardon it.—Believe me, Yours sincerely,

C. BRONTË.

617 (478). *To* JAMES TAYLOR.

November 6th, 1850.

MY DEAR SIR,—I have just finished reading the Life of Dr Arnold, but now when I wish, in accordance with your request, to express what I think of it, I do not find the task very easy; proper terms seem wanting. This is not a character to be dis-

---

[1] A *Paper Lantern for Puseyites*, by 'Will o' the Wisp,' a satire in verse, was first published by Smith, Elder & Co. in 1843: a new and revised edition of the pamphlet being issued by the same firm in 1850. See also Charlotte's letter of December 3rd, 1850.

[2] Matthew Cotes Wyatt (1777–1862), sculptor, executed equestrian statues of George III in Pall Mall East, and of the Duke of Wellington.

missed with a few laudatory words; it is not a one-sided character; pure panegyric would be inappropriate. Dr Arnold (it seems to me) was not quite saintly; his greatness was cast in a mortal mould; he was a little severe—almost a little hard; he was vehement and somewhat oppugnant. Himself the most indefatigable of workers, I know not whether he could have understood or made allowance for a temperament that required more rest, yet not to one man in twenty thousand is given his giant faculty of labour; by virtue of it he seems to me the greatest of Working Men. Exacting he might have been then on this point, and granting that he were so, and a little hasty, stern and positive, those were his sole faults (if indeed that can be called a fault which in no shape degrades the individual's own character but is only apt to oppress and overstrain the weaker nature of his neighbours). Afterwards come his good qualities. About these there is nothing dubious. Where can we find justice, firmness, independence, earnestness, sincerity, fuller and purer than in him?

But this is not all, and I am glad of it. Besides high intellect and stainless rectitude, his letters and his life attest his possession of the most true-hearted affection. Without this, however we might admire, we could not love him, but with it I think we love him much. A hundred such men, fifty, nay, ten or five such righteous men might save any country, might victoriously champion any cause.

I was struck, too, by the almost unbroken happiness of his life; a happiness resulting chiefly, no doubt, from the right use to which he put that health and strength which God had given him, but also owing partly to a singular exemption from those deep and bitter griefs which most human beings are called on to endure. His wife was what he wished; his children were healthy and promising; his own health was excellent; his undertakings were crowned with success; even Death was kind, for however sharp the pains of his last hours, they were but brief. God's blessing seems to have accompanied him from the cradle to the grave. One feels thankful to know that it has been permitted to any man to live such a life.

When I was in Westmoreland last August, I spent an evening at Fox How, where Mrs Arnold and her daughters still reside. It was twilight as I drove to the place, and almost dark ere I reached it; still I could perceive that the situation was exquisitely lovely. The house looked like a nest half buried in flowers and creepers, and, dusk as it was, I could feel that the valley and the hills round were beautiful as imagination could dream. Mrs Arnold seemed an amiable, and must once have been a very pretty, woman; her daughters I liked much. There was present also a son of Chevalier Bunsen, with his wife or rather bride. I had not then read Dr Arnold's Life; otherwise, the visit would have interested me even more than it actually did.

Mr Williams told me (if I mistake not) that you had recently visited the 'Lake Country.' I trust you enjoyed your excursion, and that our English Lakes did not suffer too much by comparison in your memory with the Scottish Lochs. —I am, my dear sir, yours sincerely,

C. Brontë.

618 (479). *To* W. S. Williams.

Nov. 9th, 1850.

My dear Sir, —I have read Lord John Russell's letter with very great zest and relish, and think him a spirited sensible little man for writing it. He makes no old womanish outcry of alarm and expresses no exaggerated wrath. One of the best paragraphs is that which refers to the Bishop of London and the Puseyites. Oh! I wish Dr Arnold were yet living or that a second Dr Arnold could be found. Were there but ten such men amongst the Hierarchs of the Church of England, she might bid defiance to all the scarlet hats and stockings in the Pope's gift. Her sanctuaries would be purified, her rites reformed, her withered veins would swell again with vital sap; but it is *not* so.

It is well that Truth is indestructible; that Ruin cannot crush nor Fire annihilate —her divine essence; while forms change and institutions perish *Truth* is great and shall prevail.

I am truly glad to hear that Miss Kavanagh's health is improved. You can send her book whenever it is most convenient. I received from Cornhill the other day a periodical containing a portrait of Jenny Lind—a sweet, natural, innocent peasant girl face —curiously contrasted with an artificial fine-lady dress. I do *like* and esteem Jenny's character; yet not long since I heard her torn to pieces by the tongue of Detraction, scarcely a virtue left —twenty odious defects imputed.

There was likewise a most faithful portrait of R. H. Horne

with his imaginative forehead and somewhat foolish looking mouth and chin—indicating that mixed character which I should think he owns. Mr Horne writes well—that tragedy on the 'Death of Marlowe' reminds me of some of the best of Dumas' dramatic pieces.—Yours very sincerely,

C. BRONTË.

619 (487). *To* ELLEN NUSSEY.

Saturday, November, 1850.

DEAR ELLEN,—I thank you for your two notes which though unanswered, have not been unregarded—There is a great deal of sickness here—though Papa continues pretty well and so do I with the exception of headaches which seem to beset me more in Autumn than at other seasons—Martha however has been very ill some days with quinsey and though better now, is still in bed —this makes me busy—as her sister is only to be had at intervals.

Take care of your cold—keep in doors on damp misty days.

Amelia's conduct to you always strikes me as giving proof of a genuinely affectionate and amiable disposition—I duly sent my card to Hunsworth—To-day's fog has brought me a sick head-ache—under the influence of which I cut short this note.—Yours faithfully,

C. BRONTË.

In November and December, 1850, Charlotte Brontë received four letters[1] from an unknown admirer of her two published novels, *Jane Eyre* and *Shirley*. He did not disclose his identity, but signed his letters only with the initials 'K. T.', and he appears to have addressed them under cover to Charlotte Brontë's publishers. As his letters are addressed to 'Currer Bell' it appears also that she did not reveal her identity to him.

His first letter begins:

MADAM,—for the 'Edinburgh Review' says it is 'Madam'—the once most famous of French novelists has commenced in his tale of 'Mary Lawson' the very vilest paraphrase of your 'Jane Eyre.'

---

[1]Now in the Bonnell Collection, at the Brontë Parsonage Museum, Haworth.

This refers to *Kitty Bell, the Orphan*,[1] by Eugene Sue, which the late Mrs Ellis H. Chadwick reprinted in 1914 as 'possibly an earlier version of Charlotte Brontë's *Jane Eyre*.'

Charlotte Brontë's reply to K. T.'s first letter has not been traced, but it is clear that she asked him to comply with his suggestion that he should send her the opinions of himself and his acquaintances of her two published novels. In reply to his second letter (dated November 13, 1850) her draft (in pencil) is as follows:

620. *To K. T. Miss Kelly's, 153, Fleet Street, London.*

MY DEAR SIR, — I read your letter with interest — it has left on my mind a pleasant and grateful impression — the task was onerous — and you have done it well — exactly what I wanted and what no professed reviewer could or would do for me — your amateur critique accomplishes — holding up a truthful glass in which I see reflected the mental features — impossible to myself to survey in their substance — Often I have been puzzled to know what 'Shirley' was like, but now I have the book's image clear in my mind's eye — distinct as others see it.

More than one touch of nice discrimination I find in what you say, and all the better for being expressed inartificially — that you are not much used to the art of composition — not at all particular about punctuation &c. is scarcely a defect, or one I feel a singular readiness to excuse — since it removes you far from the triteness of hack-writers. You have read — you can feel — you can understand — this suffices.

It requires no wizard of witch-craft to tell you one thing viz. that you are not an Englishman — but I think — an Irishman — probably too an artist. Have I ever seen you — or are you really an entire stranger to me? I remember among the small number of persons introduced to me when I was in London — were two or three artists — and one an Irishman — but that you are he — it would be somewhat rash to conclude. — Believe me, Yours sincerely,

C. B.

[1] *Kitty Bell, The Orphan.* Possibly an earlier version of Charlotte Brontë's *Jane Eyre.* Written *circa* 1844 and published as the work of Eugene Sue. With an Introduction by Mrs Ellis H. Chadwick. 1914. See also *In the Footsteps of the Brontës* by Mrs Ellis H. Chadwick, pp. 401–409.

K. T. in his reply (dated November 25th, 1850) acknowledged that Charlotte Brontë was right in her conjecture that he was an Irishman and an artist; but he confessed to a 'divided duty,' preferring Shakspere to Raphael and Milton to Michael Angelo: 'I fear it will never be in me to disquiet Maclise or make the sleep of Landseer uneasy.' 'I am not the man: never saw you: and never met with anyone who had. . . . I do not think you tall. I do not think you young. I will not swear that I think you pretty. . . . I will swear that your face is one full of thought and expression: I will swear that were you short, old and plain, I should esteem and love you as much as I do at this moment. . . .'

The draft of Charlotte's reply is as follows:

621. *To* K. T.

Your last letter must have an answer however brief. In all that you have written to me I seemed to recognise the language of a kind and loyal heart as well as an intelligent head. For your critique on 'Shirley' I do sincerely thank you—its discrimination and perfect candour gave it for me a real value—For your friendly offers of further service I thank you too—whether I should have an opportunity of accepting them or not.

Why should it annoy you that I discovered your country? Is Ireland then a Nazareth from which no prophet and no good thing can come?

I suppose from the tone of your letter that you are very young and I doubt whether life has been all sunshine to you so far—Be of good courage—you have talents—you have true feelings, and keen delicate perceptions [beyond] the ordinary—work—hope—persevere in all good resolutions—that your lot may in the end prove successful and happy is the sincere wish of

CURRER BELL.

You see I never take any notice of a certain enthusiasm which animates your letters—it is not that I either undervalue it or am in the least affected by it—I take it for what it is—the champagne-like foam of an ardent mind—a cream—a sparkle—as transient as pleasant—something in which none but the very vulgar-minded could see harm—and on which none but the ever-san-guine would rely.

A further letter from 'K. T.' (dated December 11th, 1850) closed this correspondence.

622. *To* G. H. LEWES.

HAWORTH, Novr 23rd, 1850.

MY DEAR SIR,—I am glad to hear that Miss Martineau's little story in the 'Leader' touched you and made you cry. I thought it a sample of *real* suffering; a case piteous, cureless, voiceless. It is to be feared there are many such. Life—seen in some phases—is a very dreary thing. I used to think human destinies were nearly equal, but the older I grow the weaker becomes my hold on this doctrine; it is fast slipping from me.

While I decline your offer of a fresh supply of books, believe, at the same time, that I am grateful for it.

You ask whether I am 'distilling life and thought in any new shape.' Don't goad me with such questions, my dear sir. Let it suffice to answer that I am on the worst terms with myself—alternating between a lively indignation and a brooding contempt, and that if anybody would take out a patent for a new invention enabling distressed authors to command their mood and to compel to obedience their refractory faculties—I should regard that individual as the first benefactor of his race.

As to 'recent changes of scene' I enjoyed them much at the time: they ought to do me good; my health they certainly benefited, and if their mental effect is otherwise than it ought to be—the fault is doubtless mine.

I have one pleasing duty to perform which I must not forget ere I conclude this letter—that is to congratulate you and all others whom it may concern on the pious disposition evinced by 'The Leader' to walk bodily back to the True Fold. There is something promising and touching in the tone you have lately assumed—a something which will kindle the glow of holy expectation in the heart of Cardinal Archbishop Wiseman when his chaplain reads to him your lucubrations. You ask me to write to your 'Open Council.' I couldn't presume to do such a thing—but in another year—perhaps your columns will be consecrated by contributions from the Cardinal and letters from Father John Henry Newman.

Most moving is that apostolic and evangelic declaration of the Archbishop of Westminster that he wants nothing of his See but the back courts and dark alleys and all the human poverty and misery with which they teem. There is nothing jesuitical in this, nothing whatever of the wolf-in-sheep's-clothing — and the most cursing heretic will not dare to moot the question — whether — if all Holy Church seeks be the good of the poor — she could not look after this quite as well in a curate's plain clothes as in a cardinal's robes and hat — whether the blaze and pomp of her hierarchy is absolutely necessary to the instruction of ignorance and the relief of destitution.

Wishing you and Mr Thornton Hunt and all of you much facility of speech in your first experiment in auricular confession, and a very full absolution from your awful heresies together with no heavier penance than the gravity of the case (which will be pretty stringent) shall seem absolutely to demand, — I am, Yours sincerely,

C. Brontë.

623 (480). *To* Ellen Nussey.

Novb. 26th, 1850.

Dear Ellen, — There is no chance of my getting either to Brookroyd or Hunsworth. I cannot leave home at all just now — and when I *do* go — it ought to be to see Miss Martineau — she has asked me twice — in terms so kind, considerate and yet so urgent that it would seem wrong to withstand her — Sir J. K. S.[1] has likewise asked me again — but I should only go there for a day — if at all. Do you know whether Miss Wooler is still at the Lakes? if she is — I would (in case I went) dedicate some days to her.

Papa continues pretty well; Martha is better but not quite strong. I trust and hope my headaches are going to give me a respite — they have been very annoying, not from their violence but frequency.

Is your cold quite gone?

I mean to answer Amelia's note in a day or two — at present I have other letters to write. — Yours faithfully,

C. B.

[1]Sir James Kay-Shuttleworth.

624. *To* GEORGE SMITH.

December 3rd, 1850.

MY DEAR SIR,—Your Will o' the Wisp is a very pleasant and witty sprite, and though not venomous his pungency may be none the less effective on that account. Indeed, I believe a good-natured kind of ridicule is a weapon more appropriate to the present crisis than bitter satire or serious indignation. We are in no danger. Why should we be angry? I only wish the author had rectified some of her rhymes (such as sedilia and famili*ar*, tiara and bear*er*), but critics will surely not be severe with the little book.

Mr M. A. Titmarsh holds out an alluring invitation to the Rhine. I hope thousands will take advantage of the facilities he offers to make the excursion in the 'polite society' of the Kickleburys.

As to Mr Newby, he charms me. First there is the fascinating coyness with which he shuns your pursuit. For a month, or nearly two months, have you been fondly hoping to win from him an interview, while he has been making himself as scarce as violets at Christmas, aristocratically absenting himself from town, evading your grasp like a publisher metamorphosed into a rainbow. Then when you come upon him in that fatal way in Regent Street, pin him down, and hunt him home with more promptitude than politeness, and with a want of delicate consideration for your victim's fine feelings calculated to awaken emotions of regret, that victim is still ready for the emergency. Scorning to stand on the defensive, he at once assumes the offensive. Not only has he realised no profit, he has sustained actual loss; and, to account for this, adds, with a sublime boldness of invention, that the author 'wished him to spend all possible profits in advertisements.'

Equally well acted too is the artless simplicity of his surprise at the news you communicate; and his pretty little menace of a 'Chancery injunction' consummates the picture and makes it perfect.

Any statement of accounts he may send I shall at once transmit to you. In your hands I leave him; deal with him as you list, but I heartily wish you well rid of the business.

On referring to Mr Newby's letters I find in one of them a

boast that he is 'advertising vigorously.' I remember that this flourish caused us to look out carefully for the results of his vast exertions; but though we everywhere encountered 'Jane Eyre' it was as rare a thing to find an advertisement of 'Wuthering Heights' as it appears to be to meet with Mr Newby in town at an unfashionable season of the year. The fact is he advertised the book very scantily and for a very short time. Of course we never expressed a wish or uttered an injunction on the subject; nor was it likely we should, as it was rather important to us to recover the 50*l*. we had advanced; more we did not ask.

I would say something about regret for the trouble you have had in your chase of this ethereal and evanescent ornament of '*the* Trade,' but I fear apologies would be even worse than thanks. Both these shall be left out and you shall only be request-ed to—Believe me, yours sincerely,

C. BRONTË.

The new edition of *Wuthering Heights*, prefaced by the passage concerning it in the *Palladium* article, was published on Decem-ber 10th, 1850, and Miss Brontë requested that a copy of the book, accompanied by the following note, which she forwarded to her publishers, should be sent to her friendly reviewer. For some unexplained reason, the packet did not reach its destina-tion for three or four months.[1]

625 (481).   To SYDNEY DOBELL.

HAWORTH, NEAR KEIGHLEY, YORKSHIRE,
December 8th, 1850.

I offer this little book to my critic in the 'Palladium,' and he must believe it accompanied by a tribute of the sincerest grati-tude; not so much for anything he has said of myself as for the noble justice he has rendered to one dear to me as myself—per-haps dearer—and perhaps one kind word spoken for her awak-ens a deeper, tenderer sentiment of thankfulness than eulogies heaped on my own head. As you will see when you have read the biographical notice, my sister cannot thank you herself; she

<hr>

[1] See Dobell's letter, of March 1851, to Miss Brontë.

is gone out of your sphere and mine, and human blame and praise are nothing to her now. But to me, for her sake, they are something still; it revived me for many a day to find that, dead as she was, the work of her genius had at last met with worthy appreciation.

Tell me, when you have read the introduction, whether any doubts still linger in your mind respecting the authorship of 'Wuthering Heights,' 'Wildfell Hall,' etc. Your mistrust did me some injustice; it proved a general conception of character such as I should be sorry to call mine; but these false ideas will naturally arise when we only judge an author from his works. In fairness I must also disclaim the flattering side of the portrait. I am no 'young Penthesilea *mediis in millibus*,' but a plain country parson's daughter.

Once more I thank you, and that with a full heart.

C. BRONTË.

626 (482). *To* MRS GASKELL.

December 13th, 1850.

MY DEAR MRS GASKELL,—Miss ——'s kindness and yours is such that I am placed in the dilemma of not knowing how adequately to express my sense of it. *This* I know, however, very well—that if I *could* go and be with you for a week or two in such a quiet south-country house, and with such kind people as you describe, I should like it much. I find the proposal marvellously to my taste; it is the pleasantest, gentlest, sweetest temptation possible; but, delectable as it is, its solicitations are by no means to be yielded to without the sanction of reason, and therefore I desire for the present to be silent, and to stand back till I have been to Miss Martineau's, and returned home, and considered well whether it is a scheme as right as agreeable.

Meantime the mere thought does me good. . . .

C. BRONTË.

CHAPTER XXV

CHARLOTTE MAKES NEW FRIENDS

IMMEDIATELY after the publication of the second edition of *Wuthering Heights and Agnes Grey*, Charlotte Brontë made preparations for her visit to Miss Martineau. She left Haworth on the 16th December, and remained at Ambleside for one week, returning to Yorkshire on the 23rd to spend a few days with her friend Ellen Nussey.

The two novelists had really very little in common, but Charlotte was filled with wonder and admiration for Miss Martineau's indefatigable strength and energy. Her great regard for her kind hostess is fully expressed in her letters. During Charlotte's visit, Miss Martineau was busy with the *Letters on the Laws of Man's Social Nature and Development*, which she wrote in conjunction with Henry G. Atkinson. The book was published in January, 1851, and the anti-theological views it contained gave much offence. Charlotte Brontë said that she regretted the publication for Miss Martineau's sake—'Who can trust the word, or rely on the judgment of an avowed atheist?'

However, her visit to Ambleside passed very happily and brought Charlotte new friends and new interests. She made the acquaintance of Matthew Arnold, and paid many visits to his people at Fox How. Sir James Kay-Shuttleworth also paid her a great deal of attention, and took her driving almost every day.

Charlotte spent Christmas at Brookroyd with Ellen Nussey, and then returned to Haworth, where she remained for the next five months. The letters of this period are mainly interesting on account of Mr James Taylor's assiduous courtship and its defeat, his departure from England, and Charlotte's self-analysis thereon. We are also introduced to a new friend and correspondent in the person of Sydney Dobell.

627 (483). *To* ELLEN NUSSEY.

THE KNOLL, AMBLESIDE,
Decbr 18th, 1850.

DEAR ELLEN,—I can write to you now for I am away from home and relieved, temporarily at least, by change of air and scene from the heavy burden of depression which I confess has for nearly 3 months been sinking me to the earth. I never shall forget last Autumn. Some days and nights have been cruel—but now—having once told you this—I need say no more on the subject. My loathing of solitude grew extreme; my recollection of my Sisters intolerably poignant; I am better now.

I am at Miss Martineau's for a week—her house is very pleasant both within and without—arranged at all points with admirable neatness and comfort—Her visitors enjoy the most perfect liberty; what she claims for herself she allows them. I rise at my own hour, breakfast alone—(she is up at five, takes a cold bath and a walk by starlight and has finished breakfast and got to her work by 7 o'clock) I pass the morning in the drawing-room —she in her study. At 2 o'clock we meet, work, talk, and walk together till 5—her dinner hour—spend the evening together— when she converses fluently, abundantly and with the most complete frankness—I go to my own room soon after ten—she sits up writing letters till twelve. She appears exhaustless in strength and spirit, and indefatigable in the faculty of labour. She is a great and a good woman; of course not without peculiarities but I have seen none yet that annoy me. She is both hard and warm-hearted, abrupt and affectionate—liberal and despotic. I believe she is not at all conscious of her own absolutism. When I tell her of it, she denies the charge warmly—then I laugh at her. I believe she almost rules Ambleside. Some of the gentry dislike her, but the lower orders have a great regard for her. I will not stay more than a week because about Christmas relations and other guests will come. Sir J. and Lady Shuttleworth are coming here to dine on Thursday—I mean to get off going there if I possibly can without giving downright offence. Write to me and say how you are. With kind regards to all I am—Yours faithfully,

C. BRONTË.

628 (484). *To* ELLEN NUSSEY.

AMBLESIDE, December 21st, '50.

DEAR ELLEN,—I have managed to get off going to Sir J. K. Shuttleworth's by a promise to come some other time; I thought I really should like to spend 2 or 3 days with you before going home, therefore if it is not inconvenient for you I will come on Monday and stay till Thursday. I shall be at Bradford (D.V.) at 10 minutes past 2 Monday afternoon, and can take a cab at the station forward to Birstall. I have truly enjoyed my visit. I have seen a good many people, and all have been so marvellously kind, not the least so the family of Dr Arnold. Miss Martineau I relish inexpressibly. Sir James has been almost every day to take me a drive; I begin to admit in my own mind that he is sincerely benignant to me. I grieve to say he looks to me as if wasting away. Lady S. is ill, near her confinement; she cannot go out, and I have not seen her. Till we meet, good-bye.

C. BRONTË.

629 (485). *To* The REV. P. BRONTË.

AMBLESIDE, December 21st, 1850.

DEAR PAPA,—I think I shall not come home till Thursday. If all be well I shall leave here on Monday and spend a day or two with Ellen Nussey. I have enjoyed my visit exceedingly. Sir J. K. Shuttleworth has called several times and taken me out in his carriage. He seems very truly friendly; but, I am sorry to say, he looks pale and very much wasted. I greatly fear he will not live very long unless some change for the better soon takes place. Lady Shuttleworth is ill too, and cannot go out. I have seen a good deal of Dr Arnold's family and like them much. As to Miss Martineau, I admire her and wonder at her more than I can say. Her powers of labour, of exercise, and social cheerfulness are beyond my comprehension. In spite of the unceasing activity of her colossal intellect she enjoys robust health. She is a taller, larger, and more strongly made woman than I had imagined from that first interview with her. She is very kind to me, though she must think I am a very insignificant person compared to herself. She has just been into the room to show me a chapter of her history[1] which she is now writing, relating to the Duke of Wellington's character and his proceedings in the Peninsula. She wanted an opinion on it, and I was happy to be able to give a very approving one. She seems to understand and do him justice.

You must not direct any more letters here as they will not reach me after to-day. Hoping, dear papa, that you are well, and with kind regards to Tabby and Martha, —I am, your affectionate daughter,

C. BRONTË.

Miss Martineau gave Mrs Gaskell[2] her account of the incident mentioned in Charlotte's letter to her father:

One morning I brought her the first page of the chapter on the Peninsular War in my Introductory History, and said, 'Tell me if this will do for a beginning,' &c. I read the page or two to her, as we stood before the fire, and she looked up at me and stole her hand into mine, and to my amazement the tears were running down her cheeks. She said, 'Oh! I do thank you! Oh! we are of one mind! Oh! I thank you for this justice to the man.' I saw at once there was a touch of idolatry in the case, but it was a charming enthusiasm.

630 (486). *To* ELLEN NUSSEY.

December 27th, 1850.

DEAR ELLEN,—I got home all right yesterday soon after 2 o'clock, and found papa, thank God, well and free from cold. To-day some amount of sickliness and headache is bothering me, but nothing to signify. How did you and Mr —— get on after I left you, and how is your cough? No better I fear for this misty day.

The Christmas books waiting for me were, as I expected, from Thackeray, Mrs Gaskell, and Ruskin.[3] No letter from Mr Williams. It is six weeks since I heard from him. I feel uneasy, but do not like to write. The 'Examiner' is very sore about my Pre-

---

[1] In 1849 Miss Martineau had published a *History of England during the Thirty Years' Peace*, and during 1850, she wrote an introductory volume entitled *Introduction to the History of the Peace*, which was published in 1851.

[2] *The Life of Charlotte Brontë*, by Mrs E. C. Gaskell, Haworth Edition, p. 500.

[3] See Vol. III p. 159.

face, because I did not make it a special exception in speaking of the mass of critics. The soreness is unfortunate and gratuitous, for in my mind I certainly excepted it. Another paper shows painful sensitiveness on the same account; but it does not matter —these things are all transitory. Write very soon. Love to all.—
Yours faithfully,

C. B.

631 (488). *To* JAMES TAYLOR.

January 1st, 1851.

MY DEAR SIR,—I am sorry there should have occurred an irregularity in the transmission of the papers; it has been owing to my absence from home. I trust the interruption has occasioned no inconvenience. Your last letter evinced such a sincere and discriminating admiration for Dr Arnold, that perhaps you will not be wholly uninterested in hearing that during my late visit to Miss Martineau I saw much more of Fox How and its inmates, and daily admired, in the widow and children of one of the greatest and best men of his time, the possession of qualities the most estimable and endearing. Of my kind hostess herself I cannot speak in terms too high. Without being able to share all her opinions, philosophical, political, or religious, without adopting her theories, I yet find a worth and greatness in herself, and a consistency, benevolence, perseverance in her practice such as wins the sincerest esteem and affection. She is not a person to be judged by her writings alone, but rather by her own deeds and life—than which nothing can be more exemplary or nobler. She seems to me the benefactress of Ambleside, yet takes no sort of credit to herself for her active and indefatigable philanthropy. The government of her household is admirably administered; all she does is well done, from the writing of a history down to the quietest female occupation. No sort of carelessness or neglect is allowed under her rule, and yet she is not over strict nor too rigidly exacting; her servants and her poor neighbours love as well as respect her.

I must not, however, fall into the error of talking too much about her, merely because my own mind is just now deeply impressed with what I have seen of her intellectual power and moral worth. Faults she has, but to me they appear very trivial weighed in the balance against her excellences.

Your account of Mr Atkinson tallies exactly with Miss Martineau's. She too said that placidity and mildness (rather than originality and power) were his external characteristics. She described him as a combination of the antique Greek sage with the European modern man of science. Perhaps it was mere perversity in me to get the notion that torpid veins, and a cold, slow-beating heart, lay under his marble outside. But he is a materialist: he serenely denies us our hope of immortality and quietly blots from man's future Heaven and the Life to come. That is why a savour of bitterness seasoned my feeling towards him.

All you say of Mr Thackeray is most graphic and characteristic. He stirs in me both sorrow and anger. Why should he lead so harassing a life? Why should his mocking tongue so perversely deny the better feelings of his better moods?

With every good wish of the season, —I am, my dear sir, yours very sincerely,

C. BRONTË.

632 (489). *To* W. S. WILLIAMS.

January 3rd, 1851.

MY DEAR SIR,—May I beg that a copy of 'Wuthering Heights' may be sent to Mrs Gaskell; her present address is 3 Sussex Place, Regent's Park. She has just sent me the 'Moorland Cottage.' I felt disappointed about the publication of that book, having hoped it would be offered to Smith, Elder & Co.; but it seems she had no alternative, as it was Mr Chapman himself who asked her to write a Christmas book. On my return home yesterday week I found two packets from Cornhill directed in two well-known hands waiting for me. You are all very, very good.

I trust to have derived benefit from my visit to Miss Martineau. A visit more interesting I certainly never paid. If self-sustaining strength can be acquired from example, I ought to have got good. But my nature is not hers; I could not make it so though I were to submit it seventy times seven to the furnace of affliction and discipline it for an age under the hammer and anvil of toil and self-sacrifice. Perhaps if I was like her I should not admire her so much as I do. She is somewhat absolute, though quite unconsciously so; but she is likewise kind, with an affection at once abrupt and constant, whose sincerity you cannot doubt. It was

Vol. III   o

delightful to sit near her in the evenings and hear her converse, myself mute. She speaks with what seems to me a wonderful fluency and eloquence. Her animal spirits are as unflagging as her intellectual powers. I was glad to find her health excellent. I believe neither solitude nor loss of friends would break her down. I saw some faults in her, but somehow I liked them for the sake of her good points. It gave me no pain to feel insignificant, mentally and corporeally, in comparison with her.

Trusting that you and yours are well, and sincerely wishing you all a happy new year, —I am, my dear sir, yours sincerely,

C. BRONTË.

633. *To* MRS GASKELL.

Jany. 4th, 1851.

MY DEAR MRS GASKELL, —. . . I found your note and 'The Moorland Cottage,' of which last I have only as yet read the commencement, which I find to be as sweet, as pure, as fresh as an unopened morning daisy. . . .

C. BRONTË.

634. *To* GEORGE SMITH.

HAWORTH, January 7th, 1851.

MY DEAR SIR, —Mr Thackeray ought to be condemned to build a church and therein to set up two shrines dedicated respectively to St Bungay and St Bacon, to which shrines he should, moreover, be sentenced to make a pilgrimage twice a year with peas in his shoes, and forced, in addition, to lay on each shrine the offering of a neatly-written MS., being a tale without any allusion to Belgravia in it.

As to you and Mr Williams, the honours of martyrdom must be awarded you by every well-regulated and feeling mind. Truly you have come out of great tribulation. I would offer you my whole stock of sympathy —were I not restrained by the contrast between the vast demands of the case and the feeble value of the oblation. It is an awful narrative abounding in thrilling incident; that promise 'really to set about writing' a book of which the publication was announced makes one's hair stand on end. May I ask whether, while the Christmas book, already advertised, was still unwritten, with all this guilt on his head and all this responsibility on his shoulders, Mr Thackeray managed to retain his usual fine appetite, to make good breakfasts, luncheons, and dinners, and to enjoy his natural rest; or whether he did not rather send away choice morsels on his plate untouched, and terrify Mrs Carmichael Smith, Miss Truelock, and his daughters, by habitually shrieking out in the dead of the night under the visitation of a terrible nightmare, revealing two wrathful forms at his bedside menacing him with drawn swords and demanding his MS. or his life?

Allow me to suggest an appropriate revenge. Put out of your head the cherub-vision of the 'innocent and happy Publishers' sitting on clouds in Heaven, and thence regarding with mild complacency the tortures of perjured authors. Descend from this height, turn author yourself and write 'The Lion's History of the Man' or 'A Revelation of the Crimes of popular A-th-rs by a spirited P-bl-sh-r.' Here is an idea which, properly handled, might 'mark an epoch in the history of Modern Literature.' I could almost wish you were forced to adopt it and work it out. You little know what you would make of it. You happen not quite to know yourself.

'The King of the Golden River' is a divine fairy tale. Richard Doyle has done it scant justice in his illustrations (which are rather obscurations), but it does not much matter; Mr Ruskin paints so exquisitely with his pen as to be almost independent of the designer's pencil.

I am glad 'The Kicklebury's' is likely to be successful; it has that interest and that pith without which Thackeray cannot write, yet I mentally wrung my hands as I laid it down. If Mr Titmarsh does not mind, ere long there will be a cry of Ichabod!

I think you did me a kindness in warding off that copy of 'Pendennis' intended to be discharged at my head; the necessary note of acknowledgment would have been written by me under difficulties. To have spoken my mind would have been to displease, and I know, if I had written at all, my mind would have insisted on speaking itself.

'The Stones of Venice'[1] seem nobly laid and chiselled. How grandly the 'Quarry' of vast marbles is disclosed! Mr Ruskin seems to me one of the few genuine writers (as distinguished

[1] *The Stones of Venice*, by John Ruskin, appeared in three volumes, 1851–2–3. Miss Brontë must therefore have received the first volume from Messrs Smith, Elder & Co. who then published Ruskin's works.

from book-makers) of this age. His earnestness even amuses me in certain passages; for I cannot help laughing to think how utilitarians will fume and fret over his deep, serious and (as *they* will think), fanatical reverence for Art. That pure and severe mind you ascribed to him speaks in every line. He writes like a consecrated Priest of the Abstract and Ideal.

You inquire with a certain tender anxiety about Mr Newby. I am sorry not to be in a position to soothe your solicitude respecting him. That fabulous 'Statement of Account' has never made its appearance, nor has any wind from any quarter wafted a whisper of explanation. You talk of commencing a correspondence. Let me conjure you, as you value your own peace of mind, not to risk it by hazarding such a step. The sole result will be the wasting of some good stationery-paper, ink and sealing-wax, as well as some moments of precious time, on an object that will not respond to your assiduities. It is Newby's nature to conduct himself in this manner. Nothing can change him; and I believe the best thing people who don't approve of his proceedings can do is to withdraw in due state and dignity, leaving him to his own little devices, and deeming themselves fortunate in securing their ransom at so cheap a rate as £50.

I *did* enjoy my visit to Miss Martineau very much, and I often thought, while I was with her, what a heathen R. H. Horne was, to compare her to 'a sour apple crushed with a hob-nail shoe.' She is fallible in some matters of judgment, and (as I thought) blunt on some points of feeling; but otherwise a very noble and genial being. I rather tremble at the anticipation of a work she is about to publish conjointly with a Mr Atkinson.[1] She read me some passages of it which partially mesmerised me, but she is ready to meet any shock of opposition for the sake of what she believes the Truth.

In reply to your kind enquiries after Papa, I am thankful to say he is well: wonderfully free from infirmities or failure of faculties, and looking ten years younger than his real age. I gave him your message and was charged to offer his respects in return.

Let me say this word before I bid you good-bye. Neither you nor Mr Williams should ever think of apologizing to me for not writing, however long an interval may elapse between your letters. I *do* like a friendly letter from Cornhill; I like it well and sincerely; but if a thought were to cross me that such letters were written at a sacrifice of the writer's convenience my pleasure in it would turn to grief. You need not doubt that I can wait long and quite patiently without being in the least hurt by silence. Believe this, and that I am—Yours sincerely,

C. Brontë.

635 (490). *To* Ellen Nussey.

[Jan. 8th, 1851].

Dear Nell,—I sent yesterday 'The Leader' newspaper which you must always send on to Hunsworth as soon as you have read it—I will continue to forward it as long as I get it myself.

I am trying the wet sheet and like it—I think it does me good.

Enclosed is a letter received a few days since from Mr Smith—I wish you to read it because it gives a very fine notion both of his temper and mind—read—return and tell me what you think of it.

Thackeray has given them dreadful trouble by his want of punctuality—and printers—binders—gilders and colourers have tried their patience—Williams has written also—he says if Mr Smith had not helped him out with his 'vigour, energy and method' he must have sunk under the day and night labour of the last few weeks.

How is your cough? Write soon.

C. B.

636 (491). *To* Lætitia Wheelwright.

Haworth, January 12th, 1851.

Dear Lætitia,—A spare moment must and shall be made for you, no matter how many letters I have to write (and just now there is an influx). In reply to your kind inquiries, I have to say that my stay in London and excursion to Scotland did me good—much good at the time; but my health was again somewhat sharply tried at the close of autumn, and I lost in some days of indisposition the additional flesh and strength I had previously gained. This resulted from the painful task of looking over letters and papers belonging to my sisters. Many little mementos and memoranda conspired to make an impression inexpressibly sad, which solitude deepened and fostered till I grew ill. A brief trip to Westmoreland has, however, I am thankful to say, revived me again, and the circumstance of papa being just now in good health and spirits gives me many causes for gratitude. When we have but one precious thing left we think much of it.

I have been staying a short time with Miss Martineau. As you may imagine, the visit proved one of no common interest. She is certainly a woman of wonderful endowments, both intellectual and physical, and though I share few of her opinions, and regard her as fallible on certain points of judgment, I must still accord her my sincerest esteem. The manner in which she combines the highest mental culture with the nicest discharge of feminine duties filled me with admiration, while her affectionate kindness earned my gratitude.

Your description of the magician Paxton's Crystal Palace is quite graphic. Whether I shall see it or not I don't know. London will be so dreadfully crowded and busy this season, I feel a dread of going there.

Compelled to break off, I have only time to offer my kindest remembrances to your whole circle, and my love to yourself. —
Yours ever,

C. BRONTË.

During her visit to Ambleside Charlotte Brontë had met Matthew Arnold.

'At seven,' writes Mr Arnold from Fox How (December 21, 1850),[1] 'came Miss Martineau and Miss Brontë (Jane Eyre); talked to Miss Martineau (who blasphemes frightfully) about the prospects of the Church of England, and, wretched man that I am, promised to go and see her cow-keeping miracles[2] to-morrow—I, who hardly know a cow from a sheep. I talked to Miss Brontë (past thirty and plain, with expressive grey eyes, though) of her curates, of French novels, and her education in a school at Brussels, and sent the lions roaring to their dens at half-past nine, and came to talk to you.'

By the light of this 'impression,' it is not a little interesting to see what Miss Brontë, 'past thirty and plain,' thought of Mr Matthew Arnold!

---

[1] *Letters of Matthew Arnold*, collected and arranged by George W. E. Russell.

[2] Some experiments on a farm of two acres.

637 (492). *To* JAMES TAYLOR, *Cornhill.*

January 15th, 1851.

MY DEAR SIR,—I fancy the imperfect way in which my last note was expressed must have led you into an error, and that you must have applied to Mrs Arnold the remarks I intended for Miss Martineau. I remember whilst writing about 'my hostess' I was sensible to some obscurity in the term; permit me now to explain that it referred to Miss Martineau.

Mrs Arnold is, indeed, as I judge from my own observations no less than from the unanimous testimony of all who really know her, a good and amiable woman, but the intellectual is not her forte, and she has no pretensions to power or completeness of character. The same remark, I think, applies to her daughters. You admire in them the kindliest feeling towards each other and their fellow-creatures, and they offer in their home circle a beautiful example of family unity, and of that refinement which is sure to spring thence; but when the conversation turns on literature or any subject that offers a test for the intellect, you usually felt that their opinions were rather imitative than original, rather sentimental than sound. Those who have only seen Mrs Arnold once will necessarily, I think, judge of her unfavourably; her manner on introduction disappointed me sensibly, as lacking that genuineness and simplicity one seemed to have a right to expect in the chosen life-companion of Dr Arnold. On my remarking as much to Mrs Gaskell and Sir J. K. Shuttleworth, I was told for my consolation it was a 'conventional manner,' but that it vanished on closer acquaintance; fortunately this last assurance proved true. It is observable that Matthew Arnold, the eldest son, and the author of the volume of poems to which you allude, inherits his mother's defect. Striking and prepossessing in appearance, his manner displeases, from its seeming foppery. I own it caused me at first to regard him with regretful surprise; the shade of Dr Arnold seemed to me to frown on his young representative. I was told, however, that 'Mr Arnold improved upon acquaintance.' So it was: ere long a real modesty appeared under his assumed conceit, and some genuine intellectual aspirations, as well as high educational acquirements, displaced superficial affectations. I was given to understand that his theological opinions were very vague and unsettled, and indeed he betrayed as much in the course of conversation. Most unfortunate for him, doubtless, has been the untimely loss of his father.[1]

My visit to Westmoreland has certainly done me good. Physically, I was not ill before I went there, but my mind had undergone some painful laceration. In the course of looking over my sisters' papers, mementos, and memoranda, that would have been nothing to others, conveyed for me so keen a sting. Near at hand there was no means of lightening or effacing the sad impression by refreshing social intercourse; from my father, of course, my sole care was to conceal it—age demanding the same forbearance as infancy in the communication of grief. Continuous solitude grew more than I could bear, and, to speak truth, I was glad of a change. You will say that we ought to have power in ourselves either to bear circumstances or to bend them. True, we should do our best to this end, but sometimes our best is unavailing. However, I am better now, and most thankful for the respite.

The interest you so kindly express in my sisters' works touches me home. Thank you for it, especially as I do not believe you would speak otherwise than sincerely. The only notices that I have seen of the new edition of 'Wuthering Heights' were those in the 'Examiner,' the 'Leader,' and the 'Athenæum.' That in the 'Athenæum' somehow gave me pleasure: it is quiet but respectful—so I thought, at least.

You asked whether Miss Martineau made me a convert to mesmerism? Scarcely; yet I heard miracles of its efficacy and could hardly discredit the whole of what was told me. I even underwent a personal experiment; and though the result was not absolutely clear, it was inferred that in time I should prove an excellent subject.

The question of mesmerism will be discussed with little reserve, I believe, in a forthcoming work of Miss Martineau's, and I have some painful anticipations of the manner in which other subjects, offering less legitimate ground for speculation, will be handled.

[1]Thomas Arnold (1795–1842), the famous head-master of Rugby, had been dead some years when Charlotte Brontë visited Fox How. Matthew Arnold (1822–1888), distinguished alike as a poet and a critic, was just on the eve of his appointment as an inspector of schools at this time. He had written a school-prize poem, *Alaric at Rome* (1840), won the Newdigate prize with a poem on *Cromwell* (1843), and published a small volume of verse, *The Strayed Reveller* (1849). His years of fame were all before him. He sent his *Poems* of 1853 to Miss Brontë, and his poem on 'Haworth Churchyard' was first published in *Fraser's Magazine*, May, 1855.

You mention the 'Leader'; what do you think of it? I have been asked to contribute; but though I respect the spirit of fairness and courtesy in which it is on the whole conducted, its principles on some points are such that I have hitherto shrunk from the thought of seeing my name in its columns.

Thanking you for your good wishes, — I am, my dear sir, yours sincerely,

C. Brontë.

Miss Martineau sent Mrs Gaskell[1] the following account of the 'personal experiment' referred to in the above letter:

By the way, for the mesmeric experiment on C. B. I was not responsible. She was strangely pertinacious about that, and I *most* reluctant to bring it before her at all, we being alone, and I having no confidence in her nerves. Day after day she urged me to mesmerise her. I always, and quite truly, pleaded that I was too tired for success, for we had no opportunity till the end of the day. At last, on Sunday evening, we returned from early tea somewhere; I could not say I was tired, and she insisted. I stopped the moment she called out that she was under the influence, and I would not resume it.

638 (493). *To* Ellen Nussey.

[Jan. 20th, 1851].

Dear Ellen, — Thank you heartily for the two letters I owe you. You seem very gay at present — and, provided you only take care not to catch cold with coming home at night &c. — I am not sorry to hear it; a little movement — cheerfulness, stimulus is not only beneficial — but necessary. John Taylor's manœuvres are characteristic. Let me loudly applaud your resolution not to bother your head about him; not to let him take any hold of your thoughts — not in the slightest degree to make yourself uneasy about his capricious changes. If he means anything all will go on a thousand times better for your being calm and unconcerned — if he does not — let him go to the deuce unregretted. For my own part — I have the liveliest doubts about his being half good enough for you — He may be — perhaps is — much

---

[1] *The Life of Charlotte Brontë*, by Mrs E. C. Gaskell, Haworth edition, p. 500.

better than I think; I have no great opinion of him. Joe's kindness is all very well—but would be much better if it were of a sort to be depended on, and did not partake of the family failing of whim. Accept their friendship but rely not on it; far less—their love.

Dear Nell—your last letter but one made me smile. I think you draw great conclusions from small inferences. I think those 'fixed intentions' you fancy—are imaginary—I think the 'undercurrent' amounts simply to this—a kind of natural liking and sense of something congenial. Were there no vast barrier of age, fortune &c. there is perhaps enough personal regard to make things possible which now are impossible. If men and women married because they like each others' temper, look, conversation, nature and so on—and if besides, years were more nearly equal—the chance you allude to might be admitted as a chance —but other reasons regulate matrimony—reasons of convenience, of connection, of money. Meantime I am content to have him as a friend[1]—and pray God to continue to me the commonsense to look on one so young, so rising and so hopeful in no other light.

That hint about the Rhine disturbs me; I am not made of stone —and what is mere excitement to him—is fever to me. However it is a matter for the Future and long to look forward to— As I see it now, the journey is out of the question—for many reasons—I rather wonder he should think of it—I cannot conceive either his mother or his sisters relishing it, and all London would gabble like a countless host of geese—

Good-bye, dear Nell, Heaven grant us both some quiet wisdom—and strength not merely to bear the trial of pain—but to resist the lure of pleasure when it comes in such a shape as our better judgment disapproves.

C. BRONTË.

Monday.

[1]The reference in this letter is to Mr George Smith, who was at this time only 27, whilst Charlotte was nearly 35.

639. *To* JULIA KAVANAGH.

Jany 21st, 1851.

MY DEAR MISS KAVANAGH,—I fear you will have thought hard things of me ere this—pronounced me ungrateful—uncivil and I know not what, but the fact is I only received 'Nathalie' a few days since; she has been waiting in London to come down in a parcel with some other books. At last however I have made her acquaintance, read her through from title-page to 'Finis.'

Now—do not expect me to criticise; of that ungenial office I wash my hands; it suffices for me to know and to say that I was thoroughly interested and highly pleased. Your reader is made to realize places and persons; he becomes an inmate of the old chateau of Sainville, Normandy spreads green and cultured round him. He numbers amongst his acquaintance the various personages of the tale. Some of the minor characters—the Canoness, Mdle Dantin, the femme de chambre are by no means the least cleverly drawn. Rose Montelieu is excellent; I thought those passages which refer to her illness and death amongst the very best in the book. Nathalie's perverseness as well as her final submission struck me as a little exaggerated—so did some of the traits in M. de Sainville's character—but I said I would not criticise; the contrast in their natures, and the *kind* of contrast is a happy thought; the mutual attraction to which it leads would— I doubt not, be exactly paralleled in nature and real life. In short I have to thank you for a treat; the work merits success, and the favourable notices which have been given by the various literary journals may I trust be taken as evidences that it has secured it.

I earnestly trust your health has been improved by change of air and scene; in England we have thus far had a peculiarly mild open winter; even here, in the North—no snow has yet fallen.

Perhaps ere this you may have left Boulogne; in that case I fear there is small chance of your receiving this note and thus my silence will remain unexplained. I must however trust to fortune and with every good wish for your health and happiness—I beg you to believe me,—Yours very sincerely,

C. BRONTË.

640. *To* Mrs Gaskell.

Jany. 22nd, 1851.

My dear Mrs Gaskell, — You are thrice thanked — first, for the real treat afforded by 'The Moorland Cottage.' I told you that book opened like a daisy. I now tell you it finished like a herb — a balsamic herb with healing in its leaves. That small volume has beauty for commencement, gathers power in progress, and closes in pathos; no thought can be truer than Mrs Brown's persistent, irrational, but most touching partiality for her son. The little story is fresh, natural, religious. No more need be said. . . .

C. Brontë.

641 (494). *To* Ellen Nussey.

January 30th, 1851.

Dear Nell, — I am very sorry to hear that Amelia is again so far from well — but I think both she and Joe should try and not be too anxious — even if matters do not prosper this time, all may go as well some future day. I think it is not these *early* mishaps that break the constitution, but those which occur in a much later stage. She must take heart — there may yet be a round dozen of little Joe Taylors to look after — run after — to sort and switch and train up in the way they should go — that is, with a generous use of pickled birch. From whom do you think I have received a couple of notes lately? From Amelia Walker. They are returned from the Continent it seems, and are now at Torquay. The first note touched me a little by what I thought its subdued tone — I trusted her character might be greatly improved; there were indeed traces of the 'old Adam,' but such as I was willing to overlook. I answered her soon and kindly, in reply I received to-day a longish letter — full of claptrap sentiment and humbugging attempts at fine writing, in each production the old trading spirit peeps out; she asks for autographs, it appears that she had read in some paper that I was staying with Miss Martineau, thereupon she applies for specimens of her handwriting and Wordsworth's, and Southey's, and my own. The account of her health, if given by any one else, would grieve and alarm me; she talks of fearing that her constitution is almost broken by repeated trials, and intimates a doubt as to whether she shall live long: but remembering her of old, I have good hopes that this may be a mistake. Her 'beloved Papa and Mama' and her 'precious sister' she says are living and 'gradely'—(that last is my word, I don't know whether they use it in Birstall as they do here, it means in a middling way).

You are to say no more about 'Jupiter' and 'Venus',[1] what do you mean by such heathen trash? The fact is, no fallacy can be wilder and I won't have it hinted at even in jest, because my common-sense laughs it to scorn. The idea of the 'little man' shocks me less—it would be a more likely match if 'matches' were at all in question, which *they are not*. He still sends his little newspaper—and the other day there came a letter of a bulk, volume, pith, judgment and knowledge, worthy to have been the product of a giant. You may laugh as much and as wickedly as you please—but the fact is there is a quiet constancy about this, my diminutive and red-haired friend, which adds a foot to his stature—turns his sandy locks dark, and altogether dignifies him a good deal in my estimation. However, I am not bothered by much vehement ardour—there is the nicest distance and respect preserved now, which makes matters very comfortable.

This is all nonsense—Nell—and so you will understand it. — Yours very faithfully,

C. B.

Write again soon.

The name of Miss Martineau's coadjutor is Atkinson. She often writes to me with exceeding cordiality.

---

[1]George Smith and Charlotte Brontë. It was frequently stated by Ellen Nussey and by Sir Wemyss Reid that Mr Smith proposed to Charlotte Brontë, but there is no kind of evidence of this.

642 (495). *To* W. S. WILLIAMS.

Feby 1st, 1851.

MY DEAR SIR,—I cannot lose any time in telling you that your letter—after all—gave me heartfelt satisfaction—and such a feeling of relief as it would be difficult to express in words. The fact is what goads and tortures me is—not any anxiety of my own to publish another book—to have my name before the public—to get cash &c. but a haunting fear that my dilatoriness disappoints others. Now the 'others' whose wish on the subject I really care for, reduces itself to my Father and Cornhill—and since Cornhill ungrudgingly counsels me to take my own time I think I can pacify such impatience as my dear Father naturally feels; indeed your kind and friendly letter will greatly help me.

Since writing the above, I have read your letter to Papa; your arguments had weight with him; he approves and I am content.

I now only regret the necessity of disappointing the 'Palladium' but that cannot be helped.

Good-bye, my dear Sir,—Yours very sincerely,

C. BRONTË.

643. *To* GEORGE SMITH.

February 5th, 1851.

MY DEAR SIR,—Perhaps it is hardly necessary to trouble you with an answer to your last, as I have already written to Mr Williams, and no doubt he will have told you that I have yielded with ignoble facility in the matter of 'The Professor.' Still, it may be proper to make some attempt towards dignifying that act of submission by averring that it was done 'under protest.'

'The Professor' has now had the honour of being rejected nine times by the 'Tr—de' (three rejections go to your own share); you may affirm that you accepted it this last time, but that cannot be admitted; if it were only for the sake of symmetry and effect I must regard this martyrised MS. as repulsed, or at any rate withdrawn for the ninth time! Few, I flatter myself, have earned an equal distinction, and of course my feelings towards it can only be paralleled by those of a doting parent towards an idiot child. Its merits, I plainly perceive, will never be owned by anybody but Mr Williams and me; very particular and unique must be our penetration, and I think highly of us both accordingly. You may allege that that merit is not visible to the naked eye. Granted; but the smaller the commodity the more inestimable its value.

You kindly propose to take 'The Professor' into custody. Ah, no! His modest merit shrinks at the thought of going alone and unbefriended to a spirited Publisher. Perhaps with slips of him you might light an occasional cigar, or you might remember to lose him someday, and a Cornhill functionary would gather him up and consign him to the repositories of waste paper, and thus he would prematurely find his way to the 'butter man' and trunkmakers. No, I have put him by and locked him up, not indeed in my desk, where I could not tolerate the monotony of his demure Quaker countenance, but in a cupboard by himself.

Something you say about going to London; but the words are dreamy, and fortunately I am not obliged to hear or answer them. London and summer are many months away: our moors are all white with snow just now, and little redbreasts come every morning to the window for crumbs. One can lay no plans three or four months before hand. Besides, I don't deserve to go to London: nobody merits a change or a treat less. I secretly think, on the contrary, I ought to be put in prison, and kept on bread and water in solitary confinement—without even a letter from Cornhill—till I have written a book. One of the two things would certainly result from such a mode of treatment pursued for twelve months; either I should come out at the end of that time with a 3 vol. MS. in my hand, or else with a condition of intellect that would exempt me ever after from literary efforts and expectations.

You touch upon invitations from baronets, &c. As you are well aware, a fondness for such invitations and an anxious desire to obtain them is my weak point. Aristocratic notice is what I especially covet, cultivate, and cling to. It does me so much good; it gives me such large, free and congenial enjoyment. How happy I am when counselled or commended by a baronet or noticed by a lord!

Those papers on the London Poor are singularly interesting; to me they open a new and strange world, very dark, very dreary, very noisome in some of its recesses, a world that is fostering such a future as I scarcely dare to imagine, it awakens thoughts not to be touched on in this foolish letter. The fidelity and sim-

plicity of the letterpress details harmonise well with the daguerreotype illustrations.

You must thank your Mother and sisters for their kind remembrances and offer mine in return, and you must believe me,
—Yours sincerely,

C. BRONTË.

644 (496). *To* JAMES TAYLOR.

February 11th, 1851.

MY DEAR SIR,—Have you yet read Miss Martineau's and Mr
Atkinson's new work, 'Letters on the Nature and Development
of Man.' If you have not, it would be worth your while to do so.
Of the impression this book has made on me I will not now say
much. It is the first exposition of avowed Atheism and Material-
ism I have ever read; the first unequivocal declaration of disbelief in the existence of a God or a Future Life I have ever seen.
In judging of such exposition and declaration one would wish
entirely to put aside the sort of instinctive horror they awaken,
and to consider them in an impartial spirit and collected mood.
This I find it difficult to do. The strangest thing is that we are
called on to rejoice over this hopeless blank, to receive this bitter
bereavement as great gain, to welcome this unutterable desolation as a state of pleasant freedom. Who could do this if he
would? Who would do it if he could?

Sincerely—for my own part—do I wish to find and know the
Truth, but if this be Truth, well may she guard herself with
mysteries and cover herself with a veil. If this be Truth, Man or
Woman who beholds her can but curse the day he or she was
born. I said, however, I would not dwell on what I thought; I
wish rather to hear what some other person thinks; some one
whose feelings are unapt to bias his judgment. Read the book,
then, in an unprejudiced spirit, and candidly say what you think
of it; I mean, of course, if you have time, *not otherwise*.

Thank you for your last letter; it seemed to me very good;
with all you said about the 'Leader' I entirely agree.—Believe
me, my dear sir, yours sincerely,

C. BRONTË.

645 (497). *To* Ellen Nussey.

Feby 26th, 1851.

Dear Ellen,—You ought always to conclude that when I
don't write, it is simply because I have nothing particular to say.
Be sure that ill news will travel fast enough and good news too
when any such commodity comes. If I could often *be* or *seem* in
brisk spirits—I might write oftener—knowing that any letters
would amuse—but as times go—a glimpse of sunshine now and
then is as much as one has a right to expect. However I get on
very decently. I am now and then tempted to break through my
resolution of not having you to come before summer—and to
ask you to come to this Patmos in a week or two—but it would
be dull—very dull—for you.

I also received a letter from Mary Taylor written, not in high
spirits—but still shewing hopeful prospects; also one from Ellen
Taylor by which I think her health must be better.

Is Mrs J. T. out of bed yet? and especially is she out of danger
of the apprehended mishap? I was not seriously vexed about
your telling her of my prediction only momentarily annoyed—
because I knew, of course, from her it would go to her spouse—
and it was not precisely the thing one would have said to him;
however I put a good face on it—and repeated it with additions
to herself.

I hope Mercy's trip from home will do her good both physically and mentally. I return Mrs Gorham's letter; it is very kind
and complimentary.

What would you say to coming here the week after next to
stay only just so long as you could comfortably bear the monotony—If the weather were fine and the moors dry I should not
mind it so much—we could walk for change—but if otherwise
—I know how you would flag.—Yours faithfully,

C. B.

646. *To* George Smith.

March 8th, 1851.

My dear Sir,—I have read 'Rose Douglas'[1]— read it with a tranquil but not a shallow pleasure; full well do I like it. It is a good book—so simple, so natural, so truthful, so graphic, so religious—in a word, so *Scottish* in the best and kindliest sense of the term. Surely it will succeed—for no critic can speak otherwise than well of it.

I could not refrain from writing these few lines respecting it, and you must be forgiving should my note intrude on a busy moment.—Believe me, Yours sincerely,

C. Brontë.

March 11th.

The preceding was written before I received yours; a few more lines must now be added.

Do you know that the first part of your note is most dangerously suggestive? What a rich field of subject you point out in your allusion to Cornhill, &c.—a field at which I myself should only have ventured to glance like the serpent at Paradise; but when Adam himself opens the gates and shows the way in, what can the honest snake do but bend its crest in token of gratitude and glide rejoicingly through the aperture?

But no! Don't be alarmed. You are all safe from Currer Bell— safe from his satire—safer from his eulogium. We cannot (or at least *I* cannot) write of our acquaintance with the consciousness that others will recognise their portraits, or that they themselves will know the hand which has sketched them. Under such circumstances the pencil would falter in the fingers and shrink alike from the indication of bold shades and brilliant lights (especially the last, because it would look like flattery); plain speaking would seem audacious, praise obtrusive.

Were it possible that I could take you all fearlessly, like so many abstractions, or historical characters that had been dust a hundred years, could handle, analyse, delineate you, without danger of the picture being recognised either by yourselves or others, I should think my material abundant and rich. This, however, is no more possible than that the Nurse should give

---

[1] *Rose Douglas; or, Sketches of a Country Parish: being The Autobiography of a Scotch*   *Minister's Daughter*, by Mrs Sarah R. Whitehead, 2 vols 1851.

the child the moon out of the sky. So—I repeat it—you are *very* safe.

Papa was much pleased with Mr Ruskin's Pamphlet,[1] only he thought the scheme of amalgamation suggested towards the close—impracticable. For my part I regard the *brochure* as a refreshing piece of honest writing, good sense uttered by pure lips. The Puseyite priesthood will not relish it; it strips them mercilessly of their pompous pretensions.

Was not Mr Thackeray's speech at Macready's Farewell Dinner peculiarly characteristic? I fancied so from the outline I saw of it in the papers. It seemed to me scarcely to disguise a secret sneer at the whole concern—the hero and his worshippers—and indeed Mr Macready's admirers exaggerate their enthusiasm. Your description of Mr Forster made me smile; I can well fancy him in that state of ebullient emotion.

I paused in a sort of wonder over what you say in referring to your new Indian undertaking. While earnestly wishing you all success in it I cannot but wish with at least equal earnestness that it may not bring too much additional care and labour.

May not Trade have its Alexanders as well as War?—and does not many a man begin with a modest Macedon in the City and end by desiring another world for his speculations?

But I suppose your work is your pleasure and your responsibility your strength, and very likely what a looker-on regards as a grievous burden is only the weight necessary to steady the arch. Your implied injunction to discretion is not uttered in a negligent ear, nor is Currer Bell insensible to the compliment of being told something about business; that he does not understand all the bearings of the communication by no means diminishes his gratification in receiving and looking upon it; he turns it in his hand as a savage a new trinket or tool of unknown use, and likes without fully comprehending it.

I hope Mr Taylor will bear the voyage and the change of climate well.

I am truly sorry to hear that your Mother has not been well, and especially that her indisposition arose from so harassing a cause as family annoyance of any kind; give my kind regards to her and your Sisters, and believe me,—Yours sincerely,

C. Brontë.

[1] *Notes on the Construction of Sheepfolds.* By John Ruskin, 1851.

647 (498). *To* ELLEN NUSSEY.

WELLINGTON, March 11th, 1851.

DEAR ELLEN,—Your letter made me ashamed of myself, as it reminded me how long I have neglected answering your letters. I am now going to answer it sentence by sentence as I should do if I could sit down and write the moment I read it. I am glad Joe has taken it into his head to marry some one who knows my friends and who is therefore likely to learn to think well of me. I hope you will, both you and Charlotte Brontë, keep up your acquaintance with Amelia, and each of you send news of the other as good as you can find to write.

It must be gloomy indeed for Charlotte to see her father's health declining. It is frightful to see death coming to take the last, and one can scarcely calculate the effects on a weakened, painstruck mind like Charlotte's. It seems to me as if the triumphs she has had, had only opened to her new sources of pain. She thinks or rather feels more of the criticism than the praise. In spite of her strenuous endeavour she cannot look at the cheerful side for sadness at present with her. You yourself seem in much better spirits. How do you manage it?

I wish you were sitting here by this quiet candle-light, and I would talk to you by the hour of how we were getting on. How we were looking for a ship from England—what we sold to-day. How we intend to do when the said ship comes and we have no room or next to none to put the things she is to bring. How eagerly we open the packages and scold for all the things that are not according to order. How we work! and lift, and carry, and knock boxes open as if we were carpenters by trade; and sit down in the midst of the mess when we are quite tired, and ask what time it is, and find it is the middle of the afternoon and we've forgotten our dinner! And then we settle to have some tea and eggs, and go on reading letters all the time we're eating, and don't give over working till bedtime, and take a new number of 'David Copperfield' to bed with us and drop asleep at the second page.

In quieter times we are somewhat lazy. There is not more than employment for one. As we don't keep the house particularly tidy, the other one might do a great deal. But somehow not being forced to it, we never do it. We ought to go out and draw

(ask Joe to show you our last wonders in that way), but we find
it dull going alone. Then perhaps we ought to write, but don't
like, for we might possibly be interrupted. We see some company—not much, but I think much better than we should in the
same circumstances in England. Classes are forced to mix more
here, or there would be no society at all. This circumstance is
much to our advantage, for there are not many educated people
of our standing. The women are the same everywhere, never
educated, and so far as female friends go, I think our present set
have as much principle and kindness as most of those we left,
while they have certainly more energy. You need not tell the
Birstallians my opinion of them. Probably they are not worse
than other women, but never called upon to stand alone or
allowed to act for themselves, of course they lose their wits in
time. Don't lose my letter in Church Lane or thereabouts. Some
one writes to know if it is true that Miss Brontë was jilted by a
curate—or by three in succession, I forget which—pray ask her!
I have told people of my acquaintance with the writer of 'Jane
Eyre,' and gained myself a great literary reputation thereby.
Mama has written to Waring abusing Miss Brontë for writing
'Shirley,' and Waring thereupon asked to read it. He says the
characters are all unfaithful, and stoutly denies that ever my
father talked broad Yorkshire. He seems to have forgotten
home altogether. He once described minutely how he should
like to have a room finished and furnished if he were rich; and he
described our old dining-room in every point, and said he didn't
know he'd ever seen such a room! He has a house of his own now
and wife and children, none of whom ever saw Gomersal nor
ever will do! We're getting old, Ellen, and out of date! Fare thee
well till another quiet evening.

M. TAYLOR.

648 (499). *To* JAMES TAYLOR, *Cornhill.*

March 22nd, 1851.

MY DEAR SIR,—Yesterday I despatched a box of books to
Cornhill, including the number of the 'North British Review'
which you kindly lent me. The article to which you particularly
directed my attention was read with pleasure and interest, and
if I do not now discuss it more at length, it is because I am well
aware how completely your attention must be at present en-

grossed, since, if I rightly understood a brief paragraph in Mr Smith's last note, you are now on the eve of quitting England for India.

I will limit myself, then, to the expression of a sincere wish for your welfare and prosperity in this undertaking, and to the hope that the great change of climate will bring with it no corresponding risk to health. I should think you will be missed in Cornhill, but doubtless 'business' is a Moloch which demands such sacrifices.

I do not know when you go, nor whether your absence is likely to be permanent or only for a time; whichever it be, accept my best wishes for your happiness, and my farewell, if I should not again have the opportunity of addressing you. —Believe me, sincerely yours,

C. BRONTË.

649 (500). *To* JAMES TAYLOR, *Cornhill.*

March 24th, 1851.

MY DEAR SIR,—I had written briefly to you before I received yours, but I fear the note would not reach you in time. I will now only say that both my father and myself will have pleasure in seeing you on your return from Scotland—a pleasure tinged with sadness certainly, as all partings are, but still a pleasure.

I do most entirely agree with you in what you say about Miss Martineau's and Mr Atkinson's book. I deeply regret its publication for the lady's sake; it gives a death-blow to her future usefulness. Who can trust the word, or rely on the judgment, of an avowed atheist?

May your decision in the crisis through which you have gone result in the best effect on your happiness and welfare; and indeed, guided as you are by the wish to do right and a high sense of duty, I trust it cannot be otherwise. The change of climate is all I fear; but Providence will overrule this too for the best—in Him you can believe and on Him rely. You will want, therefore, neither solace nor support, though your lot be cast as a stranger in a strange land. —I am, yours sincerely,

C. BRONTË.

When you shall have definitely fixed the time of your return southward, write me a line to say on what day I may expect you at Haworth.

C. B.

650. *To* MRS GASKELL.

HAWORTH, March 28th, '51.

MY DEAR MRS GASKELL,—I dare not but write to you with as little delay as possible. It must be confessed you have an excellent method of spurring to activity any loitering correspondent. Do you know you prove yourself thereby to be somewhat impulsive and very determined? and, indeed, I thought I discerned in you traces of both characteristics during our brief acquaintance in Westmoreland.

Your note—I think—would make Mr Smith smile—not at *me* (for he ought to set me down as a person of very bad manners to render such a note necessary—unmeritorious of smiles) but at *you*. I hope he answered it very politely—but I cannot tell what he would say as he had not heard from me for some time.

Your remarks on Miss Martineau and her book pleased me greatly from their tone and spirit: I have even taken the liberty of transcribing for her benefit one or two phrases because I know they will cheer her; she likes sympathy and appreciation (as all people do who deserve them) and most fully do I agree with you in the dislike you express of that hard contemptuous tone in which her work is spoken of by many critics.

I hope to come to Manchester before Spring is quite over and will write to you when I am at liberty—relying implicitly on the promise you give of being quite candid about the convenience or inconvenience of my visit. May I offer my respectful regards to Mr Gaskell and beg you as usual to believe me always sincerely yours,

C. BRONTË.

P.S. I shall bring with me 'The Stones of Venice'—all the Foundations of Marble and of Granite together with the mighty Quarry out of which they were hewn—and into the bargain a small assortment of crochets and dicta—the private property of one John Ruskin Esqr.

651. *To* GEORGE SMITH.

March 31st, 1851.

MY DEAR SIR,—Mrs Gaskell's letter had not remained unanswered a week, but the fact is she was taken with a little fit of impatience, whereof she has duly recorded her confession and repentance, and all is right now.

I am in very reasonably good health, thank you, and always in as good spirits as I can manage to be.

I dare offer no word of sympathy to Cornhill, hard-tasked as are its energies just now. Since you are doing right and serving with fidelity and courage in the ranks of duty, you *must* in a measure be happy — *more* happy than you have leisure to recognise. Dr Forbes will tell you and tell you truly, that successful labour to a good end is one of the best gifts of Heaven to Man, and Duty, your present Sovereign Lady, though she wears an austere brow, has also a grateful heart, and will one day repay loyal service with noble recompense.

What you say about relinquishing your proposed Continental trip stirs in me a feeble spirit of emulation. By way of imitation on a small scale I would fain give up all thoughts of going to London or elsewhere this spring or summer. Were I but as sure as you are of being able to work to some purpose, gladly, gladly would I make the sacrifice — indeed, it would be no sacrifice. I have before this found in absorbing work a curative and comforting power not to be yielded by relaxation.

The 'Stones of Venice' is a splendid and most tasteful volume, speaking of the mere outside and illustrations; the letterpress I have as yet only glanced over, catching sparkles of living eloquence here and there, but I hold in reserve the pleasure of studying it thoroughly.

You speak highly of Mr Taylor, and I think deservedly so. I believe he is a good man, firm-principled, right-minded, and reliable. His belongs to that better order of character to which it is difficult to render full justice in an early stage of acquaintance. To be appreciated he must be known. In him the kernel is not without its husk; and you must have time and opportunity to penetrate beneath the outside, to get inured to the *manner* before you even understand the *man*. So I think at least.

With inly felt wishes for your success, and renewed and earnest injunctions that you will *never* permit the task of writing to Currer Bell to add however slightly to your burdens (for, whether you think so or not, he is a disciplined person who can endure long fasting and exist on very little food—just what Fate chooses to give—and indeed can do without), I am sincerely yours,

C. Brontë.

652. *To* Miss Brontë.

Coxhorne House, near Cheltenham.
[March, 1851].

Dear Miss Brontë,—Is it possible that the packet I received from you yesterday has been lying in London since December; or has some unforeseen accident detained it in Yorkshire till now? I hope from my heart that I may believe in the last alternative. Wherever or however the delay has arisen, I shall not easily forgive a misadventure which has for three months procrastinated your letter: and if, in addition to that considerable loss, I have to reckon a malrepresentation of my own conduct and feelings, believe me I shall set down this *contretemps* among the serious misfortunes of life. That you and I should one day shake hands I have calmly taken for granted; how calmly you may perhaps remember with anything but admiration when I tell you that among the rising genius of the day there is none to whom I could so warmly give or from whom I would so gladly receive, the grasp of sympathising friendship. But I do not love to hurry the Fates in these matters. The lines of natural occurrence are usually lines of beauty; and, never doubting in our case they would in their own good time intersect I would not lessen the grace of the meeting by precipitating opportunity. Moreover, it is, or ought to be, a delicate matter to intrude upon the retirements of an author's private life; and when the sanctity of womanhood is added to more general considerations, the mere honesty of the infringing friendship can hardly compensate for the bad taste of the trespass. Therefore, I have more than once laid down a pen which, at the temptation of some new apparent occasion, I had taken up to say to you, 'Let us be friends.' But now to find that I have misread the Oracles, and that three months ago your generous hand was held out to me—'tis a very freak of destiny!

Believe me how perfectly I honour and appreciate the dignified simplicity of your letter and of that sincere disclaimer of what, in ignorance of yourself, I had been so audacious as to impute to you. I am not yet sure that the *double entendre* of which I ventured to accuse Currer Bell is at all inconsistent with the most sensitive truthfulness in Miss Brontë; and I am certain that if I had not felt such an illusion to be within the legitimate bounds of the masquerade she had chosen, I could not, even so long ago as last year, have inferred it in an authoress for whom my respect was so heartfelt, and in whom my interest already amounted to a personal regard. At some other time, we will, if you please, discuss this matter more fully. May I hope that in no future case we shall be sufficiently unacquainted for any such misconception to be possible to your reviewer?

Surely we are marked out for friendship. Entering so nearly at once the two adjoining provinces of Literature, both young, both unknown, both (and both in a first work) singularly fortunate, both the subject of many unexpected hopes and prophecies, and both possessing objects, energies and determinaations which make us independent of applause and would have carried us superior to neglect, are there not sufficient resemblances in the general features of our affairs to leave it probable that the affinity is deeper? ... Whatever are the powers and responsibilities of each, we may thank God that we were born in a day wherein they cannot be so small as to miss materials for heroic exercise, or so great as to lack worlds to subdue. Surely never was a time when one might be more grateful to live, if it were only to stand a silent spectator among the stupendous workings of the world. Never a time when more tolerable to be weak, or more sacred to be strong. When the feeble might more rejoice in the exhibition of that Strength which is made 'perfect in weakness,' and the gifted stand oftener with downcast eyes before the rebuke which humbled Pilate. To be vain-glorious, spiritually proud, drunk with applause, giddy with power, can hardly be the dangers of genius in these days. But though to an eye like yours it may be, in these times, a very humbling thing to be gifted, there never was an age perhaps in which it was and will be more dazzling to the multitude. And even as never yet in the history of the world has genius had the prospect of a work so splendid, or a consecration so divine, so never yet, I foresee, as in days which we may witness, have mankind been so ready to cry out 'It is the voice of a god,' and to re-enact the Lystra of old. Friendship, therefore, among those who share the same gifts, responsibilities and dangers becomes almost a duty of self-preservation. Truly we must keep our ears for the very fewest; but the value of the counsel which genius may receive is in the ratio of its rarity, and a poet among poets will be humble indeed. Therefore, and in all humility, I ask you to be my friend. . . .

I heard, some time since, that you were in delicate health, and I wished to beg you to try the effect of our Southern hills. . . . I waited, therefore, till E—— might be well enough to be the hostess of an invalid; but her illness turning out to be more tedious than we had hoped, I wrote to Miss Martineau about you, and I received her reply (with the gladness of unequivocal friendship) this morning. Nevertheless, you must promise me to come and stay with us some time this summer. I cannot tell you how lovely a place we live in: and will not essay it, that you may be tempted to explore for yourself. This garden-rookery, with its dreamy music; these tall old thirty-feet cypresses, over-topping the study window, from which I now look up the sloping fields; and all around our house this quiet green valley, shut in everywhere by orchard-hills—you will enjoy this contrast to your Yorkshire wolds. Strolling among these things, some day or other, we will, I hope, talk of the other subjects of your letter, and of that noble introduction to the book you were so kind as to send me. We will talk over 'Wuthering Heights' together, and I will ask you to tell me everything you can remember of its wonderful author. I see how freely I may speak to you of my estimate of her genius. If I have already spoken to you too freely of other things, my dear Miss Brontë,—if what I have written seems hardly in keeping with a first letter,—recollect that I have long been a brother to you in my thoughts, and that these honest words unconsciously betray me.—Yours sincerely,

SYDNEY DOBELL.

653. *To* SYDNEY DOBELL.

[April (?), 1851].

DEAR SIR,—My note and parcel—which it seems you have but lately received—I requested might be forwarded to your address four months back. For a little while I rather expected to hear from you; but, as this did not happen, I concluded that absorbing occupation, or some other good reason, stood in the way of your writing; and soon—ceasing to expect—I dismissed the subject from my thoughts.

Your letter is very kind—your offered friendship is very welcome; but first—you must understand me. You say, I am young. No. I daresay people still call me 'young' by courtesy, but really young I am not, and young I no longer consider myself. I feel sure you must be some years my junior, because it is evident you still view life from a point I have long out-travelled. I believe there is a morning light for you on the world, a morning-feeling of strength, enterprise and courage. I am a journeyer at noontide, desirous of some rest already, and with the dim still time of afternoon in prospect. You think chiefly what is to be done and won in life; I—what is to be suffered. The fullness, expanse and delight of existence gladden your mind; its brevity and uncertainty impress mine.

Yet this dissimilarity need not, I think, prevent us from being friends, and very true friends too. If ever we meet, you must regard me as a grave sort of elder sister.—Yours sincerely,

C. BRONTË.

654 (501). *To* ELLEN NUSSEY.

April 5th, 1851.

DEAR ELLEN,—Mr Taylor has been and is gone; things are just as they were. I only know in addition to the slight information I possessed before, that this Indian undertaking is necessary to the continued prosperity of the firm of Smith, Elder & Co., and that he, Taylor, alone was pronounced to possess the power and means to carry it out successfully—that mercantile honour, combined with his own sense of duty, obliged him to accept the post of honour and of danger to which he has been appointed, that he goes with great personal reluctance, and that he contemplates an absence of five years.

He looked much thinner and older. I saw him very near and once through my glass; the resemblance to Branwell struck me forcibly, it is marked. He is not ugly, but very peculiar; the lines in his face show an inflexibility, and I must add, a hardness of character which do not attract. As he stood near me, as he looked at me in his keen way, it was all I could do to stand my ground tranquilly and steadily, and not to recoil as before. It is no use saying anything if I am not candid—I avow then, that on this occasion, predisposed as I was to regard him very favourably—his manners and his personal presence scarcely pleased me more than at the first interview. He gave me a book at parting, requesting in his brief way, that I would keep it for his sake, and adding hastily, 'I shall hope to hear from you in India—your letters *have* been, and *will* be a greater refreshment than you can think or I can tell.'

And so he is gone, and stern and abrupt little man as he is—too often jarring as are his manners—his absence and the exclusion of his idea from my mind—leave me certainly with less support and in deeper solitude than before.

You see, dear Nell—we are still precisely on the same level—*you* are not isolated. I feel that there is a certain mystery about this transaction yet, and whether it will ever be cleared up to me I do not know; however, my plain duty is to wean my mind from the subject, and if possible to avoid pondering over it. In his conversation he seemed studiously to avoid reference to Mr Smith individually—speaking always of the 'house,'—the 'firm.' He seemed throughout quite as excited and nervous as when I first saw him. I feel that in his way he has a regard for me; a regard which I cannot bring myself entirely to reciprocate in kind, and yet its withdrawal leaves a painful blank.

Saturday Morning.

I have just got your note. I fear your journey home must have sadly fagged you, but I trust that in a day or two you will begin to feel the benefits of the change. What endless trouble that unlucky little Flossy gives you! how strange that in her trouble she should nestle into your portmanteau! little vermin!

Above you have all the account of 'my visitor'; I dare not aver that your kind wish that the visit would yield me more pleasure than pain has been fulfilled—something at my heart aches and gnaws drearily, but I must cultivate fortitude. Papa, I am thankful to say, is a little better, though he improves but slowly; he and Mr Taylor got on very well together, much better than the first time.

Write to me again *very soon*.—Yours faithfully,

C. B.

655 (502). *To* ELLEN NUSSEY.

April 9th, 1851.

DEAR NELL,—Thank you for your kind note; it was just like you to write it though it was your school-day—I never knew you to let a slight impediment stand in the way of a friendly action.

Certainly I shall not soon forget last Friday—and *never*, I think, the evening and night succeeding that morning and afternoon—evils seldom come singly—and soon after Mr T——was gone—papa who had been better grew much worse, he went to bed early and was very sick and ill for an hour and when at last he began to doze and I left him—I came down to the dining room with a sense of weight, fear and desolation hard to express and harder to endure. A wish that you were with me *did* cross my mind but I repulsed it as a most selfish wish—indeed it was only short-lived—my natural tendency in moments of this sort is to get through the struggle alone—to think that one is burdening and racking others—makes all worse.

You speak to me in soft consolatory accents, but I hold far sterner language to myself, dear Nell. An absence of five years—a dividing expanse of three oceans—the wide difference between a man's active career and a woman's passive existence—these things are almost equivalent to an eternal separation—But there is another thing which forms a barrier more difficult to pass than any of these. Would Mr T—— and I ever suit? could I ever feel for him enough love to accept of him as a husband? Friendship—gratitude—esteem I have—but each moment he came near me—and that I could see his eyes fastened on me—my veins ran ice. Now that he is away I feel far more gently towards him—it is only close by that I grow rigid—stiffening with a strange mixture of apprehension and anger—which nothing softens but his retreat and a perfect subduing of his manner. I did not want to be proud nor intend to be proud—but I was forced to be so.

Most true is it that we are ever ruled by one above us—that in his hands our very will is as clay in the hands of the potter.

Papa continues very far from well—though yesterday and I hope—this morning he is a little better. How is your mother—give my love to her and your sisters—how are you? Have you suffered from tic since you returned home—did they think you improved in looks? Write again soon.—Yours faithfully,

C. BRONTË.

656. *To* Amelia Taylor (*née* Ringrose).

HAWORTH, April 12th, 1851.

DEAR AMELIA,— . . . You kindly ask me to come and see you this summer—but I think it is very doubtful whether I shall, and I will tell you why. I don't like to carry low spirits from home . . . it costs me an effort to keep up and make a show of talking to Joe, etc.—it is a mere empty throwing about of small coin— without any real substantial fund of heartsease to keep it up, and I can't afford it. Nobody but myself knows how it tires me. . . . If ever I get a feeling of real comfort and genuine cure to my mind again—so that the faculty of spontaneous cheerfulness may return—perhaps I will come and see you. . . .—Yours sincerely,

C. BRONTË.

657 (503). *To* Ellen Nussey.

April 12th, 1851.

DEAR ELLEN,—I am truly glad that the books I sent have been of any use to your mother—it is not to be wondered at that her health should vary in this weather—I think it is a very good sign that she escapes being decidedly ill—it shews she has stamina still. I trust Papa is not worse—but he too varies—his stomach continues extremely irritable and unsettled and he frequently feels both feverish and sickly—he has never been down to break-fast but once since you left—It is not precisely the same kind of illness that he had last Spring—or rather it does not shew itself in quite the same way—the inflammatory action seems more about the stomach and less in the throat and chest—I would fain believe this is better. The circumstance of having him to think about just now is good for me in one way—it keeps my thoughts off other matters—which have become complete bitterness and ashes—for I do assure you—dear Nell—not to deceive either you or myself, a more entire crumbling away of a seeming foun-dation of support and prospect of hope—than that which I allude to—can scarcely be realized. In my own mind I am—I think— satisfied of that; we will say no more about it.

I wish Amelia had her business well over and was hearty and

happy with her chit on her knee—or yelping in that basinet you are to buy.

By the by—I meant to ask you, when you went to Leeds to do a small errand for me—but fear your hands will be too full of business to bear any addition—it was merely this—in case you chanced to be in any shop where the lace cloaks, black and white, of which I spoke, were sold, to ask their price—I suppose they would hardly like to send a few to Haworth to be looked at—and, indeed if they cost very much it would be useless—but if they are reasonable—and they would send them, I should like to see them—and also some chemisettes of small size—(the full woman's size don't fit me) both of simple style for everyday and good quality for best. Unless you have time and like the errand —don't bother yourself about it.

John Taylor is a strange enigma—comment on him I cannot venture to make. I am glad the Book-Club is going on—I think it will form an object of interest for you.—Mr Kemp seems to take it up with spirit.

I have just had another long note from Amelia Walker— complaining that I have not answered her last—and entreating me to reply to this and give her minute particulars about myself!!! She dwells a good deal on her own invalidism—which however does not seem to debar her from any sort of pleasure or enjoyment—and says how much she is an object of sympathy to all the neighbourhood—the attentions she receives—she says 'offer quite a premium on slight illness.' Hers—I trust—is only slight—for she drives about everywhere—spends her evenings in visiting &c. She requests me not to mention that they are *in England*; so be on your guard in reporting that fact. One would not be the cause of injury to them in any way.

Ought I to return Rosy Dugdale's wretched, heartless, flimsy, unsisterly scrawl? If not I'll burn it. Write, dear Nell—whenever you have time—I am keeping up as well as ever I can—but I dare not say I am happy—or see before me any very happy prospect in the future—but I must remember thousands are worse off than I am.—Yours faithfully,

C. BRONTË.

658. *To* MRS SMITH.

HAWORTH, April 17th, 1851.

MY DEAR MRS SMITH,—Before I received your note, I was nursing a comfortable and complacent conviction that I had quite made up my mind not to go to London this year: the Great Exhibition was nothing—only a series of bazaars under a magnified hot-house—and I myself was in a pharisaical state of superiority to temptation. But Pride has its fall. I read your invitation, and immediately felt a great wish to descend from my stilts. Not to conceal the truth—I should like to come and see you extremely well.

I think with you—however—that June would be the best time to name—better than an earlier period: my father, though now much better than he was—has usually somewhat variable health throughout the Spring—and till warm weather fairly sets in—I should hardly think it right or feel happy to leave him.

Mr Taylor—whose brief visit gave me great pleasure—told me to my regret—that you had all been ill of the influenza—and that Miss Smith especially had suffered. This I was very sorry to hear—because she is not one of the strongest—and I fear would not hastily lose the debilitating effects of influenza. I trust she is now quite recovered.

With kindest regards to her and all your circle, and with my Father's acknowledgment and response to your kind remembrance of him,—I am, my dear Mrs Smith, sincerely yours,

C. BRONTË.

P.S. A sudden reproach occurs to me. When I was last in London I professed to be working a cushion, of which I meant when finished to make an offering to you. That cushion—or rather the canvas which ought ere this to have matured into a cushion—lies neatly papered up in a drawer—just as it was last summer. Could even Cardinal Wiseman grant absolution for shortcomings of this description? But you shall have a cushion, and a pretty one—only you must not be too particular in asking me how I came by it.[1] You will, indeed, have the perfect goodness to suppose it of my work—the circumstance of its being

[1] See Charlotte's letter to Amelia Taylor (*née* Ringrose), June 7th, 1851, p. 244, below.

from the same pattern as the one I *intended* to manufacture will favour this benevolent delusion. On second thoughts — I might quite well have passed it off as such — if I had not gone and spoilt that plan by the above confession.

659. *To* CHARLOTTE BRONTË.

COXHORNE HOUSE, April 17th [1851].

MY DEAR MISS BRONTË, — Your frank and sisterly letter was everything I could wish; and it would be difficult to tell you how much I value it. . . . But I may say — and you will believe — that it is with a grave and sweet satisfaction I see the indefinite relationship between us at length take palpable and recognised shape.

Do not fear that I would impose upon our friendship the tax of a voluminous correspondence. My last letter was rather bulky, and this is perhaps unnecessarily prompt; but we need not take them as precedents, and I shall look for no return in kind. . . .

. . . That you are not 'young' I cannot believe, even on your own testimony. The heart of Jane Eyre will never grow old.

You are right in thinking that my 'havings in years' are but small (I claim but twenty-seven). But I have little faith in arithmetic. There is something in 'The Roman' about *age*.[1] Some rule of estimate in which, I think, death is taken as unity. Try me by my own standard, and, some day or other, I will make you look up to me as a very grey old man; showing you how often I have been by my grave; aye, have felt myself lowered into its shadow. And, for present proof that I am not altogether ignorant of sorrow, I will enclose you something which is not of the merriest.[2]

Nevertheless, you are right in thinking that I look hopefully upon a 'morning world.'

I believe that our past few thousand years of human history have been but little more than dawn. I think the east is flushing with irrepressible day, but I foretell a thunderous sunrise — the sublimest but most terrible season of the earth — and beyond it — what 'eye hath not seen.' And since we needs must mix with men, a short life in such a time seems better to me than a cycle of mediocrity.

---

[1] Age is the shadow of Death,
Cast where he standeth in the radiant
path

Of each man's immortality.
[2] 'Crazed,' which appeared first in *The Athenæum* of November 23rd, 1850.

You think these the words of youth exulting in its 'strength'; but I believe that when we know each other better, you will absolve me from 'presumptuous sins.'—Yours sincerely,

SYDNEY DOBELL.

660. *To* GEORGE SMITH.

April 19th, 1851.

MY DEAR SIR,—My scheme of emulation appears to have terminated in a somewhat egregious failure, as perhaps your mother may have told you. One can't help it. One does not profess to be made out of granite.

Your project, depend on it, has been quite providentially put a stop to. And do you really think I would have gone to the Rhine this summer? Do you think I would have partaken in all that unearned pleasure?

Now listen to a serious word. You might *possibly* have perpersuaded me to go (I do not *think* that you would, but it does not become me to be very positive on that point, seeing that proofs of inflexibility do not abound), yet had I gone I should not have been truly happy; self-reproach would have gnawed at the root of enjoyment; it is only drones and wasps who willingly eat honey they have not hived, and I protest against being classed with either of these insects. Ergo, though I am sorry for your own and your sister's sake that your castle on the Rhine has turned out a castle in the air, I am not at all sorry for mine.

May I be so egotistical as to say a word or two about my health? Two ladies, neither of them unknown to fame, whom I reverence for their talents and love for their amiability, but of whom I would beg the small favour of being allowed to remain in tolerable health, seem determined between them that I shall be a sort of invalid; and, chiefly owing to them, I am occasionally kept in hot water by people asking me how I am. If I do not answer the letters of these ladies by return of post—which, without being precisely a person overwhelmed with business, one may not always have time to do—flying rumours presently reach me derogatory to my physical condition. Twice kind but misled strangers living in southern counties have with the greatest goodness written to ask me to their houses for the benefit of a milder climate, offering every 'accommodation suitable to an invalid lady.'

This, in one sense, touches me with an almost painful gratitude, but in another it makes me a little nervous. Why may not I
be well like other people? I think I am reasonably well—not
strong or capable of much continuous exertion (which I do not
remember that I ever was), and apt, no doubt, to look haggard if
over-fatigued, but otherwise I have no ailment, and I maintain
that I am well, and hope (D. V.) to continue so awhile. I hope you
are well too. You may be sure I was very glad to see Mr Taylor,
and that he was most cordially welcomed at Haworth. Please to
tell Mr Williams that I dare on no account come to London till
he is friends with me, which I am sure he cannot be, as I have
never heard from him for nearly three months.

Will you have the goodness to forward the enclosed note to
Dr Forbes, whose address I do not know? It is an acknowledgment of his gift of his little book, the lecture, which I like very
much.—I am Yours sincerely,

C. Brontë.

661 (504). *To* Ellen Nussey.

April 23rd, 1851.

My dear Ellen,—It appears I could not rest satisfied when I
was well off. I told you I had taken one of the black lace mantles,
but when I came to try it with the black satin dress, with which I
should chiefly want to wear it, I found the effect was far from
good; the beauty of the lace was lost, and it looked somewhat
brown and rusty; I wrote to Mr Stocks, requesting him to change
it for a *white* mantle of the same price; he was extremely courteous, and sent to London for one, which I have got this morning.
The price is less, being but £1, 14s.; it is pretty, neat and light,
looks well on black; and upon reasoning the matter over, I came
to the conclusion, that it would be no shame for a person of my
means to wear a cheaper thing; so I think I shall take it, and if you
ever see it and call it 'trumpery' so much the worse.

I have heard from Mr Taylor to-day, a quiet little note; he
returned to London a week since on Saturday, he has since kindly chosen and sent me a parcel of books. He leaves England May
20th; his note concludes with asking whether he has any chance
of seeing me in London before that time. I must tell him that I
have already fixed June for my visit, and therefore, in all human
probability we shall see each other no more.

There is still a want of plain, mutual understanding in this business, and there is sadness and pain in more ways than one. My conscience, I can truly say, does not *now* accuse me of having treated Mr Taylor with injustice or unkindness. What I once did wrong in this way, I have endeavoured to remedy both to himself and in speaking of him to others, Mr Smith to wit, though I more than doubt whether that last opinion will ever reach him; I am sure he has estimable and sterling qualities, but with every disposition and with every wish, with every intention even, to look on him in the most favourable point of view at his last visit, it was impossible to me in my inward heart, to think of him as one that might one day be acceptable as a husband. It would sound harsh were I to tell even *you* of the estimate I felt compelled to form respecting him; dear Nell, I looked for something of the gentleman—something I mean of the *natural* gentleman; you know I can dispense with acquired polish, and for looks, I know myself too well to think that I have any right to be exacting on that point. I could not find one gleam, I could not see one passing glimpse, of true good-breeding; it is hard to say, but it is true. In mind too; though clever, he is second-rate; thoroughly second-rate. One does not like to say these things, but one had better be honest. Were I to marry him, my heart would bleed in pain and humiliation; I could not, *could* not look up to him. No —if Mr Taylor be the only husband fate offers to me, single I must always remain. But yet, at times I grieve for him, and perhaps it is superfluous, for I cannot think he will suffer much; a hard nature, occupation and change of scene will befriend him.

I am glad to hear that you have lost that horrid tic, and hope your cold is by this time well. Papa continues much better.— With kind regards to all, I am, dear Nell, your middle-aged friend,

C. BRONTË.

Write soon.

662. *To* SYDNEY DOBELL.

May 1st [1851].

DEAR SIR,—If I have not time to write an answer to your last, I must at least delay no longer to despatch an acknowledgment: brevity is better than (seeming) negligence.

Your letters will never indeed be at any time unacceptable to

me; on the contrary, whenever the spirit moves you to write, you
may be sure that what is written will be read with pleasure; and
for my part, I feel a true satisfaction in knowing that—should I
want to say anything to you—the way of access, by letter, is open.

I like too the calm with which you speak of patiently allowing
the course of things to teach us more of each other. I believe that
the old adage, 'the more haste the worse speed,' may be true in
friendship as in other matters. More reliable is the attachment
which grows like the oak, than that which springs like the gourd.

The piece which you enclose, and which you truly characterise as 'none of the merriest,' seems to me a piece to be kept by one
and read often. It is not 'mere sound and fury, signifying nothing'; it signifies a great deal. I saw much in it the first time of
reading, more the second, and still more on a third perusal. If I
may—I will retain it.—Yours sincerely,

C. BRONTË.

663 (505). *To* ELLEN NUSSEY.

May 5th, 1851.

MY DEAR NELL,—I hope Mercy has got well off on her travels
ere this and left you to a little repose—I wish the change may do
her good and that it may please Providence to prolong it for the
benefit of all parties. How has your Mother borne the cold weather of last week? It made Papa somewhat worse—but he is
better again now—Still I don't like to leave him and have quite
made up my mind to put off the visit to Mrs Gaskell till my return from London—though that last will depend on Papa's
health of course.

I have had a long kind letter from Miss Martineau lately—She
says she is well and happy—also I have had a very long letter
from Mr Williams—the first for many weeks—he speaks of Mr
T—— with much respect and regret—and says he will be
greatly missed by many friends.

I discover with some surprise that Papa has taken a decided
liking to Mr Taylor. The marked kindness of his manner to the
little man when he bid him good-bye—exhorting him to be 'true
to himself his Country and his God' and wishing him all good
wishes—struck me with some astonishment at the time—and
whenever he has alluded to him since it has been with significant
eulogy. When I alleged that he was 'no gentleman'—he seemed

out of patience with me for the objection. You say Papa has penetration—on this subject I believe he has indeed. I have told him nothing—yet he seems to be *au fait* to the whole business—I would think at some moments—his guesses go farther than mine. I believe he thinks a prospective union, deferred for 5 years, with such a decorous reliable personage would be a very proper and advisable affair—However I ask no questions and he asks me none, and if he did, I should have nothing to tell him—nor he me for he and Mr T—— were never long enough alone together to have had any communication on the matter.

How has your 'tic' been lately? I had one fiery night last week when this same Dragon 'Tic' held me for some hours with pestilent violence—it still comes at intervals with abated fury—owing to this and broken sleep—I am looking singularly charming—one of my true London looks. I was rather amused at Mr T—— giving such an excellent account of health &c. I do not know that I looked specially well when he was here—only not pined out and worn down as I do in London. Write soon—dear Nell—Yours faithfully,

C. BRONTË.

I enclose a letter of Mr Morgan's to Papa—written just after he had read 'Shirley.' It is curious to see the latent feeling roused in the old gentleman—I was especially struck by his remark about the chap. entitled 'The Valley of the Shadow, &c.' he must have a true sense of what he read or he could not have made it.

664 (506). *To* ELLEN NUSSEY.

May 10th, 1851.

DEAR NELL,—Poor little Flossy! I have not yet screwed up nerve to tell Papa about her fate—it seems to me so piteous. However she had a happy life with a kind mistress—whatever her Death has been.

Little hapless plague! She had more goodness and patience shown her than she deserved I fear.

John Taylor is a noodle.

I am glad to hear that J. Gorham is coming to Yorkshire—the friend at Sheffield sounds to me something like a pretext. However, keep calm and expect nothing—it is the best plan.

Mercy is as much to be pitied as little Flossy in another way. She too draws very heavily on good-nature and forbearance— you must look on her in the light of a 'cross to take up.' Comfort or pleasure—even, I fear—peace and safety—you will never have out of her; of ordeal and discipline—she has given you plenty—and will give you more. I suppose that is her use—to test and try others like a fiery furnace.

Mary Dixon's is indeed a piteous case. Were I her—I should greatly dread becoming a burden to my relatives—but I hope she is not haunted by this apprehension—is it true that she is not even able to feed herself?

Do you know that I was in Leeds on the very same day with you—last Wednesday? I had thought of telling you when I was going—and having your help and company in buying a bonnet, &c. but then I reflected this would be merely making a selfish use of you—so I determined to manage or mismanage the matter alone—I went to Hunt & Hall's for the bonnet—and got one which seemed grave and quiet there amongst all the splendours —but now it looks infinitely too gay with its pink lining—I saw some beautiful silks of pale sweet colours but had not the spirit or the means to launch out at the rate of 5*s.* per yd and went and bought a black silk at 3*s.* after all—I rather regret this—because Papa says he would have lent me a sovereign if he had known. I believe if you had been there you would have forced me to get into debt. The turtle-doves seem all right—but rather cold at Windermere—I wish the female had its nest furnished with the expected nestling—I believe it would then be more interesting —the small egotism rather repels me just now. Her faithful regard for you is one of the best points about her.

Write soon again.

C. BRONTË.

665. *To* GEORGE SMITH.

May 12th, 1851.

MY DEAR SIR,—I fear it cannot be denied that Mr Thackeray has actually gone and written a poem. The *whole* of the May-Day Ode is not poetry—*that* I will maintain; it opens with decent prose—but at the fourth stanza 'I felt a thrill of love and awe'— it begins to swell: towards the middle it waxes strong and rises high, takes a tone sustained and sweet, fills the ear with music,

the heart with glow and expansion—becomes in a word—
POETRY. Shame and sin that the man who *can* write thus—
should write thus so seldom!

How dare he sit half his life holding distaffs for the Omphales[1]
of Belgravia?—indolent intellectual Hercules—that he is—
Great image of Nebuchadnezzar's dream—made up of iron and
clay—half strength—half weakness.

Different indeed is Mr Ruskin. (I have read the Stones of
Venice through). Thackeray has no love for his Art or his Work:
he neglects it; he mocks at it; he trifles with it. Ruskin—for *his*
Art and *his* Work—has a deep serious passion. We smile sometimes at Ruskin's intense earnestness of feeling towards things
that *can* feel nothing for him in return—for instance—when he
breaks out in an apostrophe to a sepulchre 'O pure and lovely
Monument—My most beloved in Italy—that land of Mourning!' Over Thackeray's criminal carelessness of great faculties—
the gift of God—we are oftener disposed to weep—only nobody
would be such a simpleton as to weep where tears would be
worse than wasted.

I wondered to myself once or twice whether there would be
any chance of hearing his lectures. No doubt they will be blent
throughout with sarcasm calculated to vex one to the heart—
but still—just out of curiosity one would like to know what he
will say.

I do not quite understand about the 'Guild of Literature'
though I have seen it mentioned in the papers—you must be kind
enough to explain it better when I see you.

Of course I am not in the least looking forwards to going to
London—nor reckoning on it—nor allowing the matter to take
any particular place in my thoughts: no: I am very sedulously
cool and nonchalant. Moreover—I am not going to be glad to
see anybody there: *gladness* is an exaggeration of sentiment one
does not permit oneself: to be *pleased* is quite enough—and not
too well pleased either—only with pleasure of a faint tepid kind
—and to a stinted penurious amount. Perhaps—when I see your
Mother and Mr Williams again—I shall just be able to get up a
weak flicker of gratification—but that will be all. From even this
effort—I shall be exempt on seeing *you*. Authors and Publishers

---

[1]Hercules spent three years in bondage
with Omphale, Queen of Lydia. He was
degraded to female drudgery, clothed in
soft raiment and set to spin wool, while the
queen assumed the lion skin and the club.

are never expected to meet with any other than hostile feelings and on shy and distant terms. They never ought to have to shake hands: they should just bow to each other and pass by on opposite sides—keeping several yards distance between them. And besides—if obliged to communicate by Post—they should limit what they have to say to concise notes of about 3 lines apiece—which reminds me that this is too long and that it is time I thanked you for sending the Dividend—and begged with proper form to be permitted to subscribe myself—respectfully Yours,

C. BRONTË.

666. *To* MRS SMITH.

May 20th, 1851.

MY DEAR MRS SMITH,—It is pleasant to hear that Mr Thackeray still brings a lively appetite to a good dinner; I did not know whether his nervous anxiety about the forthcoming lectures might not possibly have impaired it. One of the prettiest sights of the Exhibition, I should think, would be to see Jacob Omnium[1] conducting hither and thither his tiny and fragile charge, W. M. Thackeray, Esq. You can keep your little socks for Jacob Omnium's nursling if you like. If they are too large, one might (in another year's time) knit a smaller pair for the purpose.

If all be well, and if my father continues in his present satisfactory state of health, I shall be at liberty to come to London on Thursday week, i.e. the 29th. I will not say much about being glad to see you all. Long ago, when I was a little girl, I received a somewhat sharp lesson on the duty of being glad in peace and quietness—in fear and moderation; this lesson did me good, and has never been forgotten.

Should there be any objection to the day I have fixed, you will be kind enough to tell me. If I do not hear from you, I shall conclude that it is approved. I should come by the express train which arrives in Euston Square at 10 p.m.

With kindest regards—my Father's as well as my own—to you and yours,—I am, my dear Mrs Smith, Yours very sincerely,

C. BRONTË.

[1]Matthew James Higgins (1810–1868), journalist, known as 'Jacob Omnium' from the title of his first published article, *Jacob Omnium, the Merchant Prince*.

667. *To* Charlotte Brontë.

Coxhorne, May 21st [1851].

Dear Miss Brontë,—Lifting my eyes in the sunshine of yesterday to the flowering orchards above me, the 'summer snow' that stretches away southwards to the hills, and the very Avalon of apple trees that makes an 'awful rose of dawn' towards the east—an impulse seized me to tempt you with a description of their beauty. But I threw down my pen, guiltless of a line or a word, helpless before this unapproachable world, and able only to cry out, with the Prophet, in my heart—

'Ah, Lord God! behold I cannot speak: for I am a child.'

I wish from my soul that you and I could see these things together.

And how seldom I say so much you will know when we know each other better. With how many, even of the worthiest of human kind it is simply pitiable to look at such a scene as this.

. . . But if I begin to talk of spring, this valley or you, I shall not in the time which alone is possible to me to-day (for I have been hard at work all the morning) acquit myself of a mission which by love, loyalty and inclination I am bound to fulfil. . . .

. . . I said just now that I had been 'working hard,' without being conscious of how finely the confession was *à propos* to the complaints which had preceded it. In the proof from 'The Eclectic,' which I have been correcting, a paragraph was struck out by the sapient editor. It was this:

'Yes, oh divine earth; oh incommunicable beauty, wearing thy crown of thorns, and having on the purple robe of im-memorial sunsets, we have parted thy garments among us, and for thy vesture we have cast lots.' Poor citizen—he knew not it was written in Paradise.

One question, and I must conclude. And briefly as I put it, I could write a chapter on nothing else. Is it possible that you can spare time and money to go to Switzerland this summer? E——and I hope to go in a month's time (it will not be an expensive journey—for that we authors and authoresses are not rich people, I need not tell Currer Bell; but we expect to see the noblest things in the land of marvels), and how glorious if you could accompany us!

If it is possible, come. — Yours sincerely,

SYDNEY DOBELL.

668 (507). *To* ELLEN NUSSEY.

May 21st, '51.

DEAR ELLEN, —I really can no more come to Brookroyd before I go to London than I can fly —I have lots of sewing to do — as well as household matters to arrange before I leave —as they will clean &c. in my absence; besides I am grievously oppressed with headache —which I trust to change of air for relieving —but meantime, as it proceeds from the stomach, it makes me very thin and grey —neither you nor anybody else could fatten me up or put me into good condition for the visit —it is fated otherwise —No matter.

Calm your passion —yet I am glad to see it —such spirit seems to prove health. Good bye in haste.

C. B.

Your poor Mother is like Tabby —Martha and Papa —all these fancy I am somehow —by some mysterious process to be married in London —or to engage myself to matrimony —How I smile internally! How groundless and impossible is the idea! Papa seriously told me yesterday that if I married and left him — he should give up housekeeping and go into lodgings!!!

669 (509). *To* SYDNEY DOBELL.

May 24th, 1851.

MY DEAR SIR, —I hasten to send Mrs Dobell the autograph. It was the word 'Album' that frightened me: I thought she wished me to write a sonnet on purpose for it, which I could not do.

Your proposal respecting a journey to Switzerland is deeply kind; it draws me with the force of a mighty Temptation, but the stern Impossible holds me back. No! I cannot go to Switzerland this summer.

Why did the editor of the 'Eclectic' erase that most powerful and pictorial passage? He could not be insensible to its beauty; perhaps he thought it profane. Poor man![1]

[1]See Sydney Dobell's letter to Charlotte Brontë, dated May 21st, 1851, p. 235, above.

I know nothing of such an orchard country as you describe. I have never seen such a region. Our hills only confess the coming of summer by growing green with young fern and moss, in secret little hollows. Their bloom is reserved for autumn; then they burn with a kind of dark glow, different, doubtless, from the blush of garden blossoms. About the close of next week I expect to go to London, to pay a brief and quiet visit. I fear chance will not be so propitious as to bring you to town while I am there; otherwise how glad I should be if you would call! With kind regards to Mrs Dobell, believe me sincerely yours,

C. Brontë.

670 (508). *To* Ellen Nussey.

[May 26th, 1851].

Dear Ellen,—I suppose you will have got Mercy home before this. How is she? I trust better, bodily and mentally, for her visit. I hope too that you and your mother are well. Papa's state of health gives me much cause for thankfulness—if he continues so well—I shall be able to leave him with comparatively little anxiety. For my own part—headaches and occasional sickness annoy me—I shall go to London with nothing to boast of in looks—however careful I am in diet, my stomach will not keep right.

Next Thursday is the day now fixed for my going. I have heard again from Mr S. and his mother—I would send you the notes, only that I fear your comments—you do not read them by my lights—and would see more in an impetuous expression of quite temporary satisfaction—than strict reality justifies.

Are the Hunsworth doves yet on the wing—or are they returned to the conjugal nest? They have had fine weather part of the time. I hope Amelia will gain benefit from the excursion.

I am sure Nell you did not expect me to come to Brookroyd before I went to London—I know you will be busy enough with your Spring Clean &c. preparing for the Gothams—and how in the world am I to visit you during their stay? When they are with you—I shall (D. V.) be in London. I hope we shall meet somewhere somehow—after your visitors are gone and my visit is over.—Meanwhile with regards to all,—Goodbye,

C. Brontë.

CHAPTER XXVI

CHARLOTTE'S IMPRESSIONS OF LONDON

CHARLOTTE BRONTË went to London on May 28th, 1851, and remained there until June 27th, when she left for Manchester to spend a few days with Mrs Gaskell before returning to Haworth on June 30th.

No doubt, had Charlotte been able to adopt Mr Dobell's suggestion and go to Switzerland, or even to visit the 'orchard country' near Cheltenham where he lived, it would have proved much more beneficial to her health than the excitement and fatigue of her prolonged stay in London. However, in spite of indifferent health, she clearly enjoyed her visit, which proved extremely interesting, and she took away with her many pleasant recollections of places she had seen and people she had met.

Reflecting on her visit some months afterwards, Charlotte wrote: 'What now chiefly dwells in my memory are Thackeray's lectures, Mademoiselle Rachel's acting, D'Aubigné's, Melvill's and Maurice's preaching and the Crystal Palace.' These certainly proved the main attractions, particularly Thackeray's lectures on the English Humorists.

Shortly after her return home Charlotte was kept busy with visitors at Haworth, first Ellen Nussey, then a cousin from Cornwall, and lastly Miss Wooler. Amidst all this excitement she found it almost impossible to settle down to the writing of her new novel, for which her publishers were anxiously waiting.

671 (511). *To* The Rev. P. Brontë.

76 Gloucester Terrace, Hyde Park,
London, Thursday Morning, May 29th, 1851.

Dear Papa,—I write one hasty line just to tell you that I got here quite safely at ten o'clock last night without any damage or smash in tunnels or cuttings. Mr and Mrs Smith met me at the station and gave me a kind and cordial welcome. The weather was beautiful the whole way, and warm; it is the same to-day.

I have not yet been out, but this afternoon, if all be well, I shall go to Mr Thackeray's lecture.[1] I don't know when I shall see the Exhibition, but when I do, I shall write and tell you all about it. I hope you are well, and will continue well and cheerful. Give my kind regards to Tabby and Martha, and—Believe me, your affectionate daughter,

C. BRONTË.

672 (512). *To* The REV. P. BRONTË.

76 GLOUCESTER TERRACE, HYDE PARK,
LONDON, May 31st, 1851.

DEAR PAPA,—I have now heard one of Mr Thackeray's lectures and seen the great Exhibition. On Thursday afternoon I went to hear the lecture. It was delivered in a large and splendid kind of saloon—that in which the great balls of Almack's are given. The walls were all painted and gilded, the benches were sofas stuffed and cushioned and covered with blue damask. The audience was composed of the *élite* of London society. Duchesses were there by the score, and amongst them the great and beautiful Duchess of Sutherland, the Queen's Mistress of the Robes. Amidst all this Thackeray just got up and spoke with as much simplicity and ease as if he had been speaking to a few friends by his own fireside. The lecture was truly good: he has taken pains with the composition. It was finished without being in the least studied; a quiet humour and graphic force enlivened it throughout. He saw me as I entered the room, and came straight up and spoke very kindly. He then took me to his mother, a fine, handsome old lady, and introduced me to her. After the lecture somebody came behind me, leaned over the bench, and said, 'Will you permit me, as a Yorkshireman, to introduce myself to you?' I turned round, was puzzled at first by the strange face I met, but in a minute I recognised the features. 'You are the Earl of Carlisle,'[2] I said. He smiled and assented. He went on to talk for some time in a courteous, kind fashion. He asked after you, recalled the platform electioneering scene at Haworth, and beg-

[1] Thackeray delivered a course of six lectures on the *English Humorists of the Eighteenth Century* at Willis's Rooms from May 22nd to July 3rd, 1851.
[2] This Lord Carlisle was George William Frederick Howard, 7th Earl of Carlisle (1802–1864). He won the Chancellor's prize for Latin verse and the Newdigate in 1821, succeeded his father in the earldom in 1848, and wrote *A Diary in Turkish and Greek Waters*, 1853.

ged to be remembered to you. Dr Forbes came up afterwards, and Mr Monckton Milnes,[1] a Yorkshire Member of Parliament, who introduced himself on the same plea as Lord Carlisle.

Yesterday we went to the Crystal Palace.[2] The exterior has a strange and elegant but somewhat unsubstantial effect. The interior is like a mighty Vanity Fair. The brightest colours blaze on all sides; and ware of all kinds, from diamonds to spinning jennies and printing presses, are there to be seen. It was very fine, gorgeous, animated, bewildering, but I liked Thackeray's lecture better.

I hope, dear papa, that you are keeping well. With kind regards to Tabby and Martha, and hopes that they are well too, —I am, your affectionate daughter,

C. BRONTË.

673 (513). *To* ELLEN NUSSEY.

112, GLOUCESTER TERRACE, HYDE PARK,
June 2nd [1851].

DEAR NELL,—I came here on Wednesday—being summoned a day sooner than I expected in order to be in time for Thackeray's second lecture which was delivered on Thursday afternoon. This—as you may suppose—was a genuine treat to me and I was glad not to miss it. It was given in Willis's rooms where the Almacks Balls are held—a great painted and gilded saloon with long sofas for benches — The audience was said to be of the cream of London Society and it looked so. I did not at all expect that the great Lecturer would know me or notice me under these circumstances—with admiring Duchesses and Countesses seated in rows before him—but he met me as I entered—shook hands —took me to his Mother whom I had not before seen and introduced me—She is a fine—handsome—young-looking old lady —was very gracious and called with one of her grand-daughters the next day—Thackeray called too separately—I had a long talk with him and I think he knows me now a little better than he did—but of this I cannot yet be sure—he is a great and strange man—There is quite a furor for his Lectures—they are a sort of

[1]Afterwards Lord Houghton (1809-1885). Wrote *Poems of Many Years*, 1838. *Life of Keats*, 1848, and other works.

[2]The first great international exhibition was Sir Joseph Paxton's 'Crystal Palace' which was opened by Queen Victoria in Hyde Park, London, on May 1st, 1851. It remained open until October 11th, 1851, and was visited by over six million people. The building was afterwards disposed of to a company and re-erected on its present site at Sydenham, where it was opened in 1854.

Mr George Smith
from the portrait by G.F. Watts, R.A.

essays characterized by his own peculiar originality and power —and delivered with a finished taste and ease which is felt but cannot well be described. Just before the Lecture began—somebody came behind me—leaned over and said 'Permit me—as a Yorkshireman to introduce myself'—I turned round—saw a strange not handsome face which puzzled me for half a minute and then I said—'You are Lord Carlisle.' He nodded and smiled —he talked a few minutes very pleasantly and courteously— Afterwards came another man with the same plea that he was a Yorkshireman—and this turned out to be Mr Monckton Milnes —Then came Dr Forbes whom I was sincerely glad to see. On Friday I went to the Crystal Palace—it is a marvellous, stirring, bewildering sight—a mixture of a Genii Palace and a mighty Bazaar—but it is not much in my way—I liked the Lecture better. On Saturday I saw the Exhibition at Somerset House—about half a dozen of the pictures are good and interesting—the rest of little worth. Sunday—yesterday—was a day to be marked with a white stone—through most of the day I was very happy without being tired or over-excited—in the afternoon I went to hear D'Aubigny—the great Protestant French Preacher—it was pleasant—half sweet—half sad—and strangely suggestive to hear the French language once more. For health—I have so far got on very fairly considering that I came here far from well. Mr Taylor is gone some weeks since—I hear more open complaints now about his temper than I did so long as he was in London—I am told it is unfortunately irritable. Of Mr Williams' society I have enjoyed one evening's allowance and liked it and him as usual—on such occasions his good qualities of ease, kindliness and intelligence are seen and his little faults and foibles hidden. Mr S. is somewhat changed in appearance—he looks a little older, darker and more careworn—his ordinary manner is graver—but in the evening his spirits flow back to him—Things and circumstances seem here to be as usual—but I fancy there has been some crisis in which his energy and filial affection have sustained them all—this I judge from seeing that Mother and sisters are more peculiarly bound to him than ever and that his slightest wish is an unquestioned law.

Your visitors will soon be with you—if they are not at Brookroyd already—I trust their sojourn will pass as you could wish —and bring you all pleasure. Remember me to all—especially your mother. Write soon and believe me—faithfully yours,

         C. BRONTË.

Mrs Gaskell's account of Charlotte's visit to Thackeray's lecture is very interesting:

The lady who accompanied Miss Brontë to the lecture of Thackeray's alluded to says that, soon after they had taken their places, she was aware that he was pointing out her companion to several of his friends, but she hoped that Miss Brontë herself would not perceive it. After some time, however, during which many heads had been turned round, and many glasses put up, in order to look at the author of *Jane Eyre*, Miss Brontë said, 'I am afraid Mr Thackeray has been playing me a trick'; but she soon became too much absorbed in the lecture to notice the attention which was being paid to her, except when it was directly offered, as in the case of Lord Carlisle and Mr Monckton Milnes. When the lecture was ended Mr Thackeray came down from the platform, and making his way towards her asked her for her opinion. This she mentioned to me not many days afterwards, adding remarks almost identical with those which I subsequently read in *Villette*, where a similar action on the part of M. Paul Emanuel is related.

As they were preparing to leave the room her companion saw with dismay that many of the audience were forming themselves into two lines, on each side of the aisle down which they had to pass before reaching the door. Aware that any delay would only make the ordeal more trying, her friend took Miss Brontë's arm in hers, and they went along the avenue of eager and admiring faces. During this passage through the 'cream of society' Miss Brontë's hand trembled to such a degree that her companion feared lest she should turn faint and be unable to proceed; and she dared not express her sympathy or try to give her strength by any touch or word, lest it might bring on the crisis she dreaded.

674 (514). *To* The Rev. P. Brontë.

112 Gloucester Terrace,
Hyde Park, June 7th, [1851].

Dear Papa,—I was very glad to hear that you continued in pretty good health, and that Mr Cartman came to help you on Sunday. I fear you will not have had a very comfortable week in the dining-room; but by this time I suppose the parlour reformation will be nearly completed, and you will soon be able to return to your old quarters. The letter you sent me this morning was from Mary Taylor. She continues well and happy in New Zealand, and her shop seems to answer well. The French newspaper duly arrived. Yesterday I went for the second time to the Crystal Palace. We remained in it about three hours, and I must say I was more struck with it on this occasion than at my first visit. It is a wonderful place—vast, strange, new, and impossible to describe. Its grandeur does not consist in *one* thing, but in the unique assemblage of *all* things. Whatever human industry has created, you find there, from the great compartments filled with railway engines and boilers, with mill-machinery in full work, with splendid carriages of all kinds, with harness of every description—to the glass-covered and velvet-spread stands loaded with the most gorgeous work of the goldsmith and silversmith, and the carefully guarded caskets full of real diamonds and pearls worth hundreds of thousands of pounds. It may be called a bazaar or a fair, but it is such a bazaar or fair as Eastern genii might have created. It seems as if magic only could have gathered this mass of wealth from all the ends of the earth—as if none but supernatural hands could have arranged it thus, with such a blaze and contrast of colours and marvellous power of effect. The multitude filling the great aisles seems ruled and subdued by some invisible influence. Amongst the thirty thousand souls that peopled it the day I was there, not one loud noise was to be heard, not one irregular movement seen—the living tide rolls on quietly, with a deep hum like the sea heard from a distance.

Mr Thackeray is in high spirits about the success of his lectures. It is likely to add largely both to his fame and purse. He has, however, deferred this week's lecture till next Thursday, at the earnest petition of the duchesses and marchionesses, who, on the day it should have been delivered, were necessitated to go down with the Queen and Court to Ascot Races. I told him I thought he did wrong to put it off on their account—and I think so still. The amateur performance of Bulwer's play for the Guild of Literature has likewise been deferred on account of the races. I hope, dear papa, that you, Mr Nicholls, and all at home continue well. Tell Martha to take her scrubbing and cleaning in moderation and not overwork herself. With kind regards to her and Tabby,—I am, your affectionate daughter,

C. BRONTË.

675. *To* AMELIA TAYLOR (*née* RINGROSE).

112 GLOUCESTER TERRACE,
HYDE PARK, June 7th, 1851.

DEAR AMELIA,—I want your permission to dispose of what may in some measure be considered your gift—viz. the cushion you worked for me. It is somewhat too bright and pretty for my sitting-room at home—I do not need either cushion or chair or stool or any other sitting apparatus to keep you in my recollection—it would look well in a certain apartment wherein I am now writing and would be vastly esteemed as the work of 'young Mrs Martin Yorke.'[1] May I give it?

I am truly glad to hear from Ellen Nussey that you are now much better—but I fear her own health is not in a good state and that she has too much to do and think about just now—How did she seem when you were at Brookroyd?

I have been rather more than a week in London—on the whole I am very quiet—for neither mentally or physically can I do with bustle—The Crystal Palace—you may believe is a famous and wonderful sight—I have been to it twice—and thought more of it the second time than the first—I think it requires a little consideration duly to get into the might—magic and mystery of the thing—it is hard work going over it—after some three or four hours' peregrination—you come out very sufficiently bleached and broken in bits—when you come home you drop into a chair—or better—on to a bed, and don't rise for any invitation or menace or clamorous dinner-bell—till you have had a space of rest.

What I like best are Mr. Thackeray's lectures—he was to have delivered another this week but the Duchesses and Marchionesses have petitioned him to put it off on account of Ascot Races—wearisome selfish seraphim that they are. I wonder why they like him so well—they all like him—and in his greatness—he is half their slave. His mother who—(he says) is the original of Helen Pendennis, came to see me the other day—I liked her better than I thought I should.

To-night—(if all be well) I expect to hear and see Rachel[2]—at

---

[1] Amelia's husband, Joe Taylor, was the prototype of 'Martin Yorke' in *Shirley*.

[2] Madame Rachel (1821–1858) the most famous French actress of her time, was born of poor parents of the Jewish race, and sang in the streets of Lyons and Paris before her genius was discovered. Her greatest characters were Adrienne Lecouvreur in the comedy of that name by MM. Legouvé and Scribe, and Camille in Corneille's tragedy of *Les Horaces*.

the French Theatre. I wonder whether she will fulfil reasonable expectation—as yet it has not been my lot to set eyes on any serious acting for which I cared a fig.

Mary's letter seems cheerfully written—but she does not give a very good account of Ellen's health—how is Mary Dixon? It is grievous to think of her. With respects to your Pearl of great price,—I am, dear Amelia, Sincerely yours,

C. BRONTË.

676. *To* AMELIA TAYLOR (*née* RINGROSE).

GLOUCESTER SQUARE, HYDE PARK,
June 11th, [1851].

DEAR AMELIA,—Your letter reached me quite safely and was very welcome. The account you give of Ellen pains me—I quite agree with you in wishing she might marry—if she could marry well—but I systematically avoid the subject in conversation— Nothing I think is worse than to suggest vague wishes and hopes where there is no good ground for anticipating their realization, and it is a terrible thing to be driven by a sort of despair from the evil of a solitary single life to the worse evil of an uncongenial married one. It pleases me to hear that you and Joe are happy— long may you continue so!

I have seen Rachel—her acting was something apart from any other acting it has come in my way to witness—her soul was in it —and a strange soul she has—I shall not discuss it—it is my hope to see her again—She and Thackeray are the two living things that have a spell for me in this great London—and one of these is sold to the Great Ladies—and the other—I fear—to Beelzebub.

If you send Mary's letters next week—direct them here—if later—to Haworth. With kind regards to Clara,—I am, Yours sincerely,

C. BRONTË.

677 (515). *To* ELLEN NUSSEY.

112 GLOUCESTER TERRACE, HYDE PARK,
June 11th, 1851.

DEAR NELL,—I sit down to write you this morning in an inexpressibly flat state; having spent the whole of yesterday and the day before in a gradually increasing headache, which at last grew rampant and violent, ended with excessive sickness, and this morning I am quite weak and washy. I hoped to leave my headaches behind me at Haworth; but it seems I brought them carefully packed in my trunk, and very much have they been in my way since I came. I fear you are not well. If all be well I shall leave London at the close of next week.

To come and see you while you have visitors would, I am sure, be a complete waste of time and throwing away of opportunity, therefore I *won't do it*; so that is settled. You seem to think me in such a happy, enviable position; pleasant moments I have, but it is usually a pleasure I am obliged to repel and check, which cannot benefit the future, but only add to its solitude, which is no more to be relied on than the sunshine of one summer's day. I pass portions of many a night in extreme sadness.

Since I wrote last, I have seen various things worth describing; Rachel, the great French actress, amongst the number. But to-day I really have no pith for the task. I can only wish you good-bye with all my heart. —Yours faithfully,

C. BRONTË.

Write when you have time.

678 (516). *To* The Rev. P. Brontë.

112 GLOUCESTER TERRACE, HYDE PARK,
June 14th, 1851.

DEAR PAPA, —If all be well, and if Martha can get the cleaning, etc., done by that time, I think I shall be coming home about the end of next week or the beginning of the week after. I have been pretty well in London, only somewhat troubled with headaches, owing, I suppose, to the closeness and oppression of the air. The weather has not been so favourable as when I was last here, and in wet and dark days this great Babylon is not so cheerful. All the other sights seem to give way to the great Exhibition, into which thousands and tens of thousands continue to pour every day. I was in it again yesterday afternoon, and saw the ex-royal family of France—the old Queen, the Duchess of Orleans, and her two sons, etc., pass down the transept. I almost wonder the Londoners don't tire a little of this vast Vanity Fair—and, indeed, a new toy has somewhat diverted the attention of the grandees lately, viz. a fancy ball given last night by the Queen. The great lords and ladies have been quite wrapt up in preparations for this momentous event. Their pet and darling, Mr Thackeray, of course sympathises with them. He was here yesterday to dinner, and left very early in the evening in order that he might visit respectively the Duchess of Norfolk, the Marchioness of Londonderry, Ladies Chesterfield and Clanricarde, and see them all in their fancy costumes of the reign of Charles II. before they set out for the Palace! His lectures, it appears, are a triumphant success. He says they will enable him to make a provision for his daughters; and Mr Smith believes he will not get less than four thousand pounds by them. He is going to give two courses, and then go to Edinburgh and perhaps America, but *not* under the auspices of Barnum. Amongst others, the Lord Chancellor attended his last lecture, and Mr Thackeray says he expects a place from him; but in this I think he was joking. Of course Mr 'T'. is a good deal spoiled by all this, and indeed it cannot be otherwise. He has offered two or three times to introduce me to some of his great friends, and says he knows many great ladies who would receive me with open arms if I would go to their houses; but, seriously, I cannot see that this sort of society produces so good an effect on him as to tempt me in the least to try the same experiment, so I remain obscure.

Hoping you are well, dear papa, and with kind regards to Mr Nicholls, Tabby, and Martha, also poor old Keeper and Flossie, —I am, your affectionate daughter,

C. BRONTË.

P.S.—I am glad the parlour is done and that you have got safely settled, but am quite shocked to hear of the piano being dragged up into the bedroom—there it must necessarily be absurd, and in the parlour it looked so well, besides being convenient for your books. I wonder why you don't like it.

679. *To* MRS GASKELL.

112 GLOUCESTER TERRACE, HYDE PARK,
[June, 1851].

MY DEAR MRS GASKELL,—If all be well I shall leave London at the close of next week—Friday or Saturday—how will this arrangement accord with my coming to see you for a day or two on my way home? I remember in your last you mentioned the possibility of your fetching Marianne down from school when the holidays begin—in that case a visit just now would be out of the question—to your decision then I submit the matter—relying now as ever on your perfect candour.

London has been almost as quiet for me as Haworth—I have paid but a single visit to some old friends. Thackeray's lectures and Rachel's acting are the two things in this great Babylon which have stirred and interested me most—simply because in them I found most of what was genuine whether for good or evil; two Sermons also I have liked—one preached by D'Aubigny—the other by Melville.[1] The Exhibition is no doubt a great and fine sight but not much in my way.

I have not called on Lady K. S. and indeed don't see why I should. Cui bono? Calling on people who can't possibly want you seems to me a grievous waste of exertion—besides—in my estimation—partaking of the error of obtrusiveness.

An often recurring nervous headache has much annoyed and depressed me during my stay in Town—it curtails this note.

Write me a line soon to say how you are and what I must do—remember me kindly to Mr Gaskell, and believe me—Sincerely yours,

C. BRONTË.

680 (517). *To* The Rev. P. BRONTË.

112 GLOUCESTER TERRACE, HYDE PARK, LONDON, June 17th, 1851.

DEAR PAPA,—I write a line in haste to tell you that I find they will not let me leave London till next Tuesday; and as I have promised to spend a day or two with Mrs Gaskell on my way home, it will probably be Friday or Saturday in next week before I return to Haworth. Martha will thus have a few days more time, and must not hurry or overwork herself. Yesterday I saw Cardinal Wiseman and heard him speak. It was at a meeting for the Roman Catholic Society of St. Vincent de Paul; the Cardinal presided. He is a big portly man something of the shape of Mr Morgan; he has not merely a double but a treble and quadruple chin; he has a very large mouth with oily lips, and looks as if he

[1]Henry Melvill (1798–1871), had, for many years, the reputation of being 'The most popular preacher in London,' and one of the greatest rhetoricians of his time. From 1829 to 1843 he served as incumbent of Camden Chapel, Camberwell, and in 1840 he was appointed chaplain to the Tower of London. From 1850 to 1856 he was Golden Lecturer at St Margaret's, Lothbury, and on April 21st, 1856, he was appointed Canon Residentiary of St Paul's. In 1863 he became rector of Barnes, Surrey.

would relish a good dinner with a bottle of wine after it. He came swimming into the room smiling, simpering, and bowing like a fat old lady, and sat down very demure in his chair, and looked the picture of a sleek hypocrite. He was dressed in black like a bishop or dean in plain clothes, but wore scarlet gloves and a brilliant scarlet waistcoat. A bevy of inferior priests surrounded him, many of them very dark-looking and sinister men. The Cardinal spoke in a smooth whining manner, just like a canting Methodist preacher. The audience seemed to look up to him as to a god. A spirit of the hottest zeal pervaded the whole meeting. I was told afterwards that except myself and the person who accompanied me there was not a single Protestant present. All the speeches turned on the necessity of straining every nerve to make converts to popery. It is in such a scene that one feels what the Catholics are doing. Most persevering and enthusiastic are they in their work! Let Protestants look to it. It cheered me much to hear that you continue pretty well. Take every care of yourself. Remember me kindly to Tabby and Martha, also to Mr Nicholls, and—Believe me, dear papa, your affectionate daughter,

C. BRONTË.

681 (518). *To* ELLEN NUSSEY.

June 19th, '51.

DEAR ELLEN,—I shall have to stay in London a few days longer than I intended—Sir J. K. S. has found out that I am here—at first he seemed disposed to be much hurt at my not having told him—but really I do not see what grounds he had for such a feeling—I had some trouble in warding off his wish that I should go directly to his house and take up my quarters there but Mrs Smith helped me by recounting engagements formed—and I got off with promising to spend a day there. He knew beforehand also that I was engaged to spend a day or two with Mrs Gaskell on my way home—and could not put her off — as she is going away for a portion of the summer.

Lady S. looks very delicate — he is much better— his intellect and spirits seem to have resumed their youth.

In this position of affairs Ellen—you must be reasonable and not reproach me for not coming to Brookroyd as you wish—we can none of us bend circumstances exactly to our convenience.

Papa is now very desirous I should come home—and when I have as quickly as possible paid my debts of engagements—home I must go.

Next Tuesday—I go to Manchester[1]—where I shall spend but two days—

I cannot boast that London has agreed with me well this time—the oppression of frequent head-ache—sickness and a low tone of spirits has poisoned many moments which might otherwise have been pleasant—Sometimes I have felt this hard and been tempted to murmur at Fate which condemns me to comparative silence and solitude for eleven months in the year—and in the twelveth while offering social enjoyment takes away the vigour and cheerfulness which should turn it to account. But circumstances are ordered for us, and we must submit—I still hope to see you ere long—Wishing you and your guests all happiness and pleasure—I am sincerely yours,

C. BRONTË.

682. To MRS GORE.

GLOUCESTER TERRACE,
June 21st [1851].

MY DEAR MRS GORE,—I am staying at 112 Gloucester Terrace, Hyde Park; but have now only a few days to remain—and these few seem no longer my own—each being already given to some engagement—I trust however that whenever you call—I may chance to be in; to miss the opportunity of seeing you would be no ordinary disappointment.—Believe me, Yours sincerely,

C. BRONTË.

683 (519). To ELLEN NUSSEY.

112 GLOUCESTER TERRACE,
June 24th, 1851.

DEAR ELLEN,—Your letter would have been answered yesterday but that I was already gone out before the Post-time and was out all day—Since Sir J. K. S. discovered that I was in London I have had precious little time to myself—he brings other people who are all very kind—and perhaps I shall be glad of what I have

[1]She did not go until Friday.

seen afterwards—but it is often a little trying at the time. On Thursday the Marquis of Westminster asked me to a great party—to which I was to go with Mrs Davenport—a beautiful and—(I think) a kind woman too—but this I resolutely declined—On Friday I dined at the Shuttleworth's and met Mrs Davenport and Mr Monckton Milnes—On Saturday I went to hear and see Rachel—a wonderful sight—'terrible as if the earth had cracked deep at your feet and revealed a glimpse of hell'—I shall never forget it—she made me shudder to the marrow of my bones: in her some fiend has certainly taken up an incarnate home. She is not a woman—she is a snake—she is the———. On Sunday I went to the Spanish Ambassador's Chapel—where Cardinal Wiseman in his Archiepiscopal robes and mitre held a Confirmation—The whole scene was impiously theatrical. Yesterday, Monday, I was sent for at ten to breakfast with Mr Rogers the patriarch poet—Mrs Davenport and Lord Glenelg were there—no one else—this certainly proved a most calm refined and intellectual treat. After breakfast—Sir David Brewster[1] came to take us to the Crystal Palace—I had rather dreaded this, for Sir David is a man of the profoundest science and I feared it would be impossible to understand his explanations of the mechanism &c. indeed I hardly knew how to ask him questions—I was spared all trouble—without being questioned—he gave information in the kindest and simplest manner—After two hours spent at the Exhibition and when, as you may suppose—I was *very* tired—we had to go to Lord Westminster's and spend two hours more in looking at the collection of pictures in his splendid Gallery—I cannot now leave London till Friday—To-morrow is Mr Smith's only holiday—(Mr T's. departure leaves him loaded with work—more than once since I came he has been kept in the City till 3 in the morning) he wants to take us all to Richmond and I promised last week I would stay and go with him—his Mother and Sisters. On Thursday I am also engaged—and after putting off Mrs Gaskell again and yet again it is *quite* settled that I shall go to her on Friday. Can I throw all these people

[1]Sir David Brewster (1781–1868), an eminent Scottish natural philosopher, educated at Edinburgh University. He edited the *Edinburgh Encyclopædia* 1807–29, invented the kaleidoscope in 1816, and gave permanent form to the stereoscope. In 1831 he assisted in organising the British Association for the Advancement of Science. He made important discoveries respecting the polarisation of light. His works include a *Life of Newton* 1828, *Letters on Natural Magic*, 1831, and *More Worlds than One*, 1854.

overboard—derange all plans—break all promises? Would it be rational to do this—? would it be right? *Could* it be done? Reflect —dear Nell, and be reasonable and charitable—Did I not tell you six weeks ago—that it was not likely I should see the Gorhams as they would be with you while I should be in London?

I well knew that—once in London—contingencies might arise, which I could not over-rule.—Believe me, Yours faithfully,

C. BRONTË.

684 (520). *To* The REV. P. BRONTË, *Haworth, Yorks.*

112 GLOUCESTER TERRACE,

June 26th, 1851.

DEAR PAPA,—I have not yet been able to get away from London, but if all be well I shall go to-morrow, stay two days with Mrs Gaskell at Manchester, and return home on Monday 30th *without fail.* During this last week or ten days I have seen many things, some of them very interesting, and have also been in much better health than I was during the first fortnight of my stay in London. Sir James and Lady Shuttleworth have really been very kind, and most scrupulously attentive. They desire their regards to you, and send all manner of civil messages. The Marquis of Westminster and the Earl of Ellesmere each sent me an order to see their private collection of pictures, which I enjoyed very much. Mr Rogers, the patriarch-poet, now eighty-seven years old, invited me to breakfast with him. His breakfasts, you must understand, are celebrated throughout Europe for their peculiar refinement and taste. He never admits at that meal more than four persons to his table: himself and three guests. The morning I was there I met Lord Glenelg and Mrs Davenport, a relation of Lady Shuttleworth's, and a very beautiful and fashionable woman. The visit was very interesting; I was glad that I had paid it after it was over. An attention that pleased and surprised me more I think than any other was the circumstance of Sir David Brewster, who is one of the first scientific men of his day, coming to take me over the Crystal Palace, and pointing out and explaining the most remarkable curiosities. You will know, dear papa, that I do not mention those things to boast of them, but merely because I think they will give you pleasure. Nobody, I find, thinks the worse of me for avoiding publicity and declining to go

to large parties, and everybody seems truly courteous and respectful, a mode of behaviour which makes me grateful, as it
ought to do. Good-bye till Monday. Give my best regards to
Mr Nicholls, Tabby, and Martha, and—believe me your affectionate daughter,

C. BRONTË.

685. *To* SYDNEY DOBELL.

PLYMOUTH GROVE, MANCHESTER,
June 28th, [1851].

DEAR SIR,—Your kind note reached me just as I was on the
point of leaving town; but even had it come sooner, I could not
have changed my plans without breaking sundry promises and
seriously deranging the convenience of several friends. I had
already prolonged my stay in London to the furthest available
minute for the sake of hearing one more lecture from Mr Thackeray. Nor was I disappointed; on the theme of Fielding—he put
forth his great strength—and though I could not *agree*, I was
forced to *admire*. You will be in time for his closing lecture
(Goldsmith).—I congratulate you beforehand on the treat which
I feel sure you will enjoy. Thackeray and Rachel have been the
two points of attraction for me in town: the one, being a human
creature, great, interesting, and *sometimes* good and kind; the
other, I know not what, I think a demon. I saw her in Adrienne
Lecouvreur and in Camilla[1]—in the last character I shall *never*
forget her—she will come to me in sleepless nights again and yet
again. Fiends can hate, scorn, rave, wreathe, and *agonize* as she
does, not mere men and women. I neither love, esteem, nor
admire this strange being, but (if I could bear the high mental
stimulus so long), I would go every night for three months to
watch and study its manifestations.

I thank you for 'The Eclectic Review,' and thank you twice
for the beautiful and powerful article marked S. Y. D.

Wishing you and Mrs Dobell all enjoyment and happiness in
your excursion.—I am, yours sincerely,

C. BRONTË.

I am staying with Mrs Gaskell, the authoress of 'Mary Barton
but have but two days to give her.

[1]See note on page 244, above.

686. *To* MRS GORE.

PLYMOUTH GROVE, MANCHESTER,
June 28th, [1851].

MY DEAR MRS GORE,—Your note reached me when I was on the point of leaving Town and had not time to reply to it; I now beg to acknowledge its receipt, and to say that if the *power* had been mine to comply with its injunctions—the *will* was certainly not wanting—I had however no alternative and must content myself with the hope of being able at some future day better to reconcile duty and inclination.—Believe me, Very sincerely yours,

C. BRONTË.

687 (521). *To* MRS SMITH.

HAWORTH, July 1st, 1851.

MY DEAR MRS SMITH,—Once more I am at home where—I am thankful to say—I found my Father very well. The journey to Manchester was a little hot and dusty—but otherwise pleasant enough. The two stout gentlemen who filled a portion of the carriage when I got in—quitted it at Rugby—and two other ladies and myself had it to ourselves the rest of the way.

The visit to Mrs Gaskell formed a cheering break in the journey. She is a woman of many fine qualities and deserves the epithet which I find is generally applied to her—charming. Her family consists of four little girls—all more or less pretty and intelligent—these scattered through the rooms of a somewhat spacious house—seem to fill it with liveliness and gaiety. Haworth Parsonage is rather a contrast—yet even Haworth Parsonage does not look gloomy in this bright summer weather! it is somewhat still—but with the windows open—I can hear a bird or two singing on certain thorn-trees in the garden. My Father and the Servants think me looking better than when I left home, and I certainly feel better myself for the change.

You are too much like your Son to render it advisable that I should say much about your kindness during my visit. However, one cannot help (like Captain Cuttle) making a note of these matters. Papa says I am to thank you in his name and to offer you his respects which I do accordingly. With truest regards to all your circle.—Believe me very sincerely yours,

C. BRONTË.

688. *To* GEORGE SMITH.

July 1st, 1851,

MY DEAR SIR,—After a month's voyaging I have cast anchor once more—in a rocky and lonely little cove, no doubt, but still —safe enough. The visit to Mrs Gaskell on my way home let me down easily; though I only spent two days with her they were very pleasant. She lives in a large, cheerful, airy house, quite out of Manchester smoke; a garden surrounds it, and, as in this hot weather the windows were kept open, a whispering of leaves and perfume of flowers always pervaded the rooms. Mrs Gaskell herself is a woman of whose conversation and company I should not soon tire. She seems to me kind, clever, animated, and unaffected; her husband is a good and kind man too.

I went to church by myself on Sunday morning (they are Unitarians). On my return shortly before the family came home from chapel the servant said there was a letter for me. I wondered from whom, not expecting my father to write, and not having given the address elsewhere. Of course I was not at all pleased when the small problem was solved by the letter being brought; I never care for hearing from you the least in the world. Comment on the purport of your note is unnecessary. I am glad, yet hardly dare permit myself to congratulate till the manuscript is fairly created and found to be worthy of the hand, pen, and mind whence it is to emanate. This promise to go down into the country is all very well; yet secretly I cannot but wish that a sort of 'Chamber in the Wall' might be prepared at Cornhill, furnished (besides the bed, table, stool, and candlestick which the Shunammite 'set' for Elisha) with a desk, pens, ink, and paper. There the prophet might be received and lodged, subject to a system kind (perhaps) yet firm; roused each morning at six punctually, by the contrivance of that virtuous self-acting couch which casts from it its too fondly clinging inmate; served, on being duly arrayed, with a *slight* breakfast of tea and toast; then with the exception of a crust at one, no further gastronomic interruption to be allowed till 7 p.m., at which time the greatest and most industrious of modern authors should be summoned by the most spirited and vigilant of modern publishers to a meal, comfortable and comforting—in short, a good dinner—elegant, copious, convivial (in moderation)—of which they should partake together in the finest spirit of geniality and fraternity—part at half-past nine and at that salutary hour withdraw to recreating repose. Grand would be the result of such a system pursued for six months.

Somehow I quite expect that you will let me see my 'character' though you did not promise that you would. Do not keep it back on account of my faults; remember Thackeray seems to think our faults the best part of us. I will tell you faithfully whether it seems to me true or not.

In a day or two I expect to be quite settled at home, and think I shall manage to be quite philosophic, &c. I was thankful to find my Father very well; he said that when I wrote I was to give his best respects.—I am, Sincerely yours,

C. BRONTË.

The allusion to the 'character' in the last letter is fully explained by Mr George Smith in his article on Charlotte Brontë, printed in the *Cornhill Magazine*, December, 1900:

We went together to a Dr Browne, a phrenologist who was then in vogue, using the names of Mr and Miss Fraser. Here is Dr Browne's estimate of the talents and disposition of Miss Brontë:

A PHRENOLOGICAL ESTIMATE OF THE TALENTS AND DISPOSITIONS OF A LADY.

Temperament for the most part nervous. Brain large, the anterior and superior parts remarkably salient. In her domestic relations this lady will be warm and affectionate. In the care of children she will evince judicious kindness, but she is not pleased at seeing them spoiled by over-indulgence. Her fondness for any particular locality would chiefly rest upon the associations connected with it. Her attachments are strong and enduring—indeed, this is a leading element of her character; she is rather circumspect, however, in the choice of her friends, and it is well that she is so, for she will seldom meet with persons whose dispositions approach the standard of excellence with which she can entirely sympathise. Her sense of truth and justice would be offended by any dereliction of duty, and she would in such cases express her disapprobation with warmth and energy; she would not, however, be precipitate in acting thus, and rather than live in a state of hostility with those she could wish to love she would depart from them, although the breaking off of friendship would be to her a source of great unhappiness. The careless and unreflecting, whom she would labour to amend, might deem her punctilious and perhaps exacting: not considering that their amendment and not her own gratification prompted her to admonish. She is sensitive and is very anxious to succeed in her undertakings, but is not so sanguine as to the probability of success. She is occasionally inclined to take a gloomier view of things than perhaps the facts of the case justify; she should guard against the effect of this where her affection is engaged, for her sense of her own importance is moderate and not strong enough to steel her heart against disappointment; she has more firmness than self-reliance, and her sense of justice is of a very high order. She is deferential to the aged and those she deems worthy of respect, and possesses much devotional feeling, but dislikes fanaticism and is not given to a belief in supernatural things without questioning the probability of their existence.

Money is not her idol, she values it merely for its uses; she would be liberal to the poor and compassionate to the afflicted, and when friendship calls for aid she would struggle even against her own interest to impart the required assistance — indeed, sympathy is a marked characteristic of this organisation.

Is fond of symmetry and proportion, and possesses a good perception of form, and is a good judge of colour. She is endowed with a keen perception of melody and rhythm. Her imitative powers are good, and the faculty which gives manual dexterity is well developed. These powers might have been cultivated with advantage. Is a fair calculator, and her sense of order and arrangement is remarkably good. Whatever this lady has to settle or arrange will be done with precision and taste.

She is endowed with an exalted sense of the beautiful and ideal, and longs for perfection. If not a poet her sentiments are poetical, or are at least imbued with that enthusiastic glow which is characteristic of poetical feeling. She is fond of dramatic literature and drama, especially if it be combined with music.

In its intellectual development this head is very remarkable. The forehead is at once very large and well formed. It bears the stamp of deep thoughtfulness and comprehensive understanding. It is highly philosophical. It exhibits the presence of an intellect at once perspicacious and perspicuous. There is much critical sagacity and fertility in devising resources in situations of difficulty, much originality, with a tendency to speculate and generalise. Possibly this speculative bias may sometimes interfere with the practical efficiency of some of her projects. Yet since she has scarcely an adequate share of self-reliance, and is not sanguine as to the success of her plans, there is reason to suppose that she would attend more closely to particulars, and thereby prevent the unsatisfactory results of hasty generalisation. This lady possesses a fine organ of language, and can, if she has done her talents justice by exercise, express her sentiments with clearness, precision, and force—sufficiently eloquent but not verbose. In learning a language she would investigate its spirit and structure. The character of the German language would be well adapted to such an organisation. In analysing the motives of human conduct, this lady would display originality and power, but in her mode of investigating mental science she would naturally be imbued with a metaphysical bias; she would perhaps be sceptical as to the truth of Gale's doctrine. But the study of this doctrine, this new system of mental philosophy, would give additional strength to her excellent understanding by rendering it more practical, more attentive to particulars, and contribute to her happiness by imparting to her more correct notions of the dispositions of those whose acquaintance she may wish to cultivate.

J. P. BROWNE, M.D.

367 Strand,
    June 29, 1851.

689. *To* GEORGE SMITH.

July 2nd, 1851.

MY DEAR SIR,—I send back Mr Fraser's character by return of post; but I have found time to take a careful and exact copy of the same, which (D.V.) I mean to keep always. I wanted a portrait, and have now got one very much to my mind. With the exception of that slight mistake between number and music, and the small vein of error which flows thence through the character, it is a sort of miracle—*like*—*like*—*like* as the very life itself. Destroy Mr Ford's lithograph. Transfer to fair type Dr Browne's sketch, and frame and glaze it instead. I am glad I have got it. I wanted it.

Yet if you really object to my keeping this copy tell me to burn it, and I will burn it; but I should *like* to keep it, and will show it to nobody. —With true regards to your Mother and sisters, I am,
  Yours sincerely,
                              C. BRONTË.

690. *To* GEORGE SMITH.

July 8th, 1851.

MY DEAR SIR, —I return the 'Times' and the 'Literary Gazette' with —Oh no! I forgot —*not with thanks*. Thackeray's last lecture must, I think, have been his best. What he says about Sterne is true. His observations on literary men, and their social obligations and individual duties, seem to me also true and full of mental and moral vigour. But I regret that a lecture, in other respects so worthy of his best self, should not take a more masterly, a juster view of the old question of authors and booksellers. Why did he not *speak* as —I know —he *thinks* on this subject? Why, in treating it, did he talk all the wornout cant now grown stale and commonplace? I feel sure Mr Thackeray does not quite respect himself when he runs on in that trite vein of abuse. He does not think all he says. He knows better than from his inmost heart and genuine convictions sweepingly to condemn a whole class. There may be radical evils in the *system*, meeting and courting attack, but it is time to have done with indefinable clamour against the *men*, and to cease indiscriminate aspersions which sound outrageous but mean little. Ere long Messrs Bungay and Bacon will be converted into true martyrs and very interesting characters, so innocent and so wronged that in spite of oneself one will feel obliged to pity and vindicate them. The International Copyright Meeting seems to have had but a barren result, judging from the report in the 'Literary Gazette.' I cannot see that Sir E. Bulwer and the rest *did* anything; nor can I well see what it is in their power to do. The argument brought forward about the damage accruing to American national literature from the present piratical system is a good and sound argument; but I am afraid the publishers —honest men —are not yet mentally prepared to give such reasoning due weight. I should think that which refers to the injury inflicted upon themselves, by an oppressive competition in piracy, would influence them more; but I suppose all established matters, be they good or evil, are difficult to change.

About Mr Fraser's character I must not say a word. Of your own accord you have found the safest point from which to view it; I will not say 'look higher'! I think you see the matter as it is desirable we should all see what relates to ourselves. If I had a right to whisper a word of counsel, it should be merely this: whatever your present self may be, resolve with all your strength of resolution never to degenerate thence. Be jealous of a shadow of falling off. Determine rather to look above that standard, and to strive beyond it. Everybody appreciates certain social properties, and likes his neighbour for possessing them; but perhaps few dwell upon a friend's capacity for the intellectual, or care how this might expand, if there were but facilities allowed for cultivation, and space given for growth. It seems to me that, even should such space and facilities be denied by stringent circumstances and a rigid fate, still it should do you good fully to know and tenaciously to remember, that you have such a capacity. When other people overwhelm you with acquired knowledge, such as you have not had opportunity, perhaps not application, to gain—derive not pride but support from the thought. If no new books had ever been written, some of these minds would themselves have remained blank pages: they only take an impression; they were not born with a record of thought on the brain, or an instinct of sensation on the heart. If I had never seen a printed volume, Nature would have offered my perceptions a varying picture of a continuous narrative, which, without any other teacher than herself, would have schooled me to knowledge, unsophisticated but genuine.

About the 'lady's' character I have nothing to say—not a word. For the use made of it I can quite trust you, and shall neither give directions nor impose restrictions. Show it to Mr Williams if you like, but tell him with my best regards on no account when he reads to think of Queen Elizabeth's portraits. If there be a lack of shadow, he is to be as good as not to draw attention to that fact, but kindly to supply the deficiency out of his own artistic mind. You may add that he need not be afraid to introduce the same (i.e. the shadow) in good broad masses, the 'lady' undertaking to acknowledge any defect of a not unreasonably heinous dye.

Before I received your last I had made up my mind to tell you that I should expect no letter for three months to come (intending afterwards to extend this abstinence to six months, for I am jealous of becoming dependent on this indulgence: you doubt-less cannot see why because you do not live my life). Nor shall I now expect a letter; but since you say that you would like to write now and then, I cannot say 'never write' without imposing on my real wishes a falsehood which they reject, and doing to them a violence to which they entirely refuse to submit. I can only observe that when it pleases you to write, whether seriously or for a little amusement, your notes, if they come to me will come where they are welcome.

Tell your Mother I shall try to cultivate good spirits as assidu-ously as she cultivates her geraniums. Remember me with all kindness to her and your sisters, and believe me, Sincerely yours,

C. BRONTË.

P.S.—You are not to exercise your critical *acumen* on this letter which is written in an intractable mood when the com-posing faculty will not do its duty.

691 (522). *To* MARGARET WOOLER.

HAWORTH, July 14th, 1851.

MY DEAR MISS WOOLER,—My first feeling on receiving your note was one of disappointment, but a little consideration sufficed to show me that 'all was for the best.' In truth it was a great piece of extravagance on my part to ask you and Ellen Nussey to-gether; it is much better to divide such good things. To have your visit in *prospect* will console me when hers is in *retrospect*. Not that I mean to yield to the weakness of clinging dependently to the society of friends—however dear—but still as an occasional treat I must value and even seek—such society as a necessary of life.

Let me know then whenever it suits your convenience to come to Haworth and, unless some change I cannot now foresee occurs—a ready and warm welcome will await you—Should there be any cause rendering it desirable to defer the visit, I will tell you frankly.

The pleasures of society—I cannot offer you, nor those of fine scenery, but I place very much at your command the moors—some books—a series of quiet 'curling-hair times,' and an old pupil into the bargain. E. Nussey may have told you that I have spent a month in London this summer—when you come you shall ask what questions you like on that point—and I will answer to the best of my stammering ability. Do not press me much on the subject of the 'Crystal Palace.' I went there five times—and certainly saw some interesting things—and the *coup d'œil* is striking and bewildering enough—but I never was able to get up any raptures on the subject, and each renewed visit was made under coercion rather than my own free will. It is an excessively bustling place—and after all its wonders appeal too exclusively to the eye and rarely touch the heart or head. I make an exception to the last assertion in favour of those who possess a large range of scientific knowledge. Once I went with Sir David Brewster and perceived that he looked on objects with other eyes than mine.

E. Nussey—I find—is writing, and will therefore deliver her own messages of regard. If papa were in the room he would—I know—desire his respects—and you must take both respects and a good bundle of something more cordial from yours very faithfully,

C. BRONTË.

692 (523). *To* W. S. WILLIAMS.

[July 21st, 1851].

MY DEAR SIR,—I delayed answering your very interesting letter until the box should have reached me; and now that it is come—I can only acknowledge its arrival. I cannot say at all what I felt as I unpacked its contents. These Cornhill parcels have something of the magic charm of a fairy-gift about them, as well as of the less poetical, but more substantial pleasure of a box from home received at school. You have sent me this time even more books than usual—and all good.

What shall I say about the 20 Nos. of splendid engravings—laid cozily at the bottom? the whole Vernon Gallery[1] brought to one's fireside? Indeed—indeed, I can say nothing—except that I will take care, and keep them clean, and send them back uninjured.

In reading your graphic account of a visit to Oxford after an

---

[1] In 1847 Robert Vernon presented to the nation his collection of 162 paintings by modern British artists. In 1850 they were removed from the cellars at The Royal Academy, Trafalgar Square, where they had been previously exhibited, to Marlborough House: and in 1859 they were transferred to the South Kensington Museum.

interval of 30 years since you last went there—and of the disillusion which meanwhile had taken place—I could not help wondering whether Cornhill will ever change for me as Oxford has changed for you; I have some pleasant associations connected with it now—will these alter their character some day?

Perhaps they may—though I have faith to the contrary; because—I *think*—I do not exaggerate my partialities, I *think* I take faults along with excellencies—blemishes together with beauties. And besides—in the matter of friendship—I have observed—that disappointment here arises chiefly—*not* from liking our friends too well—or thinking of them too highly—but rather from an over-estimate of *their* liking for and opinion of *us*; and that if we guard ourselves with sufficient scrupulousness of care from error in this direction—and can be content, and even happy to give more affection than we receive—can make just comparison of circumstances and be severely accurate in drawing inferences thence, and never let self-love blind our eyes—I *think* we may manage to get through life with consistency and constancy—unembittered by that misanthropy which springs from revulsions of feeling. All this sounds a little metaphysical—but it is good sense if you consider it. The Moral of it is that if we would build on a sure foundation in friendship—we must love our friends for *their* sakes rather than for *our own*, we must look at their truth to *themselves*, full as much as their truth to *us*. In the latter case—every wound to self-love would be a cause of coldness; in the former—only some painful change in the friend's character and disposition—some fearful breach in his allegiance to his better self—could alienate the heart.

How interesting your old-maiden cousin's gossip about your parents must have been to you, and how gratifying to find that her reminiscences turned on none but pleasant facts and characteristics! Life must indeed be slow in that little decaying hamlet amongst the chalk hills. After all—depend upon it, it is better to be worn out with work in a thronged community than to perish of inaction in a stagnant solitude: take this truth into consideration whenever you get tired of work and bustle.—Believe me, yours sincerely,

C. Brontë.

693. *To* CHARLOTTE BRONTË.[1]

STRONG CLOSE MILL, KEIGHLEY,
July 23rd, 1851.

DEAR MADAM,—After my departure from Haworth yesterday, I was very sorry, that I had intruded our little difference at Keighley Church upon your aged parent, the subject could in no way be interesting to him.

On my arrival at home, I asked my wife, if we had not seen a sign in Kirkby Lonsdale, bearing the name of Jane Eyre, she said that it is J. Eyre, and that she had enquired about it, and it turns out to be James Eyre, it appears that my impression has arisen from partial supposition, having stated to you what I did, I felt called upon to apologize on both accounts and also to put the matter right, especially, knowing something of the acuteness of your perceptions and powers in estimating the various characters which pass before you. May I be allowed to add, that I see you as an Angel born aloft, hovering and scanning the vicissitudes concomitant to humanity in all her various forms, I see you also landed in a heaven of rest, securely surrounded by lovers, your own, where neither flattery nor frowns dare approach.

'Tis great to possess the irresistible notes of a Swedish Nightingale, commanding any amount of Mammon's gear, but great indeed it is to possess the power registering (like you) your own immortality.

(This by the way) the writer of this, has recently combated very different opinion to his own on Shirley and Jane Eyre, expressed by a lady, in the presence of her governess; knowing the reason, tis easy to be accounted for, as the adage has it, where the shoe pinches, an outward manifestation may be expected. As to myself like a parish clerk I respond Amen to the sentiments which you have propounded, probably to all the civilized inhabitants of the earth. To conclude, inasmuch as you have afforded me many tearful and pleasing moments, may you live long to enjoy the society of those 'Wo liebe warm in hertzen sitz,' and when you have finished your earthly pilgrimage in this

---

[1]This letter was found amongst the papers left by Miss Nussey, having been sent to her by Charlotte Brontë, as appears in the next letter. Unfortunately, nothing further is known about the incident to which the letter refers.

vale of tears, may you be found, or rather, foremost amongst the number mentioned in the 7th chapter of Revelations the 9th and 3 following verses.

Dear Madam, may I indulge in the hope that I shall have your forgiveness for the liberty which I have taken—in addressing you so frankly, and that you will believe me to be yours,—With much esteem,

HNY ROBINSON.

694 (524). *To* ELLEN NUSSEY.

HAWORTH, July 27th, 1851.

DEAR NELL,—I hope you have taken no cold from your wretched journey home; you see you should have taken my advice and stayed till Saturday. Didn't I tell you I had a 'presentiment' it would be better for you to do so?

I am glad you found your mother pretty well. Is she disposed to excuse the wretched petrified condition of the bilberry preserve, in consideration of the intent of the donor? It seems they had high company while you were away. You see what you lose by coming to Haworth. No events here since your departure except a long letter from Miss Martineau. (She did not write the article on 'Woman' in the 'Westminster,' by the way, it is the production of a man, and one of the first philosophers, and political economists and metaphysicians of the day). Item, the departure of Mr Nicholls for Ireland, and his inviting himself on the eve thereof to come and take a farewell tea; good, mild, uncontentious. Item, a note from the stiff little chap who called about the epitaph for his cousin. I enclose this; a finer gem in its way it would be difficult to conceive. You need not however be at the trouble of returning it. How are they at Hunsworth yet? It is no use saying whether I am solitary or not; I drive on very well, and papa continues pretty well.—Yours faithfully,

C. BRONTË.

695. *To* GEORGE SMITH.

July 31st, 1851.

MY DEAR SIR,—As I sent a note of Miss Martineau's with a critique of Thackeray's last lecture in it, so I cannot help sending one just received from Mrs Gaskell, that you may compare the temper and judgment of the two ladies. This letter has nothing of personal interest to yourself, nothing about 'my Publishers' (I only wish it had); still I think you will like to read opinions so justly conceived and pleasantly expressed; it will be a little variety on your usual business correspondence.

I wrote to Miss Martineau immediately on the receipt of yours, communicating the full assurance you gave of your willingness to publish an anonymous work[1] from her pen, and quoting your own expression as to the best method of preserving secrecy. I wish she may try this experiment, but as far as the mystery goes I apprehend she will betray herself. I have conjured her to trust no more confidants, but I fear she will not stop at me. Should I hear from her again on the subject, I will let you know.

I have marked with red ink where you are to begin Mrs G's note; one dare not again put an index hand, you are too sarcastic. —Yours sincerely,

C. BRONTË.

696. *To* GEORGE SMITH.

August 4th, 1851.

MY DEAR SIR,—I send Miss Martineau's letter received this morning, and written for your perusal. You will see her spirit is up, and I hope and believe she will do work worthy of her. She has her faults, but she has, too, a fine mind and noble powers. She can never be so charming a woman as Mrs Gaskell, but she is a greater writer. I even begin to believe her emulation may be so wrought upon as to induce her to keep the secret. You see you will have to write to her. Her present address is West Cliff House, Norfolk.

Surely you do not intend to let this summer pass without giving yourself a holiday. I can only say that such over-devotion to business would be wrong—suicidal—it would merit punishment more than the sly peccadilloes of the erring Calcutta bookseller. Remember you cannot do without health; it is your best ally in every undertaking.

---

[1] Miss Martineau was engaged in writing a novel, which she wished to publish anonymously. Charlotte Brontë offered to get the book published by Messrs Smith Elder & Co. After various titles had been rejected the book was called *Oliver Weld*, and Miss Martineau, at Charlotte's suggestion, adopted the pseudonym of Alexander F. Murray. However, on reading the MS. Mr Smith disapproved of the book which showed favour to the Roman Catholics, and he decided to reject it. The manuscript was ultimately burnt by Miss Martineau.

Just permit me to say this: When you form resolutions about reading beware of over-tasking. Too exacting a determination alarms and impedes endeavour. Sometimes when the necessity of reading some dry and very solid book has lain heavy on my conscience, I have found that by setting myself to study it only for an hour (or perhaps in your case half an hour) each day, the last page has been reached far sooner than one could have anticipated, and one remembers it well too, read in this deliberate way.

Do I give diminutive doses of medicine in large comfits? I thought I retrenched the sugar with a very austere hand: I always intend to do so.

I am in much better health than when I was in London, during which time frequent headaches harassed me a great deal. I am not however, on good terms with myself, and have no cause to be so. My pleasantest thoughts lie in the hope that Mr Thackeray and Miss Martineau will each write a good book, and that you, they, and the public will find therein mutual benefit and satisfaction.

You had almost got another hostile manual demonstration, but on the whole I think it is better to let you alone; the blows you inflict are much more telling than those you receive. I see plainly Nature made you a critic, while Fate perversely transformed you into a publisher—in her rage against authors.—

Yours sincerely,

C. Brontë.

697 (525). *To* Mrs Gaskell.

Haworth, August 6th, 1851.

My dear Mrs Gaskell,—I was too much pleased with your letter, when I got it at last, to feel disposed to murmur now about the delay.

About a fortnight ago I received a letter from Miss Martineau: a long letter, and treating precisely the same subjects on which yours dwelt, viz. the Exhibition and Thackeray's last lecture. It was interesting mentally to place the two documents side by side—to study the two aspects of mind—to view alternately the same scene through two mediums. Full striking was the difference; and the more striking because it was not the rough contrast of good and evil, but the more subtle opposition, the more delicate diversity of different kinds of good. The excellences of one nature resembled (I thought) that of some sovereign medicine—harsh, perhaps, to the taste, but potent to invigorate; the good of the other seemed more akin to the nourishing efficacy of our daily bread. It is not bitter; it is not lusciously sweet; it pleases without flattering the palate; it sustains without forcing the strength.

I very much agree with you in all you say. For the sake of variety I could almost wish that the concord of opinion were less complete.

To begin with Trafalgar Square. My taste goes with yours and Meta's[1] completely on this point. I have always thought it a fine site (and *sight* also). The view from the summit of those steps has ever struck me as grand and imposing—Nelson Column included: the fountains I could dispense with. With respect, also, to the Crystal Palace, my thoughts are precisely yours.

Then I feel sure you speak justly of Thackeray's lecture. You do well to set aside odious comparisons, and to wax impatient of that trite twaddle about 'nothing-newness'—a jargon which simply proves, in those who habitually use it, a coarse and feeble faculty of appreciation; an inability to discern the relative value of *originality* and *novelty*; a lack of that refined perception which, dispensing with the stimulus of an ever new subject, can derive sufficiency of pleasure from freshness of treatment. To such critics the prime of a summer morning would bring no delight; wholly occupied with railing at their cook for not having provided a novel and piquant breakfast dish, they would remain insensible to such influences as lie in sunrise, dew, and breeze: therein would be 'nothing new.'

Is it Mr ——'s family experience which has influenced your feelings about the Catholics? I own I cannot be sorry for this commencing change. Good people—*very* good people—I doubt not, there are amongst the Romanists, but the system is not one which should have such sympathy as *yours*. Look at Popery taking off the mask in Naples!

I have read 'The Saint's Tragedy.'[2] As a 'work of art' it seems to me far superior to either 'Alton Locke' or 'Yeast.' Faulty it may be, crude and unequal, yet there are portions where some of the deep chords of human nature are swept with a hand which is strong even while it falters. We see throughout (I *think*) that

[1]Mrs Gaskell's daughter, Margaret Emily.

[2]*The Saint's Tragedy; or, the True Story of Elizabeth of Hungary*, by Charles Kingsley, was published in 1848.

Elizabeth has not, and never had, a mind perfectly sane. From the time that she was what she herself, in the exaggeration of her humility, calls 'an idiot girl,' to the hour when she lay moaning in visions on her dying bed, a slight craze runs through her whole existence. This is good: this is true. A sound mind, a healthy intellect, would have dashed the priest power to the wall; would have defended her natural affections from his grasp as a lioness defends her young; would have been as true to husband and children as your leal-hearted little Maggie was to her Frank. Only a mind weak with some fatal flaw *could* have been influenced as was this poor saint's. But what anguish—what struggles! Seldom do I cry over books, but here my eyes rained as I read. When Elizabeth turns her face to the wall—I stopped —there needed no more.

Deep truths are touched on in this tragedy—touched on, not fully elicited—truths that stir a peculiar pity, a compassion hot with wrath and bitter with pain. This is no poet's dream: we know that such things *have* been done; that minds *have* been thus subjected, and lives thus laid waste.

Remember me kindly and respectfully to Mr Gaskell, and though I have not seen Marianne I must beg to include her in the love I send the others. Could you manage to convey a small kiss to that dear but dangerous little person Julia? She surreptitiously possessed herself of a minute fraction of my heart, which has been missing ever since I saw her. Believe me sincerely and affectionately yours,

C. BRONTË.

698. *To* GEORGE SMITH.

August 9th, 1851.

MY DEAR SIR,—Enclosed is a letter from Miss Martineau to you. I think you will like its clearness and candour, and you will see that though she considers her own interest on the subject of terms, yet she brings to the discussion of that question none of the worldly, bargaining spirit by which I fear some minds of otherwise first-rate calibre are apt to lower their business transactions.

In reference to what she says about myself, I need hardly add that it will give me the greatest pleasure to be useful to either you or her in this matter; but it is well you do not acknowledge the 'favour I have conferred in introducing you to Miss M.' I hereby wash my hands of that charge. It was not I who did it. Fate managed the whole business, and, you see, she has known your firm of old. I trust, with you, that there is no fear of her touching on religious subjects; 'a burnt child dreads the fire,' and though she is too stoical to cry out I cannot doubt that she has been well scorched of late.

You must not be *too* sanguine about the book; for though it seems to me there are grounds for anticipating that she will produce something superior to what she has yet written in the same class, yet perhaps the nature and bent of her genius hardly warrant the expectation of first-rate excellence in fiction. She seems to be suffering from some sense of constraint from the idea of continued obligation to keep the secret; perhaps when you write to her again it may be as well to mention your own ideas on this point. I mean to say, how far do you think it desirable and important? Secret-keeping does not agree with her at all. I cannot help smiling at the kind of little bustle she makes about it.

I return the copy of your letter to Miss M. Orthography blameless. Composition well turned.

It was kind of you to write that last letter; I could hardly believe when I opened it that it was *all* for me. The 'medicine,' by the by, was accepted with a grace beyond all praise, and now, perhaps, I may venture to confess that after I had written that P.S. and sent the letter off some severe qualms came over me as to whether I had not taken a small liberty. 'It is true,' I argued with myself, 'Mr Fraser has been pronounced on authority to be without a "tincture of arrogance in his nature," but then, again, the same oracle describes him as "very sensitive;" it says "His feelings are easily wounded," and though, for my consolation, it adds, "He is of a forgiving temper," yet every sensible person knows that this is a quality which ought never to be trifled with or tried too far.' However 'all's well that ends well.' Mr Fraser kindly understood me, for which I beg to tell him I am grateful; it is pleasant to be understood.

The incident at the Guild Performance amused me; it was one of those occasions which, while startling people out of their customary smooth bearing, elicit genuine touches of character. Mr Fraser and the panic-struck young lady both revealed themselves according to their different natures. It is easy to realise the scene.

You sent about a fortnight since a volume of 'London Labour,'[1] &c. (a curiously interesting book to read); to-day you have sent Mr Ruskin's pamphlet.[2] What can one say?

I hope your mother and sisters and Alick are all enjoying themselves by the seaside this fine weather; doubtless they wish that you shared their enjoyment, but it seems as if the circle of happiness were rarely to be complete in this world; however, as long as you have good health, cheerful spirits, as long too as your operations are animated and rewarded by reasonable success, there will be abundant cause for satisfaction to those and all who wish you well. — Yours sincerely,

C. BRONTË.

699. *To* GEORGE SMITH.

[Undated].

MY DEAR SIR, — . . . I am truly glad to hear that there are good news of Mr Taylor, that he is so well, and that his business energies have so far stood the test of the Indian sun.

I hope your 'small troubles' will soon melt away; that paragraph in which you mention them brings to one's mind's eye the movements of a curbed-in, eager steed. You must be patient, you must not champ your bit and rear in that way. Good-bye. I wish there was no more reality in any evil that can possibly come near you than there is in the idea of my feeling anything but gratitude for that unjustly accused letter. — Believe me always, Sincerely yours,

C. BRONTË.

700 (526). *To* MRS GASKELL.

[Undated].

Whenever I see Florence and Julia again I shall feel like a fond but bashful suitor, who views at a distance the fair personage to whom, in his clownish awe, he dare not risk a near approach. Such is the clearest idea I can give you of my feeling towards children I like, but to whom I am a stranger. And to what children am I not a stranger? They seem to me little wonders; their talk, their ways are all matter of half-admiring, half-puzzled speculation.

---

[1] *London Labour and London Poor*, by Henry Mayhew, 1851.   [2] *Pre-Raphaelitism*, by John Ruskin, 1851.

701 (527). *To* Ellen Nussey.

August 17th, 1851.

Dear Ellen,—I write a line to you because I suppose you will be expecting me to answer your last—not because I have anything worth hearing to say.

You inquire about the plate: I have ordered none and it is very doubtful indeed whether I shall order any—certainly not at present; your Sister Ann therefore had better not wait for me.

I presume what you say about Catherine Swaine's being married is only a bit of Birstall gossip: surely it rests on no real foundation: it seems to me that for her to marry would be doing an unwise and even a wrong thing.

You will wonder about the papers not coming as usual last week—I never got the 'Leader' at all—I concluded they had given up sending it—but it has made its appearance again this morning—As to the 'Examiner'—Papa took a fancy to keep a long leading article about the Ecclesiastical Title's Bill—and also another on some other subject—accordingly he cut them out—and it was not worth while to send the paper thus mutilated—The French paper I despatch to-day.

Your account of Mr Harding possesses a certain interest from one's having often heard his name before. He seems to have impressed you rather favourably than otherwise. Joe Taylor described him as an enthusiastic man—but so coloured and turned his description as to give one the idea of a sort of spurious enthusiasm—something flighty and skin-deep. This is a low quality; as low as the genuine fire is lofty: That genuine fire is however so rare—I can scarcely believe in Harding's possessing it. His Scotch phiziognomy is however something in his favour—if Scotch it be.

I hope your Mother and all at Brookroyd continue pretty well—as Papa I am thankful to say—does—Tell me what you think of Georgiana &c. after you have paid your visit.—Yours faithfully,

C. Brontë.

702 (528). *To* ELLEN NUSSEY.

Monday Morning, September 1st, '51.

DEAR NELL,—I have mislaid your last letter and so cannot look it over to see what there is in it to be answered—but it is time it was answered in some fashion whether I have anything to say or not. Miss C. Wooler's note is very like her—all that talk about 'friendship' 'Auld-Lang syne'—'mutual friends &c.' sounds very like palaver. Mrs J. T. wrote to me a week or fortnight since—a well-meaning amiable little note—dwelling a good deal, excusably enough perhaps, on the good time that's coming—I mean to speak plain English, on her expectation of soon 'lying-in.' No doubt it is very natural in her to feel as if no woman had ever 'laid-in' before—but I could not help inditing an answer calculated to shake her up a bit. I wish however it were well over—for I suppose there really is additional doubt and hazard in the first time. A day or two since I had another note from her—quite good as usual—but I think a trifle nonplussed by the rather unceremonious fashion in which her terrors and the expected personage were previously handled—also there was a dictated note from her spouse—characteristic—how I smiled at it!

Amelia still keeps complaining much of your want of 'blooming looks' a figment I think—when—within the memory of man had you ever red cheeks? But she says that when you called there last week—you were in excellent spirits—a circumstance I was glad to hear. You will now I suppose soon be going into Sussex —so keep your courage up—

Mr Morgan was here last Monday, fat—well and hearty—he came to breakfast by nine o'clock—he brought me a lot of tracts as a present.

It is useless to tell you how I live—I endure life—but whether I enjoy it or not is another question—However I get on—The weather I think has not been good lately—or else the beneficial effects of change of air and scene are evaporating—in spite of regular exercise—the old head-aches—and starting wakeful nights are coming upon me again—But I *do* get on—and have neither wish nor right to complain. Have you yet seen your brother John? Georgiana would be the better of going out for a year as maid-of-all-work or plain cook in a respectable family.

Vol. III   t

Papa—it cheers me to say—has continued pretty well all the time of Mr Nicholls' absence—(he is now expected back before next Sunday) I hope your Mother is well—and Mercy 'blooming' (as A. says) and buxom—also Mr and Mrs Clapham—Yours faithfully,

C. BRONTË.

703. *To* GEORGE SMITH.

September 8th, 1851.

MY DEAR SIR,—I must summon courage to write a line; besides the vision of Mr Thackeray rising up, grand, with the laurel of Tasso about his brows, would rouse one out of a dead trance. Has he seen himself in this stately Italian garb, and does he like it?

Under the circumstances it is rather a singular coincidence that the same number of the 'Rivista Britannica' should contain a translation of one of Miss Martineau's tales, 'The Feats on the Fiord.' Enrichetta Martineau and Guglielmo Thackeray seem unconsciously matched against each other.

I see from the 'Leader' it is now generally known that Mr Thackeray is at work on a new novel. It was wise of him to leave England to write it; I do hope it will prove a masterpiece.

The 'John Drayton'[1] paragraph is a manœuvre worthy of the publisher of the 'Baroness von Beck's Memoirs.'[2] The book, it appears, is announced in conspicuous type as if it were to be something special. From the title I am inclined to expect an imitation of 'Mary Barton;' it sounds as if it were intended to belong to that school; but one ought not to judge from a title. I leave in your hands the treatment of all false rumours in which Currer Bell is concerned. Currer Bell has one publisher, and that is not Mr Bentley nor Mr Colburn.

I ought not to forget, and indeed have not forgotten, that your last propounds to this same Currer Bell a question about a 'serial'. My dear Sir, give Currer Bell the experience of a Thackeray or the animal spirit of a Dickens, and then repeat the question. Even *then* he would answer, 'I will publish no serial of which the last

[1] *John Drayton, being a History of the Early Life and Development of a Liverpool Engineer,* by William Wilson, 2 vols. 1851.

[2] *Adventures during the late War in Hungary,* by Baroness von Beck. 2 vols. 1850.

number is not written before the first comes out.' At present he would merely say that it is not worth your while to think of him.

I am glad you like the early rising on cold water system as prescribed by Miss Martineau. You must be sure and try it, first on yourself, and then you must coax Mr Thackeray as one of the 'authors with whom you have influence' to adopt it. Nothing can be better suited to the 'Portly Classes,' like the 'Trade;' nor perhaps, to the Anakim of Intellect, such as Miss Martineau and Mr Thackeray. But never mind the small fry, the wretched, thin, undersized scribblers; that Winter morning Walk by frosty starlight, that ice-cold bath and three tumblers of cold water would extinguish us altogether; and 'Small loss,' you would remark. Well, I incline to think so too. Meantime, believe one of them to be, Sincerely yours,

C. BRONTË.

704 (529). *To* ELLEN NUSSEY.

September 10th, 1851.

DEAR ELLEN,—I was indulging the hope that as you had not written again your mother was better; even after what you say, the impression left on my mind is that you are not to lose her yet. I think her constitutional tenacity of life will bear her through this attack, and perhaps others yet to come. We cannot be sure of this, but it is my strong persuasion; it is no doubt the turn of the year which is now trying her, and perhaps something more. The weather here has of late been peculiar; changing rapidly from hot to cold, its effects have been much felt by the old and weakly. Papa so far has borne it well. To-day is very beautiful. I trust it will favour your mother's improvement. One of the worst results of her illness may be that you will overfatigue yourself, and it is difficult to give advice on this point; you can but act for the best, and get fresh air and repose when it is in your power. I hope you will very soon write me a line however brief.—Yours faithfully,

C. BRONTË.

705 (530). *To* MARGARET WOOLER.

HAWORTH, September 13th, '51.

MY DEAR MISS WOOLER, —I have no intention of going from home during the next three weeks, but I wish you would just make up your mind to come to Haworth *now*. Miss Sarah might come too if you thought proper; and if it would be any pleasure to her, I should be glad to see her. At present the weather is fine; when it once breaks, it may be long before it settles again, and you would find the place too dull in wet weather. *Do come on Tuesday afternoon*, you and Miss Sarah.

Write a little note to me on Monday to say you will come, and I will have your room duly aired and all ready. —Sincerely and affectionately yours,

C. BRONTË.

706 (531). *To* ELLEN NUSSEY.

September 17th, 1851.

DEAR ELLEN, —I well know what you are now going through, and very sincerely in my heart do I feel with and for you, and very earnestly do I trust that the strength and patience you have so far manifested may be continued through the heavier trial which seems near. It appears to me, as to you, that those symptoms must be the precursors of dissolution. I fancy your brother will find his mother a little worse than in his cold-blooded tranquillity he seems to anticipate. Excuse the epithet 'cold-blooded' —it is richly deserved. Love him, however, as well as you can— make what allowance you can—he is your brother. Let him be brought face to face with Death as according to probabilities he seems likely to be; it will bring him a little to his senses.

I shall write no more. You need no advice. May God sustain you. —Yours faithfully,

C. BRONTË.

707 (532). *To* Ellen Nussey.

Saturday, September 20th, 1851.

Dear Ellen, — That scene you describe was truly trying and bitter, but accept it as an inevitable thing. These poor people acted, I believe, partly in dense ignorance as well as in pride. They cannot help being very vulgar in their mode of showing their feelings. Endure, pity, forgive as well as you can. But the 'unkindest cut' of all, and certainly the strangest, was your brother's conduct, yet it hardly surprised me. Illness sometimes makes an inexplicable rack of the mind, and unaccountably perverts the feelings. A seeming unkindness and ingratitude in beings tenderly loved and cherished and waited on in their sufferings with devoted patience is, I incline to believe, a species of torture oftener experienced than confessed; cruel is the anguish it strikes through the heart. I can only account for it by supposing that the soul is sick as well as the body. One knows not what the poor sufferers control and refuse in the way of peevish and unjust impulses. Alas! a sick-bed has heart-rending accompaniments. Courage, my dear Ellen. I can only wish you, in addition, comfort and peace. That your health will more or less suffer for all this must be expected.

Richard and Eliza[1] will have their overcast days sometime, and perhaps they will then see their present conduct in a different light to what they do now. — Believe me, yours faithfully,

C. Brontë.

Continue, dear Nell, to be as patient as you possibly can with ——. They are objects of pity. I could break out in strong language, but resist.

708 (533). *To* Mrs Gaskell.

September 20th, 1851.

. . . Beautiful are those sentences out of James Martineau's sermons; some of them gems most pure and genuine; ideas deeply conceived, finely expressed. I should like much to see his review of his sister's book. Of all the articles respecting which you question me I have seen none, except that notable one in the 'West-

---

[1] Mrs Richard Nussey.

minster' on the Emancipation of Women. But why are you and I to think (perhaps I should rather say to *feel*) so exactly alike on some points that there can be no discussion between us? Your words on this paper express my thoughts. Well argued it is — clear, logical — but vast is the hiatus of omission; harsh the consequent jar on every finer chord of the soul. What is this hiatus? I think I know; and knowing, I will venture to say. I think the writer forgets there is such a thing as self-sacrificing love and disinterested devotion. When I first read the paper, I thought it was the work of a powerful, clear-headed woman, who had a hard, jealous heart, and nerves of bend[1] leather; of a woman who longed for power, and had never felt affection. To many women, affection is sweet, and power conquered indifferent — though we all like influence won. I believe J. S. Mill would make a hard dry, dismal world of it; and yet he speaks admirable sense through a great portion of his article, especially when he says that if there be a natural unfitness in women for men's employment there is no need to make laws on the subject; leave all careers open; let them try; those who ought to succeed will succeed, or, at least, will have a fair chance; the incapable will fall back into their right place. He likewise disposes of the 'maternity' question very neatly. In short, J. S. Mill's head is, I dare say, very good, but I feel disposed to scorn his heart. You are right when you say that there is a large margin in human nature over which the logicians have no dominion; glad am I that it is so.[2]

I send by this post Ruskin's 'Stones of Venice,' and I hope you and Meta will find passages in it that will please you. Some parts would be dry and technical were it not for the character, the marked individuality, which pervades every page. I wish Marianne had come to speak to me at the lecture; it would have given me such pleasure. What you say of that small sprite Julia amuses me very much. I believe you don't know that she has a great deal of her mamma's nature (modified) in her, yet I think you will find she has as she grows up.

---

[1]'Bend,' in Yorkshire is strong ox leather.

[2]J. S. Mill, in a letter upon this passage says: 'I am not the author of the article. I may claim to be its editor: and I should be proud to be identified with every thought, every sentiment, and every expression in it. The writer is a woman, and the most warm-hearted woman, of the largest and most genial sympathies, and the most forgetful of self in her generous zeal to do honour to others, whom I have ever known.'

John Stuart Mill (1806–1873) married in 1851 Mrs John Taylor, the writer of the article referred to.

Will it not be a great mistake if Mr Thackeray should deliver his lectures at Manchester under such circumstances and conditions as will exclude people like you and Mr Gaskell from the number of his audience? I thought his London plan too narrow. Charles Dickens would not thus limit his sphere of action.

You charge me to write about myself. What can I say on that precious topic? My health is pretty good. My spirits are not always alike. Nothing happens to me. I hope and expect little in this world, and am thankful that I do not despond and suffer more. Thank you for inquiring after our old servant; she is pretty well; the little shawl, etc., pleased her much. Papa, likewise, I am glad to say, is pretty well. With his and my kindest regards to you and Mr Gaskell, believe me sincerely and affectionately yours,

C. BRONTË.

709. *To* GEORGE SMITH.

September 22nd, 1851.

MY DEAR SIR,—I am sure I am not low-spirited just now, but very happy, and in this mood I will write to you.

That enclosed copy of a letter (ought I to return it?) gave me great pleasure; it is comforting to be useful; it is pleasant to see a sprouting greenness where seed has been sown. I doubt not my well-intentioned preface remarks have ere this brought on you and Mr Williams the annoyance of accumulated rubbish, and it would be hard indeed if amongst all the chaff should not now and then occur a few grains of wheat. I trust this may be the case in the present instance; I wish that from these grains may spring a promising crop.

Can I help wishing you well when I owe you directly or indirectly most of the good moments I now enjoy? Or can I avoid feeling grieved—mortified—when the chance of aiding to give effect to my own wishes offers itself and, for want of strength, vitality, animal spirits, I know not what in me, passes by unimproved? Oh, that serial! It is of no use telling you what a storm in a teacup the mention of it stirred in Currer Bell's mind, what a fight he had with himself about it. You do not know, you *cannot* know, how strongly his nature inclines him to adopt suggestions coming from so friendly a quarter; how he would like to take

them up, cherish them, give them form, conduct them to a successful issue; and how sorrowfully he turns away, feeling in his
inmost heart that this work, this pleasure is not for him.

But though Currer Bell cannot do this you are still to think
him your friend, and you are still to be *his* friend. You are to
keep a fraction of yourself—if it be only the end of your little
finger—for *him*, and that fraction he will neither let gentleman
or lady, author or artist, not even Miss McCrowdie (the Scotch
gentlewoman whose portrait you so graphically depict), take
possession of, or so much as meddle with. He reduces his claim to
a minute point, and that point he monopolises.

I won't say I don't rather like Miss Girzy McCrowdie. I believe one might get on with her pretty well. After all, depend on
it, there would be a rude sort of worth in her.

What is it you say about my breaking the interval between
this and Christmas by going from home for a week? No; if there
were no other objection (and there are many) there is the pain of
that last bidding good-bye, that hopeless shaking hands, yet
undulled and unforgotten. I don't like it. I could not bear its
frequent repetition. Do not recur to this plan. Going to London
is a mere palliation and stimulant: reaction follows.

Meantime I really do get on very well; not always alike, and I
have been at intervals despondent; but Providence is kind, and
hitherto whenever depression passes a certain point some incident transpires to turn the current, to lighten the load; a cheering
sunrise so far ever followed a night of peculiar vigil and fear.
Hope, indeed, is not a plant to flourish very luxuriantly in this
northern climate, but still it throws out fresh leaves and a blos-
som now and then, proving that it is far from dead; and as for
Fortitude, Miss McCrowdie herself will tell you what tenacious
roots that shrub twines in a stony, moorish soil. Please to give
my love to your Mother and sisters, and believe me—Yours sincerely and faithfully,

C. BRONTË.

710 (534). *To* MARGARET WOOLER.

HAWORTH, September 22nd, 1851.

MY DEAR MISS WOOLER,—Our visitor (a relative from Cornwall)[1] having left us, the coast is now clear, so that whenever you

¹Mr T. Brontë Branwell, Charlotte's cousin.

feel inclined to come, papa and I will be truly glad to see you. I *do* wish the splendid weather we have had and are having may accompany you here. I fear I have somewhat grudged the fine days, fearing a change before you come.—Believe me, with papa's regards, yours respectfully and affectionately,

C. BRONTË.

Come soon; if you can, on Wednesday.

711 (535). *To* W. S. WILLIAMS.

September 26th, 1851.

As I laid down your letter, after reading with interest the graphic account it gives of a very striking scene, I could not help feeling with renewed force a truth, trite enough, yet ever impressive, viz. that it is good to be attracted out of ourselves, to be forced to take a near view of the sufferings, the privations, the efforts, the difficulties of others. If we ourselves live in fulness of content, it is well to be reminded that thousands of our fellow creatures undergo a different lot; it is well to have sleepy sympathies excited, and lethargic selfishness shaken up. If, on the other hand, we be contending with the special grief, the intimate trial—the peculiar bitterness with which God has seen fit to mingle our own cup of existence, it is very good to know that our overcast lot is not singular; it stills the repining word and thought—it rouses the flagging strength, to have it vividly set before us that there are countless afflictions in the world, each perhaps rivalling—some surpassing—the private pain over which we are too prone exclusively to sorrow.

All those crowded emigrants had their troubles—their untoward causes of banishment; you, the looker-on, had 'your wishes and regrets'—your anxieties, alloying your home happiness and domestic bliss; and the parallel might be pursued further, and still it would be true—still the same; a thorn in the flesh for each; some burden, some conflict for all.

How far this state of things is susceptible of amelioration from changes in public institutions—alterations in national habits—may and ought to be earnestly considered: but this is a problem not easily solved. The evils, as you point them out, are great, real, and most obvious: the remedy is obscure and vague; yet for such difficulties as spring from over-competition emigration must be good; the new life in a new country must give a new lease of hope; the wider field, less thickly peopled, must open a new path for endeavour. But I always think great physical powers of exertion and endurance ought to accompany such a step. . . . I am truly glad to hear that an *original* writer has fallen in your way. Originality is the pearl of great price in literature — the rarest, the most precious claim by which an author can be recommended. Are not your publishing prospects for the coming season tolerably rich and satisfactory? You inquire after 'Currer Bell.' It seems to me that the absence of his name from your list of announcements will leave no blank, and that he may at least spare himself the disquietude of thinking he is wanted when it is certainly not his lot to appear.

Perhaps Currer Bell has his secret moan about these matters; but if so he will keep it to himself. It is an affair about which no words need be wasted, for no words can make a change; it is between him and his position, his faculties and his fate, and so saying he bids you a somewhat hurried good-bye and begs to remain — Sincerely yours,

C. B.

712 (536). *To* ELLEN NUSSEY.

October 3rd, 1851.

DEAR NELL, — Do not think I have forgotten you because I have not written since your last; every day I have had you more or less in my thoughts and wondered how your mother was getting on; let me have a line of information as soon as possible. I have been busy, first with a somewhat unexpected visitor, a cousin from Cornwall who has been spending a few days with us, and now with Miss Wooler who came on Monday. The former personage we can discuss any time when we meet. Miss Wooler is and has been very pleasant. She is like good wine; I think time improves her, and really, whatever she may be in person, in mind she is younger than when at Roe Head. Papa and she get on extremely well; I have just heard papa walk into the dining-room and pay her a round compliment on her good sense. I think so far she has been pretty comfortable and likes Haworth, but as she only brought a small hand-basket of luggage with her she cannot stay long.

How are *you*? Write directly. With my love to your mother, etc., good-bye, dear Nell. — Yours faithfully,

C. BRONTË.

713. *To* MARGARET WOOLER.

HAWORTH, Octbr 21st, 1851.

MY DEAR MISS WOOLER,—I had waited somewhat impatiently for your note and was glad to get it. It had been my fear that you would be disappointed about the donkey—and would have the whole distance to accomplish by your own unaided exertions. So it appears it turned out. Well might you be tired; the walk was indeed too long; it is well you had patience to take so much time at the last; had you hurried I am sure you would have been knocked up. However since you are not made ill by the great fatigue, there is, on the whole, more reason for gratitude than regret.

You very kindly refer with pleasure to your brief stay with us. My dear Miss Wooler—the visit was an enjoyment to me too—a *true* enjoyment; your society raised my spirits in a way that surprised myself—and which you could only appreciate by seeing me as I am alone—a spectacle happily not likely to come in your way. You speak of attentions rendered: I was not sensible of having made any exertion: to make you comfortable would be to make myself happy—but you would hardly permit me the opportunity of trying to do so.

I am glad that Mrs Moore has written to you; her capacity to do this proves that she is so far spared a measure of strength to bear up under her great trial—great indeed must it be—yet who knows but a kind Providence may turn it somehow to the good of herself and family—It is true we cannot now see how—but ways that are obscure to us—may be plain to God: joys seem often to have their root in griefs—as pains are certainly the frequent and swift successors of pleasures.

Papa enjoins me to give you his best respects and to say he hopes ere long to see you at Haworth again. He would not say this unless he meant it. Tabby and Martha have each with simple sincerity expressed the same wish; in short (D.V.) you will be *obliged* to visit us again some time—but then there must be a clear understanding to begin with that when you come you will remain a fortnight or three weeks—and thus you can settle and not have your tranquillity broken by the thought that you ought to go.

Remember me kindly to Miss Sarah and believe me — my dear Miss Wooler — Yours respectfully and affectionately,

C. BRONTË.

P.S. The subject of the theme about which you enquire was 'Human Justice.'

I have heard lately from E. Nussey and from Hunsworth. Mrs Nussey continues better. I am sorry to say the little baby at Hunsworth has been ill and does not thrive — the asses' milk not agreeing with it. Mrs Joe Taylor's sister who was married shortly after herself has just got a fine little boy. Letters have been recently received from Mary and Ellen Taylor in New Zealand — I wished I could have shewn one of these to you — it gives such a thoroughly characteristic notion of their way of life. According to the description it contained of their sitting-room — neither of them were in the way of meriting the Roe-Head Neatness Prize: they deserve on the contrary loss of tickets and an early adjournment to bed. More shame to them.

C. B.

714. *To* MRS JAMES.

KNUTSFORD, Oct. 29th, 1851.

MY DEAR MRS JAMES, — ... I see that Mr Thackeray is bringing out a three-volume novel;[1] and our nice little friend Miss Mulock[2] is advertising another. I wish she had some other means of support besides writing. I think it bad in its effect upon her writing, which must be pumped up, instead of bubbling out; and very bad for her health, poor girl. I heard of your kind way of occasionally taking her a drive, and I silently thanked you for it. But I think that Miss Brontë had hold of the true idea when she said to me, last summer, 'If I had to earn my living I would go out as a governess again, much as I dislike the life; but I think one should only write out of the fulness of one's heart spontaneously.' ... — Yours most truly,

E. C. GASKELL.[3]

---

[1] In October, 1851, Messrs Smith Elder & Co. announced the forthcoming publication of A Novel. By W. M. Thackeray. This was *The History of Henry Esmond*, which was published in October, 1852.

[2] Dinah Maria Mulock (Mrs Craik), (1826–1887) wrote many novels including *The Ogilvies*, 1849: *The Head of the Family*, 1851: *Agatha's Husband*, 1852: *Bread Upon the Waters*, 1852: *John Halifax, Gentleman*, 1856: and others.

[3] This letter is printed in *Letters on Charlotte Brontë* by Mrs Gaskell, 25 copies privately printed for Clement Shorter.

715 (537). *To* ELLEN NUSSEY.

[Oct. 30th, 1851].

DEAR ELLEN,—I am not at all intending to go from home at present—I have just refused successively Miss Martineau—Mrs Gaskell and Mrs Forster—I could not go if I would—one person after another in the house has been ailing for the last month and more, first Tabby had the influenza—then Martha took it—and is ill in bed now—with quinsey (her 2nd attack) in addition—and I grieve to say, Papa too has taken cold—so far I keep pretty well—and am thankful for it—for who else could nurse them all—

Some painful mental worry I have gone through this Autumn but there is no use in dwelling on all that—At present I seem to have some respite. I feel more disinclined than ever for letter-writing.

I am glad that your Mother is better and glad that the Hunsworth people are going on well. I hope your cold will not prove a bad one. Cease to expect me at Brookroyd—I would rather you came to Haworth—I should see more of you. Life is a struggle. Good bye.—Yours sincerely,

C. B.

716 (538). *To* ELLEN NUSSEY.

November 4th, '51.

DEAR ELLEN,—Papa, Tabby, and Martha are at present all better, yet none of them well. Martha at present looks feeble, I wish she had a better constitution; as it is, one is always afraid of giving her too much to do, and yet there are many things I cannot undertake myself, and we do not like to change when we have had her so long. How are you getting on in the matter of servants? The other day I received a long letter from India. I had had one before from the same quarter which is still unanswered. I told you I did not expect to hear thence, nor did I. The letter is long, but it is worth your while to read it. In its way it has merit, that cannot be denied; abundance of information, talent of a certain kind, alloyed (I think) here and there with errors of taste. He might have spared many of the details of the bath scene, which for the rest tallies exactly with Mr Thackeray's account of the same process. This little man with all his long letters remains as much a conundrum to me as ever. Your account of the domestic joys at Hunsworth amused me much. The good folks seem very happy, long may they continue so! It somewhat cheers me to know that such happiness *does* exist on the earth. Return Mr Taylor's letter when you have read it. With love to your mother, I am, dear Nell, sincerely yours,

C. B.

717 (539). *To* W. S. WILLIAMS.

Novbr 6th, 1851.

MY DEAR SIR, —I have true pleasure in enclosing for your Son Frank—a letter of introduction to Mrs Gaskell—and earnestly do I trust the acquaintance may tend to his good. To make all sure —(for I dislike to go on doubtful grounds) I wrote to ask her if she would permit the introduction—her frank kind answer pleased me greatly.

I have received the books. I hope to write again when I have read 'the Fair Carew'[1]—the very title augurs well—it has no hackneyed sound. —Believe me, Sincerely yours,

C. BRONTË.

718 (540). *To* MRS GASKELL.

November 6th, 1851.

If anybody would tempt me from home you would; but, just now, from home I must not, will not go. I feel greatly better at present than I did three weeks ago. For a month or six weeks about the equinox (autumnal or vernal) is a period of the year which, I have noticed, strangely tries me. Sometimes the strain falls on the mental, sometimes on the physical part of me; I am ill with neuralgic headache, or I am ground to the dust with deep dejection of spirits (not, however, such dejection but I can keep to myself). That weary time has, I think and trust, got over for this year. It was the anniversary of my poor brother's death, and of my sister's failing health: I need say no more.

As to running away from home every time I have a battle of this sort to fight, it would not do: besides the 'weird' would follow. As to shaking it off, that cannot be. I have declined to go

[1] *The Fair Carew; or, Husbands and Wives,* by Miss Bigger, 1851.

to Mrs Forster, to Miss Martineau, and now I decline to go to you. But listen! do not think that I throw your kindness away, or that it fails of doing the good you desire. On the contrary, the feeling expressed in your letter—proved by your invitation— goes *right home* where you would have it to go, and heals as you would have it to heal.

Your description of Frederika Bremer tallies exactly with one I read somewhere, in I know not what book. I laughed out when I got to the mention of Frederika's special accomplishment, given by you with a distinct simplicity that, to my taste, is what the French would call 'impayable.' Where do you find the foreigner who is without some little drawback of this description? It is a pity.

C. BRONTË.

719. *To* GEORGE SMITH.

November 7th, 1851.

MY DEAR SIR,—I enclose a note just received from Miss Martineau. She wishes to put the name 'Edward Howard' on the title-page of her book. Is there any objection? I told her I could see none. I fear she is a good deal disappointed that I cannot go to see her this winter and talk the work over, as I half promised, but the fact is several people have asked me to pay them visits; it is almost impossible to select without giving offence, and if I went to all I should be continually rambling about and never at home with my father, which would not do. Besides, I should . . . unsettled as not to have the . . . chance of doing any work of my . . . may be a dreary thought, a blank . . . but I must absolutely get accustomed to a life of solitude; there is no other plan.

The enclosure in your last puzzled me a little at first, being of a larger amount than I expected; but I remember now you said something at Richmond about having some money for me. I wanted to know how that happened, and what it came from, feeling a little sceptical. You did not tell me. I did not like to ask you twice. If, however, you had any cash that was *justly* mine, you did right to put it in the Funds with the rest. I am sorry to hear that your undertakings in India are likely to be harassed by what seems scarcely honourable competition. God defend the right!—Believe me, Sincerely yours,

C. BRONTË.

720. *To* W. S. WILLIAMS.

November 10th, 1851.

MY DEAR SIR,—I have now read 'The Fair Carew.' It seems to me a delightful work and of genuine metal. Whether it has the glare and strong excitement necessary to attract the million I do not know, but I find in it the ease and repose only seen in good books. It owns both breadth of outline and delicacy of finish, sufficient force, and the most facile flow. The truth and nature of the characters are beyond praise; the satire has a keen edge, yet the temper of the work is good and genial. This writer is as shrewd as Miss Austen and not so shrewish, as interesting as Mrs Inchbald and more vigorous. Now and then I was reminded of Thackeray's wit and wisdom, but never of his vinegar and gall. The interest is strongest in the latter half of the first volume, yet for me the narrative never flagged; where I was not spellbound I was charmed and amused. Who and what is this lady? Is she young or middle-aged?—Yours sincerely,

C. BRONTË.

I return Mr Thackeray's little illustrated note. How excellent is Goldsmith issuing in full-blown complacency from Filby's shop, with Dr Johnson walking half benignant, half sarcastic by his side! Captain Steele, too, is very good. Surely if Mr Thackeray undertook to furnish illustrations he would not be troublesome and procrastinating about what he can dash off so easily and rapidly.

721 (541 and 559). *To* JAMES TAYLOR, *Bombay.*

HAWORTH, November 15th, 1851.

MY DEAR SIR,—Both your communications reached me safely —the note of the 17th September and the letter of the 2nd October. You do yourself less than justice when you stigmatise the latter as 'ill-written.' I found it quite legible, nor did I lose a word, though the lines and letters were so close. I should have been sorry if such had not been the case, as it appeared to me throughout highly interesting. It is observable that the very same information which we have previously collected, perhaps with rather languid attention, from printed books, when placed before us in familiar manuscript, and comprising the actual experience of a person with whom we are acquainted, acquires a new and vital interest: when we know the narrator we seem to realise the tale.

The BATH scene amused me much. Your account of that operation tallies in every point with Mr Thackeray's description in the 'Journey from Cornhill to Grand Cairo.' The usage seems a little rough, and I cannot help thinking that equal benefit might be obtained through less violent means; but I suppose without the previous fatigue the after-sensation would not be so enjoyable, and no doubt it is that indolent after-sensation which the self-indulgent Mahometans chiefly cultivate. I think you did right to disdain it.

It would seem to me a matter of great regret that the society at Bombay should be so deficient in all intellectual attraction. Perhaps, however, your occupations will so far absorb your thoughts as to prevent them from dwelling painfully on this circumstance. No doubt there will be moments when you will look back to London and Scotland, and the friends you have left there, with some yearning; but I suppose business has its own excitement. The new country, the new scenes too, must have their interest; and as you will not lack books to fill your leisure, you will probably soon become reconciled to a change which, for some minds would too closely resemble exile.

I fear the climate — such as you describe it — must be very trying to an European constitution. In your first letter, you mentioned October as the month of danger; it is now over. Whether you have passed its ordeal safely must yet for some weeks remain unknown to your friends in England — they can but *wish* that such may be the case. You will not expect me to write a letter that shall form a parallel with your own either in quantity or quality; what I write must be brief, and what I communicate must be commonplace and of trivial interest.

I spent a few weeks in town last summer, as you have heard, and was much interested by many things I heard and saw there. What now chiefly dwells in my memory are Mr Thackeray's lectures, Mademoiselle Rachel's acting, D'Aubigné's, Melvill's, and Maurice's preaching, and the Crystal Palace.

Mr Thackeray's lectures you will have seen mentioned and commented on in the papers; they were very interesting. I could not always coincide with the sentiments expressed, or the opinions broached; but I admired the gentlemanlike ease, the quiet humour, the taste, the talent, the simplicity, and the originality of the lecturer.

Rachel's acting transfixed me with wonder, enchained me with interest, and thrilled me with horror. The tremendous force with which she expresses the very worst passions in their strongest essence forms an exhibition as exciting as the bull-fights of Spain and the gladiatorial combats of old Rome, and (it seemed to me) not one whit more moral than these poisoned stimulants to popular ferocity. It is scarcely human nature that she shows you; it is something wilder and worse; the feelings and fury of a fiend. The great gift of genius she undoubtedly has; but, I fear, she rather abuses it than turns it to good account.

With all the three preachers I was greatly pleased. Melvill seemed to me the most eloquent, Maurice the most in earnest; had I the choice, it is Maurice whose ministry I should frequent.

On the Crystal Palace I need not comment. You must already have heard too much of it. It struck me at the first with only a vague sort of wonder and admiration; but having one day the privilege of going over it in company with an eminent countryman of yours, Sir David Brewster, and hearing, in his friendly Scotch accent, his lucid explanation of many things that have been to me before a sealed book, I began a little better to comprehend it, or at least a small part of it; whether its final results will equal expectation I know not.

My father, I am thankful to say, continues in pretty good health. I read portions of your letter to him and he was interested in hearing them. He charged me when I wrote to convey his very kind remembrances.

I had myself ceased to expect a letter from you. On taking leave at Haworth you said something about writing from India, but I doubted at the time whether it was not one of those forms of speech which politeness dictates; and as time passed, and I did not hear from you, I became confirmed in this view of the subject. With every good wish for your welfare, —I am, yours sincerely,

C. BRONTË.

722 (542). *To* ELLEN NUSSEY.

Novbr 19th, 1851.

DEAR ELLEN,—All here is pretty much as usual—and I was thinking of writing to you this morning when I received your note. I am glad to hear that your Mother bears the severe weather tolerably—as Papa does also. I had a cold—chiefly in the throat and chest—but I applied a towel dipped in cold water which relieved me of the heat and soreness—far better I think than any hot application would have done. How are you?

The only events of my life consist in that little change occasional letters bring. I have had two from Miss Wooler since she left Haworth which touched me much—She seems to think so much of a little congenial company—a little attention and kindness—that I am afraid these things are rare to her—she says she has not for many days known such enjoyment as she experienced during the ten days she stayed here—Yet you know what Haworth is—dull enough.

How could you imagine your last letter offended me? I only disagreed with you on one point—the little man's hardy disdain of the sensual pleasure of a Turkish Bath had—I must own—my approval. I thought the better of him for it.

Before answering his epistle—I got up my courage to write to Mr Williams—through whose hands or those of Mr S.—I knew the Indian letter had come—and beg him to give me an impartial judgment of Mr Taylor's character and disposition—owning that I was very much in the dark on these points and did not like to continue correspondence without further information—I got the answer which I enclose. Since receiving it—I have replied to Mr T.—in a calm civil manner. At the earliest I cannot hear from him again before Feby or March.

Return this document when you have read it. You say nothing about the Hunsworth Turtle-Doves, how are they—and how is the branch of promise? I hope doing well.—Yours faithfully,

C. BRONTË.

723. *To* ANN SHAEN.

Nov. 1851.

... Here is a note from Miss Brontë, oppressed by the monotony and solitude of her life. She has seen *no one* but her Father since 3rd of July last. ...

[E. C. GASKELL].

724. *To* GEORGE SMITH.

[Undated].

MY DEAR SIR,—Miss Martineau was much pleased with your last, which she sent me to look at. Decidedly it was not bad (I must not say it was *good*, for that would be a 'comfit'); besides, though there are many things which might be said on that head and in connection therewith, it is not necessary; yourself must speak to yourself; but I will tell you a thing to be noted, often in your letters and almost always in your conversation, a psychological thing, and not a matter pertaining to style or intellect: I mean an undercurrent of quiet raillery, an inaudible laugh to yourself, a not unkindly but somewhat subtle playing on your correspondent or companion for the time being—in short, a sly touch of a Mephistopheles with the fiend extracted. In the present instance this speciality is perceptible only in the slightest degree—quite imperceptible for the world—but it *is* there, and more or less you have it always. I by no means mention this as a *fault*, I merely tell you you have it. And I can make the accusation with comfortable impunity, guessing pretty surely that you are too busy just now to deny this or any other charge.

Miss M. has taken a little scruple into her head that she is doing rather an unhandsome thing to me in making me the instrument of engaging my publisher to publish her book. This notion entirely amuses me; but I rather prefer she should view it in that light than imagine I showed any marked eagerness in encouraging the idea of her offering you the MS.

I am glad the matter is now settled, as she says when she once begins she will work steadily. She knows nothing about my Quakerlike waiting on the spirit; that is not her plan, nor her nature. So much the better. I am very glad to find you have been to Hastings, though only for two days.—Believe me, Sincerely yours,   C. BRONTË.

725. *To* George Smith.

November 20th, 1851.

My dear Sir,—I have the pleasure of forwarding another letter from Miss Martineau. I use the word *pleasure* because you and she will recur to the notion that it must somehow be a trouble to me to act as medium. Indeed, it is no trouble; far otherwise. You will see from what she says that her plan is expanding and soaring. In a note to myself accompanying yours she expresses high and enthusiastic hopes of the success of the book. I tell her not to be too sanguine, and will venture to whisper the same to you. She is in fine spirits now, and they may last to the end, thus enabling her to achieve a great work, but she *may* also be seeing things a little too much under the rose-colour light of an excited imagination. There is something about her nature very buoyant and difficult to subdue. I think you were quite right in what you said about the name.

That anecdote in the 'Times' is evidently of Mr Thackeray's own telling. It bears his stamp upon it. In reading it I seemed to realise his look and voice. Can it be literally true?

I have been able to work a little lately, but I have quite made up my mind not to publish till Mr Thackeray's and Miss Martineau's books have had full career, so you will not think of me till next autumn, or thereabouts; is not this for the best? Meantime it is perhaps premature in me even to allude to the subject, but I do it partly to explain one of my motives for remaining at home this winter. Winter is a better time for working than summer; less liable to interruption. If I could always work, time would not be long, nor hours sad to me; but blank and heavy intervals still occur, when power and will are at variance. This, however, is talking Greek to an eminent and spirited publisher. He does not believe in such things.

'The Fair Carew,' it seems, is now fairly out. I hope it will receive from the press and the public a just and a discriminating reception. That it is really a good book, though not showy, I maintain. I have glanced at some chapters of another novel of yours—'Florence Sackville.'[1] This, too, appears to me to possess no common merit, though I have not as yet recognised in it

[1] *Florence Sackville; or, Self-Dependence.* By Mrs Burbury. 1851.

the small, quiet, sterling stamp perceptible in 'The Fair Carew,'
but I am only beginning it. — Believe me, Sincerely yours,

C. BRONTË.

726. *To* GEORGE SMITH.

HAWORTH, November 28th, 1851.

MY DEAR SIR, — I *did* see the notice of 'The Fair Carew' in the
'Leader,' and I read the 'Spectator' which you sent me. The first
struck me as a disgrace to Mr Lewes (it was evidently the production of his accomplished pen). That gentleman has, when he
chooses to use it, very good critical acumen, and even possesses
in the midst of his presumption and flippancy an instinctive
sense of justice, as well as the germ of a kind of generosity; in this
instance he shamelessly flings aside all these good properties.
But I cannot believe he really read the book. He must surely have
taken it up in some dull, sleepy mood, turned the pages three or
four at a time, and sat down to write his critique when he ought
to have put on his nightcap and gone to bed.

That in the 'Spectator' is a much more honest notice, though
infinitely stupid. The poor man used what faculties he had, but
the faculty of judging a work of fiction is not amongst his talents.
That worthy critic had no perception for originality of thought
or nicety of delineation; he is blind as a bat and profoundly satisfied with his blindness. However, if it be any consolation to Miss
Bigger, she may be told that the 'Spectator' has treated 'The
Fair Carew' with much more respect than it treated 'Jane Eyre;
of the latter its most salient remark was that the conception and
characters of the book reminded him (the critic) of nothing so
much as the grotesque and hideous masks of apes, wolves, and
griffins to be found in the carved works of certain old cathedrals.
It was in his estimation a morbid monkish fancy, a thing with the
head of an owl, the tail of a fox, and the talons of an eagle.

'Florence Sackville' is a clever book, as you say, and an interesting book of an order quite inferior to 'The Fair Carew,' yet
meriting both praise and success. What 'The Fair Carew' lacks is
the striking, the effective, the exciting — just what Mr Thackeray
lacks; and, as he once said to Currer Bell with some bitterness,
'I worked ten years before I achieved a real success,' intimating
at the same time that the said 'Currer Bell' had won his small

first-work conquest a great deal too cheaply, which would have been true only that Currer Bell had worked quite as long as Mr Thackeray, without publishing.

Mr Thackeray, by-the-bye, richly deserves what he has got in the 'Times.' He is very neatly caught in one of those elaborate nets he delights in skilfully laying for others, and there he now flounders, like the big Leviathan he is, a spectacle to England. It is his due punishment for telling your mother fictions about the Duke of Devonshire, a fact which struck me as a piece of bad manners. At his size and age he ought to have outgrown the practice of telling fibs. Dr Plumptre has put him in the corner; the proper place for him till he promises to be a good boy and 'never do so no more.'

I have no doubt that Miss Martineau's opinion of her own work, as far as it has yet advanced, may be implicitly relied on. She is no self-flatterer, but, I think, disposed to be as honest with herself as with others. The only fear is that she may be a little too sanguine in auguring from a brilliant commencement a triumphant finale.

It is not at all likely that my book will be ready at the time you mention. If my health is spared I shall get on with it as fast as is consistent with its being done, if not well, yet as well as I can do it, *not one whit faster*. When the mood leaves me (it has left me now, without vouchsafing so much as a word of a message when it will return) I put by the MS. and wait till it comes back again; and God knows I sometimes have to wait long —*very* long it seems to me.

Meantime, if I might make a request to you, it would be this; Please to say nothing about my book till it is written and in your hands. You may not like it. I am not myself elated with it as far as it has gone, and authors, you need not be told, are always tenderly indulgent, even blindly partial, to their own; even if it should turn out reasonably well, still I regard it as ruin to the prosperity of an ephemeral book like a novel to be much talked about beforehand, as if it were something great. People are apt to conceive, or at least to profess, exaggerated expectations, such as no performance can realise; then ensue disappointment and the due revenge —detraction and failure. If, when I write, I were to think of the critics who, I know, are waiting for Currer Bell, ready 'to break all his bones or ever he comes to the bottom of the den,' my hand would fall paralysed on my desk. However, I can but do my best, and then muffle my head in the mantel of Patience and sit down at her feet and wait.

Your Mother and sisters are very kind to think of my coming to see them at Christmas, but you must give them my best regards and say that such a step is not to be thought of. Tell your mother not to ask me, because I could only repeat what I have said above. This Winter I must stay at home. — Believe me always

   Sincerely yours,

C. Brontë.

CHAPTER XXVII

A DREARY WINTER

DURING the autumn of 1851 Charlotte had been in very indifferent health; she seemed to suffer from a reaction to the excitement of the previous summer, and became very depressed. In December her illness increased; she thought a little cheerful society might do her good, and invited Ellen Nussey to stay with her. She enjoyed her friend's company for a few days, during which time she seemed a little better, but the improvement was only temporary, and shortly afterwards she had a relapse and became seriously ill. By the end of January she was sufficiently recovered to make a journey to Brookroyd, where she remained for about a fortnight, carefully tended by her good friends the Nusseys. This visit cheered Charlotte immensely, her only regret being that she had not delayed her visit a few days longer in order to meet Mr George Smith, who had paid an unexpected visit to the Parsonage during her absence.

After her return home, Charlotte's health gradually improved, but in spite of repeated invitations from her friends she decided to remain quietly at Haworth. She did not leave home again until the end of May, when she decided to take a holiday on the East Coast, to visit her sister Anne's grave at Scarborough in order to have the gravestone refaced and re-lettered. She took lodgings at Filey, where she remained for a month.

Owing to her ill-health and consequent depressed spirits during the first six months of 1852, Charlotte had found it impossible to make any progress with her novel *Villette*, to the great disappointment of her publishers, who, however, had very kindly continued to send her a selection of books to cheer her isolated and lonely life.

One thing shown by the letters of this period is that Mr James Taylor had made a deeper impression on Charlotte's mind and heart than she had been conscious of hitherto; and that had 'the little man' as she so frequently termed him, come hastily over from Bombay, he might have won for his wife one of the most distinguished writers of her day.

727 (543). *To* ELLEN NUSSEY.

December, 1851.

DEAR ELLEN,—I hope you have got on this last week well. It has been very trying here. Papa so far has borne it unhurt, but these winds and changes have given me a bad cold of influenza character. However, I am better now than I was. Poor old

"KEEPER."

Keeper died last Monday morning; after being ill all night, he went gently to sleep. We laid his old faithful head in the garden. Flossy is dull and misses him. There was something very sad in losing the old dog; yet I am glad he met a natural fate; people kept hinting he ought to be put away, which neither papa nor I liked to think of. If I were near a town and could get cod-liver oil, fresh and sweet, I really would most gladly take your advice and try it, but how I could possibly procure it at Haworth I do not see. We have got curtains for the dining-room. I ordered them at the Factory to be dyed crimson, but they are badly dyed and do not please me.

I am truly glad to hear of your mother's improvement. The doctors cannot now deny that she has fairly given them the slip. I admire her, clever old lady!

You ask me about the 'Lily and the Bee.'[1] If you have read it dear Ellen, you have effected an exploit beyond me. I glanced at a few pages and laid it down hopeless, nor can I find courage to resume it. But then I never liked Warren's writings. 'Margaret Maitland'[2] is a good book I doubt not, and will just suit your mother. —I am, yours faithfully,

C. Brontë.

728 *To* Harriet Martineau.

December 10th, 1851.

My dear Miss Martineau,—Begging Mr Smith's pardon, '*Peter*' Murray, to my thinking, won't do. 'Murray' is very well, but against 'Peter' I protest with lifted hands and eyes. It reminds me of 'Peter Parley,' 'Peter Peebles,' and a dozen other 'Peters,' and in another way sounds quite as fictitious as 'Edward Howard,' with the disadvantage of being less euphonious.

Allow me to introduce and earnestly recommend to your good graces Alexander F. Murray, Esq. (F. being supposed to stand for 'Frazer'); the initial, depend on it, will tell well, coming in with the most innocent air of reality imaginable.

Do tell Mr Smith when you write again that you will be called Alexander Frazer Murray, and return him his loan of 'Peter' with compliments.

'Oliver Weld' seems to me excellent. I like the sound and the look of it.

After some deliberation, some Epicurean balancing between the comparative advantages of tasting my peach now or leaving it to hang untouched a few months longer, when it will be quite ripe, I have come to the conclusion that since 'a bird in the hand is worth two in the bush,' it will be wise to accept a bite out of the sunny side of it as soon as you think proper to put out a kind hand and hold it within my reach. So send the MS. whenever you please. Your handwriting is clear and legible. I think I shall be able to read it currently. In return you shall receive an honest account of the impression made.

[1] *The Lily and the Bee; an apologue of the Crystal Palace of* 1851. [By Samuel Warren, D.C.L.]

[2] *Margaret Maitland of Sunnyside. Written by herself.* [By Mrs Margaret Oliphant] n.d.

My Father so far has, I am glad to say, escaped injury from the late sudden change of temperature, but it brought on me a somewhat severe cold, out of the clutches of which I have not yet escaped. I shall be glad when it is over, since, with its accompaniments of influenza, headaches, and toothaches, it tends to stupefaction and depression.—Believe me, Yours sincerely and affectionately,

C. BRONTË.

729 (544). *To* ELLEN NUSSEY.

HAWORTH, Decbr 17th, 1851.

DEAR ELLEN,—I cannot at present go to see you but I should be grateful if you could come and see me—were it only for a few days. To speak truth I have put on but a poor time of it during this month past—I kept hoping to be better—but was at last obliged to have recourse to medical advice—Sometimes I have felt very weak and low and longed much for society—but could not persuade myself to commit the selfish act of asking you merely for my own relief. The doctor speaks encouragingly, but as yet I don't get better. As the illness has been coming on for a long time—it cannot—I suppose—be expected to disappear all at once. I am not confined to bed but I am weak—have had no appetite for about three weeks—and my nights are very bad. I am well aware myself that extreme and continuous depression of spirits has had much to do with the origin of the illness—and I know a little cheerful society would do me more good than gallons of medicine. If you *can* come—come on Friday—write to-morrow and say whether this be possible and what time you will be at Keighley that I may send the gig. I do not ask you to stay long—a few days is all I request.

I am sorry to hear of Mr Clapham's illness—remember me to your Mother and all at Brookroyd.—Yours faithfully,

C. BRONTË.

I have got some Cod-liver-oil but am forbidden to take it at present—The doctor says it would make me more feverish.

730 (250). *To* ELLEN NUSSEY.

HAWORTH, [Dec. 18th, 1851].

DEAR NELL,—I shall expect you on Saturday and have ordered a gig to meet you at Keighley Station at 3½ past. Don't disappoint me if you can possibly help it. I am very sorry to hear your mother is not so well but trust she will be better. Give her my love. Mercy is tiresome. At Haworth you will have a little rest at any rate. I truly long to see you.

C. B.

Thursday.

731. *To* GEORGE SMITH.

December 19th, 1851.

MY DEAR SIR,—I forward to-day the MS. of 'P. F. Murray, Esq.' I have read it, but find a little difficulty in telling you what I think about it. As a publisher's book I should think it is good— likely to attract attention and excite discussion. It touches on most of the difficult and important social topics, and abounds in evidence of the writer's high intellectual powers. As to the opinions broached or insinuated; they are not in my way, but that does not in the least signify. I wish she had kept off theology. The interest is not very enchaining. The artistic defects are many and great, but few will care for those. —Yours sincerely,

C. BRONTË.

732. *To* GEORGE SMITH.

December 31st, 1851.

MY DEAR SIR,—A note from Miss Martineau to you is enclosed. You will see she lays stress upon the third volume, but in no shape questions your right to decline the MS.

I feared you would be disappointed with 'Oliver Weld' when you read it, though I had not calculated on its proving so obnoxious in a business point of view as you seem to anticipate. I did not like to tell you how great was my own surprise on perusing the manuscript; the two notes enclosed, which are all I have on the subject, had led me to expect something very different. You will kindly return them to me when you shall have satisfied yourself by perusal that you were not mistaken in supposing that you had been led to expect a work of another tenor.

Excuse me from saying much on the subject; I am very sorry about it altogether. But I do not take it in any shape to heart, nor fear that blame can attach to you in the matter; indeed, I feel very sure Miss Martineau is much too honourable for a moment to impute it.

I scarcely feel inclined to venture on trying to influence Miss M. any more. There is a peculiar property in her which must sooner or later be recognised as a great inconvenience by such of her acquaintance as admire her intellectual powers and her many excellent personal qualities without being able to agree in her views; she is prone to mistake liking for agreement, and with the sanguine eagerness of her character thinks to sweep you along with her in her whirlwind course. This will not do.

I am somewhat relieved about my health, being assured that, notwithstanding some harassing symptoms, there is no organic unsoundness whatever, and encouraged to hope for better days if I am careful. The nervous system suffers the most, but I cannot tell how to steel it. Going from home is no cure.

Once more, be sure not to be too sensitive and anxious about this 'Oliver Weld' business. It is a disappointment, a sad disappointment, but we cannot help it.

Remember me very kindly to your mother and sisters, and believe me always — Sincerely yours,

C. BRONTË.

P.S. You did very wrong to tear up that note you said you had written to me. I should have liked it.

733 (545). *To* ELLEN NUSSEY.

Decbr 31st, 1851.

DEAR ELLEN, — Papa was quite charmed with his crimson velvet rubber — he liked the attention and besides it will really be useful to him — I am to thank you in the most polite manner possible.

Mr Ruddock came yesterday: unfortunately I was by no means so well as I had been last week — my head continued to ache all Monday — and yesterday the white tongue — parched mouth and loss of appetite were returned — accordingly I am to take more medicine. Mr R—— however repeated that there was no organic disease — only a highly sensitive and irritable condition of the liver. It was Mr R—— whom we saw in the gig on the moor that day we were walking out: he was going to a poor woman in labour. He saw us.

I am glad to hear good news from Hunsworth.

You must give my downright hearty sympathy to Mr Clapham and say I *do* hope he will be better soon. Remember me also to your Mother — Ann and Mercy —

I have just got a letter from Miss Wooler enclosing one to you — You will see she was truly pleased with yours. In haste to save the post — Yours very faithfully dear Nell,

I am better to-day.   C. Brontë.

734. *To* George Smith.

January 1st, 1852.

My dear Sir, — After all I have written a line to Miss Martineau. I grieve to think that the whole matter should be defeated through the fatal perversity of a nature on the whole great and good. I have just said these words to her, and whether they will produce any beneficial effect, or whether she will be displeased, I do not know.

'What Mr Smith wanted and expected was another "Deerbrook." He did not look for politics or theology. "Deerbrook" made you beloved wherever it was read. "Oliver Weld" will not have this effect. It is powerful; it is vivid; it must strike, but it will rarely please. You think perhaps it will do good? Not so much good as "Deerbrook" did. Better the highest part of what is in your own self than all the political and religious controversy in the world. Rest a little while; consider the matter over, and see whether you have not another "Deerbrook" in your heart to give England.'

I wish you and yours a happy New Year.   C. Brontë.

735 (546). *To* W. S. Williams.

January 1st, 1852.

My dear Sir, — I am glad of the opportunity of writing to you, for I have long wished to send you a little note, and was only deterred from doing so by the conviction that the period preceding Christmas must be a very busy one to you.

I have wished to thank you for your last, which gave me very genuine pleasure. You ascribe to Mr Taylor an excellent character; such a man's friendship, at any rate, should not be disregarded; and if the principles and disposition be what you say, faults of manner and even of temper ought to weigh light in the balance. I always believed in his judgment and good sense, but what I doubted was his kindness—he seemed to me a little too harsh, rigid, and unsympathising. Now, judgment, sense, principle are invaluable and quite indispensable points, but one would be thankful for a *little* feeling, a *little* indulgence in addition—without these, poor fallible human nature shrinks under the domination of the sterner qualities. I answered Mr Taylor's letter by the mail of the 19th November, sending it direct, for, on reflection, I did not see why I should trouble you with it.

Did your son Frank call on Mrs Gaskell? and how did he like her?

My health has not been very satisfactory lately, but I think, though I vary almost daily, I am much better than I was a fortnight ago. All the winter the fact of my never being able to stoop over a desk without bringing on pain and oppression in the chest has been a great affliction to me, and the want of tranquil rest at night has tried me much, but I hope for the better times. The doctors say that there is no organic mischief.

Wishing a happy New Year to you,   C. BRONTË.

736 (547). *To* ELLEN NUSSEY.

Tuesday Morng.
[Jan. 5th, 1852].

DEAR ELLEN,—I am sorry to say that my headache did turn out to be symptomatic of relapse—but on the whole I think I am better again now—and I do not in the least regret your going— *really* when I am downright ill—i.e. under the pressure of headache, sickness or other prostrating ailment—I would rather have it to myself and not feel it augmented by the sense of its being burdensome to others—It is when bodily ailment is gone, and the mind alone languishes that cheerful and cherished society becomes a boon. You did me great good whilst you stayed here and you went away just when your kindness would have become unavailing, and I and my liver were best left alone. All yesterday I was very very sick—to-day I feel somewhat relieved—though qualms of nausea haunt me still. I expect Mr Ruddock and shall ask him whether part of this sickness is not owing to his medicine, which I suspect and hope.

Poor Ellen Taylor! I fear hers will not be a long life—Should she die in New Zealand—it will be most sad for Mary—there are no particulars of her illness given in the letter I have seen. I had a note yesterday from Amelia—She says that when you were at Hunsworth she thought you looking *much better*—which is a great deal from *her* who is so apt to grumble about your looks. Mind—however—that the circumstance of your being pretty well just now does not make you grow careless. Ill health is sooner fallen into than got out of. I fear the changeful weather of the last day or two will have tried Mr Clapham as it tried me— but to-day is fine and I hope he will feel its good effects—With kind regards to all at Brookroyd, I am dearest Nell—Yours faithfully,

C. Brontë.

If I feel that it will do me good to go to Brookroyd for a few days I will tell you—but at present—I am certainly best at home.

737 (564). *To* Ellen Nussey.

[January, 1852].

Dear Ellen,—With regard to the pains in chest and shoulders, if they still continue there should be no delay in asking the opinion of a medical man, Mr Rayner for instance. Pains of this sort often indicate *congestion* of some organ; in *my* case it was the liver, and I had the pains at intervals for three years before I knew their origin. Have you tried a moderate dose of opening medicine? Two camomile pills might be of use, but you had better speak to a doctor.

The hand-squeezing adventure made me smile. Who was the gentleman? Could it be Mr. ——? Are you sure he was ——? Was not the squeeze probably too slight to be felt? Have you not tormented yourself about what was perceptible to yourself only?

Mary Gorham's letter is very interesting; it shows a mind one cannot but truly admire. Compare its serene, trusting strength with poor Mrs Joe Taylor's vacillating dependence. When the latter was in her first burst of happiness, I never remember the feeling finding vent in expressions of gratitude to God. There was always a continued claim upon your sympathy in the mistrust and doubt she felt of her own bliss. Mary believes, has faith, is grateful and at peace: yet while happy in herself, how thoughtful she is for others!

I enclose a letter from New Zealand which I ought to have

sent before, but forgot it until my last note was sealed. It contains nothing new, being indeed of a date prior to the one you have already seen, but somehow it tends to confirm one's fears about Ellen Taylor. With love to all at Brookroyd, —Believe me, dear Nell, yours faithfully,

C. BRONTË.

738 (548). *To* ELLEN NUSSEY.

[Jan. 14th, 1852].

MY DEAR ELLEN, —I have certainly been ill enough since I wrote to you —but do not be alarmed or uneasy —I believe my sufferings have been partly, perhaps in a great measure, owing to the medicine —the pills given me —they were alterative and contained a mixture of Mercury —this did not suit me —I was brought to a sad state —Thank God —I believe I am better —but too weak now to tell you particulars —Poor Papa has been in grievous anxiety —on the point of sending for Mr Teale, I had hard work to restrain him —Mr Ruddock was sorely flustered when he found what he had done —but I don't much blame him. Can't write more at present. Good bye dear Nell. —Yours faithfully,

C. B.

Be quite tranquil, Mr R. vows and protests I shall do perfectly well with time —and that it will even be all the better for me — but it was rough work. I return M. G.'s good and happy letter.

739 (549). *To* ELLEN NUSSEY.

Jany 16th, 1852.

DEAR ELLEN, —I wish you could have seen the coolness with which I captured your letter on its way to Papa and at once conjecturing its tenor, made the contents my own.

Be quiet. Be tranquil. It is —dear Nell —my decided intention to come to Brookroyd for a few days when I *can* come —but of this last I must positively judge for myself —and I must take my time —I am better to-day —much better —but you can have little idea of the sort of condition into which Mercury throws people to ask me to go from home anywhere in close or open carriage — and as to talking —four days since I could not well have articulated three sentences —my mouth and tongue were ulcerated —

for a week I took no sustenance except half a teacupful of liquid administered by tea-spoonfuls in the course of the day—yet I did not need nursing—and I kept out of bed. It was enough to burden myself—it would have been misery to me to have annoyed another. Mr Ruddock says he never in his whole practice knew the same effect produced by the same dose on man—woman or child—and avows it is owing to an altogether peculiar sensitiveness of constitution. He expressed great regret and annoyance at its having occurred but affirms it will do me good in the end. If this be so—the sufferings are welcome.

My appetite begins to return—my mouth and tongue are healing fast—in short—I believe I am doing well but it harasses me dear Nell—to be so urged to go from home—when I know I cannot. A week or fortnight may make all the difference—You know I generally rally pretty quickly.

With kind love and a mixture of thanks and scolding.—I am Yours faithfully,

C. BRONTË.

Poor Mr C—— has a lingering time of it; remember me to him—to your Mother &c.

740. *To* GEORGE SMITH.

January 19th, 1852.[1]

MY DEAR SIR,—The enclosed copy should have been returned ere this—if I had been able to attend to ordinary matters—but I grew worse after I wrote to you last and was very ill for some days. Weak I still continue, but believe I am getting better, and very grateful do I feel for the improvement—grateful for my Father's sake no less than for my own.

It made me sorrowful to hear that you too had been ill, but I trust you are now quite recovered. I thought you would hardly ever be ill; you looked so healthy—but over-anxiety and confining labour will undermine the strongest.

I have not heard a word from Miss Martineau and conclude her silence is of no good omen. With kind regards to your Mother and Sisters,—I am, Sincerely yours,

C. BRONTË.

[1]Charlotte wrongly dated this and the following letter 1851.

741 (550). *To* MARGARET WOOLER.

HAWORTH, Jany 20th, 1852.

MY DEAR MISS WOOLER,—Your last kind note would not
have remained so long unanswered if I had been in better health.
While Ellen Nussey was with me, I seemed to recover wonderfully—but began to grow worse again the day she left, and this
falling off proved symptomatic of a relapse. My Doctor called
the next day; he said the headache from which I was suffering
arose from inertness in the liver—prescribed some alterative
pills and promised to call again in a week. I took the pills duly and
truly—hoping for benefit—but every day I grew worse; before
the week was over I was very ill—unable to swallow any nourishment except a few teaspoonfuls of liquid per diem, my mouth
became sore, my teeth loose, my tongue swelled, raw and ulcerated while water welled continually into my mouth. I knew by
this time that Mercury had formed an ingredient in the alterative pills and that I was suffering from its effects. When my
Doctor came and found me in this condition he was much
shocked and startled, a result had been produced which he had
not intended, nor anticipated: according to him the dose of blue
pill he had given was not sufficient to salivate a child—and he
talked much about exceptional sensitiveness of constitution &c.
Strong medicines were then administered to counteract this
mistake—so that altogether I have been much reduced. Thank
God—I now feel better—and very grateful am I for the improvement—grateful no less for my dear Father's sake, than for
my own.

   Most fully can I sympathize with you in the anxiety you express about Mr Thomas. The thought of his leaving England
and going out alone to a strange country with all his natural
sensitiveness and retiring diffidence—is indeed painful—Still—
my dear Miss Wooler—should no means be found of preventing
the step—should he actually go to America—I can but then suggest to you the same source of comfort and support you have
suggested to me—and of which indeed I know you never lose
sight—namely—reliance on Providence. 'God tempers the wind
to the shorn lamb' and He will doubtless care for a good though
afflicted man amidst whatever difficulties he may be thrown.
When you write again—I should be glad to know whether your

anxiety on this subject is relieved—and also to hear how Mrs Moore and her family are getting on—I was truly glad to learn through Ellen Nussey that Ilkley still continued to agree with your health. Earnestly trusting that the New Year may prove to you a happy and tranquil time I am my dear Miss Wooler— Sincerely and affectionately yours,

C. Brontë.

Give my kind love to Miss Sarah. Papa says I am always to give his best respects when I write to you.

742 (551). *To* Ellen Nussey.

January 22nd, 1852.

Dear Ellen,—I have continued to make progress, and I think very quickly. I do not suppose I am looking much worse than when you were here, though of course I am very thin.

If all be well I hope to come to Brookroyd next week. Mr Ruddock wished me to put off for another week, but I want to see you, and my spirits sadly need some little support. I do and have done as well as I can, but the hours have been very dark sometimes. Through it all papa continues well, thank God! I intend coming by the same train you took and should therefore reach you in the course of the afternoon, but I will write again to mention the day, etc. I had a note from Amelia the other day which struck me as not being happy somehow. I don't quite like her frequent recurrence in a rather repining tone to Rosy's superior good fortune. I am glad to hear that Mr Clapham is making some progress and that Mrs Clapham is better.—Believe me, dear Nell, yours faithfully,

C. Brontë.

You must not expect me to stay one day longer than a week.

743 (552). *To* Ellen Nussey.

Haworth, Jany 24th, '52.

Dear Nell,—I hope (d.v.) to come to Brookroyd on Tuesday—and shall be at Bradford about 2 o'clock. If Mr C— *can* send the gig without inconvenience I shall be glad to have it—it will save so much trouble—but he must on no account run the risk unless the weather be fine and calm: I dare not come if it be

wet, windy or very cold —if there be the least doubt —don't let
him send —as I could get a cab if necessary.

And now my dear physician with reference to putting myself
into your hands you must take notice of this —I am to live on the
very plainest fare —to take *no butter* —at present I do not take tea —
only milk and water with a little sugar and dry bread —this with
an occasional mutton chop is my diet —and I like it better than
anything else —During the week you were at Haworth —I did
myself harm by eating too indiscriminately —but I am resolved
to be more careful now —and indeed I have no alternative if I
wish to be well: Mr Ruddock has made me take tonics which
have stimulated the appetite —but I eat little at a time.

I tell you all this to prevent you from giving yourself *one bit* of
trouble in the cooking line. It would make me miserable to see
you bother yourself —and ill besides.

Hoping Tuesday will be fine —and with kind regards to all —
I am, dear Nell —Yours faithfully,

C. BRONTË.

744. *To* GEORGE SMITH.

BROOKROYD, BIRSTALL, LEEDS,
January 29th, 1852.

MY DEAR SIR, —I have rallied very rapidly within the last week,
and, as the address of this letter will shew you, am now from
home, staying with the friend I told you of. I *do* wish now I had
delayed my departure from home a few days longer, that I
might have shared with my father the true pleasure of receiving
you at Haworth Parsonage. And a pleasure your visit would have
been, as I have sometimes dimly imagined but never ventured to
realise. I shall be returning in about a week, but if you must
make your excursion before that time, and if you came north-
wards and would call at Brookroyd, I am desired to tell you that
you would have the warmest Yorkshire welcome. My friends
would like to see you. You would find me there, but not exactly
ill now; I have only a sort of low intermittent fever which still
hangs about me, but which the doctor says will leave me as I
grow stronger.

They are hospitable people at Brookroyd, and you would be
made comfortable. I and my friend would do our best to amuse

you; it is only six miles distant from Leeds; you would have to stay all night.

Thank your mother from me for her very kind note, and tell her where I am and that I will write to her ere long. Send me a line to say whether we shall see you, and when; and believe me,

Sincerely yours,

C. BRONTË.

745. *To* MRS SMITH.

BROOKROYD, January 29th, '52.

MY DEAR MRS SMITH,—Your note and invitation are very truly kind—but as Mr Smith will have told you—I am already from home trying the effect of those remedies you recommend —change of air and scene. I am much better than I was—though I cannot expect to be well all at once.

When I bid you Good-bye in Euston Square Station—I determined in my own mind that I would not again come to London except under conditions which are yet unfulfilled. A treat must be *earned* before it can be *enjoyed*, and the treat which a visit to you affords me is yet unearned, and must so remain for a time— how long I do not know.

I will tell you about my illness and how it came on. I suffered exceedingly from depression of spirits in the Autumn. Then— at the commencement of Winter, the weather set in very severe. One day when I was walking out—I felt a peculiar pain in my right side; I did not think much of it at first—but was not well from that time. Soon after I took cold—the cold struck in, inflammatory action ensued, I had high fever at night; the pain in my side became very severe—there was a constant burning and aching in my chest—I lost my sleep and could eat nothing. My own conclusion was that my lungs were affected—but on consulting a medical man—my lungs and chest were pronounced perfectly sound, and it appeared that the inflammation had fallen on the liver. I have since varied—being better sometimes when the internal fever subsided, and again worse when it was increased by change of weather, or any other exciting cause—but I am told that there is no danger, as it is a case of functional derangement—not of organic disease. The solitude of my life I have certainly felt very keenly this winter—but every one has his own

burden to bear—and where there is no available remedy—it is
right to be patient and trust that Providence will in His own
good time lighten the load. I have wanted for no attention that
kind and faithful servants could give—and my dear father is
always kind in his way.

Give my true regards to all your circle. It is unavailing to say
how glad I shall be when I can with a good conscience once
more come and see you all. I do not, however, anticipate this
event at an early date. Good-bye, my dear Mrs Smith. —Believe
me, Yours sincerely and affectionately,

C. BRONTË.

746 (554). *To* MRS GASKELL.

February 6th, 1852.

Certainly the past winter has been to me a strange time; had I
the prospect before me of living it over again, my prayer must
necessarily be 'Let this cup pass from me.' That depression of
spirits, which I thought was gone by when I wrote last, came back
again with a heavy recoil; internal congestion ensued, and then
inflammation. I had severe pain in my right side, frequent burning and aching in my chest; sleep almost forsook me, or would
never come except accompanied by ghastly dreams; appetite
vanished, and slow fever was my continual companion. It was
some time before I could bring myself to have recourse to medical advice. I thought my lungs were affected, and could feel no
confidence in the power of medicine. When at last, however, a
doctor was consulted, he declared my lungs and chest sound,
and ascribed all my sufferings to derangement of the liver, on
which organ it seems the inflammation had fallen. This information was a great relief to my dear father, as well as to myself; but
I had subsequently rather sharp medical discipline to undergo,
and was much reduced. Though not yet well, it is with deep
thankfulness that I can say I am *greatly better*. My sleep, appetite,
and strength seem all returning.

C. BRONTË.

747. *To* GEORGE SMITH.

BROOKROYD, BIRSTALL,
February 7th, 1852.

MY DEAR SIR, — The MS.[1] reached me quite safely this morning. I shall not read it here — where I remain two or three days longer, but shall take it home with me as a comfort and pleasure in anticipation.

Alas, for Mr Thackeray's promises! Alas, for the faith of authorhood enshrined in him!

My health, though still variable, continues on the whole to improve. My spirits are certainly much better, and the capacity of sleep is being restored.

You have never told me how you are, but I do hope you are well. — Believe me, Sincerely yours,

C. BRONTË.

748 (553). *To* ELLEN NUSSEY.

[Feb. 12th, 1852].

DEAR ELLEN, — I reached home safely a little before 5 yesterday — all right but for a headache which I am sorry to say continues with me to-day. I found Papa well — he thanks you for the potted tongue and says 'old fellows get more kindness from the ladies than young ones.'

I am anxious to know how you got home and how your teeth are — I fear too you were a little ailing in yourself — be sure to write directly and tell me how Mr and Mrs Clapham your Mother and Mercy are — kind love to all. — Yours sincerely,

C. BRONTË.

I find I have stolen a pencil-case of yours. I put it away with my pen in my little box — I will take care of it till you come.

---

[1]This was the manuscript of the first volume of Thackeray's *Esmond*. Later, Charlotte Brontë received and read the manuscript of the second volume, but declined the third volume until it was printed.

749 (555). *To* GEORGE SMITH.

February 14th, 1852.

MY DEAR SIR,—It has been a great delight to me to read Mr Thackeray's work; and I so seldom now express my sense of kindness that, for once, you must permit me, without rebuke, to thank you for a pleasure so rare and special. Yet I am not going to praise either Mr Thackeray or his book. I have read, enjoyed, been interested, and, after all, feel full as much ire and sorrow as gratitude and admiration. And still one can never lay down a book of his without the last two feelings having their part, be the subject of treatment what it may. In the first half of the book what chiefly struck me was the wonderful manner in which the writer throws himself into the spirit and letters of the times whereof he treats; the allusions, the illustrations, the style, all seem to me so masterly in their exact keeping, their harmonious consistency, their nice, natural truth, their pure exemption from exaggeration. No second-rate imitator can write in that way; no coarse scene-painter can charm us with an allusion so delicate and perfect. But what bitter satire, what relentless dissection of diseased subjects! Well, and this, too, is right, or would be right, if the savage surgeon did not seem so fiercely pleased with his work. Thackeray likes to dissect an ulcer or an aneurism; he has pleasure in putting his cruel knife or probe into quivering living flesh. Thackeray would not like all the world to be good; no great satirist would like society to be perfect.

As usual, he is unjust to women, quite unjust. There is hardly any punishment he does not deserve for making Lady Castlewood peep through a keyhole, listen at a door, and be jealous of a boy and a milkmaid. Many other things I noticed that, for my part, grieved and exasperated me as I read; but then, again, came passages so true, so deeply thought, so tenderly felt, one could not help forgiving and admiring.

I wish there was any one whose word he cared for to bid him God speed, to tell him to go on courageously with the book; he may yet make it the best he has ever written.

But I wish he could be told not to care much for dwelling on the political or religious intrigues of the times. Thackeray, in his heart, does not value political or religious intrigues of any age or date. He likes to show us human nature at home, as he himself daily sees it; his wonderful observant faculty likes to be in action. In him this faculty is a sort of captain and leader; and if ever any passage in his writings lacks interest, it is when this master-faculty is for a time thrust into a subordinate position. I think such is the case in the former half of the present volume. Towards the middle he throws off restraint, becomes himself, and is strong to the close. Everything now depends on the second and third volumes. If, in pith and interest, they fall short of the first, a true success cannot ensue. If the continuation be an improvement upon the commencement, if the stream gather force as it rolls, Thackeray will triumph. Some people have been in the habit of terming him the second writer of the day; it just depends on himself whether or not these critics shall be justified in their award. He need not be the second. God made him second to no man. If I were he, I would show myself as I am, not as critics report me; at any rate I would do my best. Mr Thackeray is easy and indolent, and seldom cares to do his best. Thank you once more; and believe me yours sincerely,

C. BRONTË.

750 (556). *To* ELLEN NUSSEY.

HAWORTH, Feby 16th, '52.

DEAR NELL,—Many thanks for yours. You had a sad reception at Mrs Wards—I had quite calculated on your getting from her the relief and rest which you needed so much—however it is well that the rum proved beneficial when you at last had time to apply it.

My head-ache after continuing for two days left me, and I have continued very decent indeed ever since — *much* better than I was before leaving home—though the headache by making me look ill—robbed me of the expected congratulations on improved appearance. I do believe if the weather would but be pleasant and serene, I should be right enough—better perhaps than I was before my illness. Mr Ruddock to my dismay—came blustering in on Saturday—I had not intended to let him know of my return till this week—but somebody had caught sight of me at Keighley Station and told him I was come home. He was actually cross, that I had not immediately written—he began about the quinine directly—I told him I thought it did not suit me—but he would not listen to reason—says it is the only thing to do me permanent good &c. However I procured a respite for a week—and meantime I go on with the hop-tea which as far as I know, agrees quite well. I said nothing about it to him—but I mentioned the potass—and he laughed it to scorn—I wish I knew better what to think of this man's skill. He seems to stick like a leech: I thought I should have done with him when I came home.

I have just returned Mr T's MS. with a criticising letter which Mr Smith may shew if he likes. I said what I thought and I sometimes thought bitter things.

Do I understand rightly from your note that Mr Rayner was mistaken in his first opinion respecting the nature of your Sister Ann's illness? Is it the passing of the gallstones or bilious cholic? I hope she is better by this time but I somewhat fear that the return of stormy weather after a few days calm will be felt injuriously both by her and Mr Clapham; it has brought me back something of the pain in my side—which I had hoped gone.

Give my kind regards to your Mother, Mr C— and all the rest—Write again soon and believe me, dear Nell,—Yours faithfully,

C. BRONTË.

How is your thumb-nail? no light mischance that of turning it back.

751. *To* GEORGE SMITH.

February 17th, 1852.

MY DEAR SIR,—I do not think my note would do Mr Thackeray much good, but, as (so far as I recollect) it contains nothing I can have any objection to his seeing, you are quite at liberty to use your own discretion in the matter. What is said in that note I would, if I had nerve, and could speak without hesitating and looking like an idiot, say to himself, face to face, prepared, of course, for any amount of sarcasm in reply, prepared too for those misconstructions which are the least flattering to human pride, and which we see and take in and smile at quietly and put by sadly; little ingenuities in which, if I mistake not, Mr Thackeray, with all his greatness, excels.

I have never seen the 'Paris Sketch Book,' but you really must send nothing more for the present, at least not by Post—let your recklessly lavished 'Queen's Heads'[1] repose for awhile. I am truly glad to learn that you are better—I think, too, I grow stronger.—Believe me, Sincerely yours,

C. BRONTË.

752 (557). *To* MARGARET WOOLER.

HAWORTH, February 17th, 1852.

MY DEAR MISS WOOLER,—Your last welcome letter found me at Brookroyd, whence I am just returned after a fortnight's stay; the change has proved beneficial, not only to my health but more especially to my spirits which were so prostrated by the debility consequent on my illness, that solitude had become somewhat too trying. If serene weather were only restored—I feel as if I should soon be well again—but these long storms—these incessantly howling winds depress the nervous system much. I trust Mr Thomas has been heard of ere now; continued suspense respecting his safe arrival at Hamburg would be most painful during weather so inclement. When you write again—just mention whether you have received news of him.

If you would send me one of Mrs Moore's circulars—I could —at any rate—make the best use of it in my power—though—whether any favourable result would ensue must—as you well know—be very uncertain. Mrs Gaskell's eldest daughter is at school near London; Lady Shuttleworth has but one little girl—a child of seven—for whom, however, she has a foreign governess—and her ladyship seemed to place so little reliance on the competency of Englishwomen to train the young—and to entertain such sweeping suspicions of English schools in general that —I fear—her patronage could hardly be looked for.

During my stay at Brookroyd—I had the pleasure of seeing Miss Eliza—she had heard I was in the neighbourhood and kindly walked over one morning to make a call—bringing with her a most interesting little party—three of her nieces, Harriet, Lucy and Fanny, and her nephew John—a fine little fair-haired English-featured boy—strikingly like his uncle, Mr John Wooler. Ellen Nussey and I were to have dined at Rouse Mill—but the weather on the day appointed proved so unpropitious—it was impossible to stir out—and it was well we were prevented

---

[1]In those days a common expression for postage stamps.

—for we heard afterwards that on that day the baby was again taken very ill, so that our visit might have proved an inconvenience. I also saw Mr and Mrs Wm Wooler and Ellen who was accompanied by a Miss Rogers; they all appeared to me to be looking well—especially Mrs Wooler who grows quite stout. In the midst of it all—both E. Nussey and I could not help regretting your absence and we did regret it deeply and often.

As to the French President—it seems to me hard to say what a man with so little scruple and so much ambition will *not* attempt. I wish, however, the English Press would not prate so much about invasion; if silence were possible in a free country—would it not be far better to prepare silently for what *may* come—to place the national defences in an effective state and refrain from breathing a word of apprehension? Doubtless such is the thought of practical men like the Duke of Wellington—I can well conceive his secret impatience at the mischievous gabbling of the newspapers. Wonderful is the French Nation!

C. BRONTË.

753 (558). *To* ELLEN NUSSEY.

February 24th, 1852.

DEAR ELLEN,—I return Mary Gorham's with thanks. The time of your visit does not seem very distant; three months will soon pass. I am sorry, dear Nell, you are treating the subject of my going to Sussex as if it were at all a probable thing. Let me say distinctly, it is not at all likely; few things less so, as far as I can see.

I am glad to hear your sister, Mrs Clapham, is better; perhaps this illness may improve her general health. You do not mention Mr Clapham. I hope he still progresses. As to papa, his health has been really wonderful this winter; good sleep, good spirits, an excellent steady appetite—all seem to mark vigour; may it but continue! As for me, I yet do well; could I but get rid of indigestion and headache I should manage, but these pains pursue me.

The Indian mail brought me nothing.—I am, dear Nell, yours faithfully,

C. BRONTË.

754 (561). *To* ELLEN NUSSEY.

HAWORTH, March 4th, '52.

DEAR ELLEN, — The news of E. Taylor's death came to me last week in a letter from Mary — a long letter — which wrung my heart so — in its simple strong, truthful emotion — I have only ventured to read it once. It ripped up half-scarred wounds with terrible force — the death-bed was just the same — breath failing &c.

She fears she shall now in her dreary solitude become 'a stern, harsh, selfish woman' — this fear struck home — again and again I have felt it for myself — and what is *my* position to Mary's?

I should break out in energetic wishes that she would return to England — if reason would permit me to believe that prosperity and happiness would there await her — but I see no such prospect.

May God help her as God only can help!

I like to hear of your being cheerful — but I fear you impose on yourself too much fatigue with all this entertainment of visitors — Poor Emma Sherwood! Will she be at all provided for in case of her father's death — she will hardly like to turn governess. How are Mr and Mrs Clapham and your mother? You have not mentioned them lately. I continue better — and Papa is getting through the spring admirably.

I am sure Miss Wooler would enjoy her visit to Brookroyd — as much as you, her company. Dear Nell — I thank you sincerely for your discreet and friendly silence on the point alluded to — I had feared it would be discussed between you two — and had an inexpressible shrinking at the thought — Now — less than ever — does it seem to me a matter open to discussion. I hear nothing. And you must quite understand that if I feel any uneasiness — it is not the uneasiness of confirmed and fixed regard — but that anxiety which is inseparable from a state of absolute uncertainty about a somewhat momentous matter. I do not know — I am not sure myself that any other termination would be better than lasting estrangement and unbroken silence — yet a good deal of pain has been and must be gone through in that case. However to each — his burden.

I have not yet read the papers—D.V. I will send them to-
morrow.—Yours faithfully,

C. BRONTË.

Understand—that in whatever I have said above—I was not
fishing for pity or sympathy—I hardly pity myself. Only I wish
that in all matters in this world there was fair and open dealing—
and no underhand work.

755 (562). *To* ELLEN NUSSEY.

Mar. 5th, '52.

DEAR ELLEN,—I suppose as I have heard nothing since your
last—that the baby at Hunsworth is now better.

I do not return Amelia's letters—conceiving that they are
hardly such as you will make a point of retaining. Seldom have I
seen any from her that impressed me less favourably—the loud
—weak outcry is too much—I pity her but less than I should do
if I did not feel that she is straining her emotions to the utmost—
All that part about Hopkinson's wife and her child is sad. The
apostrophe to you 'you never were a Mother' (!!!) &c. is really
theatrical and entirely superfluous. It is well that A. has a better
side to her character than all this. If such be the sort of diet on
which she feeds Rosy—I do not wonder at the latter's occasional
silence. This kind of correspondence would do me up.

I hope you are all better at Brookroyd—the cold weather disagreed with me very much at first—I think however I am getting
used to it though I still have frequent headaches and just now a
swelled face and tic in the cheek-bone. Mr Ruddock has contra-
dicted himself about quinine—allowed that it will not do for me
and prescribed another tonic which I have taken though without
any benefit that I can perceive.

I had a letter from Miss Martineau a few days since. She has
actually suppressed her intended work calls it now 'a foolish
prank,' but it is obvious she is much chagrined.[1]

I suppose you have received your Sussex parcel ere this and I
trust its contents were satisfactory. This dry fine frosty weather
ought to suit you—dear Nell—Write soon and tell me how you
are. Papa is well.—Yours faithfully,

C. BRONTË.

---

[1] This was the cancelled novel *Oliver Weld*.

756 (563). *To* Ellen Nussey.

March 7th, 1852.

Dear Nell,—I hope both your Mother's cold and yours are quite well ere this—Papa has got something of his Spring attack of bronchitis—but so far it is in a greatly ameliorated form—very different to what it has been for three years past—I do trust it may pass off thus mildly. I continue better.

Dear Nell—I told you from the beginning that my going to Sussex was a most improbable event—I tell you now that unless want of health should absolutely compel me to give up work and leave home (which I trust and hope will not be the case) *I certainly shall not think of going.* It is better to be decided—and decided I must be, you can never want me less than when in Sussex surrounded by amusement and friends. I do not know that I shall go to Scarboro' but it might be possible to spare a fortnight to go there (for the sake of a sad duty rather than pleasure) when I could not give a month to a longer excursion. You mention '*meanness*' in connection with my going to Scarboro'—did you think I meant to sponge upon Miss Wooler?—No—I intended to take lodgings and pay for them honestly.

I have not a word of news to tell you—Many Mails have come in from India since I was at Brookroyd—and always when the day came round—(I know it now) expectation would be on the alert—but disappointment knocked her down. I have not heard a syllable—and cannot think of making inquiries at Cornhill. Well—long suspense in any matter usually proves somewhat cankering—but God orders all things for us and to his will we must submit.

Be sure to keep a calm mind when you go to Sussex!—Yours faithfully,

C. Brontë.

757. *To* George Smith.

March 11th, 1852.

My dear Sir,—I am very glad to hear that Mr Thackeray is 'getting on,' as he says—and it is to be hoped the stimulus may prove more than temporary. Is not the publication of the Lectures 'with no end of illustrations' a most commendable idea?

I should think every one who heard them delivered will like to read them over again at leisure; for my own part I can hardly imagine a greater treat, were it only for the opportunity thereby afforded of fishing for faults and fallacies—and of fuming, fretting, and brooding at ease over the passages that excited one's wrath. In listening to a lecture you have not time to be angry enough. Mr Thackeray's worship of his Baal—Bel—Bülzebub (they are all one), his false god of a Fielding—is a thing I greatly desire to consider deliberately. In that red book of yours (which I returned long ago) there was a portrait of the author of 'Jonathan Wild.' In the cynical prominence of the under-jaw one reads the man. It was the stamp of one who would never see his neighbours (especially his women neighbours) as they *are*, but as they *might* be under the worst circumstances. In Mr Thackeray's own nature is a small seasoning of this virtue, but it does not (I hope) prevail throughout his whole being.

I have read the 'Paris Sketches' slowly, and by regulated allowances of so much per diem. I was so afraid of exhausting the precious provision too quickly. What curious traces one finds (at least so it struck me) of a somewhat wild, regular, and reckless life being led at that time by the Author! And yet how good—how truthful and sagacious are many of the papers—such as touch on politics, for instance—and above all the critical articles! And then whatever vinegar and gall, whatever idle froth, a book of Thackeray's may contain, it has no dregs; you never go and wash your hands when you put it down, nor rinse your mouth to take away the flavour of a degraded soul. Perverse he may be and is, but, to do him justice, *not* degraded; no—never.

Is the first number of 'Bleak House' generally admired? I liked the Chancery part, but when it passes into the autobiographic form, and the young woman who announces that she is not 'bright' begins her history, it seems to me too often weak and twaddling; an amiable nature is caricatured, not faithfully rendered, in Miss Esther Summerson.

Did I tell you that I had heard from Miss Martineau, and that she has quite thrown aside 'Oliver Weld' and calls it now 'a foolish prank'? For the present she declines turning her attention to any other work of fiction; she says her time for writing fiction is past—this may be so.

Please to tell Mr Williams that I mean (D.V.) to look over

'Shirley' soon and to send him a list of errata, but I marvel at your courage in contemplating a reprint; I cannot conceive a score of copies being sold. — Believe me, Yours sincerely,

C. BRONTË.

758 (565). *To* MARGARET WOOLER.

HAWORTH, March 12th, 1852.

MY DEAR MISS WOOLER, — Your kind note holds out a strong temptation, but one that *must be resisted*. From home I must not go unless health or some cause equally imperative render a change necessary. For nearly four months now (*i.e.* since I first became ill) I have not put pen to paper — my work has been lying untouched and my faculties have been rusting for want of exercise; further relaxation is out of the question, and I *will not permit myself to think of it*. My publisher groans over my long delays; I am sometimes provoked to check the expression of his impatience with short and crusty answers.

Yet the pleasure I now deny myself I would fain regard as only deferred. I heard something about your purposing to visit Scarbro' in the course of the summer, and could I — by the close of July or August bring my task to a certain point — how glad should I be to join you there for awhile!

Ellen Nussey will probably go to the south about May to make a stay of two or three months — she has formed a plan for my accompanying her and taking lodgings on the Sussex coast — but the scheme seems to me impracticable for many reasons — and moreover my medical man doubts the advisability of my going Southward in Summer — he says it might prove very enervating — whereas Scarbro' or Burlington would brace and strengthen. However — I dare not lay plans at this distance of time — for me so much must depend first on Papa's health (which — throughout the winter — has been — I am thankful to say — really excellent), and 2nd, on the progress of work — a matter not wholly contingent on wish or will — but lying in a great measure beyond the reach of effort and out of the pale of calculation.

I am truly glad to learn that satisfactory tidings have been received regarding Mr Thomas — he may prosper better than could be anticipated, foreign scenes and faces may prove a salutary stimulus; ere now I have observed that persons of diffident, self-doubting character are more at ease amongst total strangers than with those to whom they are partially known.

I will not write more at present, as I wish to save this post. All in the house would join in kind remembrances to you if they knew I was writing; Tabby and Martha both frequently enquire after 'Miss Wooler,' and desire their respects when an opportunity offers of presenting the same. — Believe me, yours always affectionately and respectfully,

C. BRONTË.

759. *To* GEORGE SMITH.

March 21st, 1852.

MY DEAR SIR, —I have read and now return Mr Thackeray's second volume. The complaint, I suppose, will be that there is too little story. I thought so myself in reading the first part of this packet of MS. I felt tedium in the first campaign of Harry Esmond; the second and third seemed to me to kindle the spirit. The character of Marlborough I thought a masterly piece of writing. But where is the use of giving one's broken impressions of such a book? It ought not to be judged piecemeal.

You are kind enough to inquire after Currer Bell's health. Thank you; he is better; latterly he has been much better; if he could continue so well he would look up yet; but—I say again, expect no good of him this summer.

I suppose that Mr Forster,[1] about whom you inquire, is a Mr F. from the neighbourhood of Bradford; he wrote an answer to Macaulay's attack on Penn on the Marshes; he is, or *was*, a Quaker himself; he has published also letters in the 'Leader' on Communion or the Associative Principle. — I trust you are better. Yours sincerely,

C. BRONTË.

I return the MS. by this Post.

[1]William Edward Forster (1818–1886), statesman, was educated at Quaker schools in Bristol and Tottenham, and in 1842 entered the woollen trade at Bradford. In 1849 he re-issued Clarkson's *Life of Penn* with a preface defending the quakers from the charges made against them by Macaulay in his *History of England*. In 1850 Forster married the eldest daughter of Dr Arnold, and visited Haworth with his wife in 1852; (see letter of October 5th, 1852). He was for many years Liberal M.P. for Bradford.

760 (566). *To* ELLEN NUSSEY.

HAWORTH, March 23rd, '52.

DEAR ELLEN,—Let me fulfil in this note a duty I forgot in the last—to thank you for the pretty d'oyley and to enclose payment in postage stamps.

I gave your Mother 'The Women of Christianity.'[1]

I have not been to visit Miss Wooler—she asked me very kindly and I should have liked it—but felt it incumbent on me to refuse as I often feel it incumbent on me to refuse you.

My health has been decidedly better lately—less headache—pain in the side sometimes but not often—Papa now begins to say I am looking better: he—thank God—is well and looks well.

H. Cockhill's account of J. Nussey is beautiful—if I were a man—that is the sort of family I would not marry into—the sort of father-in-law I would not have. I don't envy Mr Richardson. You may well indeed felicitate yourself that such relations in the flesh do not find you kindred in the spirit—and *that* they never will.

Did you go to Rouse Mill on Friday? How did you enjoy yourself and whom did you see?

You say, dear Nell—that you often wish I would chat on paper as you do. How can I?— Where are my materials?—is my life fertile in subjects of chat?— What callers do I see—what visits do I pay? No—you must chat and I must listen and say yes and no and thank you for five minutes recreation.

I don't know what that dear Mrs Joe T—— will make of her little one in the end: between port-wine and calomel and Mr Bennet and Mr Anderson—I should not like to be in its socks. Yet I think it will live—that it will ever be a good life—I do *not* think.

I am amused at the interest you take in politics—don't expect to rouse me—to me all ministries and all oppositions seem to be pretty much alike. D'Israeli was factious as Leader of the Opposition—Lord J. Russell is going to be factious now that he has stepped into D'I's shoes—Confound them all. Lord Derby's 'christian tone and spirit' is worth 3 halfpence ¼.—Yours sincerely,

C. BRONTË.

[1] By Julia Kavanagh.

761 (567). *To* W. S. WILLIAMS.

March 25th, 1852.

MY DEAR SIR,—Mr Smith intimated a short time since that he had some thoughts of publishing a reprint of 'Shirley.' Having revised the work, I now enclose the errata. I have likewise sent off to-day per rail a return box of Cornhill books.

I have lately read with great pleasure 'The Two Families.'[1] This work, it seems, should have reached me in January—but owing to a mistake it was detained at the Dead-Letter Office and lay there nearly two months. I liked the commencement very much; the close seemed to me scarcely equal to 'Rose Douglas.' I thought the authoress committed a mistake in shifting the main interest from the two personages on whom it first rests— viz Ben Wilson and Mary—to other characters of quite inferior conception. Had she made Ben and Mary her hero and heroine, and continued the development of their fortunes and characters in the same truthful natural vein in which she commences it—an excellent—even an original book might have been the result. As for Lilias and Ronald—they are mere romantic figments—with nothing of the genuine Scottish peasant about them; they do not even speak the Caledonian dialect; they palaver like a fine lady and gentleman. I ought long since to have acknowledged the gratification with which I read Miss Kavanagh's 'Women of Christianity.' Her charity and (on the whole) her impartiality are very beautiful. She touches indeed with too gentle a hand the theme of Elizabeth of Hungary—and in her own mind—she evidently misconstrues the fact of Protestant Charities *seeming* to be fewer than Catholic. She forgot or does not know that Pro-testantism is a quieter creed than Romanism—as it does not clothe its priesthood in scarlet, so neither does it set up its good women for Saints, canonize their names and proclaim their good works—In the records of man their almsgiving will not perhaps be found registered—but Heaven has its Account as well as Earth.

With kind regards to yourself and family who—I trust—have all safely weathered the rough Winter lately past—as well as the East Winds which are still nipping our Spring in Yorkshire— I am—my dear Sir, Yours sincerely,   C. BRONTË.

[1] *The Two Families*, 1852. By Mrs S. R. Whitehead, author of *Rose Douglas*. See the letter of 8th March, 1851, p. 210, above.

762 (568). *To* W. S. WILLIAMS.

April 3rd, 1852.

MY DEAR SIR,—The box arrived safely and I very much thank you for the contents which are most kindly selected.

As you wished me to say what I thought of 'The School for Fathers'[1]—I hastened to read it. The book seems to me clever, interesting, very amusing and likely to please generally. There is a merit in the choice of ground which is not yet too hackneyed; the comparative freshness of subject, character and epoch give the tale a certain attractiveness. There is also—I think—a graphic rendering of situation, and a lively talent for describing whatever is visible and tangible—what the eye meets on the *surface* of things. The humour appears to me such as would answer well on the Stage: most of the scenes seem to demand dramatic accessories to give them their full effect. But I think one cannot with justice bestow higher praise than this. To speak candidly—I felt in reading the tale—a wondrous hollowness in the moral and sentiment; a strange dilettante shallowness in the purpose and feeling. After all—'Jack' is not much better than a 'Tony Lumpkin,' and there is no very great breadth of choice between the clown he *is* and the fop his father would have made him. The grossly material life of the Old English Foxhunter—and the frivolous existence of the Fine Gentleman present extremes, each in its way, so repugnant—that one feels half-inclined to smile when called upon to sentimentalize over the lot of a youth forced to pass from one to the other—torn from the stables to be ushered perforce into the ballroom. Jack dies mournfully indeed and you are sorry for the poor fellow's untimely end—but you cannot forget that if he had not been thrust into the way of Colonel Penruddock's weapon—he might possibly have broken his neck in a fox-hunt. The character of Sir Thomas Warren is excellent—consistent throughout. That of Mr Addison—not bad but sketchy—a mere outline—wanting colour and finish. The Man's portrait is there and his costume and fragmentary anecdotes of his life—but where is the man's nature—soul and self?

I say nothing about the female characters—not one word—

[1] *The School for Fathers* was written by Josepha Gulston under the pseudonym of 'Talbot Gwynne.' She also wrote *Young Singleton, The School for Dreamers, Silas Barnstarke,* and *Nanette and her Lovers.*

only that Lydia seems to me like a pretty little actress, prettily dressed, gracefully appearing and disappearing and reappearing in a genteel comedy; assuming the proper sentiment of her part with all due tact and naïveté, and—that is all.

Your description of the Model Man of Business is true enough, I doubt not—but we will not fear that Society will ever be brought quite to this standard; Human Nature—(bad as it is) has, after all, elements that forbid it. But the very tendency to such a consummation—the marked tendency—I fear of the day —produces no doubt cruel suffering—Yet when the evil of Competition passes a certain limit—must it not in time work its own cure? I suppose it will—but then through some convulsed crisis—shattering all around it like an earthquake. Meantime for how many is Life made a struggle—enjoyment and rest curtailed —labour terribly enhanced beyond almost what Nature can bear —I often think that this World would be the most terrible of enigmas were it not for the firm belief that there is a World to come where conscientious effort and patient pain will meet their reward.—Believe me—my dear Sir, Sincerely yours,

C. BRONTË.

763 (459). *To* MISS BRONTË.

WELLINGTON, N.Z. [April 1852].

DEAR CHARLOTTE,—I began a letter to you one bitter cold evening last week, but it turned out such a sad one that I have left it and begun again. I am sitting all alone in my own house, or rather what is to be mine when I've paid for it. I bought it of Henry, when Ellen died, shop and all, and carry on by myself. I have made up my mind not to get any assistance; I have not too much work, and the annoyance of having an unsuitable companion was too great to put up with without necessity. I find now that it was Ellen that made me so busy, and without her to nurse I have plenty of time. I have begun to keep the house very tidy; it makes it less desolate. I take great interest in my trade— as much as I could do in anything that was not *all* pleasure. But the best part of my life is the excitement of arrivals from England. Reading all the news, written and printed, is like living another life separate from this one. The old letters are strange, very, when I begin to read them, but quite familiar notwithstanding. So are all the books and newspapers though I never

see a human being to whom it would ever occur to me to mention anything I read in them. I see your *nom de guerre* in them
sometimes. I saw a criticism on the preface to the second edition
of 'Wuthering Heights.' I saw it among the notables who
attended Thackeray's lectures. I have seen it somehow connected with Sir J. K. Shuttleworth. Did he want to marry you
or only to lionise you? *Or was it somebody else?*

Your life in London is a 'new country' to me which I cannot
even picture to myself. You seem to like it—at least some things
in it, and yet your late letters to Mrs Joe Taylor talk of low spirits
and illness. 'What's the matter with you now?' as my mother
used to say, as if it were the twentieth time in a fortnight. It is
really melancholy that now, in the prime of life, in the flush of
your hard-earned prosperity, you can't be well! Did not Miss
Martineau improve you? If she did, why not try her and her plan
again? But I suppose if you had hope and energy to try, you
would be well. Well, it's nearly dark, and you will surely be well
when you read this, so what's the use of writing? I should like
well to have some details of your life, but how can I hope for it?
I have often tried to give you a picture of mine, but I have not
the skill. I get a heap of details, most paltry in themselves and not
enough to give you an idea of the whole. O for one hour's talk!
You are getting too far off and beginning to look strange to me.
Do you look as you used to do, I wonder? What do you and
Ellen Nussey talk about when you meet? There! it's dark.

Sunday night.—I have let the vessel go that was to take this. As
there are others going soon I did not much care. I am in the
height of cogitation whether to send for some worsted stockings,
etc. They will come next year at this time, and who can tell what
I shall want then, or shall be doing! Yet hitherto we have sent
such orders and have guessed or known pretty well what we
should want. I have just been looking over a list four pages long
in Ellen's handwriting. These things ought to come by the next
vessel or part of them at least. Then, tired of that, I began to read
some pages of 'my book,' intending to write some more, but
went on reading for pleasure. I often do this and find it very interesting indeed. It does not get on fast tho'. I have written
about one volume and a half. It's full of music, poverty, disput-
ing, politics, and original views of life. I can't for the life of me
bring the lover into it, nor tell what he's to do when he comes.
Of the men generally I can never tell what they'll do next. The

women I understand pretty well, and rare tracasserie there is among them; they are perfectly feminine in that respect at least.

I am just now in a state of famine. No books and no news from England for this two months. I am thinking of visiting a circulating library from sheer dulness. If I had more time I should get melancholy. No one can prize activity more than I do, little interest though there is in it. I never long am without it but a gloom comes over me. The cloud seems to be always there behind me, and never quite out of sight but when I keep on at a good rate. Fortunately the more I work the better I like it. I shall take to scrubbing the floor before it's dirty, and polishing pans on the outside in my old age. It is the only thing that gives me an appetite for dinner.

I suppose if the vessel coming from England is not lost I shall soon be too busy to write if the last vessel were sailing that ever was to go. So take this in anticipation, as I can't write an answer to your letters until they get too old to answer.

PAG.

Give my love to Ellen Nussey.

764 (569). *To* LÆTITIA WHEELWRIGHT.

HAWORTH, April 12th, 1852.

DEAR LÆTITIA,—Your last letter gave me much concern. I had hoped you were long ere this restored to your usual health, and it both pained and surprised me to hear that you still suffer so much from debility. I cannot help thinking your constitution is naturally sound and healthy. Can it be the air of London which disagrees with you? For myself, I struggled through the winter and the early part of spring often with great difficulty. My friend[1] stayed with me a few days in the early part of January[2] —she could not be spared longer. I was better during her visit, but had a relapse soon after she left me, which reduced my strength very much. It cannot be denied that the solitude of my position fearfully aggravated its other evils. Some long, stormy days and nights there were when I felt such a craving for support and companionship as I cannot express. Sleepless, I lay awake night after night; weak and unable to occupy myself, I sat in my chair

[1] Miss Ellen Nussey who never met Miss Wheelwright.

[2] No: it was the end of December.

day after day, the saddest memories my only company. It was a
time I shall never forget, but God sent it and it must have been
for the best.

I am better now, and very grateful do I feel for the restoration
of tolerable health; but, as if there was always to be some affliction, papa, who enjoyed wonderful health during the whole winter, is ailing with his spring attack of bronchitis. I earnestly trust
it may pass over in the comparatively ameliorated form in which
it has hitherto shown itself.

Let me not forget to answer your question about the cataract.
Tell your papa my father was seventy[1] at the time he underwent
an operation; he was most reluctant to try the experiment—
could not believe that at his age and with his want of robust
strength it would succeed. I was obliged to be very decided in
the matter and to act entirely on my own responsibility. Nearly
six years have now elapsed since the cataract was extracted (it
was not merely depressed). He has never once, during that time,
regretted the step, and a day seldom passes that he does not express gratitude and pleasure at the restoration of that inestimable privilege of vision whose loss he once knew.

I hope the next tidings you hear of your brother Charles will
be satisfactory for his parents' and sisters' sake as well as his own.
Your poor mamma has had many successive trials, and her un-
complaining resignation seems to offer us all an example worthy
to be followed. Remember me kindly to her, to your papa, and
all your circle, and—Believe me, with best wishes to yourself,
yours sincerely,

C. BRONTË.

765 (571). *To* ELLEN NUSSEY.

April 22nd, 1852.

DEAR ELLEN,—I have forgotten whether the 22nd is your
birthday or mine; whichever it be, I wish you many happy
returns.

Poor Mr ——. I am very sorry to hear of his illness, especially
as I fear he will never be strong.

You seem to be quite gay, in paying and receiving visits; take
care of your health in the midst of it all. Papa, I think, is pretty

[1]He was 69.

well again; the attack was comparatively very slight. I, too, am keeping better; a little pain sometimes; I keep thin; but I am thankful to be so well.

When I read to papa Mrs Joe Taylor's account of her system with the poor little water-patient, he said if that child died, its parents ought to be tried for infanticide! I think they go too far, yet she says it is stronger. It is quite unlikely that you will get to Haworth before you go into Sussex. I deny myself pleasure just now.—Yours sincerely enough (as you see),

C. BRONTË.

'I had given Miss Brontë, in one of my letters,' says Mrs Gaskell, 'an outline of the story on which I was then engaged.' This would be *Ruth*, published in 1853.

766 (570). *To* MRS GASKELL.

April 26th, 1852.

I have lately got hold of a bound copy of Dickens's 'House-hold Words' for 1851. Therein, I have, as yet, only read three articles—to wit, 'Society at Cranford,' 'Love at Cranford,' 'Memory at Cranford.' Before reading them I had received a hint as to the authorship, which hint gave them special zest. The best is the last—Memory. How good I thought it—I must not tell *you*.

The sketch you give of your work (respecting which I am, of course, dumb) seems to me very noble; and its purpose may be as useful in practical result as it is high and just in theoretical tendency. Such a book may restore hope and energy to many who thought they had forfeited their right to both, and open a clear course for honourable effort to some who deemed that they and all honour had parted company in this world.

Yet—hear my protest!

Why should she die? Why are we to shut up the book weeping?

My heart fails me already at the thought of the pang it will have to undergo. And yet you must follow the impulse of your own inspiration. If *that* commands the slaying of the victim, no bystander has a right to put out his hand to stay the sacrificial knife; but I hold you a stern priestess in these matters.

C. BRONTË.

767 (572). *To* ELLEN NUSSEY.

HAWORTH, May 11th, '52.

DEAR ELLEN,—I must adhere to my resolution of neither visiting nor being visited at present—Stay you quietly at Brookroyd till you go into Sussex—as I shall stay at Haworth; as sincere a farewell can be taken with the heart as with the lips and perhaps less painful.

I am glad the weather is changed—this return of the South-West Wind suits me—but I hope you have no cause to regret the departure of your favourite East wind.

What you say about A. does not surprise me; I have had many little notes (whereof I answer about 1 in three) breathing the same spirit—Self and child the sole all absorbing topics on which the changes are rung even to weariness. But I suppose one must not heed it—or think the case singular—nor, I am afraid, must one expect her to improve; I read in a French book lately a sentence to the effect that 'Marriage might be defined as the state of twofold selfishness.' Let the single therefore take comfort.

Thank you for M. G.'s letter. She *does* seem most happy—and I cannot tell you how much more real, lasting and better-warranted her happiness seems than ever A's did. I think so much of it is in herself and her own serene, pure, trusting, religious nature —A. always gave one the idea of a vacillating unsteady rapture entirely dependant on circumstances with all their fluctuations. If Mary lives to be a Mother—you will then see a still greater difference.

I wish you—dear E. all health—enjoyment and happiness in your visit—And as far as one can judge—at present there seems a fair prospect of the wish being realised. — Yours faithfully,

C. BRONTË.

768 (573). *To* ELLEN NUSSEY.

HAWORTH, May 18th, '52.

DEAR ELLEN,—I enclose Mary's letter announcing Ellen's death and Ellen's two last letters—sorrowful documents—all of them. I received them this morning from Hunsworth without any note or directions where to send them, but I think—if I mistake not—Amelia in a previous note told me to transmit them to you.

What you say about your sister Ann concerns me much — every time I have seen her for some years past I have been struck by her sickly and weary look — Most certainly there must be something seriously wrong — either derangement or disease of some organ — it is very many years now since she has enjoyed good health. I hope you will write again very soon and let me know particularly how she gets on.

Do not fear — dear Nell — that I shall think you conceited in what you say about Mr ———, and do not apprehend either that I shall trouble you with advice — I always think that the two persons most concerned in these matters are those who alone can rightly judge the expediency or inexpediency of their own case. That they always *do* rightly judge I will not affirm — but if *their* bias is to error — no other hand can rectify it.

It seems desirable that you should have been able to start from home at once and without impediment — but who knows? A temporary delay may turn out for the best after all. It is really too bad of Mercy to give trouble just now.

Be sure to write soon and believe me — Yours faithfully,

C. B.

769. *To* GEORGE SMITH.

May 22nd, 1852.

MY DEAR SIR, — Your note enclosing a Bank Post Bill for the amount of my dividend reached me safely.

Occupied as you are — I will not at present detain you by more than an acknowledgment.

Should you write to me in the course of the next fortnight or three weeks, my address will be Cliff House, Filey, East-Riding, Yorkshire. It is a small watering-place on the coast where I propose going for change of air. — Yours sincerely,

C. BRONTË.

770. *To* MRS GASKELL.

May 22nd, 1852.

. . . I read 'Visiting at Cranford' with that sort of pleasure which seems always too brief in its duration — I wished the paper had been twice as long. . . .

C. BRONTË.

771. *To* MRS GORE.

FILEY, May 28th, 1852.

DEAR MRS GORE,—I have no thoughts of visiting Town this Summer. The past Winter and Spring proved somewhat trying to me, and I am now at the Seaside endeavouring to regain lost ground. Already I am very much better—and if the weather were a little milder—no doubt should be better still.

With thanks for your kind note,—I am, dear Mrs Gore, Yours sincerely,

C. BRONTË.

772 (574). *To* The REV. P. BRONTË, *Haworth, Yorks.*

CLIFF HOUSE, FILEY, June 2nd, 1852.

DEAR PAPA,—Thank you for your letter, which I was so glad to get that I think I must answer it by return of post. I had expected one yesterday, and was perhaps a little unreasonably anxious when disappointed, but the weather has been so *very* cold that I feared either you were ill or Martha worse. I hope Martha will take care of herself. I cannot help feeling a little uneasy about her.

On the whole, I get on very well here, but I have not bathed yet, as I am told it is much too cold and too early in the season. The sea is very grand. Yesterday it was a somewhat unusually high tide, and I stood about an hour on the cliffs yesterday afternoon watching the tumbling in of great tawny turbid waves, that made the whole shore white with foam and filled the air with a sound hollower and deeper than thunder. There are so very few visitors at Filey yet that I and a few sea-birds and fishing-boats have often the whole expanse of sea, shore, and cliff to ourselves. When the tide is out the sands are wide, long, and smooth, and very pleasant to walk on. When the high tides are in, not a vestige of sand remains. I saw a great dog rush into the sea yesterday, and swim and bear up against the waves like a seal. I wonder what Flossy would say to that.

On Sunday afternoon I went to a church which I should like Mr Nicholls to see. It was certainly not more than thrice the length and breadth of our passage, floored with brick, the walls green with mould, the pews painted white, but the paint almost all worn off with time and decay. At one end there is a little gallery for the singers, and when these personages stood up to perform, they all turned their backs upon the congregation, and the congregation turned *their* backs on the pulpit and parson. The effect of this manœuvre was so ludicrous, I could hardly help laughing; had Mr Nicholls been there he certainly would have laughed out. Looking up at the gallery and seeing only the broad backs of the singers presented to their audience was excessively grotesque. There is a well-meaning but utterly inactive clergyman at Filey, and Methodists flourish.

I cannot help enjoying Mr Butterfield's defeat; and yet in one sense this is a bad state of things, calculated to make working people both discontented and insubordinate. Give my kind regards, dear papa, to Mr Nicholls, Tabby, and Martha. Charge Martha to beware of draughts, and to get such help in her cleaning as she shall need. I hope you will continue well.—Believe me, your affectionate daughter,

C. BRONTË.

773 (575). *To* ELLEN NUSSEY.

CLIFF HOUSE, FILEY, June 6th, 1852.

DEAR ELLEN,—I am at Filey utterly alone. Do not be angry. The step is right. I considered it and resolved on it with due deliberation. Change of air was necessary; there were reasons why I should *not* go to the South and why I should come here. On Friday I went to Scarboro', visited the church-yard and stone[1]—it must be refaced and re-lettered—there are 5 errors. I gave the necessary directions—*that* duty then is done—long has it lain heavy on my mind—and that was a pilgrimage I felt I could only make alone.

I am in our old lodgings at Mrs Smith's—not however in the same rooms—but in less expensive apartments—they seemed glad to see me—remembered you and me very well and seemingly with great good will. The Daughter who used to wait on us is just married. Filey seems to me much altered—more lodging-houses—some of them very handsome—have been built—the sea has all its old grandeur—I walk on the sands a good deal and try *not* to feel desolate and melancholy. How sorely my heart

---

[1]The inscription on Anne's tombstone. See Vol. II, p.336, note.

longs for you I need not say. I have bathed once — it seemed to do me good — I may perhaps stay here a fortnight. There are as yet scarcely any visitors. A Lady Wenlock is staying at the large house of which you used so vigilantly to observe the inmates. One day I set out with intent to trudge to Filey Bridge but was frightened back by two cows. I mean to try again some morning. Mrs Smith in talking about Mr and Mrs Hudson yesterday — observed that they were now in quite reduced circumstances. I was very sorry to hear this.

Dear Nell — a part of your letter touched me to the heart — but you should have been more explicit — what makes you so *certain*? Have you just grounds for your present conclusion? Not that I would wish to revive deceptive hopes — you know I am always for facing the stern truth — but still — life seems hard and dreary for some of us, and yet — it *must* be accepted — and with submission.

I left papa well — I have been a good deal troubled with headache and with some pain in the side since I came here but I feel that this has been owing to the cold wind — for very cold has it been till lately — at present I feel better — Shall I send the papers to you as usual? Write again directly and tell me this — and anything and everything else that comes into your mind. Georgiana wants whipping. — Believe me — dearest Nell, Yours faithfully,

C. BRONTË.

774 (576). *To* ELLEN NUSSEY.

FILEY, June 16th, [1852].

DEAR ELLEN, — I send you the 'Examiner' with this: the 'Leader' — I imagine will be out of place at Cakeham: it had better not go.

Be quite easy about me. I really think I am better for my stay at Filey — that I have derived indeed more benefit from it than I dared to anticipate — I believe could I stay here two months and enjoy something like social cheerfulness as well as exercise and good air — my health would be quite renewed. This — however — cannot possibly be — but I am most thankful for the good received. I may stay another week.

Tell me no particulars, dear Nell — that would give you pain — I only asked because I thought you might be viewing the subject too hardly for yourself.

Vol. III   z

Notice this. A visit that opens very pleasantly often closes in pain and disappointment—and vice versa. Be of good courage. I fancy somehow you will be more comfortable when the wedding[1] is over.

Your plan about the school-girls—the little caps—the flower-scattering &c. made me smile—and still more the idea of my aiding and advising in it were I on the spot—Not at all—I should not relish it in the least—Do it if you like—your motive is kind and excellent—Mary and her Spouse may like that sort of thing —you know best.

I return E. Sherwood's letter. I am sorry for her; I believe she suffers—but—I do not like her style of expressing herself, it absolutely reminds me of Amelia Walker. Grief as well as joy manifests itself in most different ways in different people—and I doubt not she is sincere and in earnest when she talks of her 'sainted, precious father'; but I could wish she used simpler language.

Write again soon and believe me—Yours faithfully,

C. BRONTË.

I have calculated that it takes two posts to reach you—if am wrong—tell me as I would not put you to useless expense.

775 (577). *To* LÆTITIA WHEELWRIGHT.

FILEY, June 16th, 1852.

DEAR LÆTITIA,—I return that most precious document—the letter of Maria Miller.[2] Selfish indeed is the policy which has dictated it—worldly the adroitness with which the suggestion has been carried out. The impudent pretence of revived interest (under the circumstances, *it is sheer impudence*), the sly postponement of her real motive to the postscript, are too bad; yet the whole is but clumsily managed—being quite transparent. If you wish to have my opinion about answering it—I can only say it seems to me you are bound to consult nothing in the world in this matter but your own inclination and convenience. No deference is due to Mrs W. P. Robertson. Alas! she proves herself too unmistakably selfish.

I think the less you have to do with her or any of her affairs —

[1]Mary Gorham married the Rev. Thomas Swinton Hewitt.   [2]See Vol. I, p. 255.

the better. The residence at Boulogne does not sound very well; Boulogne is the asylum of a not very respectable class. The publication of a work by subscription is a decidedly objectionable, shifty, shabby expedient. Wash your hands clean of them, Lætitia: keep out of the mess. It grieves me much that your state of health is still so far from satisfactory.

I am now staying at Filey—a small bathing-place on the east coast of Yorkshire; I have been here three weeks and thus far think I have derived real benefit from the change. I earnestly wish you could say as much. Of all merely material blessings I think health is the greatest.

Well can I sympathise with you all on the subject of your Papa's state. I have watched the progress of that calamity, and know how sad is the gradual darkening.

With kindest regards to your dear parents and all your sisters —with hopes that strength needful for the day will be given to all—and with sincere solicitude for yourself.—I am dear Lætitia,

Yours affectionately,

C. BRONTË.

776 (578). *To* MARGARET WOOLER.

FILEY BAY, June 23rd, 1852.

MY DEAR MISS WOOLER,—Your kind and welcome note reached me at this place where I have been staying three weeks— *quite alone*. Change and sea-air had become necessary; distance and other considerations forbade my accompanying Ellen Nussey to the South—much as I should have liked it—had I felt quite free and unfettered; Ellen told me some time ago that you were not likely to visit Scarbro' till the Autumn—so I forthwith packed my trunk and betook myself here.

The first week or ten days—I greatly feared the seaside would not suit me—for I suffered almost constantly from headache and other harassing ailments; the weather too was dark, stormy, and excessively—*bitterly* cold; my Solitude, under such circumstances, partook of the character of Desolation; I had some dreary evening hours and night-vigils. However—that passed; I think I am now better and stronger from the change, and in a day or two hope to return home.

E. Nussey told me that Mr Wm Wooler said—people with my tendency to congestion of the liver—should walk three or

four hours every day; accordingly I have walked as much as I
could since I came here, and look almost as sunburnt and wea-
ther-beaten as a fisherman or a bathing-woman with being out in
the open air.

As to my work — it has stood obstinately still for a long while:
certainly a torpid liver makes torpid brains: no spirit moves me.
If this state of things does not entirely change — my chance of a
holiday in the Autumn is not worth much. Yet I should be very
sorry not to be able to meet you for a little while at Scarbro'.

The duty to be discharged at Scarbro' was the chief motive
that drew me to the East Coast: I have been there — visited the
churchyard, seen the stone — there were five errors — consequently I had to give directions for its being re-faced and re-
lettered.[1]

My dear Miss Wooler — I do most truly sympathise with you
on the success of your kind efforts to provide for your young
kinsman — I know what your feelings would be under the circumstances. To me — the decision of his uncles seems *too* hard —
too worldly, and I am glad that Providence saw fit to make you
the means of awarding him a milder doom. Poor youth! such
banishment might have been justifiable in the case of a rough,
reckless, unmanageable boy — but for one whose disadvantages
had their source in over-timidity and weak nerves — it would
have been really cruel. Very grateful must be his mother's feelings towards you.

Give my kind regards to Mr and Mrs Carter — tell me about
Ellen and Susan when you write. . . .

C. BRONTË.

777 (579). *To* ELLEN NUSSEY.

HAWORTH, July 1st, 1852.

DEAR ELLEN, — I am again at home, where (thank God) I
found all well. I certainly feel much better than I did, and would
fain trust that the improvement may prove permanent. Do not
be alarmed about the pains in your chest and shoulders, they are
certainly not desirable, but, I believe, not dangerous nor indica-
tive of serious ailment. The weather no doubt has much to do
with them; certain states of the atmosphere produce more or less

---

[1]Pencil note by Miss Wooler: 'Anne B.'s tomb.'

of visceral congestion, and these pains are the result; such is my theory, gathered from experience. The first fortnight I was at Filey I had constantly recurring pain in the right side, just in the middle of the chest, burning and aching between the shoulders, and sick headache into the bargain. My spirits at the same time were cruelly depressed, prostrated sometimes. I feared the misery and the sufferings of last winter were all returning, consequently I am now indeed thankful to find myself so much better. Tell me particularly how you are?

You ask about India. Let us dismiss the subject in a few words and not recur to it. All is silent as the grave. Cornhill is silent too. There has been bitter disappointment there at my having no work ready for this season. We must not rely upon our fellow-creatures, only on ourselves, and on Him who is above both us and them. My labours as you call them stand in abeyance, and I cannot hurry them. I must take my own time, however long that time may be.

I was amused to learn from Miss Martineau that Joe Taylor and suite during their late visit to Ambleside waited actually on *her* under the plea of being *my* friends. I fancy she received them very kindly. She terms Amelia a tranquil little Dutch woman. Joe's organ of combativeness and contradiction amused and amazed her. She liked the baby best. How inconsistent of Joe to make this call. He who railed at Lord John Manners and Mr Smythe, and accused them of insolence in calling on me.

I send the 'Examiner.' Let me hear from you soon, and believe me, yours faithfully,

C. BRONTË.

END OF VOLUME III

The Brontë Sisters
from the painting by Branwell Brontë
in the National Portrait Gallery

Emery Walker Ltd. ph sc.

THE BRONTËS: THEIR LIVES, FRIEND-
SHIPS & CORRESPONDENCE

VOLUME THE FOURTH

1852 - 1928

THIS EDITION OF THE WORKS AND LIVES
OF THE BRONTËS IS DEDICATED TO
SIR JAMES AND LADY ROBERTS
OF FAIRLIGHT HALL AND
OF STRATHALLAN CASTLE SCOTLAND
BY WHOSE GENEROSITY
THE BRONTË PARSONAGE AT HAWORTH
HAS BEEN ESTABLISHED AS
ONE OF OUR NATIONAL
LITERARY SHRINES

THE ILLUSTRATIONS

FACSIMILES

CONTENTS OF VOLUME IV

Contents

A BRONTË CHRONOLOGY

Volume IV. 1852–1928

Mr Brontë's illness	July, 1852
Mr Nicholls's Proposal of Marriage	December, 1852
Charlotte in London	January, 1853
Publication of *Villette*	January 28, 1853
Charlotte visits Mrs Gaskell in Manchester	April, 1853
Mr Nicholls leaves Haworth	May, 1853
Charlotte's trip to Scotland with Mr and Mrs Joe Taylor	August, 1853
Mrs Gaskell's visit to Haworth	September, 1853
Charlotte visits Miss Wooler at Hornsea	October, 1853
Charlotte's engagement to the Rev. A. B. Nicholls	April, 1854
Charlotte visits Mrs Gaskell in Manchester	May, 1854
Visits Mr and Mrs J. Taylor at Hunsworth	May, 1854
Charlotte's Marriage	June 29, 1854
Her Death	March 31, 1855
Publication of the *Professor*	1857
Publication of Mrs Gaskell's *Life of Charlotte Brontë*	March, 1857
Death of the Rev. Patrick Brontë	June 7, 1861
Publication of the first illustrated edition of the Brontë Works	October, 1872
Publication of Sir T. Wemyss Reid's *Charlotte Brontë: a Monograph*	1877
Memorial Tablet to the Brontës erected in Haworth Church by Sidney Biddell of London	1882
Publication of A. Mary F. Robinson's *Emily Brontë*	April, 1883
Stained glass window erected in Haworth Church in memory of Charlotte Brontë by Thomas Hockley of Philadelphia	May, 1884
Foundation of the Brontë Society	December 16, 1893
First Brontë Museum opened	May 18, 1895
Publication of Clement K. Shorter's *Charlotte Brontë and Her Circle*	1896
Death of the Rev. A. B. Nicholls	December 3, 1906
Opening of the Brontë Parsonage Museum, Haworth	August 4, 1928

CHAPTER XXVIII
THE WRITING OF *VILLETTE*

THE writing of *Villette* proved one of the hardest tasks of Charlotte Brontë's life. She had returned from Filey renewed in health and vigour, fully determined to make good progress with her book, but the work proved onerous, and she felt that she could not get on. Then to add to her difficulties Mr Brontë had a seizure, and was again threatened with the loss of his sight. Another fact which made *Villette* lie heavy on her hands was that there was now no one from whom she might ask advice. The nightly discussions between the three sisters had been a great help during the writing of the earlier novels, but now Charlotte had to work quite alone, and she began to lose confidence in her own judgment.

The letters of the next few months give a painful picture of the nerve-wracked little authoress, increasingly harassed by her father's illness, yet determined to forego all enjoyment and diversion in a gigantic effort to finish her book. The strain proved too heavy, and she was at length compelled to permit herself a short respite, by receiving a visit from her friend Ellen Nussey.

The first two volumes of the manuscript of *Villette* were sent to the publishers at the end of October, and Charlotte was much gratified to receive a favourable criticism from them. The third volume, however, proved much more difficult. She seems to have encountered some difficulty in the final disposing of her characters and the winding up of the story. She left the conclusion so vague that readers must decide for themselves whether Paul Emanuel married Lucy Snowe or not. At last it was finished and posted to her publishers on November 20th. Her task thus completed, Charlotte went to Brookroyd for a change and rest. She was very anxious to hear her publishers' views of the last volume of her book, and when a letter did not arrive so soon as could be reasonably expected, she was prepared to set off to London at once to see her Cornhill friends.

Vol. IV   b

778 (580). *To* ELLEN NUSSEY.

HAWORTH, July 26th, 1852.

DEAR ELLEN, —I return Mrs T. H.'s letter. It is the language of happiness which dares not trust itself to full expression. A kind of suppressed buoyancy is obvious throughout.

I should not have written to you to-day by choice; lately I have again been harassed with headache, the heavy electric atmosphere oppresses me much, yet I am less miserable just now than I was a little while ago. A severe shock came upon me about papa. He was suddenly attacked with acute inflammation of the eye. Mr Ruddock was sent for, and after he had examined him, he called me into another room, and said papa's pulse was bounding at 150 per minute, that there was a strong pressure of blood upon the brain, that in short the symptoms were decidedly apoplectic.

Active measures were immediately taken, by the next day the pulse was reduced to 90. Thank God he is now better, though not well. The eye is a good deal inflamed. He does not know his state, to tell him he had been in danger of apoplexy would almost be to kill him at once, it would increase the rush to the brain and perhaps bring about rupture; he is kept very quiet.

Dear Nell, you will excuse a short note. Write again soon, tell me all concerning yourself that can relieve you. — Yours faithfully,

C. B.

779 (581). *To* W. S. WILLIAMS.

July 28th, 1852.

MY DEAR SIR, — Is it in contemplation to publish the new edition of 'Shirley' soon? Would it not be better to defer it for a time? In reference to a part of your letter, permit me to express this wish — and I trust in so doing I shall not be regarded as stepping out of my position as an author, and encroaching on the arrangements of business — viz. that no announcement of a new work by the author of 'Jane Eyre' shall be made till the MS. of such work is actually in my publisher's hands. Perhaps we are none of us justified in speaking very decidedly where the future is concerned; but for some too much caution in such calculations can scarcely be observed: amongst this number I must class my-self. Nor in doing so can I assume an apologetic tone. He does right who does his best.

Last autumn I got on for a time quickly. I ventured to look forward to spring as the period of publication: my health gave way; I passed such a winter as, having been once experienced, will never be forgotten. The spring proved little better than a protraction of trial. The warm weather and a visit to the sea have done me much good physically; but as yet I have recovered neither elasticity of animal spirits nor flow of the power of com-position. And if it were otherwise the difference would be of no avail; my time and thoughts are at present taken up with close attendance on my father, whose health is just now in a very critical state, the heat of the weather having produced determin-ation of blood to the head. —I am, yours sincerely,

C. BRONTË.

780 (582). *To* ELLEN NUSSEY.

August 3rd, 1852.

DEAR ELLEN, —I write a line to say that papa is now consider-ed out of danger, his progress to health is not without relapse, but I think he gains ground, if slowly, surely. Mr Ruddock says the seizure was quite of an apoplectic character; there was partial paralysis for two days, but the mind remained clear, in spite of a high degree of nervous irritation. One eye still remains inflamed, and papa is weak, but all muscular affection is gone, and the pulse is accurate. One cannot be too thankful that papa's sight is yet spared, it was the fear of losing that which chiefly distressed him.

With best wishes for yourself, dear Ellen, I am, yours faith-fully,

C. BRONTË.

My headaches are better. I have needed no help, but I thank you sincerely for your kind offers.

781 (584). *To* ELLEN NUSSEY.

HAWORTH, August 13th, 1852.

DEAR ELLEN, —Papa has varied occasionally since I wrote to you last—Monday was a very bad day—his spirits sunk pain-fully—Tuesday and yesterday however were much better and to-day he seems wonderfully well. The prostration of spirits which accompanies anything like a relapse is almost the most difficult point to manage. Dear Nell, you are tenderly kind in offering your society — but rest very tranquil where you are — be fully assured that it is not now nor under present circumstances that I feel the lack either of society or occupation — my time is pretty well filled and my thoughts appropriated — Mr Ruddock seems quite satisfied that there is now no present danger whatever — he says Papa has an excellent constitution and may live many years yet — the true balance is not yet restored to the circulation of the blood — but I believe that impetuous and dangerous determination to the head is quite obviated.

A letter has just been received from Mary Taylor which no doubt will be duly sent you — She seems to write in somewhat better spirits — she had got the box containing the bonnets &c. which you selected and expresses herself most thoroughly satisfied, with Ellen Nussey's choice — She says Amelia could not have put the affair in better hands.

I cannot permit myself to comment much on the chief contents of your last — advice is not necessary — as far as I can judge you seem hitherto enabled to take these trials in a good and wise spirit — I can only pray that such combined strength and resignation may be continued to you.

Submission — courage — exertion when practicable — these seem to be the weapons with which we must fight life's long battle. — Yours faithfully,

C. BRONTË.

782. *To* GEORGE SMITH.

August 19th, 1852.

MY DEAR SIR, — I am thankful to say that my Father is now much better, though still weak. The danger is, I trust, subsided, but I am warned that the attack has been of an apoplectic character, a circumstance which, at his age, brings anxieties not easily dispelled. His mind, however, has not been in the least clouded, and the muscular paralysis which existed for a time seems quite gone now. I am assured that with his excellent constitution there is every prospect that a return of the seizure may be long delayed.

I am glad to hear that your Mother is at Woodford, as I know how much she is attached to the country and its quiet pleasures; your sisters also will, no doubt, enjoy the change at this season. I do not wonder that you all felt regret at parting from Alick; he seemed to me an amiable boy. It is to be hoped, however, that the climate of Bombay will agree with him, and if it should not less than a month will bring him once more home.

I had better refrain from commenting on the brief glimpse you give of what your own labours have lately been. Surely you will now take some rest. Such systematic overtasking of mind and body may be borne for a time by some constitutions, but in the end it tells on the most vigorous. If physical strength stands it out, the brain suffers, and where the brain is continually irritated I believe both peace of mind and health of body are endangered.

'Shirley'[1] looks very respectable in her new attire.

Do not send the third volume of Mr Thackeray's MS. I would rather wait to see it in print. It will be something to look forward to.

My stay at the seaside was of great use. As to last winter and spring, they are quite gone, and I have no wish to dwell upon their passage.

Give my kind remembrances to your Mother and sisters when you see them. — Yours sincerely,

C. Brontë.

783 (583). *To* Ellen Nussey.

Haworth, Augt 25th, '52.

Dear Ellen, — I am thankful to say that Papa's convalescence seems now to be quite confirmed. There is scarcely any remainder of the inflammation in his eyes and his general health progresses satisfactorily. He begins even to look forward to resuming his duty ere long — but caution must be observed on that head. Martha has been very willing and helpful during Papa's illness — Poor Tabby is ill herself at present with English Cholera which complaint together with influenza has lately been almost universally prevalent in this district; of the last I have myself had a touch — but it went off very gently on the whole — affecting my chest and liver less than any cold has done for the last three years.

I trust, dear Ellen, you are well in health yourself — this visit

[1]The first one-volume edition, 1852.

to the south has not so far been productive of unmingled present pleasure—yet it may bring you future benefit in more ways than one.

I write to you about yourself rather under constraint and in the dark—for your letters—dear Nell—are most remarkably oracular—dropping nothing but hints—which tie my tongue a good deal. What for instance can I say to your last postscript? It is quite Sybilline. I can hardly guess what checks you in writing to me—There is certainly no one in this house or elsewhere to whom I should show your notes—and I do not imagine they are in any peril in passing through the Post-Offices.

Perhaps you think that as I generally write with some reserve —you ought to do the same. *My* reserve, however, has its found-ation not in design, but in necessity—I am silent because I have literally *nothing to say*. I might indeed repeat over and over again that my life is a pale blank and often a very weary burden—and that the Future sometimes appals me—but what end could be answered by such repetition except to weary you and enervate myself?

The evils that now and then wring a groan from my heart—lie in position—not that I am a *single* woman and likely to remain a *single* woman—but because I am a *lonely* woman and likely to be *lonely*. But it cannot be helped and therefore *imperatively must be borne*—and borne too with as few words about it as may be.

I write all this—just to prove to you that whatever you would freely *say* to me—you may just as freely write.

Understand—that I remain just as resolved as ever not to allow myself the holiday of a visit from you till I have done my work. After labour—pleasure—but while work was lying at the wall undone I never yet could enjoy recreation.—Yours very faithfully,

C. BRONTË.

784 (586). *To* MARGARET WOOLER.

HAWORTH, Septbr 2nd, 1852.

MY DEAR MISS WOOLER,—I have delayed answering your very kind letter till I could speak decidedly respecting Papa's health. For some weeks after the attack there were frequent variations—and once a threatening of relapse, but I trust his convalescence may now be regarded as confirmed. The acute inflammation of the eye, which distressed Papa so much as threatening loss of sight, but which, I suppose, was merely symptomatic of the rush of blood to the brain—is now quite subsided; the partial paralysis has also disappeared, the appetite is better; weakness with occasional slight giddiness seem now the only lingering traces of disease. I am assured that with Papa's excellent constitution—there is every prospect of his still being spared to me for many years.

For two things I have reason to be most thankful—viz. that the mental faculties have remained quite untouched, and also that my own health and strength have been found sufficient for the occasion. Solitary as I certainly was at Filey—I yet derived great benefit from the change.

It would be pleasant at the seaside this fine warm weather, and I should dearly like to be there with you; to such a treat, however, I do not now look forward at all. You will fully understand the impossibility of my enjoying peace of mind during absence from Papa under present circumstances; his strength must be very much more fully restored before I can think of leaving home.

My dear Miss Wooler—in case you should go to Scarbro' this season—may I request you to pay one visit to the churchyard and see if the inscription on the stone has been altered as I directed—We have heard nothing since on the subject, and I fear the alteration may have been neglected.

Ellen Nussey has made a long stay in the South, but I believe she will soon return now, and I am looking forward to the pleasure of having her company in the course of the autumn.

Your account of the Carters[1] interested me much: Susan seems a good, dear girl; I liked that trait of her choosing rather to spend the holidays at home than to give part of the precious time to a visit amongst comparative strangers; such a preference speaks volumes; I wish she may grow up such a character as will please you; I wish she may always retain some genuine feeling, something congenial and consolatory in her disposition, something you can turn to with reliance, esteem, affection—I wish in short that she may prove a dutiful and tender niece.

With kind regards to all old friends, and sincere love to yourself,—I am, my dear Miss Wooler, yours affectionately and respectfully,   C. BRONTË.

[1]See Vol. I, p. 84, note.

785 (587). *To* ELLEN NUSSEY.

September 9th, 1852.

DEAR ELLEN,—I did not send the 'Examiner' last week, not knowing how to address; I send it however this week as usual.

Thank you for Ann's notes, I like to read them, they are so full of news, but they are illegible, a great many words I really cannot make out. It is pleasing to hear that Mercy is doing so well, and the tidings about your mother seem also good. What she said about 'mending her *manners*' when Ellen came home made me laugh.

Papa continues pretty well, but his spirits often flag, and he complains much of weakness.

I get a note from Hunsworth every now and then, but I fear my last reply has not given much satisfaction; it contained a taste of that unpalatable commodity called *advice*, such advice too as might be, and I dare say was, construed into faint reproof.

I can scarcely tell what there is about Amelia that in spite of one's conviction of her amiability, in spite of one's sincere wish for her welfare, palls upon one, satiates, stirs impatience. She *will* complacently put forth opinions and tastes as her own, which are *not her own*, nor in any sense natural to her. She pretentiously talks Taylorism with a Ringrose air and voice. My patience can really hardly sustain the test of such a jay in borrowed plumes. She prated so much about the fine wilful spirit of her child, whom she describes as a hard brown little thing who will do nothing but what pleases herself, that I hit out at last, not very hard, but enough to make her think herself ill-used, I doubt not. Can't help it. She often says she is not 'absorbed in self,' but the fact is, I have seldom seen any one more unconsciously, thoroughly, and often weakly egotistic. Then too she is inconsistent. In the same breath she boasts her matrimonial happiness and whines for sympathy. Don't understand it. With a paragon of a husband and child, why that whining, craving note? Either her lot is not all she professes it to be, or she is hard to content. The fact is she makes me a little savage. How does she write to you? Answer soon and believe me, yours faithfully,   C. BRONTË.

If you be waited on by lady's-maids you'll have to pay them — for which reason I refuse.

786 (585). *To* ELLEN NUSSEY.

Friday [September 24th, 1852].

DEAR NELL,—I did not think you would at all expect to hear from me again till you got home, so little as I have to communicate, it did not seem to me worth while to write.

I do hope and believe the changes you have been having this summer will do you permanent good—notwithstanding the pain with which they have been too often mingled—Yet I feel glad that you are soon coming home—and I really must not trust myself to say how much I wish the time were come when without let or hindrance I could once more welcome you to Haworth.

But oh Nell! I don't get on—I feel fettered—incapable—sometimes very low—However—at present the subject must not be dwelt upon—it presses me too hardly—nearly and painfully.

Less than ever can I taste or know pleasure till this work is wound up. And yet—I often sit up in bed at night—thinking of and wishing for you.

Thank you for the 'Times'—what it said on the mighty and mournful subject was *well* said—All at once the whole Nation seems now to take a just view of that great character.[1]

There was a review too of an American book which I was glad to see. Read 'Uncle Tom's Cabin';[2] probably though you have read it.

Papa's health continues satisfactory thank God! As for me—my wretched liver has been disordered again of late—but I hope it is now going to be on better behaviour—it hinders me in working—depresses both power and tone of feeling. I must expect this derangement from time to time.

Write as soon as you can—I hope this letter will reach you before you start from Town—Good bye.—Yours faithfully,

C. BRONTË.

Your hint about Mrs Gorham does not in the least surprise me—I felt sure that with her alone you would not be comfortable. Mary is a genuine pearl of pure water.

[1]The Duke of Wellington died on 14th September, 1852, and after lying in state at Chelsea Hospital, was buried in St Paul's Cathedral.

[2]Harriet Beecher Stowe (1811-1896) wrote *Uncle Tom's Cabin* in 1851.

787 (589). *To* ELLEN NUSSEY.

October 5th, 1852.

DEAR ELLEN,—I must write a line to accompany the two letters which I return with thanks. Mary's is very pleasant and cheerful. I hope you are safe at home by this time. Write very soon and tell me how you are, and how you found all.

Dear Nell, you know very well I should as soon think of going to the moon as of setting off to Brookroyd at present; no, I trust when we meet it will be at Haworth.

Mr and Mrs Forster[1] made another of their sudden calls here yesterday. They came in a fly in the midst of dreadful drenching weather. A lady accompanied them, a Miss Dixon from Dublin; it seems there is some distant connection between her family and that of the Birmingham Dixons, but they have no personal intercourse. They wanted to take me back with them; of course, vainly. Papa and I are both under pressure of colds at present. I was very uneasy about Papa on Sunday—but I trust he is better now, and so I think am I. Do you escape pretty well?

I send the newspapers. Write soon.—Yours faithfully,

C. BRONTË.

788 (590). *To* ELLEN NUSSEY.

October 9th, 1852.

DEAR NELL,—Papa expresses so strong a wish that I should ask you to come, and I feel some little refreshment so absolutely necessary myself, that I really must beg you to come to Haworth for one single week. I thought I would persist in denying myself till I had done my work, but I find it won't do, the matter refuses to progress, and this excessive solitude presses too heavily, so let me see your dear face, Nell, just for one reviving week.

Could you come on Wednesday? Write to-morrow and let me know by what train you would reach Keighley, that I may send for you.

I am right glad that you keep up your courage so nobly, how much better, how much wiser than to sink in bodily and mental weakness. The effort will have its reward.

We will leave all other matters to talk about.—Yours faithfully,

C. BRONTË.

[1] See letter dated March 21, 1852, Vol. III, p. 324.

789 (650). *To* ELLEN NUSSEY.

Monday morning.
[October 11th, 1852].

DEAR ELLEN,—I find I cannot have the gig till Friday—On that day (D. V.) it shall be at the station at the hour you mention viz. 43m. past 3 o'clock—and then I hope it will bring you safe to me. The prospect of seeing you already cheers. One reason which I may tell you when you come partly reconciles me to this temporary delay. If I do not hear anything from you to the contrary—I shall consider the matter settled. May no other hindrance arise either here or at Brookroyd—kind regards to all Dear Nell,—Yours faithfully,

C. BRONTË.

790 (588). *To* MARGARET WOOLER.

HAWORTH, October 21st, 1852.

MY DEAR MISS WOOLER,—I was truly sorry to hear that when Ellen Nussey called at the Parsonage at Heckmondwike you were suffering under influenza: I know that an attack of this debilitating complaint is no trifle in your case as its effects linger with you long. It has been very prevalent in this neighbourhood; I did not escape, but the sickness and fever only lasted a few days, and the cough was not severe—Papa—I am thankful to say—continues pretty well; Ellen Nussey thinks him little, if at all, altered.

And now for your kind present.[1] The book will be precious to me—chiefly perhaps for the sake of the giver, but also for its own sake—for it is a good book—and I wish I may be enabled to read it with some approach to the spirit you would desire; its perusal came recommended in such a manner as to obviate danger of neglect—its place shall always be on my dressing-table.

As to the other part of the present—it arrived under these circumstances. For a month past an urgent necessity to buy and make some chemises[2] for winter-wear had been importuning my conscience; the *buying* might be soon effected, but the *making*

[1] 'The Gospel,' by the Rev. H. White, inscribed Miss Brontë from her affectionate friend, M. W. Sept. 3rd 1852.

[2] 'Chemises' scratched out; 'things' added in pencil.

was a more serious consideration. At this juncture Ellen Nussey
arrives with a good-sized parcel which—when opened—dis-
closes these excellent chemises[1] perfectly made and of capital
useful fabric—adorned also with cambric frills—which seemly
decoration it is but too probable I might myself have foregone as
an augmentation of trouble not to be lightly incurred. I felt
strong doubts as to my right to profit by this sort of fairy-gift,
so unlooked-for and so curiously opportune: on reading a note
accompanying the garments—I am told that to accept will be to
confer a favour (!). The doctrine is too palatable to be rejected;
I even waive all nice scrutiny of its soundness—in short—I submit with as good a grace as may be.

Ellen Nussey has only been my companion one little week—
I would not have her any longer—for I am disgusted with myself and my delays—and consider it was a weak yielding to
temptation in me to send for her at all—but in truth my spirits
were getting low—prostrate sometimes, and she has done me
inexpressible good. I wonder when I shall see you at Haworth
again; both my father and the servants have again and again
insinuated a distinct wish that you should be requested to come
in the course of the Summer and Autumn, but I always turned
rather a deaf ear: 'Not yet,' was my thought, 'I want first to be
free—work first—then pleasure.'

I venture to send by E. N. a book which may amuse an hour—
a Scotch tale by a Minister's wife—it seems to me well told—and
may serve to remind you of characters and manners you have
seen in Scotland. When you have time to write a line—I shall
feel anxious to hear how you are. With kind regards to all old
friends—and truest affection to yourself—in which E. N. joins
me,—I am, my dear Miss Wooler, yours gratefully and respectfully,

C. BRONTË.

791 (591 and 527). *To* ELLEN NUSSEY.

Tuesday, [October 26th, '52].

DEAR NELL,—Your note came only this morning, I had expected it yesterday and was beginning actually to feel uneasy,
like you. This won't do, I am afraid of caring for you too much.

[1]'These excellent chemises' deleted and 'the things I require' added in pencil.

You must have come upon Hunsworth at an unfavourable moment; seen it under a cloud. Surely they are not always or often thus, or else married life is indeed but a slipshod paradise. I am glad, however, that the child is, as we conjectured, pretty well.

Miss Wooler's note is indeed kind, good, and characteristic.

I only send the 'Examiner,' not having yet read the 'Leader.' I was spared the remorse I feared. On Saturday I fell to business, and as the welcome mood is still decently existent, and my eyes consequently excessively tired with scribbling, you must excuse a mere scrawl. You left your smart shoes. Papa was glad to hear you had got home well, as well as myself. Regards to all. Good-bye. — Yours faithfully,   C. BRONTË.

I do miss my dear bed-fellow. No more of that calm sleep.

I have been very well ever since you were here and am really fatter now, though I don't know how long it will last. Papa continues as usual, but he frequently complains of weakness, and needs often renewed encouragement. It is now getting dark.

792 (592). *To* GEORGE SMITH.

October 30th, 1852.

MY DEAR SIR, — You must notify honestly what you think of 'Villette' when you have read it. I can hardly tell you how I hunger to hear some opinion beside my own, and how I have sometimes desponded, and almost despaired, because there was no one to whom to read a line, or of whom to ask a counsel. 'Jane Eyre' was not written under such circumstances, nor were two-thirds of 'Shirley.' I got so miserable about it, I could bear no allusion to the book. It is not finished yet; but now I hope. As to the anonymous publication, I have this to say: If the withholding of the author's name should tend materially to injure the publisher's interest, to interfere with booksellers' orders, etc., I would not press the point; but if no such detriment is contingent I should be much thankful for the sheltering shadow of an incognito. I seem to dread the advertisements — the large-lettered 'Currer Bell's New Novel,' or 'New Work by the Author of "Jane Eyre."' These, however, I feel well enough, are the transcendentalisms of a retired wretch; so you must speak frankly. ... I shall be glad to see 'Colonel Esmond.' My objection to the second volume lay here: I thought it contained decidedly too much History—too little Story.

You will see that 'Villette' touches on no matter of public interest. I cannot write books handling the topics of the day; it is of no use trying. Nor can I write a book for its moral. Nor can I take up a philanthropic scheme, though I honour philanthropy; and voluntarily and sincerely veil my face before such a mighty subject as that handled in Mrs Beecher Stowe's work, 'Uncle Tom's Cabin.' To manage these great matters rightly they must be long and practically studied—their bearings known intimately, and their evils felt genuinely; they must not be taken up as a business matter and a trading speculation. I doubt not Mrs Stowe had felt the iron of slavery enter into her heart, from childhood upwards, long before she ever thought of writing books. The feeling throughout her work is sincere and not got up. Remember to be an honest critic of 'Villette,' and tell Mr Williams to be unsparing: not that I am likely to alter anything, but I want to know his impressions and yours.

793 (595). *To* ELLEN NUSSEY.

Octr 31st, 1852.

DEAR ELLEN,—Mrs Upjohn's[1] letter—which I return—interested me a good deal. It reads like the production of a warm-hearted good-natured woman—there is a sort of vivacity of temperament and feeling about it which seems to have had genuineness to survive such a catalogue of afflictions as rarely fall in succession on one human being. Poor woman! She has been sorely tried. Her proposal to you is peculiar. If I rightly understand it—it amounts to this. That you should go and spend some time with them on a sort of experiment visit—that if the result were mutually satisfactory—they would wish in a sense to adopt you—with the prospect of leaving you property—amount of course indefinite.

The affectionate remembrance which has suggested this idea says much both to your credit and hers. It seems to me that the experiment visit should be paid, if not now—as you have so lately and so long been absent—yet next spring for instance—and this is all you are called upon to decide for the present—the rest may be left for future consideration. After you shall have

[1]The Rev. Francis Upjohn, M.A., was Vicar of Gorleston, Suffolk.

seen them both and know what it is to live with them—your
way will be clearer. I cannot help wishing that something permanently advantageous to you may spring from this incident.
Yet it is a case which presents difficulties. To leave your own
home and Mother for the society of two elderly invalids is a step
demanding caution.

Mrs J.T.'s epistle is characteristic enough—'sitz-bath'—'alum
and water' and all! She seems to have got into the way of perpetually messing with something or other.

I have just got a letter from New Zealand which I enclose—it
made me sad—I cannot help earnestly wishing that Mary were
back in England—if one could but see the slightest chance of an
opening for her making her way.

I am quite glad to hear Mercy is such a good girl—long may
she continue so—both for your sake and her own. Give my love
both to her and your Mother and believe me dear Nell—Yours
faithfully,

C. BRONTË.

Write again soon.

794 (616). *To* ELLEN NUSSEY.

[Undated].

DEAR NELL,—Forgive a mere scrap of writing, I am hurried.
I send your shoes by this post. Thanks for your letter, you are
right to go, and to go soon. I somehow wish you to get it over;
I hope you won't be *very* long away this time, whatever you
eventually decide on. I am not sanguine. If your affections bind
or incline you to Mr and Mrs Upjohn you *ought* to stay; if they do
not, I know from your nature you never will be able to get on.
I feel certain that for the mere prospect of 'future advantage' you
could no more live with them than I could, you will see how it is.
I quite anticipate difficulties, but *you will see* I wish the 'future
advantage' were more defined; would it be a legacy of £40 or
£50 per ann. or what? When I mentioned it to papa, he remarked
that it was not *delicately* expressed. I could not but agree in this
remark. He seems, however, most specially solicitous that you
should try the adventure, and thinks unimportant objections
ought not lightly to weigh with you.—Yours faithfully,

C. BRONTË.

795 (593). *To* GEORGE SMITH.

November 3rd, 1852.

MY DEAR SIR, —I feel very grateful for your letter; it relieved me much, for I was a good deal harassed by doubts as to how 'Villette' might appear in other eyes than my own. I feel in some degree authorised to rely on your favourable impressions, because you are quite right where you hint disapprobation. You have exactly hit two points at least where I was conscious of defect—the discrepancy, the want of perfect harmony, between Graham's boyhood and manhood—the angular abruptness of his change of sentiment towards Miss Fanshawe. You must remember, though, that in secret he had for some time appreciated that young lady at a somewhat depressed standard—held her a *little* lower than the angels. But still the reader ought to have been better made to feel this preparation towards a change of mood. As to the publishing arrangements, I leave them to Cornhill. There is, undoubtedly, a certain force in what you say about the inexpediency of affecting a mystery which cannot be sustained; so you must act as you think is for the best. I submit, also, to the advertisements in large letters, but under protest, and with a kind of ostrich longing for concealment. Most of the third volume is given to the development of the 'crabbed Professor's' character. Lucy must not marry Dr. John; he is far too youthful, handsome, bright-spirited, and sweet-tempered; he is a 'curled darling' of Nature and of Fortune, and must draw a prize in life's lottery. His wife must be young, rich, pretty; he must be made very happy indeed. If Lucy marries anybody it must be the Professor—a man in whom there is much to forgive, much to 'put up with.' But I am not leniently disposed towards Miss *Frost*;[1] from the beginning I never meant to appoint her lines in pleasant places. The conclusion of this third volume is still a matter of some anxiety: I can but do my best, however. It would speedily be finished, could I ward off certain obnoxious headaches, which whenever I get into the spirit of my work, are apt to seize and prostrate me. . . .

Colonel Henry Esmond[2] is just arrived. He looks very antique

[1] In the original manuscript, 'Lucy Frost' may be seen with the name of 'Frost' erased and 'Snowe' substituted.

[2] Thackeray sent Miss Brontë a copy of *The History of Henry Esmond*, inscribed 'Miss Brontë, with W. M. Thackeray's grateful regards. October 28, 1852.'

and distinguished in his Queen Anne's garb; the periwig, sword, lace, and ruffles are very well represented by the old 'Spectator' type.

C. BRONTË.

796 (594). *To* GEORGE SMITH.

HAWORTH.

The third volume[1] seemed to me to possess the most sparkle, impetus, and interest. Of the first and second my judgment was that parts of them were admirable; but there was the fault of containing too much History—too little Story. I hold that a work of fiction ought to be a work of creation: that the *real* should be sparingly introduced in pages dedicated to the *ideal*. Plain household bread is a far more wholesome and necessary thing than cake; yet who would like to see the brown loaf placed upon the table for dessert? In the second volume the author gives us an ample supply of excellent brown bread; in his third, only such a portion as gives substance, like the crumbs of bread in a well-made, not too rich, plum-pudding.

C. BRONTË.

797 (596). *To* W. S. WILLIAMS.

November 6th, 1852.

MY DEAR SIR,—I must not delay thanking you for your kind letter, with its candid and able commentary on 'Villette.' With many of your strictures I concur. The third volume may, perhaps, do away with some of the objections; others still remain in force. I do not think the interest culminates anywhere to the degree you would wish. What climax there is does not come on till near the conclusion; and even then I doubt whether the regular novel-reader will consider the 'agony piled sufficiently high' (as the Americans say), or the colours dashed on to the canvas with the proper amount of daring. Still, I fear, they must be satisfied with what is offered; my palette affords no brighter tints; were I to attempt to deepen the reds, or burnish the yellows, I should but botch.

Unless I am mistaken the emotion of the book will be found

[1] Of Thackeray's *Esmond*.

to be kept throughout in tolerable subjection. As to the name of the heroine, I can hardly express what subtlety of thought made me decide upon giving her a cold name; but at first I called her 'Lucy Snowe' (spelt with an 'e'), which Snowe I afterwards changed to 'Frost.' Subsequently I rather regretted the change, and wished it 'Snowe' again. If not too late I should like the alteration to be made now throughout the MS. A *cold* name she must have; partly, perhaps, on the *'lucus a non lucendo'* principle —partly on that of the 'fitness of things,' for she has about her an external coldness.

You say that she may be thought morbid and weak, unless the history of her life be more fully given. I consider that she *is* both morbid and weak at times; her character sets up no pretensions to unmixed strength, and anybody living her life would necessarily become morbid. It was no impetus of healthy feeling which urged her to the confessional, for instance; it was the semi-delirium of solitary grief and sickness. If, however, the book does not express all this, there must be a great fault somewhere. I might explain away a few other points, but it would be too much like drawing a picture and then writing underneath the name of the object intended to be represented. We know what sort of a pencil that is which needs an ally in the pen.

Thanking you again for the clearness and fulness with which you have responded to my request for a statement of impressions, I am, my dear sir, yours very sincerely,

C. BRONTË.

I trust the work will be seen in MS. by no one except Mr Smith and yourself.

798 (597). *To* W. S. WILLIAMS.

November 10th, 1852.

MY DEAR SIR,—I only wished the publication of 'Shirley' to be delayed till 'Villette' was nearly ready; so that there can now be no objection to its being issued whenever you think fit. About putting the MS. into type I can only say that, should I be able to proceed with the third volume at my average rate of composition, and with no more than the average amount of interruptions, I should hope to have it ready in about three weeks. I leave it to you to decide whether it would be better to delay the printing that space of time, or to commence it immediately. It would certainly be more satisfactory if you were to see the third volume before printing the first and the second; yet, if delay is likely to prove injurious, I do not think it is indispensable. I have read the third volume of 'Esmond.' I found it both entertaining and exciting to me; it seems to possess an impetus and excitement beyond the other two; that movement and brilliancy its predecessors sometimes wanted never fail here. In certain passages I thought Thackeray used all his powers; their grand, serious force yielded a profound satisfaction. 'At last he puts forth his strength,' I could not help saying to myself. No character in the book strikes me as more masterly than that of Beatrix; its conception is fresh, and its delineation vivid. It is peculiar; it has impressions of a new kind—new, at least, to me. Beatrix is not, in herself, all bad. So much does she sometimes reveal of what is good and great as to suggest this feeling; you would think she was urged by a Fate. You would think that some antique doom presses on her house, and that once in so many generations its brightest ornament was to become its greatest disgrace. At times what is good in her struggles against this terrible destiny, but the Fate conquers. Beatrix cannot be an honest woman and a good man's wife. She 'tries and she *cannot*.' Proud, beautiful, and sullied, she was born what she becomes, a king's mistress. I know not whether you have seen the notice in the 'Leader'; I read it just after concluding the book. Can I be wrong in deeming it a notice tame, cold, and insufficient? With all its professed friendliness it produced on me a most disheartening impression. Surely another sort of justice than this will be rendered to 'Esmond' from other quarters. One acute remark of the critic is to the effect that Blanche Amory and Beatrix are identical— sketched from the same original! To me they are about as identical as a weasel and a royal tigress of Bengal; both the latter are quadrupeds, both the former women. But I must not take up either your time or my own with further remarks. —Believe me yours sincerely,

C. BRONTË.

799. *To* GEORGE SMITH.

Novb. 20th, 1852.

MY DEAR SIR,—I send the 3rd Vol. of 'Villette' to-day, having been able to get on with the concluding chapters faster than I anticipated. When you shall have glanced over it—speak, as before, frankly.

I am afraid Mr Williams was a little disheartened by the tranquillity of the 1st and 2nd Vols.: he will scarcely approve the former part of the 3rd, but perhaps the close will suit him better. Writers cannot choose their own mood: with them it is not always high-tide, nor—thank Heaven!—always Storm. But then—the Public must have 'excitement': the best of us can only say: 'Such as I have, give I unto thee.'

Glad am I to see that 'Esmond' is likely to meet something like the appreciation it deserves. That was a genial notice in the 'Spectator.' That in the 'Examiner' seemed to me—not perhaps so genial, but more discriminating. I do not say that *all* the 'Examiner' says is true—for instance the doubt it casts on the enduring characters of Mr Thackeray's writings must be considered quite unwarranted—still the notice struck me as containing much truth. I wonder how the 'Times' will treat 'Esmond.'

Now that 'Villette' is off my hands—I mean to try to wait the result with calm. Conscience—if she be just—will not reproach me, for I have tried to do my best.—Believe me, Yours sincerely,

C. BRONTË.

800 (598). *To* ELLEN NUSSEY.

Nov. 22nd, 1852, Monday morning.

DEAR ELLEN,—Truly thankful am I to be able to tell you that I finished my long task on Saturday; packed and sent off the parcel to Cornhill. I said my prayers when I had done it. Whether it is well or ill done, I don't know. D.V. I will now try to wait the issue quietly. The book, I think, will not be considered pretentious, nor is it of a character to excite hostility.

As papa is pretty well, I may, I think, dear Nell, do as you wish me and come for a few days to Brookroyd. Miss Martineau has also urgently asked me to go and see her. I promised if all were well to do so, the close of November or beginning of December, so that I could go from Brookroyd to Westmoreland. Would Wednesday suit you? I should leave Keighley by the 2 o'clock train—reach Bradford by 20 minutes after 2. I should get to Heckmondwike by 8 minutes past 3. Thence, if it were not convenient to send the gig to meet me, I would walk, and get my luggage sent on. Whether would it be better to stop at Heckmondwike or Liversedge?

'Esmond' shall come with me, that is, Thackeray's novel. Yours in cruel haste,   C. BRONTË.

801. *To* GEORGE SMITH.

Novb. 23rd, 1852.

MY DEAR SIR,—I like the type of the Proof-sheets much. I have corrected them in some haste—being on the point of starting from home. I may be absent about a fortnight; the next sheets should be directed to me at Brookroyd, Birstall, Leeds. Thence I may perhaps go on to Ambleside for a few days.

I sent the 3rd Vol. of 'Villette' on Saturday. The cash for the copyright may be invested in the funds with the rest—except 20£.—for which I have a present use and which perhaps you will be kind enough to send me in a Bank bill.

Give my best regards to your Mother and Sisters and believe me, in great haste—Yours very sincerely,   C. BRONTË.

802. *To* MRS SMITH.

BROOKROYD, Novb. 25th, '52.

MY DEAR MRS SMITH,—Your kind note reached me just when I was on the point of leaving home. I have promised to stay with my friends here for a week, and afterwards I have further promised to spend a week with Miss Martineau at Ambleside: a fortnight is as long a time as—for the present—I should like to be absent from my Father.

You must then permit me to defer my visit to you. I own I do not at all wish to be in a hurry about it; it pleases me to have it in prospect—it is something to look forward to and to anticipate; I keep it, on the principle of the school-boy who hoards his choicest piece of cake.

When I mentioned your invitation to my Father—he suggested another reason for delay: he said I ought to wait and see what the critics would do to me—and indeed I think myself, that in case of the great 'Times' for instance—having another Field-Marshal Haynau[1] castigation in store for me—I would rather undergo that infliction at Haworth than in London.

I was glad to hear of your long stay at Woodford during the summer—for I felt sure you would enjoy it much. I trust that ere this you have heard good news from Alick. Mr Smith mentioned last August that he was gone out to India; no doubt—you will have heard before now of his safe arrival, and whether he is likely to settle comfortably in his new and distant quarters.

Remember me very kindly to all your circle, and believe me my dear Mrs Smith—Yours sincerely and affectionately,

C. BRONTË.

803 (599). *To* GEORGE SMITH.

December 6th, 1852.

MY DEAR SIR,—The receipts have reached me safely. I received the first on Saturday, enclosed in a cover without a line, and had made up my mind to take the train on Monday, and go up to London to see what was the matter, and what had struck my publisher mute. On Sunday morning your letter came, and you have thus been spared the visitation of the unannounced and unsummoned apparition of Currer Bell in Cornhill. Inexplicable delays should be avoided when possible, for they are apt to urge those subjected to their harassment to sudden and impulsive steps.

I must pronounce you right again, in your complaint of the transfer of interest in the third volume from one set of characters to another. It is not pleasant, and it will probably be found as unwelcome to the reader as it was, in a sense, compulsory upon the writer. The spirit of romance would have indicated another course, far more flowery and inviting; it would have fashioned a paramount hero, kept faithfully with him, and made him su-

---

[1] Julius Jacob, Baron von Haynau (1786–1853), an Austrian general, whose atrocious severity towards the defeated enemies in both the Italian and Hungarian campaigns excited the detestation of Europe. In 1850, when visiting the brewery of Messrs Barclay & Perkins in London, he was assaulted by the draymen and escaped with his life, but the loss of his moustache.

premely worshipful; he should have an idol, and not a mute, unresponding idol either; but this would have been unlike real life—inconsistent with truth—at variance with probability. I greatly apprehend, however, that the weakest character in the book is the one I aimed at making the most beautiful; and, if this be the case, the fault lies in its wanting the germ of the *real*—in its being purely imaginary. I felt that this character lacked substance; I fear that the reader will feel the same. Union with it resembles too much the fate of Ixion, who was mated with a cloud. The childhood of Paulina is, however, I think, pretty well imagined, but her . . . [the remainder of this interesting sentence is torn off the letter]. A brief visit to London becomes thus more practicable, and if your mother will kindly write, when she has time, and name a day after Christmas which will suit her, I shall have pleasure, papa's health permitting, in availing myself of her invitation. I wish I could come in time to correct some at least of the proofs; it would save trouble.

C. BRONTË.

804 (600). *To* MARGARET WOOLER.

BROOKROYD, Decbr 7th, 1852.

MY DEAR MISS WOOLER,—Since you were so kind as to take some interest in my small tribulation of Saturday—I write a line to tell you that on Sunday morning a letter came which put me out of pain and obviated the necessity of an impromptu journey to London.[1]

The *money transaction*, of course, remains the same—and perhaps is not quite equitable—but when an author finds that his work is cordially approved—he can pardon the rest; indeed my chief regret now lies in the conviction that Papa will be disappointed—he expected me to earn £700—nor did I—myself—anticipate that a lower sum would be offered; however, £500 is not to be despised.

Your sudden departure from Brookroyd left a legacy of consternation to the bereaved breakfast-table: Ellen was not easily

[1]Pencil note (by Miss Wooler?) at the top of the letter: 'Great anxiety about Shirley had determined C. to set off to London instanter a letter not arriving as expected— She was prevailed upon to wait another post, when the letter came.' Miss Wooler evidently added this note at a later date: the incident to which she refers did not concern *Shirley* but *Villette*.

to be soothed, though I diligently represented to her that you had quitted Haworth with the same inexorable haste. I am commissioned to tell you, first that she has decided not to go to Yarmouth till after Christmas—her mother's health having within the last few days betrayed some symptoms not unlike those which preceded her former illness—and though it is to be hoped that these may pass without untoward result—yet they naturally increase Ellen's reluctance to leave home for the present.

Secondly—I am to say—that when the present you left—came to be examined—the costliness and beauty of the cambric inspired some concern. Ellen thinks you are too kind—as I also think every morning when I put on my frilled under-raiment, for I am now benefiting by your kind gift.

With sincere regards to all at the Parsonage—and especially I think to Mr Carter as a friend who, having temporarily been lost is again found,—I am, my dear Miss Wooler, yours respectfully and affectionately,

C. BRONTË.

P.S.—I shall direct that 'Esmond' (Mr Thackeray's work) shall be sent on to you as soon as the Hunsworth party have read it. It has already reached a second edition.

805 (601). *To* ELLEN NUSSEY.

Dec. 9th, 1852, Thursday Morning.

DEAR NELL,—I got home safely at five o'clock yesterday afternoon, and, I am most thankful to say, found papa and all the rest well. I did my business satisfactorily in Leeds, the head-dress rearranged as I wished; it is now a very different matter to the bushy, tasteless thing it was before.

On my arrival I found no proof-sheets, but a letter from Mr Smith, which I would have enclosed, but so many words are scarcely legible, you would have no pleasure in reading it: he continues to make a mystery of his 'reason'—something in the third volume sticks confoundedly in his throat, and as to the 'female character' about which I asked, he responds crabbedly that, 'She is an odd, fascinating little puss,' but affirms that he is 'not in love with her.' He tells me also that he will answer no more questions about 'Villette.'

This morning I have a brief note from Mr Williams intimating that he has 'not yet been permitted to read the 3rd vol.' Also there is a note from Mrs Smith, very kind, I almost wish I could still look on that kindness just as I used to do: it was very pleasant to me once.

Write *immediately*, Dear Nell, and tell me how your mother is. Give my kindest regards to her and all at Brookroyd. Everybody was very good to me this last visit, I remember them with corresponding pleasure. Papa seems glad on the whole to hear you are not going to Yarmouth just yet; he thinks you should be cautious. — Yours faithfully,

C. Brontë.

I enclose a postage stamp for the $\frac{1}{2}$d. you were to pay for me at the station. Don't forget it.

806. *To* Mrs Smith.

Decb. 10th, 1852.

My dear Mrs Smith, — Since you leave the question of time to my decision — I will — if all be well — write to you again within a short period after Christmas, when the holiday week shall be well over — and name the day and train of arrival.

Meantime there is pleasure in looking forward to seeing once more you and yours. It will be about eighteen months since I bid you good-bye in Euston-Square: the interim has not always been one of good health to me, and I must expect that friends who have not seen me for a year and a half, will find some change. Latterly, however, I have felt much better: a brief stay with some kind old friends has proved specially beneficial. I am thankful to say my Father's health seems now very satisfactory.

With best wishes and kindest regards to your family, — I am my dear Mrs Smith, Yours sincerely and affectionately,

C. Brontë.

CHAPTER XXIX

ARTHUR BELL NICHOLLS

IN December, 1852, Charlotte Brontë received her fourth proposal of marriage, the suitor this time being her father's curate the Rev. A. B. Nicholls.

Arthur Bell Nicholls was born of Scottish parents at Crumlin, Co. Antrim, Ireland, on January 6th, 1818. He was left an orphan at the age of seven, and taken charge of by his uncle, Dr Alan Bell, headmaster of the Royal High School, Banagher, who brought him up with his own family. In 1840 Mr Nicholls entered Trinity College, Dublin, and five years later he was ordained, after graduating in the Trinity term of 1844. In 1845 he succeeded the Rev. James William Smith as curate of Haworth, and for the next sixteen years was closely associated with the home of the Brontës.

The first reference to Mr Nicholls in Charlotte's letters is contained in a note addressed to Mrs Rand on May 26th, 1845, wherein she writes: 'Papa has got a new curate lately, a Mr Nicholls from Ireland — he did duty for the first time on Sunday — he appears a respectable young man, reads well, and I hope will give satisfaction.' At a later date, however, she writes to her friend Ellen Nussey:[1] 'Mr Nicholls is returned just the same; I cannot for my life see those interesting germs of goodness in him you discovered; his narrowness of mind always strikes me chiefly. I fear he is indebted to your imagination for his hidden treasure.'

Mr Nicholls lived at the house of John Brown the sexton of Haworth, and father of Martha Brown, the Brontë's servant. Mrs Gaskell tells us that Mr Nicholls was 'a grave, reserved, conscientious man, with a deep sense of religion, and of his duties as one of its ministers.' He was somewhat brusque in manner, which rather prejudiced people against him, and it was only after a long and close acquaintanceship that the true depth and

[1]October 15th, 1847, Vol. II, p. 148.

sincerity of his character could be discovered. He appears to have been attracted to Charlotte Brontë from the first, for before he had been at Haworth very long, Ellen Nussey wrote to ask if it was really true that Charlotte was engaged to her father's curate. Charlotte gave an emphatic denial to the rumour, stating that all the curates in the neighbourhood looked upon her as an old maid. This was long before Mr Nicholls proposed to Charlotte, and before she had made a name in the literary world. It was decidedly the woman rather than the authoress who attracted Mr Nicholls. At home she was not shy and nervous as she was amongst strangers, so that she appeared to much greater advantage. It was probably a great blow to Mr Nicholls's hopes when Charlotte became famous and was visited by titled people, for his small salary of £100 a year made it exceedingly difficult for him to approach her with an offer of marriage, but he no doubt felt greatly encouraged by the kindly reference to him as Mr Macarthey in *Shirley*:

'Perhaps I ought to remark that, on the premature and sudden vanishing of Mr Malone from the stage of Briarfield parish . . . there came as his successor another Irish curate, Mr Macarthey. I am happy to be able to inform you, *with truth*, that this gentleman did as much credit to his country as Malone had done it discredit; he proved himself as decent, decorous and conscientious as Peter was rampant, boisterous and — (this last epithet I choose to suppress, because it would let the cat out of the bag). He laboured faithfully in the parish; the schools both Sunday and day schools, flourished under his sway like green bay-trees. Being human, of course he had his faults; these, however, were proper, steady-going, clerical faults: the circumstance of finding himself invited to tea with a dissenter would unhinge him for a week; the spectacle of a Quaker wearing his hat in the church, the thought of an unbaptized fellow-creature being interred with Christian rites — these things could make sad havoc in Mr Macarthey's physical and mental economy: otherwise he was sane and rational, diligent and charitable.'

Mr Nicholls appears to have been pleased with this portrait of himself, for on January 28th, 1850, Charlotte wrote to Ellen Nussey:

'Mr. Nicholls has finished reading "Shirley," he is delighted with it. John Brown's wife seriously thought he had gone wrong in the head as she heard him giving vent to roars of laughter as he sat alone, clapping his hands and stamping on the floor. He would read all the scenes about the curates aloud to papa, he triumphed in his own character.'

Mr Nicholls had been Mr Brontë's curate for some seven and a half years before he proposed for his daughter's hand. During the year 1852 he had watched with great admiration Charlotte's valiant struggle to get on with her work though constantly hindered by ill-health. He seems to have waited until she had finished writing *Villette* before he proposed. The story of his proposal and its rejection is related in Charlotte's letters. Mr Brontë's attitude was very definitely adverse, and Mr Nicholls himself felt that the old man was in a sense justified. Charlotte had already refused the Rev. Henry Nussey, who became Vicar of Hathersage, and Mr James Taylor, a man of good status in London and Bombay. Mr Brontë felt strongly that the curate with only £100 a year was not at all a good match for his gifted daughter.

The relations between Mr Brontë and his curate became very strained, and Charlotte found the situation intolerable. She felt very sorry for Mr Nicholls but would not act in direct opposition to her father's wishes. In the circumstances, she was pleased to receive from Mrs Smith an invitation to London, which she gladly accepted. Mr Nicholls sent in his resignation from the curacy of Haworth, and eventually obtained an appointment as curate at Kirk-Smeaton near Pontefract.

807 (602). *To* ELLEN NUSSEY.

December 15th, 1852.

DEAR NELL,—I return Mrs Upjohn's note which is highly characteristic, and not, I fear, of good omen for the comfort of your visit. There must be something wrong in herself as well as in her servants. I enclose another note which, taken in conjunction with the incident immediately preceding it, and with a long series of indications whose meaning I scarce ventured hitherto to interpret to myself, much less hint to any other, has left on my mind a feeling of deep concern. This note, you will see, is from Mr Nicholls.

I know not whether you have ever observed him specially when staying here, your perception is generally quick enough, *too* quick I have sometimes thought, yet as you never said anything, I restrained my own dim misgivings, which could not claim the sure guide of vision. What papa has seen or guessed I will not inquire though I may conjecture. He has minutely noticed all Mr Nicholls's low spirits, all his threats of expatriation, all his symptoms of impaired health, noticed them with little sympathy and much indirect sarcasm. On Monday evening Mr Nicholls was here to tea. I vaguely felt without clearly seeing, as without seeing, I have felt for some time, the meaning of his constant looks, and strange, feverish restraint. After tea I withdrew to the dining-room as usual. As usual, Mr Nicholls sat with papa till between eight and nine o'clock, I then heard him open the parlour door as if going. I expected the clash of the front-door. He stopped in the passage: he tapped: like lightning it flashed on me what was coming. He entered—he stood before me. What his words were you can guess; his manner—you can hardly realise—never can I forget it. Shaking from head to foot, looking deadly pale, speaking low, vehemently yet with difficulty—he made me for the first time feel what it costs a man to declare affection where he doubts response.

The spectacle of one ordinarily so statue-like, thus trembling, stirred, and overcome, gave me a kind of strange shock. He spoke of sufferings he had borne for months, of sufferings he could endure no longer, and craved leave for some hope. I could only entreat him to leave me then and promise a reply on the morrow. I asked him if he had spoken to papa. He said, he dared not. I think I half led, half put him out of the room. When he was gone I immediately went to papa, and told him what had taken place. Agitation and anger disproportionate to the occasion ensued; if I had *loved* Mr Nicholls and had heard such epithets applied to him as were used, it would have transported me past my patience; as it was, my blood boiled with a sense of injustice, but papa worked himself into a state not to be trifled with, the veins on his temples started up like whipcord, and his eyes became suddenly bloodshot. I made haste to promise that Mr Nicholls should on the morrow have a distinct refusal.

I wrote yesterday and got his note. There is no need to add to this statement any comment. Papa's vehement antipathy to the bare thought of any one thinking of me as a wife, and Mr Nicholls's distress, both give me pain. Attachment to Mr Nicholls you are aware I never entertained, but the poignant pity inspired by his state on Monday evening, by the hurried revelation of his sufferings for many months, is something galling and irksome. That he cared something for me, and wanted me to care for him, I have long suspected, but I did not know the degree or strength of his feelings. Dear Nell, good-bye.—Yours faithfully,

C. BRONTË.

I have letters from Sir J. K. Shuttleworth and Miss Martineau, but I cannot talk of them now.

808 (603). *To* ELLEN NUSSEY.

HAWORTH, December 18th, '52.

DEAR NELL,—You may well ask, How is it? for I am sure I don't know. This business would seem to me like a dream, did not my reason tell me it has long been brewing. It puzzles me to comprehend how and whence comes this turbulence of feeling.

You ask how papa demeans himself to Mr Nicholls. I only wish you were here to see papa in his present mood: you would know something of him. He just treats him with a hardness not to be bent, and a contempt not to be propitiated. The two have had no interview as yet: all has been done by letter. Papa wrote, I must say, a most cruel note to Mr Nicholls on Wednesday. In his state of mind and health (for the poor man is horrifying his landlady, Martha's mother, by entirely rejecting his meals) I felt that the blow must be parried, and I thought it right to accompany the pitiless despatch by a line to the effect that, while Mr Nicholls must never expect me to reciprocate the feeling he had expressed, yet at the same time I wished to disclaim participation in sentiments calculated to give him pain; and I exhorted him to maintain his courage and spirits. On receiving the two letters, he set off from home. Yesterday came the enclosed brief epistle.

You must understand that a good share of papa's anger arises from the idea, not altogether groundless, that Mr Nicholls has behaved with disingenuousness in so long concealing his aim, forging that Irish fiction, etc. I am afraid also that papa thinks a little too much about his want of money; he says that the match would be a degradation, that I should be throwing myself away, that he expects me, if I marry at all, to do very differently; in short, his manner of viewing the subject is, on the whole, far from being one in which I can sympathise. My own objections arise from a sense of incongruity and uncongeniality in feelings, tastes, principles.

How are you getting on, dear Nell, and how are all at Brookroyd? Remember me kindly to everybody. Yours, wishing devoutly that papa would resume his tranquillity, and Mr N. his beef and pudding,

C. Brontë.

I am glad to say that the incipient inflammation in papa's eye is disappearing.

809. Mrs Gaskell *to* Tottie Fox.

December 20th, 1852.

. . . Miss Brontë has been ill —*very* ill I'm afraid, but I only heard of it yesterday morning thro' the Shaens, who had asked her there, and she gave that as her excuse, or rather reason, for not coming to them. I wrote to her directly—though I don't know that *that* did much good—only one felt how lonely and out of the world she must be, poor creature. I've a great mind to go and see her uninvited some day. I cd (that's to say if I'd the money) stay at the Inn so as not to be in Mr Brontë's road. However, I don't mean to stir from home this long time when I get back, but write, write, write; I really do mean to do something good and virtuous. . . .

810. *To* Mrs Smith.

December 30th, 1852.

My dear Mrs Smith,—I can now name Wednesday, the 5th of January, as the day when I hope to see you if all be well. Should there by any objection to this day—you will kindly let me know. My Father is, thus far, passing the winter so well that I can look forward to leaving home for a little while with a comparatively easy mind: he seems also pleased that I should have a little change. I should leave Leeds at 25 m. past 10 in the morn-

ing, and, if I understand 'Bradshaw' aright — should arrive in
Euston Square at 15 m. past 4 in the afternoon.

It grieved me to see that the 'Times' has shown its teeth at
'Esmond' with a courteously malignant grin which seems to say
that it never forgets a grudge.

I want to know what Mr Smith thinks about 'Villette' coming
out so nearly at the same time with Mrs Gaskell's new work
'Ruth.' I am afraid he will not regard the coincidence as auspi-
cious; but I hope soon to be able to hear his verbal opinion.

Trusting that all in 'Gloucester Terrace' have spent a merry
Christmas — and wishing to each and every one, by anticipation,
a happy New Year, believe me, my dear Mrs Smith, — Yours
sincerely and affectionately,

C. BRONTË.

811 (604). *To* ELLEN NUSSEY.

Jany 2nd, 1853.

DEAR NELL, — I thought of you on New Year's night and hope
you got well over your formidable tea-making. I trust that Tuesday and Wednesday will also pass pleasantly. I am busy too in
my little way — preparing to go to London this week — a matter
which necessitates some little application to the needle. I find it is
quite necessary that I should go to superintend the press as Mr
S[mith] seems quite determined not to let the printing get on till
I come. I have actually only recd 3 proof sheets since I was at
Brookroyd. Papa wants me to go too — to be out of the way —
I suppose — but I am sorry for one other person whom nobody
pities but me. Martha is bitter against him. John Brown says *he
should like to shoot him.* They don't understand the nature of his
feelings — but I see now what they are. Mr N[icholls] is one of
those who attach themselves to very few, whose sensations are
close and deep — like an underground stream, running strong
but in a narrow channel. He continues restless and ill — he carefully performs the occasional duty — but does not come near the
church, procuring a substitute every Sunday.

A few days since he wrote to Papa requesting permission to
withdraw his resignation. Papa answered that he should only do
so on condition of giving his written promise never again to
broach the obnoxious subject either to him or to me. This he has
evaded doing, so the matter remains unsettled.

I feel persuaded the termination will be—his departure for Australia. Dear Nell—without loving him—I don't like to think of him, suffering in solitude, and wish him anywhere so that he were happier. He and Papa have never met or spoken yet.

I am very glad to hear that your Mother is pretty well—and also that *the* shirts are progressing. I hope you will not be called away to Norfolk before I come home: I should like you to pay a visit to Haworth first. Write again soon.—Yours faithfully,

C. BRONTË.

812 (605). *To* ELLEN NUSSEY.

GLOUCESTER TERRACE, HYDE PARK,
Jany 11th, '53.

DEAR NELL,—I came here last Wednesday—I had a delightful day for my journey and was kindly received at the close. My time has passed pleasantly enough since I came—yet I have not much to tell you—nor is it likely I shall have—I do not mean to go out much or see many people. Sir J. K. S. wrote to me two or three times before I left home—and made me promise to let him know when I should be in Town but I reserved to myself the right of deferring the communication till the latter part of my stay. I really so much dread the sort of excited fuss into which he puts himself—that I only wish to see just as much of him as civility exacts.

All in this house appear to be pretty much as usual and yet I see some changes—Mrs S[mith] and her daughters look well enough—but on Mr S[mith] hard work is telling early—both his complexion, his countenance and the very lines of his features are altered—it is rather the remembrance of what he was than the fact of what he is which can warrant the picture I have been accustomed to give of him. One feels pained to see a physical alteration of this kind—yet I feel glad and thankful that it is *merely* physical: as far as I can judge mind and manners have undergone no deterioration—rather, I think, the contrary. His Mother's account of the weight of work bearing upon him is really fearful. In some of his notes to me I half suspected exaggeration; it was no exaggeration—far otherwise.

Mr T[aylor] is said to be getting on well in India—but there are complaints of his temper and nerves being rendered dreadfully excitable by the hot climate; it seems he is bad to live with

—I never catch a pleasant word about him; except that his probity and usefulness are held in esteem.

No news yet from home—and I feel a little uneasy to hear how Papa is—I left him well—but at his age one specially feels the uncertainty of health.

Remember me affectionately to all at Brookroyd. Write again soon and believe me dear Nell—Yours faithfully,

C. BRONTË.

I hope you enjoyed yourself at Mrs Burnley's: you must tell me how you got on.

813 (606). *To* MRS GASKELL.

LONDON, January 12th, 1853.

MY DEAR MRS GASKELL,—It is with *you* the ball rests. I have not heard from you since I wrote last; but I thought I knew the reason of your silence, viz. application to work—and therefore I accept it, not merely with resignation, but with satisfaction.

I am now in London, as the date above will show; staying very quietly at my publisher's, and correcting proofs, etc. Before receiving yours I had felt, and expressed to Mr Smith, reluctance to come in the way of 'Ruth'; not that I think *she* (bless her very sweet face. I have already devoured Vol. I) would suffer from contact with 'Villette'—we know not but that the damage might be the other way—but I have ever held comparisons to be odious, and would fain that neither I nor my friends should be made subjects for the same. Mr Smith proposes, accordingly, to defer the publication of my book till the 24th inst.; he says that will give 'Ruth' the start in the papers, daily and weekly, and also will leave free to her all the February magazines. Should this delay appear to you insufficient, speak! and it shall be protracted.

I dare say, arrange as we may, we shall not be able wholly to prevent comparisons; it is the nature of some critics to be invidious; but we need not care: we can set them at defiance; they *shall* not make us foes, they *shall* not mingle with our mutual feelings one taint of jealousy: there is my hand on that: I know you will give clasp for clasp.

'Villette' has indeed no right to push itself before 'Ruth.' There is a goodness, a philanthropic purpose, a social use in the latter, to which the former cannot for an instant pretend; nor can it claim precedence on the ground of surpassing power: I think it much quieter than 'Jane Eyre.' As far as I have got in 'Ruth' I think it excels 'Mary Barton' for beauty, whatever it does for strength. As to the style I found it such as my soul welcomes. Of the delineation of character I shall be better able to judge when I get to the end, but may say in passing—that Sally, the old servant, seems to be an 'apple of gold,' deserving to be 'set in a picture of silver.'

I wish to see *you*, probably at least as much as you can wish to see *me*, and therefore shall consider your invitation for March as an engagement; about the close of that month, then, I hope to pay you a brief visit. With kindest remembrances to Mr Gaskell and all your precious circle, I am, etc.,

C. BRONTË.

814 (607). *To* ELLEN NUSSEY.

112 GLOUCESTER TERRACE,
HYDE PARK GARDENS, Jany 19th, '53.

DEAR NELL,—I return Mrs Hewitt's letter which I read with pleasure; it is so truly kind and friendly.

Thank you for your brief account of the party. I can hardly tell what to say about J[oe] T[aylor] and Mr R[ingrose] in a letter: it is a subject rather to talk than write about.

I still continue to get on very comfortably and quietly in London—in the way I like—seeing rather things than persons— Being allowed to have my own choice of sights this time—I selected rather the *real* than the *decorative* side of Life—I have been over two prisons ancient and modern—Newgate and Pentonville—also the Bank, the Exchange, the Foundling Hospital, —and to-day if all be well—I go with Dr Forbes to see Bethlehem Hospital. Mrs S[mith] and her daughters are—I believe—a little amazed at my gloomy tastes, but I take no notice.

Papa—I am glad to say—continues well—I enclose portions of two notes of his which will show you—better than anything I can say—how he treats a certain subject—one of the notes purports to be written by Flossy!

I think of staying here till next Wednesday. What are your present plans with regard to Mrs Upjohn? You *must* if possible come to Haworth before you go into Norfolk.

My book is to appear at the close of this month. Mrs Gaskell wrote so pitifully to beg that it should not clash with her 'Ruth' that it was impossible to refuse to defer the publication a week or two.

I hope your Mother continues pretty well and also Ann, Mercy and Mr Clapham. Give my best love to all. Are the shirts getting on?[1]

Write very soon and believe me — Yours faithfully,

C. Brontë.

You may burn Papa's notes when read.

---

[1]There was a little wager arising out of some nonsense about this work as to the possibility of doing such an amount in a certain time, Mr C. thinking E. was incapable of such close plain work—C. knew better and challenged him. [Note by Ellen Nussey].

CHAPTER XXX

THE LAST NOVEL

AS the day arranged for the publication of *Villette* drew near, Charlotte Brontë became increasingly anxious about the fate of her book. She had sacrificed much health and peace of mind in writing it, and her publisher's adverse criticism of the last volume made her all the more eager to hear the opinion of her literary friends and the public.

Villette was published on January 28th, 1853, and was received with loud acclamations of praise. George Eliot wrote enthusiastically to Mrs Bray, 'I am only just returned to a sense of the real world about me, for I have been reading *Villette*, a still more wonderful book than *Jane Eyre*. There is something almost preternatural in its power,' and a few days later, '*Villette* —*Villette*—have you read it?' The reviews came in fast, and Charlotte was immensely gratified by the favourable reception accorded to her book. She was therefore much chagrined to receive an unfavourable criticism from her friend Harriet Martineau, to whom she had written asking for a candid opinion of the novel. Miss Martineau also wrote a review of *Villette* for the *Daily News*, in which she contended that the book made love too general and too absorbing a factor in women's lives, and protested against the assumption that 'events and characters are to be regarded through the medium of one passion only.' Charlotte strongly resented this, and a difference arose between the two writers, with the result that they ceased to correspond.

The story of *Villette* is drawn from Charlotte Brontë's sojourn in Brussels, and nearly all the persons and places in the book have been identified.[1] It has been surmised that Bretton is Burlington or Bridlington, the Yorkshire watering-place that Miss Brontë had twice visited, and where she and her sisters had contemplated opening a school. Villette is of course Brussels,

[1]See *Persons and Places of the Brontë Novels—Villette and The Professor*, by Herbert E. Wroot. *Brontë Society Transactions*, Vol. III.

and the Pensionnat Heger in the Rue d'Isabelle is minutely described in the novel as the school of Madame Beck in the Rue Fossette. The Church of St Jean the Baptiste, whose bell was heard from the school, was the Church of St Jacques-sur-Caudenberg, and the church of Lucy Snowe's confession was the Cathedral of Ste Gudule. M. Paul Emanuel of the novel was undoubtedly suggested by Charlotte's beloved master, M. Heger, while Madame Heger served as the prototype for Madame Beck. Many of the people mentioned in the book were still alive when it was published, and for that reason Charlotte was most anxious that it should not be translated into French. However, only a few months after its appearance, a copy of *Villette* found its way to Brussels, and was there read by one of Charlotte's schoolfellows, who had no difficulty in identifying both the main characters and the places portrayed in the novel.

815 (609) *To* HARRIET MARTINEAU.

January 21st, 1853.

I know that you will give me your thoughts upon my book, as frankly as if you spoke to some near relative whose good you preferred to her gratification. I wince under the pain of condemnation, like any other weak structure of flesh and blood; but I love, I honour, I kneel to truth. Let her smite me on the one cheek—good! the tears may spring to the eyes; but courage! there is the other side; hit again, right sharply.

C. BRONTË.

816 (608). *To* MARGARET WOOLER.

112, GLOUCESTER TERRACE, Jany 27th, 1853.

MY DEAR MISS WOOLER,—I received your letter here in London where I have been staying about three weeks—and shall probably remain a few days longer. 'Villette' is to be published to-morrow—its appearance has been purposely delayed hitherto—to avoid discourteous clashing with Mrs Gaskell's new work 'Ruth.' Your name was one of the first on the list of presentees—and consequently your copy will be sent off immediately directed to the Parsonage, Heckmondwike—where I shall also send this letter — as you mention that you are to leave Halifax at the close of this week. I will bear in mind what you say about Mrs Moore, and should I ever have an opportunity of serving her — will not omit to do so — I only wish my chance of being useful were greater. Schools seem to be considered almost obsolete in London. Ladies' colleges, with Professors for every branch of instruction, are superseding the old-fashioned Seminary. How this system will work, I can't tell: I think the College classes might be very useful for finishing the education of ladies intended to go out as Governesses; but what progress little girls will make in them — seems to me another question.

My dear Miss Wooler — I read attentively all you say about Miss Martineau; the sincerity and constancy of your solicitude touches me very much; I should grieve to neglect or oppose your advice, and yet I do not feel that it would be right to give Miss Martineau up entirely. There is, in her nature, much that is very noble; hundreds have forsaken her[1] — more — I fear — in the apprehension that their fair names may suffer if seen in connection with hers — than from any pure convictions such as you suggest — of harm consequent on her fatal tenets. With these fair-weather friends I cannot bear to rank — and for her sin — is it not one of those which God and not man must judge?

To speak the truth — my dear Miss Wooler — I believe if you were in my place, and knew Miss Martineau as I do — if you had shared with me the proofs of her rough but genuine kindliness, and had seen how she secretly suffers from abandonment, you would be the last to give her up; you would separate the sinner from the sin, and feel as if the right lay rather in quietly adhering to her in her strait — while that adherence is unfashionable and unpopular — than in turning on her your back when the world sets the example — I believe she is one of those whom opposition and desertion make obstinate in error; while patience and tolerance touch her deeply and keenly, and incline her to ask of her own heart whether the course she has been pursuing may not possibly be a faulty course — However — I have time to think of this subject — and I shall think of it seriously.

---

[1] In reference to this passage Miss Martineau writes thus; 'There is the unaccountable delusion that I was "deserted" on account of the Atkinson Letters. . . . Facts are best, so I will only say that I am not aware of having lost any friends whatever by that book, while I have gained a new world of sympathy.'

Miss Wooler has written the following pencil note on the letter; 'C. did eventually give up Miss M. from sincere conviction.'

As to what I have seen in London during my present visit —
I hope one day to tell you all about it by our fireside at home.
When you write again will you name a time when it would suit
you to come and see me — everybody in the house would be glad
of your presence — your last visit is pleasantly remembered by
all.

With kindest regards to Mr and Mrs Carter and all their circle
I am always, affectionately and respectfully yours,

C. BRONTË.

817 (612). *To* ELLEN NUSSEY.

112 GLOUCESTER TERRACE, HYDE PARK,
Jany 28th, '53.

DEAR NELL, — I have been longing to write to you every day
this week and have not once been able — my time is much taken
up — In the three hours of leisure afforded me this morning — I
have four letters to write and therefore must be brief.

I have got the parcel of books for you — Edward and Georgiana brought it in propria persona — and I saw them — They behaved very nicely — Georgiana has certainly a striking appearance — but I believe her brother (with, no doubt, some faults and
weaknesses) — has the better heart of the two — the most of the
Nussey goodness — for there *is* a goodness I like in the better
members of your family. The next day Madame herself thought
fitting to call, very stately in her carriage — I was not in — but she
left her card — and the next day came a note asking me to dine at
4 Cleveland Row on Tuesday next — I declined dinner — but
promised to call to-morrow morning — which D.V. I hope to do.

Don't you think you have been shamefully impatient about
'Villette'? To-day is the first day of publication — but the gift-
copies were sent off yesterday — yours among the number — and
I hope you have got it by this time —

If all be well I go home on Wednesday next without fail — I
shall reach Keighley at 44 m. past 3 o'clock, afternoon — and I
want you to meet me there and then we can go home together —
You must be so kind, dear Nell, as to write directly and tell me
whether this arrangement will suit — as I earnestly hope it will —
as I should wish to write a line of notification to Martha that she
may be prepared with a comfortable welcome.

My visit has on the whole passed pleasantly enough with some sorrowful impressions—I have seen a good deal of Sir J. K. S.— he has been very kind—so has Dr Forbes—and indeed every- body. But I must stop—Be sure to write immediately—Give my kind love to all and believe me—Yours faithfully,

C. Brontë.

818 (613). *To* Martha Brown.

Gloucester Terrace,
London, January 28th, 1853.

Dear Martha,—If all be well I hope to come home next Wednesday. I have asked Miss Nussey to come with me. We shall reach Haworth about half-past four o'clock in the after- noon, and I know I can trust you to have things comfortable and in readiness. The tablecloths had better be put on the dining- room tables; you will have something prepared that will do for supper—perhaps a nice piece of cold boiled ham would be as well as anything, as it would come in for breakfast in the morn- ing. The weather has been very changeable here, in London. I have often wondered how you and papa stood it at home; I felt the changes in some degree, but not half so much as I should have done at Haworth, and have only had one really bad day of headache and sickness since I came. I hope you and Tabby have agreed pretty well, and that you have got help in your work whenever you have wanted it. Remember me kindly to Tabby, and believe me, dear Martha, your sincere friend,

C. Brontë.

819 (610). *To* Charlotte Brontë.

As for the other side of the question, which you so desire to know, I have but one thing to say; but it is not a small one. I do not like the love, either the kind or the degree of it; and its pre- valence in the book, and effect on the action of it, help to explain the passages in the reviews which you consulted me about, and seem to afford *some* foundation for the criticisms they offered.

H. Martineau.

820 (611). *To* HARRIET MARTINEAU.

MY DEAR MISS MARTINEAU,—I think I best show my sense of the tone and feeling of your last, by immediate compliance with the wish you express that I should send your letter. I enclose it, and have marked with red ink the passage which struck me dumb. All the rest is fair, right, worthy of you, but I protest against this passage; and were I brought up before the bar of all the critics in England to such a charge I should respond, 'Not guilty.'

I know what *love* is as I understand it; and if man or woman should be ashamed of feeling such love, then is there nothing right, noble, faithful, truthful, unselfish in this earth, as I comprehend rectitude, nobleness, fidelity, truth, and disinterestedness.—Yours sincerely,

C. B.

To differ from you gives me keen pain.

With reference to this correspondence Mrs Gaskell writes:[1]

Miss Martineau, both in an article on *Villette* in the *Daily News* and in a private letter to Miss Brontë, wounded her to the quick by expressions of censure which she believed to be unjust and unfounded, but which, if correct and true, went deeper than any merely artistic fault. An author may bring himself to believe that he can bear blame with equanimity, from whatever quarter it comes; but its force is derived altogether from the character of this. To the public one reviewer may be the same impersonal being as another; but an author has frequently a far deeper significance to attach to opinions. They are the verdicts of those whom he respects and admires, or the mere words of those for whose judgment he cares not a jot. It is this knowledge of the individual worth of the reviewer's opinion which makes the censures of some sink so deep, and prey so heavily upon an author's heart. And thus, in proportion to her true, firm regard for Miss Martineau did Miss Brontë suffer under what she considered her misjudgment not merely of writing, but of character.

She had long before asked Miss Martineau to tell her whether

[1] *The Life of Charlotte Brontë*, by Mrs E. C. Gaskell, Haworth Edition, pp. 595–98.

she considered that any want of womanly delicacy or propriety was betrayed in *Jane Eyre*. And on receiving Miss Martineau's assurance that she did not, Miss Brontë entreated her to declare it frankly if she thought there was any failure of this description in any future work of 'Currer Bell's.' The promise then given of faithful truth-speaking Miss Martineau fulfilled when *Villette* appeared. Miss Brontë writhed under what she felt to be injustice.

It is but due to Miss Martineau to give some of the particulars of this misunderstanding, as she has written them down for me. It appears that on Miss Brontë's first interview with Miss Martineau in December 1849, she had expressed pleasure at being able to consult a friend about certain strictures of the reviewers, which she did not understand, and by which she had every desire to profit. 'She said that the reviews sometimes puzzled her, and that some imputed to her what made her think she must be very unlike other people, or cause herself to be misunderstood. She could not make it out at all, and wished that I could explain it. I had not seen that sort of criticism then, I think, but I had heard *Jane Eyre* called "coarse." I told her that love was treated with unusual breadth, and that the kind of intercourse was uncommon, and uncommonly described, but that I did *not* consider the book a coarse one, though I could not answer for it that there were no traits which, on a second leisurely reading, I might not dislike on that ground. She begged me to give it that second reading, and I did on condition that she would regard my criticisms as made through the eyes of her reviewers. . . .'

Miss Martineau has also allowed me to make use of the passage referring to the same fault, real or supposed, in her notice of *Villette* in the *Daily News*.

'All the female characters, in all their thoughts and lives, are full of one thing, or are regarded by the reader in the light of that one thought—love. It begins with the child of six years old, at the opening—a charming picture—and it closes with it at the last page; and so dominant is this idea—so incessant is the writer's tendency to describe the need of being loved—that the heroine, who tells her own story, leaves the reader at last under the uncomfortable impression of her having either entertained a double love, or allowed one to supersede another without notification of the transition. It is not thus in real life. There are substantial, heartfelt interests for women of all ages, and, under

ordinary circumstances, quite apart from love: there is an absence of introspection, an unconsciousness, a repose in women's
lives—unless under peculiarly unfortunate circumstances—of
which we find no admission in this book; and to the absence of it
may be attributed some of the criticism which the book will
meet with from readers who are no prudes, but whose reason
and taste will reject the assumption that events and characters
are to be regarded through the medium of one passion only.
And here ends all demur.'

821. *To* GEORGE SMITH.

HAWORTH, February 7th, 1853.

MY DEAR SIR,—I have received and read the Reviews. I think I
ought to be, and feel that I *am*, very thankful. That in the
'Examiner' is better than I expected, and that in the 'Literary
Gazette' is as good as any author can look for. Somebody also
sent me the 'Nonconformist' with a favourable review. The
notice in the 'Daily News' was undoubtedly written by Miss
Martineau (to this paper she contributed her Irish letters). I have
received a letter from her precisely to the same effect, marking
the same point, and urging the same objections, similarly sug-
gesting, too, a likeness to Balzac, whose works I have not read.[1]
Her letter only differs from the reviews in being severe to the
point of injustice; her eulogy is also more highly wrought. On
the whole, if Cornhill is content thus far, so am I.—Yours
sincerely,

C. BRONTË.

822. *To* GEORGE SMITH.

HAWORTH, NEAR KEIGHLEY,
February 7th, 1853.

MY DEAR SIR,—I know not whether you are in the habit of
canvassing for your publication the suffrages of the provincial
press. There is, however, one provincial editor to whom it
might be advisable to send a copy of my daughter's work,
'Villette,' viz. Mr Baines, editor of the 'Leeds Mercury.' His
paper enjoys a wide circulation and considerable influence in the

[1]See her letter to G. H. Lewes, dated
October 17th, 1850, in which she thanks
him for lending her two of Balzac's works,
and comments on them.

north of England, and as I am an old subscriber, and occasional contributor, to the 'Mercury,' a fair notice, I think of 'Villette' might be counted upon. Offer my kind regards to Mrs Smith, and also my acknowledgments for her late friendly hospitality to my daughter. —I am Yours faithfully,

P. BRONTË.

823 (614). *To* MARGARET WOOLER.

HAWORTH, Feby 11th, 1853.

MY DEAR MISS WOOLER, —Excuse a very brief note—for I have time only to thank you for your last kind and welcome letter—and to say that in obedience to your wishes, I send you by to-day's post two reviews—the 'Examiner' and the 'Morning Advertiser'—which perhaps you will kindly return at your leisure. E. Nussey has a third—the 'Literary Gazette'—which she will likewise send. The reception of the book has been favourable thus far—for which I am thankful—less, I trust, on my own account—than for the sake of those few real friends who take so sincere an interest in my welfare as to be happy in my happiness.

Remember me very kindly to all at Heckmondwike—and believe me, yours affectionately and respectfully,

C. BRONTË.

824 (615). *To* ELLEN NUSSEY.

HAWORTH, Feby 15th, 1853.

DEAR ELLEN, —I am very glad to hear that you got home all right and that you managed to execute your commissions in Leeds so satisfactorily—you do not say whether you remembered to order the Bishop's Dessert—I shall know however by to-morrow morning. You had a very tolerable day after all for your journey.

I got a budget of no less than 7 papers yesterday and to-day—the import of all the notices is such as to make my heart swell with thankfulness to Him who takes note both of suffering and work and motives—Papa is pleased too. As to friends in general—I believe I can love them still without expecting them to take any large share in this sort of gratification. The longer I live—the more plainly I see that gentle must be the strain on fragile human nature—it will not bear much.

Give my kind regards to your Mother, Sisters and Mr C. and believe me — Yours faithfully,

C. Brontë.

Papa continues to improve. He came down to breakfast this morning.

825. *To* George Smith.

Haworth, February 16th, 1853.

My dear Sir, — I do not, of course, expect to have a letter from you at present, because I know that this is the busy time at Cornhill; but after the weary mail is gone out I should like much to hear what you think of the general tone of the notices, whether you regard them as reasonably satisfactory. My father seems pleased with them, and so am I, as an evidence that the book is pretty well received. I must not tell you what I think of such reviews as that in the 'Athenæum,' lest you should pronounce me fastidious and exacting. On the whole the critique I like best yet is one I got at an early stage of the work, before it had undergone the 'Old Bailey,' being the observations of a respected amateur critic, one A. Fraser Esq. I am bound to admit, however, that this gentleman confined his approving remarks to the two first volumes, tacitly condemning the third by the severity of a prolonged silence. — Yours sincerely,

C. Brontë.

826 (617). *To* Ellen Nussey.

[February, 1853].

Dear Ellen, — The parcel is come, and the contents seem good and all right. I enclose 6s. 6d. in postage stamps. Mrs Upjohn is really too trying. I do hope before this time you have heard from her. What weather for you to travel so far! Your crotchet about papa, dear Nell, made me angry; never was fancy more groundless.

I have heard from Mrs Gaskell, very kind, panegyrical and so on. Mr Smith tells me he has ascertained that Miss Martineau *did* write the notice in the 'Daily News.'

Joe Taylor offers to give me a regular blowing up and setting-down for £5; but I tell him the 'Times' will probably let me have the same gratis. I write in haste this morning. I shall be anxious to hear from you again, to know what is decided. This suspense, and this constant change of plan is very wearisome and wearing. Love to all. —Yours faithfully,

C. BRONTË.

827 (618). *To* ELLEN NUSSEY.

February 21st, 1853.

DEAR NELL, —The accompanying letter was brought here by the post this morning, with the explanation that it was left last Tuesday, February 15th, at *Hainworth* Vicarage (the church between Keighley and Haworth), and that Mrs Mayne, the clergyman's wife, kept it there till this day, for which she deserves the ducking-stool. She must have known that Miss E. Nussey was not one of her acquaintance. I do trust no serious injury will accrue from the delay. —Yours in haste,

C. BRONTË.

828 (619). *To* GEORGE SMITH.

HAWORTH, February 26th, 1853.

MY DEAR SIR, —At a late hour yesterday evening I had the honour of receiving, at Haworth Parsonage, a distinguished guest, none other than W. M. Thackeray, Esq. Mindful of the rites of hospitality, I hung him up in state this morning. He looks superb in his beautiful, tasteful gilded gibbet. For companion he has the Duke of Wellington (do you remember giving me that picture?) and for contrast and foil Richmond's portrait of an unworthy individual who, in such society, must be nameless. Thackeray looks away from the latter character with a grand scorn, edifying to witness. I wonder if the giver of these gifts will ever see them on the walls where they now hang; it pleases me to fancy that one day he may. My father stood for a quarter of an hour this morning examining the great man's picture. The conclusion of his survey was, that he thought it a puzzling head; if he had known nothing previously of the original's character, he could not have read it in his features. I wonder at this. To me the broad brow seems to express intellect. Certain lines about the nose and cheek betray the satirist and cynic; the mouth indicates a childlike simplicity —perhaps even a degree of irresoluteness, inconsistency —weakness, in short, but a weakness not unamiable. The engraving seems to me very good. A certain not quite Christian expression — 'not to put too fine a point upon it' — an expression of *spite*, most vividly marked in the original, is here softened, and perhaps a little — a very little — of the power has escaped in this ameliorating process. Did it strike you thus?

I have not quite settled it yet whether thanks or remonstrance is the due meed of the prompt reply I received to my last. I had concluded that Monday, the 28th, would be the earliest day when an answer could reasonably be expected, whereas one arrived Saturday, 19th. It must have been written in the very crisis of the cruel 'mail.' Well, I won't say anything. 'A bird in the hand is worth two in the bush' and the letter was very welcome, that is certain. — Yours sincerely,

C. BRONTË.

829 (620). *To* MRS GASKELL.

February 24th, 1853.

For my part I have thus far borne the cold weather well. I have taken long walks on the crackling snow, and felt the frosty air bracing. This winter has, for me, not been like last winter. December, January, February '51-2 passed like a long stormy night, conscious of one painful dream, all solitary grief and sickness. The corresponding months in '52-3 have gone over my head quietly and not uncheerfully. Thank God for the change and the repose! How welcome it has been He only knows! My father, too, has borne the season well; and my book and its reception thus far have pleased and cheered him.

C. BRONTË.

830. *To* MRS GASKELL.

[February, 1853].

. . . The beauty of 'Ruth' seems to me very great. Your style never rose higher, nor — I think — have you ever excelled the power of certain passages. The brutal dismissal of Ruth by Mr Bradshaw, the disclosure of her secret to her son, his grief and humiliation, the mother's sacrifices, efforts, death — these, I think, are passages which must pierce every heart.

I anticipate that a certain class of critics will fix upon the mis-

take of the good Mr Benson and his sister—in passing off Ruth
as a widow—as the weak part of the book—fix and cling there.
In vain is it explicitly shown that this step was regarded by the
author as an error, and that she unflinchingly follows it up to its
natural and fatal consequences—there—I doubt not—some
critics will stick like flies caught in treacle. These, however, let
us hope will be few in number; and clearer-sighted commenta-
tors will not be wanting, to do justice....

C. BRONTË.

831 (621). *To* ELLEN NUSSEY.

March 4th, 1853.

DEAR ELLEN,—I return Mrs Upjohn's letter. She is really a
most inconclusive person to have to do with. Have you come to
any decision yet? The Bishop[1] has been, and is gone. He is certainly a most charming little Bishop; the most benignant little
gentleman that ever put on lawn sleeves; yet stately too, and
quite competent to check encroachments. His visit passed capitally well; and at its close, as he was going away, he expressed
himself thoroughly gratified with all he had seen. The Inspector
also has been in the course of the past week; so that I have had a
somewhat busy time of it. If you could have been at Haworth to
share the pleasures of the company, without having been inconvenienced by the little bustle of the preparation, I should have
been *very* glad. But the house was a good deal put out of its way,
as you may suppose; all passed, however, orderly, quietly, and
well. Martha waited very nicely, and I had a person to help her in
the kitchen. Papa kept up, too, fully as well as I expected, though
I doubt whether he could have borne another day of it. My penalty came on in a strong headache and bilious attack as soon as
the Bishop was fairly gone: how thankful I was that it had politely waited his departure! I continue mighty stupid to-day: of
course, it is the reaction consequent on several days of extra
exertion and excitement. It is very well to talk of receiving a
Bishop without trouble, but you *must* prepare for him. We had
the parsons to supper as well as to tea. Mr Nicholls demeaned
himself not quite pleasantly. I thought he made no effort to

[1]Dr Longley. Charles Thomas Longley
(1794–1868) became the first Bishop of
Ripon in 1836, Bishop of Durham in 1856,
Archbishop of York in 1860, and Archbishop of Canterbury in 1862.

struggle with his dejection, but gave way to it in a manner to draw notice; the Bishop was obviously puzzled by it. Mr Nicholls also showed temper once or twice in speaking to papa. Martha was beginning to tell me of certain 'flaysome' looks also, but I desired not to hear of them. The fact is, I shall be most thankful when he is well away; I pity him, but I don't like that dark gloom of his. He dogged me up the lane after the evening service in no pleasant manner, he stopped also in the passage after the Bishop and the other clergy were gone into the room, and it was because I drew away and went upstairs that he gave that look which filled Martha's soul with horror. She, it seems, meantime, was making it her business to watch him from the kitchen door. If Mr Nicholls be a good man at bottom, it is a sad thing that nature has not given him the faculty to put goodness into a more attractive form. Into the bargain of all the rest he managed to get up a most pertinacious and needless dispute with the Inspector, in listening to which all my old unfavourable impressions revived so strongly, I fear my countenance could not but show them.

Dear Nell, I consider that on the whole it is a mercy you have been at home and not at Norfolk during the late cold weather. Love to all at Brookroyd. — Yours faithfully,

C. BRONTË.

832 (627). *To* W. S. WILLIAMS.

HAWORTH, March 9th, '53.

MY DEAR SIR, — I thank you for the 'Eclectic Review' and the 'Guardian' which I have duly received and read. And now I can only say — surely few authors would be so weak as to be shaken by reviews like these!

My dear Sir — were a review to appear inspired with treble their animus — *pray* do not withhold it from me. I like to see the satisfactory notices — especially I like to carry them to my Father — but I *must* see such as are *un*satisfactory and hostile — these are for my own especial edification — it is in these I best read public feeling and opinion. To shun examination into the dangerous and disagreeable seems to me cowardly — I long always to know what really *is*, and am only unnerved when kept in the dark.

And now I smile at my friends with their little notes of condolence, with their hints about 'unmanly insult.' Surely the poor

Guardian Critic has a right to lisp his opinion that Currer Bell's female characters do not realize his notion of ladyhood—and even 'respectfully to decline' the honour of an acquaintance with 'Jane Eyre' and 'Lucy Snowe' without meriting on that account to be charged with having offered an 'unmanly insult.'

Ah! I forgive the worthy critic very freely—his acquaintance and his standard of refinement are two points that will not trouble me much: perhaps ere to-morrow I shall even have forgiven my 'Kyind friends' their false alarm.

I received Miss Lupton's letter, and felt at once on reading it that it formed an exception to the general rule of complimentary effusions—that delicacy of feeling you speak of—appeared to me perceptible throughout. I answered her a few days ago. From what she said I conclude she is an authoress—what works has she written?

I have tried to read 'Daisy Burns'; at the close of the 1st Vol. I stopped. I must not give an opinion of it for I should seem severe. Miss Kavanagh's intentions are thoroughly good—her execution in this case seems to me disastrous. 'Madeleine' her first quiet, unpretending book—is worth a hundred such tawdry deformities as 'Daisy Burns'—I find in it no real blood or life; it is painted and cold.

With kind regards to Mrs W. and your family,—I am my dear Sir, Yours sincerely,

C. Brontë.

833 (622). *To* Ellen Nussey.

Haworth, March 10th, '53.

Dear Ellen,—I only got the 'Guardian' Newspaper yesterday morning and have not yet seen either the 'Critic' or 'Sharpe's Mag.'

The 'Guardian' does not wound me much—I see the motive—which indeed there is no attempt to disguise—still I think it a choice little morsel for foes—(Mr Grant was the first person to bring the news of the review to Papa) and a still choicer for 'friends' who—bless them! while they would not perhaps positively do me an injury—still take a dear delight in dashing with bitterness the too sweet cup of success. Is 'Sharpe's' small article like a bit of sugar-candy too Ellen? or has it the proper wholesome wormwood flavour?

Of course I guess it will be like the 'Guardian.' It matters precious little. My dear 'friends' will weary of waiting for the 'Times' 'O Sisera! —why tarry the wheels of thy chariot so long!'

How is your sister Ann? In a note I had from Miss Wooler lately she mentions that Mrs C. had lately been ill—confined to her bed—As your last makes no special mention of her illness— I trust she is now better. I hope Mercy is also convalescent and that your Mother is pretty well. Give my love to them all.

Mrs Upjohn is really a strange person—but I begin to think that when you actually go to Gorleston, you will find her better than expectation—she cannot be much worse.—I am dear Ellen, Yours faithfully,

C. BRONTË.

834 (624). *To* ELLEN NUSSEY.

Tuesday Morning
[March 22nd, 1853].

DEAR ELLEN,—Mrs Upjohn really carries her protractions and vacillations a little too far—and I am truly sorry that your movements should thus inevitably be hampered by her fluctuations. It is a trial of Job to be thus moved backward and forward by this most luckless of Mistresses and her tribe of reprobate servants.

Thank you for sending Amelia's notes; though I have not alluded to them lately they always amuse me—I like to read them; one gets from them a clear enough idea of her sort of life. Joe's attempts to improve his good partner's mind make me smile. I think it all right enough and doubt not they are happy in their way—only the direction he gives his efforts seems of rather problematic wisdom—Algebra and Optics! Why not rather enlarge her views by a little well-chosen general reading? However —they do right to amuse themselves in their own way.

The rather dark view you seem inclined to take of the general opinion about 'Villette'—surprizes me the less, dear Nell, as only the more unfavourable reviews seem to have come in your way. Some reports reach me of a different tendency; but no matter—Time will shew. As to the character of 'Lucy Snowe' my intention from the first was that she should not occupy the pedestal to which 'Jane Eyre' was raised by some injudicious admirers. She is where I meant her to be, and where no charge of self-laudation can touch her.

I cannot accept your kind invitation. I must be at home at Easter on two or three accounts connected with Sermons to be preached, parsons to be entertained—Mechanics' Institute Meetings and tea-drinkings to be solemnized—and ere long I have promised to go and see Mrs Gaskell—but till this wintry weather is passed I would rather eschew visiting anywhere. I trust that bad cold of yours is *quite* well and that you will take good care of yourself in future. That night-work is always perilous.—Yours faithfully,

C. BRONTË.

835. CATHERINE WINKWORTH *to* EMMA SHAEN.[1]

ALDERLEY, March 23rd, 1853.

I made up my mind not to write to you again till I had read 'Villette,' and now I have just finished it, and don't wonder at all you say about it. It is a thorough enjoyment to read it, so powerful everywhere, no rant, as there were bits of in her other books, so deep and true in its appreciation of character. . . . I like him [Graham Bretton] so much, though he didn't appreciate Lucy Snowe. To be sure she scarcely gave him a chance. Should you have fallen in love with the fiery little Professor for scolding so abominably? One can see very well how Lucy did it, when he alone had the power to see anything of her heart.

'Villette' makes one feel an extreme reverence for any one capable of so much deep feeling and brave endurance and truth, but it makes one feel 'eerie,' too, to be brought face to face with a life so wanting in *Versöhnung*, as Germans would say. I wonder whether Miss B. is so, and I wonder, too, whether she ever was in love; surely she could never herself have made love to any one, as all her heroines, even Lucy Snowe, do. To be sure Paulina does not; how well she and Ginevra are contrasted; only it annoys one at last that that Nun, who really has frightened one all through the book, turns out a trick of such a stupid creature. How finely done—though very improbable, one can't help fancying—is that fête-night when she wanders out;—just like a wild bad dream; but, as Selina says 'one wouldn't for the sake of

[1] Sister of William Shaen who married Emily Winkworth.

a stupid probability miss all that beautiful piece.' No, indeed! Yes: there are bits that go very deep into one's heart; more especially with me all she says about facing and accepting some evil fate. And yet, yet, it never goes *quite* deep enough; it comes to an heroic Stoicism which is grand, but not the best.

I have been reading another book, as unlike 'Villette' as possible, whereof there are many parts that *do* go to 'the innermost depths,' and sink into them like water into the dry ground, and that's Bunsen's 'Hippolytus and His Age.' Have you seen it? I wonder whether you would even care for it at all. I have not seen the fourth volume yet, and the other three I have read in a partial and desultory manner very unbefitting such a work, but I shall go back to it again. Then there is a great deal of Greek and Latin in it, and discussions concerning MSS., which are unintelligible to the unlearned, and some of the English is not over-easy, but it is *worth* thinking about. . . .

836 (627). *To* W. S. WILLIAMS.

[March, 1853].

The note you sent this morning from Lady Harriet St Clair[1] is precisely to the same purport as Miss Mulock's request—an application for exact and authentic information respecting the fate of M. Paul Emanuel! You see how much the ladies think of this little man, whom you none of you like. I had a letter the other day announcing that a lady of some note, who had always determined that whenever she married her husband should be the counterpart of 'Mr Knightley' in Miss Austen's 'Emma,' had now changed her mind, and vowed that she would either find the duplicate of Professor Emanuel or remain for ever single! I have sent Lady Harriet an answer so worded as to leave the matter pretty much where it was. Since the little puzzle amuses the ladies, it would be a pity to spoil their sport by giving them the key.

C. BRONTË.

[1]Lady Harriet Elizabeth St Clair, daughter of the third Earl of Rosslyn, and sister of the poet. She married Count Münster, German Ambassador to the Court of St James's, and died in 1867.

837. *To* GEORGE SMITH.

March 26th, 1853.

MY DEAR SIR, — The 'Mail' being now fairly gone out (at least I hope so) I venture to write to you.

I trust the negotiations to which you allude in your last will be brought to an early and successful conclusion, and that their result will really be a division and consequent alleviation of labour. That you had too much to do, too much to think about, nobody of course can know so well as yourself; therefore it might seem superfluous to dwell on the subject, and yet a looker-on could not but experience a painful prescience of ill sooner or later ensuing from such exertions if continued. That week of overwork which occurred when I was in London was a thing not to be forgotten. Besides 'cultivating the humanities' be resolved to turn to account some part of your leisure in getting fresh air and exercise. When people think too much, and sit too closely, the circulation loses its balance, forsakes the extremities, and bears with too strong a current on the brain; I suppose exercise is the best means of counteracting such a state of things. Pardon me if I speak too much like a doctor. You express surprise that Miss Martineau should apply to *you* for news of *me*. The fact is, I have never written to her since a letter I received from her about eight weeks ago, just after she had read 'Villette.' What is more, I do not know when I can bring myself to write again. The differences of feeling between Miss M. and myself are very strong and marked; very wide and irreconcilable. Besides, I fear language does not convey to her apprehension the same meaning as to mine. In short, she has hurt me a good deal, and at present it appears very plain to me that she and I had better not try to be close friends; my wish, indeed, is that she should quietly forget me. Sundry notions that she considers right and grand strike me as entirely monstrous; it is of no use telling her so. I don't want to quarrel with her, but I want to be let alone. The sketch you enclose is indeed a gem; I suppose I may keep it? 'Miss Eyre' is evidently trying to mesmerise 'Pilot' by a stare of unique fixity, and I fear I must add, stolidity. The embodiment of 'Mr Rochester' surpasses anticipation and strikes panegyric dumb.

With regard to that momentous point M. Paul's fate, in case any one in future should request to be enlightened thereon, he may be told that it was designed that every reader should settle the catastrophe for himself, according to the quality of his disposition, the tender or remorseless impulse of his nature: Drowning and Matrimony are the fearful alternatives. The merciful—like Miss Mulock, Mr Williams, Lady Harriet St Clair, and Mr Alexander Frazer—will of course choose the former and milder doom—drown him to put him out of pain. The cruel-hearted will, on the contrary, pitilessly impale him on the second horn of the dilemma, marrying him without ruth or compunction to that — person — that — that — individual — 'Lucy Snowe.'—

    Yours sincerely,

C. Brontë.

838 (623). *To* Ellen Nussey.

Haworth, April 6th, 1853.

Dear Ellen,—I return Mrs Upjohn's letter. She has indeed acted very strangely, but it is evident to me that there is something very wrong either in herself, her husband, or her domestic arrangements, or (what is perhaps most probable) in all three, and it may be that on the whole, provoking as this conclusion appears, it is the best for you that could well be arrived at. The grounds for expecting permanent good some time ago assumed a very unsubstantial appearance; the hope of present pleasure, I fear, would have turned out equally fallacious. Indeed I now feel little confidence in either comfort or credit ensuing from the connection in any shape.

    My visit to Manchester is for the present put off by Mr Morgan having written to say that since papa will not go to Buckingham to see him, he will come to Yorkshire to see papa; when, I don't yet know, and I trust in goodness he will not stay long, as papa really cannot bear putting out of his way. I must wait, however, till the infliction is over.

    You ask about Mr Nicholls. I hear he has got a curacy, but do not yet know where. I trust the news is true. He and papa never speak. He seems to pass a desolate life. He has allowed late circumstances so to act on him as to freeze up his manner and overcast his countenance not only to those immediately concerned but to every one. He sits drearily in his rooms. If Mr Croxton or Mr Grant, or any other clergyman calls to see, and as they think, to cheer him, he scarcely speaks. I find he tells them nothing, seeks no confidant, rebuffs all attempts to penetrate his mind. I own I respect him for this. He still lets Flossy go to his rooms and takes him to walk. He still goes over to see Mr Sowden sometimes, and, poor fellow, that is all. He looks ill and miserable. I think and trust in Heaven that he will be better as soon as he gets away from Haworth. I pity him inexpressibly. We never meet nor speak, nor dare I look at him, silent pity is just all I can give him, and as he knows nothing about that, it does not comfort. He is now grown so gloomy and reserved, that nobody seems to like him, his fellow-curates shun trouble in that shape, the lower orders dislike it. Papa has a perfect antipathy to him, and he, I fear, to papa. Martha hates him. I think he might almost be *dying* and they would not speak a friendly word to or of him. How much of all this he deserves I can't tell, certainly he never was agreeable or amiable, and is less so now than ever, and alas! I do not know him well enough to be sure there is truth and true affection, or only rancour and corroding disappointment at the bottom of his chagrin. In this state of things I must be, and I am, *entirely passive*. I may be losing the purest gem, and to me far the most precious life can give—genuine attachment—or I may be escaping the yoke of a morose temper. In this doubt conscience will not suffer me to take one step in opposition to papa's will, blended as that will is with the most bitter and unreasonable prejudices. So I just leave the matter where we must leave all important matters.

Remember me kindly to all at Brookroyd, and believe me, yours faithfully,

C. BRONTË.

839 (625). *To* ELLEN NUSSEY.

DEAR ELLEN,—I have the pleasure of forwarding you a racy review in the 'Morning Herald.' When read, be so good as to send the paper to Hunsworth, whence it came.—Yours faithfully.

C. BRONTË.

840 (626). *To* MARGARET WOOLER.

HAWORTH, April 13th, '53.

MY DEAR MISS WOOLER,—Your last kind letter ought to have been answered long since, and would have been—did I find it practicable to proportion the promptitude of the response to the value I place upon my correspondents and their communications: You will easily understand, however, that the contrary rule often holds good, and that the epistle which importunes often takes precedence of that which interests.

My publishers express entire satisfaction with the reception which has been accorded to 'Villette.' And indeed the majority of the reviews have been favourable enough; you will be aware however that there is a minority — small in number but influential in character which views the work with no favourable eye. Currer Bell's remarks on Romanism have drawn down on him the condign displeasure of the High Church Party — which displeasure has been unequivocally expressed through their principal organs the 'Guardian,' the 'English Churchman,' and the 'Christian Remembrancer.' I can well understand that some of the charges launched against me by these publications will tell heavily to my prejudice in the minds of most readers — but this must be borne, and for my part — I can suffer no accusation to oppress me much which is not supported by the inward evidence of Conscience and Reason.

'Extremes meet,' says the proverb; in proof whereof I would mention that Miss Martineau finds with 'Villette' nearly the same fault as the Puseyites — She accuses me with attacking Popery 'with virulence' — of going out of my way to assault it 'passionately.' In other respects she has shown with reference to the work a spirit so strangely and unexpectedly acrimonious — that I have gathered courage to tell her that the gulf of mutual difference between her and me is so wide and deep — the bridge of union so slight and uncertain — I have come to the conclusion that frequent intercourse would be most perilous and unadvisable — and have begged to adjourn *sine die* my long projected visit to her — Of course she is now very angry — and I know her bitterness will not be short-lived, but it cannot be helped.

Two or three weeks since I received a long and kind letter from Mr Wm Wooler[1] — which I answered a short time ago. I believe Mr Wooler thinks me a much hotter advocate for *change* and what is called 'political progress' than I am. However — in my reply — I did not touch on these subjects. He intimated a wish to publish some of his own MSS. I fear he would hardly

[1]Miss Wooler's eldest brother—a physician in Derby until he retired in middle life.

like the somewhat dissuasive tendency of my answer—but really
—in these days of headlong competition—it is a great risk to
publish.

If all be well—I purpose going to Manchester next week to
spend a few days with Mrs Gaskell. Ellen Nussey's visit to Yarmouth seems for the present given up—and really—all things
considered—I think the circumstance is scarcely to be regretted
—it seemed a doubtful kind of prospect.

Do you not think—my dear Miss Wooler, that you could
come to Haworth before you go to the Coast? I am afraid that
when you once get settled at the seaside, your stay will not be
brief. I must repeat that a visit from you would be anticipated
with pleasure—not only by me, but by every inmate of Haworth
Parsonage. Papa has given me a general commission to send his
respects to you whenever I write—accept them, therefore, and
Believe me, yours affectionately and sincerely,

C. BRONTË.

841 (628). *To* MRS GASKELL, *Manchester*.

HAWORTH, April 14th, 1853.

MY DEAR MRS GASKELL,—Would it suit you if I were to
come next Thursday, the 21st?

If that day tallies with your convenience, and if my father continues as well as he is now, I know of no engagement on my part
which need compel me longer to defer the pleasure of seeing you.

I should arrive by the train which reaches Manchester at
7 o'clock P.M. That, I think, would be about your tea-time, and,
of course, I should dine before leaving home. I always like evening for an arrival; it seems more cosy and pleasant than coming
in about the busy middle of the day. I think if I stay a week that
will be a very long visit; it will give you time to get well tired of
me.

Remember me very kindly to Mr Gaskell and Marianne. As to
Mesdames Flossy and Julia, those venerable ladies are requested
beforehand to make due allowance for the awe with which they
will be sure to impress a diffident admirer. I am sorry I shall not
see Meta.—Believe me my dear Mrs Gaskell, yours affectionately and sincerely,

C. BRONTË.

842 (629). *To* ELLEN NUSSEY.

HAWORTH, April 18th, '53.

DEAR ELLEN,—It seems they are in great trouble again at Hunsworth; I have had two or three notes from Amelia giving sad accounts of little Tim. Do you know anything certain on the subject? A's communications as usual seem a good deal coloured by alarm—natural enough no doubt under the circumstances— but still involving inconsistencies of statement which leave one somewhat in the dark. Symptoms seem attributed to the poor child which would indicate scarlet fever, brain fever and croup all in one. The Parents watch all night, the doctor stays till 12 o'clock. Still I hope Tim will get through it.

You seem quite gay at Birstall. I hope you continue well and hearty through all your visiting—and indeed—I think the variety quite advisable, provided you keep duly on your guard against the night-air.

If all be well—I think of going to Manchester about the close of this week. I only intend staying a few days—but I can say nothing about coming back by way of Brookroyd; do not expect me; I would rather see you at Haworth by and by.

Two or three weeks since Miss Martineau wrote to ask why she did not hear from me—and to press me to go to Ambleside. Explanations ensued—the notes on each side were quite civil— but having deliberately formed my resolution on substantial grounds—I adhered to it. I have declined being her visitor— and bid her good-bye. Of course some bitterness remains in her heart. It is best so, however; the antagonism of our natures and principles was too serious a thing to be trifled with.

I have no news for you: things at Haworth are as they were. Remember me kindly to all at Brookroyd and believe me,—
Yours faithfully,

C. BRONTË.

Mr Morgan did *not* come, and if he had, the subject you mention would not have been touched on. Papa alludes to it to nobody; he calls it 'degrading' and would not have it hinted at or known. This circumstance serves as a tolerably pointed illustration of his painful way of viewing the matter.

Mrs Gaskell's address is Plymouth Grove, Manchester.

CHAPTER XXXI

FRIENDSHIP WITH MRS GASKELL

THE friendship of Elizabeth Cleghorn Gaskell and Charlotte Brontë was destined to be brief, but it seems to have been of the most genuine character. Never, anywhere, do we find a single jarring note. Mrs Gaskell gave a whole-hearted admiration to the novels of her friend, and Miss Brontë keenly enjoyed *Mary Barton, Cranford, and Ruth*, the three important books by Mrs Gaskell that were written before Charlotte Brontë's death. Mrs Gaskell has of late obtained a far greater reputation in literature than could have been anticipated by her contemporaries,[1] and it is pleasant to be able to bind together the two names in this correspondence.

Charlotte Brontë paid her second visit to the home of Mrs Gaskell at Plymouth Grove, Manchester, in April, 1853. Mrs Gaskell was an admirable hostess, and although Charlotte, through her extreme self-consciousness, was rather a difficult guest to entertain, the visit passed off very well. Mrs Gaskell arranged one or two small parties for her, and also took her to the theatre to see *Twelfth Night*.

Mrs Gaskell thus records her impression of this visit:[2]

She came, at the close of April, to visit us in Manchester. We had a friend, a young lady, staying with us. Miss Brontë had expected to find us alone; and although our friend was gentle and sensible after Miss Brontë's own heart, yet her presence was enough to create a nervous tremor. I was aware that both of our guests were unusually silent; and I saw a little shiver run from time to time over Miss Brontë's frame. I could account for the modest reserve of the young lady; and the next day Miss Brontë told me how the unexpected sight of a strange face had affected her.

[1] One complete edition of her *Works*, edited by Dr A. W. Ward, was issued in 1906 by Smith, Elder & Co.; and another, published by Henry Frowde in the 'World's Classics.' See also *Mrs. Gaskell and Her Friends*, by Elizabeth S. Haldane (Hodder & Stoughton, 1930).

[2] *The Life of Charlotte Brontë*, by Mrs. E. C. Gaskell, Haworth Edition, pp. 607-9.

It was now two or three years since I had witnessed a similar effect produced on her, in anticipation of a quiet evening at Fox How; and since then she had seen many and various people in London: but the physical sensations produced by shyness were still the same; and on the following day she laboured under severe headache. I had several opportunities of perceiving how this nervousness was ingrained in her constitution, and how acutely she suffered in striving to overcome it. One evening we had, among other guests, two sisters[1] who sang Scottish ballads exquisitely. Miss Brontë had been sitting quiet and constrained till they began 'The Bonnie House of Airlie,' but the effect of that and 'Carlisle Yetts,' which followed, was as irresistible as the playing of the Piper of Hamelin. The beautiful clear light came into her eyes; her lips quivered with emotion; she forgot herself, rose, and crossed the room to the piano where she asked eagerly for song after song. The sisters begged her to come and see them the next morning, when they would sing as long as ever she liked; and she promised gladly and thankfully. But on reaching the house her courage failed. We walked some time up and down the street; she upbraiding herself all the while for folly, and trying to dwell on the sweet echoes in her memory rather than on the thought of a third sister who would have to be faced if we went in. But it was of no use; and dreading lest this struggle with herself might bring on one of her trying head-aches, I entered at last and made the best apology I could for her non-appearance. Much of this nervous dread of encountering strangers I ascribed to the idea of her personal ugliness, which had been strongly impressed upon her imagination early in life, and which she exaggerated to herself in a remarkable manner. 'I notice,' said she, 'that after a stranger has once looked at my face he is careful not to let his eyes wander to that part of the room again!' A more untrue idea never entered into any one's head. Two gentlemen who saw her during this visit, without knowing at the time who she was, were singularly attracted by her appearance; and this feeling of attraction towards a pleasant countenance, sweet voice, and gentle timid manners was so strong in one as to conquer a dislike he had previously enter-tained to her works.

[1]Probably the Misses Susanna and Catherine Winkworth, who were great friends of the Gaskells.

There was another circumstance that came to my knowledge at this period which told secrets about the finely strung frame. One night I was on the point of relating some dismal ghost story, just before bedtime. She shrank from hearing it, and confessed that she was superstitious, and prone at all times to the involuntary recurrence of any thoughts of ominous gloom which might have been suggested to her. She said that on first coming to us she had found a letter on her dressing-table from a friend in Yorkshire, containing a story which had impressed her vividly ever since—that it mingled with her dreams at night and made her sleep restless and unrefreshing.

One day we asked two gentlemen to meet her at dinner, expecting that she and they would have a mutual pleasure in making each other's acquaintance. To our disappointment she drew back with timid reserve from all their advances, replying to their questions and remarks in the briefest manner possible, till at last they gave up their efforts to draw her into conversation in despair, and talked to each other and my husband on subjects of recent local interest. Among these Thackeray's Lectures (which had lately been delivered in Manchester) were spoken of, and that on Fielding especially dwelt upon. One gentleman objected to it strongly as calculated to do moral harm, and regretted that a man having so great an influence over the tone of thought of the day as Thackeray should not more carefully weigh his words. The other took the opposite view. He said that Thackeray described men from the inside, as it were; through his strong power of dramatic sympathy he identified himself with certain characters, felt their temptations, entered into their pleasures, etc. This roused Miss Brontë, who threw herself warmly into the discussion; the ice of her reserve was broken, and from that time she showed her interest in all that was said, and contributed her share to any conversation that was going on in the course of the evening.

From Manchester Charlotte went to Birstall to stay with Ellen Nussey and then returned to Haworth. In June, Mrs Gaskell was invited to stay at Haworth Parsonage, but owing to Charlotte's ill-health, the visit was deferred until the following September.

843 (630). *To* ELLEN NUSSEY.

PLYMOUTH GROVE,
MANCHESTER, April 23rd, 1853.

DEAR ELLEN,—I came here yesterday, and found your letter. There is something in its tone which makes me apprehend that you are rather low spirited, so that I shall manage to do as you wish and return by Birstall. I expect to leave here next Thursday, and return home on Saturday, but I will write again, D.V. before Thursday.

I only scratch this hasty line now to give you an idea of my movements. With kind regards to all at Brookroyd, and best birthday wishes to yourself,—I am, dear Ellen, yours faithfully,

C. BRONTË.

844 (631). *To* ELLEN NUSSEY.

April 26th, 1853.

DEAR ELLEN,—I hope to reach Birstall on Thursday at 5 o'clock, if all be well, and stay till Saturday or Monday, as we shall decide when we meet. I have had a very pleasant visit here, but we can chat about it anon. I have only just time to pen this notification. Kind regards.—I am, yours faithfully,

C. BRONTË.

845 *To* MRS GASKELL.

[April 1853].

MY DEAR MRS GASKELL,— The week I spent in Manchester has impressed me as the very brightest and healthiest I have known for these five years past. . . .   [C. BRONTË].

846 (632). *To* ELLEN NUSSEY.

May 16th, 1853.

DEAR ELLEN,—Habituated by this time to Mrs Upjohn's fluctuations, I received the news of this fresh put off without the slightest sentiment of wonder. Indeed, I keep all my powers of surprise for the intelligence that you are safely arrived at Gorleston, and still more for the desired but very moderately expected tidings that you are happy there.

The east winds about which you inquire have spared me wonderfully till to-day, when I feel somewhat sick physically, and not very blithe mentally. I am not sure that the east winds are entirely to blame for this ailment. Yesterday was a strange sort of a day at church. It seems as if I were to be punished for my doubts about the nature and truth of poor Mr Nicholls's regard. Having ventured on Whit-Sunday to stop to the sacrament, I got a lesson not to be repeated. He struggled, faltered, then lost command over himself, stood before my eyes and in the sight of all the communicants, white, shaking, voiceless. Papa was not there, thank God! Joseph Redman spoke some words to him. He made a great effort, but could only with difficulty whisper and falter through the service. I suppose he thought this would be the last time; he goes either this week or the next. I heard the women sobbing round, and I could not quite check my own tears. What had happened was reported to papa either by Joseph Redman or John Brown; it excited only anger, and such expressions as 'unmanly driveller.' Compassion or relenting is no more to be looked for from Papa than sap from firewood.

I never saw a battle more sternly fought with the feelings than Mr Nicholls fights with his, and when he yields momentarily, you are almost sickened by the sense of the strain upon him. However he is to go, and I cannot speak to him or look at him or comfort him a whit, and I must submit. Providence is over all, that is the only consolation. — Yours faithfully,

C. Brontë.

847 (633). *To* Ellen Nussey.

Haworth, May 19th, 1853.

Dear Ellen, — It is almost a relief to hear that you only think of staying at Yarmouth a month, though of course one must not be selfish in wishing you to come home soon, and you will be guided in your final decision by the state of things as you find it at Mrs Upjohn's. There cannot, I think, be any disappointment in the business. I really do hope causes may be discovered of agreeable surprise. At any rate for a month you surely may be made comfortable, unless the house be really haunted, as Mr Clapham supposed.

You do not mention how you got on on Whit-Tuesday. Tell me when you write again.

Vol. IV   f

I cannot help feeling a certain satisfaction in finding that the people here are getting up a subscription to offer a testimonial of respect to Mr Nicholls on his leaving the place.[1] Many are expressing both their commiseration and esteem for him. The Churchwardens recently put the question to him plainly. Why was he going? Was it Mr Brontë's fault or his own? 'His own,' he answered. Did he blame Mr Brontë? 'No! he did not: if anybody was wrong it was himself.' Was he willing to go? 'No! it gave him great pain.' Yet he is not always right. I must be just. He shows a curious mixture of honour and obstinacy; feeling and sullenness. Papa addressed him at the school tea-drinking, with *constrained* civility, but still with *civility*. He did not reply civilly; he cut short further words. This sort of treatment offered in public is what papa never will forget or forgive; it inspires him with a silent bitterness not to be expressed. I am afraid both are unchristian in their mutual feelings. Nor do I know which of them is least accessible to reason or least likely to forgive. It is a dismal state of things.

The weather is fine now, dear Nell. We will take these sunny days as a good omen for your visit to Yarmouth. With kind regards to all at Brookroyd, and best wishes to yourself. —I am, yours sincerely,

C. BRONTË.

If you have time before you go, I wish you would get me 1 lb. of plain biscuits like those you had at Brookroyd, and ½ lb. of invalid biscuits, and send them per rail. I can pay for them in postage stamps. They are things I cannot get here, nor good, at Keighley.

848 (634). *To* W. S. WILLIAMS.

HAWORTH, May —, 1853.

MY DEAR SIR, —The 'Lectures'[2] arrived safely; I have read them through twice. They must be studied to be appreciated. I thought well of them when I heard them delivered, but now I see their real power, and it is great. The lecture on Swift was

---

[1] It took the form of a gold watch, which Mr Nicholls showed to the late Clement K. Shorter with natural pride, forty years later, while walking over his farm at Banagher. The following inscription was engraved upon it:—'Presented to the Rev. A.

B. Nicholls, B.A., by the teachers, scholars, & congregation of St Michael's, Haworth, Yorkshire, May 25, 1853.'

[2] Thackeray's *Lectures on the English Humorists of the Eighteenth Century*.

new to me; I thought it almost matchless. Not that by any means I always agree with Mr Thackeray's opinions, but his force, his penetration, his pithy simplicity, his eloquence—his manly, sonorous eloquence—command entire admiration. I deny and must deny that Mr Thackeray is very good, or very amiable, but the man is great—great, but mistaken, full of errors—against his errors I protest, were it treason to do so. I was present at the Fielding lecture; the hour spent in listening to it was a painful hour. That Thackeray was wrong in his way of treating Fielding's character and vices my conscience told me. After reading that lecture I trebly felt that he was wrong—dangerously wrong. Had Thackeray owned a son, grown or growing up, and a son brilliant but reckless—would he have spoken in that light way of courses that lead to disgrace and the grave? He speaks of it all as if he theorised; as if he had never been called on, in the course of his life to witness the actual consequences of such failings; as if he had never stood by and seen the issue, the final result of it all. I believe, if only once the prospect of a promising life blasted at the outset by wild ways had passed close under his eyes, he never *could* have spoken with such levity of what led to its piteous destruction. Had I a brother yet living, I should tremble to let him read Thackeray's lecture on Fielding. I should hide it away from him. If, in spite of precaution, it should fall into his hands, I should earnestly pray him not to be misled by the voice of the charmer, let him charm never so wisely. Not that for a moment I would have had Thackeray to *abuse* Fielding, or even pharisaically to condemn his life; but I do most deeply grieve that it never entered into his heart sadly and nearly to feel the peril of such a career, that he might have dedicated some of his great strength to a potent warning against its adoption by any young man. I believe temptation often assails the finest manly natures, as the pecking sparrow or destructive wasp attacks the sweetest and mellowest fruit, eschewing what is sour and crude. The true lover of his race ought to devote his vigour to guard and protect; he should sweep away every lure with a kind of rage at its treachery. You will think this far too serious, I dare say; but the subject is serious, and one cannot help feeling upon it earnestly.—Believe me, Sincerely yours,

C. BRONTË.

849 (635). *To* Ellen Nussey.

Haworth, May 27th, 1853.

Dear Ellen,—I was right glad to get your letter this morning and to find that you really were safely arrived at last. How strange it seems though that there should have been a sort of miscalculation up to the very last! I am afraid you would feel a little damped on your arrival to find Mrs Upjohn from home. However, I *do* think it is well you are gone, the experiment was worth trying, and according to present appearances really promises very fairly. If tempers, etc., are only right, there seem to be many other appliances and means for enjoyment! I do not much like to hear of that supposed affection of the brain. If there be any thing wrong there, it is to be feared that with time it will rather increase than diminish; however let us hope for the best. I trust Mr Upjohn may prove a pleasant, well-informed companion.

The biscuits came all right, but I believe you have sent about twice the quantity I ordered. You *must* tell me how much they cost, dear Nell, or I shall never be able to ask you to render me a similar service again.

I send by this post the 'Examiner' and French paper. I suppose I had better suppress the 'Leader' while you are at Gorleston. I don't think it would suit Mr Upjohn.

You will want to know about the leave-taking; the whole matter is but a painful subject, but I must treat it briefly. The testimonial was presented in a public meeting. Mr T. and Mr Grant were there. Papa was not very well and I advised him to stay away, which he did. As to the last Sunday, it was a cruel struggle. Mr Nicholls ought not to have had to take any duty.

He left Haworth this morning at 6 o'clock. Yesterday evening he called to render into Papa's hands the deeds of the National School, and to say good-bye. They were busy cleaning, washing the paint, etc., in the dining-room, so he did not find me there. I would not go into the parlour to speak to him in Papa's presence. He went out thinking he was not to see me, and indeed, till the very last moment, I thought it best not. But perceiving that he stayed long before going out at the gate, and remembering his long grief, I took courage and went out trembling and miserable. I found him leaning against the garden door in a paroxysm of anguish, sobbing as women never sob. Of course I went straight to him. Very few words were interchanged, those few barely articulate. Several things I should have liked to ask him were swept entirely from my memory. Poor fellow! But he wanted such hope and such encouragement as I *could* not give him. Still I trust he must know now that I am not cruelly blind and indifferent to his constancy and grief. For a few weeks he goes to the South of England — afterwards he takes a curacy somewhere in Yorkshire,[1] but I don't know where.

Papa has been far from strong lately. I dare not mention Mr Nicholls's name to him. He speaks of him quietly and without opprobrium to others, but to me he is implacable on the matter. However, he is gone — gone — and there's an end of it. I see no chance of hearing a word about him in future, unless some stray shred of intelligence comes through Mr Sowden or some other second-hand source. In all this it is not I who am to be pitied at all, and of course nobody pities me. They all think, in Haworth, that I have disdainfully refused him, etc. If pity would do Mr Nicholls any good, he ought to have and I believe has it. They may abuse me if they will; whether they do or not I can't tell.

Write soon and say how your prospects proceed. I trust they will daily brighten. — Yours faithfully,

C. BRONTË.

850 (636). *To* W. S. WILLIAMS.

HAWORTH, May 28th, 1853.

MY DEAR SIR, — The box of books arrived safely yesterday evening, and I feel especially obliged for the Selection as it includes several that will be acceptable and interesting to my Father.

I despatch to-day a box of return books: among them will be found two or three of those just sent, being such as I had read before — i.e. Moore's 'Life and Correspondence,' 1st and 2nd Vols., Lamartine's 'Restoration of the Monarchy,' etc.

I have thought of you more than once during the late bright weather knowing how genial you find warmth and sunshine. I trust it has brought this season its usual cheering and beneficial effect.

Remember me kindly to Mrs Williams and her Daughters — and believe me, Yours sincerely,

C. BRONTË.

[1]At Kirk Smeaton, six miles south-east of Pontefract.

851 (637). *To* MRS GASKELL.

HAWORTH, June 1st, 1853.

DEAR MRS GASKELL,—June is come, and now I want to know if you can come on Thursday, the 9th inst.

Ever since I was at Manchester I have been anticipating your visit. Not that I attempt to justify myself in asking you; the place has no attractions, as I told you, here in this house. Papa too takes great interest in the matter. I only pray that the weather may be fine, and that a cold, by which I am now stupefied, may be gone before the 9th, so that I may have no let and hindrance in taking you on to the moors—the sole, but, with one who loves nature as you do, not despicable, resource.

When you take leave of the domestic circle and turn your back on Plymouth Grove to come to Haworth, you must do it in the spirit which might sustain you in case you were setting out on a brief trip to the backwoods of America. Leaving behind your husband, children, and civilisation, you must come out to barbarism, loneliness, and liberty. The change will perhaps do good, if not too prolonged. . . . Please, when you write, to mention by what train you will come, and at what hour you will arrive at Keighley; for I must take measures to have a conveyance waiting for you at the station; otherwise, as there is no cab-stand, you might be inconvenienced and hindered.

C. BRONTË.

852 (638). *To* ELLEN NUSSEY.

June 6th, '53.

DEAR ELLEN,—At present, I will comment on nothing you have told me. I am so unlucky as to have got a very bad influenza cold, and to-day I am so miserably sick, I cannot bear out of bed. Write to me again when you get to your Brother's.—Yours faithfully,

C. BRONTË.

Mrs Gaskell has written to say she will come on Thursday and stay till Monday. Unless I alter very much and very rapidly, I shall be constrained to send her back word not to come.

853 (639). *To* Ellen Nussey.

June 13th, 1853.

Dear Ellen, — You must still excuse a few scant lines. I have been suffering most severely for ten days with continued pain in the head, on the nerves it is said to be; blistering at last seems to have done it some good, but I am yet weak and bewildered. Of course I could not receive Mrs Gaskell; it was a great disappointment. I now long to be better, to get her visit over if possible, and then to ask you; but I must wait awhile yet. Papa has not been well either, but I hope he is better now. You have had a hard time of it and some rough experience. Good-bye for the present. I wish much to talk with you about these strange, unhappy people at Gorleston, — Yours faithfully,

C. Brontë.

854 (640). *To* Ellen Nussey.

June 16th, 1853.

Dear Ellen, — I am better now — as usual the reduction of strength was rapid — and the convalescence equally so. The very dreadful pain in my head is almost gone and so is the influenza. Papa too is better — but I was frightened about him — not that he has in the least lost appetite or thought himself ill in body — but the eyes, &c. betrayed those symptoms that fill me with alarm.

I have written to Mrs Gaskell to ask her for next week — I do not know however whether she will now be at liberty before August or Septb. but when I get her answer I will tell you what is its purport — and your coming can be arranged accordingly.

I am glad dear Nell, you are having a little enjoyment. Stay at Oundle if you can till you hear from me again — as if Mrs Gaskell does *not* come — you had better come direct here — but we shall see. — Yours faithfully,

C. Brontë.

855 (641). *To* ELLEN NUSSEY.

June 20th, '53.

DEAR ELLEN,—I have been very much vexed to find that
Martha forgot to post my letter of Saturday till too late, consequently as we have no post on Sunday it will not reach you till
to-day at the earliest. I now write a line to tell you to be sure and
arrange your departure from Oundle according to your own
convenience. My health has nothing to do with the question, as
I am now about in my usual condition, only thin, as I always am
after illness. Be sure, however, to let me know the time of your
arrival that I may arrange to send for you.

.   .   .   .   .

I do trust it may be fine healthy weather while you are here.
The enclosed is from Amelia to you. I have not read it, though
it was sent to me open. It takes two posts from O. to Haworth.

I shall expect you by next Thursday.—Yours faithfully,

C. BRONTË.

I trust you will get through your journey all right.

It will be remembered that Miss Nussey had contemplated the
post of companion to a Mrs Upjohn at Gorleston upon conditions which made her consult her two friends. We have seen
Charlotte Brontë's letters upon the point. Here is Mary Taylor's
sarcastic treatment of the matter.

856 (677). *To* ELLEN NUSSEY.

[WELLINGTON, July 21st, 1853].[1]

MY DEAR MR CLERGYMAN AND MRS CLERGYMAN,—I
have received your letter expressing a wish to have my services
as companion. Your terms are so indefinite and so low that I had
rather have nothing to do with you. As I understand your proposal, you offer me board and lodging, but no clothes or means
of getting any. If you intend providing my dress, I should like
to know what liberty I should have in the choice and make, and
who had worn the things before me, tho' I must say this would
not alter my refusal of your offer, as I should still not be so well

[1]Postmark. The letter was written in May, June, and July.

off as a servant-girl. The pecuniary advantages you offer at some future time I consider worth nothing. They are quite indefinite; the time when I am to receive them is too far off, and the condition that you make—that you must be dead before I can profit by them—decides me to refuse them altogether.

Your letter is as indefinite about the services you require as about the wages you offer. As to the companionship, affection, etc., I have very little to offer to a stranger, and it strikes me I should never have much for you. Your coarseness of feeling that allows you to pay me the greater part of my wages only after your death, your evident dishonesty in leaving the engagement so indefinite that I might do two women's work for twenty years to come and then have no legal claim on you or your heirs, your evident notion that an expensive dress and diet is to compensate for the absence of money wages, all make me think that your feelings, principles, and pleasures are very different to mine, and there could be no companionship in the case. As to my services, I would not give them without certain money wages paid quarterly, and certain time to be at my own disposal. These are what every servant gets! and I should want something more.—Yours.

May.

DEAR ELLEN,—Here's my opinion on the impudent proposal you mention in your letter, which I received this morning along with one from Amelia. All your news is very interesting, particularly that concerning Amelia, Joe, and Charlotte. My last letters told quite a contrary tale. They were none of them well, and that was proved more by their low spirits than their complaints. I've no doubt Tim is a little pest, as Joe says, but that is no reason why it should not be brought up healthily if possible. I am sorry to hear its intellect is so forward; it ought to look stupid and get fat.

June 26.

I have kept my letter back because I had not said all I had to say, and now it's gone out of my head. Since then I have received a letter from you, dated 7th October 1852. It came along with some from Hunsworth of 20th and 23rd February 1853, and one from John, dated 20th October, 1852. You mention Mr Brontë's illness and Charlotte Brontë's liver complaint. I had heard of them both, but not from her. I did not know her liver complaint still continued, and since the date of yours I hear from Amelia that you and she have been at Hun., and Charlotte Brontë was very well indeed. How are you all now I wonder?

I hear—I mean read—that there is a box full of treasures on the way to me per *Maori*, now at Nelson. All the sailors have run away—very sensible of them when they are probably [working] for £2 a month, and by keeping out of sight till the *Maori* is gone, can hire themselves here for £7. They—I don't mean the sailors—have got some Maoris to land the cargo, but as they can't persuade them to go up aloft, there is no knowing when the ship can come on here.

Well, in the said box is a pair of lace cuffs from you for me to wear 'when I go to a dance.' Do you think I go once a week to a dance? I am very curious to see them, and particularly to know if the fashion of them is still unknown here—in which case they will certainly set me up for a twelvemonth. It is a great mercy and a particular favour of Providence that they were not sent in the *Mahomet Shah*.

I go to a dance now and then. I get an invitation from somebody in the name of some 'party' or parties unknown. We dance at the Hall of the Athenæum, hired and decorated with flags and green stuff for the occasion. We muster about 25 couples, dance with great gravity, and call ourselves *very select*. The thing is managed by some second- and third-rate bachelors who don't know how to give their invites properly in a body, and individually had rather not 'come forward.'

My best amusement is to put on a hood—such as children wear, and very common here for grown people—and go after I've shut up at night, and gossip with a neighbour. I have four or five houses where I do this, and talk more *real talk* in an hour than all the night at a dance.

July 2.

I have just found out it was not you but Amelia that sent me the lace cuffs, and you and Charlotte Brontë concocted the rest of the box. I have no doubt I shall approve of your choice, as Amelia says. Were you all together in the little room at Hunsworth? Giving her your advice? Mind, if the dress is scarlet or pale green, I'll never forgive you.

I folded this letter once without putting my name to [it].

Don't go and live with Mrs Clergyman.

M. TAYLOR.

857. *To* GEORGE SMITH.

HAWORTH, July 3rd, 1853.

MY DEAR SIR,—Nobody could read your last note without experiencing a sense of concern. Such a feeling indeed was inspired by a former letter of yours received in May; but you then spoke of being better; the concluding lines were hopeful. Better it seems you are not; at least your spirits are not improved, and I write a line because whoever wishes you well can hardly rest satisfied without making some little effort to cheer you.

Permit me to say that it is wise to anticipate better days with even sanguine confidence. I do not think your health is undermined, but your nerves have been so frightfully overstrained with too much work that now they are relaxed, and both *time* and *repose* are absolutely necessary to the recovery of a healthy tone.

I suppose a very phlegmatic, heavy nature would not feel the evils from which you are now suffering; but where the nervous system is delicately constructed, and either from overwork or other causes has to undergo ...[1]

Thank you for your kind inquiries about my father; there is no change for the worse in his sight since I wrote last; rather, I think, a tendency to improvement. He says the sort of veil between him and the light appears thinner; his general health has, however, been lately a good deal affected, and, desirable as it might appear in some points of view to adopt your suggestions with reference to seeking the best medical advice, I fear that at present there would be a serious hazard in undertaking a long journey by rail. He must become stronger than he appears to be just now, less liable to sudden sickness and swimming in the head, before such a step could be thought of.

Your kind offer of attention in case he should ever come to town merits and has my best acknowledgments. I know, however, that my father's first and last thought would be to give trouble nowhere, and especially to infringe on no precious time. He would, of course, take private lodgings.

As for me, I am and have been for some weeks pretty much as usual again. That is to say, no object for solicitude whatever.

[1]Incomplete.

You do not mention whether your mother and sisters are well, but I hope they are, and beg always to be kindly remembered to them. I hope too your partner, Mr King, will soon acquire a working faculty, and leave you some leisure and opportunity effectually to cultivate health.—Believe me, yours sincerely,

C. BRONTË.

858. *To* the Revd [WELBURY] MITTON, *Bradford, Yorkshire.*

HAWORTH, NR KEIGHLEY,
July 8th, 1853.

REVD AND DEAR SIR,—I have heard, that you are so obliging as sometimes to preach for charitable Institutions—I therefore venture to request that you will be so kind as to preach for us, on Sunday the twenty fourth Inst. a sermon in the Afternoon, and another in the Evening—in behalf of our Sunday School— The service in the afternoon will begin at a quarter past two o'Clock, and in the Evening at six.

An early answer will oblige.—Yours very faithfully,

P. BRONTË.

859 (642). *To* Mrs GASKELL.

HAWORTH, July 9th, 1853.

MY DEAR MRS GASKELL,—Thank you for your letter—it was as pleasant as a quiet chat, as welcome as spring showers, as reviving as a friend's visit; in short, it was very like a page of 'Cranford.'

That book duly reached me—coming on the very morning you should have come in person—had Fate been propitious. I have read it over twice; once to myself, and once aloud to my Father. I find it pleasurable reading—graphic, pithy, penetrating, shrewd, yet kind and indulgent.

A thought comes to me. Do you, who have so many friends —so large a circle of acquaintance—find it easy, when you sit down to write, to isolate yourself from all those ties, and their sweet associations, so as to be quite *your own woman*, uninfluenced unswayed by the consciousness of how your work may affect other minds; what blame, what sympathy it may call forth? Does no luminous cloud ever come between you and the severe Truth as you know it in your own secret and clear-seeing soul? In a word, are you never tempted to make your characters more amiable than the Life, by the inclination to assimilate your thoughts to the thoughts of those who always *feel* kindly, but sometimes fail to *see* justly? Don't answer the question; it is not intended to be answered. . . . Your account of Mrs Stowe was stimulatingly interesting. I long to see you, to get you to say it, and many other things, all over again.

My Father continues better. I am better too; but to-day I have a headache again, which will hardly let me write coherently. Give my kind love to Marianne and Meta, dear happy girls as they are. Remember me too to Mr Gaskell. You cannot now transmit my message to Flossy and Julia. I prized the little wild-flower—not that I think the sender cares for me; she *does* not, and *cannot*, for she does not know me; but no matter. In my reminiscences she is a person of a certain distinction. I think hers a fine little nature, frank and of genuine promise. I often see her, as she appeared, stepping supreme from the portico towards the carriage, that evening we went to see 'Twelfth Night.' I believe in Julia's future; I like what speaks in her movements, and what is written upon her face. —Yours with true attachment,

C. BRONTË.

860. *To* GEORGE SMITH.

HAWORTH, July 14th, 1853.

MY DEAR SIR,—Mr Ruskin's beautiful book[1] reached me safe-ly this morning; its arrival was a pleasant surprise, as I was far from expecting to see it so soon after publication. Of course I have not yet read it, but a mere glance over the pages suffices to excite anticipation and to give a foretaste of excellence.

Acknowledgment is also due for the great pleasure I derived from reading Dr Forbes's 'Memorandum' (sent in the last Corn-hill parcel). Without according with every opinion broached, or accepting as infallible every inference drawn or every conclu-sion arrived at, one cannot but like the book and sincerely respect the author on account of the good sense, good feeling, good nature, and good humour everywhere obvious in his 'Memorandum.'

[1] *Lectures on Architecture and Painting*, by John Ruskin, 1853.

About a fortnight since I observed in the 'Examiner' an intimation that Mr Thackeray is about to issue a new serial.[1] Is this good news true? and if so, do you at all know the subject, and are you to publish it? I hope so.

Mrs Gaskell was in town a few weeks ago, and gave a most propitious account of the great man's present mood and spirits, but I am afraid, after all his fêting in America, he will find it rather a dull change to sit down again to his desk, especially when he is in some sense bound to refrain from the very subject which must still be uppermost in his thoughts.

My father's half-formed project of visiting London this summer for a few days has been rather painfully frustrated. In June he had a sudden seizure, which, without seeming greatly to affect his general health, brought on for a time total blindness. He could not discern between day and night. I feared the optic nerve was paralysed, and that he would never see more. Vision has, however, been partially restored, but it is now very imperfect.

He sometimes utters a wish that he could see the camp at Cobham, but that would not be possible under present circumstances. I think him very patient with the apprehension of what, to him, would be the greatest of privations hanging over his head. I can but earnestly hope that what remains of sight may be spared him to the end.

I trust your mother and sisters are well, and that you have ere now secured assistance and are relieved from some part of your hard work, and consequently that your health and spirits are improved. — Yours sincerely,

C. BRONTË.

The review which seemed to affect Miss Brontë most of all was one in *The Christian Remembrancer* of April 1853, in which the author of *Villette* was described as 'having gained both in amiability and propriety since she first presented herself to the world — soured, coarse, and grumbling; an alien, it might seem, from society, and amenable to none of its laws.' Dr Robertson Nicoll unearthed a protest from Charlotte Brontë to the editor of *The Christian Remembrancer*, in which the author of *Villette*

[1] *The Newcomes: Memoirs of a most respectable Family, edited by Arthur Pendennis, Esq.*, by W. M. Thackeray, first issued in twenty-four monthly numbers from October 1853 to August 1855. Published in two volumes, illustrated by R. Doyle, 1854–55.

resents the suggestion of her critic that she is an alien from society.[1]

861 (643). *To* the Editor of 'THE CHRISTIAN REMEM-
BRANCER.'

HAWORTH, July 18th, 1853.

SIR,—To him I would say that no cause of seclusion such as he would imply has ever come near my thoughts, deeds, or life. It has not entered my experience. It has not crossed my observation.

Providence so regulated my destiny that I was born and have been reared in the seclusion of a country parsonage. I have never been rich enough to go out into the world as a participator in its gaieties, though it early became my duty to leave home, in order partly to diminish the many calls on a limited income. That income is lightened of claims in another sense now, for of a family of six I am the only survivor.

My father is now in his seventy-seventh year; his mind is clear as it ever was, and he is not infirm, but he suffers from partial privation and threatened loss of sight; and his general health is also delicate—he cannot be left often or long: my place consequently is at home. There are reasons which make retirement a plain duty; but were no such reasons in existence, were I bound by no such ties, it is very possible that seclusion might still appear to me, on the whole, more congenial than publicity; the brief and rare glimpses I have had of the world do not incline me to think I should seek its circles with very keen zest—nor can I consider such disinclination a just subject for reproach.

This is the truth. The careless, rather than malevolent insinuations of reviewers have, it seems, widely spread another impression. It would be weak to complain, but I feel that it is only right to place the real in opposition to the unreal.

Will you kindly show this note to my reviewer? Perhaps he cannot now find an antidote for the poison into which he dipped that shaft he shot at 'Currer Bell,' but when again tempted to take aim at other prey, let him refrain his hand a moment till he has considered consequences to the wounded, and recalled the 'golden rule.'

CURRER BELL.

[1] *The Bookman*, November 1899.

It was fated that the two reviews of her work which most offended Miss Brontë should have been written by women—the *Quarterly Review* article by Miss Rigby, and *The Christian Remembrancer* article by Miss Anne Mozley.

The following letter is interesting, because it shows the Rev. Patrick Brontë in a more genial frame of mind than was usual with him, for as a rule he was rather a stiff and formal correspondent. We know that he kept a pistol at the Rectory, but it was never suspected that he had in his younger days been in the habit of shooting on the moors.

When this letter was written he was 76 years old. He always took a great interest in politics—even when his children were quite young he was in the habit of discussing political matters with them. Charlotte was probably away on a short visit to Scotland when her father received the present of game.

In 1853 Mr Ferrand was 44 years of age. He was the representative of a family which had held extensive estates in Bingley and the Harden Valley for many centuries. William Busfeild Ferrand was a typical country squire; powerful in physique, a great sportsman, and a popular landlord. He figured largely in the political history of his time, for, besides being a J.P. and Deputy Lieutenant, he was a member of Parliament for many years, and took an active part in supporting the Ten Hours' Factory legislation, exposing the truck system, and the harsh conditions of Poor Law administration. Mr Halliwell Sutcliffe, in his now rare book, *The Eleventh Commandment*, and also in his *Man of the Moors*, draws a fine portrait of Mr Ferrand as a genial country squire.

There is a reference to the Ferrands in Charlotte's letter to Ellen Nussey, dated August 26, 1850.[1]

862. *To* W. B. Ferrand, *Bingley*.

HAWORTH, Nr KEIGHLEY,
Augt. 23rd, 1853.

DEAR SIR,—I thank you for your kind remembrance of me, through your presents of game—they remind me of my youth-

[1]Vol. III, p. 149.

ful days, when I often traversed the moors and fields myself, and in a quick and steady aim, might have been not an unworthy competitor, even with you, though from what I learn, that would have been no easy matter; since I hear, you scarcely ever miss — Well — you have strong nerves, quick sight, and a steady hand, good, and necessary qualifications for hitting the mark. I had the curiosity to weigh one of the birds — it weighed nearly twenty-six ounces — which was the greatest weight, I ever knew.

But, to pass from moorcocks to statesmen, from powder to politics. What think ye of the materials of our present Government, and their proceedings. Was there ever so heterogeneous a Mass, under the sun? — Whig, and Tory — Conservative and Radical, Romanist, and Puritan — all jumbled together![1] Are these the men, to make a long pull, a strong pull, and a pull, all together, for the public good? Where there must be so much sacrifice, of principle and consistency, it is not difficult to foresee, the inglorious and disastrous issue.

Hoping that you, your Lady and family are well, — I remain, Dear Sir, Yours respectfully and truly,

                                        P. BRONTË.

863 (644). *To* MARGARET WOOLER.

                    HAWORTH, Augst 30th, 1853.

MY DEAR MISS WOOLER, — I was from home when your kind letter came, and as it was not forwarded — I did not get it till my return. All the summer I have felt the wish and cherished the intention to join you for a brief period at the seaside; nor do I yet entirely relinquish the purpose, though its fulfilment must depend on my father's health. At present he complains so much of weakness and depressed spirits — no thoughts of leaving him can be entertained. Should he improve however — I would fain come to you before Autumn is quite gone.

My late absence was but for a week, when I accompanied Mr

[1]This was the Coalition Ministry of Peelites and Whigs which came into office in December 1852, with Lord Aberdeen, the leader of the Peelites, as Prime Minister. It was a heterogeneous Ministry as Mr Brontë says, and its lack of cohesion soon became apparent. Called upon to face the Eastern problem it adopted a half-hearted policy and drifted into the Crimean War, its conduct of which was a tale of woeful disasters. It is probably to the imminence of war that the letter makes reference. Certainly its forebodings proved justified. The long, strong, and united pull was not forthcoming, and after two years of mismanagement the Ministry fell 'unwept, unhonoured, and unsung.'

and Mrs Joe Taylor and baby on a trip to Scotland. They went with the intention of taking up their quarters at Kirkcudbright or some watering-place on the Solway Firth. We barely reached that locality, and had stayed but one night—when the baby (that rather despotic member of modern households) exhibited some symptoms of indisposition. To my unskilled perception its ailments appeared very slight—nowise interfering with its appetite or spirits, but parental eyes saw the matter in a different light: the air of Scotland was pronounced unpropitious to the child— and consequently we had to retrace our steps. I own I felt some little reluctance to leave 'bonnie Scotland' so soon and so abruptly, but of course I could not say a word, since however strong on my own mind the impression that the ailment in question was very trivial and temporary (an impression confirmed by the issue—as the slight diarrhœa disappeared in a few hours), I could not be absolutely certain that such was the case—and had any evil consequences followed a prolonged stay—I should never have forgiven myself.

Ilkley was the next place thought of. We went there, but I only remained three days—for in the hurry of changing trains at one of the stations—my box was lost and without clothes, I could not stay. I have heard of it since—but have not yet regained it. In all probability it is now lying at Kirkcudbright, where it was directed.

Notwithstanding some minor trials—I greatly enjoyed this little excursion—the scenery through which we travelled from Dumfries to Kirkcudbright (a distance of 30 miles performed outside a stage-coach) was beautiful, though not all of a peculiarly Scottish character, being richly cultivated, and well-wooded. I liked Ilkley too exceedingly, and shall long to revisit the place. On the whole—I thought it for the best that circumstances obliged me to return home so soon, for I found Papa far from well: he is something better now, yet I shall not feel it right to leave him again till I see a more thorough re-establishment of health and strength.

With some things to regret and smile at—I saw many things to admire in the small family party with which I travelled. Mr Joe makes a most devoted father and husband. I admired his great kindness to his wife—an amiable though not a clever or cultivated woman, but I rather groaned (inwardly) over the unbounded indulgence of both parents towards their only child.

The world does not revolve round the Sun—that is a mistake; certain babies I plainly perceive—are the important centre of all things. The Papa and Mamma could only take their meals, rest and exercise at such times and in such measure as the despotic infant permitted. While Mrs J. eat [*sic*] her dinner, Mr J. relieved guard as nurse. A nominal nurse indeed accompanied the party, but her place was a sort of anxious, waiting sinecure, as the child did not fancy her attendance. Tenderness to offspring is a virtue, yet I think I have seen Mothers—the late Mrs Allbutt[1] for instance—who were most tender and thoughtful—yet in very love for their children—would not permit them to become tyrants either over themselves or others.

I shall be glad and grateful—my dear Miss Wooler, to hear from you again whenever you have time or inclination to write —though—as I told you before—there is no fear of my misunderstanding silence.

Should you leave Hornsea before Winter sets in—I trust you will just come straight to Haworth, and pay your long-anticipated visit there before you go elsewhere.

Papa and the servants send their respects. I always duly deliver your kind messages of remembrance because they give pleasure.—Believe me always, yours affectionately and respectfully,

C. Brontë.

864 (645). *To* Mrs Gaskell.

September —, 1853.

Dear Mrs Gaskell,—I was glad to get your little note, glad to hear you were at home again. Not that, practically, it makes much difference to me whether you are in Normandy or Manchester: the shorter distance separates perhaps as effectually as the longer, yet there is a mental comfort in thinking that but thirty miles intervene.

Come to Haworth as soon as you can; the heath is in bloom now; I have waited and watched for its purple signal as the forerunner of your coming. It will not be quite faded before the 16th, but after that it will soon grow sere. Be sure to mention the day and hour of your arrival at Keighley.

Wife of the Rev.T. Allbutt, Vicar of Dewsbury, mother of Sir Clifford Allbutt.

My father has passed the summer, not well, yet better than I expected. His chief complaint is of weakness and depressed spirits; the prospect of your visit still affords him pleasure. I am surprised to see how he looks forward to it. My own health has been much better lately.

I suppose that Meta is ere this returned to school again. This summer's tour will no doubt furnish a lifelong remembrance of pleasure to her and Marianne. Great would be the joy of the little ones at seeing you all home again.

I saw in the papers the death of Mr S., of scarlet fever, at his residence in Wales. Was it not there you left Flossy and Julia? This thought recurred to me, with some chilling fears of what might happen; but I trust that all is safe now. How is poor Mrs S.?

Remember me very, very kindly to Mr Gaskell and the whole circle. Write when you have time; come at the earliest day, and believe me yours very truthfully,

C. BRONTË.

865. *To* MRS GASKELL.

[September 7th, 1853].

MY DEAR MADAM,—From what my daughter has told me and from my perusal of your able, moral, and interesting literary works, I think that you and she are congenial spirits, and that a little intercourse between you might, under the strange vicissitudes and frequent trials of this mortal life and under providence be productive of pleasure and profit to you both. We are gregarious beings and cannot always be comfortable if alone, and a faithful and intellectual friend . . . . [incomplete.]

[P. BRONTË].

866 (646). *To* MARGARET WOOLER.

HAWORTH, September 8th, '53.

MY DEAR MISS WOOLER,—Your letter was truly kind and made me warmly wish to join you. My prospects however of being able to leave home continue very unsettled. I am expecting Mrs Gaskell next week or the week after—the day being yet undetermined. She was to have come in June—but then my severe attack of influenza rendered it impossible that I should receive or entertain her; since that time she has been absent on the continent with her husband and 2 eldest girls—and just before I had received yours I had a letter from her volunteering a visit at a vague date which I requested her to fix as soon as possible. My Father has been much better during the last three or four days.

When I know anything certain I will write to you again.— Believe me, my dear Miss Wooler, yours respectfully and affectionately,   C. BRONTË.

Mrs Gaskell thus describes her visit in a letter written from Haworth at the time and afterwards published in her biography of Charlotte Brontë:[1]

867 (647). Mrs GASKELL *to a* Friend.

It was a dull, drizzly, Indian-inky day all the way on the railroad to Keighley, which is a rising wool-manufacturing town, lying in a hollow between hills—not a pretty hollow, but more what the Yorkshire people call a 'bottom,' or 'botham.' I left Keighley in a car for Haworth, four miles off—four tough, steep, scrambling miles, the road winding between the wave-like hills that rose and fell on every side of the horizon, with a long, illimitable, sinuous look, as if they were a part of the line of the Great Serpent which the Norse legend says girdles the world. The day was lead-coloured; the road had stone factories alongside of it; grey, dull-coloured rows of stone cottages belonging to these factories; and then we came to poor, hungry-looking fields—stone fences everywhere, and trees nowhere. Haworth is a long, straggling village: one steep narrow street— so steep that the flagstones with which it is paved are placed endways, that the horses' feet may have something to cling to, and not slip down backwards, which if they did they would soon reach Keighley. But if the horses had cats' feet and claws they would do all the better. Well, we (the man, horse, car, and I) clambered up this street, and reached the church dedicated to

---

[1] *The Life of Charlotte Brontë*, by Mrs E. C. Gaskell, Haworth Edition, pp. 617-20.

St Autest (who was he?),[1] then we turned off into a lane on the left, past the curate's lodging at the sexton's, past the school-house, up to the Parsonage yard-door. I went round the house to the front door, looking to the church;—moors everywhere beyond and above. The crowded graveyard surrounds the house and small grass enclosure for drying clothes.

I don't know that I ever saw a spot more exquisitely clean; the most dainty place for that I ever saw. To be sure the life is like clockwork. No one comes to the house; nothing disturbs the deep repose; hardly a voice is heard; you catch the ticking of the clock in the kitchen, or the buzzing of a fly in the parlour, all over the house. Miss Brontë sits alone in her parlour, break-fasting with her father in his study at nine o'clock. She helps in the housework; for one of their servants, Tabby, is nearly ninety, and the other only a girl. Then I accompanied her in her walks on the sweeping moors; the heather bloom had been blighted by a thunderstorm a day or two before, and was all of a livid brown colour, instead of the blaze of purple glory it ought to have been. Oh! those high, wild, desolate moors, up above the whole world, and the very realms of silence! Home to dinner at two. Mr Brontë has his dinner sent in to him. All the small table arrange-ments had the same dainty simplicity about them. Then we rested, and talked over the clear bright fire; it is a cold country, and the fires gave a pretty warm dancing light all over the house. The parlour has been evidently refurnished within the last few years, since Miss Brontë's success has enabled her to have a little more money to spend. Everything fits into, and is in harmony with, the idea of a country parsonage, possessed by people of very moderate means. The prevailing colour of the room is crimson, to make a warm setting for the cold grey landscape without. There is her likeness by Richmond, and an engraving from Lawrence's picture of Thackeray; and two recesses, on each side of the high, narrow, old-fashioned mantelpiece, filled with books—books given to her, books she has bought, and which tell of her individual pursuits and tastes; *not* standard books.

[1]Mrs Gaskell was misinformed as to 'St Autest.' The church at Haworth is dedi-cated to St Michael. It is a perpetual curacy, and the net value is stated to be £170 per annum. The name of 'Eutest' is found in a Latin inscription in the tower, but this was probably (J. Horsfall Turner's *Haworth*, *Past and Present*) a stonemason's spelling of Eustat, a contraction of Eustatius. On another stone is the inscription 'Pray for ye Soul of Autest—600'—probably the rough and ready translation of a seventeenth-century incumbent, ambitious for the an-tiquity of his church.

She cannot see well, and does little beside knitting. The way she weakened her eyesight was this: When she was sixteen or seventeen, she wanted much to draw; and she copied nimini-pimini copper-plate engravings out of annuals ('stippling' don't the artists call it?), every little point put in, till at the end of six months she had produced an exquisitely faithful copy of the engraving. She wanted to learn to express her ideas by drawing. After she had tried to *draw* stories, and not succeeded, she took the better mode of writing, but in so small a hand that it is almost impossible to decipher what she wrote at this time.

But now to return to our quiet hour of rest after dinner. I soon observed that her habits of order were such that she could not go on with the conversation if a chair was out of its place; everything was arranged with delicate regularity. We talked over the old times of her childhood; of her elder sister's (Maria's) death—just like that of Helen Burns in 'Jane Eyre'—of the desire (almost amounting to illness) of expressing herself in some way, writing or drawing; of her weakened eyesight, which prevented her doing anything for two years, from the age of seventeen to nineteen; of her being a governess; of her going to Brussels; whereupon I said I disliked Lucy Snowe, and we discussed M. Paul Emanuel; and I told her of ———'s admiration of 'Shirley,' which pleased her, for the character of Shirley was meant for her sister Emily, about whom she is never tired of talking, nor I of listening. Emily must have been a remnant of the Titans, great-granddaughter of the giants who used to inhabit the earth. One day Miss Brontë brought down a rough, common-looking oil painting, done by her brother, of herself—a little rather prim-looking girl of eighteen—and the two other sisters, girls of sixteen and fourteen, with cropped hair, and sad, dreamy-looking eyes. . . . Emily had a great dog—half mastiff, half bulldog—so savage, etc. . . . This dog went to her funeral, walking side by side with her father; and then, to the day of its death, it slept at her room door, snuffing under it, and whining every morning.

We have generally had another walk before tea, which is at six; at half-past eight prayers; and by nine all the household are in bed, except ourselves. We sit up together till ten, or past; and after I go I hear Miss Brontë come down and walk up and down the room for an hour or so.

E. C. Gaskell.

A longer and more detailed description of this visit is contained in another letter from Mrs Gaskell, written after her return home.

868. Mrs Gaskell *to a* Friend.

[September, 1853].

... We turned up a narrow bye-lane near the church—past the curate's, the schools and skirting the pestiferous churchyard we arrived at the door into the Parsonage yard. In I went,—half blown back by the wild vehemence of the wind which swept along the narrow gravel walk—round the corner of the house into a small plot of grass enclosed within a low stone wall, over which the more ambitious grave-stones towered all round. There are two windows on each side the door and steps up to it. On these steps I encountered a ruddy tired-looking man of no great refinement,—but I had no time to think of him; in at the door into an exquisitely clean passage, to the left into a square parlour looking out on the grass plot, the tall headstones beyond, the tower end of the church, the village houses and the brown moors.

Miss Brontë gave me the kindest welcome, and the room looked the perfection of warmth, snugness and comfort, crimson predominating in the furniture, which did well with the bleak cold colours without. Every thing in her department has been new within the last few years; and every thing, furniture appointments, &c. is admirable for its consistency. All simple, good, sufficient for every possible reasonable want, and of the most delicate and scrupulous cleanliness. She is so neat herself I got quite ashamed of any touches of untidiness—a chair out of its place,—work left on the table were all of them, I could see, annoyances to her habitual sense of order; not annoyances to her temper in the least; you understand the difference. There was her likeness by Richmond, given to her father by Messrs Smith & Elder, the later print of Thackeray, and a good likeness of the Duke of Wellington, hanging up. My room was above this parlour, and looking on the same view, which was really beautiful in certain lights, moon-light especially. Mr Brontë lives almost entirely in the room opposite (right hand side) of the front door; behind his room is the kitchen, behind the parlour a store room kind of pantry. Mr Brontë's bedroom is over his sitting-room, Miss Brontë's over the kitchen. The servants over the pantry. Where the rest of the household slept when they were all one large family, I can't imagine. The wind goes piping and wailing and sobbing round the square unsheltered house in a very strange unearthly way.

We dined—she and I together—Mr Brontë having his dinner sent to him in his sitting-room according to his invariable custom, (fancy it! and only they two left,) and then she told me that the man whom I met on the steps was a Mr Francis Bennock, something Park, Black Heath, who had written the previous day to say he was coming to call on her on his way from Hull where he had been reading a paper on currency. His claim for coming to call on Miss Brontë was 'that he was a patron of Authors and literature.' I hope he belongs to your Guild; Miss Brontë sent to the address he gave to say she had rather not see him, but he came all the same, captivated Mr Brontë, who would make his daughter come in; and abused us both for 'a couple of proud minxes' when we said we would rather be without individual patronage if it was to subject us to individual impertinence. (Oh, please burn this letter as soon as you have read it.) This Mr Bennock produced a MS. dedication of some forthcoming work of Miss Mitford's[1] to himself, as a sort of portable certificate of his merits and it sounded altogether very funny—but still a good natured person evidently, and really doing a good deal of kindness I have no doubt. Mrs Toulmin or Crosland,[2] and Mr Charles Swain[3] of our town were two authors to whom he hoped to introduce Miss Brontë at some future time.

Mr Brontë came in to tea—an honour to me I believe. Before tea we had had a long delicious walk right against the wind on Penistone Moor which stretches directly behind the Parsonage going over the hill in brown and purple sweeps and falling softly down into a little upland valley through which a 'beck' ran, and beyond again was another great waving hill—and in the dip of that might be seen another yet more distant, and beyond that the said Lancashire came; but the sinuous hills

[1]Mary Russell Mitford (1787–1855), novelist and dramatist, wrote much for magazines. Published amongst other works, *Recollections of a Literary Life*, 1852; and *Atherton*, 1854.
[2]Camilla Dufour Toulmin, afterwards Mrs Newton Crosland (1812–95), mis-cellaneous writer, contributed to periodicals, and published novels and translations.
[3]Charles Swain (1801–74) published several volumes of poetry, including *The Mind and Other Poems*, 1832. Many of his songs were set to music.

seemed to girdle the world like the great Norse serpent, and for
my part I don't know if they don't stretch up to the North Pole.
On the Moors we met no one. Here and there in the gloom of the
distant hollows she pointed out a dark grey dwelling—with
Scotch firs growing near them often,—and told me such wild
tales of the ungovernable families who lived or had lived therein
that Wuthering Heights even seemed tame comparatively. Such
dare-devil people,—men especially,—and women so stony and
cruel in some of their feelings and so passionately fond in others.
They are a queer people up there. Small landed proprietors,
dwelling on one spot since Q. Eliz.—and lately adding marvellously to their incomes by using the water power of the becks in
the woollen manufacture which had sprung up during the last
50 years:—uneducated—unrestrained by public opinion—for
their equals in position are as bad as themselves, and the poor,
besides being densely ignorant are all dependent on their em-
ployers. Miss Brontë does not what we should call 'visit' with
any of them. She goes to see the poor—teaches at the Schools
most gently and constantly—but the richer sort of people despise her for her poverty,—and they would have nothing in
common if they did meet. These people build grand houses, and
live in the kitchens, own hundreds of thousands of pounds and
yet bring up their sons with only just enough learning to qualify
them for over-lookers during their father's lifetime and greedy
grasping money-hunters after his death. Here and there from
the high moorland summit we saw newly built churches,—
which her Irish curates see after—every one of those being
literal copies of different curates in the neighbourhood, whose
amusement has been ever since to call each other by the names
she gave them in Shirley.

In the evening Mr Brontë went to his room and smoked a
pipe,—a regular clay,—and we sat over the fire and talked—
talked of long ago when that very same room was full of children; and how one by one they had dropped off into the churchyard close to the windows. At $\frac{1}{2}$ past 8 we went in to prayers,—
soon after nine every one was in bed but we two;—in general
there she sits quite alone thinking over the past; for her eyesight prevents her reading or writing by candle-light, and knitting is but very mechanical and does not keep the thoughts from
wandering. Each day—I was 4 there—was the same in outward
arrangement—breakfast at 9, in Mr Brontë's room—which we

left immediately after. What he does with himself through the day I cannot imagine! He is a tall fine looking old man, with silver bristles all over his head; nearly blind; speaking with a strong Scotch accent (he comes from the North of Ireland), raised himself from the ranks of a poor farmer's son—and was rather intimate with Lord Palmerston at Cambridge, a pleasant soothing reflection now, in his shut-out life. There was not a sign of engraving, map, writing materials, beyond a desk, &c. no books but those contained on two hanging shelves between the windows—his two pipes, &c. a spittoon, if you know what that is. He was very polite and agreeable to me; paying rather elaborate old-fashioned compliments, but I was sadly afraid of him in my inmost soul; for I caught a glare of his stern eyes over his spectacles at Miss Brontë once or twice which made me know my man; and he talked at her sometimes; he is very fearless; has taken the part of the men against the masters,—and vice versa just as he thought fit and right; and is consequently much respected and to be respected. But he ought never to have married. He did not like children; and they had six in six years, and the consequent pinching and family disorder—(which can't be helped), and noise &c. made him shut himself up and want no companionship—nay be positively annoyed by it. He won't let Miss Brontë accompany him in his walks, although he is so nearly blind; goes out in defiance of her gentle attempts to restrain him, speaking as if she thought him in his second childhood; and comes home moaning and tired:—having lost his way. 'Where is my strength gone?' is his cry then. 'I used to walk 40 miles a day,' &c. There are little bits of picturesque affection about him—for his old dogs for instance—when very ill some years ago in Manchester, whither he had come to be operated upon for cataract, his wail was, 'I shall never feel Keeper's paws on my knees again!' Moreover to account for my fear—rather an admiring fear after all—of Mr Brontë, please to take into account that though I like the beautiful glittering of bright flashing steel I don't fancy firearms at all, at all—and Miss Brontë never remembers her father dressing himself in the morning without putting a loaded pistol in his pocket, just as regularly as he puts on his watch. There was this little deadly pistol sitting down to breakfast with us, kneeling down to prayers at night to say nothing of a loaded gun hanging up on high, ready to pop off on the slightest emergency. Mr Brontë has a great fancy for arms of all kinds. He begged Miss Brontë (Oh, I can't condense it more than I do, and yet here's my 4th sheet!) to go and see Prince Albert's armoury at Windsor; and when he is unusually out of spirits she tells him over and over again of the different weapons &c. there. But all this time I wander from the course of our day, which is the course of her usual days. Breakfast over, the letters come; not many, sometimes for days none at all. About 12 we went out to walk. At 2 we dined, about 4 we went out again; at 6 we had tea; by nine every one was in bed but ourselves. Monotonous enough in sound, but not a bit in reality. There are some people whose stock of facts and anecdotes are soon exhausted; but Miss B. is none of these. She has the wild, strange facts of her own and her sisters' lives, —and beyond and above these she has most original and suggestive thoughts of her own; so that, like the moors, I felt on the last day as if our talk might be extended in any direction without getting to the end of any subject. There are 2 servants; one Tabby, aged up-wards of 90;[1] sitting in an arm-chair by the kitchen fire, —and Martha, the real active serving maiden, who has lived with them 10 years. I asked this last one day to take me into the Church and show me the Brontë graves: so when Miss Brontë was engaged we stole out. There is a tablet put up in the communion railing —Maria Brontë, wife of the Revd Patrick B. died 1821 aged 39.[2] Maria Brontë—May 1825 aged 12[2] (the original of Helen Burns in 'Jane Eyre.' She and the next sister died of the fever at the Clergy School). Elizabeth Brontë died June, 1825, aged 11.[2] Patrick Branwell Brontë died Sept. 24, 1848, aged 30.[2] Emily Jane Brontë died Decr 18, 1848 aged 29[2] —Anne Brontë May 28, 1849, aged 27.[2] 'Yes!' said Martha. 'They were all well when Mr Branwell was buried; but Miss Emily broke down the next week. We saw she was ill, but she never would own it, never would have a doctor near her, never would breakfast in bed— the last morning she got up, and she dying all the time—the rattle in her throat while she would dress herself; and neither Miss Brontë nor I dared offer to help her. She died just before Xmas—you'll see the date there—and we all went to her funeral. Master and Keeper, her dog, walking first side by side, and then

[1] Aged 82 at this time.
[2] The ages given are incorrect, and should be as follows: Mrs Brontë 38, Maria 11, Elizabeth 10, Patrick Branwell 31, Emily Jane 30, Anne 29.

Miss Brontë and Miss Anne, and then Tabby and me. Next day Miss Anne took ill just in the same way—and it was "Oh, if it was but Spring and I could go to the sea,"—"Oh, if it was but Spring." And at last Spring came and Miss Brontë took her to Scarborough—they got there on the Saturday and on the Monday she died. She is buried in the old church at Scarboro'. For as long as I can remember—Tabby says since they were little bairns—Miss Brontë and Miss Emily and Miss Anne used to put away their sewing after prayers and walk all three one after the other round the table in the parlour till near eleven o'clock. Miss Emily walked as long as she could, and when she died Miss Anne and Miss Brontë took it up—and now my heart aches to hear Miss Brontë walking, walking, on alone.'And on enquiring I found that after Miss Brontë had seen me to my room she did come down every night, and begin that slow monotonous incessant walk in which I am sure I should fancy I heard the steps of the dead following me. She says she could not sleep without it—that she and her sisters talked over the plans and projects of their whole lives at such times.

About Mr Branwell Brontë the less said the better—poor fellow. He never knew 'Jane Eyre' was written although he lived a year afterwards; but that year was passed in the shadow of the coming death, with the consciousness of his wasted life. But Emily—poor Emily—the pangs of disappointment as review after review came out about 'Wuthering Heights' were terrible. Miss B. said she had no recollection of pleasure or gladness about 'Jane Eyre,' every such feeling was lost in seeing Emily's resolute endurance, yet knowing what she felt. . . .

E. C. Gaskell.

Mrs Gaskell thus continues in the *Life* her reminiscences of that visit:[1]

I asked her whether she had ever taken opium, as the description given of its effects in 'Villette' was so exactly like what I had experienced—vivid and exaggerated presence of objects, of which the outlines were indistinct or lost in golden mist, etc. She replied that she had never, to her knowledge, taken a grain

[1]*The Life of Charlotte Brontë*, by Mrs E. C. Gaskell, Haworth Edition, pp. 620-1.

of it in any shape, but that she had followed the process she always adopted when she had to describe anything which had not fallen within her own experience; she had thought intently on it for many and many a night before falling to sleep—wondering what it was like, or how it would be—till at length, sometimes after the progress of her story had been arrested at this one point for weeks, she wakened up in the morning with all clear before her, as if she had in reality gone through the experience, and then could describe it, word for word, as it had happened. I cannot account for this psychologically; I only am sure that it was so because she said it.

She made many inquiries as to Mrs Stowe's personal appearance; and it evidently harmonised well with some theory of hers to hear that the author of 'Uncle Tom's Cabin' was small and slight. It was another of her theories that no mixtures of blood produce such fine characters, mentally and morally, as the Scottish and English.

I recollect, too, her saying how acutely she dreaded a charge of plagiarism when, after she had written 'Jane Eyre,' she read the thrilling effect of the mysterious scream at midnight in Mrs Marsh's story of 'The Deformed.'[1] She also said that, when she read 'The Neighbours,' she thought every one would fancy that she must have taken her conception of Jane Eyre's character from that of 'Francesca,' the narrator of Miss Bremer's story. For my own part, I cannot see the slightest resemblance between the two characters, and so I told her; but she persisted in saying that Francesca was Jane Eyre married to a good-natured 'Bear' of a Swedish surgeon.

We went, not purposely, but accidentally, to see various poor people in our distant walks. From one we had borrowed an umbrella; in the house of another we had taken shelter from a rough September storm. In all these cottages her quiet presence was known. At three miles from her home the chair was dusted for her, with a kindly 'Sit ye down, Miss Brontë'; and she knew what absent or ailing members of the family to inquire after. Her quiet, gentle words, few though they might be, were evidently

---

[1] Mrs Marsh (1799–1874), whose maiden name was Anne Caldwell, wrote many novels and some historical works. Of *Mordaunt Hall*, the *Sun* of 1849 wrote that it was 'the most beautiful of many beautiful tales yet written by its author. It fascinates the attention of the reader like Scott's never to be forgotten story of "Lucy Ashton," ' and the *Spectator* wrote of *Norman's Bridge* that it 'surpasses anything that this writer—or perhaps any other writer—has done, if we except Godwin's chef-d'œuvre.'

grateful to those Yorkshire ears. Their welcome to her, though rough and curt, was sincere and hearty.

We talked about the different courses through which life ran. She said in her own composed manner, as if she had accepted the theory as a fact, that she believed some were appointed beforehand to sorrow and much disappointment; that it did not fall to the lot of all — as Scripture told us — to have their lines fall in pleasant places; that it was well for those who had rougher paths to perceive that such was God's will concerning them, and try to moderate their expectations, leaving hope to those of a different doom, and seeking patience and resignation as the virtues they were to cultivate. I took a different view: I thought that human lots were more equal than she imagined; that to some happiness and sorrow came in strong patches of light and shadow (so to speak), while in the lives of others they were pretty equally blended throughout. She smiled, and shook her head, and said she was trying to school herself against ever anticipating any pleasure; that it was better to be brave and submit faithfully; there was some good reason, which we should know in time, why sorrow and disappointment were to be the lot of some on earth. It was better to acknowledge this, and face out the truth in a religious faith.

In connection with this conversation she named a little abortive plan which I had not heard of till then: how, in the previous July, she had been tempted to join some friends (a married couple and their child) in an excursion to Scotland. They set out joyfully; she with special gladness, for Scotland was a land which had its roots deep down in her imaginative affections, and the glimpse of two days at Edinburgh was all she had yet seen of it. But, at the first stage after Carlisle, the little yearling child was taken with a slight indisposition; the anxious parents fancied that strange diet had disagreed with it, and hurried back to their Yorkshire home as eagerly as, two or three days before, they had set their faces northward in hopes of a month's pleasant ramble.

We parted with many intentions, on both sides, of renewing very frequently the pleasure we had had in being together. We agreed that when she wanted bustle, or when I wanted quiet, we were to let each other know, and exchange visits as occasion required.

I was aware that she had a great anxiety on her mind at this time; and being acquainted with its nature, I could not but deeply admire the patient docility which she displayed in her conduct towards her father.

When Mrs Gaskell returned home she took with her a little book for her youngest daughter: 'New Friends, or a Fortnight at the Rectory,' containing the inscription: 'To Julia, with my love, C.B.' Mrs Gaskell added the following: 'This book was given to Julia Gaskell by Charlotte Brontë, who lost her heart to the child.'

869. *To* MRS GASKELL.

[HAWORTH, September 25th, 1853].

. . . After you left, the house felt very much as if the shutters had been suddenly closed and the blinds let down. One was sensible during the remainder of the day of a depressing silence, shadow, loss, and want. However, if the going away was sad, the stay was very pleasant and did permanent good. Papa, I am sure, derived real benefit from your visit; he has been better ever since. . . .

[C. BRONTË].

Arthur Bell Nicholls
From a photograph made about 1861

CHAPTER XXXII

MARRIAGE

AFTER Mrs Gaskell's return to Manchester, Charlotte paid a visit to Ellen Nussey at Brookroyd, and a little later she went to stay with Miss Wooler at Hornsea.

During the past few months, Mr Nicholls had not been forgotten. After leaving Haworth for Kirk-Smeaton in May, he had written a few times to Charlotte Brontë, and at last she replied. This led to a regular correspondence, which continued unknown to her father throughout the summer of 1853. Mr Nicholls had also visited Haworth a few times, staying with Mr Grant, incumbent of Oxenhope. Charlotte was harassed at the thought of keeping her association with Mr Nicholls secret from her father, but owing to his violent opposition, it seemed the wisest course to take.

Meanwhile a Mr de Renzy had taken Mr Nicholls's place at Haworth, but Mr Brontë missed the diligent care of his former curate. This, combined with his failing health, probably made him rather doubtful as to whether he had acted wisely in objecting so strongly to Mr Nicholls's proposal. However, it was not until the following January that any definite move was made. Charlotte, unable to keep the secret any longer, told her father of her correspondence with Mr Nicholls and her desire to become better acquainted. Mr Brontë's opposition was gradually broken down, and Mr Nicholls was allowed to return to Haworth.

Charlotte Brontë and Mr Nicholls became engaged early in April and were married on June 29th, 1854.

870 (649). *To* ELLEN NUSSEY.

HAWORTH—Thursday Morng.
[October 6th, 1853].

DEAR ELLEN,—I duly and safely reached home with my purchases at about 5 o'clock yesterday afternoon. I found Papa &c. very well. The Mops, carpet and rug all give satisfaction—the

Vol. IV h

crockery and glass I kept out of sight—but they will be appreciated I daresay when they appear in their proper time and place. I hope you also reached home all right—but I fear the fatigue you underwent will leave its effects to-day—it was not a very good preparation for the long walk to Scholes.[1]

Write a line soon and tell me how you are. I have some headache to-day but not violent—a general jaded, weary feeling was to be expected. With love to your Mother and Mercy and kind regards to Mr C.—I am, dear Ellen, Yours fagged but faithfully,

C. BRONTË.

871 (648). *To* MARGARET WOOLER.

HAWORTH, Octbr 8th, 1853.

MY DEAR MISS WOOLER,—I wished much to write to you immediately on my return home, but I found several little matters demanding attention, and have been kept busy till now. Mr Cartman could not come to preach the sermons, and consequently Mr Fawcett was applied to in his stead; he arrived on Saturday and remained till yesterday.

My journey home would have been pleasant enough had it not been spoilt in the commencement by one slight incident. About half-way between Hull and Hornsea a respectable looking woman and her little girl were admitted into the coach. The child took her place opposite me: she had not sat long before—without any previous warning, or the slightest complaint of nausea—sickness seized her and the contents of her little stomach—consisting apparently of a milk breakfast—were unceremoniously deposited in my lap! Of course I alighted from the coach in a pretty mess, but succeeding in procuring water and a towel at the station with which I managed to make my dress and cloak once more presentable.

I reached home about 5 o'clock in the afternoon and the anxiety which is inseparable from a return after absence was pleasantly relieved by finding Papa well and cheerful. He inquired after you with interest. I gave him your kind regards and he specially charged me whenever I wrote to present his in return, and to say also that he hoped to see you at Haworth at the earliest date which shall be convenient to you.

[1] A little place two miles from Birstall, and eleven miles from Leeds.

The week I spent at Hornsea was a happy and pleasant week. Thank you, my dear Miss Wooler—for the true kindness which gave it its chief charm. I shall think of you often especially when I walk out—and during the long evenings. I believe the weather has at length taken a turn: to-day is beautifully fine. I wish I were at Hornsea and just now preparing to go out with you to walk on the sands or along the lake.

I would not have you to fatigue yourself with writing to me when you are not inclined, but yet I should be glad to hear from you some day ere long. When you *do* write, tell me how you liked 'The Experience of Life,' and whether you have read 'The Newcomes,' and what you think of it.—Believe me always yours with true affection and respect,

C. Brontë.

In November Charlotte was planning another visit to London, but at the last moment her plans were frustrated.

872. *To* Emily Shaen (*née* Winkworth).

Haworth, Novbr 21st, '53.

My dear Mrs Shaen,—Thank you cordially for your very kind note—I should have answered it by return—had I not previously written for lodgings at Mrs Gaskell's recommendation (Mrs Dove, 36, Bloomsbury Sq.) and been expecting a reply. No answer comes however—and as I have little time to lose—I think it better at once to avail myself of the information you have so kindly collected for me. I am quite sure I can trust your opinion better than my own, and shall therefore be truly obliged if you will engage for me the front sitting room and bedroom at 30s. a week at Mrs Joyce's, 37 Bedford Place, for next Thursday. I should probably want them a week. If these cannot now be had—I should like the airy and clean but old-fashioned rooms at Mrs Wetherall's, 41, Gt Ormond St. Should these be engaged I must then beg you to decide on any others you think suitable and of which the terms would not exceed 30s. per week.

I too feel as if I knew you through Mrs Gaskell—and I look forward with sincere pleasure to the prospect of soon seeing you. Were my business in town more engrossing than it is at all likely to be I should still have contrived to make room for that qualification.

If you could write to me by return of post—I should get your letter on Wednesday morning. Perhaps it would be better to mention at the lodgings that I could not arrive earlier than 10 o'clock on Thursday evening.—Believe me my dear Mrs Shaen,

Very sincerely yours,

C. BRONTË.

873. *To* EMILY SHAEN (*née* WINKWORTH).

HAWORTH, Thursday morning.
[November 24th, 1853].

MY DEAR MRS SHAEN,—Man *pro*poses but Another *dis*poses. At the last moment when my portmanteau was packed and all ready—circumstances have taken a turn which will prevent my intended journey to London. I had pleased myself much with the thought of seeing you, but it cannot be at present. I can only trust that the pleasure is but deferred.

I have written to Mrs Dove, and have told her of course that I shall transmit at once any charge she may choose to make for the apartments taken in my name.

I feel very sorry for the useless trouble you have had. Forgive it and believe me,—Sincerely yours,

C. BRONTË.

874 (651). *To* W. S. WILLIAMS.

December 6th, 1853.

MY DEAR SIR,—I forwarded last week a box of return books to Cornhill, which I trust arrived safely. To-day I received the 'Edinburgh Guardian,'[1] for which I thank you.

Do not trouble yourself to select or send any more books. These courtesies must cease some day, and I would rather give them up than wear them out.—Believe me, yours sincerely,

C. BRONTË.

[1] This contained an article by Sir John Skelton, K.C.B. (1831–97), who, under the pseudonym of 'Shirley,' made a consider-able reputation in literature. He was Chairman of the Local Government Board for Scotland.

875 (652). *To* MARGARET WOOLER.

HAWORTH, Decbr 12th, 1853.

MY DEAR MISS WOOLER,—I wonder how you are spending these long winter evenings. Alone—probably—like me. The thought often crosses me, as I sit by myself—how pleasant it would be if you lived within a walking distance, and I could go to you sometimes, or have you to come and spend a day and night with me. Yes; I did enjoy that week at Hornsea. I remember it with pleasure and I look forward to Spring as the period when you will fulfil your promise of coming to visit me.

I fear you must be very solitary at Hornsea. How hard to some people of the world it would seem to live your life—how utterly impossible to live it with a serene spirit and an unsoured disposition! It seems wonderful to me—because you are not like Mrs Ruff—phlegmatic and impenetrable—but received from nature feelings of the very finest edge. Such feelings when they are locked up—sometimes damage the mind and temper. They don't with you. It must be partly principle—partly self-discipline, which keeps you as you are.

Do not think that your kind wish respecting E. Nussey and myself does not touch or influence me; it does both; yet I hardly know how to take the step you recommend. My heart....[1]

C. BRONTË.

876. *To* the Rev. W. CARTMAN, *Schoolhouse, Skipton.*

HAWORTH, near KEIGHLEY, Jany 27th, 1854.

MY DEAR SIR,—I have safely received the Ice Apparatus which fits me admirably, and for which I sincerely thank you—and which I value, as much for the sake of the Donor, as its own intrinsic worth—It will serve as another prop to Old Age.

Charlotte joins me in very kind regards,—Yours, very sincerely and truly,

P. BRONTË.

[1] This letter is incomplete.

877 (653). *To* SYDNEY DOBELL.

HAWORTH, near KEIGHLEY, February 3rd, 1854.
MY DEAR SIR,—I can hardly tell you how glad I am to have an
opportunity of explaining that taciturnity to which you allude.
Your letter came at a period of danger and care, when my father
was very ill, and I could not leave his bedside. I answered no
letters at that time, and yours was one of three or four that, when
leisure returned to me, and I came to consider their purport, it
seemed to me that the time was past for answering them, and I
laid them finally aside. If you remember, you asked me to go to
London; it was too late either to go or to decline. I was sure
you had left London. One circumstance you mentioned—your
wife's illness—which I have thought of many a time, and wondered whether she is better. In your present note you do not
refer to her, but I trust her health has long ere now been quite
restored.

'Balder'[1] arrived safely. I looked at him, before cutting his
leaves, with singular pleasure. Remembering well his elder brother, the potent 'Roman,' it was natural to give a cordial welcome to a fresh scion of the same house and race. I have read
him. He impresses me thus: He teems with power; I found in
him a wild wealth of life, but I thought his favourite and favoured
child would bring his sire trouble—would make his heart ache.
It seemed to me that his strength and beauty were not so much
those of Joseph, the pillar of Jacob's age, as of the Prodigal
Son, who troubled his father, though he always kept his love.

How is it that while the first-born of genius often brings
honour the second almost as often proves a source of depression
and care? I could almost prophesy that your third will atone for
any anxiety inflicted by this his immediate predecessor.

There is power in that character of 'Balder,' and to me a certain horror. Did you mean it to embody, along with force, any
of the special defects of the artistic character? It seems to me that
those defects were never thrown out in stronger lines. I did not
and could not think you meant to offer him as your cherished

[1]"Sydney Dobell's *Balder*, published in
1853, was, with the general public and the
majority of critics less fortunate than *The
Roman*. It is harder to read as it was harder
to write . . . but it exhibits the highest
flights of the author's imagination and his
finest pictures of nature.'—Professor
Nichol in the *Dictionary of National Biography*.

ideal of the true great poet; I regard him as a vividly coloured picture of inflated self-esteem, almost frantic aspiration; of a nature that has made a Moloch of intellect—offered up, in pagan fires, the natural affections—sacrificed the heart to the brain. Do we not all know that true greatness is simple, self-oblivious, prone to unambitious, unselfish attachments? I am certain you feel this truth in your heart of hearts.

But if the critics err now (as yet I have seen none of their lucubrations) you shall one day set them right in the second part of 'Balder.' You shall show them that you too know—better, perhaps, than they—that the truly great man is too sincere in his affections to grudge a sacrifice; too much absorbed in his work to talk loudly about it; too intent on finding the best way to accomplish what he undertakes to think great things of himself —the instrument. And if God places seeming impediments in his way—if his duties sometimes seem to hamper his powers— he feels keenly, perhaps writhes under, the slow torture of hindrance and delay; but if there be a true man's heart in his breast he can bear, submit, wait patiently.

Whoever speaks to me of 'Balder'—though I live too retired a life to come often in the way of comment—shall be answered according to your suggestion and my own impression. Equity demands that you shall be your own interpreter. Good-bye for the present, and believe me, faithfully and gratefully,

CHARLOTTE BRONTË.

878. *To* ELLEN NUSSEY.

EAST MARSDEN, 21st Feby [1854].

MY DEAR ELLEN,—I was glad to receive your second letter telling me you had heard from Miss Brontë—glad for her as well as you—for it seemed unnatural that she could so throw off all her old friendship that she did not evince some little return of it when you were ill—I was very glad she did—it must have comforted you very much and you had suffered so much pain about her evidently. Now you are ready to forget all I can see— and that is kind and right—but she will not quite forget I hope —but will remember enough to see how your true friendship was shown in it—and be guided by you—her thoughts—and affections must really need control. It is an example of the dangerous gift such a mind as hers must be, and I trust it *will* overcome temptations, and shine out brightly at last—That will be a happiness to you indeed.

Your third note too I must thank you for, I am glad of any thing that gives you occasion to write—but sorry to hear of Mrs ·Richard Nussey's serious illness. They have lived together but a few years—after their long engagement, have they—I trust however she may yet recover for a longer time than you antici- pate. . . .

I hope Miss Mercy's foot is well again and herself recovered from the jar. I shall be glad to hear Mrs Clapham is better, it is very satisfactory to have a competent opinion in a case like hers —she has been an invalid a long long time. Mama unites with me in very kind love to Mrs Nussey of whom we are very glad to hear so well—and with best love and regards from us all to you all—dear Ellen,—believe me ever Your most affec. friend,

MARY HEWITT.[1]

This is a most shabby letter, the most so I have ever sent you I think.

879 (654). To ELLEN NUSSEY.

WELLINGTON, February 24th, '54.

DEAR ELLEN,—I got a letter from you some time ago Pr. Con- stantin, dated Brookroyd, Aug. 12/53, just about six months ago. Thank you for your trouble concerning my dress and bon- net. You may have the satisfaction of knowing it was not in vain, as they both turned out wonderfully well, and I shall cer- tainly accept your kind offer and get another in time for next winter but one. How ever did you manage to make the dress so heavy? and then call it not a winter dress! It fitted well, tho' it was too long; a very small fault. The bonnet just suited me. The thermometer just now rises to about 80° every day, wherefore the fine things are put by. I shall bring them out in due time. You cannot imagine the importance they give; the peak behind is the object of universal admiration.

I am glad you approved of my lecture to Joe on diet; tho' you are mistaken in thinking that I follow my own advice. In sum- mer I never eat six dinners in the week, seldom more than three. My health suffers less from low living than it would from bilious-

---

[1] Née Mary Gorham, who has often been mentioned in Charlotte's letters.

ness were I to eat more. Luckily winter comes, and I can keep up my strength and have an easy mind and clear head at the same time I seldom taste anything stronger than tea, either in hot weather or cold.

You talk wonderful nonsense about Charlotte Brontë in your letter. What do you mean about 'bearing her position so long, and enduring to the end'? and still better, 'bearing our lot, whatever it is.' If it's Charlotte's lot to be married, shouldn't she bear that too? or does your strange morality mean that she should refuse to ameliorate her lot when it is in her power. How would she be inconsistent with herself in marrying? Because she considers her own pleasure? If this is so new for her to do, it is high time she began to make it more common. It is an outrageous exaction to expect her to give up her choice in a matter so important, and I think her to blame in having been hitherto so yielding that her friends can think of making such an impudent demand. . . . Your account of your trip to Yarmouth is amusing. I am right glad you came back again.

All your gossip is very interesting. Mrs Joe Taylor sends me very little, being used, I think, to spend her time too much at home. Perhaps when her health improves she will take more interest in her neighbours.

I wish you could see how busy I am going to be. I have got such a lot of things coming. Finery of all kinds. It will take me a fortnight's hard work to get them all arranged and ticketed. And then the people that will come to see them! I always find myself wondering at these people with one eye, while I wait on them with the other. It gives them such evident pain to see anything they can't buy, and it is so impossible for them not to look at the most expensive things, even when they can't buy any but the cheapest. Then the tricks they play on their husbands' head, or heart, or purse, to get the money! And then the coolness with which they'll say they don't care a bit about it, only thought they might as well have it! There are some silk mantles coming, about which more lies will be told than would make a lawyer's fortune, to me, their husbands, friends, and neighbours. Don't think all my customers answer to this description. Yet it's wonderful how many do.

I've got an addition to my store, by which you may see I'm getting on in the world. It has 20 feet frontage and is 16 feet deep. I could let it for £50 or £60 Pr. an., but then the ground is not paid for. I intend to pay for it this winter. My coming home seems just as far off as ever; that is, two or three years more. In that time I expect this town and colony to advance wonderfully. There will be steam communication *viâ* Panama — perhaps I'll come home that way. There will be a large export of wool to England and provisions to Australia. Then there are signs of a mania for emigration to N. Zealand coming on — a sort of fever which will injure those who get it, but will benefit the colony generally. All settlers of course encourage this mania, as it is to their own advantage. Indeed, so long as people come of their judgment there is no doubt they will do well. Labouring men get six shillings a day, and every other kind of work is paid in proportion. But once let it be understood that a man can get rich just by coming here and we shall have such cargoes of helpless, silly people!

There was a family of that kind came here once and settled in the country. They brought a man-servant for the gentleman and a maid for the lady and a few more servants. They went into the country, about two days' journey from Wellington, after making themselves remarkable for a while in the town with their extraordinary ringlets, ribbons, fly-away hats, and frippery of all kinds. After a few months I heard they were in great distress — nearly starving. All their servants had left them, and they were all ill in bed. 'Why, what's the matter with them?' 'Oh, the mosquitoes have bitten them so!'

I wish you would send me some more particular account of yourself in your next letter. You write twice a year and I quite lose the thread of your wanderings between the letters. One newspaper sent me is addressed to you at *Oundle* vicarage. Where in the world is *Oundle*? And what have you been doing there? You appear to travel about a good deal. When I see you again you will have travelled much more than I have, though people won't think so. You don't mention Miss Wooler. Have you seen her, or rather do you see her when you come home from your peregrinations?

Good-bye, dear Ellen, I have written to the last minute, March 3d/54. — Yours affectionately,

MARY TAYLOR.

880 (655). *To* ELLEN NUSSEY.

HAWORTH, March 1st, 1854.

MY DEAR ELLEN,—I am sorry to hear that Mrs Richard Nussey has had a paralytic stroke. Is this true, or is it an exaggerated account? At her age one would scarcely have expected an attack of that nature, but I believe paralysis attacks more persons and younger persons than formerly. A clergyman of not more than thirty-five, in the neighbourhood of Skipton, is entirely disabled from duty by the effects of a paralytic stroke. How does your mother continue to get on? Papa has so far borne the winter surprisingly well on the whole, though now and then he still complains of muscular weakness, and other slight symptoms which renew anxiety. Still I have more reason for gratitude than fear in his case. Your sister Ann it seems has consulted Mr Teale —is she better for his advice? Last, but not least, how are you yourself?—Yours affectionately,

C. BRONTË.

881 (656). *To* ELLEN NUSSEY.

HAWORTH, March 7th, '54.

MY DEAR ELLEN,—I am very glad to hear that Mrs Richard is pronounced out of danger for I think her loss would probably be severely felt by your brother—and he could not be much disturbed, without the evil coming more or less home to you all at Brookroyd.

It is well too that the brain has so far escaped serious injury— it seems to me, perhaps, the worst of all dooms for the death of the mind to anticipate that of the body. Yet sometimes when these attacks fall chiefly on the nervous system a state of irritation follows which is found very trying not only for the poor patient —but most especially for friends. You do not mention that such is the case in the present instance, and I hope it will not prove so.

I trust and believe your brother John is right in his opinion of your own ailment. On no account let it alarm you—for I imagine that comparatively few people are wholly free from some such inconvenience as you describe. An over-sedentary life producing a confined state of the bowels—I suppose is at the root of it. Remembering the effect that iodine produced on you

long since—I cannot help being glad that you have given up
that remedy. It seems to me that those reducing drugs must be
hazardous where the constitution is not robust. It is strange I
have never heard of you as looking ill; but I have no doubt it
was owing to the low state to which the pills &c. had brought
you—that that cold you caught in the winter took such hold on
your system. So far I have been so favoured as to escape *severe*
colds—but my headaches &c. still at times harass me and keep
me thin. I am truly glad to hear that your Mother, Mr Clapham
and Mercy are well and that your Sister Ann is better. Mr Teale
will really do a good deed if he succeeds in curing her. Papa still
continues well. Believe me my dear Ellen,—Yours affectionately,

C. BRONTË.

882 (657). *To* LÆTITIA WHEELWRIGHT.

HAWORTH, March 8th, 1854.

MY DEAR LÆTITIA,—I was very glad to see your handwriting
again; it is, I believe, a year since I heard from you. Again and
again you have recurred to my thoughts lately, and I was beginning to have some sad presages as to the cause of your silence.
Your letter happily does away with all these; it brings, on the
whole, good tidings both of your papa, mamma, your sister,
and, last but not least, your dear respected English self.

My dear Father has borne the severe winter very well, a circumstance for which I feel the more thankful, as he had many
weeks of very precarious health last summer, following an
attack from which he suffered last June, and which for a few
hours deprived him totally of sight, though neither his mind,
speech, nor even his powers of motion were in the least affected.
I can hardly tell you how thankful I was, dear Lætitia, when,
after that dreary and almost despairing interval of utter darkness, some gleam of daylight became visible to him once more.
I had feared that paralysis had seized the optic nerve. A sort of
mist remained for a long time, and indeed his vision is not yet
perfectly clear, but he can read, write, and walk about, and he
preaches *twice* every Sunday, the curate only reading the prayers.
You can well understand how earnestly I pray that sight may be
spared him to the end; he so dreads the privation of blindness.
His mind is just as strong and active as ever, and politics interest

him as they do *your* papa. The Czar, the war, the alliance between France and England—into all these things he throws himself heart and soul. They seem to carry him back to his comparatively young days, and to renew the excitement of the last great European struggle. Of course, my Father's sympathies (and mine too) are all with Justice and Europe against Tyranny and Russia.

Circumstanced as I have been, you will comprehend that I had neither the leisure nor inclination to go from home much during the past year. I spent a week with Mrs Gaskell in the spring, and a fortnight with some other friends more recently, and that includes the whole of my visiting since I saw you last. My life is indeed very uniform and retired—more so than is quite healthful either for mind or body; yet I find reason for often renewed feelings of gratitude—in the sort of support which still comes and cheers me from time to time. My health—though not unbroken—is, I sometimes fancy, rather stronger on the whole than it was three years ago; headaches and dyspepsia are my worse ailments. Whether I shall come up to town this season for a few days I do not yet know; but if I do I shall hope to call in Phillimore Place. With kindest remembrances to your papa, mamma, and sisters, —I am, dear Lætitia, affectionately yours,

C. BRONTË.

883 (658). *To* ELLEN NUSSEY.

Wednesday morng. [Mar. 22nd, 1854].

MY DEAR ELLEN,—I put off writing yesterday because I had a headache—I have it again to-day—not severe but depressing—however I will write a few lines—and if they are inefficient you will know the reason.

Miss Wooler kindly asked me likewise to go and see her at Hornsea—but I had a prior engagement this month—which, however, it now seems very doubtful whether I shall keep—it would have given me true pleasure to have joined Miss Wooler —had not my previous promise stood in the way.

I was very glad to hear of Miss Cockhill's engagement—offer her my sincere congratulations on the subject. I don't know John Battye—but if he only prove as kind a husband as I feel sure she will be a good wife—they have a good chance of happiness.

Mrs Rd Nussey's convalescence was good news also—I trust

she will now steadily improve—and many years may elapse before she has any return. The third stroke of paralysis or apoplexy is generally said to be fatal—but there is an instance in this neighbourhood of three strokes occurring within a period of 20 years—and the patient lives still and is indeed almost entirely recovered from the effects of the 3rd attack. One leg only is stiff and unmanageable but he can walk pretty well.

Be sure and look after yourself dear Ellen—take exercise—keep your spirits up—mind cold and the night-air. Tell me if you are in pretty good spirits when you write again.—Yours affectionately,

C. BRONTË.

How does your sister Ann go on?—and what treatment is prescribed by Mr Teale.

884 (659). *To* ELLEN NUSSEY.

HAWORTH, March 28th, '54.

MY DEAR ELLEN,—The enclosure in yours of yesterday puzzled me at first, for I did not immediately recognise my own handwriting; when I did, the sensation was one of consternation and vexation, as the letter ought by all means to have gone on Friday. It was intended to relieve him of great anxiety. However, I trust he will get it to-day, and on the whole, when I think it over, I can only be thankful that the mistake was no worse, and did not throw the letter into the hands of some indifferent and unscrupulous person. I wrote it after some days of indisposition and uneasiness, and when I felt weak and unfit to write. While writing to him, I was at the same time intending to answer your note, which I suppose accounts for the confusion of ideas, shown in the mixed and blundering address.

I wish you could come about Easter rather than at another time, for this reason—Mr Nicholls, if not prevented, proposes coming over then. I suppose he will stay at Mr Grant's as he has done two or three times before, but he will be frequently coming here, which would enliven your visit a little. Perhaps, too, he might take a walk with us occasionally. Altogether it would be a little change; such as, you know, I could not always offer.

If all be well he will come under different circumstances to any that have attended his visits before; were it otherwise I should not ask you to meet him, for when aspects are gloomy and un-propitious, the fewer there are to suffer from the cloud the better.

He was here in January and was then received, but not plea-santly. I trust it will be a little different now.

Papa has breakfasted in bed to-day, and has not yet risen; his bronchitis is still troublesome. I had a bad week last week, but am greatly better now, for my mind is a little relieved, though very sedate and rising only to expectations the most moderate.

Sometime, perhaps in May, I may be in your neighbourhood and shall then hope to come to Brookroyd! but as you will understand from what I have now stated, I could not come before.

Think it over, dear Nell, and come to Haworth if you can. Write as soon as you can decide. —Yours affectionately,

C. Brontë.

885 (660). *To* Ellen Nussey.

April 1st, '54.

My dear Ellen,—You certainly were right in your second interpretation of my note; I am too well aware of the dulness of Haworth for any visitor, not to be glad to avail myself of the chance of offering even a slight change. But this morning my little plans have been disarranged by an intimation that Mr Nicholls is coming on Monday. I thought to put him off, but have not succeeded. As Easter now consequently seems an un-favourable period both from your point of view and mine, we will adjourn it till a better opportunity offers. Meantime, I thank you, dear Ellen, for your kind offer to come in case I wanted you. Papa is still very far from well, his cough very troublesome and a good deal of inflammatory action in the chest. To-day he seems somewhat better than yesterday, and I earnestly hope the improvement may continue.

With kind regards to your mother and all at Brookroyd,—I am, dear Ellen, yours affectionately,

C. Brontë.

886 (661). *To* ELLEN NUSSEY.

HAWORTH, April 11th, 1854.

DEAR ELLEN,—Thank you for the collar; it is very pretty, and I will wear it for the sake of her who made and gave it.

Mr Nicholls came on Monday, and was here all last week. Matters have progressed thus since July. He renewed his visit in September, but then matters so fell out that I saw little of him. He continued to write. The correspondence pressed on my mind. I grew very miserable in keeping it from Papa. At last sheer pain made me gather courage to break it—I told all. It was very hard and rough work at the time—but the issue after a few days was that I obtained leave to continue the communication. Mr N[icholls] came in Jan[uary]; he was ten days in the neighbourhood. I saw much of him. I had stipulated with Papa for opportunity to become better acquainted—I had it, and all I learnt inclined me to esteem and if not love—at least affection. Still papa was very, very hostile—bitterly unjust.

I told Mr Nicholls the great obstacles that lay in his way. He has persevered. The result of this, his last visit, is, that Papa's consent is gained—that his respect, I believe, is won, for Mr Nicholls has in all things proved himself disinterested and forbearing. He has shown, too, that while his feelings are exquisitely keen—he can freely forgive. Certainly I must respect him, nor can I withhold from him more than mere cool respect. In fact, dear Ellen, I am engaged.

Mr Nicholls, in the course of a few months, will return to the curacy of Haworth. I stipulated that I would not leave Papa, and to Papa himself I proposed a plan of residence which should maintain his seclusion and convenience uninvaded and in a pecuniary sense bring him gain instead of loss. What seemed at one time impossible is now arranged, and papa begins really to take a pleasure in the prospect.

For myself, dear Ellen, while thankful to One who seems to have guided me through much difficulty, much and deep distress and perplexity of mind, I am still very calm, very inexpectant. What I taste of happiness is of the soberest order. I trust to love my husband—I am grateful for his tender love to me. I believe him to be an affectionate, a conscientious, a high-principled man; and if, with all this, I should yield to regrets, that fine talents, congenial tastes and thoughts are not added, it seems to me I should be most presumptuous and thankless.

Providence offers me this destiny. Doubtless then it is the best for me. Nor do I shrink from wishing those dear to me one not less happy.

It is possible that our marriage may take place in the course of the Summer. Mr Nicholls wishes it to be in July. He spoke of you with great kindness, and said he hoped you would be at our wedding. I said I thought of having no other bridesmaid. Did I say rightly? I mean the marriage to be literally *as quiet as possible*.

Do not mention these things just yet. I mean to write to Miss Wooler shortly. Good-bye. There is a strange half-sad feeling in making these announcements. The whole thing is something other than imagination paints it beforehand; cares, fears, come mixed inextricably with hopes. I trust yet to talk the matter over with you. Often last week I wished for your presence, and said so to Mr Nicholls, Arthur as I now call him, but he said it was the only time and place when he could not have wished to see you. Good-bye. — Yours affectionately,

C. BRONTË.

887 (662). *To* MARGARET WOOLER.

HAWORTH, April 12th, 1854.

MY DEAR MISS WOOLER, — The truly kind interest which you have always taken in my affairs makes me feel that it is due to you to transmit an early communication on a subject respecting which I have already consulted you more than once.

I must tell you then — that since I wrote last — Papa's mind has gradually come round to a view very different to that which he once took, and that after some correspondence, and as the result of a visit Mr Nicholls paid here about a week ago — it was agreed that he is to resume the curacy of Haworth, as soon as Papa's present assistant is provided with a situation, and in due course of time he is to be received as an inmate into this house.

It gives me unspeakable content to see that — now my Father has once admitted this new view of the case — he dwells on it complacently. In all arrangements his convenience and seclusion will be scrupulously respected. Mr Nicholls seems deeply to feel the wish to comfort and sustain his declining years. I think—from Mr N.'s character—I may depend on this not being a mere transitory, impulsive feeling, but rather that it will be accepted steadily as a duty—and discharged tenderly as an office of affection.

The destiny which Providence in His goodness and wisdom seems to offer me will not—I am aware—be generally regarded as brilliant—but I trust I see in it some germs of real happiness. I trust the demands of both feeling and duty will be in some measure reconciled by the step in contemplation—It is Mr Nicholls's wish that the marriage should take place this Summer he urges the month of July—but that seems very soon.

When you write to me—tell me how you are. It is probable I may be at Brookroyd before very long, and then I trust to see you and fix the time for your coming here. I have now decidedly declined the visit to London: the ensuing three months will bring me abundance of occupation—I could not afford to throw away a month.

Ellen and I are—I think—*quite* friends again—thanks, in a great measure to the kind mediating word which 'turned away wrath.' 'Blessed are the peace-makers!'

Remember me kindly to Mr and Mrs Carter and their household circle—and believe me—my dear Miss Wooler—Yours with true affection and respect,

C. BRONTË.

Papa has just got a letter from the good and dear Bishop—which has touched and pleased me much. It expresses so cordial an approbation of Mr N's return to Haworth (respecting which he was consulted) and such kind gratification at the domestic arrangements which are to ensue. It seems his penetration discovered the state of things when he was here in Jany 1853—while his benevolence sympathized with Mr N.—*then* in sorrow and dejection. I saw him press his hand and speak to him very kindly at parting.

888 (663). *To* ELLEN NUSSEY.

April 15th, '54.

MY OWN DEAR NELL,—I hope to see you somewhere about the second week in May.

The Manchester visit is still hanging over my head. I have deferred it, and deferred it, but have finally promised to go about the beginning of next month. I shall only stay three days, then I spend two or three days at Hunsworth, then come to Brook-royd. The three visits must be compressed into the space of a fortnight, if possible.

I suppose I shall have to go to Leeds. My purchases cannot be either expensive or extensive. You must just resolve in your head the bonnets and dresses; something that can be turned to decent use and worn after the wedding-day will be best I think.

I wrote immediately to Miss Wooler and received a truly kind letter from her this morning. If you think she would like to come to the marriage, I will not fail to ask her.

Papa's mind seems wholly changed about the matter, and he has said both to me and when I was not there, how much happier he feels since he allowed all to be settled. It is a wonderful relief for me to hear him treat the thing rationally, and quietly and amicably, to talk over with him themes on which once I dared not touch. He is rather anxious things should get forward now, and takes quite an interest in the arrangement of preliminaries. His health improves daily, though this east wind still keeps up a slight irritation in the throat and chest.

The feeling which had been disappointed in Papa was *ambition*, paternal pride—ever a restless feeling, as we all know. Now that this unquiet spirit is exorcised, justice, which was once quite forgotten, is once more listened to; and affection, I hope, resumes some power.

My hope is that in the end this arrangement will turn out more truly to Papa's advantage than any other it was in my power to achieve. Mr Nicholls only in his last letter refers touchingly to his earnest desire to prove his gratitude to Papa, by offering support and consolation to his declining age. This will not be mere *talk* with him; he is no talker, no dealer in professions.

Dear Nell, I will write no more at present. You can of course tell your mother, Mrs Clapham, etc., the Healds, too, if you judge proper: indeed, I now leave the communication to you. I know you will not obtrude it where no interest would be taken. —Yours affectionately,

C. BRONTË.

889. *To* Mrs. GASKELL.

April 18th, 1854.

MY DEAR MRS GASKELL,—I should have deferred writing to you till I could fix the day of coming to Manchester, but I have a thing or two to communicate which I want to get done with.

You remember—or perhaps you do not remember—what I told you when you were at Haworth. Towards the end of autumn the matter was again brought prominently forward. There was much reluctance, and many difficulties to be overcome. I cannot deny that I had a battle to fight with myself; I am not sure that I have even yet conquered certain inward combatants. Be this as it may—in January last papa gave his sanction for a renewal of acquaintance. Things have progressed I don't know how. It is of no use going into detail. After various visits and as the result of perseverance in one quarter and a gradual change of feeling in others, I find myself what people call 'engaged.' Mr Nicholls returns to Haworth. The people are very glad—especially the poor and old and very young—to all of whom he was kind, with a kindness that showed no flash at first, but left a very durable impression. He is to become a resident in this house. I believe it is expected that I shall change my name in the course of summer—perhaps in July. He promises to prove his gratitude to papa by offering faithful support and consolation to his age. As he is not a man of fine words, I believe him. The Rubicon once passed, papa seems cheerful and satisfied; he says he has been far too stern; he even admits that he was unjust—terribly unjust he certainly was for a time, but now all this is effaced from memory—now that he is kind again and declares himself happy—and talks reasonably and without invective. I could almost cry sometimes that in this important action in my life I cannot better satisfy papa's perhaps natural pride. My destiny will not be brilliant, certainly, but Mr Nicholls is conscientious, affectionate, pure in heart and life. He offers a most constant and tried attachment—I am very grateful to him. I mean to try and make him happy, and papa too. . . .

C. BRONTË.

890. MRS GASKELL *to* JOHN FORSTER.

April 23rd, 1854.

... Ah! did you not cheat me with your ('now don't tell') at the bottom of the page! I turned over, thinking you really had pressed, and for that and previous misconduct on the same affair I have half a mind not to tell you. Yes! she is going to be married! to Mr Nicholls, who has returned to Haworth. He made some kind of renewed application to her father to be allowed to see them from time to time as an acquaintance in January; in February he again spoke to her; and she says she cannot tell me all the details in a letter, but 'events have so flowed out of each other that now she finds herself what people call engaged.' Mr Nicholls returns to Haworth to be curate to her father, himself only a perpetual curate under the vicar of Bradford with £250 a year *pour tout potage*, out of which he pays Mr Nicholl's salary. They are all three, father, daughter, and husband, to live together; she says her father seems now anxious to make up for former injustice, and is so kind that at times she 'could cry that she has not been able more to gratify his natural pride.' The 'old, the poor, the very young' among the Haworth people are delighted, which speaks well for Mr Nicholls, I'm sure. I am terribly afraid he won't let her go on being intimate with us heretics. I see she is, too, a little. However, she is coming to us in May, and I must make the most of her then, and hope for the future. I fancy him very good, but *very* stern and bigoted; but I daresay that is partly fancy. Still, it arises from what she told me. He sounds vehemently in love with her. And I like his having known her dead sisters and dead brother and all she has gone through of home trials, and being no person who has just fancied himself in love with her because he was dazzled by her genius. Mr N. never knew till long after 'Shirley' was published that she wrote books, and came in cold and disapproving one day to ask her if the report he had heard at Keighley was true, etc. Fancy him, an Irish curate, loving her even then, reading that beginning of 'Shirley!' However, with all his bigotry and sternness it must be charming to be loved with all the strength of his heart as she sounds to be. Mr Shaen accuses me always of being 'too much of a woman' in always wanting to obey somebody — but I am sure that Miss Brontë could never have borne not to be well ruled and ordered. Well, I think I have got into a fiasco, and I have hardly any right to go on discussing what she could or she could not do—but I mean that she would never have been happy but with an exacting, rigid, law-giving, passionate man —only, you see, I am afraid one of his laws will be to shut us out, so I am making a sort of selfish moan over it, and have got out of temper, I suppose, with the very thing I have been wanting for her this six months past....

E. C. GASKELL.

891. *To* ELLEN NUSSEY.

EAST MARSDEN, April 24th [1854].

MY DEAREST ELLEN,—I am so sorry for not having written to you—some time back I might have done so—but I then did not feel very well and thought I would wait till I was better. Then I really became ill and this is the first for many days that I have felt at all equal to writing. I cannot do much now—but must thank you for your letters very much—for all your news —congratulate you and Miss Brontë especially on the at length happy conclusion—I am so glad of your reconcilement! How many marriages around you—You will certainly be married yourself someday whether you will or no. I must tell you too all is well with us except this ailment of mine. Mama recovered from her attack better than I could expect but has had another slight illness since—she is better and coming to us to-day I am thankful to say for it will be a great comfort and do me a great deal of good....

MARY HEWITT.

892. *To* GEORGE SMITH.

April 25th, 1854.

MY DEAR SIR,—Thank you for your congratulations and good wishes; if these last are realised but in part—I shall be very thankful. It gave me also sincere pleasure to be assured of your happiness though of that I never doubted. I have faith also in its permanent character—provided Mrs George Smith is— what it pleases me to fancy her to be. You never told me any particulars about her, though I should have liked them much, but did not like to ask questions, knowing how much your mind and time would be engaged. What *I* have to say is soon told.

The step in contemplation is no hasty one; on the gentleman's side, at least, it has been meditated for many years, and I hope that, in at last acceding to it, I am acting right; it is what I earnestly wish to do. My future husband is a clergyman. He was for eight years my Father's curate. He left because the idea of this marriage was not entertained as he wished. His departure was regarded by the parish as a calamity, for he had devoted himself to his duties with no ordinary diligence. Various circumstances have led my Father to consent to his return, nor can I deny that my own feelings have been much impressed and changed by the nature and strength of the qualities brought out in the course of his long attachment. I fear I must accuse myself of having formerly done him less than justice. However, he is to come back now. He has foregone many chances of preferment to return to the obscure village of Haworth. I believe I do right in marrying him. I mean to try to make him a good wife. There has been heavy anxiety—but I begin to hope all will end for the best. My expectations however are very subdued—very different, I dare say, to what *yours* were before you were married. Care and Fear stand so close to Hope, I sometimes scarcely can see her for the shadows they cast. And yet I am thankful too, and the doubtful Future must be left with Providence.

On one feature in the marriage I can dwell with unmingled satisfaction, with a *certainty* of being right. It takes nothing from the attention I owe to my Father. I am not to leave him—my future husband consents to come here—thus Papa secures by the step a devoted and reliable assistant in his old age.

There can, of course, be no reason for withholding the intelligence from your Mother and sisters; remember me kindly to them whenever you write.

I hardly know in what form of greeting to include your wife's name, as I have never seen her. Say to her whatever may seem to you most appropriate and most expressive of goodwill. I sometimes wonder how Mr Williams is, and hope he is well. In the course of the year that is gone, Cornhill and London have receded a long way from me; the links of communication have waxed very frail and few. It must be so in this world. All things considered, I don't wish it otherwise.—Yours sincerely,

C. BRONTË.

893 (664). *To* ELLEN NUSSEY.

April 28th, 1854.

MY DEAR ELLEN, —I have delayed writing till I could give you
some clear notion of my movements. If all be well, I go to Manchester on the 1st of May. Thence, on Thursday, to Hunsworth
till Monday, when (D.V.) I come to Brookroyd. I must be at
home by the close of the week. Papa, thank God! continues to
improve much. He preached twice on Sunday and again on
Wednesday and was not tired; his mind and mood are different
to what they were, so much more cheerful and quiet. I trust the
illusions of ambition are quite dissipated, and that he really sees
it is better to relieve a suffering and faithful heart, to secure in
its fidelity a solid good, than unfeelingly to abandon one who is
truly attached to *his* interests as well as mine, and pursue some
vain empty shadow.

I thank you, dear Ellen, for your kind invitation to Mr
Nicholls. He was asked likewise to Manchester and Hunsworth.
I would not have opposed his coming had there been no real
obstacle to the arrangement; certain little awkwardnesses of
feeling I would have tried to get over for the sake of introducing
him to old friends; but it so happens that he cannot leave on
account of his Rector's absence. Mr C.[1] will be in town with his
family till June, and he always stipulates that his Curate shall
remain at Kirk-Smeaton while he is away.

How did you get on at the Oratorio? And what did Miss
Wooler say to the proposal of being at the wedding? I have
many points to discuss when I see you. I hope your mother and
all are well. With kind remembrances to them, and true love to
you, —I am, dear Nell, faithfully yours,

C. BRONTË.

When you write, address me at Mrs Gaskell's, Plymouth
Grove, Manchester.

894 (665). *To* ELLEN NUSSEY.

HUNSWORTH, May 6th, '54.

MY DEAR ELLEN, —I came to Hunsworth on Thursday afternoon. I shall stay over Saturday and Sunday —and if all be well

---

[1] The Rev. T. Cator became Incumbent of Kirk-Smeaton in 1829.

I hope to come to Brookroyd on Monday after dinner and just
in time for tea. I leave you to judge by your own feelings whether
I long to see you or not. Amelia tells me you are looking well.
She tells me also that I am not—rather ugly as usual; but never
mind that, dear Nell—as indeed you never did: On the whole I
feel very decently at present—and within the last fortnight have
had much respite from headache.

You are kind to be so much in earnest in wishing for Mr
Nicholls to come to Brookroyd—and I am sorry that circumstances do not favour such a step—but knowing how matters
stood—I did not repeat the proposal to him—for I thought it
would be like tempting him to forget duty.

No more at present—dear Nell except love to all at Brookroyd.—Yours affectionately,

C. BRONTË.

895. MRS GASKELL *to* JOHN FORSTER.

[May, 1854].

. . . I troubled you with my groans, my dear Mr Forster, so
now you see I am going to send you my reliefs—selfish the first
is. I don't believe Miss Brontë will *soon* become bigoted, or *ever*
lose her true love for me, but I do fear a *little* for her happiness
just because he is narrow and she is not. Good, true, pure and
affectionate he is, but he is also narrow, and she can never be
so. . . .

E. C. GASKELL.

896. CATHERINE WINKWORTH *to* EMMA SHAEN.[1]

ALDERLEY EDGE, May 8th, 1854.

. . . I meant to have written to you last week, but finding that
I was to see Miss Brontë[2] this week I determined to wait till I
could write about her, and her *marriage*. I suppose you will have
heard that she is to be married in a few weeks to a clergyman, a
Mr Nicholls, who was for eight years curate to her father, was
then sent off in a hurry for his audacity in falling in love with
the rector's daughter, but is now coming back to be curate and

---

[1]Sister of William Shaen, who married Emily Winkworth.   [2]Miss Brontë was staying with the Gaskells at Manchester.

son-in-law. Alas! alas! I am very glad for Miss Brontë's sake, but sorry for ours, for we can never reckon on seeing her much again when she is 'a married woman.' Emily and I both went over on Tuesday to see her; Emily some hours first, so as to have some talk to herself. When I came in, Lily[1] took me in to Miss Brontë's bedroom and left me for a little bit, intending that I should speak of her marriage. I, not knowing whether I was supposed to know of it, held my tongue on that subject, but we talked friendlily, chiefly she asking me questions about myself, till I thought she looked tired, so I took myself off; but at parting Miss Brontë said to me: 'I hope I shall see you again.' So I went in on Wednesday. Lily drew me in directly to the room, whispering: 'Say something about her marriage.' . . . When she was summoned away I began: 'I was very glad to hear something Mrs Gaskell told me about you.' 'What was it?' 'That you are not going to be alone any more.' She leant her head on her hand and said very quickly: 'Yes, I am going to be married in June.' 'It will be a great happiness for you to have some one to care for, and make happy.' 'Yes; and it is a great thing to be the first object with any one.' 'And you must be very sure of that with Mr Nicholls; he has known you and wished for this so long, I hear.' 'Yes, he has more than once refused preferment since he left my father, because he knew he never could marry me unless he could return to Haworth; he knew I could not leave my father.' She stopped, and then went on: 'But, Katie, it has cost me a good deal to come to this.' 'You will have to care for his things, instead of his caring for yours, is that it?' 'Yes, I can see that beforehand.' 'But you have been together so long already that you know what his things are, very well. He is very devoted to his duties, is he not?—and you can and would like to help him in those?' 'I have always been used to those, and it is one great pleasure to me that he is so much beloved by all the people in the parish; there is quite a rejoicing over his return. But those are not everything, and I cannot conceal from myself that he is *not* intellectual; there are many places into which he could not follow me intellectually.' 'Well; of course every one has their own tastes. For myself, if a man had a firm, constant, affectionate, reliable nature, with tolerable practical sense, I should be much better satisfied with him than if he had an intellect far

---

[1] Mrs Gaskell, who was always so called by her husband and familiar friends.

beyond mine, and brilliant gifts without that trustworthiness.
I care most for a calm, equable atmosphere at home.' 'I do believe Mr Nicholls is as reliable as you say, or I wouldn't marry
him.' 'And you have had time to prove it; you are not acting in
a hurry.' 'That is true; and, indeed, I am quite satisfied with my
decision; still'—here Lily came in, and Miss Brontë repeated
what I had been saying, ending with—'still such a character
would be far less amusing and interesting than a more impulsive
and fickle one; it might be dull!' 'Yes, indeed,' said Lily. 'For a
day's companion, yes,' I said, 'but not for a life's: one's home
ought to be the one fixed point, the one untroubled region in
one's lot; at home one wants peace and settled love and trust,
not storm and change and excitement; besides such a character
would have the advantage that one might do the fickleness required one's self, which would be a relief sometimes.' 'Oh,
Katie, if *I* had ever said such a wicked thing,' cried Lily; and
then Miss Brontë: 'Oh, Katie, I never thought to hear such a
speech from *you*!' 'You don't agree with it?' 'Oh, there is truth
in it; so much that I don't think *I* could ever have been so candid,' Miss Brontë said; 'And there is danger, too, one might be
led on to go too far.' 'I think not,' I said; 'the steadiness and
generosity on the other side would always keep one in check.'
But they made a great deal of fun and laughing about this, and
then Lily was called away again, and Miss Brontë went on: 'He
is a Puseyite and very stiff; I fear it will stand in the way of my
intercourse with some of my friends. But I shall always be the
same in my heart towards them. I shall never let him make me
a bigot. I don't think differences of opinion ought to interfere
with friendship, do you?' 'No.' And we talked about this a little,
and then I said: 'Perhaps, too, you may do something to introduce him to goodness in sects where he has thought it could
not be.' 'That is what I hope; he has a most sincere love of goodness wherever he sees it. I think if he could come to know Mr
Gaskell it would change his feeling.' Then, quite suddenly, she
said: 'Tell me about your sister. Is she happy in her married
life?' 'Yes, very happy indeed.' 'Sincerely?' 'Yes, she not only
says so, but it shines out in everything that she is happier than
ever before in her life.' 'And what is your brother-in-law like?'
So I had to describe Will, thinking privately that it did not sound
as though Mr Nicholls would make half such a good husband,
but did not say so, and to tell her a good deal about their en-

gagement. What she cared most about hearing about Will was, whether he was selfish about small things, whether he took his share of small economies, or whether he appreciated Emily's endeavours and small self-denials, &c. Concerning which he had been praising Emily to me the last time he was here, so I edified her with reporting that, and gave him generally 'an excellent character,' as people say of servants. About Emily she wanted to know what variations of mood, what doubts and fears, she had felt about her marriage beforehand. Had she felt any, or was she always light-hearted during the time? So I said that no one could be exactly always light-hearted, I thought, who was not very young and thoughtless, whereat it came out that she thought Emily not twenty-five now. And then we talked over all the natural doubts that any thoughtful woman would feel at such a time, and my own mother's early married life, and when Lily returned she said she felt greatly comforted; and thereupon Lily set off praising *her* husband for being a good sick nurse and so good to the children, and how very winning that was to the mother. Afterwards, Miss Brontë asked me a good deal about you, with a great deal of kindly interest.

What I hear from Lily of Mr Nicholls is all good. She [Miss Brontë] knew him well all those eight years, and has the greatest trust in his temper and principles. He loved her, but she refused him; he went on, but her father discovered it, went into a rage, and sent him away. He wrote to her very miserably; wrote six times, and then she answered him—a letter exhorting him to heroic submission to his lot, &c. He sent word it had comforted him so much that he must have a little more, and so she came to write to him several times. Then her father wanted a curate, and never liked anyone so well as Mr Nicholls, but did not at first like to have him; sent for him, however, after a time. This was about Christmas. Miss Brontë had not then made up her mind; but when she saw him again, she decided that she could make him happy, and that his love was too good to be thrown away by one so lonely as she is; and so they are to be married. He thinks her intellectually superior to himself, and admires her gifts, and likes her the better, which sounds as though he were generous. And he has very good family connections, and he gets on with her father, and all the parishioners adore him; but they will be very poor, for the living is only £250 a year. If only he is not altogether far too narrow for her, one can fancy her much more really happy with such a man than with one who might have made her more in love, and I am sure she will be really good to him. But I *guess* the true love was Paul Emanuel after all, and is dead; but I don't know, and don't think that Lily knows....

897 (666). *To* ELLEN NUSSEY.

HAWORTH, May 14th, 1854.

MY DEAR ELLEN,—I took the time of the Leeds-Keighley-Skipton trains from Mr Clapham's Feby Time-Table—and when I got to Leeds found myself all wrong. The trains on that line were changed—one had that moment left the station—indeed it was just steaming away—there was not another till a quarter after 5 o'clock; so I had just four hours to sit and twirl my thumbs. I got over the time somehow, but I was vexed to think how much more pleasantly I might have spent it at Brook-royd.

It was just 7 o'clock when I reached home. I found Papa well. It seems he has been particularly well during my absence—but to-day he is a little sickly and only preached once: however he is better again this evening. He has already given Mr de Renzy the legal notice: that gentleman is still perfectly smooth and fairspoken to Papa; he never told him a word of what he has written to Mr Nicholls—nor does he make any objection before Papa—but has the deplorable weakness to go and pour out acrimonious complaints to John Brown, the National Schoolmaster and other subordinates. This only exposes himself to disrespectful comment from those exalted personages. For his own and his office-sake I wish he would be quiet.

Dear Ellen, I could not leave you with a very quiet mind—or take away a satisfied feeling about you—Not that I think that bad cough lodged in a dangerous quarter—but it shakes your system, wears you out and makes you look ill.

Take care of it—do dear Ellen avoid the evening air for a time—and even in the day-time—keep in the house when the weather is cold. Observe these precautions till the cough is quite gone—and you regain strength and feel better able to bear chill and change. Believe me it does not suit you at present to be much exposed to variations of temperature. I send the mantle with this—but have made up my mind not to let you have the

cushion now —lest you should sit stitching over it too closely —
it will do any time and whenever it comes, will be your present
all the same. Write soon say how you are—and believe me—
faithfully yours,

C. BRONTË.

Remember me to them all at Brookroyd and thank them all
for their kindness of word and deed.

898 (667). *To* ELLEN NUSSEY.

May 22nd, 1854.

DEAR ELLEN,—I wonder how you are, and whether that
harassing cough is better; but I am afraid the variable weather of
last week will not have been favourable to improvement. I *will*
not and *do* not believe the cough lies on any vital organ. Still it is
a mark of weakness, and a warning to be scrupulously careful
about undue exposure. Just now, dear Ellen, an hour's inadver-
tence might derange your whole constitution for years to come
—might throw you into a state of chronic ill-health which would
waste, fade, and wither you up prematurely. So, once and again,
TAKE CARE. If you go to ——, or any other evening party, pack
yourself in blankets and a feather-bed to come home, also fold
your boa twice over your mouth, to serve as a respirator. Since I
came home I have been very busy stitching; the little new room
is got into order, and the green and white curtains are up; they
exactly suit the paper, and look neat and clean enough. I had a
letter a day or two since announcing that Mr Nicholls comes to-
morrow. I feel anxious about him, more anxious on one point
than I dare quite express to myself. It seems he has again been
suffering sharply from his rheumatic affection. I hear this not
from himself, but from another quarter. He was ill while I was at
Manchester and Brookroyd. He uttered no complaint to me,
dropped no hint on the subject. Alas! he was hoping he had got
the better of it, and I know how this contradiction of his hopes
will sadden him. For unselfish reasons he did so earnestly wish
this complaint might not become chronic. I fear, I fear. But,
however, I mean to stand by him now, whether in weal or woe.
This liability to rheumatic pain was one of the strong arguments
used against the marriage. It did not weigh somehow. If he is

doomed to suffer, it seems that so much the more will he need care and help. And yet the ultimate possibilities of such a case are appalling. You remember your aunt. Well, come what may, God help and strengthen both him and me. I look forward to to-morrow with a mixture of impatience and anxiety. Poor fellow! I want to see with my own eyes how he is.

It is getting late and dark. Write soon, dear Ellen. Good-night and God bless you. — Yours affectionately,

C. BRONTË.

899 (668). *To* ELLEN NUSSEY.

HAWORTH, May 27th, 1854.

DEAR ELLEN, — Your letter was very welcome and I am glad and thankful to hear that you are better. Still beware of pre-suming on the improvement — don't let it make you careless.

Mr Nicholls has just left me this morning. Your hopes were not ill-founded. At first I was thoroughly frightened by his look when he came on Monday last — It was wasted and strange, and his whole manner nervous. My worst apprehensions — I thought were in the way of being realized. However — inquiry gradu-ally relieved me. In the first place — he could give his ailment no name. He had not had one touch of rheumatism — that report was quite groundless — He was going to die, however, or some-thing like it, I took heart on hearing this — which may seem paradoxical — but you know — dear Nell — when people are real-ly going to die — they don't come a distance of some fifty miles to tell you so.

Having drawn in the horns of my sympathy — I heard further that he had been to Mr Teale — and was not surprised to receive the additional intelligence that that gentleman informed him that he had no manner of complaint whatever except an over-excited mind — In short I soon discovered that my business was — instead of sympathizing — to rate him soundly. He had whole-some treatment while he was at Haworth — and went away sin-gularly better. Perfectly unreasonable however on some points — as his fallible sex are not ashamed to be — groaning over the prospect of a few more weeks of bachelorhood — as much as if it were an age of banishment or prison. It is probable he will fret himself thin again in the time — but I certainly shall not pity him if he does—there is not a woman in England but would have more sense—more courage—more sustaining hope than to behave so.

Man is indeed an amazing piece of mechanism when you see —so to speak—the full weakness—of what he calls—his strength. There is not a female child above the age of eight but might rebuke him for the spoilt petulance of his wilful nonsense.

I bought a border for the table-cloth and have put it on. If your Sister Ann really wishes to do, what is very uncalled for, in the shape of making a present—let her give me a neat *inexpensive* ink-stand—to stand on a table. I have not one and it is a convenient thing.

As to the cards I wish now I had ordered a hundred of each instead of 50. Mr N. has such a string of clerical acquaintances to whom he wishes to send. I ought to have reminded you to get some white wax proper for sealing—when you get the envelopes—I have none and it is not sold here.

Good-bye—dear Nell—write again soon and mind and give a bulletin,—Yours faithfully,

C. Brontë.

900 (669). *To* Ellen Nussey.

Haworth, June 7th, 1854.

My dear Ellen,—I am very glad and thankful to hear that you continue better, though I am afraid your cough will have returned a little during the late chilly change in the weather. Are you taking proper care of yourself and either staying in the house or going out warmly clad and with a boa doing duty as a respirator? On this last point I incline particularly to insist—for you seemed careless about it and unconscious how much atmospheric harm the fine thick hairs of the fur might ward off.

I was very miserable about Papa again some days ago—while the weather was so sultry and electric about a week since—he was suddenly attacked with deafness and complained of other symptoms which shewed the old tendency to the head. His spirits too became excessively depressed—it was all I could do to keep him up and I own I was sad and apprehensive myself— However he took some medicine which did him good. The change to cooler weather too has suited him—the temporary deafness has quite disappeared for the present—and his head is again clear and cool. I can only earnestly trust he will continue better. That unlucky Mr de Renzy continues his efforts to give what trouble he can—and I am obliged to conceal and keep things from Papa's knowledge as well as I can to spare him that anxiety which hurts him so much. Mr de R's whole aim is to throw Papa into the dilemma of being without a curate for some weeks. Papa has every legal right to frustrate this at once by telling him he must stay till his quarter is up—but this is just the harsh decided sort of measure which it goes against Papa's nature to adopt and which I *can* not and *will* not urge upon him while he is in delicate health. I feel compelled to throw the burden of the contest upon Mr Nicholls who is younger—more pugnacious and can bear it better. The worst of it is Mr N. has not Papa's rights to speak and act or he would do it to purpose— I should then have to mediate not rouse, to play the part of 'feather-bed t'wixt castle-wall and heavy brunt of cannon-ball.'

You did quite right, dear Nell, about the cards—it was better not to put 'Haworth' in the corner. Thank you too for ordering another 50. Good bye for the present. My kind regards to all at Brookroyd.—Yours faithfully,

C. BRONTË.

901 (670). *To* ELLEN NUSSEY.

June 11th, 1854.

DEAR ELLEN,—Papa preached twice to-day as well and as strongly as ever. It is strange how he varies, how soon he is depressed and how soon revived. It makes me feel so thankful when he is better. I am thankful too that you are stronger, dear Nell. My worthy acquaintance at Kirk-Smeaton refuses to acknowledge himself better yet. I am uneasy about not writing to Miss Wooler. I fear she will think me negligent, while I am only busy and bothered. I want to clear up my needlework a little, and have been sewing against time since I was at Brookroyd. Mr Nicholls hindered me a full week.

I like the card very well, but not the envelope. I should like a perfectly plain envelope with a silver initial.

I got my dresses from Halifax a day or two since, but have not had time to have them unpacked, so I don't know what they are like.

Next time I write, I hope to be able to give you clear information, and to beg you to come here without further delay. Good-bye, dear Nell.—Yours faithfully,

C. BRONTË.

902 (671). *To* ELLEN NUSSEY.

June 16th, '54.

MY DEAR ELLEN,—Can you come next Wednesday or Thursday? I am afraid circumstances will compel me to agree to an earlier day than I wished. I sadly wished to defer it till the 2nd week in July, but I fear it must be sooner, the 1st week in July, possibly the last week in June, for Mr de Renzy has succeeded in obtaining his holiday, and whereas his quarter will not be up till the 20th of August, he leaves on the 25th June. This gives rise to much trouble and many difficulties as you may imagine, and Papa's whole anxiety now is to get the business over. Mr Nicholls with his usual trustworthiness takes all the trouble of providing substitutes on his own shoulders.

I write to Miss Wooler to-day. Would it not be better, dear Nell, if you and she could arrange to come to Haworth on the same day, arrive at Keighley by the same train, then I could order the cab to meet you at the station and bring you on with your luggage. In this hot weather, walking would be quite out of the question, either for you or her, and I know she would persist in doing it if left to herself, and arrive half-killed. I thought it better to mention this arrangement to *you* first, and then if you liked it, you could settle the time, etc., with Miss Wooler and let me know. Be sure to give me timely information that I may write to the Devonshire Arms about the cab.

Mr Nicholls is a kind considerate fellow, with all his masculine faults in some points; he enters into my wishes about having the thing done quietly in a way which makes me grateful, and if nobody interferes and spoils his arrangements, he will manage so that not a soul in Haworth shall be aware of the day. He is so thoughtful too about 'the ladies,' *i.e.* you and Miss Wooler,—anticipating the very arrangements I was going to propose to him about providing for your departure, etc.

He and Mr Sowden[1] will come to Mr Grant's the evening

[1]The Rev. Sutcliffe Sowden, who officiated at the marriage ceremony. He and his brother, the Rev. George Sowden (1822–99), Canon of Wakefield Cathedral and Vicar of Hebden Bridge, Yorks., were the most intimate friends of Mr Nicholls at the time of his marriage.

before; write me a note to let me know they are there. Precisely at 8 in the morning they will be in the Church, and there we are to meet them. Mr and Mrs Grant are asked to the breakfast, not the ceremony.

Let me hear from you as soon as possible, dear Nell, and believe me faithfully yours,

C. BRONTË.

I had almost forgotten to mention about the envelopes. Mr Nicholls says I have ordered far too few, he thinks sixty will be wanted. Is it too late to remedy this error? There is no end to his string of parson-friends. My own list I have not made out.

903. *To* MARGARET WOOLER.

HAWORTH, June 16th, 1854.

MY DEAR MISS WOOLER,—Owing to certain untoward proceedings—matters have hitherto been kept in such a state of uncertainty that I could not make any approach towards fixing the day; and now if I would avoid inconveniencing Papa—I must hurry. I believe the commencement of July is the furthest date upon which I can calculate—*possibly* I may be obliged to accept one still nearer—the close of June. I cannot quite decide till next week. Meantime—will you—my dear Miss Wooler—come as soon as you possibly can—and let me know at your earliest convenience the day of your arrival. I have written to Ellen N. begged her to communicate with you and mentioning an arrangement which I think might suit you both. On second thoughts—if you saw her soon—*she* might write and save you the trouble of a letter. I earnestly hope nothing will happen to prevent your coming. Your absence would be a real and grievous disappointment. Papa also seems much to wish your presence. Mr Nicholls enters with true kindness into my wish to have all done quietly and he has made such arrangements as—I trust— will secure literal privacy. Yourself, E. Nussey and Mr Sowden will be the only persons present at the ceremony. Mr and Mrs Grant[1] are asked to the breakfast afterwards. I know you will kindly excuse this brief note—for I am and have been *very* busy —and must still be busy up to the very day. Give my sincere

[1] The name 'Grant' is underlined and 'Mr Donne in Shirley' written below.

love to all Mr Carter's family. I hope Mr Carter[1] and Mr Nicholls
may meet some day—I believe mutual acquaintance would, in
time, bring mutual respect—but one of them at least requires
knowing to be *appreciated*—and I must say that I have not yet
found him to lose with closer knowledge—I make no grand
discoveries—but I occasionally come on a quiet little nook of
character which excites esteem. He is always reliable, truthful,
faithful, affectionate; a little unbending perhaps—but still per-
suadable—and open to kind influence. A man never indeed to be
driven—but who may be led. Good-bye my dear Miss Wooler.
—Yours now and always I trust affectionately and respectfully,

C. BRONTË.

Charlotte Brontë's list of friends, to whom wedding-cards
were to be sent, is in her own handwriting, and is not without
interest:

The Rev. W. Morgan, Rectory, Hulcott, Aylesbury, Bucks.
Joseph Branwell, Esq., Thamar Terrace, Launceston, Corn-
wall.
Wheelwright, 29 Phillimore Place, Kensington, London.
George Smith, Esq., 65 Cornhill, London.
Mrs and Misses Smith,   — do. —
W. S. Williams, Esq.,   — do. —
R. Monckton Milnes, Esq.
Mrs Gaskell, Plymouth Grove, Manchester.
Francis Bennoch, Esq., Park, Blackheath, London.[2]
George Taylor, Esq., Stanbury.
Mrs and Miss Taylor, Haworth.
H. Merrall, Esq., Lea Sykes, Haworth.
E. Merrall, Esq., Ebor House, Haworth.
R. Butterfield, Esq., Woodlands, Haworth.
R. Thomas, Esq., Haworth.
J. Pickles, Esq., Brow Top, Haworth.
Wooler Family.
Brookroyd.[3]

[1] Vicar of Heckmondwike, whose wife (a sister of Margaret Wooler) about this time gave Charlotte Brontë a small book, *The Golden Grove*, inscribed 'Miss Brontë, with the kind love and best wishes for her happi-ness here and hereafter of her affectionate friend, Susan Carter, July, 1854.'
[2] See Mrs Gaskell's letter, September, 1853, p. 89 above.
[3] The Nusseys.

Here is Mrs Gaskell's account of the wedding. One wishes she had actually been present as has been erroneously stated by one of her biographers:[1]

It was fixed that the marriage was to take place on June 29. Her two friends arrived at Haworth Parsonage the day before; and the long summer afternoon and evening were spent by Charlotte in thoughtful arrangements for the morrow, and for her father's comfort during her absence from home. When all was finished—the trunk packed, the morning's breakfast arranged, the wedding dress laid out—just at bedtime, Mr Brontë announced his intention of stopping at home while the others went to church.[2] What was to be done? Who was to give the bride away? There were only to be the officiating clergyman, the bride and bridegroom, the bridesmaid, and Miss Wooler present. The Prayer Book was referred to; and there it was seen that the rubric enjoins that the minister shall receive 'the woman from her father's or *friend's* hand' and that nothing is specified as to the sex of the 'friend.' So Miss Wooler, ever kind in emergency, volunteered to give her old pupil away.

The news of the wedding had slipt abroad before the little party came out of church, and many old and humble friends were there, seeing her look 'like a snowdrop,' as they say. Her dress was white embroidered muslin, with a lace mantle, and white bonnet trimmed with green leaves, which perhaps might suggest the resemblance to the pale wintry flower.

The following letter was written on her wedding-day, June 29, 1854:

904 (672). *To* ELLEN NUSSEY.

Thursday Evening.

DEAR ELLEN,—I scribble one hasty line just to say that after a pleasant enough journey—we have got safely to Conway—the evening is wet and wild, though the day was fair chiefly with

[1]Mr A. W. Ward, in the *Dictionary of National Biography*. The error is repeated in the Introduction to the Knutsford edition of the *Works of Mrs Gaskell*.

[2]This is probably incorrect. Miss Wooler had been informed in the letter dated June 16th 1854 that only she and Ellen Nussey and the officiating clergyman would be present at the ceremony.

some gleams of sunshine. However, we are sheltered in a comfortable inn. My cold is not worse. If you get this scrawl tomorrow and write by return—direct to me at the Post-Office, Bangor, and I may get it on Monday. Say how you and Miss Wooler got home. Give my kindest and most grateful love to Miss Wooler whenever you write. On Monday, I think, we cross the Channel. No more at present.—Yours faithfully and lovingly,

C. B. N.

905 (673). *To* Margaret Wooler.

Banagher, July 10th, '54.

My dear Miss Wooler,—I know that in your kindness you will have thought of me some-times since we parted at Haworth—and I feel that it is time to give some account of myself.

We remained in Wales till Tuesday. If I had more leisure I would tell you my impressions of what I saw there—but I have at this moment six letters to answer and my friends are waiting for me to take a drive. I snatch a moment to devote to you and Ellen Nussey to whom you must kindly forward this note—as I long to let her know how I am getting on—and cannot write to her to-day or indeed this week.

Last Tuesday we crossed from Holyhead to Dublin—the weather was calm—the passage good. We spent two days in Dublin—drove over great part of the city—saw the College library, museum, chapel &c. and should have seen much more—had not my bad cold been a restraint upon us.

Three of Mr Nicholls' relatives met us in Dublin—his brother and 2 cousins. The 1st (brother) is manager of the Grand Canal from Dublin to Banagher—a sagacious well-informed and courteous man—his cousin is a student of the University and has just gained 3 premiums. The other cousin was a pretty lady-like girl with gentle English manners. They accompanied us last Friday down to Banagher—his Aunt—Mrs Bell's residence, where we now are.

I cannot help feeling singularly interested in all about the place. In this house Mr Nicholls was brought up by his uncle Dr Bell. It is very large and looks externally like a gentleman's country-seat—within most of the rooms are lofty and spacious and some—the drawing-room—dining-room &c. handsomely and commodiously furnished.

The passages look desolate and bare—our bed-room, a great room on the ground-floor would have looked gloomy when we were shewn into it but for the turf-fire that was burning in the wide old chimney. The male members of this family—such as I have seen seem thoroughly educated gentlemen. Mrs Bell is like an English or Scotch Matron quiet, kind and well-bred—It seems she was brought up in London.

Both her daughters are strikingly pretty in appearance—and their manners are very amiable and pleasing. I must say I like my new relations. My dear husband too appears in a new light here in his own country. More than once I have had deep pleasure in hearing his praises on all sides. Some of the old servants and followers of the family tell me I am a most fortunate person for that I have got one of the best gentlemen in the country. His Aunt too speaks of him with a mixture of affection and respect most gratifying to hear. I was not well when I came here—fatigue and excitement had nearly knocked me up—and my cough was become very bad—but Mrs Bell has nursed me both with kindness and skill, and I am greatly better now.

I trust I feel thankful to God for having enabled me to make what seems a right choice—and I pray to be enabled to repay as I ought the affectionate devotion of a truthful, honourable, un-boastful man.

Remember me kindly to all Mr Carter's family—When you write—tell me how you got home and how you are.

I received Ellen Nussey's last welcome letter—when she reads this she must write to me again. We go in a few days to Kilkee a watering-place on the South-West Coast. The letters may be addressed. Mrs Arthur Nicholls, Post-Office, Kilkee, County Clare, Ireland.

Believe me my dear Miss Wooler—Always yours with affec-tion and respect,

C. B. Nicholls.

906. *To* Catherine Wooler.[1]

July 18th, 1854.
Kilkee, Co. Clare, Ireland.

My dear Miss Catherine,—Your kind letter reached me in a wild and remote spot—a little watering-place on the South West Coast of Ireland.

[1] The second of the Wooler sisters.

Thank you for your kind wishes. I believe my dear husband to be a good man, and trust I have done right in marrying him. I hope too I shall be enabled always to feel grateful for the kindness and affection he shews me.

On the day of our marriage we went to Wales. The weather was not very favourable there—yet by making the most of opportunity we contrived to see some splendid Scenery—one drive indeed from Llanberis to Beddgelert surpassed anything I remember of the English Lakes.

We afterwards took the packet from Holyhead to Dublin. If I had time I would tell you what I saw in Dublin—but your kind letter reached me in a parcel with about a dozen more, and they are all to be answered—and my husband is just now sitting before me kindly stretching his patience to the utmost, but wishing me very much to have done writing, and put on my bonnet for a walk.

From Dublin we went to Banagher where Mr Nicholls' relations live—and spent a week amongst them. I was very much pleased with all I saw—but I was also greatly surprised to find so much of English order and repose in the family habits and arrangements. I had heard a great deal about Irish negligence &c. I own that till I came to Kilkee—I saw little of it. Here at our Inn—splendidly designated 'the West-End Hotel'—there is a good deal to carp at if one were in a carping humour—but we laugh instead of grumbling—for out of doors there is much indeed to compensate for any indoor shortcomings; so magnificent an ocean—so bold and grand a coast—I never yet saw. My husband calls me—Give my love to all who care to have it and believe me dear Miss Catherine,—Your old pupil,

C. B. NICHOLLS.

Mrs Gaskell was reluctant to write to Charlotte while she was on her honeymoon. In a letter to Miss Geraldine Endsor Jewsbury, dated July 21st, 1854, she says:

'. . . Miss Brontë is married, and I ought to write to her, but I've a panic about the husband seeing my letters. Bridegrooms are always curious; husbands are not. . . .'

Their common friend Miss Winkworth, however, had no such scruples, and Charlotte's reply to her letter is, perhaps, the most interesting of the 'honeymoon' series.

Miss Catherine Winkworth was the daughter of Henry Winkworth, a silk manufacturer. She first met Charlotte Brontë at the home of Mrs Gaskell, in April, 1853, and again in May, 1854. In the letter to Miss Shaen, dated May 8th, 1854 (see p. 121 above), she relates her conversation with Charlotte Brontë about her forthcoming marriage with Mr Nicholls. It was in the course of this conversation that Charlotte expressed her doubts as to whether she and her future husband had 'congenial tastes.' She said to Miss Winkworth 'I cannot conceal from myself that he is *not* intellectual; there are many places into which he could not follow me intellectually.' In the letter to Miss Winkworth written after her marriage Charlotte refers to these 'grand doubts,' and expresses her appreciation of Mr Nicholls's kind indulgence.

907. *To* CATHERINE ('KATIE') WINKWORTH.[1]

CORK, July 27th, 1854.

DEAR KATIE,—It was at a little wild spot on the South West Coast of Ireland that your letter reached me; of course I did not at first recognize the handwriting—and when I saw the signature and afterwards read the full and interesting communication—I was touched—you are very good—Katie—very thoughtful for others.

Yes—I am married—a month ago this very day I changed my name—the same day we went to Conway—stayed a few days in Wales—then crossed from Holyhead to Dublin—after a short sojourn in the capital—went to the coast—such a wild, iron-bound coast—with such an ocean-view as I had not yet seen and such battling of waves with rocks as I had never imagined.

My husband is not a poet or a poetical man—and one of my grand doubts before marriage was about 'congenial tastes' and so on. The first morning we went out on to the cliffs and saw the Atlantic coming in all white foam, I did not know whether

[1]The letter is addressed to:—Miss K.   Grove, Manchester, England, and re-addressed 'Alderley Edge, near Manchester.'
Winkworth, care of Mrs Gaskell, Plymouth

I should get leave or time to take the matter in my own way. I did not want to talk — but I *did* want to look and be silent. Having hinted a petition, licence was not refused — covered with a rug to keep off the spray I was allowed to sit where I chose — and he only interrupted me when he thought I crept too near the edge of the cliff. So far he is always good in this way — and this protection which does not interfere or pretend is I believe a thousand times better than any half sort of pseudo sympathy. I will try with God's help to be as indulgent to him whenever indulgence is needed.

We have been to Killarney — I will not describe it a bit. We saw and went through the Gap of Dunloe. A sudden glimpse of a very grim phantom came on us in the Gap. The guide had warned me to alight from my horse as the path was now very broken and dangerous — I did not feel afraid and declined — we passed the dangerous part — the horse trembled in every limb and slipped once but did not fall — soon after she (it was a mare) started and was unruly for a minute — however I kept my seat — my husband went to her head and led her — suddenly without any apparent cause — she seemed to go mad — reared, plunged — I was thrown on the stones right under her — my husband did not see that I had fallen — he still held her — I saw and felt her kick, plunge, trample round me. I had my thoughts about the moment — its consequences — my husband — my father — When my plight was seen, the struggling creature was let loose — she sprung over me. I was lifted off the stones neither bruised by the fall nor touched by the mare's hoofs. Of course the only feeling left was gratitude for more sakes than my own.

I can write no more at present. Only this under the circumstances — I can't see that Mrs Gaskell is one whit in error. Mr Dickens, I think, may have been somewhat too exacting — but if she found or thought her honour pledged — she does well to redeem it to the best of her ability — as she will — and I have no doubt it will be worthily done. I go home soon; goodbye, dear Katie. I direct this to P. Grove not being sure of your address.

C. B. NICHOLLS.

Park. July 27th 185?

Dear Katie

It was at a little wild spot
on the South-West Coast of Ireland
that your letter reached me; of
course I did not at first recognize
the handwriting - and when I saw
the signature and afterwards read the
full and interesting communication: I
was touched - you are very good -
Katie - very thoughtful for others.

Yes - I am married - a month ago this
very day I changed my name -
The same day we went to Conway -
stayed a few days in Wales - then

crossed from Holyhead to Dublin —
after a short sojourn in the capital —
went to the coast — such a wild,
iron-bound coast — with such an
ocean-view as I had not yet seen
— and such battling of waves with rocks
as I had never imagined.

My husband is not a poet or a poetical
man — and one of my grand doubts before
marriage was about "congenial tastes"
and so on. The first morning we went
out on to the cliffs and saw the Atlantic
coming in all white foam, I did not
know whether I should get leave or time
to take the matter in my own way. I did
not want to talk — but I did want to
look and be silent. Having hinted a petition, licence was not refused — covered
with a rug to keep off the spray I was
allowed to sit where I chose — and he
only interrupted me when he thought I

crept too near the edge of the cliff
So far he is always good in this
way – and this protection which does
not interfere, or pretend, is I believe a thousand
times better than any half sort of
pseudo sympathy. I will try with
God's help to be as indulgent to him
whenever indulgence is needed

We have been to Killarney – I will not
describe it a bit. We saw and went
through the Gap of Dunloe. A sudden
glimpse of a very grim phantom came on us.
in the Gap. The guide had warned me to
alight from my horse as the path was now
very broken and dangerous – I did not feel
afraid and declined – we passed the danger
ous part – the horse trembled in every limb
and slipped once but did not fall – soon
after she (it was a mare) started and was unruly for a
minute – however I kept my seat – my
husband went to her head and led her –
suddenly without any apparent cause –

She seemed to go mad – reared, plunged –
I was thrown. on the stones right under her –
My husband did not see that I had fallen
– he still held her – I saw and felt her
kick, plunge, trample. round me. I had my
thoughts about the moment – its consequences –
my husband – my father – When my flight was
seen, the struggling creature was let loose – she
sprung over me. I was lifted off the stones
neither bruised by the fall nor touched by
the mare's hoofs. Of course the only feeling
left was gratitude for more sakes than my
own.

I can write no more at present. Only this
under the circumstances – I can't see that
Mrs Gaskell is one whit in error. Mr
Dickens, I think, may have been somewhat
too exacting – but if she found or thoughts
her honour pledged – she does mean to redeem it to the best of her ability – as
she will – and I have no doubt it will
be worthily done. I go home soon; good-
bye, dear Katie. I direct this to P– Grove
not being sure of your address

(P Nicholls

908. *To* MARTHA BROWN.

DUBLIN, July 28th, 1854.

DEAR MARTHA,—I write a line to tell you that if all be well, we shall come home on Tuesday, August 1st at about seven o'clock in the evening. I feel very anxious about Papa—the idea of his illness has followed me all through my journey and made me miserable sometimes when otherwise I should have been happy enough. I longed to come home a fortnight since—though perhaps it would not have done much good—and I was sure that you would do your best for him.

Have things ready for tea on Tuesday Evening—and you had better have a little cold meat or ham as well—as we shall probably get no dinner—and Mr Nicholls will want something.

I hope you and Tabby have been and are well—and I do earnestly hope to find Papa better.

I am in haste, and can only bid you good-bye for the present. Yours faithfully,   C. B. N.

909. *To* ELLEN NUSSEY.

DUBLIN, July 28th, 1854.

DEAR ELLEN,—I really cannot rest any longer without writing you a line, which I have literally not had time to do during the last fortnight. We have been travelling about, with only just such cessation as enabled me to answer a few of the many notes of congratulation forwarded, and which I dared not suffer to accumulate till my return, when I know I shall be busy enough. We have been to Killarney, Glen Gariffe, Tarbert, Tralee, Cork, and are now once more in Dublin again, on our way home, where we hope to arrive next week. I shall make no effort to describe the scenery through which we have passed. Some parts have exceeded all I ever imagined. Of course, much pleasure has sprung from all this, and more, perhaps, from the kind and ceaseless protection which has ever surrounded me, and made travelling a different matter to me from what it has heretofore been.

Still, Nell, it is written that there shall be no unmixed happiness in this world. Papa has not been well, and I have been longing, *longing intensely* sometimes, to be at home. Indeed, I could enjoy and rest no more, and so home we are going.

I can't write another line—the post is going out.—Yours,

C. B. N.

CHAPTER XXXIII

MARRIED LIFE

THE letters written during the first few months of Charlotte Brontë's married life show the novelist entirely happy in her new rôle as a busy clergyman's wife, and increasingly fond of her husband.

Mr and Mrs Nicholls returned to Haworth on August 1st, 1854, and Charlotte soon found her life entirely changed. Her time was now fully occupied in entertaining visitors, and in assisting her husband in various ways, especially in visiting and helping the poor of the parish. She no longer had time for long hours of reading and writing. Many of the neighbouring clergy called to offer their congratulations to the newly-married couple, and return calls had to be made.

One of Charlotte's most important visitors during her brief married life, was Sir James Kay-Shuttleworth, who, with a friend, spent a week-end at Haworth Parsonage. The main purpose of his visit was to offer Mr Nicholls the living of Padiham, near Burnley, Lancashire, but Mr Nicholls's promise to remain with Mr Brontë prevented him from accepting the appointment. No doubt Charlotte would have derived much benefit from the healthier house and surroundings which Padiham offered, and with Sir James, who had been a doctor, close at hand, she might have been persuaded to take more care of her health.

Mr Nicholls was very practical and methodical, and a lover of fresh air and exercise. He was fond of taking brisk walks over the moors, and on these Charlotte sometimes accompanied him. In a letter to Ellen Nussey towards the end of November, she describes a long walk over the moors to the waterfall, with her husband, during which they were caught in a rain-storm. As a result Charlotte developed a severe cold, which lasted throughout the winter, and which was the forerunner of her last illness.

910 (674). *To* ELLEN NUSSEY.

HAWORTH, Augt 9th 1854.

DEAR ELLEN,—I earnestly hope you are by yourself now—
and relieved from the fag of entertaining guests. You do not
complain, but I am afraid you have had too much of it.

E. Sherwood will probably end by accepting Lionel Knowles
—and judging from what you say—it seems to me that it would
be rational to do so. If—indeed—some one else whom she preferred *wished* to have her—and had duly and sincerely come forward—matters would be different—but this it appears is not the
case—and to cherish any *ungrounded* and unsanctioned preference is neither right nor wise.

Since I came home I have not had an unemployed moment;
my life is changed indeed—to be wanted continually—to be
constantly called for and occupied seems so strange: yet it is a
marvellously good thing. As yet I don't quite understand how
some wives grow so selfish—As far as my experience of matrimony goes—I think it tends to draw you out of, and away from
yourself.

We have had sundry callers this week. Yesterday Mr Sowden
and another gentleman dined here and Mr and Mrs Grant joined
them at tea.

I do not think we shall go to Brookroyd soon—on Papa's
account. I do not wish again to leave home for a time—but I
trust you will ere long come here.

I really like Mr Sowden very well. He asked after you. Mr
Nicholls told him we expected you would be coming to stay
with us in the course of 3 or 4 weeks—and that he should then
invite him over again as he wished us to take sundry rather long
walks—and as he should have his wife to look after—and she
was trouble enough—it would be quite necessary to have a
guardian for the other lady. Mr S—— seemed perfectly acqui-
escent.

Dear Nell—during the last 6 weeks—the colour of my
thoughts is a good deal changed: I know more of the realities of
life than I once did. I think many false ideas are propagated perhaps unintentionally. I think those married women who indiscriminately urge their acquaintance to marry—much to blame.
For my part—I can only say with deeper sincerity and fuller sig-

nificance—what I always said in theory—Wait God's will. Indeed—indeed Nell—it is a solemn and strange and perilous thing for a woman to become a wife. Man's lot is far—far different. Tell me when you think you can come. Papa is better but not well. How is your Mother? Give my love to her and Ann and Mr Clapham—and Mercy if she is good.—Yours faithfully,

C. B. NICHOLLS.

Have I told you how much better Mr Nicholls is? He looks quite strong and hale—he gained 12 lbs. during the 4 weeks we were in Ireland. To see this improvement in him has been a main source of happiness to me, and to speak truth—a subject of wonder too.

911 (678). *To* ELLEN NUSSEY.

WELLINGTON, August 10th, 1854.

DEAR ELLEN,—My conscience has been reproaching me for this last month for neglecting my correspondence. I have done neither that nor anything else except what I could not shirk. Without being positively ill, I have been dull and indifferent to everything but new arrivals or something equally important. I have cured myself, or at least bettered myself for the present, having a 'clean down,' and have just taken out a bundle that ought to have been answered long since.

I am very well content with my dresses and bonnets, and more thankful than you would think to be saved the trouble and responsibility of dressing myself. Neither of the dresses fit—it would be a wonder if they did. They are rather too expensive for my habits, and make rather a contrast to my usual wear. The last bonnet fitted my face to a T, and was altogether a hit, being neither too good nor too flimsy, nor too wintry nor too summery. The one before it (blue satin) I sold; it being only fit for winter, and likely to last me, at the rate I should wear it, about six years.

I thank you for your information in medical matters. It is so difficult a thing for women to get, that it is particular favour to come by any at a less expense than an illness of one's own. From Amelia's last letter I learn that you had been, or were, ill, and she could not see you, being confined herself to the sofa. I am afraid myself that you have more courage than good fortune, and that your illness has not been so temporary as you hoped in your letter that it would be.

We have lately had a wonder here — viz. a steamer. Not a war steamer, but a merchant vessel. We thought so much of it that the authorities agreed with the owners to hire it for twelve months certain, to ply between the N.Z. ports. Two days ago came another wonder on the top of the first one — another steamer walked in, coming from Sydney *viâ* Auckland. This one is likely to be a trader between here and Australia. This last one coming in met the other going out, so we had two in sight at once, a thing that has never happened before.

We are in general thriving — that is, commercially, for as to health the place is worse off than usual. I suppose it is time for the cholera to have come round to us, and though we have not got it, we have some change in the air or climate which makes the place unhealthy. We have scarlatina, influenza, etc. Your last letter has little news, and that not lively. I fear the confinement and dulness of illness will cast down your spirits in spite of your good intentions. I wish this letter could raise them for you. You are certainly better at home when out of health, even when without any definite illness to complain of. It is in this state that one feels the misery of that service that requires you not to do anything, but to be at the beck of another person, and no liberty even to be alone. Ten hours' work at breaking stones is not such a burden as this, if you only have the other fourteen to yourself, with or without the 'comforts of a home.'

Amelia's letter speaks of little but illness — and Tim; she calls Tim of a *forgiving disposition*. It is amusing to think of her not venturing to vex the child for fear it should be angry, and then, when the baby fit of passion was over, breaking out into praise of its *forgiving* disposition! Children don't forgive, they forget. And many full-grown people who get praise for being placable are children in this respect. To forgive requires a mind full grown, which does not always exist in a full-grown body.

MARY TAYLOR.

912. *To* The Rev. GEORGE SOWDEN.

HAWORTH, KEIGHLEY, Augt, 1854.

MY DEAR SOWDEN,—I feel that I have indeed been guilty of great negligence in not sooner replying to your kind letter of Congratulation on the occasion of my marriage—I trust however that you will accept the novelty of my position and the multiplicity of my engagements as an excuse for my silence. We had a delightful tour over nearly the same ground as you and your brother travelled, only we took the Shannon in our progress to Limerick: we also diverged to Kilkee, a glorious watering place, with the finest shore I ever saw—Completely girdled with stupendous cliffs—it was most refreshing to sit on a rock and look out on the broad Atlantic boiling and foaming at our feet—

Your brother spent Tuesday last with us—He seems in good case. Mrs Nicholls joins with me in the request that you will not fail to pay us a visit on your next appearance in Yorkshire—I need scarcely say how glad I shall be to see you.—Believe me My dear Sowden, Very sincerely yours,

A. B. NICHOLLS.

913 (676). *To* MARGARET WOOLER.

HAWORTH, August 22nd, 1854.

MY DEAR MISS WOOLER,—I found your letter with many others awaiting me on my return home from Ireland. I thought to answer it immediately, but I reckoned without my host. Marriage certainly makes a difference in some things and amongst others the disposition and consumption of time. I really seem to have had scarcely a spare moment since that dim quiet June Morning when you, E. Nussey and myself all walked down to Haworth Church—Not that I have been hurried or oppressed—but the fact is my time is not my own now; Somebody else wants a good portion of it—and says we must do so and so. We *do* 'so and so' accordingly, and it generally seems the right thing—only I sometimes wish that I could have written the letter as well as taken the walk.

We have had many callers too—from a distance—and latterly some little occupation in the way of preparing for a small village entertainment. Both Mr Nicholls and myself wished much to make some response for the hearty welcome and general good-will shewn by the parishioners on his return; accordingly the Sunday and day-scholars and Teachers—the church ringers, singers, &c. to the number of 500 were asked to Tea and Supper in the schoolroom. They seemed to enjoy it much, and it was very pleasant to see their happiness. One of the villagers in proposing my husband's health described him as '*a consistent Christian and a kind gentleman.*' I own the words touched me—and I thought—(as I know *you* would have thought—had you been present)—that to merit and win such a character was better than to earn either Wealth or Fame or Power. I am disposed to echo that high but simple eulogium *now*. If I can do so with sincerity and conviction *seven years—or even a year hence*—I shall esteem myself a happy woman. Faultless my husband is not—faultless no human being is; but as you well know—I did not expect perfection.

My dear father was not well when we returned from Ireland—I am however most thankful to say that he is better now—May God preserve him to us yet for some years! The wish for his continued life—together with a certain solicitude for his happiness and health seems—I scarcely know why—stronger in me now than before I was married. So far the understanding between Papa and Mr Nicholls seems excellent—if it only continues thus I shall be truly grateful. Papa has taken no duty since we returned—and each time I see Mr Nicholls put on gown or surplice—I feel comforted to think that this marriage has secured Papa good aid in his old age.

Are you at Richmond alone my dear Miss Wooler? Are you well and enjoying some share of that happiness you so thoroughly deserve? I wonder when I shall see you again—now you are once at Richmond you will stay there a long time I fear. As I do not know your address I enclose this under cover to Mr Carter, answering his kind note at the same time. Yours always with true respect and warm affection,

C. B. NICHOLLS.

914 (675). *To* ELLEN NUSSEY.

HAWORTH, Augt 29th [1854].

DEAR ELLEN,—Can you come here on Wednesday week (Septb. 6th)? Try to arrange matters to do so if possible—for it will be better than to delay your visit till the days grow cold and short. I want to see you again dear Nell—and my husband too will receive you with pleasure—and he is not diffuse of his courtesies or partialities—I can assure you. One friendly word from him means as much as twenty from most people.

We have been busy lately giving a supper and tea-drinking to the Singers, ringers, Sunday-School Teachers and all the Scholars of the Sunday and National Schools—amounting in all to some 500 souls. It gave satisfaction and went off well.

Papa, I am thankful to say is much better; he preached last Sunday. How does your Mother bear this hot weather? Write soon dear Nell and say you will come.—Yours faithfully,

C. B. N.

915 (679). *To* ELLEN NUSSEY.

HAWORTH, September 7th, 1854.

DEAR ELLEN,—I send a French paper to-day. You would almost think I had given them up, it is so long since one was despatched. The fact is they had accumulated to quite a pile during my absence. I wished to look them over before sending them off, and as yet I have scarcely found time. That same Time is an article of which I once had a large stock always on hand; where it is all gone now it would be difficult to say, but my moments are very fully occupied. Take warning, Ellen, the married woman can call but a very small portion of each day her own. Not that I complain of this sort of monopoly as yet, and I hope I never shall incline to regard it as a misfortune, but it certainly exists. We were both disappointed that you could not come on the day I mentioned. I have grudged this splendid weather very much, the moors are in glory, I never saw them fuller of purple bloom. I wanted you to see them at their best; they are just turning now, and in another week, I fear, will be faded and sere. As soon as ever you can leave home, be sure to write and let me know.

I am afraid Amelia continues to get on but poorly. At least I had a grievous letter from her a day or two since detailing a visit from Dr Henriquez, whom it appears she felt herself under the necessity of summoning down from London. I wish her nervous system, or whatever is wrong with her, could get into better order.

Papa continues greatly better; my husband flourishes, he begins indeed to express some slight alarm at the growing improvement in his condition. I think I am decent, better certainly than I was two months ago; but people don't compliment me as they do Arthur, excuse the name, it has grown natural to use it now. I trust, dear Nell, that you are all well at Brookroyd, and that your visiting stirs are pretty nearly over. I compassionate you from my heart for all the trouble to which you must be put, and I am rather ashamed of people coming sponging in that fashion one after another; get away from them and come here. — Yours faithfully,

C. B. NICHOLLS.

How does the romance of real life between E. S. and L. K. get on?

916 (680). *To* ELLEN NUSSEY.

HAWORTH, September 14th, 1854.

DEAR ELLEN, — Mr Nicholls and I have a call or two to make in the neighbourhood of Keighley; we wish so to arrange as to meet you there and bring you back with us in the cab. On Wednesday Mr Nicholls is always engaged, as it is a lecture day, but on Thursday next (the 21st) we will D. V. expect you at the station by the 6.11 train. We shall be very, very glad to see you, dear Nell, and I want the day to come.

E. S. does not seem to me one of the wise virgins, and I must candidly add that L. K. strikes me also as one of the slightly infatuated; it must be outside which chiefly attracts him, and then her reluctance stimulates his pursuit. However, I trust we shall have plenty of time to talk them and others over ere long. Good-bye, dear Nell. — Yours very faithfully,

C. B. NICHOLLS.

917 (681). *To* MARGARET WOOLER.

HAWORTH, Septbr 19th, 1854.

MY DEAR MISS WOOLER,—You kindly tell me not to write while Ellen Nussey is with me; I am expecting her this week; and as I think it would be wrong—long to defer answering a letter like your last—I will reduce to practice the maxim 'there is no time like the present;' and do it at once.

It grieves me that you should have had any anxiety about my health; the cough left me before I quitted Ireland, and since my return home I have scarcely had an ailment, except occasional head-aches. My dear Father too continues much better. Dr Burnet was here on Sunday—preaching a sermon for the Jews, and he gratified me much by saying that he thought Papa not at all altered since he saw him last—nearly a year ago. I am afraid this opinion is rather flattering, but still it gave one pleasure—for I had feared that he looked undeniably thinner and older.

You ask what visitors we have had?—a good many amongst the clergy &c. in the neighbourhood, but none of note from a distance. Haworth is—as you say—a very quiet place; it is also difficult of access and unless under the stimulus of necessity or that of strong curiosity—or finally that of true and tried friendship—few take the courage to penetrate to so remote a nook. Besides, now that I am married I do not expect to be an object of much general interest. Ladies who have won some prominence (call it either *notoriety* or celebrity) in their single life —often fall quite into the background when they change their names; but if true domestic happiness replace Fame—the exchange will indeed be for the better.

Yes—I am thankful to say—my dear Miss Wooler—that my Husband is in improved health and spirits. It makes me content and grateful to hear him from time to time avow his happiness in the brief plain phrase of sincerity.

My own life is more occupied than it used to be: I have not so much time for thinking: I am obliged to be more practical, for my dear Arthur is a very practical as well as a very punctual, methodical man. Every morning he is in the National School by nine o'clock; he gives the children religious instruction till $\frac{1}{2}$ past 10. Almost every afternoon he pays visits amongst the poor parishioners. Of course he often finds a little work for his wife to do, and I hope she is not sorry to help him.

I believe it is not bad for me that his bent should be so wholly towards matters of real life and active usefulness—so little inclined to the literary and contemplative. As to his continued affection and kind attentions—it does not become me to say much of them but as yet they neither change nor diminish.

I wish, my dear Miss Wooler—*you* had some kind, faithful companion to enliven your solitude at Richmond—some friend to whom to communicate your pleasure in the scenery, the fine weather, the pleasant walks. You never complain, never murmur, never seem otherwise than thankful, but I know you must miss a privilege none could more keenly appreciate than yourself.

Both my Father and my Husband desire me, whenever I write to offer their kind regards to you, and both say that whenever you can come here they will be truly happy to see you.—Believe me always, Yours with truest affection and respect,

C. B. NICHOLLS.

918. *To* Mrs GASKELL.

HAWORTH, September 30th, '54.

MY DEAR MRS GASKELL,—Do not suffer yourself to be either vexed or in low spirits about what you have 'gone and done.'

We all know that it is not precisely advantageous to a really good book to be published piecemeal in a periodical—but still —such a plan has its good side. 'North and South' will thus be seen by many into whose hands it would not otherwise fall.

What has appeared I like well, and better and better each fresh number; best of all the last (to-day's). The subject seems to me difficult; at first, I groaned over it. If you had any narrowness of views or bitterness of feeling towards the Church or her Clergy, I should groan over it still; but I think I see the ground you are about to take as far as the Church is concerned; not that of attack on her, but of defence of those who conscientiously differ from her, and feel it a duty to leave her fold.

Well—it is good ground, but still rugged for the step of Fiction; stony—thorny will it prove at times—I fear. It seems to me you understand well the Genius of the North. Where the Southern Lady and the Northern Mechanic are brought into contrast and contact, I think Nature is well respected. Simple, true and good did I think the last number—clear of artificial trammels of style and thought. ...Yours truly and affectionately,

C. B. NICHOLLS.

919 (683). *To* ELLEN NUSSEY.

HAWORTH, October 11th, '54.

DEAR ELLEN,—I cannot say I was surprised when I received yours to learn that you had had to wait at Keighley Station two long hours without fire or company, but I was truly vexed and concerned. On looking at the clock after you were gone, I feared how it would be, so did Arthur, and we were both exceedingly grieved that you had not stayed for the later train. I must say Mr E.'s behaviour was very creditable to him, the man must have the germ of innate politeness in his nature. I return his courteous little note.

You will ask how we got on with the party yesterday. Read the enclosed which I received on Monday morning, and it will tell you. Amelia is really a simpleton in some things, she will now be worshipping Mrs ——, fine clothes, open pink muslin gown, worked petticoat, velvet cape, and carriage and pairs included. I do not say that she should show or feel one shade of jealousy of her husband's former flames, but that assiduous cultivation of their society and countenance seems strained, odd, unnatural. Arthur is very strong upon it and much out of patience with Amelia.

I don't know whether I shall be able to keep him at home now whenever she does come. He threatens to bolt. He flourishes, and desires his kind regards to you. He also often says he wishes you were well settled in life. He is just gone out this morning in a rather refractory mood about some Dissenters. On Sunday, we had a pair of very sweet sermons indeed, really good, and touching the better springs of our nature. Just before going to Church he menaced me with something worse than the preceding Sunday. I was agreeably disappointed.

I cannot say I wonder at Mr Heald's resignation. It seems to me that all who truly believe the doctrines and trust the promises of Christianity must, after watching the sufferings of sickness and agonies of death in one they love, feel, in the first instance, a sort of peace in their release, and resignation to their loss. It is some time afterwards that the dark and durable regrets arise, and perhaps, surrounded by his family and parishioners, he may be spared these.

With love to your dear mother, and all at Brookroyd, most to yourself, Nell, — I am, yours faithfully,

C. B. NICHOLLS.

Papa, I am sorry to say, is still a good deal troubled with his cough, though better than he has been.

920 (684). *To* ELLEN NUSSEY.

[October 20th, '54] Friday Morning.

DEAR NELL, — You would have been written to before now if I had not been very busy. Amelia and Joe [Taylor] and the child came on Tuesday morning. Joe only stayed till the same evening, we had the others till yesterday. We got on with them better than I expected. Amelia seemed pleased and content and forgot her fancies for the time; she looked not at all pretty but stronger and in better health. Tim behaved capitally on the whole. She amused papa very much — chattering away to him very funnily — his white hair took her fancy. She announced a decided preference for it over Arthur's black hair, and coolly advised the latter to 'go to the barber and get his whiskers cut off.' Papa says she speaks as I did when I was a child — says the same odd unexpected things. Neither Arthur nor papa liked Amelia's looks at first, but she improved on them, I think.

Arthur will go to the Consecration of Heptonstall Church, D.V., but I don't mean to accompany him. I hardly like coming in contact with all the Mrs Parsons; if you were here I should go.

Arthur heard from Mr Sowden lately — an uninteresting letter, no remark on our vote of thanks etc. A brother of his is coming over. Arthur means to invite them both here for a night. I shall take stock of them and tell you what I think.

Arthur is impatient for his walk. I am obliged to scrawl hurriedly. When I go to Brookroyd, if I hear Mr Clapham or anybody else say anything to the disparagement of single women, I shall go off like a bomb shell, and as for *you*, — but I won't prophesy.

Arthur has just been glancing over this note. He thinks I have written too freely about Amelia, &c. Men don't seem to understand making letters a vehicle of communication, they always seem to think us incautious. I'm sure I don't think I have said anything rash; however, you must BURN it when read. Arthur says such letters as mine never ought to be kept, they are dangerous as lucifer matches, so be sure to follow a recommendation he has just given, 'fire them' or 'there will be no more,' such is his resolve. I can't help laughing, this seems to me so funny. Arthur, however, says he is quite 'serious' and looks it, I assure you; he is bending over the desk with his eyes full of concern. I am now desired 'to have done with it,' so with his kind regards and mine, good-bye, dear Ellen. — Yours affectionately,

C. B. Nicholls.

921 (685). *To* Ellen Nussey.

Haworth, October 31st, 1854.

Dear Ellen, — I wrote my last in a hurry, and as soon as I had sealed it, remembered that it contained no comment on what you had said about Elizabeth's illness. I was sorry, for the news had impressed me painfully, and I wished much to know how she was getting on. Does the slight improvement continue? Her particular wish for champagne might imply a turn either for the better or the worse. I trust it was the former in her case, though I have known where such a caprice of the appetite has been of fatal augury. You will kindly remember to give me information respecting her when you write again.

The Consecration of Heptonstall Church took place last Thursday; Arthur fully intended to go, but a funeral kept him at home. I regretted this as the day happened to be very fine. Mr Grant went. He said there was a good attendance of the laity, but very few clergy, this was owing to the fact of invitations not having been sent.

I return Mrs ——'s letter; it bears that character of unassuming goodness and sense which mark all her letters, but I should fear her illness has perhaps been more serious than she allows. She is evidently not one to make much of her own ailments.

Dear Ellen, Arthur complains that you do not distinctly promise to burn my letters as you receive them. He says you must give him a plain pledge to that effect, or he will read every line I write and elect himself censor of our correspondence.

He says women are most rash in letter-writing, they think only of the trustworthiness of their immediate friend, and do not look to contingencies; a letter may fall into any hand. You must give the promise, I believe, at least he says so, with his best regards, or else you will get such notes as he writes to Mr Sowden, plain, brief statements of facts without the adornment of a single flourish, with no comment on the character or peculiarities of any human being, and if a phrase of sensibility or affection steals in, it seems to come on tiptoe, looking ashamed of itself, blushing 'pea-green' as he says, and holding both its shy hands before its face. Write him out his promise on a separate slip of paper, in a legible hand, and send it in your next. Papa, I am glad to say, continues pretty well. I hope your mother prospers, and that Ann is better, with love to all, Mr Clapham included.—I am, yours faithfully,

C. B. NICHOLLS.[1]

922. *To the* REVD. THE MAGISTER.

[November, 1854].

MY DEAR MR NICHOLLS,—As you seem to hold in great horror the ardentia verba of feminine epistles, I pledge myself to the destruction of Charlotte's epistles, henceforth, if you pledge yourself to *no* authorship in the matter communicated.—Yours very truly,

E. NUSSEY.[2]

923 (686). *To* ELLEN NUSSEY.

HAWORTH, November 7th, 1854.

DEAR ELLEN,—The news of an acquaintance's death always seems to come suddenly. I thought ill of the previous accounts you had given of poor Elizabeth ——, but still I did not expect she would die so soon. And theirs is a family into which it is

---

[1]Upon this letter Miss Nussey had written a note to the effect that Mr Nicholls and Mr Brontë were the very first to break his (Mr Nicholls's) objections—by requesting the use of Charlotte Brontë's Letters for Mrs Gaskell.

[2]The following note is written at the head of the letter: 'Mr N. continued his authorship so the pledge was void.'

difficult to realise the entrance of death. They seemed so cheerful, active, sanguine. How does S. bear her loss? Will she not
feel companionless, almost sisterless? I should almost fear so,
for a married sister can hardly be to her like the other. I should
like to know too how Mrs Hewitt[1] is. Did she ever lose a child
before?

Arthur wishes you would burn my letters. He was out when I
commenced this letter, but he is just come in. On my asking
whether he would give the pledge required in return, he says,
'Yes, we may now write any dangerous stuff we please to each
other'; it is not 'old friends' he mistrusts, but the chances of war,
the accidental passing of letters into hands and under eyes for
which they were never written.

All this seems mighty amusing to me: it is a man's mode of
viewing correspondence. Men's letters are proverbially uninteresting and uncommunicative. I never quite knew before why
they made them so. They may be right in a sense. Strange
chances do fall out certainly. As to my own notes, I never
thought of attaching importance to them or considering their
fate, till Arthur seemed to reflect on both so seriously.

Mr Sowden and his brother were here yesterday, stayed all
night, and are but just gone. George Sowden is six or seven
years the junior of Sutcliffe Sowden (the one you have seen); he
looks very delicate and quiet, a good sincere man, I should think,
Mr Sowden asked after Miss Nussey.

I will write again next week if all be well, to name a day for
coming to see you. I am sure you want, or at least ought to have
a little rest before you are bothered with more company: but
whenever I come, I suppose, dear Nell, under present circumstances, it will be a quiet visit, and that I shall not need to bring
more than a plain dress or two. Tell me this when you write. —
Believe me, faithfully yours,

                                        C. B. NICHOLLS.

I intend to write to Miss Wooler shortly.

924 (687). *To* ELLEN NUSSEY.

HAWORTH, November 14th, 1854.

DEAR ELLEN, —I am only just at liberty to write to you: guests
have kept me very busy during the last two or three days. Sir J.
Kay-Shuttleworth and a friend of his came here on Saturday

---

[1] Mrs Thomas Swinton Hewitt, *née* Mary Gorham.

afternoon, and stayed till after dinner on Monday. His chief errand was to see my husband, and when he had seen him he took a fancy to him, and before his departure made him a formal offer of the living of Padiham (near his house at Gawthorpe), now vacant, or on the point of becoming so. Arthur of course is tied to Haworth so long as papa lives, and was obliged to decline for that reason, had there been none other. Sir James then begged him to name some other clergyman of his acquaintance and in whom he had confidence. Arthur has thought of Mr Sowden, and would have gone over to-day to propose the matter to him and talk over pros and cons; but it is very wet, and he means consequently to write and summon Mr Sowden here to-morrow. I wish it might be arranged. Mr Sowden would suit Sir James better than any man I know. The living it seems is £200 per ann. Mr Sowden's present income is only £130; £80 fixed, the rest quite uncertain. There is a beautiful Church at Padiham, and a parsonage is about to be erected.

When I go to Brookroyd, Arthur will take me there and stay one night, but I cannot yet fix the time of my visit. Joe and Amelia, it seems, are off to Scarbro'; they mean to stay a fortnight, and Amelia has written in great anxiety that I should wait till they come home. Indeed I have so long promised to visit them when I go to Brookroyd that it would not be right to fall off. You are aware of the inconvenience and expense of making Hunsworth the subject of a second visit direct from Haworth. I am sorry too to be obliged to defer seeing you, very sorry, but I hope to manage the matter before Christmas.—Good-bye for the present, dear Nell. Yours faithfully,

C. B. Nicholls.

925 (682). *To* Margaret Wooler.

Haworth, Novbr 15th, 1854.

My dear Miss Wooler,—I should have acknowledged your last kind and interesting letter before now, had I not waited in the hopes of being able to give a definite answer to your inquiry respecting the probable date of my visit to Brookroyd. I had fixed for next week, but am now obliged to defer it for a short time, as I had promised a brief stay at Hunsworth after the visit to Ellen Nussey—and at present Mr and Mrs J. Taylor are absent at Scarbro' where they are gone by medical advice in consequence of Joe's very delicate state of health. He is said to have gastric fever—a complaint which has been strangely prevalent and often fatal this autumn. I feel anxious to hear how he is getting on—for I fear his constitution has not much stamina to resist disease—and he has now been suffering from prostration of strength for some time.

You kindly inquire after Papa. He is better—and seems to gain strength as the weather gets colder; indeed of late years his health has always been better in Winter than in Summer.

We are all—indeed—pretty well—and for my own part—it is long since I have known such comparative immunity from head-ache, sickness and indigestion, as during the last three months.

My life is different to what it used to be. May God make me thankful for it! I have a good, kind attached husband and every day makes my own attachment to him stronger.

Do you remember, my dear Miss Wooler—my speaking of Sir J. K. Shuttleworth when you were here last and mentioning the frightful accident by which sight and life were emperilled together? I am glad to say that, after much suffering, he is better—indeed quite recovered—with the exception of the lost eye which can never be restored. He has been our guest within the last few days; he came on Saturday and remained till Monday afternoon—I mention this—partly for the purpose of introducing what was to me a gratifying proof of respect for my dear Arthur. Sir James seemed to take quite a fancy to him—and before his departure, offered him his living of Habergham or Padiham. It is worth £200 per ann. and in many ways would have been advantageous—could Arthur have accepted it—but, of course, during Papa's life, he is bound to Haworth. He has therefore no alternative but to decline. Sir James then requested Arthur to recommend some clerical friend, and this he will try to do.

I am glad to hear good accounts of all Mr Carter's family. I trust Susan will one day repay your kindness to her, and that Ellen may derive benefit moral and physical from her sojourn abroad. She is making good discoveries—it appears—respecting the advantages of regular employment and rational repasts: 'Better late than never.'

With kindest regards to Mr and Mrs Carter and all old friends —and in the hopes of seeing you ere long,—I am—my dear Miss Wooler, Yours faithfully and affectionately,

C. B. NICHOLLS.

926 (688). *To* ELLEN NUSSEY.

HAWORTH, November 21st, 1854.

DEAR ELLEN,—I hope you will write very soon and let me know how Mercy is getting on, and how you all are. I trust the fever will soon be allayed in Mercy's case, and, above all, that it will be confined to her, and not spread to others of the family, and, indeed I quite hope this will not be the case, because the fever was not generated at Brookroyd, proving miasma in the neighbourhood, but was imported it seems from Leeds. Mrs —— was indeed thoughtless. I fear you will have much to do, too much; but yet I hope and believe you will be supported.

You ask about Mr Sowden's matter. He walked over here on a wild rainy day. We talked it over. He is quite disposed to entertain the proposal, but of course there must be close inquiry and ripe consideration before either he or the patron decide. Meantime, Mr Sowden is most anxious that the affairs should be kept absolutely quiet; in the event of disappointment it would be both painful and injurious to him if it should be rumoured at Hebden Bridge that he has had thoughts of leaving. Arthur says if a whisper gets out, these things fly from parson to parson like wild-fire. I cannot help somehow wishing that the matter should be arranged, if all on examination is found tolerably satisfactory.

Papa continues pretty well, I am thankful to say; his deafness is wonderfully relieved. Winter seems to suit him better than summer, besides he is settled and content, as I perceive with gratitude to God.

Dear Ellen, I wish you well through every trouble. Arthur is not in just now or he would send a kind message. With love to Mercy and all at Brookroyd, and in the hope that you will, as soon as possible, let me know how she is doing.—Believe me, yours faithfully,

C. B. NICHOLLS.

927 (689). *To* ELLEN NUSSEY.

HAWORTH, November 29th, 1854.

DEAR ELLEN,—I intended to have written a line yesterday, but just as I was sitting down for the purpose Arthur called to me to take a walk. We set off not intending to go far, but though wild and cloudy it was fair in the morning. When we had got about half a mile on the moors, Arthur suggested the idea of the water-fall—after the melted snow he said it would be fine. I had often wanted to see it in its winter power, so we walked on. It was fine indeed—a perfect torrent raving over the rocks white and beautiful. It began to rain while we were watching it, and we returned home under a stormy sky. However I enjoyed the walk inexpressibly, and would not have missed the spectacle on any account.

How is Mercy now? I hope she will get forward with her convalescence in clever style, and not linger half-fondly over the business. How are you? Can you get out now and take a walk sometimes? Let me know soon, dear Ellen, about your welfare and hers.

Arthur somewhat demurs about my going to Brookroyd as yet: fever, you know, is a formidable word. I cannot say I entertain any apprehensions myself—further than this—that I should be terribly bothered at the idea of being taken ill from home and causing trouble, and strangers are sometimes more liable to infection than persons living in the house.

Mr Sowden has seen Sir J. K. Shuttleworth, but I fancy the matter is very uncertain as yet. It seems the Bishop of Manchester stipulates that the clergyman chosen should if possible be from his own Diocese, and this, Arthur says, is quite right and just. An exception would be made in Arthur's favour, but the case is not so clear with Mr Sowden. However no harm will have been done if the matter does not take wind, as I trust it will not. Write very soon, dear Nell, and believe me yours faithfully,

C. B. NICHOLLS.

928. *To* AMELIA TAYLOR (*née* RINGROSE).

[December, 1854].

DEAR AMELIA,—You never were more thoroughly right in your thoughts than when you believed I cared for yourself and Joe—*that* I do with my whole heart. I have known Joe above twenty years and differed from him and been enraged with him and liked him and cared for him as long—and *you* dear Amelia— well, I will just say this—I can now realise how Joe will appreciate the value of a nature genuinely affectionate—which will adhere to him the closer and love him the better because there is something to be done for him—In high health—there might have been women who would give life more brilliancy, in sickness—no wife could be better than Joe's own actual wife.

Continue to keep as strong in heart as you can, dear Amelia, and believe as well as you can in the better time which we will still hope is coming. Dear little Tim—I did not name her in my last as I remembered after closing the envelope. Give her a kiss from grandmamma and the wish that the many Christmasses which probably are yet in store for her may be as happy as the changing nature of this life will permit.

Whenever you are low, dear Amelia, comfort yourself with this thought—that when Joe gets better he will certainly value you more and love you better than ever he has done.... —[Faithfully yours,

C. B. NICHOLLS].

929 (682). *To* MARGARET WOOLER.

HAWORTH, Decbr 6th, 1854.

MY DEAR MISS WOOLER,—I thank you very much for your truly kind warning—and I believe my husband thanks you still more. He is quite of your opinion—indeed before we received your note—and when I was ignorant that Miss Mercy Nussey's case was anything more than one of ordinary low fever—he was averse to my going—Now his wish is so decided—that for the present I think it will be right to defer the visit at least till Miss Mercy is well. I am very sorry to hear that her illness is of so serious a nature, and I earnestly trust Ellen, as well as the other inmates of Brookroyd may be preserved from infection. I believe Ellen does not know her sister's illness to be typhus—of course *I* shall say nothing to her on the subject—but it seems to me that medical men ought to be more candid in these matters.

It pains me to disappoint Ellen and nearly as much to dis-appoint myself—I have long been looking forward to the visit both on her account and yours. When do you think—my dear Miss Wooler—that you can come to see us at Haworth? The disadvantages of weather, roads &c. make me diffident of urg-ing invitations in the Winter Season, but whenever it may suit your convenience and inclination to undertake the journey—let me know—for all in this house will be glad to see you.

With kindest regards to Mr and Mrs Carter and all old friends, —Believe me always, Yours faithfully and affectionately,

C. B. NICHOLLS.

I say nothing about the War—but when I read of its horrors —I cannot help thinking that it is one of the greatest curses that can fall upon mankind. I trust it may not last long—for it really seems to me that no glory to be gained can compensate for the sufferings which must be endured. This tone may seem a little ignoble and unpatriotic—but I think that as we advance towards middle age—nobleness and patriotism bear a different significa-tion to us to that which we accept while young.

I still hope to go to Brookroyd soon after Christmas, and then I trust I shall have the true pleasure of seeing you. Good-bye.

C. B. N.

930 (690). To ELLEN NUSSEY.

HAWORTH, December 7th, 1854.

DEAR ELLEN,—I shall not get leave to go to Brookroyd before Christmas now, so do not expect me. For my own part I really should have no fear, and if it just depended on me, I should come; but these matters are not quite in my power now, another must be consulted, and where his wish and judgment have a decided bias to a particular course, I make no stir, but just adopt it. Arthur is sorry to disappoint both you and me, but it is his fixed wish that a few weeks should be allowed yet to elapse before we meet. Probably he is confirmed in this desire by my having a cold at present. I did not achieve the walk to the waterfall with impunity, though I changed my wet things immediately on returning home, yet I felt a chill afterwards, and the same night had sore throat and cold; however, I am better now, but not quite well.

I am truly glad to hear that Mercy is recovering so nicely. I trust for your sake as well as hers there will be no drawback, and that you will soon have some complete rest, which you must need.

It is good news about Mrs Hewitt. The affair seems to have got over admirably. Was it not a little sooner than she expected?

Did I tell you that our poor little Flossy is dead? He drooped for a single day, and died quietly in the night without pain. The loss even of a dog was very saddening, yet perhaps no dog ever had a happier life or an easier death.

Papa continues pretty well, I am happy to say, and my dear boy flourishes; I do not mean that he continues to grow stouter, which one would not desire, but he keeps in excellent condition.

You would wonder I dare say at the long disappearance of the French paper. I had got such an accumulation of them unread that I thought I would not wait to send the old ones. Now you will receive them regularly. I am writing in haste. It is almost inexplicable to me that I seem so often hurried now, but the fact is, whenever Arthur is in, I must have occupations in which he can share, or which will not at least divert my attention from him; thus a multitude of little matters get put off till he goes out, and then I am quite busy. Good-bye, dear Ellen, I hope we shall meet soon. — Yours faithfully,

C. B. NICHOLLS.

931. *To* AMELIA TAYLOR (*née* RINGROSE).

[December, 1854].

DEAR AMELIA, — If there is no tubercular ulceration of the bowels or lungs — I should think there *is* hope. The case may look bad; its lingering character and the frequent relapses dishearten, yet for my part I could not cease to hope yet.

Still Joe is very right to prepare himself in that quiet and firm spirit which few can possess at such a time — and very right are you to share that spirit and preparation with him. Whatever happens — perhaps the keenest pang is felt when we first allow to ourselves that what we so well love — so dearly value — is passing from us. I don't want him to go yet—*you* don't want him to go. May God keep him a little longer! I cannot help praying this.

You cannot probably write long letters—but send me an envelope with a word in it as often as you can. Come what will Joe has a nurse tender and faithful.—Good-bye.

C. B. NICHOLLS.

The strong probability that Joe may yet recover returns upon me. It is astonishing how much debilitating wasting functional derangement the human frame can bear when there is nothing of, what the doctors call, organic change—no tubercles—no ulcers. I wonder if Joe would be better away from Hunsworth—at Birmingham for instance, could he travel so far? Can he still take nourishment regularly? Has he the least cough—or has he any pain?

Though it is right Joe should be, as he is, tranquilly prepared for what is—at least possible—yet he must not quit his hold upon life in thought nor entirely relax his *will* to live. A mental tendency inherited from his mother will dispose him to do this too soon. He must remember it is better for his wife, better for his child—better for many that he should live. *He* may feel that he can already lie down serene and fearless by his Father and Grandfather—but others may find it too difficult and dreary to live on after he has left them.

I shall hope both for him and you a little longer yet. But write a line soon—to-morrow if possible—though indeed he will not change from day to day. A week hence you might be able to say whether he is better or worse—weaker or stronger—but a week is a long time to wait.

932 (691). To ELLEN NUSSEY.

HAWORTH, December 26th, '54.

DEAR ELLEN,—I return Mrs. Hewitt's letter. It is as you say, very genuine, truthful, affectionate, maternal, without a taint of sham or exaggeration. Mary will love her child without spoiling it, I think. She does not make an uproar about her happiness either: the longer I live, the more I suspect exaggerations. I fancy it is sometimes a sort of fashion for each to vie with the other in protestations about their wonderful felicity, and sometimes they — FIB. I am truly glad to hear you are all better at Brookroyd. In the course of three or four weeks more, I expect to get leave to come to you. I certainly long to see you again; one circumstance reconciles me to this delay, the weather. I do not know whether it has been as bad with you as with us, but here for three weeks we have had little else than a succession of hurricanes.

In your last, you asked about Mr Sowden and Sir James. I fear Mr Sowden has little chance of the living; he had heard nothing more of it the last time he wrote to Arthur, and in a note he had from Sir James, yesterday, the subject is not mentioned.

You inquire too after Mrs Gaskell. She has not been here, and I think I should not like her to come now till summer. She is very busy with her story of 'North and South.'

I must make this note short that it may not be overweight. Arthur joins me in sincere good wishes for a happy Christmas, a many of them to you and yours. He is well, thank God, and so am I, and he is 'my dear boy' certainly, dearer now than he was six months ago. In three days we shall actually have been married that length of time! Good-bye, dear Nell. — Yours faithfully,

C. B. NICHOLLS.

933 (692). *To* ANN CLAPHAM (*née* NUSSEY).

HAWORTH, December 28th, 1854.

MY DEAR MRS CLAPHAM, — Ellen will have already received a note from me which partly answers your kind note of yesterday. I hope to visit Brookroyd about the beginning of February, but before that time, I do not think it likely I shall get off. Do not therefore postpone any engagements that may offer for yourself on my account. As to infection, I have not the slightest fear on my own account, but there are cases, as I need not remind you, where wives have just to put their own judgment on the shelf and do as they are bid.

I am truly glad to hear through you that Ellen has borne her late fatigues pretty well, for I know that much anxiety or over-exertion does not suit her, and she must have had a good deal of both lately.

It would be cheering to see your mother and Mercy both

down on Christmas Day. Give my love to Mercy. I hope she will be a very good girl, eat nourishing things and get strong as fast as she can. You do not mention your own health, but I trust you are now quite recovered from your late painful attack.

Tell Mr Clapham I have long been wanting to pay my bride-visit to Brookroyd and that I shall be sincerely glad to shake hands with him once more. I want to introduce him to my husband too, and I have an idea that they would not disagree, that is, if they had time to know each other, which, however, could scarcely be done in a day.

With love to your mother, Ellen, Mercy, and yourself.— Believe me, my dear Mrs Clapham, affectionately yours,

C. B. NICHOLLS.

934. *To* AMELIA TAYLOR (*née* RINGROSE).

[December, 1854].

DEAR AMELIA,—I would not be a false comforter if I knew it, but I certainly think from your report of this morning—a far better report than I had ventured to expect—you are justified in hoping that Joe will get better. His quiet pulse proves that there is no feverish hectic: from what you say I can gather evidence of no ailment but debility. Keep yourself as calm, as steadily cheerful—as reliant on a good issue as you can dear Amelia. If one single sign of mortal disease were apparent—I would not say this—I should just think it right that you should make up your mind to part with your husband, but nature tells us to hope while grounds for hope are seen—and I think that the fortitude which is voluntarily put in the place of *hope yet justifiable*—is an artificial kind of fortitude different from that strange and powerful feeling which accompanies true, inevitable despair. You would know that feeling when it came—and it is not to be met or made except in the awful exigency. We then feel that he is a fool who struggles—and are perfectly quiet.

I *think* Joe will not get better as long as the turmoil of this stormy damp weather lasts—exciting irritation in all weak points of weak frames—He will relapse probably every time a fresh hurricane brews—When a steady calm returns to the atmosphere and bracing frost sets in—I believe he will change for the better and perhaps in two months time he will be well enough to argue with all imaginable perversity and even to wear that expression seen in his daguerreotype Portrait.

I am glad you have got to Spen—Hurry yourself as little as you can and get what help you can. — Yours faithfully,

C. B. NICHOLLS.

935. Mrs GASKELL *to* CATHERINE WINKWORTH.

January 1st, 1855.

... Thanks for your note; and best and kindest wishes for you at the New Year; 'best wishes' leave *happiness* in the hands of God, to come or not at His good pleasure. I think 'best wishes' means to me a deeper sense of His being above all in His great peace and wisdom, and yet loving me with an individual love, tenderer than my mother's. Oh Katie, that fall has made me ill—a constant feeling of coming faintness which never comes and has done with it. . . .

Miss Brontë's letter is very nice; I wish she'd write to me — should I to her? Last time I wrote it was a sort of explanation of my way of looking at her Church (the Establishment) and religion; intended for her husband's benefit. She has never answered it. I'm glad she likes 'North and South'—I did not think Margaret was so *over* good. What would Miss B. say to Florence Nightingale I can't imagine! for there is intellect such as I never came in contact with before in woman!—only two in men— great beauty, and of her holy goodness, who is fit to speak? . . .

[E. C. GASKELL].

CHAPTER XXXIV

LAST DAYS

THE letters of the next few weeks tell their own sad story. Early in the new year Mr and Mrs Nicholls spent three days with Sir James Kay-Shuttleworth at Gawthorpe. Mrs Gaskell informs us that:

Soon after her return she was attacked by new sensations of perpetual nausea and ever-recurring faintness. After this state of things had lasted for some time she yielded to Mr Nicholls's wish that a doctor should be sent for. He came, and assigned a natural cause for her miserable indisposition—a little patience and all would go right. She, who was ever patient in illness, tried hard to bear up and bear on. But the dreadful sickness increased and increased, till the very sight of food occasioned nausea. 'A wren would have starved on what she ate during those last six weeks,' says one. Tabby's health had suddenly and utterly given way, and she died in this time of distress and anxiety respecting the last daughter of the house she had served so long. Martha tenderly waited on her mistress, and from time to time tried to cheer her with the thought of the baby that was coming. 'I dare say I shall be glad some day,' she would say; 'but I am so ill—so weary——' Then she took to her bed, too weak to sit up!

Charlotte Brontë died on March 31, 1855.

936 (693). *To* ELLEN NUSSEY.

HAWORTH, Jany 19th, 1855.

DEAR ELLEN,—Since our return from Gawthorpe we have had a Mr Bell—one of Arthur's cousins—staying with us—It was a great pleasure: I wish you could have seen him and made his acquaintance: a true gentleman by nature and cultivation is not after all an everyday thing.

As to the living of Habergham or Padiham—it appears the chance is doubtful at present for anybody. The present incumbent wishes to retract his resignation and declares his intention

of appointing a curate for two years. I fear Mr S. hardly produced a favourable impression; a strong wish was again expressed that Arthur could come—but *that* is out of the question.

I very much wish to come to Brookroyd—and I hoped to be
able to write with certainty and fix Wednesday the 31st Jany as
the day—but the fact is I am not sure whether I shall be well
enough to leave home. At present I should be a most tedious
visitor. My health has been really very good ever since my return from Ireland till about ten days ago, when the stomach
seemed quite suddenly to lose its tone—indigestion and continual faint sickness have been my portion ever since. Don't
conjecture—dear Nell—for it is too soon yet though I certainly
never before felt as I have done lately. But keep the matter
wholly to yourself—for I can come to no decided opinion at
present. I am rather mortified to lose my good looks and grow
thin as I am doing—just when I thought of going to Brookroyd.
Poor Joe Taylor! I still hope he will get better—but Amelia
writes grievous though not always clear or consistent accounts.
Dear Ellen I want to see you and I hope I shall see you well. My
love to all.—Yours faithfully,

C. B. NICHOLLS.

Thank Mr Clapham for his hospitable wish—but it would be
quite out of Arthur's power to stay more than one night or two
at the most.

937. *To* Dr INGHAM, Surgeon.

HAWORTH, Tuesday Afternoon.
[January, 1855].

DEAR SIR,—I regret to have to disturb you at a time when you
are suffering from illness, but I merely wish to ask if you can
send any medicine for our old servant Tabby.—Yours faithfully,

C. B. NICHOLLS.

938. *To* AMELIA TAYLOR (*née* RINGROSE).

[January 21st, 1855].

DEAR AMELIA,—I have long wanted to see Joe, and both
Arthur and Papa have of their own accord suggested my going
over for the purpose—but I know quite well, from the simple

directness of your character, that whenever you thought a visit advisable you would say so—and I knew also by sorrowful experience that visits even from dear friends are rarely advisable during serious sickness. Ellen Nussey used, with a good intention enough, to volunteer her presence when my sisters were ill; it was impossible for me to do with her—except during the last fortnight when we went from home—and an acquaintance was absolutely indispensable to witness and help in the event which I knew too well was about to befall amongst total strangers.

I think if all be well, of going to Brookroyd in the course of a fortnight—My stay will not be very long there—and I can spend one night and one day with you on my road home—if you then think it right that I should do so. This arrangement will obviate any awkwardness of the kind to which you allude about E. N.

It is well indeed that you are sustained so far with both husband and child to nurse; but affection has its peculiar strength, and sorrow is sometimes its own stay. There is one comfort in the nature of poor little Tim's ailment—I hope it may ultimately do good—external eruption sometimes relieves the system of irritation for a long time.

As the year turns I still believe and hope Joe will gather strength.

When I go to Brookroyd I hope to be better than I am now— till about a fortnight since I have scarcely had an ailment since I was married—but latterly my health has been a good deal disordered—only however by indigestion—loss of appetite and such like annoyances.

Papa continues much better—and Arthur is well and flourishing. His cousin has been here and the visit was a real treat—He is a cultivated, thoroughly educated man with a mind stored with information gathered from books and travel—and what is far rarer—with the art of conversing appropriately and quietly and never pushing his superiority upon you. His name is James Adamson Bell and he is a clergyman.

It is an hourly happiness to me dear Amelia to see how well Arthur and my Father get on together now—there has never been a misunderstanding or wrong word.

I wish you continued strength, and I hope comfort may soon come to you dear A.—Faithfully yours,

                                        C. B. NICHOLLS.

939 (694). *To* ELLEN NUSSEY.

HAWORTH, KEIGHLEY,
Jany 23rd, 1855.

DEAR MISS NUSSEY,—As Charlotte is not well, she requests me to answer your letter, and say that it will not be possible for her to visit you earlier than the 31st. I should say that unless she improve very rapidly, it will not be advisable for her to leave home even then.

She will be obliged to you to keep 2 lbs of honey for her—she does not know of a customer for the Queens of Scotland. The remainder of your note she will answer, I hope, soon.—Believe me, sincerely yours,

A. B. NICHOLLS.

940 (695). *To* ELLEN NUSSEY.

HAWORTH, KEIGHLEY,
Jany 29th, 1855.

DEAR MISS NUSSEY,—As Charlotte continues unwell I again write a line for her—She has been confined to bed for some days. I have sent for Dr MacTurk[1] to-day, as I wish to have better advice than Haworth affords. Under these circumstances you will see that it is quite impossible to name any date for our visit to you.

Charlotte sends her love, and says she will write as soon as she is able.—Believe me, faithfully yours,

A. B. NICHOLLS.

941 (696). *To* ELLEN NUSSEY.

HAWORTH, Feby 1st, 1855.

DEAR MISS NUSSEY,—Dr MacTurk saw Charlotte on Tuesday. His opinion was that her illness would be of some duration, but that there was no immediate danger. I trust therefore that in a few weeks she will be well again.

We were very much concerned to hear of your sister's continued illness, both on your account and hers—Charlotte begs

[1] Dr MacTurk was the most able physician in Bradford at this period.

you will write a line soon to let her know how Miss Mercy gets on—and she is sure she can trust you to excuse her from answering until she is able.—Believe me, Yrs faithfully,

A. B. NICHOLLS.

942 (697). *To* ELLEN NUSSEY.

HAWORTH, Feb. 14th, 1855.

DEAR MISS NUSSEY,—It is difficult to write to friends about my wife's illness, as its cause is yet uncertain—at present she is completely prostrated with weakness and sickness and frequent fever—all may turn out well in the end, and I hope it will; if you saw her you would perceive that she can maintain no correspondence at present.

She thinks of you and sympathizes with you in your present affliction, and longed much to hear from you.—Believe me, Sincerely yrs.

A. B. NICHOLLS.

P. S. Till lately Mr Brontë was very [well], he is now however suffering from bronchial irritation.

There are a few more letters, all written in faint pencil, from the bed of sickness:

943 (698). *To* LÆTITIA WHEELWRIGHT.

February 15th, 1855.

DEAR LÆTITIA,—A few lines of acknowledgment your letter *shall* have, whether well or ill. At present I am confined to my bed with illness, and have been so for 3 weeks. Up to this period, since my marriage, I have had excellent health—my husband and I live at home with my Father—of course I could not leave *him*. He is pretty well—better than last summer. No kinder, better husband than mine, it seems to me, can there be in the world. I do not want now for kind companionship in health and the tenderest nursing in sickness.

Deeply I sympathise in all you tell me about Dr Wheelwright—and your excellent Mamma's anxiety—I trust he will not risk another operation. I cannot write more now for I am much reduced and very weak—God bless you all!—Yours affectionately,

C. B. NICHOLLS.

944 (699). *To* ELLEN NUSSEY.

HAWORTH [February 21st, 1855].

MY DEAR ELLEN,—I must write one line out of my weary bed. The news of Mercy's probable recovery came like a ray of joy to me. I am not going to talk about my sufferings, it would be useless and painful—I want to give you an assurance which I know will comfort you—and that is that I find my husband the tenderest nurse, the kindest support—the best earthly comfort that ever woman had. His patience never fails, and it is tried by sad days and broken nights. Write and tell me about Mrs Hewitt's case, how long she was ill and in what way.

Papa, thank God! is better. Our poor old Tabby is *dead* and *buried*.[1] Give my truest love to Miss Wooler. May God comfort and help you.

C. B. NICHOLLS.

945 (700). *To* ELLEN NUSSEY.

[February, 1855].

MY DEAR ELLEN,—Thank you very much for Mrs Hewitt's sensible clear letter. Thank her too. In much, her case was wonderfully like mine—but I am reduced to greater weakness—the skeleton emaciation is the same, &c., &c., &c. I cannot talk—even to my dear, patient, constant Arthur, I can say but few words at once.

These last two days I have been somewhat better and have taken some beef-tea—spoonsful of wine and water—a mouthful of light pudding at different times.

Dear Ellen, I realise full well what you have gone through, and will have to go through with poor Mercy—O may you continue to be supported and not sink! Sickness here has been terribly rife. Papa is well now. Kindest regards to Mr and Mrs C., your mother, Mercy.

Write when you can.—Yours,

C. B. NICHOLLS.

[1] Tabitha Aykroyd died on 17th February, 1855, aged 84 years.

946. *To* AMELIA TAYLOR (*née* RINGROSE).

[February, 1855].

DEAR AMELIA, — Let me speak the plain truth — my sufferings
are very great — my nights indescribable — sickness with scarce a
reprieve — I strain until what I vomit is mixed with blood. Medicine I have quite discontinued. If you can send me anything that
will do good — *do*.

As to my husband — my heart is knit to him — he is so tender,
so good, helpful, patient.

Poor Joe! long has he to suffer. May God soon send him, you,
all of us health, strength — comfort.

C. B. NICHOLLS.

947. *To* AMELIA TAYLOR (*née* RINGROSE).

[February, 1855].

DEAR AMELIA, — I'll try to write a line myself.

The medicines produced no perceptible effect on me but I
thank you for them all the same.

I would not let Arthur write to Dr Hemingway — I know it
would be wholly useless.

For 2 days I have been something better — owing to the
milder weather.

We all grieve that there is no better news of Joe. Oh for happier times! My little Grandchild[1] — when shall I see her again?
God bless you!

C. B. NICHOLLS.

Write when you can. I think of you all very much.

948 (701). *To* ELLEN NUSSEY.

HAWORTH, KEIGHLEY,
March 15th, 1855.

MY DEAR MISS NUSSEY, — Be assured you have all our sympathies in the awful and painful event which has just befallen
your household. I broke the sad news to Charlotte as gently as I
could but it was a great shock. She is much concerned both on

---

[1] 'Tim,' the little daughter of Joseph and Amelia Taylor, who called Mrs Nicholls
'granny.'

your account, and that of poor Mrs Clapham, and also at the thought that she shall never see again one whom she greatly respected.

These seem troubled times, my dear Miss Nussey. May God support you through them.

Charlotte was better last week — This week I am sorry to say she has again suffered much. The bad weather has thrown her back. You do not mention Miss Mercy, but we should be glad to know how she is getting on, when you can write again. — Believe me, Yrs very sincerely,

A. B. NICHOLLS.

949. *To* ELLEN NUSSEY, *Brookroyd, Birstall.*

HAWORTH, nr KEIGHLEY,
March 30th, 1855.

MY DEAR MADAM, — We are all in great trouble, and Mr Nicholls so much so that he is not so sufficiently strong and composed as to be able to write. I therefore devote a few moments to tell you that my dear Daughter is very ill, and apparently on the verge of the grave. If she could speak she would no doubt dictate to us while answering your kind letter, but we are left to ourselves to give what answer we can. The Doctors have no hope of her case, and fondly as we a long time cherished hope that hope is now gone, and we have only to look forward to the solemn event with prayer to God that He will give us grace and strength sufficient unto our day.

Will you be so kind as to write to Miss Wooler, and Mrs Joe Taylor, and inform them that we requested you to do so, telling them of our present condition? — Ever truly and respectfully yours,

P. BRONTË.

950 (702). *To* ELLEN NUSSEY.

HAWORTH, March 31st, 1855.

DEAR MISS NUSSEY, — Mr Brontë's letter would prepare you for the sad intelligence I have to communicate. Our dear Charlotte is no more. She died last night of exhaustion. For the last two or three weeks we had become very uneasy about her, but it

was not until Sunday evening that it became apparent that her
sojourn with us was likely to be short. We intend to bury her on
Wednesday morning.—Believe me, sincerely yours,

A. B. Nicholls.

Mrs Gaskell is our only other authority for the last sad days.

Long days and longer nights went by; still the same relentless
nausea and faintness, and still borne on in patient trust. About
the third week in March there was a change; a low, wandering
delirium came on; and in it she begged constantly for food and
even for stimulants. She swallowed eagerly now; but it was too
late. Wakening for an instant from this stupor of intelligence she
saw her husband's woe-worn face, and caught the sound of
some murmured words of prayer that God would spare her.
'Oh!' she whispered forth, 'I am not going to die, am I? He will
not separate us, we have been so happy.'

Early on Saturday morning, March 31st, the solemn tolling of
Haworth church bell spoke forth the fact of her death to the
villagers who had known her from a child, and whose hearts
shivered within them as they thought of the two sitting desolate
and alone in the old grey house.

951 (703). *To* Mary Hewitt (*née* Gorham)?[1]

Haworth Parsonage, Keighley,
Apl 11th, 1855.

My dear Madam,—Mr Brontë and myself thank you very
sincerely for your sympathy with us in our sad bereavement—
our loss is indeed great—the loss of one as good as she was
gifted. Altho' she had been ill from the beginning of January, it
was only a few days previous to her death that we became
alarmed for her safety—On [the] whole she had not much
suffering—she spoke little during the last few days, but continued quite conscious. Mr Brontë is pretty well, tho' of course
the present trial is a great shock to him. I return your letter as I
do not know the address. Again thanking you for your sympathy.—I am, dear Madam, Yrs faithfully,

A. B. Nicholls.

[1]Under cover to Ellen Nussey.

952. *To* ELLEN NUSSEY.

HAWORTH, KEIGHLEY,
Apl 16th, 1855.

DEAR MISS NUSSEY, — We thank you for your kind enquiries after our health. We are, thank God, no worse than when you left us. Will you be so kind as to thank your Mother and sister on our behalf for their sympathy for us in our affliction.

I trust that Miss Wooler is better — I was glad to hear that Mr Taylor was not so bad as was expected. I understand he continues to be rather better. — Believe me, Yrs sincerely,

A. B. NICHOLLS.

953. *To* GEORGE SMITH.

HAWORTH, near KEIGHLEY,
April 20th, 1855.

MY DEAR SIR, — I thank you for your kind sympathy. Having heard my dear daughter speak so much about you and your family, your letter seemed to be one from an old friend. Her husband's sorrow and mine is indeed very great. We mourn the loss of one whose like we hope not ever to see again, and, as you justly state, we do not mourn alone. That you may never experimently know sorrow such as ours, and that when trouble does come you may receive due aid from Heaven, is the sincere wish and ardent prayer of — Yours very respectfully and truly,

P. BRONTË.

One of the noblest tributes to Charlotte Brontë was written by Harriet Martineau:[1]

---

[1] In the *Daily News*, April, 1855.

DEATH OF CURRER BELL

By HARRIET MARTINEAU

'Currer Bell' is dead! The early death of the large family of whom she was the sole survivor prepared all who knew the circumstances to expect the loss of this gifted creature at any time: but not the less deep will be the grief of society that her genius will yield us nothing more. We have three works from her pen which will hold their place in the literature of our country; and, but for her frail health, there might have been three times three, —for she was under forty—and her genius was not of an exhaustible kind. If it had been exhaustible, it would have been exhausted some time since. She had every inducement that could have availed with one less high-minded to publish two or three novels a year. Fame waited upon all she did; and she might have enriched herself by very slight exertion: but her steady conviction was that the publication of a book is a solemn act of conscience—in the case of a novel as much as any other kind of book. She was not fond of speaking of herself and her conscience; but she now and then uttered to her very few friends things which may, alas! be told now, without fear of hurting her sensitive nature; things which ought to be told in her honour. Among these sayings was one which explains the long interval between her works. She said that she thought every serious delineation of life ought to be the product of personal experience and observation of a normal, and not of a forced or special kind. 'I have not accumulated, since I published "Shirley",' she said, 'what makes it needful for me to speak again, and, till I do, may God give me grace to be dumb!' She had a conscientiousness which could not be relaxed by praise or even sympathy—dear as sympathy was to her sensitive nature. She had no vanity which praise could aggravate or censure mortify. She calmly read all adverse reviews of her books, for the sake of instruction; and when she could not recognise the aptness of criticism, she was more puzzled than hurt or angry. The common flatteries which wait upon literary success she quizzed with a charming grace; and any occasional severity, such as literary women are favoured with at the beginning of their course, she accepted with a humility which was full of dignity and charm. From her feeble constitution of body, her sufferings by the death of her whole family, and the secluded and monotonous life she led, she became morbidly sensitive in some respects; but in her high vocation, she had, in addition to the deep intuitions of a gifted woman, the strength of a man, the patience of a hero, and the conscientiousness of a saint. In the points in which women are usually most weak—in regard to opinion, to appreciation, to applause, —her moral strength fell not a whit behind the intellectual force manifested in her works. Though passion occupies too prominent a place in her pictures of life, though women have to complain that she represents love as the whole and sole concern of their lives, and though governesses especially have reason to remonstrate, and do remonstrate, that their share of human conflict is laid open somewhat rudely and inconsiderately and sweepingly to social observation, it is a true social blessing that we have had a female writer who has discountenanced sentimentalism and feeble egotism with such practical force as is apparent in the works of Currer Bell. Her heroines love too readily, too vehemently, and sometimes after a fashion which their female readers may resent; but they do their duty through everything, and are healthy in action, however morbid in passion.

How admirable this strength is—how wonderful this force of integrity—can hardly be understood by any but the few who know the story of this remarkable woman's life. The account of the school in 'Jane Eyre' is only too true. The 'Helen' of that tale is—not precisely the eldest sister, who died there—but more like her than any other person. She is that sister, 'with a difference.' Another sister died at home soon after leaving school, and in consequence of its hardships; and 'Currer Bell' (Charlotte Brontë) was never free while there (for a year and a half) from the gnawing sensation or consequent feebleness of downright hunger; and she never grew an inch from that time. She was the smallest of women; and it was that school which stunted her growth. As she tells us in 'Jane Eyre', the visitation of an epidemic caused a total change and radical reform in the establishment, which was even removed to another site. But the reform came too late to reverse the destiny of the doomed family of the Brontës.

These wonderful girls were the daughters of a clergyman who, now very aged and infirm, survives his wife and all his many children. The name Brontë (an abbreviation of Bronterre) is Irish and very ancient. The mother died many years ago, and several of her children. When the reading world began to have an interest in their existence, there were three sisters and a brother living with their father at Haworth, near Keighley, in Yorkshire. The girls had been out as governesses—Charlotte, at Brussels, as is no secret to the readers of 'Villette.' They rejoiced to meet again at home Charlotte, Emily, and Ann[1] ('Currer,' 'Ellis,' and 'Acton'). In her obituary notice of her two sisters 'Currer' reveals something of their process of authorship, and their experience of failure and success. How terrible some of their experience of life was, in the midst of the domestic freedom and indulgence afforded them by their studious father, may be seen by the fearful representations of masculine nature and character found in the novels and tales of Emily and Ann. They considered it their duty, they told us, to present life as they knew it; and they gave us 'Wuthering Heights,' and 'The Tenant of Wildfell Hall.' Such an experience as this indicates is really perplexing to English people in general; and all that we have to do with it is to bear it in mind when disposed to pass criticism on the coarseness which, to a certain degree, pervades the works of all the sisters, and the repulsiveness which makes the tales by Emily and Ann really horrible to people who have not iron nerves.

'Jane Eyre' was naturally and universally supposed to be Charlotte herself; but she always denied it, calmly, cheerfully, and with the obvious sincerity which characterised all she said. She declared that there was no more ground for the assertion than this. She once told her sisters that they were wrong—even morally wrong—in making their heroines beautiful, as a matter of course. They replied that it was impossible to make a heroine interesting on other terms. Her answer was, 'I will prove to you that you are wrong. I will show you a heroine as small and as plain as myself who shall be as interesting as any of yours.' 'Hence, "Jane Eyre",' said she in telling the anecdote; 'but she is not myself, any further than that.' As the work went on the interest deepened to the writer. When she came to 'Thornfield' she could not stop. Being short-sighted to excess, she wrote in little square paper books, held close to her eyes, and (the first copy) in pencil. On she went, writing incessantly for three weeks; by which time she had carried her heroine away from Thornfield,

[1]Anne is meant.

and was herself in a fever, which compelled her to pause. The rest was written with less vehemence, and more anxious care. The world adds, with less vigour and interest. She could gratify her singular reserve in regard to the publication of this remarkable book. We all remember how long it was before we could learn who wrote it, and any particulars of the writer, when the name was revealed. She was living among the wild Yorkshire hills, with a father who was too much absorbed in his studies to notice her occupations, in a place where newspapers were never seen (or where she never saw any), and in a house where the servants knew nothing about books, manuscripts, proofs, or the post. When she told her secret to her father, she carried her book in one hand, and an adverse review in the other, to save his simple and unworldly mind from rash expectations of a fame and fortune which she was determined should never be the aims of her life. That we have had only two novels since shows how deeply grounded was this resolve.

'Shirley' was conceived and wrought out in the midst of fearful domestic griefs. Her only brother, a young man of once splendid promise which was early blighted, and both her remaining sisters, died in one year. There was something inexpressibly affecting in the aspect of the frail little creature who had done such wonderful things, and who was able to bear up, with so bright an eye and so composed a countenance, under such a weight of sorrow, and such a prospect of solitude. In her deep mourning dress (neat as a quaker's), with her beautiful hair, smooth and brown, her fine eyes blazing with meaning, and her sensible face indicating a habit of self-control, if not of silence, she seemed a perfect household image—irresistibly recalling Wordsworth's description of that domestic treasure. And she was this. She was as able at the needle as the pen. The household knew the excellence of her cookery before they heard of that of her books. In so utter a seclusion as she lived in—in those dreary wilds, where she was not strong enough to roam over the hills,[1] in that retreat where her studious father rarely broke the silence—and there was no one else to do it; in that for-

---

[1]On reading this a friend wrote to Mrs Gaskell: 'They are mistaken in saying she was too weak to roam the hills for the benefit of the air. I do not think any one, certainly not any woman, in this locality, went so much on the moors as she did, when the weather permitted.' (See *The Life of Charlotte Brontë*, by Mrs E. C. Gaskell, Haworth Edition, p. 485.)

lorn house, planted on the very clay of the churchyard, where the graves of her sisters were before her window; in such a living sepulchre her mind could not prey upon itself; and how it did suffer, we see in the more painful portions of her last novel — 'Villette.' She said, with a change in her steady countenance, that she should feel very lonely when her aged father died. But she formed new ties after that. She married; and it is the old father who survives to mourn her. He knows, to his comfort, that it is not for long. Others now mourn her, in a domestic sense; and, as for the public, there can be no doubt that a pang will be felt in the midst of the strongest interests of the day, through the length and breadth of the land, and in the very heart of Germany (where her works are singularly appreciated), France, and America, that the 'Currer Bell,' who so lately stole a shadow into the field of contemporary literature had already become a shadow again — vanishing from our view, and henceforth haunting only the memory of the multitude whose expectation was fixed upon her.

CURRER BELL[1]

We recently quoted from the *Daily News* an interesting article on this gifted authoress, or rather on the person known to the reading public by that pseudonym. We have since learnt some particulars respecting her father's family which will be more especially interesting to our readers, when they learn, probably for the first time, that they were natives of the county Down. The father of the authoress was Mr Patrick Prunty, of the parish of Ahaderg, near Loughbrickland. His parents were of humble origin, but their large family were remarkable for physical strength and personal beauty. The natural quickness and intelligence of Patrick Prunty attracted the attention of the Rev. Mr Tighe, rector of Drumgooland parish, who gave him a good education in England, and finally procured him a curacy in   . In his new sphere he was not unmindful of the family claims, for he settled £20 per annum on his mother. The writer of the article in the *Daily News*, in giving the real name of the authoress as Bronti[2], derives it from Bronterre, and declares that the family was of ancient Irish extraction. The latter statement

---

[1]From the *Belfast Mercury*, April, 1855.   [2]Bronti and Bronte are here printed without the diaeresis.

may or may not be the fact, but we have excellent authority for mentioning that Prunty was the name which the family bore in their own neighbourhood of the county Down. The patron of Mr Patrick Prunty, disliking the name, requested him to take that of Bronte, from the fanciful idea that the Greek word *Bronte* would appositely signify the singular quickness and intelligence of his intellect. After Mr Bronte had assumed the duties of his clerical office, he married, and the issue of that marriage were the three talented women who delighted the reading world under the titles of Currer, Acton, and Ellis Bell. Of this triad, Currer was the 'bright, particular star,' and her fictitious title of Currer Bell was not less revered by her readers, than was her real name of Charlotte Bronte by her aged relatives in the county Down, to whom she presented very lately the sum of £120, with copies of her works.

CHAPTER XXXV

MRS GASKELL'S BIOGRAPHY

THERE have been few biographies that have secured a more widespread interest than the *Life of Charlotte Brontë* by Mrs Gaskell. It has held a position of singular popularity, and while biography after biography has come and gone, it still commands a place side by side with Boswell's *Johnson* and Lockhart's *Scott*. There were obvious reasons for this success. Mrs Gaskell was herself a popular novelist, who commanded a very wide audience, and *Cranford*, at least, has taken a place among the classics of our literature. She brought to bear upon the biography of Charlotte Brontë some of those literary gifts which made the charm of her eight volumes of romance. And these gifts were employed upon a romance of real life, not less fascinating than anything which imagination could have furnished. Charlotte Brontë's success as an author turned the eyes of the world upon her. Thackeray had sent her his *Vanity Fair* before he knew her name or sex, and Thackeray did not send many inscribed copies of his books even to successful authors. Speculation concerning the author of *Jane Eyre* was sufficiently rife during those seven sad years of literary renown to make a biography imperative when death came to Charlotte Brontë in 1855. All the world had heard something of the three marvellous sisters, daughters of a poor parson in Yorkshire, going one after another to their death with such melancholy swiftness, but leaving—two of them, at least—imperishable work behind them. The old father and the bereaved husband read the confused eulogy and criticism, sometimes with a sad pleasure at the praise, oftener with a sadder pain at the grotesque inaccuracy. Small wonder that it became impressed upon Mr Brontë's mind that an authoritative biography was desirable. His son-in-law, Mr Arthur Bell Nicholls, who lived with him in the Haworth parsonage during the six weary years which succeeded Mrs Nicholls's death, was not so readily won to the unveiling of his wife's inner life; and although we, who read Mrs Gaskell's *Memoir*, have every reason to be thankful for Mr Brontë's decision, peace of mind would undoubtedly have been more assured to Charlotte Brontë's surviving relatives had the most rigid silence been maintained. The book, when it appeared in 1857, gave infinite pain to a number of people, including Mr Brontë and Mr Nicholls; and Mrs Gaskell's subsequent experiences had the effect of persuading her that all biographical literature was intolerable and undesirable.

She would seem to have given instructions that no biography of herself should be written.

A journey in the footsteps, as it were, of Mrs Gaskell reveals to us the remarkable conscientiousness with which she set about her task. It would have been possible, with so much fame behind her, to have secured an equal success, and certainly an equal pecuniary reward, had she merely written a brief monograph with such material as was voluntarily placed in her hands. Mrs Gaskell possessed a higher ideal of a biographer's duties. She spared no pains to find out the facts; she visited nearly every spot associated with the name of Charlotte Brontë—Thornton, Haworth, Cowan Bridge, Birstall, Brussels—and she wrote countless letters to the friends of Charlotte Brontë's earlier days.

But why, it may be asked, was Mrs Gaskell selected as biographer? The choice was made by Mr Brontë, and it would have been difficult to have named any other practised writer with equal qualifications. When Mr Brontë had once decided that there should be an authoritative biography—and he alone was active in the matter—there could be but little doubt upon whom the task would fall. Among all the friends whom fame had brought to Charlotte, Mrs Gaskell stood prominent for her literary gifts and her large-hearted sympathy. She had made the acquaintance of Miss Brontë when the latter was on a visit to Sir James Kay-Shuttleworth, in 1850; and a letter from Charlotte to her father, and others to Mr W. S. Williams, which will be found in due chronological order, indicate the beginning of a friendship which was to leave so striking a record in literary history.

But the friendship, which commenced so late in Charlotte Brontë's life, never reached the stage of downright intimacy. Of this there is abundant evidence in the biography; and Mrs Gaskell was forced to rely upon the correspondence of older friends of Charlotte's. Mr George Smith, the head of the firm of Smith and Elder, furnished some twenty letters. Mr W. S. Williams, to whom is due the credit of 'discovering' the author of *Jane Eyre*, lent others; and another member of Messrs Smith and Elder's staff, Mr James Taylor, furnished half-a-dozen more; but the best help came from another quarter.

Of the two schoolfellows with whom Charlotte Brontë regularly corresponded from childhood till death, Mary Taylor and Ellen Nussey, the former had destroyed nearly every letter; and thus it came about that by far the larger part of the correspondence in Mrs Gaskell's biography was addressed to Miss Ellen Nussey, now as 'My dearest Nell,' now simply as 'E.' The correspondence which refers to the biography, relates how, in accordance with a request from Mr Brontë, Mrs Gaskell undertook to write the work, and went over to Haworth. There she made the acquaintance of Mr Nicholls for the first time. She told Mr Brontë how much she felt the difficulty of the task she had undertaken. Nevertheless, she sincerely desired to make his daughter's character known to all who took a deep interest in her writings. Both Mr Brontë and Mr Nicholls agreed to help to the utmost, although Mrs Gaskell was struck by the fact that it was Mr Nicholls, and not Mr Brontë, who was more intellectually alive to the attraction which such a book would have for the public. His feelings were opposed to any biography at all; but he had yielded to Mr Brontë's 'impetuous wish,' and he brought down all the materials he could find, in the shape of about a dozen letters. Mr Nicholls, moreover, told Mrs Gaskell that Miss Nussey was the person of all others to apply to; that she had been the friend of his wife ever since Charlotte was fifteen, and that he was writing to Miss Nussey to beg her to let Mrs Gaskell see some of the correspondence.

From the letters written shortly after Charlotte's death it appears that it was really a suggestion from Miss Nussey that produced the application to Mrs Gaskell. She desired that some attempt should be made to furnish a biography of her friend — if only to set at rest, once and for all, the speculations of the gossiping community with whom Charlotte Brontë's personality was still shrouded in mystery.

954. *To* the REV. A. B. NICHOLLS.

BROOKROYD, June 6th, 1855.

DEAR MR NICHOLLS,—I have been much hurt and pained by the perusal of an article in 'Sharpe' for this month, entitled 'A Few Words about "Jane Eyre."' You will be certain to see the article, and I am sure both you and Mr Brontë will feel acutely the misrepresentations and the malignant spirit which characterises it. Will you suffer the article to pass current without any refutations? The writer merits the contempt of silence, but there will be readers and believers. Shall such be left to imbibe a tissue of malignant falsehoods, or shall an attempt be made to do justice to one who so highly deserved justice, whose very name those who best knew her but speak with reverence and affection? Should not her aged father be defended from the reproach the writer coarsely attempts to bring upon him?

I wish Mrs Gaskell, who is every way capable, would undertake a reply, and would give a sound castigation to the writer. Her personal acquaintance with Haworth, the Parsonage, and its inmates, fits her for the task, and if on other subjects she lacked information I would gladly supply her with facts sufficient to set aside much that is asserted, if you yourself are not provided with all the information that is needed on the subjects produced. Will you ask Mrs Gaskell to undertake this just and honourable defence? I think she would do it gladly. She valued dear Charlotte, and such an act of friendship, performed with her ability and power, could only add to the laurels she has already won. I hope you and Mr Brontë are well. My kind regards to both.— Believe me, yours sincerely,

E. NUSSEY.

955. *To* ELLEN NUSSEY.

HAWORTH, June 11th, 1855.

DEAR MISS NUSSEY,—We had not seen the article in 'Sharpe,' and very possibly should not, if you had not directed our attention to it. We ordered a copy, and have now read the 'Few Words about "Jane Eyre."' The writer has certainly made many mistakes, but apparently not from any unkind motive, as he professes to be an admirer of Charlotte's works, pays a just tribute

to her genius, and in common with thousands deplores her untimely death. His design seems rather to be to gratify the curiosity of the multitude in reference to one who had made such a
sensation in the literary world. But even if the article had been of
a less harmless character, we should not have felt inclined to
take any notice of it, as by doing so we should have given it an
importance which it would not otherwise have obtained. Charlotte herself would have acted thus; and her character stands too
high to be injured by the statements in a magazine of small circulation and little influence — statements which the writer prefaces
with the remark that he does not vouch for their accuracy. The
many laudatory notices of Charlotte and her works which appeared since her death may well make us indifferent to the detractions
of a few envious or malignant persons, as there ever will be such.

The remarks respecting Mr Brontë excited in him only amusement — indeed, I have not seen him laugh as much for some
months as he did while I was reading the article to him. We are
both well in health, but lonely and desolate.

Mr Brontë unites with me in kind regards. — Yours sincerely,

A. B. NICHOLLS.

956. *To* MRS GASKELL.

HAWORTH, near KEIGHLEY,
July 16th, 1855.

MY DEAR MADAM, — Finding that a great many scribblers, as
well as some clever and truthful writers, have published articles
in newspapers and tracts respecting my dear daughter Charlotte
since her death, and seeing that many things that have been
stated are untrue, but more false; and having reason to think that
some may venture to write her life who will be ill-qualified for
the undertaking, I can see no better plan under the circumstances than to apply to some established author to write a brief
account of her life and to make some remarks on her works. You
seem to me to be the best qualified for doing what I wish should
be done. If, therefore, you will be so kind as to publish a long or
short account of her life and works, just as you may deem expedient and proper, Mr Nicholls and I will give you such information as you may require.

I should expect and request that you would affix your name,
so that the work might obtain a wide circulation and be handed

down to the latest times. Whatever profits might arise from the sale would, of course, belong to you. You are the first to whom I have applied. Mr Nicholls approves of the step I have taken, and could my daughter speak from the tomb I feel certain she would laud our choice.

Give my respectful regards to Mr Gaskell and your family, and—Believe me, my dear Madam, Yours very respectfully and truly,

P. Brontë.

Mrs Gaskell visited Haworth Parsonage on July 23rd.

957. *To* Ellen Nussey.

Haworth, Keighley,
July 24, 1855.

Dear Miss Nussey,—Some other erroneous notices of Charlotte having appeared, Mr Brontë has deemed it advisable that some authentic statement should be put forth. He has therefore adopted your suggestion and applied to Mrs Gaskell who has undertaken to write a life of Charlotte. Mrs Gaskell came over yesterday and spent a few hours with us. The greatest difficulty seems to be in obtaining materials to shew the development of Charlotte's character. For this reason Mrs G. is anxious to see any of her letters,—Especially those of any early date—I think I understood you to say that you had some—if so we should feel obliged by your letting us have any that you may think proper—not for publication, but merely to give the writer an insight into her mode of thought—of course they will be returned after a little time.

I confess that the course most consonant with my own feelings would be to take no steps in the matter, but I do not think it right to offer any opposition to Mr Brontë's wishes. We have the same object in view, but should differ in our mode of proceeding. Mr Brontë has not been very well—Excitement on Sunday (our rush-bearing) and Mrs Gaskell's visit yesterday have been rather much for him.—Believe me, Sincerely yrs,

A. B. Nicholls.

958. *To* ELLEN NUSSEY.

PLYMOUTH GROVE, MANCHESTER,
July 24th, 1855.

. . . I don't know if you have heard of Mr Brontë's request to me that I would write the life of his daughter, Mrs Nicholls, who was, I am well aware, your dear and long-tried friend. But if you have been informed of this wish of Mr Brontë's you will not be surprised to hear that I went over to Haworth yesterday to see him and make the acquaintance of Mr Nicholls. I told Mr Brontë how much I felt the difficulty of the task I had undertaken, yet how much I wished to do it well, and make his daughter's most unusual character (as taken separately from her genius) known to those who from their deep interest and admiration of her writings would naturally, if her life was to be written, expect to be informed as to the circumstances which made her what she was. Both he and Mr Nicholls agreed to this, Mr Brontë not perceiving the full extent of the great interest in her personal history felt by strangers, but desirous above all things that her life should be written, and written by me. (His last words were, 'No quailing, Mrs Gaskell. No drawing back.')

Mr Nicholls was far more aware of the kind of particulars which people would look for, and saw how they had snatched at every gossiping account of her, and how desirable it was to have a full and authorized history of her life, if it were done at all. His feeling was against its being written, but he yielded to Mr Brontë's impetuous wish; and brought me down all the materials he could furnish me with, in the shape of about a dozen letters, addressed principally to her sister Emily, one or two to her father and her brother, and one to her aunt. The dates extend from 1839 to 1843. But Mr Nicholls said that he thought that you were the person of all others to apply to; that you had been a friend of his wife's ever since she was 15; and that he would write to you to-day, and ask if you would allow us to see as much of her correspondence with you as you might feel inclined to trust me with. But recalling since how often she had spoken of you to me, I should like very much to make your personal acquaintance, if you will allow me; and if agreeable to you I would come over from Manchester on either Friday, July 27th, or Saturday, July 28th next, whichever was most convenient to you, by the train that arrives at Birstall at ¾ past 10 in the morning. I do not know if your old schoolmistress, Miss Wooler, is yet alive and living in Birstall, but if so I shall endeavour to see her, and Mr and Mrs Taylor....

E. C. GASKELL.

959. *To* MRS GASKELL, *Manchester.*

ILKLEY, July 26th, 1855.

MY DEAR MADAM,—Owing to my absence from home your letter has only just reached me. I had not heard of Mr Brontë's request, but I am most heartily glad that he has made it. A letter from Mr Nicholls was forwarded along with yours, which I opened first, and was thus prepared for your communication, the subject of which is of the deepest interest to me. I will do everything in my power to aid the righteous work you have undertaken, but I feel my powers very limited, and apprehend that you may experience some disappointment that I cannot contribute more largely the information which you desire. I possess a great many letters (for I have destroyed but a small portion of the correspondence), but I fear the early letters are not such as to unfold the character of the writer except in a few points. You perhaps may discover more than is apparent to me. You will read them with a purpose—I perused them only with interests of affection. I will immediately look over the correspondence, and I promise to let you see all that I can confide to your friendly custody. I regret that my absence from home should have made it impossible for me to have the pleasure of seeing you at Brookroyd at the time you propose. I am engaged to stay here till Monday week, and shall be happy to see you any day you name after that date, or, if more convenient to you to come Friday or Saturday in next week, I will gladly return in time to give you the meeting. I am staying with our school-mistress, Miss Wooler, in this place. I wish her very much to give me leave to ask you here, but she does not yield to my wishes; it would have been pleasanter to me to talk with you among these hills than sitting in my home and thinking of one who had so often been present there.—I am, my dear madam, yours sincerely,

ELLEN NUSSEY.

Vol. IV   o

960. *To* MRS GASKELL.

HAWORTH, August 27th, 1855.

... The people here are poor, but whether rich or poor they have always been not only civil to me and mine but friendly when an opportunity offered for showing their disposition. On a solemn occasion I saw this clearly exhibited. My children generally, and my dear daughter Charlotte in particular, were both kind, liberal and affable with the inhabitants. A thorough sense of this proceeding was not wanting on the death of each of them—and when the last death took place, when my dear Charlotte was no more, both rich and poor throughout the village and the neighbourhood, both publicly and privately, gave sure proofs of genuine sorrow. The poor have often been accused of ingratitude—I think wrongfully. There was no instance of this when my dear Charlotte died. A case or two I might mention as an illustration of what I say. One moral and amiable girl who had been deceived and deserted by a deceitful man who had promised her marriage, when she heard of my daughter's hopeless illness, without our knowing it at the time, she spent a week of sleepless distress, and ever since deeply mourns her loss, and all this because my daughter had kindly sympathised with her in her distress and given her good advice and helped her in her time of need and enabled her to get on till she made a prudent marriage with a worthier man. Another case which I would speak of, which is only one amongst many—a poor blind girl who received an annual donation from my daughter, after her death required to be led four miles to be at my daughter's funeral, over which she wept many tears of gratitude and sorrow. In her acts of kindness my dear daughter was, as I thought, often rather impulsive. Two or three winters ago a poor man fell on the ice and broke his thigh, and had to be carried home to his comfortless cottage, where he had a wife with twins and six other small children. My daughter having heard of their situation sent the servant to see how they were. On her return she made a very eloquent and pathetic report. My daughter being touched, got up directly and sent them a sovereign, to their great astonishment—and pleasure—for which they have been ever afterwards grateful. Though I could not help being pleased with this act—though hardly in accordance with my daughter's means—I observed to her that women were often impulsive in deeds of charity. She jocularly replied 'In deeds of charity men reason much and do little; women reason little and do much, and I will act the woman still.'

P. BRONTË.

961. *To* CATHERINE WINKWORTH.

LINDETH TOWER, SILVERDALE,
August, 1855.

. . . Here I arrived yesterday, and find the weather, which I left fine and soft, just as blustering and showery as it used to be, so that a fire is welcome in the sitting-room. Lily[1] received me most affectionately, and I am glad to find that her quest for materials [for Miss Brontë's 'Life'] has been most successful, and I really think now she will make a capital thing of the 'Life' and show people how lives ought to be written.

SUSANNA WINKWORTH.

962. *To* MARGARET WOOLER.

PLYMOUTH GROVE, MANCHESTER,
Monday, Novr 12th [1855].

MY DEAR MISS WOOLER,—I am sure you will be glad to hear that your valuable parcel of letters was received in safety, and that I promise that the utmost care shall be taken of them, and that they shall be returned to you before very long. I hardly know how it is, but I like them better than any other series of letters of hers that I have seen; (a few to 'Emily' those to Miss Nussey, and some to Mr Smith); I am sure you will allow me to apply to you with any questions that may suggest themselves to me in the course of my work, which is getting on but slowly, owing to the pressure of business of other kinds that has been weighing upon me.

I hope you and your hostess continue as well satisfied with each other, as you spoke of being when I had the pleasure of seeing you at Brookroyd.—Believe me ever to remain dear Madam, Yours respectfully and truly,

E. C. GASKELL.

[1]Mrs. Gaskell.

963. *To* MRS GASKELL.

BROOKROYD, Nov. 15th, [1855].

MY DEAR MRS GASKELL,—I should not have been thus long in answering your last very welcome epistle but I waited to hear from Miss Wooler to whom I had sent for perusal the present enclosure—I had never spoken much with her of dear Anne Brontë's death and I thought I should like her to see the copy I had made of a few notes pencilled in my pocket-book shortly after our return from Scarbro'—I brought the pocket-book in my hand as we sat at work the eveng you were here thinking at the moment I could read to you what I had written but I had not courage to execute my purpose. The record of those few days is very slightly, and, I am conscious, very feebly portrayed, still I prefer giving you exactly the impressions and recollections of the time. In truth there was not much to note down, for they were silent days—days of patience anxiety and fears to at least two of the little party and little did I think of any eye but my own ever viewing the remembrance there in my book.

I enclose also a notice which dear C. made in a letter of the death of a young lady who was a pupil at the time Anne Brontë was at School, a pupil who attached herself strongly to Anne B. and Anne bestowed upon her a great deal of quiet affection and genial notice. I think the young lady's friends would most probably be gratified if dear C.'s comments on her decease were inserted—they are monied and influential people in this neighbourhood, some of them not very friendly to Currer Bell's emanations. Would they not be won by her kindly thought of one of their own? ...

ELLEN NUSSEY.

964. *To* W. S. WILLIAMS.

PLYMOUTH GROVE, December 15th, 1855.

DEAR SIR,—I am extremely obliged to you for the packet of Miss Brontë's letters which I found here on my return home, too late for Friday's post for me to acknowledge them. I have read them hastily over and I like the tone of them very much; it is curious how much the spirit in which she wrote varies according to the correspondent whom she is addressing, I imagine. I like the series of letters which you have sent better than any other, excepting one, that I have seen. The subjects, too, are very interesting; how beautifully she speaks, for instance, of her wanderings on the moors after her sister's death! I am extremely obliged to you, sir, for your kindness in sending them to me, and I will take great care of them as long as they are in my keeping.

I can fancy from the way you speak that your son's career in Australia has not been so prosperous as at one time perhaps both you and he hoped it might have been, but if you lived in such a town as this, you would see how terribly injurious to young men mere worldly prosperity too often becomes. Still, Australia is a long way off, and his prolonged absence from you and his mother must, I am sure, be a trial to both you and him. Will you remember me to him when you write? Mr Gaskell thought he recognised him again in another Mr Williams, whom he met with at Chamounix this summer; he still thinks it must have been Mr Frank Williams's[1] brother to whom he spoke, the likeness was so great. —Believe me to remain, Yours truly and obliged,

E. C. GASKELL.

965. *To* ELLEN NUSSEY.

HAWORTH, Dec. 24, 1855.

DEAR MISS NUSSEY, —Mr Brontë and myself are much obliged to you for your kind enquiries; we are both thank God well in general. Mr Brontë suffers occasionally from a cough, otherwise he enjoys as good health as is usual for persons of such advanced age.

We have neither heard nor seen anything of Mrs Gaskell—I have every confidence that she will do ample justice to Charlotte —but I am quite sensible that she has undertaken a very difficult task with only slender material. Nor do I fear that Miss Martineau will write anything derogatory to Charlotte's memory— as I know from her letters that she entertained the highest opinion of her abilities, and was fully sensible of her many virtues.

I am glad that Mrs Gaskell has seen Miss Wooler—Mr Brontë knew nothing of your paragraph in 'The Mercury' until he saw

[1]Charlotte Brontë gave Mr Williams's son Frank a letter of introduction to Mrs Gaskell. See letter dated November 6th, 1851, Vol. III, p. 286.

it in print—it is however no secret that Mrs Gaskell has undertaken the biography.

If Mrs Gaskell wishes to see Mrs Brontë's letters and will
communicate that wish to Mr Brontë I dare . . .[1]

[A. B. NICHOLLS].

966 (704). To ELLEN NUSSEY.

WELLINGTON, April 19th, '56.

DEAR ELLEN,—I got your letter a week ago, that is 5 months
after it was written. It has been the same with those from John
and from Amelia. It is quite old-fashioned to be so long without
news from England! There were 3 mails due at once. Your letter
is most interesting concerning poor Charlotte's 'Life.' If, for the
sake of those who behaved ill to her, the truth cannot be spoken,
still people should not tell lies. The fact reached me even here
that Mr Brontë did not choose his daughter should marry—she
wrote to me that she once dismissed Mr Nicholls because he
(her papa) was so angry that she was frightened—frightened for
him. It was long after, years I think, that she told him that she
had determined to see Mr Nicholls again, and without positively saying yes, to retract her refusal. I can never think without
gloomy anger of Charlotte's sacrifices to the selfish old man.
How well we know that, had she left him entirely and succeeded
in gaining wealth, and name, and influence, she would have had
all the world lauding her to the skies for any trivial act of generosity that would have cost her nothing! But how on earth is all
this to be set straight! Mrs Gaskell seems far too able a woman to
put her head into such a wasp nest, as she would raise about her
by speaking the truth of living people. How she will get through
with it I can't imagine. Charlotte once wrote to me that Miss
Martineau had no bump of secretiveness at all, and that she
(Charlotte) had dropped her acquaintance on that account. I am
very curious about Miss Martineau's life. What do you mean
about her having written it—is it published? Otherwise how do
you know what she has said of Charlotte?[2]

Your account of Joe and Amelia agrees with the impression
Amelia's letters give me. She writes late at night and seems to
have spent her time nursing until every other idea has gone out

---

[1]The remainder of this letter is lost.
[2]Harriet Martineau wrote her Autobiography in 1855, but it was not published
until 1877.

of her head. She gives no news, mentions no friends, and seems to know nothing but how unhappy she is. This want of power to turn her thoughts abroad shows more depression than she herself is aware of. But what remedy? No one can take her place, even if they had the authority to send her away. Her very mind gets warped by the constant strain on it. I begin now to incline to John's opinion that Joe's hopelessness is a symptom of his disorder and not to be believed in. John seems to think he will get better by slow degrees.

We have been in danger of a terrible misfortune here. A fire broke out in a lot of warehouses at 2 o'clock in the morning a week ago (3rd May) and was not subdued till five. It was so calm (a most unusual thing) that the smoke and flame rose perpendicularly. If there had been any wind at all, all our end of the town must have been burnt. We roof our houses with thin pieces of wood put on like slates, and a slight breeze would have set a dozen roofs on fire at once. Waring's place is about 200 yds off, mine 300 yds more; but there are wooden buildings all the way, and I should only have had the favour of being burnt last. In three hours the fire destroyed the value of £15,000, and then we were much indebted to a brick wall, the only one about the whole clump of buildings, that delayed the fire a little and gave the engines power over it. Twelve years ago there was a fire and raging wind, and buildings as distant as mine were set on fire by the sparks and embers. Nearly the whole town was burnt. *Du-reste*, I am plodding on as usual. I have good health and pleasant times, though no great pleasures; yet little unhappiness except the recollection that I am getting old and shall soon be solitary, for my friends are slipping away. I cannot say I make no new ones, but somehow I don't believe in them. I suppose I get selfish and suspicious. I suppose you know that in the last 18 months I have not prospered in wealth, being just where I was in that respect a year and a half ago. I have no right to call this a misfortune, but having been improving several years before made me unreasonable. I do not work hard enough to justify me in expectations of getting rich. Just now I have more to do and probably shall have. I wish I could set the world right on many points, but above all respecting Charlotte. It would do said world good to know her and be forced to revere her in spite of their contempt for poverty and helplessness. No one ever gave up more than she did and with full consciousness of what she sacrificed. I

don't think myself that women are justified in sacrificing themselves for others, but since the world generally expects it of
them, they should at least acknowledge it. But where much is
given we are all wonderfully given to grasp at more. If Charlotte
had left home and made a favour of returning, she would have
got thanks instead of tyranny — wherefore take care of yourself
Ellen, and if you choose to give a small modicum of mention of
other people, *grumble hard.* — Yours affectionately,

MARY TAYLOR.

In 1856 Mrs Gaskell was energetically engaged upon a biography of her friend which should lack nothing of thorough-
ness, as she hoped. She claimed to have visited the scenes of all
the incidents in Charlotte's life, 'the two little pieces of private
governess-ship excepted.' She went one day with Mr Smith to
the Chapter Coffee-House, where the sisters first stayed in London. Another day she visited Yorkshire, where she made the
acquaintance of Miss Wooler, which permitted, as she said, 'a
more friendly manner of writing towards Charlotte Brontë's old
school-mistress.' Again, she went to Brussels, where Madame
Heger refused to see her, although M. Heger was kind and
communicative, 'and very much indeed I both like and respect
him.' Her countless questions were exceedingly interesting.
They covered many pages of note-paper. 'Did Branwell Brontë
know of the publication of *Jane Eyre*,' she asks, 'and how did he
receive the news?' Mrs Gaskell was persuaded in her own mind
that he had never known of its publication. Charlotte had distinctly informed her, she said, that Branwell was not in a fit condition at the time to be told. 'Where did the girls get the books
which they read so continually? Did Emily accompany Charlotte
as a pupil when the latter went as a teacher to Roe Head? Why
did not Branwell go to the Royal Academy in London to learn
painting? Did Emily ever go out as a governess? What were
Emily's religious opinions? Did *she* ever make friends?' Such
were the questions which came quick and fast to Miss Nussey.

967 (705). *To* ELLEN NUSSEY.

PLYMOUTH GROVE, MANCHESTER,
July 9th, '56.

MY DEAR MISS NUSSEY, — You must excuse any kind of writing, for my girls are all from home, and I suppose I have between thirty and forty notes and letters to answer this morning, *if possible* (which it is *not*), and yet I want to write you a long letter, and tell you all my adventures. Brussels, where Mme Heger, understanding that I was a friend of Miss Brontë's, refused to see me; but I made M. Heger's acquaintance, and very much indeed I both like and respect him. Mr and Mrs Smith, junr, and Mrs Smith, senr (*exactly* like Mrs Bretton). Mr Smith said (half suspiciously, having an eye to Dr John, I *fancied*), 'Do you know, I sometimes think Miss Brontë had my mother in her mind when she wrote Mrs Bretton in "Villette"?' As I had not then seen Mrs Smith I could only answer, 'Do you?' a very safe reply. I went with Mr Smith to see the Chapter Coffee-House in Paternoster Row, where she and Anne Brontë took up their abode that first hurried rush up to London. In fact, I now think I have been everywhere where she ever lived, except of course her two little pieces of private governess-ship. I still want one or two things to complete my materials, and I am very doubtful if I can get them — at any rate, I think they will necessitate my going to Haworth again, and I am literally *afraid* of that. I will tell you the things I should *like* to have, and shall be glad if, knowing the parties, you could give me advice. First of all, I promised M. Heger to ask to see his letters to her; he is sure she would keep them, as they contained advice about her character, studies, mode of life. I doubt much if Mr Nicholls has not destroyed them. Then again, Mr Smith suggests — and I think with great justice — that if I might see the MS. of 'The Professor' (which Mr Nicholls told me last July that he had in his possession), I might read it, and express my opinion as to its merits and demerits as a first work. He says that much of it — whole pieces of it, as far as he remembers — are so interwoven with 'Villette' that it could never be published, nor would it be worth while to give extracts, even if Mr N. would allow it; but if I might read it, I could give the kind of criticism and opinion upon it that Mr Brontë was anxious I should give on those published works of hers, on which (I told him) public opinion had already pronounced her fiat, and set her seal. So much for 'The Professor' and M. Heger's letters. Now another of Mr Smith's suggestions is this: Might I, do you think, see the beginning (fifty pages, Mr Nicholls said) of the new story[1] she had commenced? Reasons why desirable. Her happy state of mind during her married life would probably give a different character of greater hope and serenity to the fragment.

One thing more. Mr Smith says that her letters to her father from London, giving an account of places and persons she saw, were long, constant, and minute; they would not refer to any private affairs, but to the impressions celebrated strangers made upon her, etc.

I agree with Mr Smith that it would be a great advantage to me, as her biographer, and to her memory also, for I am convinced the more her character and talents are known the more thoroughly will both be admired and reverenced. But I doubt much if Mr Nicholls won't object to granting me the sight of these things; and all the remains, etc., appear to be in his hands. Read (and return, please) this note of Mr Brontë's to Mr Smith in reply to his application to be allowed to have a copy *for himself* (he thought it best to ask for this *only, which he had promised him*) at first. It seems as if Mr Brontë's own consent or opinion on these matters had very little weight with Mr Nicholls. I found Mr Smith an agreeable, genial-mannered man, with a keen eye to business; he is rather too stout to be handsome, but has a very pretty, Paulina-like little wife, and a little girl of eighteen months old. Mr Williams dined there when I did: grey-haired, silent, and refined.

Now for questions I should be much obliged to you if you would answer—I am afraid to say by return of post, but I should *like* that! Did *Emily* accompany C. B. as a pupil when the latter went as teacher to Roe Head? This was evidently the *plan*; yet afterwards it seems as if it were *Anne* that went. Why did not Branwell go to the Royal Academy in London to learn painting? Did Emily ever go out as a governess? I know Anne and Charlotte did.

I wrote twenty pages yesterday because it rained perpetually, and I was uninterrupted; such a good day for writing may not come again for months. All August I shall be away. But I am thoroughly interested in my subject, and Mr Smith, who looks at the affair from the experienced man of business point of view,

[1] *Emma*. A fragment of a story, first published in the *Cornhill Magazine*, pp. 485–498, 1860.

says, 'There is no hurry; there would be a great cry of indelicacy if it were published too soon. Do it well, and never fear that the public interest in her will die away.' But a note of his (written after reading as much of my MS. which was then written, which you remember, I read to you), and which I enclose for your own *private* reading, makes me rather uncomfortable. See the passage I have marked at the side. Now I thought that I carefully preserved the reader's respect of Mr Brontë, while truth and the desire of doing justice to her compelled me to state the domestic peculiarities of her childhood, which (as in all cases) contributed so much to make her what she was; yet you see what Mr Smith says, and what reviews, in their desire for smartness and carelessness for scrupulous consideration, would be sure to say, even yet more plainly. May I call you simply 'Ellen' in the book? Initials give so little personality — they are so like a mathematical proposition. I should not even put an initial to your surname.

I have written you a terribly long letter, because, as somebody says, 'I have not time to write you a short one,' but I both wanted answers to my questions, and also wanted you to know how I am going on. We look forward to seeing you in the autumn. Mr Gaskell desires his kind regards; every one else is from home. Your sister must not forget me, for I do not forget her and her kind reception of me. — Yours faithfully,

E. C. GASKELL.

968. *To* MRS GASKELL, *Manchester.*

BROOKROYD, [July, 1856].

MY DEAR MRS GASKELL, — If you go to London pray try what may be done with regard to a portrait of dear Charlotte. It would greatly enhance the value and interest of the memoir, and be such a satisfaction to people to see something that would settle their ideas of the personal appearance of the dear departed one. It has been a surprise to every stranger, I think, that she was so gentle and lady-like to look upon.

Emily Brontë went to Roe Head as pupil when Charlotte went as teacher; she stayed there but two months; she never settled, and was ill from nothing but home-sickness. Anne took her place and remained about two years. Emily was a teacher for one six months in a ladies' school in Halifax or the neighbourhood. I do not know whether it was conduct or want of finances that prevented Branwell from going to the Royal Academy. Probably there were impediments of both kinds.

I am afraid if you give me my name I shall feel a prominence in the book that I altogether shrink from. My very last wish would be to appear in the book more than is absolutely necessary. If it were possible, I would choose not to be known at all. It is my friend only that I care to see and recognise, though your framing and setting of the picture will very greatly enhance its value. — I am, my dear Mrs Gaskell, yours very sincerely,

ELLEN NUSSEY.

969. *To* MRS GASKELL.

[July, 1856].

MY DEAR MRS GASKELL, — I was quite pleased to see your handwriting again this morng and thank you very much for all the details you kindly give, all of which are deeply interesting to me. I have often had a wish to know if you had reached Brussels and what was your reception. If Madame Heger did not feel the justice of her portrait she would never shrink from observation. She herself fits the cap more than is wise or politic. I feel pleasure in your account of Monsieur. He would do dear C. justice for he could understand her nature and the intensity of how it was never more manifested than during her sojourn at Brussels and for some time subsequent to that sojourn. I hope these letters are not destroyed, as many have been found still to be in existence, but I fear, as C. told me before her marriage that she had destroyed all correspondence. This however must have been said with some limit or there was a mistake on my part, since some letters have been given to you, that were not likely to be spared if others were assigned to destruction. I think Mr N. ought to have no reserve with you, his very affection should make him see it is wisest, best, and kindest to tell the whole truth to you in everything that regards her literary life or her domestic virtues — I wish I could talk to him half an hour and convince him that the more she is known the more highly will she shine and be the means of good to the readers of her Memoir. If you go to Haworth I hope you may be able to open his heart, he spoke in one of his notes to me last year of having implicit confidence in you I think you may win him by your own heartiness in the

work—at any rate you will Mr B., and for a quiet life Mr N. will
have to yield where Mr B. is urgent and impatient. It is very
desirable that you should see the last labour of her pen for what
can be of more interest than the glimpse it would give of her
new life—I enclose a few letters written after marriage for the
sake of the remarks on marriage. They unexpectedly turned up
in the pocket of a dress which had been laid by.

I am very sorry about the refusal of the portrait. Though
there would always have been regret for its painful expression to
be perpetuated. Mr N. had too much reserve and Mr B. would
have scarcely any. Did you obtain any of dear C.'s letters to
Monsieur Heger. Your description of Mr B. made an impression
on me which I always meant to describe to you when I saw you
next—The anecdote of the little coloured shoes produced a
mental sting that no time would obliterate and I felt that all
commonplace readers would fail to see the Spartan nature of the
act unless you plainly pointed it out to them, and I was intending
to ask you to make very clear and distinct comments on Mr B.'s
character—I do not wish anything you have said suppressed
only I think your readers will have to be taught to think kindly
of Mr B. . . .

E. NUSSEY.

970. To MARTHA BROWN.

HAWORTH, July 18th, 1856.

The Money contained in this little Box, consists of sums,
given by me, to Martha Brown, at different times, for her faithful
services to me and my children. And this money I wish her to
keep ready for a time of need.

P. BRONTË, A.B.,
Incumbent of Haworth, Yorkshire.

971. To LÆTITIA WHEELWRIGHT.

WM EWART'S ESQ. M.P., BROADLEAS,
DEVIZES, WILTS.

Augt 22nd, [1856].

MY DEAR MISS WHEELWRIGHT,—I am going to avail myself of your kind permission to ask you any further questions
about Miss Brontë. I am just come in her life to the part she spent

at Brussels. If I remember rightly you went to Mme Heger's at the beginning of the quarter that succeeded to the first September holidays of her stay there. I forget whether you told me about those holidays, or how much you remembered. You would greatly oblige me if you would have the kindness to write and tell me if she spent them entirely in the rue d'Isabelle, or if she had invitations from any friends during the vacation. It must have been before Mrs Wheelwright's arrival in Brussels, so that she cannot have experienced her kindness as on future occasions in taking her away from the school in the holidays. I want to know where and how they were spent. And if you could give me any details about Charlotte and Emily's school life—their exact position in the school—their duties and occupations—If they had a bedroom to themselves—even the school hours—all these details would be invaluable—as any others you might remember.

I distinctly recollect your account of Emily's appearance and manners—but I forget what you said was the first impression made by Charlotte on any casual observer. I suppose she was extremely shy?

I shall be very much obliged to you if you will answer all my questions, and can only regret that some of them are repetitions of those whose answers I have forgotten.

With kind remembrances to Mrs Wheelwright and your sister from my daughter and myself, I remain, yrs truly,

E. C. Gaskell.

My address after Wedy will be
                    Plymouth Grove,
                         Manchester,
till then the present.

972. *To* Ellen Nussey.

September 6th, 1856.

My dear Miss Nussey,—I have read *once* over all the letters you so kindly entrusted me with, and I don't think even you, her most cherished friend, could wish the impression on me to be different from what it is, that she was one to study the path of duty well, and, having ascertained what it was right to do, to follow out her idea strictly. They gave me a very beautiful idea of her character. I like the one you sent to-day much. I shall be glad to see any others you will allow me to see. I am sure the more fully she—Charlotte Brontë—the *friend*, the *daughter*, the *sister*, the *wife*, is known, and known where need be in her own words, the more highly will she be appreciated.—Yours faithfully,

E. C. GASKELL.

973. *To* EMILY SHAEN (*née* WINKWORTH).

P. GROVE, Sunday Morning,
[Sep. 8, 1856].

MY DEAREST EMILY,—I was so sorry when I got your note last night darling, that I had not written the day after I got home: that is, I could not have written, but I could have made one of the girls do it—but I wanted so very much to write to you myself, and that literally was impossible till I did. I am writing my last letters to-day: to-morrow I set to and fag away at Miss Brontë again. You see in general you hear (and I like to feel you do), all sorts of things about *me and us* from Katie and Susanna so that I always feel you are *au courant*,—and now it seems as if I had such a great deal to say to you. I think I had better begin about Miss B. You would hear before you left Alderley that I had been to Haworth, with Sir J. P. K. S. He had not the slightest delicacy or scruple: and asked for an immense number of things, literally taking no refusal. Hence we carried away with us a whole heap of those minute writings of which William showed you one or two at Alderley: the beginning (only about 20 pages) of a new novel[1] which she had written at the end of 1854, before marriage, and I dare say when she was anxious enough. This fragment was excessively interesting: a child left at a school by a rich flashy man, who pretended to be her father; the school mistresses deference to the rich child—her mysterious reserved character evidently painfully conscious of the imposition practised; the non-payment of bills; the enquiry—no such person to be found, and just when the child implores mercy and confesses her complicity to the worldly and indignant schoolmistress the story stops—for ever. Besides these things we carried off the

'Professor'—that *first* novel, rejected by all the publishers. This Sir James took away with him intending to read it first and then forward to me. He wrote to me before he forwarded it, praising it extremely—saying it would add to her reputation—objecting to 'certain coarse and objectionable phrases'—but offering to *revise* it,—'and expunge and make the necessary alterations,'—and begging me to forward his letter to Mr Smith. I dreaded lest the Prof. should involve anything with M. Heger—I had heard her say it related to her Brussels life,—and I thought if he were again brought before the public what would he think of me? I believed him to be too good to publish those letters[1]—but I felt that his friends might really with some justice urge him to do so —so I awaited the arrival of the Prof. (by Mr Gaskell at Dumbleton) with great anxiety. It does relate to the school, but not to M. Heger, and Mme or Madame Beck, is only slightly introduced; so on *that* ground there would be no objection to publishing it. I don't think it will *add* to her reputation,—the interest will arise from its being the work of so remarkable a mind. It is an autobiography—of a *man*, the *English* Professor at a Brussels school—there are one or two remarkable portraits—the most charming woman she ever drew, and a glimpse of that woman as a mother—very lovely: otherwise little or no story: and disfigured by more coarseness and profanity in quoting texts of scripture disagreeably than in any of her other works. However I had nothing to do except to be a medium—so I sent Sir J. P. K. S's letter on to Mr Nicholls, and told him I was going to send a copy of it to Mr Smith, if he had no objection; that I did not think so highly of the book as Sir J. P. K. S.: although I thought that she herself having prepared it for the press Sir J. P. K. S. ought not to interfere with it—as, although to my mind there certainly were several things that had better be expunged, yet that he (Mr N.) was, it seemed to me, the right person to do it. I did not know what Mr N. might say to this, as he certainly is under obligation to Sir James for the offer of a living &c., but I don't know if you remember some of the passages I copied out in her letters relating to Sir J. and there were others I did *not* all making me feel she would have especially disliked *him* to meddle with her writings. However Mr N. quite agreed with me, and wrote to Sir James declining his proposal, saying privately to me that he feared Sir J. would be hurt (he, Sir J., evidently wants to appear to the world in intimate connexion with her), but that

[1]Mrs Gaskell had evidently seen Charlotte's letters to M. Heger.

knowing his wife's opinion on the subject, he could not allow any such revisal, but that he would himself look over the 'Professor' and judge as well as he could with relation to the passages Sir J. and I had objected to. So there it rests with Mr Nicholls, to whom the MS. of the Prof. was returned a fortnight ago. With regard to Mr Smith of course he jumped at the idea; whatever sum I fixed on as the price should be cheerfully paid—(I declined the responsibility—but I said I thought it ought to be paid for like her other works in proportion to the length). Would I edit it? (No for several reasons). When would the Life be ready. Michaelmas? The time of publishing the Prof. would have to be guided by that.[1] All I could say in reply was that I would make haste, but that it could not be ready by Michaelmas *possibly*. Since then (about 10 days ago) I have heard nothing either from Mr Smith, or from Mr Nicholls. Now as to the Life. Among that mass of minute writing I found quantities of fragments very short but very graphic written when she was about 12, giving glimpses of her life at that time, all of which I had to decipher, and interweave with what I had already written—in fact I had to re-write about 40 pages. They give a much pleasanter though hardly less *queer* notion of the old father—moreover Mrs Wordsworth sent me a letter of Branwell's to Mr W. and altogether it was dreary work, looking over, correcting, interweaving, &c. &c. &c. and besides that I *wrote* 120 *new* pages while we were absent on one holiday, which was no holiday to me. I used to go up at Dumbleton and Boughton to my own room, directly after 9 o'clock breakfast; and came down to lunch at $\frac{1}{2}$ p. 1, up again and write without allowing any temptation to carry me off till 5 —or past: having just a run of a walk before 7 o'clock dinner. I got through an immense deal: but I found head and health suffering—I could not sleep for thinking of it. So at Broad Leas (the Ewarts) I only wrote till lunch: and since then, not at all. I have been too busy since I came home. I enjoyed Broad Leas for the most of my visit, perhaps owing to my not having the sick wearied feeling of being over-worked: and Mr Gaskell being very jolly; and delicious downs (Salisbury Plain) get-at-able in our afternoon drives great sweeps of green turf, like emerald billows stretching off into the blue sky miles and miles away,— with here and there a 'barrow' of some ancient Briton, and

[1] *The Professor, a Tale*, by Currer Bell, was published by Messrs Smith, Elder & Co. in 1857. It contains a preface by the Rev. A. B. Nicholls, dated September 22nd, 1856.

Wansdyke, and Silbury Hill, and the great circle of Avebury all
to be seen, while the horses went noisily over the thick soft vel-
vety grass high up over blue misty plains, and villages in nests of
trees, and church spires which did not reach nearly up to where
we were in our beautiful free air, and primitive world. . . .
—Ever your most affec.

E. C. G[ASKELL].

974. *To* George Smith.

42, Plymouth Grove,
September 10th, 1856.

My dear Sir,—In the preface to the revised edition of
'Wuthering Heights and Agnes Grey' by Ellis, and Acton Bell,
Miss Brontë says speaking of the difficulty of obtaining answers
from Publishers:

'Being greatly harassed by this obstacle, I ventured to apply to
the Messrs Chambers of Edinburgh, *they* may have forgotten the
circumstances but *I* have not, for from them I received a brief
and business-like, but civil and sensible reply, on which we
acted, and at last made way.' This was in the autumn of 1845, or
beginning of the following year. I mentioned this to you at
Cheltenham, and you kindly promised me to look through your
papers for the desired letters.

If you could forward me the correspondence, as soon as convenient to you, I should esteem it a very great favour and would
return the letters immediately after copying them.—I remain,
Yours very truly,

E. C. Gaskell.

975. *To* George Smith.

Plymouth Grove,
Monday [October, 1856].

My dear Sir,—I suspect I see your writing on the heading of
the pages—would it be giving you much trouble?—and would it
not be saving trouble to the printers, if, instead of waiting to
insert the accompanying extract in the proof, I requested you to
place it in the MS. It relates to the period when Miss Brontë went
as *teacher* to Miss Wooler's school (1836 and '37[1]) and her sister

[1] July 29th, 1835, is the correct date.

Emily accompanied her at her first going as a *pupil*. I found out from the letters that she did not remain long, by the substitution of *Anne's* name in Miss Brontë's letters for that of *Emily*; but I could not quite satisfactorily account for it, when I was writing the MS. In looking over the second notice of Emily (prefixed to one or two of her poems) at the end of 2nd edition of 'Wuthering Heights,'—I found this extract; which exactly fills up a little blank and accounts for what wanted accounting for.

I will give you the date of the change of the sisters,—I am sorry I cannot refer you to the exact page of MS. (in looking over the letters I am sorry I cannot find the date, but I think you will easily see when it is to be inserted) Miss Nussey was here last week reading the MS. I was gratified to hear her repeatedly say how completely the life at the Parsonage appeared to her reproduced. Much of this was owing to the remarkable extracts from letters; but she said several times how exactly and accurately I had written about the life and characters.—Yours very truly,

E. C. GASKELL.

976. *To* WILLIAM STORY.

. . . I hope to have finished my Life of Miss Brontë by the end of February, and then I should like to be off and away out of the reach of reviews, which, in this case, will have a double power to wound, for if they say anything disparaging of *her* I know I shall not have done her, and the circumstances in which she was placed, justice; that is to say that, in her case more visibly than in most, her circumstances made her faults, while her virtues were her own.

[E. C. GASKELL].

977 (706). *To* ELLEN NUSSEY.

January 8th, '57.

DEAR ELLEN,—A few days ago I got a letter from you dated 2nd May '56 along with some patterns and a fashion book. They seem to have been lost somehow, as the box ought to have come by the 'Hastings' and only now makes its appearance by the 'Philip Lang.' It has come very *à propos* for a new year's gift, and the patterns were not opened twenty-four hours before a silk cape was cut out by one of them. I think I made a very impertinent request when I asked you to give yourself so much trouble. I thought you would just look out a few paper patterns which you might happen to have. Your being from home made the matter give you still more trouble. The poor woman for whom I wanted them is now our first-rate dressmaker; her drunken husband, who was her main misfortune, having taken himself off and not been heard of lately. Your account of Joe and Amelia, like all that I get of them, is very melancholy — more melancholy than illness even. It seems to show them absorbed in themselves and their misfortunes so as to shut other people out by their own miseries. That Amelia should want to keep Tim's affection all to herself I can well imagine. I often see the feeling here, especially where there is only one child. It needs to have half a dozen and plenty to do, for the Mama to find out that she may as well let any one love the children who will take the trouble even if the children should love them in return. Poor Amelia has a hard life of it, for her one hope is so delicate, and the care they take of it is so little successful in its results, that I am afraid there is more pain than pleasure on the whole.

I am glad to hear that Mrs Gaskell is progressing with the 'Life.' I wish I had kept Charlotte's letters now, though I never felt safe to do so until latterly that I have had a home of my own. They would have been much better evidence than my imperfect recollection, and infinitely more interesting. A settled opinion is very likely to look absurd unless you give the grounds for it, and even if I could remember them, it looks as if there might be other facts which I have neglected which ought to have altered it. Your news of the 'neighbours' is very interesting; especially of Miss Wooler and my old school-fellows. Why on earth has Susan Ledgard had an attack of paralysis? She is still in the thirties. There must have been some strong cause for it. Was it mental or bodily? I wish I knew how to give you some account of my ways and doings here and the effect of my position on me. First of all, it agrees with me. I am in better health than at any time since I left school. This difference won't seem much to other people, since I never was *ill* since then; but it is very great to me, for it is just the difference between everything being a burden and everything being more or less a pleasure. Half from physical weakness and half from depression of spirits my judgment in former days was always at war with my will. There was always plenty to do, but never anything that I really felt was worth the labour of doing. My life now is not overburdened with work, and what I do has interest and attraction in it. I should think it is that part that I shall think most agreeable when I look back on my death-bed — a number of small pleasures scattered over my way, that, when seen from a distance, will seem to cover it thick. They don't cover it by any means, but I never had so many.

I look after my shopwoman; make out bills; decide who shall have 'trust' and who not. Then I go a-buying; not near such an anxious piece of business now that I understand my trade and have, moreover, a good 'credit.' I read a good deal; sometimes on the sofa; a vice I am much given to in hot weather. Then I have some friends. Not many and no geniuses — which fact pray keep strictly to yourself, for somehow the doings and sayings of Wellington people in England always come out again to N.Z. I do not think my acquaintances are inferior to what I should have had elsewhere, even with more means and a higher position of my own. They are most of them narrow-minded and ignorant. Those of the higher class only differ by being less practical and more exacting. They are not very interesting anyway. This is my fault in part, for I can't take an interest in their concerns. It would be dreadful to me to spend as much time as they do on the details of dressing and eating — at least providing the eating. Then their children, of course, concern me but little. A book is worth any of them and a good book worth them put together Mamas included.

Our place is thriving on the whole, though there is an attempt making just now to get up a rage for emigrating and exporting to N. Zealand. Such rages always go too far, and we shall likely get a bad character among you in consequence. It's all the same to us. I wish I had better news of your own health. I think pain in the chest a serious thing. Our east winds are much the pleasantest and healthiest we have; the soft moist north-west brings headache and depression, it even blights the trees. — Yours affectionately,

MARY TAYLOR.

978. *To* LÆTITIA WHEELWRIGHT.

PLYMOUTH GROVE, MANCHESTER,
Saturday, Febry 7, 1857.

MY DEAR MISS WHEELWRIGHT, —I have to-day finished my Life of Miss Brontë; and next week we set out for Rome. Before I go however I must return you your precious letters, with my best thanks, not merely for the loan of them, although their value has been great, but for the kind readiness with which you all, (especially you and your mother), met my wishes about giving me information.

I hope sometime or other to be able to call upon you, and express all this personally, if you will allow me.

Meanwhile I trust you will accept a copy of the Memoir, which will be forwarded to you on publication; and with kind compliments, ever believe me, dear Miss Wheelwright, — Yours most truly,

E. C. GASKELL.

The book was published in two volumes, under the title of *The Life of Charlotte Brontë*, in March, 1857. At first all was well. Mr Brontë's earliest acknowledgment of the book was one of approbation. Sir James Kay-Shuttleworth expressed the hope that Mr Nicholls would 'rejoice that his wife would be known as a Christian heroine who could bear her cross with the firmness of a martyr saint.'

It was a short-lived triumph, however, and Mrs Gaskell soon found herself, as she expressed it, 'in a veritable hornets' nest.' Mr Brontë, to begin with, did not care for the references to himself and the suggestion that he had treated his wife unkindly, although it is clear from the correspondence that he did not find anything wrong on his first perusal of the book. Mrs Gaskell had associated him with numerous eccentricities and ebullitions of temper, which during his later years he always asserted, and undoubtedly with perfect truth, were, at the best, the fabrications of a dismissed servant.[1] Mr Nicholls had also his grievance. There was just a suspicion implied that he had not been quite the

[1] See Vol. I, pp.46–52.

most sympathetic of husbands. The suspicion was absolutely ill-founded, and arose from Mr Nicholls's intense shyness. But neither Mr Brontë nor Mr Nicholls gave Mrs Gaskell much trouble. They, at any rate, were silent. Trouble, however, came from many quarters. Yorkshire people resented the air of patronage with which, as it seemed to them, a good Lancashire lady had taken their county in hand. They were not quite the savages, they retorted, which some of Mrs Gaskell's descriptions in the beginning of her book seemed to suggest. Between Lancashire and Yorkshire there is always a suspicion of jealousy. It was intensified for the moment by these sombre pictures of 'this lawless, yet not unkindly population.'[1] A son-in-law of Mr Redhead wrote to deny the account of that clergyman's association with Haworth. 'He gives another as true,' wrote Mrs Gaskell, 'in which I don't see any great difference.' Miss Martineau wrote sheet after sheet explanatory of her relations with Charlotte Brontë. 'Two separate householders in London *each* declare that the first interview between Miss Brontë and Miss Martineau took place at *her* house,' is another of Mrs Gaskell's despairing cries. In one passage Mrs Gaskell had spoken of wasteful young servants, and the servants in question came upon Mr Brontë for a testimonial.[2]

Three whole pages were devoted to the dramatic recital of a scandal at Haworth, and this entirely disappears from the third edition. A casual reference to a girl who had been seduced, and had found a friend in Miss Brontë, gave further trouble. 'I have altered the word "seduced" to "betrayed," ' writes Mrs Gaskell to Martha Brown, 'and I hope that this will satisfy the unhappy girl's friends.' But all these were small matters compared with the Cowan Bridge controversy and the threatened legal proceedings over Branwell Brontë's suggested love affairs. Mrs Gaskell defended the description in *Jane Eyre* of Cowan Bridge with peculiar vigour. Mr Carus Wilson, the Brocklehurst of *Jane Eyre*, and his friends were furious. They threatened an action.

[1] 'Some of the West Ridingers are very angry, and declare they are half a century in civilisation before some of the Lancashire folk, and that this neighbourhood is a paradise compared with some districts not far from Manchester.'—Ellen Nussey to Mrs Gaskell, April 16th, 1859.
[2] See page 226 below.

There were letters in the *Times* and letters in the *Daily News*. Mr Nicholls broke silence—the only time that he did so during the forty years that followed his wife's death—with five letters to the *Halifax Guardian*.[1] The Cowan Bridge controversy was a drawn battle, in spite of numerous and glowing testimonials to the virtues of Mr Carus Wilson. Most people who know anything of the average private schools of that time are satisfied that Charlotte Brontë's description was substantially correct. 'I want to show you many letters,' writes Mrs Gaskell, 'most of them praising the character of our dear friend as she deserves, and from people whose opinion she would have cared for, such as the Duke of Argyll, Kingsley, Greg, etc. Many abusing me. I should think seven or eight of this kind from the Carus Wilson clique.'

The Branwell matter was more serious. Mrs Gaskell published the full story of Branwell's affair with Mrs Robinson, which, although her account was, in the main, true, was indiscreet considering that the lady was still alive. Mrs Gaskell wrote:[2]

The story must be told. If I could, I would have avoided it; but not merely is it so well-known to many living as to be, in a manner, public property, but it is possible that, by revealing the misery, the gnawing, life-long misery, the degrading habits, the early death of her partner in guilt—the acute and long-enduring agony of his family—to the wretched woman, who not only survives, but passes about in the gay circles of London society, as a vivacious, well-dressed, flourishing widow, there may be awakened in her some feelings of repentance. . . .

All the disgraceful details came out. Branwell was in no state to conceal his agony of remorse, or, strange to say, his agony of guilty love, from any dread of shame. He gave passionate way to his feelings; he shocked and distressed those loving sisters inexpressibly; the blind father sat stunned, sorely tempted to curse the profligate woman, who had tempted his boy—his only son —into the deep disgrace of deadly crime. . . .

The pitiable part, as far as he was concerned, was the yearning love he still bore to the woman who had got so strong a hold upon him. It is true, that she professed equal love; . . . The case

[1]See Appendix I.
[2]*The Life of Charlotte Brontë*, by Mrs E. C. Gaskell, first edition, pp. 316, 317, 328, 330–332.

presents the reverse of the usual features; the man became the victim; the man's life was blighted, and crushed out of him by suffering, and guilt entailed by guilt; the man's family were stung by keenest shame. The woman—...— she goes flaunting about to this day in respectable society; a showy woman for her age kept afloat by her reputed wealth. I see her name in county papers, as one of those who patronize the Christmas balls; and I hear of her in London drawing-rooms. . . .

A few months later (I have the exact date, but, for obvious reasons, withhold it) the invalid husband of the woman with whom he had intrigued, died. Branwell had been looking forward to this event with guilty hope. After her husband's death, his paramour would be free; strange as it seems, the young man still loved her passionately, and now he imagined the time was come when they might look forwards to being married, and might live together without reproach or blame. She had offered to elope with him; she had written to him perpetually; she had sent him money—twenty pounds at a time; he remembered the criminal advances she had made; she had braved shame, and her children's menaced disclosures, for his sake; he thought she must love him; he little knew how bad a depraved woman can be. Her husband had made a will, in which what property he left to her was bequeathed solely on the condition that she should never see Branwell Brontë again. At the very time when the will was read, she did not know but that he might be on his way to her, having heard of her husband's death. She despatched a servant in hot haste to Haworth. He stopped at the Black Bull, and a messenger was sent up to the parsonage for Branwell. He came down to the little inn, and was shut up with the man for some time. . . . he was forbidden by his paramour ever to see her again, as, if he did, she would forfeit her fortune. Let her live and flourish! He died, his pockets filled with her letters, which he had carried perpetually about his person, in order that he might read them as often as he wished.

These statements regarding Mrs Robinson which were published in the First and Second Editions of the *Life of Charlotte Brontë*, nearly resulted in an action at law. Mrs Robinson (who had since become Lady Scott), threatened to sue Mrs Gaskell for libel unless the passages relating to her were withdrawn from subsequent editions of the book, and a public apology made.

Mrs Gaskell agreed to withdraw the statements referred to, not because they were untrue, but because she had not sufficient evidence to substantiate them. Her account, which was gleaned mainly from Charlotte's letters or from what Ellen Nussey could tell her of the affair, was fairly correct. Charlotte and her sisters were thoroughly persuaded that Mrs Robinson was the cause of their brother's ruin, and Mr Nicholls believed the story to have some truth in it, as he could not otherwise account for Anne's acceptance of her brother's version of the affair, she being all the time in the same family, but all actual evidence had no doubt been discreetly destroyed by Mr Brontë after Branwell's death.

Mrs Gaskell certainly made one or two inaccurate statements. She was not correct in saying that Branwell's pockets were full of letters from Mrs Robinson,[1] nor was she right in her statement regarding Mr Robinson's will, which was a story circulated by Mrs Robinson herself, in order to prevent Branwell from pressing his attentions upon her, when she already had prospects of a more advantageous match.[2]

However, Mrs Gaskell agreed to suppress the obnoxious passages in subsequent editions of her book, and a letter was sent to the *Times* by her solicitors.[3]

Yet when all is said, Mrs Gaskell had done her work as thoroughly and well as the documents before her permitted. Lockhart's *Scott* and Froude's *Carlyle* are examples of great biographies which called for abundant censure upon their publication; yet both these books will live as classics of their kind. To be interesting, it is perhaps indispensable that the biographer should be indiscreet, and certainly the Branwell incident—a matter of two or three pages—is the only part of Mrs Gaskell's biography in which indiscretion becomes indefensible. And for this she suffered cruelly. 'I did so try to tell the truth,' she said to a friend, 'and I believe *now* I hit as near to the truth as any one could do.' 'I weighed every line with my whole power and

---

[1] 'To this bold statement (*i.e.* that love-letters were found in Branwell's pockets) Martha Brown gave to me a flat contradiction, declaring that she was employed in the sick-room at the time, and had personal knowledge that not one letter, nor a vestige of one, from the lady in question, was so found.'—Leyland, *The Brontë Family*, Vol.II, p. 284.

[2] Mrs Robinson married Sir Edward Scott in November, 1848.

[3] See p. 223 below.

heart,' she said on another occasion, 'so that every line should go to its great purpose of making *her* known and valued, as one who had gone through such a terrible life with a brave and faithful heart.' And that clearly Mrs Gaskell succeeded in doing. It is quite certain that Charlotte Brontë would not stand on so splendid a pedestal to-day but for the single-minded devotion of her accomplished biographer.

It has sometimes been implied that the portrait drawn by Mrs Gaskell was far too sombre, that there are passages in Charlotte's letters which show that ofttimes her heart was merry and her life sufficiently cheerful. That there were long periods of gaiety for all the three sisters, surely no one ever doubted. To few people, fortunately, is it given to have lives wholly without happiness. And yet, when this is acknowledged, how can one say that the picture was too gloomy? Taken as a whole, the life of Charlotte Brontë was among the saddest in literature. At a miserable school, where she herself was unhappy, she saw her two elder sisters stricken down and carried home to die. She had, in the years when that was most essential, no mother's care; and perhaps there was a somewhat too rigid disciplinarian in the aunt who took the mother's place. Her second school brought her, indeed, two kind friends; but her shyness made that school-life in itself a prolonged tragedy. Two experiences as a private governess were periods of torture to her sensitive nature. The ambition of the three girls to start a school on their own account failed ignominiously. The suppressed vitality of childhood and early womanhood made Charlotte unable to enter with sympathy and toleration into the life of a foreign city, and Brussels was for her a further disaster. Then within two years, just as literary fame was bringing its consolation for the trials of the past, she saw her two beloved sisters taken from her. And, finally, when at last a good man won her love, there were left to her only nine months of happy married life. 'I am not going to die. We have been so happy.' These words to her husband on her death-bed are not the least piteously sad in her tragic story. That her life was a tragedy, was the opinion of Mary Taylor, the friend with whom on the intellectual side she had most in common.

979. *To* GEORGE SMITH.

HAWORTH, near KEIGHLEY,
March 30th, 1857.

DEAR SIR,—I thank you and Mrs Gaskell for the biographical books you have sent me. I have read them with a high degree of melancholy interest, and consider them amongst the ablest, most interesting, and best works of the kind. Mrs Gaskell, though moving in what was to her a new line—a somewhat critical matter—has done herself great credit by this biographical work, which I doubt not will place her higher in literary fame even than she stood before. Notwithstanding that I have formed my own opinion, from which the critics cannot shake me, I am curious to know what they may say. I will thank you, therefore, to send me two or three newspapers containing criticisms on the biography, and I will remit the price of them to you in letter stamps.—I remain, dear Sir, yours respectfully and truly,

P. BRONTË.

980. *To* MRS GASKELL.

HAWORTH, near KEIGHLEY,
April 2nd, 1857.

MY DEAR MADAM,—I thank you for the books you have sent me containing the Memoir of my daughter. I have perused them with a degree of pleasure and pain which can be known only to myself. As you will have the opinion of abler critics than myself I shall not say much in the way of criticism. I shall only make a few remarks in unison with the feelings of my heart. With a tenacity of purpose usual with me, in all cases of importance, I was fully determined that the biography of my daughter should, if possible, be written by one not unworthy of the undertaking. My mind first turned to you, and you kindly acceded to my wishes. Had you refused I would have applied to the next best, and so on; and had all applications failed, as the last resource, though above eighty years of age and feeble, and unfit for the task, I would myself have written a short though inadequate memoir, rather than have left all to selfish, hostile, or ignorant scribblers. But the work is now done, and done rightly, as I wished it to be, and in its completion has afforded me more satisfaction than I have felt during many years of a life in which has been exemplified the saying that 'man is born to trouble, as the sparks fly upwards.' You have not only given a picture of my dear daughter Charlotte, but of my dear wife, and all my dear children and such a picture, too, as is full of truth and life. The picture of my brilliant and unhappy son is a masterpiece. Indeed, all the pictures in the work have vigorous, truthful, and delicate touches in them, which could have been executed only by a skilful female hand. There are a few trifling mistakes, which, should it be deemed necessary, may be corrected in the second edition. Mr Nicholls joins me in kind and respectful regards to you, Mr Gaskell, and your family, wishing you greatest good in both the words. —I remain, my dear Madam, Yours respectfully and truly,

P. BRONTË.

981. *To* MRS GASKELL.

HAWORTH, April 7th, 1857.

... The principal mistake in the memoir which I wish to mention is that which states that I laid my daughters under restriction with regard to their diet, obliging them to live chiefly on vegetable food. This I never did. After their aunt's death, with regard to the housekeeping affairs they had all their own way. Thinking their constitutions to be delicate the advice I repeatedly gave them was that they should wear flannel, eat as much wholesome animal food as they could digest, take air and exercise in moderation, and not devote too much time and attention to study and composition. I should wish this to be mentioned in the second edition. ...

P. BRONTË.

982 (707). *To* ELLEN NUSSEY.

PLYMOUTH GROVE,
April 15th, 1857.

MY DEAR MISS NUSSEY,—Among a huge heap of letters awaiting me on my arrival from Newcastle last night (where I had been since Thursday) was the enclosed. As you may suppose, it was anything but agreeable to think what you must have been setting me down as—an unlettered, unmannered, ungrate-

ful, good-for-nothing sort of brute. I send the envelope by way
of exculpation, though perhaps it leaves me open to the charge
of defect—but I was obliged to write in a hurry, and was not
sure whether to put on Halifax or Leeds. I hope your copy of the
'Life' and the one for Miss Wooler came safe. All the notices that
I have seen have been favourable, and some of the best exceedingly so. I have had a considerable number of letters too from
distinguished men expressing high approval. Mr Brontë, too, I
am happy to say, is pleased, and I can only hope that Mr Nicholls
will (as Sir J. K. Shuttleworth says) 'learn to rejoice that his wife
will be known as a Christian heroine, who could bear her cross
with the firmness of a martyr saint.' I have not time to give you
any long account of the travellers. They were to leave Rome for
Florence yesterday, after going through all the crushing and
excitement of the Holy Week. I only hope they won't be kilt and
spilt entirely. They intend to get as far as Venice, and then I suppose will turn their steps homeward. My two chickens here are
very well, and if they were not gone to school could send their
love.

Hoping your mother is better, I am, my dear Miss Nussey,
yours very hastily, but sincerely,

WM GASKELL.

983. CHARLES KINGSLEY *to* MRS GASKELL.

ST LEONARDS, May 14th, 1857.

Let me renew our long interrupted acquaintance by compli-
menting you on poor Miss Brontë's 'Life.' You have had a
delicate and a great work to do, and you have done it admirably.
Be sure that the book will do good. It will shame literary people
into some stronger belief that a simple, virtuous, practical home
life is consistent with high imaginative genius; and it will shame,
too, the prudery of a not over cleanly though carefully white-
washed age, into believing that purity is now (as in all ages till
now) quite compatible with the knowledge of evil. I confess that
the book has made me ashamed of myself. 'Jane Eyre' I hardly
looked into, very seldom reading a work of fiction—yours,
indeed, and Thackeray's are the only ones I care to open. 'Shirley' disgusted me at the opening, and I gave up the writer and
her books with a notion that she was a person who liked coarseness. How I misjudged her! and how thankful I am that I never

put a word of my misconceptions into print, or recorded my misjudgements of one who is a whole heaven above me.

Well have you done your work, and given us the picture of a valiant woman made perfect by sufferings. I shall now read carefully and lovingly every word she has written, especially those poems, which ought not to have fallen dead as they did, and which seem to be (from a review in the current 'Fraser') of remarkable strength and purity.

I must add that Mrs Kingsley agrees fully with all I have said, and bids me tell you that she is more intensely interested in the book than in almost any which she has ever read.

CHARLES KINGSLEY.

984. *To* Messrs NEWTON & ROBINSON, *Solicitors, York.*

8 BEDFORD ROW, LONDON,
May 26th, 1857.

DEAR SIRS,—As solicitor for and on behalf of the Rev. W. Gaskell and of Mrs Gaskell, his wife, the latter of whom is authoress of the 'Life of Charlotte Brontë,' I am instructed to retract every statement contained in that work which imputes to a widowed lady, referred to, but not named therein, any breach of her conjugal, or of her maternal, or of her social duties, and more especially of the statement contained in chapter 13 of the first volume, and in chapter 2 of the second volume, which imputes to the lady in question a guilty intercourse with the late Branwell Brontë. All those statements were made upon information which at the time Mrs Gaskell believed to be well founded, but which, upon investigation, with the additional evidence furnished to me by you, I have ascertained not to be trustworthy. I am therefore authorised not only to retract the statements in question, but to express the deep regret of Mrs Gaskell that she should have been led to make them.—I am, dear sirs, yours truly,

WILLIAM SHAEN.

A certain 'Note' which appeared in the *Athenæum* a few days later is not without interest now:

We are sorry to be called upon to return to Mrs Gaskell's 'Life of Charlotte Brontë,' but we must do so, since the book has gone forth with our recommendation. Praise, it is needless to point out, implied trust in the biographer as an accurate collector of facts. This, we regret to state, Mrs Gaskell proves not to have been. To the gossip which for weeks past has been seething and circulating in the London *coteries*, we gave small heed; but the 'Times' advertises a legal apology, made on behalf of Mrs Gaskell, withdrawing the statements put forth in her book respecting the cause of Branwell Brontë's wreck and ruin. These Mrs Gaskell's lawyer is now fain to confess his client advanced on insufficient testimony. The telling of an episodical and gratuitous tale so dismal as concerns the dead, so damaging to the living, could only be excused by the story of sin being severely, strictly true; and every one will have cause to regret that due caution was not used to test representations not, it seems, to be justified. It is in the interest of Letters that biographers should be deterred from rushing into print with mere impressions in place of proofs however eager and sincere those impressions may be. They *may* be slanders, and as such they may sting cruelly. Meanwhile the 'Life of Charlotte Brontë' must undergo modification ere it can be further circulated.

985. *To* Martha Brown.

PLYMOUTH GROVE,
Saturday, July 11th, [1857].

MY DEAR MARTHA,—I should be very much obliged to you indeed if you would be so kind as to send me the letters you speak of. I will take great care of them and return them to you quite safely. I am very glad you thought of it.—Yours truly,

E. C. GASKELL.

986. *To* Ellen Nussey, *Brookroyd, Birstall.*

LONDON, July 28th, 1857.

DEAR MADAM,—In consequence of my absence from home I did not receive your note of the 23rd instant until my return home yesterday. I have this morning seen a friend of Mrs Gaskells to whom that lady has referred me with reference to the new edition of her book, but I am not yet aware what course will

be taken with reference to the alterations to be made for the new edition, and indeed, as I am without direct replies to my letters to Mrs Gaskell (who has, I believe, been so much engaged by preparations for her daughter's marriage as to be unable to attend to anything else) I am able to give you but little information on the subject. With reference however to your enquiry as to when we shall require the corrections which you wish to have made before the new edition is printed, I must reply in the course of two or three days—as I hope that the communication which will be made to Mrs Gaskell by her friend this evening, will induce her either to furnish us with such alterations as she has to make forthwith, or to sanction our reprinting the book without further alterations than the omission of the passages which it has become necessary to withdraw.—I beg to remain,
        Your very faithful servant,
                                        G. SMITH.

987. *To* MRS GASKELL.

WELLINGTON, 30th July, 1857.

MY DEAR MRS GASKELL,—I am unaccountably in receipt by post of two vols containing the 'Life of C. Brontë.' I have pleasure in attributing this compliment to you; I beg, therefore, to thank you for them. The book is a perfect success, in giving a true picture of a melancholy life, and you have practically answered my puzzle as to how you would give an account of her, not being at liberty to give a true description of those around. Though not so gloomy as the truth, it is perhaps as much so as people will accept without calling it exaggerated, and feeling the desire to doubt and contradict it. I have seen two reviews of it. One of them sums it up as 'a life of poverty and self-suppression,' the other has nothing to the purpose at all. Neither of them seems to think it a strange or wrong state of things that a woman of first-rate talents, industry, and integrity should live all her life in a walking nightmare of 'poverty and self-suppression.' I doubt whether any of them will.

It must upset most people's notions of beauty to be told that the portrait at the beginning is that of an ugly woman.[1] I do not altogether like the idea of publishing a flattered likeness. I had

[1] Mrs Gaskell had described Charlotte Brontë's features as 'plain, large, and ill-set,' and had written of her 'crooked mouth and large nose'—while acknowledging the beauty of hair and eyes.

rather the mouth and eyes had been nearer together, and shown the veritable square face and large disproportionate nose.

I had the impression that Cartwright's mill was burnt in 1820, not in 1812. You give much too favourable an account of the black-coated and Tory savages that kept the people down, and provoked excesses in those days. Old Roberson said he 'would wade to the knees in blood rather than the then state of things should be altered,'—a state including Corn law, Test law, and a host of other oppressions.

Once more I thank you for the book—the first copy, I believe, that arrived in New Zealand.—Sincerely yours,

MARY TAYLOR.

988. The Rev. P. BRONTË.
Signed testimonial for Nancy and Sarah Garrs.

HAWORTH, Augt 17th, 1857.

I beg leave to state to all whom it may concern, that Nancy and Sarah Garrs, during the time they were in my service, were kind to my children, and honest; and not wasteful, but sufficiently careful in regard to food, and all other articles committed to their charge.

P. BRONTË, A.B.,
Incumbent of Haworth, Yorkshire.

989. *To* MRS GASKELL.

HAWORTH, August 24th, 1857.

... Why should you disturb yourself concerning what has been, is, and ever will be the lot of eminent writers? But here, as in other cases, according to the old adage, 'The more cost the more honour.' Above three thousand years since Solomon said, 'He that increaseth knowledge increaseth sorrow'; 'Much study is a weariness of the flesh.' So you may find it, and so my daughter Charlotte found it, and so thousands may find it till the end of the world should this sinful, perverse world last so long as to produce so many authors like you and my daughter Charlotte. You have had and will have much praise with a little blame. Then drink the mixed cup with thankfulness to the great Physician of souls. It will be far more salutary to you in the end, and even in the beginning, than if it were all unmixed sweetness....

P. BRONTË.

990. *To* MARTHA BROWN.

PLYMOUTH GROVE, Sept. 3rd [1857].

MY DEAR MARTHA,—I am very much obliged to you indeed for letting me see these letters of your dear mistress. I am sending you a copy of the third edition of her life; and you will find that in that book I have made use of two or three of these valuable letters.

I was very sorry indeed that I was out when you called here, for I should like to have seen you very much.

I altered the word 'seduced' to 'betrayed' in this edition, which I hope will satisfy the poor young woman's friends.

With kindest regards to Mr Brontë, believe me to remain,—Your sincere friend,

E. C. GASKELL.

991. *To* GEORGE SMITH.

HAWORTH, near KEIGHLEY,
Sept. 4th, 1857.

MY DEAR SIR,—I thank you for the books which I have just received; Mr Nicholls also sends his thanks for those you have given to him. As far as I have gone through the third edition of the 'Memoir' I am much pleased with it. I hope it will give general satisfaction. Should you see any reviews worth notice be so kind as to let me have them, as I am rather anxious to know what the sage critics may deem it expedient in their wisdom to say. I hope that by this time Mrs Smith has fully recovered her health. Your anxiety on her account must be very great. Mr Nicholls joins me in kind and respectful regards.—Yours very respectfully and truly,

P. BRONTË.

992 (708). *To* ELLEN NUSSEY.

1857.

MY DEAR MISS ELLEN,—I must not detain your letter any longer, and now thank you for the loan of it. Many changes have occurred since Mary left England, and if a year must elapse before she again treads its shores, there may be many others.

Yesterday I met Mrs Marshall, and who do you think had been her guest and had just left Hornsea for Edinburgh? Mrs Joe Taylor! I did not hear that she was inconsolable;[1] but I am to take tea there soon and shall then hear more. The third edition has at length ventured out—our curate tells me he is assured it is quite inferior to the former ones—so you see Mrs Gaskell displayed worldly wisdom in going out of her way to furnish gossip for the discerning public. Did I name to you that Mrs E. Gibson knows two or three young ladies in Hull who finished their education at Madame Heger's pension? Mrs Gaskell said they read 'Villette' with keen interest—of course they would. I had a nice walk with a Mrs Goldsmith, a Suffolk lady, a visitor of the Marshalls, who was evidently delighted to meet with one who had personally known our dear Charlotte Brontë, and would not soon have wearied of a conversation in which she was the topic. Mrs Palmer says she was more interested in her biography than in any she ever perused. I am truly sorry to hear that the vicars of Birstall and Dewsbury are both incapacitated for duty. Mr A[llbutt]'s attack has been more severe than I had any idea of, and it is not the first. The loss of their papa would indeed be a severe trial to dear Clifford and Marianne. May it please God to avert it for a few years at least! During the last six weeks I have been almost free from indigestion. *How thankful should I be!*

M. WOOLER.

993. *To* Sir JOSEPH PAXTON, Bart., *Hardwick Hall, Chesterfield.*

HAWORTH, NEAR KEIGHLEY,
January 16th, 1858.

SIR,—Your letter, whch I have received this morning, gives both Mr Nicholls and me great uneasiness. It would seem that application has been made to the Duke of Devonshire for money to aid the subscription in reference to the expense of apparatus for heating our church and schools. This has been done without our knowledge, and most assuredly, had we known it, would have met with our strong opposition. We have no claim on the duke. His Grace honoured us with a visit in token of his respect

[1] Joseph Taylor died in March, 1857.

for the memory of the dead, and his liberality and munificence are well and widely known; and the mercenary, taking an unfair advantage of these circumstances, have taken a step which both Mr Nicholls and I utterly regret and condemn.

In answer to your query, I may say that the whole expense for both the schools and church is about one hundred pounds, and that after what has been and may be subscribed, there may fifty pounds remain as a debit, but this may, and ought to be raised by the inhabitants in the next year after the depression in trade shall, it is hoped, have passed away. I have written to his Grace on the subject.

I remain, Sir, Your obedient Servant,

P. BRONTË.

994. *To* ELLEN NUSSEY.

January 28th, 1858.

DEAR ELLEN, — Your account of Mrs Gaskell's book was very interesting. She seems a hasty, impulsive person, and the needful drawing back after her warmth gives her an inconsistent look. Yet I doubt not her book will be of great use. You must be aware that many strange notions as to the kind of person Charlotte really was will be done away with by a knowledge of the true facts of her life. I have heard imperfectly of farther printing on the subject. As to the mutilated edition that is to come, I am sorry for it. Libellous or not, the first edition was all true, and except the declamation all, in my opinion, useful to be published. Of course I don't know how far necessity may make Mrs Gaskell give them up. You know one dare not always say the world moves. — Yours affectionately,

MARY TAYLOR.

995 (710). *To* MRS NUNN, *near Eye, Suffolk.*[1]

HAWORTH, near KEIGHLEY,
February 1st, 1858.

MY DEAR MADAM, — I thank you for your kind offer of the excellent newspaper you have mentioned, but there is no necessity of sending to me, since, owing to the newspapers I take, and

---

[1]The Rev. John Nunn was Mr Brontë's old college friend who was curate at Shrewsbury when Mr Brontë was at Wellington. See Vol.I,p. 5.

the various institutions in the village, I can see the 'Record,' or any other I may choose, daily. And truly, in this changeable and ever-changing world, this state of our probation, we clergymen ought to read and know what is passing, and to discern the signs of the times, so that we may be able to speak a word in season to the people committed to our charge. I have forgotten the age of my dear old friend Mr Nunn—will you be so kind as to mention it when you next write. I am now in the eighty-first year of my age. I think he must be six or seven years younger; but it appears that his bodily strength has considerably failed him, and that it is now his duty not to exert himself, as formerly, but to be a little cautious, so that by Divine aid his useful life may be spared long for the benefit of the flock of our blessed Lord and Saviour. I preach once every Sabbath afternoon, but I cannot do more. Mr Nicholls joins me in kind regards.—I remain, my dear madam, yours in the best of bonds,

P. BRONTË.

996. *To* a HAWORTH GENTLEMAN.

HAWORTH, February 4th, 1858.

DEAR SIR,—I thank you and Mrs——— for your kind invitation but I never go out at night, nor indeed by day, to any parties. Mr Nicholls will, however, do himself the pleasure of visiting you at the time specified.—I remain, Yours respectfully and truly,

P. BRONTË.

997 (709). *To* ELLEN NUSSEY.

WELLINGTON, June 4th, '58.

DEAR ELLEN,—I have lately heard through Amelia that you have lost your mother and that you are leaving Brookroyd. Where to? And how will you be situated? I imagine you now with plenty of leisure and independence, but with a sense of desolation arising from the strange place you are in, and even from the want of your accustomed work and anxiety. I shall not even see Brookroyd again, and one of the people who lived there and one whom I used to see there, I shall never see more. Keep yourself well, dear Ellen, and gather round you as much happiness and interest as you can, and let me find you cheery and thriving when I come. When that will be I don't yet know; but one thing is sure, I have given over ordering goods from England, so that I must sometime give over for want of anything to sell. The last things ordered I expect to arrive about the beginning of the year 1859. In the course of that year therefore I shall be left without anything to do or motive for staying. Possibly this time twelve-month I may be leaving Wellington. Amelia writes that Tim has got her last tooth through, so that I suppose the danger is over. Certainly Amelia's life does not impress me favourably as to the happiness of even a suitable marriage. I think (my choice being free) that I would rather not have my all of earthly pleasure hang on so slender a thread, though it might be that my enjoyment were less intense. The absorption of her letters makes one tremble for her. I can well imagine that she will gradually drop all her friends out of sheer forgetfulness and be quite unconscious of her selfishness owing to the disguise it takes. I should not like to be the one to advise her to think now and then of something else, for were the poor thing to die, she would certainly think it had got its mortal injury in the time she was not thinking of it.

We are here in the height of a political crisis. The election for the highest office in the province (Superintendent) comes off in about a fortnight. Moreover, we have just got a judge landed, for the first time these two years, and one of the members of our provincial council has been waiting for the Supreme Court to sit to go to law with the late Superintendent, who is also a candidate for re-election. There is altogether a small storm going on in our teacup, quite brisk enough to stir everything in it. My principal interest therein is the sale of election ribbons; though I am afraid, owing to the bad weather, there will be little display. Besides the elections there is nothing interesting. We all go on pretty well. I have got a pony about four feet high that carries me about ten miles from Wellington, which is much more than walking distance, to which I have been confined for the last ten years. I have given over most of the work to Miss Smith, who will finally take the business, and if we had fine weather I think I should enjoy myself. We have a very wet and early winter, and have had no earthquakes for a long time, which is always thought a bad sign. People expect a sharp one when one comes after a long interval of quiet. My main want here is for books enough to fill up my idle time. It seems to me that when I get home I will spend half

my income on books, and sell them when I have read them, to
make it go farther. I know this is absurd, but people with an un-
satisfied appetite think they can eat enormously. It rains just
now five days out of six.

Remember me kindly to Miss Wooler, and tell me more about
her in your next. You must by no means give over writing to me
until I tell you. If I don't sail till next year at this time you may
safely write until April, *i.e.* by the March mail. Fill your letter
with gossip. You are mistaken in thinking I hear much.

Describe your new dwelling and employment—where you
will go or what you will do, without work. Write quickly and
fully, and tell me all about it.—Yours affectionately,

MARY TAYLOR.

998. *To* FRANKLIN BACHELLER, *Lynn, Mass., U.S.A.*

HAWORTH, NEAR KEIGHLEY, ENGLAND,
December 22, 1858.

DEAR SIR,—Owing to the many demands upon me, I can send
you only a small piece of my dear Charlotte's handwriting, which
is herewith enclosed.—I remain, dear Sir, Very respectfully
yours,

P. BRONTË.

Attached to this letter is the beginning of one from Charlotte
Brontë to her father:

DEAR PAPA,—I left...
having settled all...

999. *To* MR MILLIGAN, *Surgeon, Keighley.*

HAWORTH, Nr. KEIGHLEY,
Jany 25th, 1859.

DEAR SIR,—I thank you for the able scientific work which you
have sent me, and which I hope will make a useful addition to
many important discoveries and improvements since the days of
Galen.

Yet, I apprehend, that the Healing Art is but in its infancy,
and that the time may not be far distant when the vital principles

will be better understood, and antidotes, and remedies, and specifics, more numerous than at present. The Author of every Good and perfect Gift, will I trust throw light upon a subject so important, and necessary for the comfort and happiness of his creatures.

I should have written sooner, had it not been that I have been confined to bed by an attack of bronchitis. However I thank God I am better. Give my kind regards to Mrs Milligan, and believe me, — Yours respectfully and truly,

P. BRONTË.

1000. *To* JOHN STUART MILL.

July 14, 1859.

SIR, — When you look at the signature of this letter you will probably be surprised at receiving it, as the only communication I ever received from you was couched in terms which I then thought impertinent, unjust and inexcusable; which I now think simply unjust. For after reading the dedication of your Essay on Liberty I can understand how any word expressing a meaning only conjectured that was derogatory to your wife would wound you most deeply. And therefore I now write to express my deep regret that you received such pain through me. I still think you were unreasonable; but I like you better than if you had been reasonable under such circumstances. You used hard words towards me; I hardly expect now to be able to change your opinion of me; indeed I write now more with the intention of relieving my own mind by expressing sorrow for having given pain, than with the idea of clearing myself in your opinion. But still it would be but fair in you to listen to my view of the case. I knew nothing of the writer of the article in question: I had not even read the article. Miss Brontë knew nothing either;[1] but the impression produced on her mind by it made her imagine that such and such must have been the disposition and character of the person who wrote it. This imagination told as much of *her* mind and judgment — if not more, than it could be held to reveal of the writer's. I do not express myself very clearly in this way.

---

[1]The reference is to a letter of Charlotte Brontë's (published in the *Life*, 1st ed. Vol. ii, pp. 229-230) referring to J. S. Mill, in which Charlotte presumes him to be the author of an article on the Emancipation of Women. The author was actually Mrs J. S. Mill, formerly Mrs John Taylor. She died in 1858. *See* Vol. III of this edition, p. 278.

I will try and take an analogous case. I see a great picture, the painter of which is utterly unknown to me even by name. As well as my opinion of the picture I unconsciously form some idea of the painter. His choice of treatment of a subject is either pleasing or displeasing to me, individually; and I try and discover why it is so, and to conjecture what qualities he must possess to have made it so. In speaking of these and of his character, as conjectured from his work, I believe that I should reveal as much of my own character as of his. It seemed to me that in publishing that part of Miss Brontë's letter which gave you such acute pain that no one would receive any impression of the writer of the article in question; while to some a good deal might be learnt of Miss Brontë's state of mind and thought on such subjects.

But I will not trouble you further with recurring to a subject which I fear still must give you pain. I will not even give you my address for I do not want you to answer this. Only please do not go on thinking so badly of me, as you must have done before you could have written that letter. —Yours respectfully and truly,

E. C. GASKELL.

1001. *To* MRS GASKELL.

[July, 1859].

You entirely mistake the motive which actuated the letter to which you refer. It was not hurt feelings on a sensitive point, but a sense of truth and justice which I flatter myself would have been the same in any other case. Even now I should feel that I was acting contrary to her wishes and character by any partiality or unreasonable sensitiveness, much more than at a time when I could afford to regard these things with indifference.

The case being simply that in the exercise of the discretion of an editor you neglected the usual and indispensable duty which custom (founded on reason) has imposed, of omitting all that might be offensive to the feelings of individuals. Had what was said referred only to myself the publication of it would have been equally unjustifiable. Miss Brontë was entitled to express any foolish impression that might occur to her in a private letter. It is the editor who publishes what may give just offence who is alone to blame.

[J. S. MILL].

1002. *To* A. HOLROYD, *Westgate, Bradford.*

HAWORTH PARSONAGE, Augt 10th, 1859.

DEAR SIR,—I hope you will forgive my not writing to you sooner, the reason is I have been very buisey (*sic*) preserving fruit. I have duly received eight numbers of the Cottage in the wood,[1] for which I return you my thanks. I have given one with the cover on to Mr Brontë—he sends you his respects—and thinks that for the price they are neatly got up.—I remain,

Yours respectfully,

MARTHA BROWN.

1003. *To* JOHN STUART MILL.

42, PLYMOUTH GROVE, MANCHESTER,
August 11th, 1859.

SIR,—You do me an injustice, I think, and I shall try once more to set myself partially right in your opinion, because I value it; but I do not believe in any good result arising from this final attempt.

I wrote from Scotland, where I was away from books, and had no power of referring to the passage in the Life of Miss Brontë. I am now at home, and have it and your letter by me. Where I think you do me an injustice is in saying that 'in publishing letters not written for publication you disregarded the obligation which custom founded on reason has imposed, of omitting what would be offensive to the feelings and perhaps injurious to the moral reputation of individuals . . . and the notion you seem to entertain that everything said or written by any one, which could possibly throw light on the character of the sayer or writer, may, justifiably be published by a biographer, is one which the world, and those who are higher and better than the world, would, I believe, perfectly unite in condemning.'

I have expressed myself badly if you think that I intentionally disregarded the 'obligation which custom or reason has imposed &c.'—I certainly did not think that 'a foolish opinion,' a mere conjecture, obviously formed on insufficient grounds for having any weight affixed to it by the most careless reader could

[1] This was the sixteen-page pamphlet reprinted from the second edition of *The Cot-* *tage in the Wood*, and published by M. Nelson and A. Holroyd of Bradford, 1859.

have been 'offensive to the feelings, or injurious to the moral reputation.' That is the point on which we differ; *not* on the duty of a biographer to omit whatever can reasonably be expected to 'be offensive' &c. I acknowledge that duty, and I believe that you are the only person who has made any complaint or remonstrance to me about the publication of any part of Miss Brontë's 'Letters.' I tried to be very careful and it was difficult to exactly tell where the limit (the necessity for which, let me say once again, I fully acknowledge) was to be drawn.

Now, having endeavoured to set you right as to my recognition of the duty you seem to think I ignore — (and some hasty expression in my last letter may have given rise to this misconception on your part) I will candidly say that on reading the offensive part over again, I believe that I *ought* to have omitted some part of what I inserted, in fulfilment of the duty which I acknowledge as much as you do. It may be that your letters, and the sense of having given pain has awakened my conscience; it may be that in two or three years one's perception of right and wrong becomes juster and keener, — but, if it were to be re-edited now, I should *certainly* omit the final paragraph relating to yourself. 'In short J. S. Mill's head is I dare say, very good, but I feel disposed to scorn his heart.' It was, I see, morally wrong to have published that. But I am not so sure about the rest.

Do you understand? I acknowledge the duty as much as you do. I have failed in this duty, as I now perceive in *one* part. As to the *other* part, that is a matter of opinion. I do not yet clearly see that I have failed in this duty with regard to that. I do not believe that a just and reasonable person ought to have been offended by the publication of such a mere conjecture as to possible character. As I said I do *not* believe that this letter will alter your opinion of me, and of the transaction which has brought us thus unpleasantly into contact. But I write it for the chance. — Yours respectfully and truly,

E. C. GASKELL.

1004 (711). *To* MRS NUNN, *Rectory, near Eye.*

HAWORTH, near KEIGHLEY,
October 26th, 1859.

MY DEAR MADAM, — I thank you for the picture of the Rectory. It is *well* executed, and shows a very respectable and convenient building, which is, I hope and believe, only the *earnest* and fore-runner of '*that* House, not made with hands, eternal in the Heavens.' But large and commodious as your house is, I think it has no room for a third person as a lodger, who would prob-ably be a discordant string that would spoil your domestic har-mony. You inquired whether your parcels and letters cost me anything; they all come free, and I pay for all I send to you. The newspaper account of the idle and ostentatious pageantry got up in the church, where the Gospel was once faithfully preached, grieves me. But, my dear madam, a bad spirit, some call it the spirit of the age (I fear it might rather be called the spirit of revo-lution, vanity, scepticism, and Romish idolatry), this ominous spirit of the age is actuating numbers; and the young, thought-less, and vain have looked upon, loved, and greedily embraced the delusion. But Christ, who conquers death and hell, will give his followers the victory, and make all things work together for good to those who enlist in his service, and fight the good fight of Faith, in his name, and by his wisdom and power. All things work together for good to those who love God. Yes, for good, in reference to *both* the worlds. I hope that you will be able to read this miserable scrawl. My sight is very scanty, and the day is dim. Mr Nicholls joins me in kind regards to you and my dear old friend. —Yours very truly, in the best of bonds,

P. Brontë.

I have posted for you a picture of my house and church.

1005. *To* Mr Rand, *Ipswich*.

Haworth, Nr Keighley,
Octr 29th, 1859.

Dear Sir, —I am much pleas'd to learn that through Divine mercy, you are again able to see. I know what it is to be unable to behold the sight of the sun, and again, to see his beams. You have had your trials, and I have had mine—May the Lord sanctify them, and make them tend to our happiness in time and eternity!

Give my kind regards to Mrs Rand, Mrs Bacon, and your son —I remain, Yours very truly,

P. Brontë.

1006. *To* GEORGE SMITH.

HAWORTH, near KEIGHLEY,
March 26th, 1860.

MY DEAR SIR,—Though writing is to me now something of a task I cannot avoid sending you a few lines to thank you for sending me the magazines, and for your gentlemanly conduct towards my daughter in all your transactions with her, from first to last. All the numbers of the magazines were good; the last especially attracted my attention and excited my admiration. The 'Last Sketch' took full possession of my mind. Mr Thackeray in his remarks in it has excelled even himself. He has written *multum in parvo, dignissima cedro*. And what he has written does honour both to his head and heart. Thank him kindly both in Mr Nicholls's name and mine. Amongst the various articles that have been written in reference to my family and me it has pleased some of the writers, for want of more important matter, to set up an ideal target for me as a mark to shoot at. In their practice a few have drawn the long bow with a vengeance, and made declensions very ridiculously wide; others have used the surer rifle and come nearer the mark; but all have proved that there is still space left for improvement, both in theory and practice. Had I but half Mr Thackeray's talents in giving a photograph likeness of human nature I might have selected and might yet select a choice number of these practising volunteers, and, whether they like it or not, give their portraits to the curious public. If organless spirits see as we see, and feel as we feel, in this material clogging world, my daughter Charlotte's spirit will receive additional happiness on scanning the remarks of her Ancient Favourite. In the last letter I received from you you mentioned that Mrs Smith was in delicate health; I hope that she is now well. I need scarcely request you to excuse all faults in this hasty scrawl, since a man in his eighty-fourth year generally lets his age plead his apology.—I remain, my dear Sir, Yours very respectfully and truly,

P. BRONTË.

1007 META GASKELL *to* EMILY SHAEN (*née* WINKWORTH).

[November 6th, 1860.]

MY DEAREST EMILY,—. . . What I want really to tell you about, is a visit which Mama and I paid to old Mr Brontë to-day. We were talking about him on Thursday, and I was expressing a great wish to see him, out of which conversation sprung a plan for my going alone to call on him—Mama saying that she fancied he would not like to see her; because so many reviews, letters in newspapers, etc., which she knew had reached him, had dwelt on the way in which, while pretending to have been his daughter's friend, she had held up his character to ridicule, etc. etc. But, however, at length it seemed better that she'd go too; to brave his displeasure if there were any, and to please him by the attention if there were none. So she wrote on Thursday evening to ask him if we might go. This she did, thinking that then, if he really had any objection to seeing her, it would give him the opportunity of preventing our visit. However, this morning there came a few tremulous, feeble lines to say he should be glad to see us; and we scuttled through our breakfast and caught the 8.40 train, which took us to Keighley, and then we got a fly that brought us to Haworth by about 11.15. 'Martha,' such a blooming, bright, clean young woman, gave us a hearty welcome; and took us into the parlour (Miss B's sitting-room), where we waited for about $\frac{1}{4}$ of an hour; when she came to fetch us to Mr B.—Mama had no idea that he was confined to bed, as he is now—we were taken into his bedroom; where everything was delicately clean and white, and there he was sitting propped up in bed in a clean nightgown, with a clean towel laid just for his hands to play upon—looking Oh! very different from the stiff scarred face above the white walls of cravat in the photograph— he had a short soft white growth of beard on his chin; and such a gentle, quiet, sweet, half-pitiful expression on his mouth, a good deal of soft white hair, and spectacles on. He shook hands with us, and we sat down, and then said how glad he was to see Mama—and she said how she had hesitated about coming,— feeling as if he might now have unpleasant associations with her —which never seemed to have entered into his head—then he asked her how, since he last saw her, she had passed through this weary and varied world—in a sort of half grandiloquent style—

and then interrupting himself he said, 'but first tell me how is that young lady, whose friend went to the Massacres in India?' I thought he meant the Ewarts, or something, and was quite surprised (besides other things) when Mama pointed to me, and said I was here, and then he prosecuted his inquiries about the engagement, and its breaking off;[1] and then turned round and told me that he hoped I would forget the past; and would hope —that we ought all to live on hope. —Then he told Mama how many, many applications he had for bits of Miss B's handwriting,—how he had to cut up her letters into strips of a line each. —He talked of her as simply 'Charlotte' without any hesitation—He said to Mama—'As I told you in my first letter, the Memoir is a book which will hand your name down to posterity,' and that there was only one fault he had to find with it; might he speak out openly before me? Mama told him he might, and we both sat expecting some allusion to the Lady S[cott] but —but what he said was that the statement that he had not allowed his children to have meat till they were (a certain age) had been quoted by either Mr Carus Wilson, or his defenders, as more likely to have been the cause of their delicacy than the fare they subsequently had at Cowan's Bridge. Now—this statement was a mistake. His children had always been allowed meat; but he said he had chosen not to defend himself at the expense of proving Mama inaccurate: and so giving a handle to those who accused her of mis-statements—I wish I could remember more of what he said. He very soon turned the conversation to politics: asked Mama whether she thought the English ought to interfere in Italian affairs at present, or wait till the Italians asked for help; and seemed very much pleased when she said she thought we ought to hold back for the present. 'You see we agree in politics as in everything else.' He had been very pleased with Thackeray's notice in the Cornhill[2] —he thought it showed 'heart, but Thackeray was an odd man, a very odd man.' He alluded to his own 'eccentricity' with a certain pride; and his 'independence,' too, of other people's opinion; not but what he valued the opinion of good people—Mama said: 'Yes—I was just telling my daughter as we came up the hill, that I thought you had always done what you thought right.'—'And so I have,'

---

[1] Miss Meta Gaskell's engagement to an officer, which was broken off.

[2] The Last Sketch (Emma a fragment of a story by Charlotte Brontë) in the Cornhill Magazine, April, 1860.

he said, 'and I appeal to God.' There was something very solemn in the way he said it; and in him altogether—None of the sternness I had fancied—Mama said something about our not staying too long to tire him and that we were going, for me to make a sketch; And he said, 'There are certain circumstances, you see,' looking very knowing, 'which make it desirable that when you leave in 5 minutes or so, we should shake hands—and I give your daughter free leave to make a sketch, or do anything *outside* the house. Do you understand Latin? Mrs Gaskell does at any rate, well, *verbum sap.*, a word to the wise,' and then he chuckled very much; the gist of it was, as Mama saw, and I guessed, that he feared Mr Nicholls' return from the school—and we were to be safely out of the house before that. Mama is telling Mr Shaen all about the sexton. Just before leaving Haworth we went to call on John Greenwood; and whilst Mama was talking to him, his wife volunteered to me how she disliked Mr N., as they all seemed to do—(The sexton said, 'Aye, Mester Brontë and Mr Nicholls live together still *ever near* but *ever separate*,' and he told us how when the fresh monument was put up in the church, Mr N. made him take the old tablet-stone, and with a hammer break it into small pieces, which he then bade, and saw, him bury 4ft deep in the garden: for fear any one should get hold of a piece for a relic). Well—Mrs Greenwood had a puny, precocious little lad clinging to her dress, about $1\frac{1}{2}$ years old[1]—so of course I asked its name, and she said 'Brontë, Miss. Eh, Mr Nicholls was angry a' that.' He heard they were going to give it the name; and said in Mr B's hearing that he wouldn't christen the child, whereupon Mr B. sent word by Martha of his determination to the Greenwoods, to spare them the annoyance of a direct refusal, so they kept the child unchristened till it was 6 months old when it became so ailing that they thought it wouldn't live; and Mr B. hearing of this, sent for it (as far as I understand) to his own bedroom (it is a year since his health began to fail) and christened it there; having the Register-book for baptisms, and writing down its name with his own hand. It was years since he had christened a child. Of course the next baby Mr N. condescended to christen, he went to write its name down, and there saw Mr B's registration of the christening of little Brontë Greenwood. Mrs G. said that there and then he strode straight back to the Parsonage, and up into Mr B's bedroom; and 'So I see you have christened your

[1] Brontë Greenwood born May, 1859 now (1932) living in Wyncot, Pa., U.S.A.

namesake.' And Mr B. got out of it by saying that he had done it to save Mr N. from the terrible scrape in which he would have found himself, had the child died unchristened, etc. But this is a specimen of Mr N's sullen, obstinate rooted objection to any reverence being paid to Miss B. one might almost say at any rate to people caring to remember her as an authoress . . .

M. E. GASKELL.

1008. *To* W. S. WILLIAMS.

46, PLYMOUTH GROVE, MANCHESTER,
December 20th, 1860.

MY DEAR SIR,—When I was abroad this summer, I was introduced to a Miss Burnett, who asked me for an introduction to Messrs Smith, Elder & Co., with a view to the publication of an MS. which she had then in hand. The other day she wrote to claim the fulfilment of my promise; and I have thought it best to perform it by writing direct to yourself, as I have been sending Mr Smith lately so many similar introductions that I have some scruples in troubling him further in that way. Besides you have always been so kind to me, however and whenever I have applied to you, that I think you will forgive me, if my bringing this MS. under your notice should uselessly waste your time.

We had the pleasure of seeing Mr Lowes Dickinson last Saturday week, and a real pleasure it was to us. Mr Gaskell missed his share, however, owing to his inevitable Saturday night's sermon, but we hope that Mr Dickinson will come and see us again when he returns to Manchester, and then Mr Gaskell will make up for lost time.

About six weeks ago I paid a visit to Mr Brontë, and sat for about an hour with him. He is completely confined to bed now, but talks hopefully of leaving it again when the summer comes round. I am afraid that it will not be leaving it as he plans, poor old man! He is touchingly softened by illness; but still talks in his pompous way, and mingles moral remarks and somewhat stale sentiments with his conversation on ordinary subjects. Mr Nicholls seems to keep him rather *in terrorem*. *He* is more unpopular in the village than ever; and seems to have even a greater aversion than formerly to any strangers visiting his wife's grave; or, indeed, to any reverence paid to her memory, even by those who knew and loved her for her own sake. He refused to christen Mr Greenwood's last child when he heard that it was to be named 'Brontë' after her, and the child remained unchristened for six months in consequence, when its great delicacy coming to Mr Brontë's knowledge, he sent for it privately and christened it in his own room. When Mr Nicholls came upon its name upon the register book Mr Greenwood says that he stormed and stamped, and went straight home to the Parsonage to Mr Brontë to ask him for his reasons in going so directly against his wishes. Fortunately Mr Brontë had the excellent defence of saying that if the child had died unchristened Mr Nicholls's case would have been extremely awkward, and that he had thus saved him from a great scrape. —Believe me yours most sincerely,

E. C. GASKELL.

There still remain some interesting facts to add to the Brontë story. By her will, which runs as follows, Mrs Nicholls left her husband the very small property that she had derived from her novels:

Extracted from the District Probate Registry at York attached to Her Majesty's High Court of Justice.

In the name of God. Amen. I, CHARLOTTE NICHOLLS, of Haworth, in the parish of Bradford and county of York, being of sound and disposing mind, memory, and understanding, but mindful of my own mortality, do this seventeenth day of February, in the year of our Lord one thousand eight hundred and fifty-five, make this my last Will and Testament in manner and form following, that is to say: In case I die without issue I give and bequeath to my husband all my property to be his absolutely and entirely, but, In case I leave issue I bequeath to my husband the interest of my property during his lifetime, and at his death I desire that the principal should go to my surviving child or children; should there be more than one child, share and share alike. And I do hereby make and appoint my said husband, Arthur Bell Nicholls, clerk, sole executor of this my last Will and Testament; In witness whereof I have to this my last Will and Testament subscribed by my hand, the day and year first above written—Charlotte Nicholls. Signed and acknowledged by the said testatrix Charlotte Nicholls, as and for her last Will and Testament in the presence of us, who, at her request, in her presence and in presence of each other, have at the same time hereunto subscribed our names as witnesses thereto: Patrick Brontë, B.A., Incumbent of Haworth, Yorkshire; Martha Brown.

The eighteenth day of April 1855, the Will of Charlotte Nicholls, late of Haworth, in the parish of Bradford in the county of York (wife of the Reverend Arthur Bell Nicholls, Clerk in Holy Orders) (having *bona notabilia* within the province of York) Deceased was proved in the prerogative court of York by the oath of the said Arthur Bell Nicholls (the husband), the sole executor to whom administration was granted, he having been first sworn duly to administer.

Testatrix died 31st March 1855.

Mr Nicholls stayed on at Haworth for the six years that followed his wife's death. When Mr Brontë died he returned to Ireland—to Banagher in King's County. On August 25th, 1864, he married again—a cousin, Miss Bell by name. Mr Shorter found him, on March 31st 1895, in a home of supreme simplicity and charm, esteemed by all who knew him and idolised in his own household. It was not difficult to understand that Charlotte Brontë had loved him and had fought down parental opposition in his behalf. The qualities of gentleness, sincerity, unaffected piety, and delicacy of mind were his. He lived for years as a country farmer, attending the neighbouring markets and looking after his stock. He wrote once or twice to English newspapers when questions arose concerning his wife's fame—otherwise he broke no silence.

Martha Brown went to stay with him and his wife for a time, but the only visitors from England who were Brontë enthusiasts whom he consented to receive were Mr Clement K. Shorter, Mr Reginald Smith of the firm of Smith, Elder, and Mr Field of the Brontë Society. He read every word written about the Brontës with keenest interest, and his house was full of mementos. There were drawings on the walls by the three sisters, and books in the cases that they had handled. Assuredly the Brontë tradition was well maintained in that quiet little Irish town.[1]

Mr Brontë died on June 7, 1861, and his funeral in Haworth Church is described in the *Bradford Review* of the following week:

Great numbers of people had collected in the churchyard, and a few minutes before noon the corpse was brought out through the eastern gate of the garden leading into the churchyard. The Rev. Dr Burnet, Vicar of Bradford, read the funeral service, and led the way into the church, and the following clergymen were the bearers of the coffin: The Rev. Dr Cartman of Skipton; Rev. Mr Snowden of Hebden Bridge; the Incumbents of Cullingworth, Oakworth, Morton, Oxenhope, and St John's Ingrow. The chief mourners were the Rev. Arthur Bell Nicholls, son-in-law of the deceased; Martha Brown, the housekeeper; and her sister; Mrs Brown, and Mrs Wainwright. There were several gentlemen followed the corpse whom we did not know. All the shops in Haworth were closed, and the people filled every pew, and the aisles in the church, and many shed tears during the impressive reading of the service for the burial of the dead, by the vicar. The body of Mr Brontë was laid within the altar rails, by the side of his daughter Charlotte. He is the last that can be interred inside of Haworth Church. On the coffin was this inscription: 'Patrick Brontë, died June 7th, 1861, aged 84 years.'

His will, which was proved at Wakefield, left the bulk of his property, as was natural, to the son-in-law who faithfully served and tended him for the six years which succeeded Charlotte Brontë's death:

Extracted from the Principal Registry of the Probate Divorce and Admiralty Division of the High Court of Justice.

Being of sound mind and judgment, in the name of God the Father, Son, and Holy Ghost, I, PATRICK BRONTË, B.A., Incumbent of Haworth, in the Parish of Bradford and county of

---

[1]Arthur Bell Nicholls died on Monday, December 3, 1906, and was buried in the new churchyard of Banagher.

York, make this my last Will and Testament: I leave forty pounds to be equally divided amongst all my brothers and sisters to whom I gave considerable sums in times past; And I direct the same sum of forty pounds to be sent for distribution to Mr Hugh Brontë, Ballinasceaugh, near Loughbrickland, Ireland; I leave thirty pounds to my servant, Martha Brown, as a token of regard for long and faithful services to me and my children; To my beloved and esteemed son-in-law, the Rev. Arthur Bell Nicholls, B.A., I leave and bequeath the residue of my personal estate of every description which I shall be possessed of at my death for his own absolute benefit; And I make him my sole executor; And I revoke all former and other Wills, in witness whereof I, the said PATRICK BRONTË, have to this my last Will, contained in this sheet of paper, set my hand this twentieth day of June, one thousand eight hundred and fifty-five.

PATRICK BRONTË. — Signed and acknowledged by the said PATRICK BRONTË as his Will in the presence of us present at the same time, and who in his presence and in the presence of each other have hereunto subscribed our names as witnesses: JOSEPH REDMAN, ELIZA BROWN.

CHAPTER XXXVI
THE AFTERMATH

AFTER the publication of Mrs Gaskell's biography, we find that a wealth of information concerning the subsequent history of Charlotte Brontë's letters and the writing of other works on the Brontës is contained in the correspondence of Miss Ellen Nussey.

Miss Nussey was much chagrined that she received no monetary reward from Mrs Gaskell for the help she had given her, and also she was hurt that none of the reviews referred to her. In a letter to a friend she writes:[1] 'It is curious how nearly all reviewers leave out of account the *source* from which Mrs Gaskell and others have gained their knowledge of the Brontë family. . . . It seems hardly fair does it, that the ore should have been so well used as it has been, and the mine forgotten as it were?' She therefore decided to try to make some use of the letters herself, for her own financial benefit, and in 1863, two years after the death of the Rev. Patrick Brontë, she wrote to M. Constantin Heger, Charlotte's former professor in Brussels, asking his advice regarding the publication, and subsequent translation into French, of the letters of Charlotte Brontë in her possession. It is interesting to read his reply.

1009. *To* ELLEN NUSSEY.

BRUXELLES, 7 Septembre, 1863.

MADEMOISELLE, —Deux mois expliqueront et me feront pardonner je l'espère le retard que j'ai, bien malgré moi, mis à vous répondre. Votre lettre ne m'a pas trouvé à Spa, je n'en ai pris connaissance qu'à mon retour des vacances.

Vous daignez Mademoiselle, me consulter sur trois points: 1°. la publication de près de 500 lettres de Charlotte Brontë, votre amie; 2°. la traduction en français de cette correspondance; 3°. ma participation éventuelle à cette traduction.

[1]Letter to Mrs Flower, June 29th, 1883.

M'expliquer sincèrement sur ces trois points, est à mes yeux un devoir.

Je crois, comme vous Mademoiselle, que votre amie sera plus fidèlement peinte par elle-même, que par autrui. Je crois que ces lettres intimes, où rien ne déguise le mouvement intime de sa pensée et en quelque sorte les battements de ce pauvre cœur malade, peuvent offrir encore un vif intérêt, même après la biographie développée de Mrs Gaskell; je suis convaincu de cela, et cependant il s'élève du fond de ma conscience, certaines objections que je soumets humblement à la vôtre. J'ai longtemps hésité à parler, parceque je sens combien est délicate la question que je vais aborder, mais cette hésitation que je ne veux point céler, je la regarde comme une faiblesse et je passe outre. Quelque chose me dit que ma sincérité ne saurait vous blesser. Vous parler comme je vais le faire, c'est rendre hommage à votre loyauté, à votre cœur.

Je me suis donc posé cette question? Pourrais-je, sans l'assentiment de mon ami, publier ses lettres intimes, c'est à dire ses confidences? — Ne m'a-t-il pas laissé voir de lui-même, plus qu'il ne voulait montrer au premier venu? Ce qu'il m'a dit à voix baissé, à l'oreille de mon cœur, puis-je aller le crier aux passants sur la place publique? Ces impressions fugitives, ces appréciations irréfléchies, jetées à cœur ouvert, dans une causerie à deux, où la plume trotte la bride sur le cou, puis-je les livrer en pâture à la curiosité maligne des lecteurs. . . . Je n'ai pas, Mademoiselle, l'injurieuse prétention de resoudre pour vous, cette question: je vous sais trop de délicatesse pour pouvoir supposer que votre raison et votre cœur aient ici besoin d'aide. Mais j'en appelle à votre propre experience: Il doit vous être arrivé, comme à moi, comme à tout le monde, de retrouver, après plusieurs années, le brouillon de quelqu'une de nos lettres. Certes je crois pouvoir affirmer que nous n'eussions pas livré ces lettres, sans modification aucune, à la publicité, quand l'expérience et les années avaient sur plus d'un point, modifié nos sentiments et nos idées.

Par la publication de cette correspondance, votre pieuse affection croit et veut ajouter à la gloire, à la considération de votre amie. Je le comprends, mais, pour vous mettre en garde contre vous-même, pour ne rien faire que votre amie n'approuve delà Haut, en triant ses lettres, supposez toujours votre amie présente et consultez-la.

Voilà, Mademoiselle, sans reticence ce que je pense de la publication des lettres originales en anglais.

Quant à la traduction en français quelque soit le mérite du traducteur, il me parait que, de toutes les œuvres littéraires, ce sont *les lettres* qui perdent le plus à être traduites. Dans la correspondance intime, l'à-propos, la liberté de l'allure, l'allusion voilée, les demi-mots, même les charmantes negligences d'une forme toute spontanée donnent, aux moindres choses, une grâce, un charme *intraduisibles*. Je ne sache pas qu'on ait songé à traduire les lettres de Madame de Sévigné, pas plus qu'on n'a tenté de peindre le vol, ou de noter le chant de l'oiseau. Certaines lettres résistent à la traduction, je le sais, mais c'est parce que, traitant de politique, de voyager, de critique littéraire, de morale, &c., elles ont un fond solide, et une valeur réelle indépendante de la forme. — Peut-être les lettres de votre amie sont-elles dans ce cas? — Je l'ignore et vous seule en pouvez juger.

Après avoir exprimé mon opinion sur la traduction, et confessé implicitement ainsi mon impuissance à faire ce que vous paraissez désirer de moi, je crois inutile d'ajouter qu'il me serait impossible, dans tous les cas, faute de loisir, de coopérer à la publication dont vous avez pieusement rassemblé les matériaux.

Veuillez, Mademoiselle, peser avec une indulgente bienveillance, les motifs de mon abstention, et agréer l'hommage de mes meilleurs sentiments.

C. Heger.

Translation.

Madam, — *Two words will explain, and I hope excuse, the delay which I have, much against my will, made in replying to you. Your letter did not find me at Spa; I only knew of it on my return from the holidays.*

You condescend, Madam, to consult me on three points: (1) The publication of nearly 500 letters of Charlotte Brontë, your friend: (2) The translation into French of this correspondence: (3) My eventual participation in this translation.

To explain myself sincerely on these three points is in my eyes a duty.

I think, like you, Madam, that your friend will be more faithfully depicted by herself than by another. I think that these intimate letters, in which nothing disguises the innermost movement of her thoughts, and in a way, the beatings of this poor sick heart, can still offer a lively interest, even after Mrs Gaskell's detailed biography. I am convinced of that, and yet it raises from the depths of my conscience certain objections which I humbly submit to yours. I have, for a long time, hesitated to speak, because I feel how delicate is the question which I am about to broach, but this hesitation, which I do not wish to hide, I regard as a weakness and I pass it by. Something tells me that my sincerity cannot wound you. To speak to you as I am going to do, is to pay homage to your loyalty, to your heart.

I therefore asked myself this question: Could I, without the consent of my friend, publish his intimate letters —that is to say, his confidences? Has he not allowed me to see more of himself than he would wish to show to the first comer? What he has whispered to me at the ear of my heart, can I go and cry it to passers-by in the public street? Those fugitive impressions, those unguarded appreciations, thrown with an open heart, in private talk, when the pen runs with a free rein, can I deliver them up as food for the malignant curiosity of readers? . . . I make no unconscionable claim, Madam, to settle this question for you. I know that you have too much delicacy for me to be able to suppose that your reason and your heart have need of help in this. But I appeal to your own experience. It must have happened to you, as to me, as to everyone, to come across, after many years, the rough draft of some letters of ours. I think I can surely say that we should not have made these letters public without some modification, after experience and the lapse of years had, on more than one point, modified our sentiments and our ideas.

By the publication of this correspondence, your affectionate love thinks and wishes to add to the glory and reputation of your friend. I understand that, but, to put you on your guard against yourself, so that you will do nothing of which your friend would not approve from Above, in sorting out her letters, always suppose that your friend is present, and consult her.

There, Madam, without reserve, is what I think of the publication of the original letters in English.

As for the translation into French, whatever may be the merit of the translator, it seems to me that of all literary work it is letters which lose most by being translated. In intimate correspondence, the associations, the freedom of expression, the veiled allusion, the half-hints, even the charming carelessness of their entire spontaneity, give the smallest things an untranslatable *grace and charm. I don't suppose any one ever dreamed of translating the letters of Madame de Sévigné any more than one would attempt to paint the flight or to write down the song of a bird. Certain letters stand translation, I know, but that is because, treating of politics, travel, literary criticism, morals, etc. they have a solid foundation and a real value independent of style. Perhaps your friend's letters belong to this class? I don't know, and you alone can judge.*

After having expressed my opinion on the translation, and thus tacitly confessed my inability to do what you appear to desire of me, I think it unnecessary to add that it would be impossible for me, in any case, for want of spare time, to join in the publication for which you have lovingly collected the materials.

Kindly weigh with an indulgent benevolence, Madam, the motives for my abstention, and accept my sincere regards.

C. HEGER.

After this, Miss Nussey appears to have taken no further steps in the matter until 1869, when she applied to George Smith of Messrs Smith, Elder & Co. regarding the publication of Charlotte's letters. Again she was doomed to disappointment, as the copyright in the letters belonged to Mr Nicholls, who, since leaving Haworth, had ceased to correspond with her, and who was strongly opposed to the publication by her of his wife's letters. He no doubt realised and strongly resented the commercial element behind Miss Nussey's endeavours to get the letters into print, and maybe, too, he considered that Miss Nussey was intellectually incapable of doing justice to them. Charlotte herself said of Ellen 'She is no more than a conscientious, observant, calm, well-bred Yorkshire girl,' and possibly Mr Nicholls shared this opinion.

Mr Smith handled Miss Nussey very kindly as the following letters indicate.

1010. *To* ELLEN NUSSEY.

45 PALL MALL, S.W., February 19th, 1868.

MY DEAR MADAM, —I have succeeded in finding a copy of the first edition of 'Villette' and have sent it to your address by book post. It gives me much pleasure to beg your acceptance of the book. I am much obliged to you for your kind enquiry about my mother and sisters. I lost one of my sisters, Sarah, about two years ago from consumption. Mother and remaining two sisters are quite well, my wife and children are also well, my wife is much stronger and better in health than she was some years ago.

If you should ever come to London it will give her and myself much pleasure to see you.

If you know what has become of Mr Nicholls and how he is I should be very glad to hear something of him when you have leisure to write to me. —I beg to remain, Yours very faithfully,

G. SMITH.

1011. *To* GEORGE SMITH.

LANESIDE, GOMERSAL, Feb. 20th, '68.

MY DEAR SIR,—I had the pleasure of receiving 'Villette' by this morg's post and feel very much indebted to you for it—as you kindly wish me to accept it as a gift I have much pleasure in letting it replace the lost and much-regretted original copy.

It is little I can tell you of Mr Nicholls—he left Haworth after Mr Brontë's decease and went to Ireland, and shortly after he married a cousin there, I accidentally heard lately, that not very long ago he was in England but only visiting, I think—I have not had a line from him since Mr Brontë died and then it was an ungracious reply to inquiries which I made, being then in the Isle of Wight and out of reach of all hearing about Mr Brontë—he seems to have been in a savage humour with me ever since the 'Life' came out—but he had no just reason for such conduct. I hope to make an expedition to Haworth some day and then I shall know more of many things that interest me in connection with the Brontës.

I am pleased to hear your mother keeps well and your sisters, and Mrs Smith, but very sorry to hear your sister Sarah is gone, for if I remember rightly she was the one who was in Scotland with Charlotte.

If the Leeds Exhibition should attract you and Mrs Smith to Leeds I hope you will let me know that I may see you here for a few hours at least.

We are only an hour from Leeds. . . .

[E. NUSSEY].

1012. *To* ELLEN NUSSEY.

15, WATERLOO PLACE, S.W.

January 18th, 1869.

MY DEAR MADAM,—I am afraid that I must suggest a difficulty in regard to the publication of Miss Brontë's letters to you which may not have occurred to your mind. The right to print those letters (otherwise the copyright in those letters) belongs to Mr Nicholls not to you. The letters themselves are your property and Mr Nicholls cannot claim them from you, but you cannot print them without his permission. That permission would not,

I fear, be easy to obtain, but if the letters are suitable for publication it might at all events be worth while to endeavour to get Mr Nicholls's consent to their publication, and I shall be very glad to see the letters you have copied if you will do me the favour of sending them to me.—Believe me, My dear Madam,
Yours very faithfully,

G. SMITH.

1013. *To* ELLEN NUSSEY.

15, WATERLOO PLACE, S.W.

January 21st, 1869.

MY DEAR MADAM,—You will perhaps be glad to have a few lines to inform you of the safe arrival of the parcel of MS. which you sent to me through the post office. I shall read the letters with much interest, and I am obliged to you for allowing me to have them.

The portrait of Miss Brontë by George Richmond was exhibited at South Kensington and the authorities of the Museum must have discovered the address of Mr Nicholls in order to obtain the loan of it—I shall endeavour to get his address from them as we may wish to communicate with him about the letters. —Believe me, My dear Madam, Yours very faithfully,

G. SMITH.

1014. *To* ELLEN NUSSEY.

15, WATERLOO PLACE, S.W.

February 12th, 1869.

MY DEAR MADAM,—I need scarcely say that I have been very much interested in reading the letters of Charlotte Brontë with which you have favoured me, as they express without reserve her inmost feelings. How these revelations of her emotions would strike the public mind if they were published separately, and whether they would heighten the impression of her character made by Mrs Gaskell's biography, appears to me an important consideration.

And it occurs to me that if you were to select some of the most characteristic letters, or passages from them and incorporate them in a brief and simple narrative of your friendship with Charlotte Brontë giving also your impressions of her and her family, with such other details from your own letters as would complete the picture of your early friendship, the letters would be more valuable and interesting for such additions to the biography.

Should this suggestion accord with your views, I think that Mr Nicholls could not make any objection to such a publication, especially if it took place in the 'Cornhill Magazine.' Indeed I would venture to print your articles in the Magazine without communicating with him. — Believe me, My dear Madam, Yours sincerely,

G. SMITH.

1015. *To* GEORGE SMITH.

[February, 1869].

... I was very glad to receive your letter and I will at once reply to suggestions at the close of it, at the present I feel in no position to give it even *consideration* for I am pledged to do what involves work almost night and day till after Easter, namely furnish a stall along with one other lady for the sale of work of which I send you a circular as a complete warrant of my excuse.

It is kind of you to make the proposal of printing in the Cornhill for me. Would you mind giving me an idea of the possible remunerations if I could write any thing practicable which I feel very diffident about. Could you learn for me if Mr N. has any of my letters to his wife in his possession — if I could procure them, if in existence, they would materially help me if I write when I am free to do so. There is one point in C. B.'s character which Mrs G. sadly marred in the biography — the religious element — so many people have expressed themselves as shocked by its absence — it was not *absent* which Mrs G. failed to see, or her peculiar favour for another creed made her. . . .

[E. NUSSEY].

1016. *To* GEORGE SMITH.

[Feb. 20, 1869].

... I have some letters which most people in his [Mr Nicholls's] place would give almost a fortune to possess — besides one from Mr Brontë written under the soubriquet of the old favourite dog.[1]

---

[1] See Charlotte's letter dated January 19, 1853, Vol. IV, p. 35.

If you think it right you can give him a hint that he has not all the power on his side—and that there is an obligation in kindness which is never ignored by true-hearted people.

If you on the chance of my being able to do something by and byewill kindly give me any information or suggestions that may occur to you I shall be greatly obliged. You must regard me as one quite ignorant of the ways and requirements of the press.

I was sorry to see a black border to your letter. How are your mother and your sister? are your own family well? As I said before you are not as strangers to me in idea.

I do not like to ask you for we have no claim upon you, but if ladies do ever beg contributions from your place of business for their Bazaars, and you do give to them, I think I may say I should be as grateful as any of them for a favour of the kind.

[E. NUSSEY].

1017. *To* ELLEN NUSSEY.

15, WATERLOO PLACE, S.W.
February 24th, 1869.

MY DEAR MADAM,—As you are so pressingly occupied at the present moment I need only say that there is plenty of time to think over the suggestion I offered for your consideration. At the same time I may say that the doubt I felt as to Mr Nicholls's approving the publication of some portions of these letters is confirmed by the tone of your allusions to him. I have not had any communication with Mr Nicholls for some time and should not have thought of writing to him on the subject of your letters, as any application to him would more properly come from you; especially as you desire to get back any letters of yours. But I think that we might venture to print such articles as I suggested without applying to Mr Nicholls on the subject.

With respect to the terms on which we should print your articles, it is of course difficult to name any sum without seeing the articles, but assuming that two or three articles would appear in the 'Cornhill Magazine' I think you might expect to receive £50 or thereabouts.

I find myself in a difficulty as to the contributions of books for your Bazaar, as applications of a similar kind are of such frequent occurrence that I have been compelled to withhold them, even from intimate friends.

Thank you for your kind reference to the border of my note paper. I am in mourning for the mother of my wife who died a few days ago. —Believe me, My dear Madam, Yours very faithfully,

G. SMITH.

1018. *To* GEORGE SMITH.

LANESIDE, GOMERSAL, Feb. 27th, '69.

MY DEAR SIR,—I must just thank you for your letter of the 24th inst and ask you to be kind enough to return me the copied letters when quite convenient.

I am sorry I took so much for granted with regard to them, but the allusion to my own letters led me to think you had some knowledge of their existence through Mr N. Charlotte said before her marriage that she would destroy all former correspondence but I was led very seriously to doubt her having carried out this intention from some little episodes in Mr N.'s subsequent behaviour. He discovered something about your Mr Taylor which sent him over hither in an excited state about a month after his wife's death: he did not find me at home, happily —but he wrote to Miss Wooler on the subject, fortunately she knew little. His next move was to get me into his neighbourhood to stay with some intimate friend of his, which I declined. It was a shock to me discovering that he had been ransacking his wife's things, so speedily after losing her, unfavourable impressions deepened still more, afterwards, by what seemed a most selfish appropriation of everything to himself, and when there were near relatives living both of Mr and Mrs Brontë's side. His notes to me became less and less civil in time till the time of Mr B.'s death when I ceased to write at all. I feel an insuperable aversion to write to him even for the obtaining (if I could) of my own letters. I procured his address or rather read his address sent from Haworth to Miss Gaskell not long ago, but I do not know it myself.

I am sorry you find a difficulty in sending us a contribution to our sale, for after paying off the debt, we shall yet want about £3,000 to finish the interior of our church. . . .

[E. NUSSEY].

1019. *To* ELLEN NUSSEY.

15, WATERLOO PLACE, S.W.
March 5th, 1869.

MY DEAR MADAM, —I had intended to write to you to advise you of the dispatch of your manuscript, but I have been so much pressed by work that I was obliged to defer doing so. Your note received this morning brings me intelligence of its safe arrival. From what you say of Mr Nicholls in your former letter I should fear there is no prospect of your receiving from him your letters to Miss Brontë.

You may judge how stringent is the necessity I am under to withhold contributions of books for your sale, since it compels me to resist your forcible appeal. —Believe me, My dear Madam, Yours very faithfully,

G. SMITH.

Having failed to get the letters published in England, Miss Nussey next applied, early in 1870, to the American publishers, Messrs Charles Scribner. A certain John Bigelow agreed to edit the letters and arranged for them to be published in *Hours at Home* at the rate of six or eight pages per month, on the understanding that if the letters were well received, Messrs Scribner should offer Miss Nussey such terms as they could afford for bringing them out in book form. Miss Nussey therefore sent copies of her Brontë letters, with her own biographical notes and data, to Messrs Scribner for perusal, but when the editor and publishers came to compare the MS with Mrs Gaskell's *Life* they discovered that practically the whole of the letters had been used. They therefore decided to extract from the MS the unpublished letters, and publish these in sections in *Hours at Home*[1] while Ellen Nussey's *Reminiscences* were printed in *Scribner's Monthly* in the following year.[2] It was however deemed inadvisable to publish the letters in volume form, and the scheme was again abandoned.

[1] *Unpublished Letters of Charlotte Brontë* in *Hours at Home*, Vol. II, June—September, 1870.

[2] *Reminiscences of Charlotte Brontë* by E. [Ellen Nussey] in *Scribner's Monthly*, Vol. II, May, 1871, pp. 18–31.

Vol. IV   s

In her preface to the *Reminiscences* Ellen Nussey states that her object in bringing these further letters before the public was to defend her friend from the charge of irreligion which had been made against her. This was a criticism of Charlotte Brontë which Miss Nussey as a staunch Christian and church-worker resented strongly. Here is a letter which she wrote in reply to some such criticism.

1020. *To the* EDITOR *of* 'THE STANDARD.'

MR EDITOR,—Having seen an extract in the 'Yorkshire Post' from an Article published in the 'Standard' on the 9th inst I beg to offer a few remarks on the passage referring to the order of Bishops—The writer of the article is much too fervent an ad-mirer of the Brontës (I am sure) to take any offence at being set right where he is wrong—I should be glad for him to see what I have to say simply as a matter of justice to C. B. and her sisters and also to the Ecclesiastical order supposed to be held by them in something like contempt. Such was not the case—for none could have greater respect or reverence for the clerical office where ever it was personally maintained in consistent life and reverend performance of duties. Their contempt was for *such Ecclesiastics* as the three curates described in 'Shirley'—Men who were neither of Oxford or Cambridge but Literates who brought the irreverence and vulgarity of their cast into their work and daily life, and thus earned the sarcasm lashed upon them— Bishop Longley was at that time Bishop of Ripon and so far was he from feeling any cut at his order or any disapprobation of the Brontë writings that he proposed a visit to Haworth Parsonage and spent 2 nights and 3 days there to the great satisfaction of himself and the inmates of the Parsonage.[1]

I do not wish my name to appear but I should rejoice for the writer of the article to say something in correction of the mistake he has unwittingly fallen into as a matter of justice to both sides —one of the three curates is still living near Haworth and he has become a worker in his way, and an improved man from the very fact of seeing himself depicted in 'Shirley'—if he had failed to do that Mr Brontë would have enlightened him for he some-times humorously addressed him or spoke of him as Mr Donne.

[1] See Charlotte's letter of March 4, 1853, Vol. IV. p. 49.

The writer of the article is unknown to me—Could I have his name. He has won admirers for his courage and independent stand up against the vandalism of dense minds and still denser taste that would obliterate mementos of a world-famed genius who was as great in her worth as in her genius.

[E. NUSSEY].

In 1872–1873, Messrs Smith, Elder & Co. published the first illustrated edition of the Works of the Brontës, and in this connection they were indebted to Miss Nussey for her assistance in the correct identification of the places portrayed in the novels.

1021. *To* ELLEN NUSSEY.

15, WATERLOO PLACE, S.W.
March 30th, 1872.

MY DEAR MADAM,—Being desirous of illustrating the works of your friend Charlotte Brontë and her sisters with views of the scenery and places depicted in their stories, I have commissioned a skilful artist to visit Haworth and its neighbourhood and make drawings on the spot.

The places named by Mrs Gaskell in her memoir are found on the map, but those described in the stories have fictitious names, though probably representing actual scenes, and the artist requires a clue to identify them.

It has occurred to me that you may possibly know the real names of some of the places so vividly described in 'Jane Eyre,' 'Shirley,' and 'Wuthering Heights' and if my conjecture be right, you would very much oblige me by indicating any you know.

To give you as little trouble as possible I enclose a list of the most prominent places mentioned in the novels, with reference to the pages in the volumes I send herewith, and if you could kindly note down on the side of the list the names of the actual places, so that the artist may be able to find them, I should esteem it a favour.

The interest you have always felt in Charlotte Brontë and her sisters, will, I hope, induce you to excuse my thus troubling you.—I remain, My dear Madam, Yours very faithfully,

GEO. SMITH.

1022. *To* ELLEN NUSSEY.

15, WATERLOO PLACE, S.W.
May 28th, 1872.

DEAR MISS NUSSEY,—I should have replied to your note before this, but was in daily expectation of the return of Mr Wimperis,[1] whom I did not see until Saturday last. He then showed me his clever and characteristic sketches, and I am now able fully to appreciate the value of the information you gave him.

In thanking you very much for the interest you have so kindly taken in this matter, I may add that the thanks of all the admirers of the Brontë sisters will also be due to you.

With regard to your suggestion of a series of large photographs, I think you will agree with me, when you see the engravings, in preferring a plan, which will place the views within the reach of every reader of 'Jane Eyre.'

I am glad to say that Mr Wimperis succeeded in making a sketch of Kirklees. — Believe me to remain, Dear Miss Nussey, Yours truly obliged,

G. SMITH.

1023. *To* ELLEN NUSSEY.

15, WATERLOO PLACE, LONDON, S.W.
October 30th, 1872.

DEAR MADAM,—We have now the pleasure of begging your acceptance of the first volume of the illustrated edition of the 'Life and works of Charlotte Brontë and her sisters' and we hope the engravings will satisfy you that the artist and engraver have profited to the best of their abilities by the information you kindly afforded them in the search for the places described by the authors. We have thought it best to retain the names given to the different places in the novels, without stating the actual names. —We remain Dear Madam, Yours obliged, and faithfully,

SMITH, ELDER & CO.

---

[1] Edmund Morison Wimperis (1835–1900), water-colour painter and wood-engraver.

For the next ten to fifteen years the letters remained in Miss Nussey's possession, although it appears from her correspondence that she considered disposing of them to the British Museum. Meanwhile several authors were preparing books on the Brontës, and they were continually applying to Miss Nussey for help and information. Among these were Sir T. Wemyss Reid, author of *Charlotte Brontë: A Monograph;* Miss Mary F. Robinson, who was the first to write a biography of Emily Brontë; William Scruton, author of *The Birthplace of Charlotte Brontë;* J. Horsfall Turner, author of *Haworth: Past and Present;* and Dr J. A. Erskine Stuart, author of *The Brontë Country,* and other works.

Extracts from Miss Nussey's extensive correspondence will illustrate the widespread interest taken in the Brontës at this time, and the active part played by her in the compilation of Brontë literature. The first writer on the Brontës from whom Miss Nussey received any financial reward for her help was Sir T. Wemyss Reid, who was at that time editor of *The Leeds Mercury.* He agreed to pay Miss Nussey one third of the amount he received from Messrs Macmillan for his book *Charlotte Brontë: A Monograph.*

1024. *To* ELLEN NUSSEY.

'MERCURY OFFICE,' LEEDS,
May 11, 1876.

DEAR MISS NUSSEY, —I was unable to write yesterday to acknowledge the receipt of your packet and its most valuable contents. I am glad to say that they came safely to hand and shall be most carefully preserved.

With regard to your letter received this morning, I must say at once that I feel very grateful to you for the mark of confidence which you are so good as to favour me with. I should esteem it a very great pleasure and privilege to be able to give the world a 'life' of Charlotte Brontë wch should be free from some of the defects in Mrs Gaskell's admirably written story.

My idea has been rather to publish a monograph than a memoir—to write and print a sketch of her life and character which shall be faithful as a portrait, and not necessarily a mere repetition of Mrs Gaskell's book. To do that, I should weave as many of her letters as possible into the narrative, so that C. B. might speak for herself, and tell her own story to the world.

I have written this morning to a very intimate friend of mine (William Black the author of the 'Princess of Thule' &c.) asking him what he thinks of the matter, and begging him to take the opinion of W. Macmillan the publisher regarding it. As soon as I hear from him I shall write to you again, and in the meantime I shall be delighted to have any further hints or help you can give me, so that I may be enabled to judge better than I can yet do as to the extent of new material which could be made use of in such a memorial as we are thinking of.

You told me I remember when I last saw you at Gomersal how many of your letters Mrs Gaskell had been allowed to make use of, and how many others you had in your possession.

Could you kindly give me this information again?—Yours very sincerely,

T. WEMYSS REID.

1025. *To* ELLEN NUSSEY.

'MERCURY OFFICE,' LEEDS,
May 26th, 1876.

DEAR MISS NUSSEY,—... I have completed my reading of the letters. They are charming! The day I hope will come when these letters will be given to the world, almost without the omission of a single word, and 'Charlotte Brontë and her friends' will become as well known as Dr Johnson and his friends now are. But that will not be in your time—or in mine. I have put aside a certain number of letters (about 100) from which I proposed to make extracts. In the meantime I have arranged that the first article shall appear in 'Macmillan' in August. The sketch there is to occupy three numbers of the magazine—Aug. Sept. and Oct. and then I shall enlarge the monograph so as to make a volume of 250 pages which Macmillan will publish. The latter part of the arrangement is not yet concluded, for I must make terms with the publisher wch. will protect me against loss, but he seems zealous and friendly, and I trust therefore that the matter is as good as settled. You shall see proofs of everything, and any statement I have obtained from you or any extract I have made from any of the letters, shall be omitted or altered at your request. To that I pledge myself. I am at some loss as to the manner in which I shall allude to you. I should like to give your name in full. May I at any rate be permitted to call you 'Ellen' instead of simply 'E'? I forward to you by this post, the first page or two of MS. as that refers so particularly to yourself, to Mrs Gaskell and to the letters. Please say how you like it, and whether you can suggest any correction or addition, and kindly return as soon as possible.

I have many questions I should like to ask you; but I shall only put one at present: can you tell me when Charlotte first told you of her authorship, either of 'Jane Eyre' or the poems? Had you any idea that the latter were written by your friends?—Believe me, Yours very truly,

T. WEMYSS REID.

1026. *To* ELLEN NUSSEY.

'MERCURY OFFICE,' LEEDS.

Nov. 2, 1876.

DEAR MISS NUSSEY,—... I am sorry you have had any annoyance because of the monograph. I have had a peremptory letter from Mr Nicholls, desiring me to inform you of his displeasure. Poor man! I have written him a civil answer wch I hope may turn away his wrath. Certainly I think I may say both of you and myself that we have done our best to avoid offence.

One or two very nice letters wch have been sent to me by people who have read the monograph have greatly encouraged me. They show that it has not quite failed in its purpose.

I am extremely busy at present, but hope in a day or two to begin the additions of the sketch for the volume, and then I shall write to you again.

I have written to Macmillans reminding them to send you the usual copies of the magazine.

Please excuse haste and believe me,—Yours very sincerely,

T. WEMYSS REID.

1027. *To* ELLEN NUSSEY.

'MERCURY OFFICE,' LEEDS,
Nov. 8th, 1876.

MY DEAR MISS NUSSEY,—I must apologise to you for having neglected to write by return. Your letter reached me quite safely, and I intended to acknowledge it immediately; but in the fuss of work I somehow allowed it to escape my recollection. I was very much obliged for it. I am writing an entirely new chapter for the Book, which I hope may interest you. It is partly critical and partly biographical. I shall of course send you a proof.

I have had another letter from Mr Nicholls; much more moderate in tone than the first and 'thanking me very sincerely for all I have written about his wife'! ...—Yours very sincerely,

T. WEMYSS REID.

1028. *To* ELLEN NUSSEY.

'MERCURY OFFICE,' LEEDS.
Nov. 13th, 1877.

DEAR MISS NUSSEY,—. . . I have been laid up by a sharp attack of illness which is still hanging about me or I should have sent you the reviews earlier. Indeed I have come down to the office this morning mainly to write this letter. You will see among the notices a very good one which appeared in the 'Times' a few days ago, and also two letters from a Mrs Firth and myself which will amuse you. They are advertising a second edition of the monograph but it will do me no good. Two editions of it have also been published in America, but I have not even seen a copy of them.

A number of forged 'autograph' letters of C. B. have lately been shown to me. They have been sold by the forger as genuine letters, though the clumsiness of their execution ought to have deceived nobody.

I hope you are well. I am not letting the British Museum matter rest, but I am forced to act very cautiously because of the possibility of Mr Nicholls appearing on the scene.—With kind regards, Yours very sincerely,

T. WEMYSS REID.

It is evident that Miss Nussey also consulted Mr George Smith regarding the advisability of disposing of her Brontë letters to the British Museum.

1029. *To* ELLEN NUSSEY.

15, WATERLOO PLACE, S.W.

May 10th, 1878.

DEAR MADAM, —I have hesitated a little before answering your letter of the 3rd instant.

As to the particular enquiry you make in it, respecting the marketable value of the private letters from the late Miss Brontë in your possession, I can offer no opinion. It however occurs to me to suggest to you, that if the Revd Mr Nicholls be alive, or if, in the event of his death, he has left an executor, it is doubtful if you can legally sell his late wife's letters to the Trustees of the British Museum without his sanction; and I think the officials of the British Museum, if they were willing to purchase the letters, might probably require the sanction of Mr Nicholls's legal representative, before purchasing them.

Your reference to Mr Williams indicates that you suppose him to be still alive. I am sorry to have to inform you that he died about two years ago.—I beg to remain, Dear Madam, Yours faithfully,

G. SMITH.

The next letter is from a correspondent in Norfolk, whose book on the Brontës unfortunately never matured. He makes particular enquiries regarding the Woolers and Roe Head School.

1030. *To* ELLEN NUSSEY.

NEW WALSINGHAM, NORFOLK.

Nov. 2nd, 1878.

MY DEAR MISS NUSSEY, —. . . Will you kindly send me by return of post your valuable account of your early friendship with Charlotte Brontë published in the American magazine. The magazine in which it was contained is in a very dilapidated condition. You may remember that I gave it back to you when I called upon you at Easter.

266 Miss Nussey and a new Writer

Mrs Rayner has written me a nice letter; no reminiscences, she says that Mrs Clarks died more than 20 years ago.

I am now hard at work on my book. I think my dear Miss Nussey that you have told me that you never wrote a book; if you had done so, you could understand that nothing is ready to read until all is done. At Christmas I hope to have all done in a rough way; and then I shall have much to interest you.

I thank you very much indeed for your interesting letter and for such information as you have been able to give me. Of course I am very sorry indeed if your formation of my acquaintance has caused your friends to desert you, and does it not become a question whether I ought to act so as to deprive you of them?

Would you be so kind as to tell me who the teachers were when you and C. B. were at Roehead and what the distribution of subjects, and hours of work were. In 1831 and 1832 am I right in supposing that Miss Wooler and Miss Catherine Wooler were the only teachers resident but that Mrs Carter was then married and came over from Mirfield at stated times to teach drawing, or was Mrs Allbutt unmarried, and a teacher at that time. Miss Eliza was not was she?

What subject did each teach? Miss Catherine taught French and Mrs Carter drawing, that is all I know. Were there any subjects that Charlotte did not learn except music and singing — Why pray, did she not learn singing, which would not require eyesight? I never could make out. I am also at a loss to know what Branwell was doing and where he spent his time when from 1832 to 1835 between the time Charlotte left Roehead as a pupil and went as a teacher — you and the three girls at Haworth Parsonage were tramp, tramp, tramping and talking in your wild way after the elders had gone to bed.

I hope my work will delight you — I think it will. Kindly answer all my points as soon as you can. — With our united kind regards, Yours very sincerely,

A. WILKES.

There were so many admirers of the genius of the Brontës, that it is not surprising to find that the question of erecting suitable memorials to the gifted sisters was already entertained. The old church at Haworth had lately been rebuilt, and it was felt desirable that some special identification should be made of the fact that the Brontë family were buried there. It was due to the generosity of Mr Sidney Biddell of London that the first memorial to the Brontës was erected in the new church at Haworth.

Mr Biddell took keen interest in everything pertaining to the Brontës, and particularly in any new books or articles on the subject. Miss Nussey consulted him regarding an application for information which she had received from Miss Mary F. Robinson, who was busy preparing her biography of Emily Brontë, which was published in 1883. In spite of Mr Biddell's and Miss Nussey's forebodings, Miss Robinson's work met with great success, but it is interesting to read some of the letters that passed between them.

1031. *To* ELLEN NUSSEY.

NEW UNIVERSITY CLUB,
ST JAMES'S STREET, S.W.
Monday, 28th Feby, 1881.

MY DEAR MISS NUSSEY,—I return you very sincere thanks for your kind letter.

The work you speak of 'Two Great Englishwomen'—is by Mr Peter Bayne, and so far as Charlotte Brontë is concerned, is merely a transcript of what you are now reading in the pages of the 'Literary World.' Immediately the work is published I will send you a copy.

I am about taking a house and shooting in North Wales, and sometime during the spring or summer I will do myself the pleasure of calling upon you.

But for your not wishing to see me till after Easter, I should have asked you to allow me to call within the next week or so, as I have to go and see this place before taking it. I am in correspondence with Mr Wade, Rector of Haworth, about erecting a Memorial to the Brontë family in his new Church. Mr Nicholls, I believe, contemplates erecting a memorial to his wife *only*, but probably he would not object to its being a memorial to the *three* sisters, so that the outside Public might take a part in it.

When I see you I will ask you kindly to allow me to see Emily's letter, as I fear my chance of possessing one is now very small.

It does seem to me so strange that now, after an interval of very nearly twenty-six years since the death of Charlotte Brontë it should be my privilege to be writing to one who was the life-long friend of that great woman. I value it much. —Believe me, dear Madam, Yours faithfully,

SIDNEY BIDDELL.

1032. *To* ELLEN NUSSEY.

84, GOWER STREET, W.C.

[March 23rd, 1882].

MY DEAR MADAM, —I am about to ask you so great a favour that I should have no expectation of your granting it in any degree, if I did not know that your interest in all belonging to the Brontës must be even greater than my own.

I am writing a Life of Emily Brontë; the first, I believe which has yet been attempted; and, in the endeavour to make it as good as possible, I venture to ask you for any details you may remember concerning her. If you would lend me her letters, or any letters in which she is mentioned, I assure you I would guard them as among my most precious possessions.

As for my qualifications to undertake this work, the greatest is a sincere and long established admiration for that remarkable and passionate spirit. I have published two volumes of poems (A Handful of Honeysuckle, 1879; The Crowned Hippolytus, 1881, Kegan Paul) and have written several stories and criticisms.

I am very anxious to give as clear an impression of the character of Emily Brontë as I can; for I have always believed that, had she lived longer and seen more, the integrity and passion of that character would have shown itself in a completer work than any she has left. When people die, having accomplished much, but with the capacity for accomplishing infinitely more, it seems to me a sort of duty to give the impression of that capacity as clearly as we can, and not to rest content with estimating the work that is printed and published.

So, dear Madam, you see I shall be very grateful for even the slightest memoranda you can give me of your friend's sister. There is no one else who can help me as you could.

Forgive me for troubling you so much, and believe me—, Sincerely yours,

A. MARY F. ROBINSON.

1033. *To* ELLEN NUSSEY.

35, REDCLIFFE GARDENS,
S. KENSINGTON, S.W.
Monday, 27th March, 1882.

MY DEAR MISS NUSSEY,—... Miss or Mrs Robinson's letter
is an enigma to me. She says 'I *am* writing a life of E. B.' therefore the work is progressing; but with such slight material to
work upon, who could have suggested such a work? Does she
know anything at all about the Brontë family, I wonder? No
great woman who ever lived has left so little behind her that can
be written about as Emily Brontë. Charlotte has given us her
life in 'Jane Eyre'; Anne in 'Agnes Grey,' but beyond Shirley
Keeldar what do we know of the inner life of Emily? As for her
letters, where are they? Miss Robinson has set herself an impossible task, and the sooner she extinguishes it the better. *You* and
you alone have the knowledge necessary for such a work, and I
wish you would solemnly set to work and write down everything your memory serves you in regarding the three sisters. I do
not think the world wants a literary work exactly, so much as the
home lives of the sisters. We know their literary merits by their
works, but what do we know of their daily lives?

When they were seated round the fire in the dining room of
Haworth Parsonage on winter nights, what did they talk about?
From the time they left their chambers in the morning till they
returned to them at night, how did they pass their time?

It is trivial details of this kind that make biographies so interesting, and give such insight into the characters of great men and
women.

As for Miss Robinson what can she know? She can but produce a posthumous portrait, but the Emily Brontë who wrote
'Wuthering Heights' and your friend, she is as ignorant of as I
am.

I have not had the heart to do much in reply to Mr Wade's
letters.

There is such a wheel within a wheel in every thing in connection with Haworth, its Rector and its new church that I have
not the courage to attempt more than a simple memorial cross or
plate. I wrote to Lord Houghton from my Club, imploring him
to take initiatory steps to secure three windows, but on reading

the letter a second time, it seemed so positively tame and weak that I committed it to the flames. I then thought of writing to Mr Wemyss Reid, but here again my courage failed me, so I contented myself with calling at the offices of Messrs Smith, Elder & Co., hoping to have an interview with Mr George Smith. I saw one of the head men there, but no entreaties of mine would ever persuade him to interest himself in procuring me an interview with Mr George Smith, who even then was in the building.

He assured me Mr Smith (the one Charlotte knew) would have nothing whatever to do with any memorial, and was far too busy to be troubled on such matters.

In fact this fellow looked upon me very much as a Rip Van Winkle—a man out of date—out of his time, and meddlesome to boot, so I left the room downhearted and disconsolate with the resolve to do nothing further in the matter.

If people who knew her, have pressed her hand and looked into her soulful eyes will do nothing, what can I do?

The simple brass Memorial is another thing and shall be sent.

If anything could shew up Mr Nicholls as being a monster, it surely would be his luke-warmness in the matter. He cares to do nothing, and in one respect I am glad of it, for if he did, I certainly would have nothing to do with it—I send you two photographs shewing the position of the tablet and the spot where the graves are—the tablet being at the West end and the graves at the East end of the Church.

I see there is an article in 'The Modern Review' on Jane Austen and Charlotte Brontë. I will get the magazine and send it you immediately I have read it myself.

On looking over my numbers of 'The Literary World' you were so good as to annotate for me, I find the 1st number is missing. Have you it? I trust I have not lost it. With our united kind regards, believe me, —dear Miss Nussey, Yours sincerely,

SIDNEY BIDDELL.

1034. *To* ELLEN NUSSEY.

84 GOWER STREET, April 5th, [1882].

DEAR MADAM, —... Let me thank you earnestly for your kind offer to correct the MS. of my primer on Emily Brontë. If you will indeed look through the rough proofs when they are ready in the summer, I shall not know how to thank you enough, and will gratefully consider any alteration that you may propose. But at present there is nothing but a chaotic mass of notes. Before I cast them into shape, I must go for a day or two to Haworth to see with my own eyes the scene that is so closely related to the character of Emily Brontë's work.

Dear Madam, you have wished to know who I am. There is little to say. I am an architect's daughter and, like the Brontë's finished my schooling in Brussels. But long before then I had read and re-read their books. On my twenty-first birthday I published a book of verses which had a sort of vogue and gained me many friends among poets and writers. They were not, however, very strong or original verses. Three years later (last summer) I brought out a translation from Euripides with some much soberer verses, they also had a far soberer welcome. I have written many articles in German, Italian and English reviews and journals; but the only thing I can think of to send you is a little story which came out in 'Fraser' last September. That is really all there is to tell about me.

I enclose several questions which it would make me very happy to have answered; if you think fit. I must again apologize for this untidy letter; I am sure you would excuse it if you knew how sharply a tooth is aching.

Questions. Mrs Gaskell and to a certain degree—Mr Wemyss Reid, describe Mr Brontë as a man of wild, extraordinary character. But even from particulars they give he seems to me to belong to a not uncommon and easily recognized type of Irish character; intensely self-important, rigidly upright, kind and even generous to dependants, utterly intolerant of equality; not naturally passionate but willing to assume violence as a means of governing others; facile in courtesy but cold to his familiars; facile in conversation but without any real depth of insight, imagination, or sympathy. Did Mr Brontë belong to this type?

To what degree may 'Shirley' be taken as a likeness of Emily? I imagine Emily rather different to Mr Swinburne's 'austere vestal.' I imagine her to have been a brilliant, sarcastic, deep-natured, proud, loving and undemonstrative person; naturally reserved, more inaccessible by circumstances; especially because having passed through the darkest and loneliest Valley of the Shadow of disbelief, she had lacked the courage or the will to unburden herself to friend or sister and henceforth imagined herself separated from them by an invisible gulf. How far is this true?

Do you not believe that the gloom and wickedness of the persons in 'Wuthering Heights' are not to be traced to a perverse choice on Emily's part but rather to the fact that (leading a most secluded life) she heard the village gossip and the village tragedies without having the intimate knowledge of their daily trivialities, amusements, businesses necessary to balance these darker facts. Being lonely and sensitive and pondering things in her head she exaggerated these characteristics, from undeliberate preference of gloomy and startling effects, but with the sincerest wish to make a truthful picture of the world she lived in.

This sentence is very ill expressed but will you kindly tell me if there is any truth in my notion?

Was not Emily, in daily life, rather dependent on Charlotte; instead of the intensely selfish and wayward character usually represented?

And thanking you for your letter,—I remain, Dear Madam, Truly yours,

MARY ROBINSON.

1035. *To* ELLEN NUSSEY.

84 GOWER STREET, April 16th, [1882].

DEAR MADAM,—It was a great satisfaction to get your kind letter with its most welcome information about Emily Brontë, and the offer to see me on my way to Haworth which I most thankfully accept. It will indeed be a priceless advantage to me. I think I shall go to Haworth on Tuesday week if I am successful in finding a suitable lodging; and, if I may, I will come over one afternoon from Haworth to Drighlington; for (as I am not very strong and should be tired) I am unwilling that my interview with you should occupy the weary interval between two journeys. If indeed it is very far, or a difficult journey, from Haworth to Birstall, I might stay one night at Meanwood with Mrs Mapleton, my Mother's cousin, or with my sister's friends the Fords at Adel; but as I personally am a stranger at either house I would much rather come over from Haworth if that be possible.

I am about to tell you a great secret in order that you may think me less audacious. An enterprising publisher intends bringing out a series of primers on Representative women, of much the same size and quality as 'English Men of Letters.'

Last month, as soon as I was back from Italy, the editor came to see me with a list and asked me to choose some one of the included representative women. I do not greatly approve of Primers but I was anxious to write something about Emily Brontë, and as it is certain she would have been selected for the series, if not by me by some one else, I offered to write a short Primer of about 200 pages on Emily Brontë; determining as far as possible to tell the truth and avoid mere picturesque tradition. The publisher is very anxious to keep the whole scheme very quiet, so I tell it you, dear Madam, throwing myself on your confidence.

With very many thanks for the kindness you have taken in answering my letters and the further help you promise, —Believe me, Very truly yours,

MARY ROBINSON.

I told my bookseller to send you 'Fraser's Magazine.' I will see to it to-morrow.

1036. *To* ELLEN NUSSEY.

35 REDCLIFFE GARDENS,
SOUTH KENSINGTON, S.W.
Monday, 18th April, 1882.

MY DEAR MISS NUSSEY, —From this time henceforth consider me no longer responsible for my actions—Your letter this morning gave me real alarm, as I had begun to think that after all, you had found the letters, when I learned however that they were still missing I was thrown into utter despair. To the roll I flew, undid it, examined carefully the two outer wraps and the engraving, but no letters.

A bright thought dawned upon me! I peeped inside the roll when lo and behold there were the letters!!! You may imagine my delight! I shouted for my wife and daughter and shewed them my discovery, and then instantly sent you off a telegram. But what a goose I have been. A goose indeed! it is a shame to malign so respectable a bird—Although I have repeatedly examined the roll, I have hitherto always taken it to be solid; in fact I thought it was a wooden roll.

I will read them, and select two or three for sale.

I have given up all thought of calling on Miss Robinson, and for this reason, that I really am unable to be of the slightest assistance to her.

I thought however there would be no harm in my sending her a letter giving her my impression of Emily Brontë's character, formed after repeated conversations with Martha; Her indomitable courage, iron will, and strong purpose, her intense fondness for animal life. Her unconquerable shyness and reserve. Her love of home and her love of her native Moors.

I told Miss Robinson that unless she saw these characteristics clearly she would miss Emily Brontë altogether.

Was I not right?

I also said, I looked forward to the publication of her work with anxiety and interest, anxiety because I considered good as they are, Mrs Gaskell's Life and Wemyss Reid's monographs were both failures—and interest, because I trusted she might have something new to reveal, that I knew not of, in the home history of the most wonderful family the world has record of. You know what I mean by the word 'failures' as applied to the two works mentioned, and I told Miss R. I meant that you learnt little or nothing of the home-life of the three sisters, their joys and sorrows, their actual every day experiences, the books they read, their conversations and thoughts at the hour of night when they commenced 'making out' their wondrous stories.

I took the liberty of mentioning your name, but only so far as this, that you would, I felt sure, assist her in the work. She knows my name, but nothing more as I purposely with-held my address, as I am quite aware I can be of no real service to her in the matter. . . .

SIDNEY BIDDELL.

1037. *To* ELLEN NUSSEY.

35 REDCLIFFE GARDENS,
SOUTH KENSINGTON, S.W.
Thursday, 20th April, 1882.

MY DEAR MISS NUSSEY,—I had not read Charlotte Brontë's letters until after I had sent my last letter to you.

How charming, how delightful they are, how brimful they are of humour and fun. I have learnt more of her inner nature from them, than I got in reading all previous literature concerning her.

I have continually wished for some record of this kind to give me an insight into her character. What has always struck me in reading her letters (published ones) is that she is such a perfect letter-writer. It is an art that of letter-writing, and she stands facile princeps. There is such a smooth rhythm about her sentences, and the right word is always in the right place.

I think it very kind of you to place such confidence in me as to allow me to read them, particularly as they are not for the public eye. It is a sacred trust you have reposed in me, and no one shall see them.

But reading these letters, how it makes me wish you had a like number of Emily's. How priceless they would be. Do look among your papers and see if you cannot unearth a few. I should so like to see one. . . .

SIDNEY BIDDELL.

Miss Nussey lent so much of her Brontë material to her various correspondents that she could not always keep track of it, and sometimes feared that everything had not been duly returned to her. Mr Wilkes, who was in correspondence with her in 1878, regarding a work he was preparing on the Brontës, was much offended by Miss Nussey's suggestion that he had retained some of her property.

1038. *To* ELLEN NUSSEY.

NEW WALSINGHAM, NORFOLK,
June 2nd, 1882.

DEAR MADAM,—I have just received your letter, and am pained beyond my power to write, by your accusation, and by the tone of your letter.

I have never professed for the Brontës greater regard than I have ever felt, and still feel; and I have never proposed to write what I do not now wish, and still hope, in time, to be able to write.

Allow me to say that I scrupulously and religiously returned to you *every letter* written by the Brontës, which you were kind enough to lend me. I did not retain one:—nor do I possess one line of their writing which ever belonged to you.

You may remember telling me when I remarked to you that I had not received from you all the letters which were in print, in the 'Life'; that you had reason to believe that some of the letters had been taken away (without your consent and knowledge at the time) by some person who had been living under your roof. I think you said she had been your servant, or had perhaps occupied a somewhat higher position. You also mentioned the name of another person who had not returned to you all the letters which had been lent.

I have never wavered in my intention to write the work which you know I had in hand; but because, since I saw you, I have been extremely busy as a Tutor, and otherwise; and also because I was not very strongly encouraged, I have not finished my work.

On account of my intention, I retained (by your permission) a few pencil sketches, by Charlotte Brontë, and two copies of 'Scribner's Magazine,' which belong to you; but if you request me to give them up to you before I have accomplished my purpose, I cannot refuse to comply with your request, seeing that they are your own property and not mine.

Will you allow me, dear Madam, to say that I never before in my life, received such a letter as the one you have sent me; and, as I am, in no respect, different from what you formerly supposed me to be, I cannot admit that you ought to have written to me, in the least degree in such a strain.—Believe me, Dear Madam, With many thanks for your past kindness, Yours very truly,

A. WILKES.

1039. *To* ELLEN NUSSEY.

ST JOHN'S HOUSE, WARWICK,
15th August, [1882].

MY DEAR MISS NUSSEY,—I am very sorry you are disappointed with my work, because I think a great deal of your opinion, and because I know how much you have my success at heart. But let me explain myself a little. You see, I wish to deal a death-blow, once for all, to the absurd supposition that Branwell Brontë wrote 'Wuthering Heights,' and this can only be done by showing him gradually to the reader as he was, brilliant and clever but very weak and vain, utterly incapable of the sustained power and passion of Emily's book. It is a much more artistic and I think a surer way than to trust entirely to my powers of emphasis and denial—of course I will omit anything regarding

yourself that you may wish, but (pardon me) you are so necessary as a relief to the grey loneliness of Haworth that it will be
like taking the sunshine out of my landscape — But if absolutely
your decree, I will do it.

Of course I shall be very grateful for any suggestions you
make — any details I can alter I will — but as to the general scheme
of one's book, one can only put down what one sees.

No, I don't think people can object to the quotations, so
much had to be re-told which had been told before and in such
cases it is scarcely fair to take the fact without any acknowledgement. — Your very tired and affectionate,

Mary Robinson.

1040. *To* Ellen Nussey.

Warwick, Aug. 17th, [1882].

My dear Miss Nussey, — I am indeed very grieved that you
do not recognize the portrait I have been working at so long;
perhaps it would have been better had I not shown it you until
it was at least completely blocked in, so that you should see the
proportions of the thing at once. But that can't be now — however such of your suggestions as I can adopt, I will gratefully
acquiesce in; and those that I reject you must believe are not dis-
carded from caprice, but because they are not consistent with
my very strong mental vision of the situation I am trying to
depict, or because, as regards construction, it would be like
taking a brick from the middle of a wall. To take your objections
point by point.

My reputation must take care of itself, it is (such as it is) the
reputation of an artist, and not of an accomplished young lady
with talents d'agréments for her decoration. The best reputation
I desire is that of a sincere, unflinching and (as far as may be)
scientific exponent of the things that are given me to declare in
poetry or prose; and I should feel it a staining cowardice if it
seemed to me that such and such a cause explained such and
such a result, to say nothing about it because it was unpleasant.

So much for me — and thank you none the less, dear Miss
Nussey for being more ready to consider me than I am to consider myself, but now for Emily — How can I let people think
that the many basenesses of her hero's character are the gratuitous inventions of an inexperienced girl? How can I explain the

very existence of 'Wuthering Heights'? How show the reason why the tree grew with all its branches bent one way? Only by explaining Branwell. You tell me Mrs Scott has daughters living, that is another thing, and I will faithfully do all I can to rub out any too obvious clue to identification—I have nothing to do with her.—But, without Branwell, with a good brother or with no brother at all, like Shirley Keeldar, do you think Emily would have written 'Wuthering Heights'? As for yourself, *soit*, you shall exist as little as you please in the narrative. I am very sorry, but I acknowledge your right of jurisdiction. You say you have other materials. I should be so grateful for them, if you can send me any notes of them. You cannot think how grieved I am to vex you, and perhaps to seem rash and obstinate in your eyes, after all your kindness—You must remember that Emily's work has not yet been touched on and that in describing that, and there alone, can I introduce my own theories.—Yours affectionately,

MARY ROBINSON.

1041. *To* ELLEN NUSSEY.

6 BOLTON GARDENS, S.W.
Friday, 24th Nov. [1882].

DEAR MISS NUSSEY,—You never uttered truer words than when you said 'I have been the mine whence writers on the Brontës have drawn their ore.'

What should we know of the sisters but for you? As little as we do of the man in the Iron Mask, or the murder of the Young Princes in the Tower—I wish I had it in me to write such an article as you suggest. The world should soon know who Miss Ellen Nussey is, and what we owe to her for the revelations she has so kindly and unselfishly made to those writers who have attempted lives of Charlotte and Emily Brontë. But it would be folly in me to undertake such a task, which, if done, ought to be done by a well-known critic. If Miss Robinson acknowledges her debt of gratitude to you in the only way she ought to, there will surely be some one who will do you justice, but it would never do for a weak pen to take up your cause. Some months ago you were kind enough to send me for perusal several letters of Charlotte's. I return them now with many many thanks— eleven in number.

They plainly indicate that though the course of her life ran in a somewhat sad groove, yet there were times when she was full of fun.

Her letters always appear to me so perfect in their language. Whether in good spirits, or low and dejected, she clothes her thoughts in words that could not by any possibility be altered or improved upon. Has this ever struck you? Writing to you, as she must have done, with no sort of mask to conceal her feelings or thoughts, one would sometime expect to find a slip of the pen, or some remark not particularly pregnant with meaning, but no, all is pure gold.

Even when she is light and playful she gives in a *morceau* that neither Thackeray nor Dickens could improve upon — 'Has anything tumbled into the basinet at Hunsworth yet — or is all there as yet hushed emotion and solemn expectation?' Even in such a trifle as this, the master hand is conspicuously present.

Why not prepare a little volume containing nothing but her letters to you, keeping back nothing? — a short preface from yourself, with notes to doubtful passages, and I am sure the work would have a great sale.

The risk would be nil, because in all probability a publisher would pay you a good sum for publication.

I would be the go-between and arrange all business matters, and you should have nothing to do but write a short preface and collect the letters.

Besides this would entirely penetrate any plan of Mr Wilkes of giving out a garbled edition of Charlotte's letters to the world at some future date. The idea is a new one, for I had not thought of it when I commenced this letter. You must have in your possession many more letters than have as yet appeared in either Mrs Gaskell's or Mr Reid's work. *Suppress none*, but give out to the world her immortal ipsissima verba. I have lately been much interested in reading Rossetti's Life of Shelley and I will close this by transcribing the last passage of his work — 'My task here terminates. — I have written of the immortal poet, and the man alike loveable and admirable, with one all-dominating desire — that of stating the exact truth, as far as I can ascertain or infer it, whatever may be its bearing — Any judgment pronounced upon Shelley ought to be that of a sympathizing and grateful as well as an equitable man; sympathizing, for history records no more beautiful nature, — grateful, for how much do

we not all owe him! Our sympathy and gratitude entitle us to be
fearless likewise; and for myself I should have felt any slurring-
over of dubious or censurable particulars to be so much deroga-
tion from my reverence for Shelley.

'The meaning of slurring-over (apart from motives of obligation and delicacy) is unmistakable: it must imply that the person
who adopts that course feels a little ashamed of his hero, and to
justify his professed admiration in the eyes of others, presents
that hero to them as something slightly other than he really was.
But I feel not at all ashamed of Shelley. He asks for no suppres-
sions, he needs none, and from me he gets none. After everything has been stated, we find that the man Shelley was worthy
to be the poet Shelley, and praise cannot reach higher than that;
We find him to call forth the most eager and fervent homage,
and to be one of the ultimate glories of our race and planet.' —
Now my dear Miss Nussey, I am not going to spoil that eloquent
tribute to Shelley's memory by another word of mine, further
than to ask you to reconsider my suggestion well over and to
assert your prerogative of being the friend and school-fellow of
Charlotte and Emily Brontë.

With our united kind regards, — Yours sincerely,

SIDNEY BIDDELL.

1042. *To* ELLEN NUSSEY.

20 EARL'S TERRACE, KENSINGTON, W.

April 29th, '83.

MY DEAR MISS NUSSEY, — At last I am able to send off to you
the earliest copy of Emily Brontë. Please believe that the binding
is not my choice; but the whole series is doomed, it seems, to
wear these yellow Gaberdines and no exception could be made
for me or for the Brontës.

If you will kindly let me have Mr Biddell's address I should
like to send him a copy too. . . .

Let me hear how you are, dear Miss Nussey. — And believe
me, Affectionately yours,

MARY ROBINSON.

1043. *To* Ellen Nussey.

18 Manor Road, Folkestone,
Tuesday, 15th May, 1883.

Dear Miss Nussey,—Miss Robinson's 'Emily Brontë' is prettily enough written, and will, I think, add a fresh spray of laurel to her brows.

But I confess to being a little disappointed, as my knowledge of that great woman is not one jot increased by anything Miss R. has written. I prefer Mrs Gaskell's work as being more versatile; Mr Reid's as being more vivacious, and Mr Bayne as being more stern and real.

Miss Robinson is straining after effect in every page, and certainly her language is at times very forcible and telling.

The great blot in the book however, in my opinion, is the constant mention of Branwell Brontë.

She has set Emily in a frame and he is the frame. Better far that she had written a separate book about him altogether.

It confirms me in the conclusion I have long ago arrived at, that only one person in existence can give to the world a true and faithful likeness of the Author of 'Wuthering Heights'—yourself. Considering however that Miss Robinson had no personal knowledge of the Brontë family; that she had only one solitary letter of Emily's to work upon, and that she had only one reliable friend of Emily's she could consult, I think we may be well satisfied with what we have.

It's a pity she did not make her more a psychological study, and have gone a little deeper into the hidden recesses of her mind.

Knowledge is denied to us, and we have still to learn how Emily Brontë came to write 'Wuthering Heights,' the hidden spring within her that at last found vent in that awful book. It is not usual in this world for a perfect untrained inexperienced man suddenly to present to the world an Apollo Belvidere or a transfiguration. Such work may ultimately result from years of toil and thought, but suddenly without preparation or effort, inspiration can alone account for their conception.

We owe Miss Robinson a debt of gratitude if only for the beautiful poem she has unearthed and given in at the end of her work, commencing 'No coward Soul is mine'—

It is new to me, at least I don't remember it. As we shall be seeing you so shortly I will say no more.

Altogether we may consider that if Miss R. has not enlightened us very much, she has at all events helped us to pass a pleasant
hour or two under the shadow of Haworth Parsonage. With our
united kind regards, believe me, dear Miss Nussey,—Yours
sincerely,

SIDNEY BIDDELL.

1044. To ELLEN NUSSEY.

20 EARL'S TERRACE, KENSINGTON,
June 16th, [1883].

MY DEAR MISS NUSSEY,—. . . I was so stupid as to leave Mr
Reid's pleasant notice at Kensington (we are spending Sunday
at Epsom) but I will send it back to you this week when I send
the 'Spectator.' I hear there is a very good review in one of the
late numbers, so I have sent for the paper which I do not generally see. More American reviews keep dropping in. By this post
I send you the 'Athenaeum,' for I am sure Mr Swinburne's
beautiful and eloquent praise of your dead friend, will give more
pleasure to no one than to you—Perhaps also you will like to see
the kind words said of me. You see he agrees with you about
the letter; though Mr Watts (Swinburne's great friend and
guardian Angel as one might say) the chief critic of the 'Athenaeum' thinks I was in the right to print it, and that without it the
beautiful charity of Emily would have been far less apparent.
Mr Watts, also, greatly likes the book and was to have reviewed
it when Swinburne, who very rarely writes criticisms, declared
he should like to write of it himself. So Mr Watts made way for
him. It is a great honour for me; and as much for your sake,
because I know you still love the Brontës as warmly as living
sisters, as for my sake, I am very very glad it has come. . . .
—Affectionately yours,

MARY ROBINSON.

1045. To ELLEN NUSSEY.

20 EARL'S TERRACE, KENSINGTON, W.
July 17th, [1883].

MY DEAR MISS NUSSEY,—I at once return the little cutting
which I have so long forgotten to enclose. Your letter came this
morning, and surprised me not a little. Why should I be suffer-

ing? Here at least my book has been, to my great pleasure and surprise, a most brilliant success. The principal critics not only of London, but of Rome and Paris have sent me through different friends messages of congratulation. The Roman 'Fanfulla,' I hear, is to devote two or three of its principal reviews to noticing all my works and chiefly 'Emily Brontë.' An American publisher sends me a message to say that having read 'Emily Brontë', he will in future take any work I like to send him at a liberal price. Several Editors of Magazines have written to ask me to write for their papers. I am constantly getting letters and invitations from people I do not know. When I go out every one begins talking to me about it, till I get a little bored sometimes. All this sounds very vainglorious, and nothing would have induced me to have written it except the discovery that you were really anxious and dispirited on my account. I assure you that I have had the kindest, warmest and most generous praise on all hands, and from all quarters for my little book, of course here and there a few notes of blame; but in a great minority. You at first, like everyone else, were pleased with Mr Swinburne's letter; and if you read it again I think you will see that there is much more praise than blame in it. The 'Academy,' 'Spectator,' Provincial and American papers have been, almost every one, most favourable, — So, dear Miss Nussey, don't trouble your kind and anxious heart for me. . . . —Very sincerely yours,

MARY ROBINSON.

1046. *To* MARY F. ROBINSON.

FIELDHEAD, BIRSTALL,
July 24th, '83.

MY DEAR MISS ROBINSON, —I was glad to find you could write in such good spirits —Have you seen the 'Athenaeum' of the 21st? Who is Mr Francis Leyland?[1] No friend of yours certainly for he cuts the ground from under your feet as the biographer of Emily Brontë —he is most unfair and uninformed in what he says, and illogical in the assumptions he makes —Mr

---

[1]Brother of Branwell Brontë's friend, J. B. Leyland, and author of *The Brontë Family with Special Reference to Patrick Branwell Brontë*, 1886. Mr Leyland objected to Miss Robinson's account of Branwell Brontë, which was contained in her work on Emily, and wrote a letter to the *Athenaeum* after the appearance of Swinburne's review of her book.

Brontë might well express his sorrow and amazement that his
son's failings should have been so published and handled, this is
the last thing he says, but *who* were the authors of these revelations? Certainly, not his sisters, nor yet his sister's friend in any
sense — The *Letters do not make known* Branwell's defects, beyond
naming them, as slightly as was possible with the acknowledgement of the sorrow they caused — The friend so far from giving
her consent to all that Mrs G. published, expressly stipulated
that only such *extracts* should be made as were necessary for the
correction of mistatements, and truthful delineation of the sisters — Mrs Gaskell did not keep her promise — and for that not
only herself, but her *publisher* was to blame — for he never let
Mrs G. rest till she gave in to his wish for 2 vols. — the extension
of the work led to all the mischief — Smith & Elder's desire for
gain — I entirely repudiate any blame whatever in the matter of
the Letters or of B. Brontë. No one could be more opposed than
I was to the Letters being given to the public, and much I suffered at the time, and have done since. All that I desired and
suggested when Mrs Gaskell was asked to undertake the
memoirs — was a *lengthy article* in the leading Periodicals — sufficient to set the Public right as to real facts, and the prominent
characteristic features in the sisters — If Mr Leyland can't defend
Branwell B. on any ground but that of aspersing his relatives and
their friend — he has indeed a bad case in hand. Mr Leyland has
demonstrated in this article a very hasty and ill-considered judgment as his own special possession. — Yours affect.

E. NUSSEY.

1047. *To* ELLEN NUSSEY.

20 EARL'S TERRACE, KENSINGTON, W.
[July, 1883].

MY DEAR MISS NUSSEY, — It is indeed a great shame that you
should be annoyed and worried by such twistings and distort-
ings of the fact. Mr Leyland is, I have heard, a tailor or small
printer (accounts differ) who some day means to write a Life of
Branwell. Heaven forbid! In your case I should write a letter to
the 'Athenaeum'; you might quote my preface which distinctly
repudiates any information concerning Branwell being obtained
through you. And you could either send it: N. Maccoll Esq.
'Athenaeum' Office, Wellington Street, Strand, or I would forward it for you. I believe Mr Leyland has absolutely no first-

hand knowledge of Branwell; at least he could give none to Mr
Ingram who applied on my behalf. I return your letter (which
please return) because all the last part would do almost word for
word as it stands — for 'Mr Leyland.' — Affectionately yours,

MARY ROBINSON.

Please let me have your letter back when you have done with it.

Mr Biddell was not the only admirer who wished to see some
permanent memorial to the Brontës established at Haworth. In
August 1883 the rector received a letter from Mr Thomas
Hockley of Philadelphia, offering to provide a stained glass
window for Haworth Church in memory of Charlotte Brontë.
His offer was gratefully and immediately accepted, and the win-
dow was beautifully executed by Messrs Clayton & Bell of
London. The subjects of the window represent the six acts of
Mercy as set forth in St Matthew's Gospel, Chapter xxv. verses
35–36:

> I was a stranger, and ye took me in:
> I was sick, and ye visited me:
> I was in prison, and ye came unto me:
> I was an hungered, and ye gave me meat
> I was thirsty, and ye gave me drink:
> Naked, and ye clothed me.

As Mr Hockley did not wish his name to appear in connection
with the gift, the following inscription was chosen:

TO THE GLORY OF GOD IN PLEASANT
MEMORY OF CHARLOTTE BRONTË
BY AN AMERICAN CITIZEN.

The window was placed in position in May, 1884.

1048. The Rev. J. WADE *to* THOMAS HOCKLEY, *Philadelphia*.

HAWORTH RECTORY, KEIGHLEY,
9th Aug., 1883.

DEAR SIR, — I have the pleasure to acknowledge the receipt of
your letter of 24 July kindly offering to place a stained glass
window in Haworth Church to the memory of Charlotte Brontë.
With the concurrence of the Churchwarden I gratefully accept

of your proposed gift, which is what we have long desired to have. With the exception that a gentleman in London offered us a brass memorial to lay down upon the grave of the Brontës we have had no offer of any memorial to that gifted family until now, and I am sorry to say with regard to the alternative mentioned in your letter that as we have no knowledge of any person's willingness to share in a joint memorial we shall be obliged to close with that part of your proposal which throws the whole cost of the window on yourself.

There are already 9 stained memorial windows in the Church, and perhaps those which are most admired have been executed by Messrs Clayton & Bell of 311 Regent Street, London, to whose skill and care I should wish to commit your window if agreeable to you. I believe they are the largest stained glass makers in England and are thoroughly reliable. All the existing windows represent some portion of the Holy Scriptures and we should hardly like to deviate from this plan. If you were willing to employ Messrs Clayton & Bell in the execution of the window they would prepare an original design, but they will not enter into competition for such work, nor make a design free of charge, if the work is not committed to them. But they would of course submit the design for your suggestions and approval. Believe me, Dear Sir, — Yours faithfully,

J. WADE.

In 1884 Miss Nussey again approached Sir T. Wemyss Reid for advice regarding the ultimate disposal of her collection of Brontë letters, but he found it somewhat difficult to advise her on this point.

1049. *To* ELLEN NUSSEY.

THORN LEA, CARDIGAN ROAD,
LEEDS, March 24th, 1884.

MY DEAR MISS NUSSEY, —. . . You ask about the Brontë letters and their future appropriation. Some time ago you spoke or wrote to me on the subject of handing them over to the British Museum, and I saw Lord Houghton and spoke to him about it—he being a trustee. He, however, did not encourage the idea that the Museum would buy the letters from you, and therefore I did not mention the matter to you.

I feel it is very difficult to advise you on the subject. If they went to the British Museum, they would be open to everybody and perhaps an unscrupulous use might be made of them. I have always felt that something more could be made out of them when Mr Nicholls died, but not before; but even then it would need to be done very tenderly and discreetly.

I am of course greatly touched by your thought of leaving them to me; but even if it were not for the fact that, after all, there is not so great a disparity in our ages as to make me altogether a suitable legatee (indeed there are many reasons that seem to point to you as the probable survivor) I should like you to take no step of this kind without the fullest consideration of it from all sides. Curiously enough a lady (Mrs Jeaffreson) has made me her legatee for a chair once belonging to Charlotte Brontë which she bought some years ago. But she is younger than I am, so I look upon the intended legacy as a kindly compliment and nothing more. — With kind regards, believe me, Yours very sincerely,

T. WEMYSS REID.

The next letter is from Sidney Biddell who gives some interesting extracts from Cross's *Life of George Eliot*.[1]

1050. *To* ELLEN NUSSEY.

32, THE GROVE,
BOLTON GARDENS, S.W.
15th Feby, 1885.

MY DEAR MISS NUSSEY, — I have been too long in returning the letters. Reading them has been most interesting to me. I am having a great treat in Cross's 'Life of George Eliot.' Most wonderful woman! — At 34 years of age she became *Editor* of the 'Westminster Review,' the most intellectual Review of the day, numbering among its contributors such minds as Lewes, Carlyle, Froude, John Stuart Mill, &c. &c. — She, a young girl, who up to this time had lived a quiet country life near Coventry, to have the management and control of such a work as this and to be daily in the Society of our greatest men, on a par with them intellectually if not a notch beyond them!! At 24 years of age this

---

[1] *The Life of George Eliot*, by J. W. Cross, 1884.

most wonderful of girls translated from the German Strauss's
'Leben Jesu' after only 4 years study of the language! —When
Sonie has finished the first volume I will send it you. —I am
nearly through this vol. myself, and as yet she (George Eliot)
only makes mention of one of Charlotte Brontë's works —'Jane
Eyre.'

Writing to a Correspondent in June 1848, she says, 'I have
read "Jane Eyre," and shall be glad to know what you admire in
it. —All self-sacrifice is good, but one would like it to be in a
somewhat nobler cause than that of a diabolical law which
chains a man soul and body to a putrefying carcase. However the
book *is* interesting; only I wish the characters would talk a little
less like the heroes and heroines of police reports.'

Qualified praise you will say; and feeling sure she will speak
more favourably of Charlotte's later works, I have had the curiosity to look at the index to the third volume for 'Villette' and I
find that in 1853 she writes to Mrs Bray as follows: 'I am only
just returned to a sense of the real world about me, for I have
been reading "Villette," a still more wonderful book than "Jane
Eyre." —There is something almost preternatural in its power,'
and again in a letter four days later she writes to the same correspondent: '"Villette," "Villette," have you read it?' Of Mrs
Gaskell's 'Life' she writes to a friend in 1857: 'But there is *one*
new book we have been enjoying and, so I hope, have you, —the
"Life of Charlotte Brontë" &c. &c.'

I will not quote more or it may deprive you of interest in her
own Life. . . . With our united love believe me, dear Miss
Nussey, —Yours sincerely,

SIDNEY BIDDELL.

I return C. B.'s letters by this post.

The question of publishing Miss Nussey's collection of Charlotte Brontë's letters was again revived in 1887, when Mr Horsfall Turner of Idel, Bradford, projected a series of works entitled
Brontëana;[1] *The Story of the Brontës: Their Home, Haunts, Friends
and Works*, including a volume of Charlotte's letters. He discussed the matter with Miss Nussey, who entrusted to him her
collection of Brontë letters. During the years 1887 and 1888 the
letters were being set up in type, and Miss Nussey assisted with

---

[1] The only volume of the series to mature was *The Rev. Patrick Brontë, A.B. His Works
and Life*, which appeared in 1898.

the revising and correcting of the proofs. In April, 1887, Mr Turner wrote to Miss Nussey: 'The "Haunts and Friends" are already compiled in a measure, but I hope to get a few questions answered by you in a short time. The letters are as fully an epitome of your life as your friend's.' The sheets for the volume containing Charlotte's letters were finally printed in 1889 with the title *The Story of the Brontës: Their Home, Haunts, Friends and Works, Part Second—Charlotte's Letters*, but before it was absolutely completed and issued, news of the scheme reached the ears of Mr Nicholls, who caused the book to be suppressed. The whole issue was destroyed but for some ten or twelve copies, which were retained by Miss Nussey and Mr Turner.

The following letter, addressed to Clement Shorter, conveys an interesting account of the end of the unfortunate venture.

PULHAM RECTORY,
DORCHESTER.

DEAR SIR, — The sight of your book on the Brontës has recalled a chapter in their Story.

You are acquainted with the fact that the letters of Charlotte written to Miss Nussey were printed but never published, and that most of the copies were eventually destroyed. I destroyed them. When Miss Nussey found that they could not be published her difficulty was what to do with them. My wife and I were among her intimate friends, and she consulted us as to what she should do. I told her that if she would have them conveyed to my house I would see that they were destroyed. She accepted the offer, and also consented to my keeping three complete copies of the volume. A few others were retained by Miss Nussey. Her own was interleaved for notes. What became of her copies I do not know; probably they went to her relations, though you had one, I think. In all probability the man who saw the work through the press had at least one. The whole edition was brought to me in a hurry from the loft where it had been stored for some time.

When I saw the great bundles I felt that I had made a rash offer. They were packed away in a garden house until I could devise some plan to get rid of them. After a time I had the courage to open some of the packages. One contained sheets all ready folded for binding; in another part only were folded. All the others held sheets unfolded as they came from the press.

After removing my three copies I commenced to burn the remainder. I never appreciated before that closely packed paper took so much burning. The martyrdom was exceedingly prolonged; there were probably more than 30,000 sheets to get rid of. It took weeks of my spare time. My garden was at the top of a hill and the Yorkshire winds were fierce. Often when I thought whole heaps were cinders I would run a pole through them, only to find that complete volumes were not even smoke-stained except at the edges. But not all the doomed sheets passed through the fire; many went through water instead. Whilst some were burning, many were steeped almost to pulp in the largest tub I could find, and then buried. I don't think a single sheet ever escaped the bounds of that back garden. I began the work of destruction with regret, but as the work went on I gleefully watched the pile diminish.

I was glad for my own sake when my task was done, but more so for Miss Nussey's peace of mind. I really believe that the whole transaction, the printing and subsequent difficulties connected with it, worried her into weakened health. Poor old lady! The last years of her life had many disappointments, most of them arising entirely from her warped views of life. She had a kind heart, and she was an interesting companion, with many memories of things local and otherwise.

Pray excuse this long story. — Yours faithfully,

J. RIDLEY.

In 1890, Miss Nussey, on the suggestion of Mr Augustine Birrell, again entered into correspondence with Messrs Charles Scribner & Son of New York, regarding the publication of the letters in America, but they were unable to come to any satisfactory arrangements, and the scheme again fell through.

Miss Nussey then began to dispose of her letters, and many of them found their way into the hands of various collectors. However, she did not abandon the idea of having the correspondence published, and in 1895 she sent a copy of Mr Horsfall Turner's suppressed volume to Mr Clement K. Shorter, who thus relates the story of the part he played in placing the letters of Charlotte Brontë before the public.

Miss Ellen Nussey placed in my hands a printed volume of some 400 pages, which bore no publisher's name, but contained upon its title-page the statement that it was *The Story of Charlotte Brontë's Life, as told through her Letters*. These are the Letters which Miss Nussey had lent to Mrs Gaskell and to Sir Wemyss Reid. Of these letters Mrs Gaskell published about 100, and Sir Wemyss Reid added a few more. It was explained to me that the volume had been privately printed by Mr J. Horsfall Turner of Idel, Bradford, under a misconception, and that only some dozen copies were extant. Miss Nussey asked me if I would write something around what might remain of the unpublished letters, and if I saw my way to do anything which would add to the public appreciation of the friend who from early childhood until then had been the most absorbing interest of her life. A careful study of the volume made it perfectly clear to me that there were still some letters which might with advantage be added to the Brontë story, although Mr Augustine Birrell had advised to the contrary, and Mr John Morley declined, on behalf of Messrs Macmillan, to accept a book on the subject. At the same time arose the possibility of a veto being placed upon the publication of these letters. An examination of Charlotte Brontë's will, which was proved at York by her husband in 1855, suggested an easy way out of the difficulty. I made up my mind to try and see Mr Nicholls. I had heard of his disinclination to be in any way associated with the controversy which had gathered round his wife for all these years; but I wrote to him nevertheless, and received a cordial invitation to visit him in his Irish home.

It was exactly forty years to a day after Charlotte died— March 31st, 1895—when I alighted at the station in the quiet little town of Banagher in Ireland, to receive the cordial hand-clasp of the man into whose keeping Charlotte Brontë had given her life. It was one of many visits, and the beginning of an interesting correspondence. Mr Nicholls placed all the papers in his possession in my hands. They were more varied and more abundant than I could possibly have anticipated. They included countless manuscripts written in childhood, and bundles of letters. Here were the letters Charlotte Brontë had written to her family during her second sojourn in Brussels—to 'Dear Branwell' and 'Dear E. J.,' as she calls Emily Jane Brontë—letters that even to handle was calculated to give a thrill to the Brontë enthusiast. Here also were the love-letters of Maria Branwell to her lover Patrick Brontë, which were referred to in Mrs Gaskell's biography, but had never hitherto been printed.

'The four small scraps of Emily and Anne's manuscript,' writes Mr Nicholls, 'I accidentally found squeezed into the little box I send you. They are sad reading, poor girls! The others I found in the bottom of a cupboard tied up in a newspaper, where they had lain for nearly thirty years, and where, had it not been for your visit, they must have remained during my lifetime, and most likely afterwards have been destroyed.'

Some slight extracts from Brontë letters in *Macmillan's Magazine*, signed 'E. Baumer Williams,' brought me into communication with a gifted daughter of Mr W. S. Williams, who had first discovered the merit of the novelist. Mrs Williams and her husband generously placed the whole series of these letters of Charlotte Brontë to their father at my disposal. It was of some of these letters that Mrs Gaskell wrote in enthusiastic terms when she had read them, and she was only permitted to see a few. Then I have to thank Mr Joshua Taylor, the nephew of Miss Mary Taylor, for permission to publish his aunt's letters. Mr James Taylor,[1] again, who wanted to marry Charlotte Brontë, and who died twenty years afterwards in Bombay, left behind him a bundle of letters which I found in the possession of a relative in the north of London.[2] I discovered through a letter addressed to Miss Nussey that the 'Brussels friend' referred to by Mrs Gaskell was a Miss Lætitia Wheelwright, and I determined to write to all the Wheelwrights in the London Directory. My first effort succeeded, and *the* Miss Wheelwright kindly lent me all the letters that she had preserved. It is scarcely possible that time will reveal any more unpublished letters from the author of *Jane Eyre*. Several of those already in print are forgeries, and I have already seen a letter addressed from Paris, a city which Miss Brontë never visited.[3]

Mr Shorter's first book on the Brontës — *Charlotte Brontë and Her Circle* — was published in 1896 both in England and America, and proved extremely popular. In 1900 Mr Shorter edited the

[1] Who was in no way related to Mary Taylor and her family.
[2] Mrs Lawry of Muswell Hill. These letters were afterwards purchsed by Mr Thomas Wise, and are now in the Wrenn Library, Texas.

[3] There is also a letter purporting to be written and signed by Charlotte Brontë, and dated from Rome, in the possession of the Historical Society of Pennsylvania, Philadelphia.

Life for the Haworth Edition of *The Life and Works of Charlotte Brontë and Her Sisters*, and in 1905 he contributed a volume entitled *Charlotte Brontë and Her Sisters* to the 'Literary Lives' series, edited by W. Robertson Nicoll. The most complete of Mr Shorter's works on the Brontës was *The Brontës: Life and Letters*, published in 1908, which was followed by *The Brontës and Their Circle*, a smaller compilation embodying many of the letters: this was published in 'The Wayfarers' Library' in 1914. Meanwhile another lasting influence in Brontë history had sprung up in Yorkshire. This was the Brontë Society, which was founded on the 16th December, 1893, by a few enthusiastic admirers of the Brontës, who wished to establish a Museum of relics at Haworth. Their efforts to collect material met with great success, and on May 18, 1895, the first Brontë Museum was opened in two rooms situated over the Yorkshire Penny Bank in Main Street, Haworth. Many books, manuscripts, drawings and letters, as well as furniture from Haworth Parsonage and personal relics, were loaned or given to the Brontë Museum, and the membership of the Society rapidly increased. Thousands of visitors every year, from all parts of the world, climbed the steep hill to the little Museum. The two small rooms soon became quite inadequate to house the large collection of relics, but it was not for some years that the ideal home for them was secured.

In 1927 the opportunity presented itself of acquiring the Haworth Parsonage, which was accomplished by the very kind and generous offer of Sir James and Lady Roberts, who most thoughtfully provided means for a new Rectory, thus enabling the Ecclesiastical Commissioners to dispose of the old Parsonage.

The long-cherished hope of all Brontë lovers was realised on August 4th, 1928, when the title deeds of the old Haworth Parsonage were officially handed over by Sir James Roberts, a native of Haworth, to Lord Brotherton, the President of the Brontë Society, and thus the home of the Brontës was founded as a permanent and national Museum and Library of Brontë Memorials.

In handing over the title deeds of the property of Haworth

Parsonage, now known as the Brontë Parsonage Museum, Sir James said:

... In performing this duty I am returning to the well-remembered scenes of my childhood and youth, and to-day is an occasion when, standing on the verge of fourscore years, these early memories are vividly reproduced.

I was born in this parish in the same week in which the unhappy Branwell died; an event followed at intervals of distressing brevity by the deaths of Emily and Anne. . . . It is to me a somewhat melancholy reflection that I am one of the fast narrowing circle of Haworth veterans who remember the Parsonage family. I heard Mr Brontë preach, in the pathetic blindness of his old age. Mr Nicholls frequently visited the old school-house as we children ate the mid-day meal in the interval of our elementary studies; while Martha Brown, the faithful servant to whom Mr Brontë gave the money box, the contents of which she was 'to keep ready for a time of need,' is still to me a well-remembered figure. . . .

Above all these memorabilia there rises before me the frail, the unforgettable figure of Charlotte Brontë, who more than once stopped to speak a kindly word to the little lad who now stands a patriarch before you. I remember her funeral one Easter-tide, and, some six years afterwards, that of her father.

These early associations, still very dear to me, and which I am proud to revive in your presence to-day, were followed in after years by an exceeding delight in those creations of imaginative genius which Charlotte and her sisters have left to us. . . .

I humbly stand in the ranks of that unnumbered and world-wide multitude who have found not only delight but inspiration from these sisters, who, encumbered with many adversities, rose to such great and shining heights of endeavour, and discovered to the world their extraordinary literary powers. Those gifts, matured within these walls, and under the wide horizon of the Haworth moor, have made of our little moorland village a shrine to which pilgrims from many lands wend every year their way.

Therefore, when there was so pressing a necessity to secure adequate and honourable accommodation for the Brontë treasures, and when it appeared that the purchase of the property of the Parsonage was possible, it seemed to me that here, and here alone, where for forty years the family had its hearth and home, was their true resting-place. . . . The presentation of these title deeds is to me an act of homage, alike to their genius and to the nobility of their courageous lives.

Since the opening of the Brontë Parsonage Museum, many interesting and valuable relics have been added to the exhibits, and some of the original Brontë furniture has been restored. In January, 1929, the collection was greatly enhanced by the addition of the books, manuscripts and other relics collected by the late Henry H. Bonnell of Philadelphia, and bequeathed by him to the Brontë Museum. Mr Bonnell owned one of the finest collections of Brontëana, including copies of first editions of all the novels, and many fine manuscripts and autograph letters. Not the least treasured of the relics in the Bonnell Collection is Emily Brontë's rosewood writing desk, which is now restored to its original home.

Thus through the establishment of the Brontë Parsonage Museum, the grey house on the windswept moors will for ever belong to the unforgettable and tragic family who lived and suffered there a century ago. It is indeed a house of memories and a shrine to the immortal genius of the Brontës.

> Now the high gates lift up their head,
>   Now stormier music than the blast
> Swells over the immortal dead,
>   Silent and sleeping, free at last! . . .
>
> But from the tempest and the gloom
>   The stars, the fires of God, steal forth,
> Dews fall upon your heather bloom
>   O Royal sisters of the North![1]

[1] *Poems* by Lionel Johnson, London, Elkin Matthews, 1895, pp. 90–92.

THE END

APPENDIX I

MR A. B. NICHOLLS AND MR CARUS WILSON

From 'The Daily News,' April 24th, 1857.

JANE EYRE.

SIR,—Allow me to make a few remarks on *The Life of Charlotte Brontë* by Mrs Gaskell, now one of the most popular works of the day.

I chiefly wish to call attention to the unfounded statements made on the Clergy Daughters' School, where Miss Brontë commenced her school career, when it was at Cowan Bridge.

I have seen letters from teachers and pupils, who were there with her, denying all that she stated regarding that valuable institution; and the lady who was superintendent at the time sent to a Review a long letter which was published condemning the whole account in *Jane Eyre*.

Miss Brontë left the school at the age of nine, Mrs Gaskell tells us. So what judgement could she form? And her father being an austere and peculiar man, denying his children animal food, etc. and they all being naturally very delicate, as we read also in Mrs Gaskell's work, is it fair to trace all her sufferings in after life, as Mrs Gaskell does, to the very short time she was at that establishment?

My father has spent a long lifetime for the good of others, and though, from his independent position in life and the wonderful way in which God has prospered every work he has undertaken for the good of the church and his fellow creatures, he might have much to boast of, yet I can truly say there lives not a man with a lower opinion of himself or more opposite to the character Mrs Gaskell has sketched of him.—I am, etc.

W. W. CARUS WILSON.

From 'The Leeds Mercury,' May 16th, 1857.

CHARLOTTE BRONTË.

GENTLEMEN,—May I ask for a corner for the following taken out of a Review, which is a complete answer to the statements in *The Life of Charlotte Brontë* regarding my father's charitable institutions.—Yours,

W. W. CARUS WILSON.

'Now, we are in a position to state that, when *Jane Eyre* came out, many old pupils and teachers, who were at Cowan Bridge when Miss Brontë was there, wrote to Mr Wilson's family, denying and grieving over her statements as to "bad diet and treatment, etc.", and the lady who was superintendent of that institution in 1824 (whose husband now heads a college in America) wrote in 1855 a long and complete answer to all the assertions in *Jane Eyre*, and her able letter appeared in a Review. We wish we could have inserted all this important letter, but we have only space for the following extract. She says:

'"The columns of the leading papers have for some time past been occupied with obituary notices of the late Miss Brontë, and many conveying the impression that her treatment at the Clergy Daughters' School when at Cowan Bridge, was of a character not only to affect her health but to darken her prospects in after life. Now, as I have it in my power to refute these charges, I should consider myself guilty in a measure concerning them, did I not make known to the world the truth of the case, and thereby exonerate an excellent and eminently useful clergyman from the imputations cast on him in *Jane Eyre*, as well as vindicate an institution which has been to the poverty-stricken clergy a blessing of inestimable value." She then goes on to say:—"In July 1824, Mr. Brontë arrived at Cowan Bridge with two of his daughters, Maria and Elizabeth; the children were so delicate that there were doubts whether they could be admitted into the school. They were received, and went on so well that their father brought in September two more, Charlotte and Emily. During both these visits Mr Brontë stayed at the school, sat at the table with the pupils, and saw the whole routine of the establishment.

'"They all inherited consumption from their mother, and were taken home; none of them, as has been stated, had any attack of fever or died at the school. I can truly say that none of the pupils were denied a sufficient quantity of good food; they were never limited: meat, vegetables, and puddings daily in abundance; any statement to the contrary is most false. Charlotte was a bright, clever, happy little girl, never in disgrace. In size remarkably diminutive, and if, as has been asserted, she never grew an inch after leaving school, she must have been a literal dwarf. . . . Let us hope that in caricaturing an institution which has been such a blessing to the daughters of her own church, she had no injurious motives, but, misled by a vivid imagination, and a dim recollection of thirty years, when she was but a child, she published in an unguarded moment, unmindful of the consequences, misstatements, the tendency of which has been to calumniate a most excellent institution, and to bring disgrace on religion. ... When it is known that I have been absent twelve years from my native land, and ten previously had withdrawn from conscientious motives from the Church of England, I think I need not fear being considered a partisan. My only object is to do justice, and to state to the public things as they have been and are."'

The whole of this letter Mrs Gaskell must have seen as she quotes one sentence out of it word for word, but has carefully suppressed all in it that bears so favourably on the school. She allows 'it is a subject she approaches with the greatest difficulty,' and, admitting an improvement in the school, seems greatly puzzled how to do this and yet defend her friend's assertions in *Jane Eyre*.

With the above we would take the testimony of hundreds of pupils, who with their parents have gratefully acknowledged the advantages they received at these institutions, rather than the account of one, however talented, who when but a child of nine left the establishment, and has so ungenerously cast an odium upon him who first planned such a help to our poorer clergy, and who has yearly undertaken the risk of the support of near 300 pupils and teachers, for, including a preparatory school, there are about 150 daughters of clergymen boarded, clothed, and educated, at only £14 a year each, including everything, and in the 'Servants' School,' above 100 girls trained for service, each paying only £10 a year.

The schools are situated in Westmoreland, built on Mr Carus Wilson's property, half a mile from Casterton Hall, his residence. They stand amid beautiful scenery, on high and healthy situations. They require above £1,000 a year, in addition to the payments of the pupils, to cover all expenses.

From 'The Halifax Guardian,' May 23rd, 1857.

VINDICATION OF CHARLOTTE BRONTË.

ALTHOUGH we did not insert the letters to which the following refers (having confidence that the late eminent writer, whose memory they sought to darken, was not the woman to pen what she knew to be untrue), we willingly give insertion to the Rev. Mr Nicholls's vindication of his lost wife's character, which, dear as it will be to him must also be dear to all the readers of her wonderful works:

To the Editors of 'The Leeds Mercury.'

GENTLEMEN,—On Saturday last you published, by request of Mr W. W. Carus Wilson, an extract from a review, containing, he says, 'a complete answer to the statements regarding his father's charitable institutions.'

The statements referred to are, I presume, the following:—That the unhealthy situation of Cowan Bridge, unwholesome food, and exposure to cold, etc., enfeebled the girls, and predisposed them to disease; that fever broke out among them; that about forty of them suffered from it; that the surgeon, who was called in, condemned the girls' daily food by the expressive action of spitting out a portion of it, which he had taken in order to taste it; that the school was removed to a new situation, and a committee of management appointed.

Now let us examine the 'complete answer,' and see how these charges are disposed of. And first, the reviewer assumes that these statements rest solely on the testimony 'of one who, when but a child of nine, left the establishment'; a reference, however, to the *Life of Charlotte Brontë* will show that this is a *false* assumption. He praises the situation of the school, 'on Mr Carus Wilson's property, half a mile from Casterton Hall, high and healthy'; but he has not the candour to state that this description applies to the *present* site, and *not to that referred to in 'Jane Eyre.'*

He eulogises Mr Wilson's liberality, but omits to state that funds are raised from the public for the support of the establishment which Mr W. W. Carus Wilson modestly calls his 'father's charitable institutions.'

He makes *no mention whatever* of the condemnation of the girls' daily food by the medical man, of the fever which scourged the school, and the consequent change of site and reformation of the establishment.

But surely the former superintendent, 'whose able letter appeared in a review,' will supply the gentleman's omissions, and in her 'long and complete answer to the assertions in *Jane Eyre*,' make some reference to this eventful period in the existence of 'The Clergy Daughters' School.' She does no such thing; at least as quoted in the review. She eulogises Mr Wilson;

asseverates her own impartiality; refers to her apostasy from her church and expatriation from her country; makes a somewhat erroneous statement respecting Mr Brontë's family; hazards some conjectures about the intentions of the author of *Jane Eyre*; and lays before us a bill of fare at Cowan Bridge— 'Meat, vegetables, and puddings, daily in abundance.' Very good, madam! But what about the *cooking* that spoiled these provisions, boiled the puddings in unclean water, compounded the Saturday's nauseous mess from the fragments accumulated in a dirty larder during the week, and too often sent up the porridge, not merely burnt, but with offensive fragments of other substances discoverable in it?

The Reviewer says: 'The whole of this letter Mrs Gaskell must have seen, as she quotes one sentence out of it word for word.' Whether Mrs Gaskell has seen this letter, I do not know; but if the Reviewer will refer to the *Life*, vol. i, p. 78, he will find that Mrs Gaskell quotes from a letter which she had *herself* received from the same lady, who evidently, in both instances, used the same form of expression—identical, however, in only *three* words, 'bright, clever, happy'—in reference to the same child. May I not justly retort the charge of disingenuousness on the Reviewer, who must have known this when he charged Mrs Gaskell with making a garbled quotation.

Jane Eyre was published in 1847; Lowood was almost immediately identified with Cowan Bridge, yet 'the lady, who was superintendent in 1824,' was discreetly silent for more than *seven* years, in fact until the author was laid in her grave. So were Mr W. W. Carus Wilson and the Reviewer, for aught I know. Their present proceedings are merely an illustration of a very old fable.

To the day of her death 'Currer Bell' maintained that the picture drawn in *Jane Eyre* was on the whole a true picture of Cowan Bridge School, as she knew it by experience: that the institution was subsequently greatly improved she knew and stated in the same work in which she exposed its former mismanagement.

I am told that the Reviewer, referred to in this letter, has with *exquisite taste* and *great charity* alluded to the closing hours of my wife's life, describing them as painful. *Painful* indeed they were, but not in his sense of the term. On this subject I would say to him, 'Who art thou that judgest another? Judge not that ye be not judged. First cast out the beam out of thine own eye; and then shalt thou see clearly to pull out the mote that is in thy brother's eye.'

Trusting to your sense of justice to give this letter a place in your Saturday's impression, I am, gentlemen, your obedient servant,

A. B. NICHOLLS.

HAWORTH PARSONAGE, May 20th, 1857.

From 'The Leeds Mercury,' May 28th, 1857.

CHARLOTTE BRONTË.

GENTLEMEN,—If the Rev. A. Nicholls will refer to the refutation which in your paper of last Thursday he endeavours to answer, he will see that the reviewer particularly stated that he wished there had been space to have inserted *all* the letter of the lady who was over the Cowan Bridge School when C. Brontë was there. In a former letter to you, the statements as to the 'half-starved' condition of the pupils were disposed of. If you will kindly give the room, I will quote for your readers that part of the letter which bears on the subject Mr N. says has been evaded, viz., the fever and the spoiling of food:

'During the Spring of 1825 a low fever, though not an alarming one, (Mr N. says it "scourged the school") prevailed, and the managers, naturally anxious to know if any local cause occasioned it, asked the doctor's opinion of the food that had happened to be on the table. I recollect he spoke rather scornfully of a baked rice pudding, but as the ingredients were rice, sugar and milk, its effects could hardly have been so serious as have been affirmed. I thus furnish you with the simple fact from which these statements have been manufactured. I have not the least hesitation in saying that the comforts were as many and the privations as few at Cowan Bridge as can well be found in so large an establishment. How far young and delicate children are able to contend with the necessary evils of a public school is, in my opinion, a very grave question, and does not enter into the present discussion. Then, again, thoughtless servants will spoil food even in private families.'

In addition to the above, my father has denied the accounts in *Jane Eyre*, and declared he was most particular about the food at Cowan Bridge.

I leave your readers to form their own judgment between the testimony of this lady and my father, and a child who left the institution when but nine years old.

If there are any besides, perhaps a dismissed pupil or teacher, who can bear out C. Brontë's assertions, there are many more Cowan Bridge pupils who have written to me during the last month saying 'how happy they were there, how all loved my father, how entirely false the character Mrs Gaskell has sketched of him, and how good the food was, better (some have said) than they got at their own home.'

Mr Nicholls complains of the expression 'My father's charitable institutions.' It was my father who first established them, had them built on his own property, collected single-handed for thirty years all subscriptions for them, running the risk himself of their yearly support, and thereby doing for his brother clergy what no other man has done. No 'Committee of management was formed' till about six years ago, when ill-health obliged my father to live abroad. Mr Nicholls complains that in the refutation no mention is made of funds being raised yearly for the schools and their removal to Casterton. Both these facts are well known and sufficiently alluded to in the review.

Mr N. is surprised that no defence was made on the publication of *Jane Eyre*. But that was a novel, and persons and places were not publicly and certainly identified till the obituary notices of the press in 1855 and the memoir of C. Brontë appeared. It was in 1855 that the letter of refutation was sent to a Review by the lady who was over Cowan Bridge School, when C. Brontë was there; who from conscientious motives left the Church of England, and who married the head of a college in America, which Mr N. charitably calls 'apostasy' and 'expatriation.'

It is only natural that Mr N. should seek to defend his wife's assertions, but considering that to add force to her fiction she casts odium on an invaluable institution, and a public benefactor to mankind, which as Mrs Gaskell says she often afterwards regretted, I think Mr N. should be the first to share in that regret and to repair the great injury that has been done.—Yours, etc.,

W. W. CARUS-WILSON.

WESTON-SUPER-MARE, May 20th.

From 'The Halifax Guardian,' June 6th, 1857.

CHARLOTTE BRONTË.

To the Editor of 'The Halifax Guardian.'

SIR,—I was aware that the Reviewer had expressed the wish, referred to by Mr W. Carus Wilson, and I now see that, while inserting all that was favourable to the management of the school, the writer carefully omitted whatever told against it.

Let me, however, thank Mr Wilson for his last letter. In his former statement all was perfection at Cowan Bridge, now we have the following points *admitted*: That 'during the spring of 1825 there prevailed a low fever, though not an alarming one' (what would *alarm* Mr W. if the illness of about forty girls failed to do so?); that 'the doctor rather scornfully' condemned the girls' food; that 'thoughtless servants spoiled it'; that there were 'privations'; that the schools were removed to a new site—from what cause Mr Wilson does not say.

But mark how easily Mr Wilson disposes of adverse testimony; 'if there *are* any besides (C. Brontë), perhaps a dismissed pupil or teacher.'

Now even at the risk of incurring such a summary dismissal I cannot forbear giving him the following extract from a letter which I have received from a former pupil at Cowan Bridge:

'On first reading *Jane Eyre* several years ago I recognised immediately the picture there drawn, and was far from considering it any way exaggerated; in fact, I thought at the time, and still think the matter rather understated than otherwise. I suffered so severely from the treatment that I was never in the schoolroom during the last three months I was there, until about a week before I left, and was considered to be far gone in consumption. My mother (whose only child I was) was never informed of my illness, and I might certainly have died there without her being informed of it, had not a severe illness of her own caused her hastily to summon me home. She was so much shocked at my appearance that she refused to allow me to return, though pressed to do so. . . . I attribute my illness to the unhealthy situation of the school, the long walks to church in bad weather (for in winter our feet were often wet during the whole of the service), and the scanty and ill-prepared food. . . . The housekeeper was very dirty with the cooking. I have frequently seen grease swimming on the milk and water we had for breakfast, in consequence of its having been boiled in a greasy copper, and I perfectly remember once being sent for a cup of tea for a teacher, who was ill in bed, and no spoon being at hand, the housekeeper stirred it with her finger, she being engaged in cutting up raw meat at the time. I could give you scores of such instances as these which fell under my own observation. Our food was almost always badly cooked, and besides that we certainly had not enough of it, whatever may be said to the contrary. . . . In a word, the system at Cowan Bridge was a very harsh one, and I was very glad to hear that an improvement took place after the school was removed to Casterton, for it was much needed. I had no knowledge whatever of Mrs Nicholls personally, therefore my statement may fairly be considered an impartial one. You are quite welcome to make what use you think proper of this letter.'

If Mr Wilson's friends had confined themselves to a legitimate review of Mrs Gaskell's work I should never have written a line on this subject, but when they attacked the dead, and adopted the questionable course of disseminating their vile slander anonymously through the post-office (actually sending a copy to Mr Brontë), I should indeed have been inexcusable had I allowed their assertions to pass unchallenged.

Mr W. W. Carus Wilson published a refutation (as he called it) of the assertions in *Jane Eyre*. I pointed out that it was nothing of the sort. His subsequent admissions, with the testimony I have furnished in this letter, more than justify all that was said in that work respecting the management of Cowan Bridge School. To bandy further arguments with Mr Wilson I have neither time nor inclination; besides I am quite sure you and your readers would soon be as tired of us and our discussions as the poor girls were of their burnt porridge with 'mixture as before.'—Apologising for again trespassing on your space, I am, sir, your obedient servant,

                                                        A. B. NICHOLLS.
HAWORTH PARSONAGE, June 3rd, 1857.

P.S.—Will Mr Wilson give the *maiden* name of the superintendent who 'married the head of a college in America'? For, if she is, as I suspect, *most intimately* acquainted with the 'Miss Scratcherd' of *Jane Eyre*, there is strong reason why she should wish to disparage the testimony of the avenging sister of 'Helen Burns' (Maria Brontë), who was so cruelly treated by that *amiable* lady.

From 'The Halifax Guardian,' June 13th, 1857.
'JANE EYRE' AND THE COWAN BRIDGE SCHOOL.
To the Editor of 'The Halifax Guardian.'

SIR,—My attention has been called to two letters recently published in your paper, purporting to be rejoinders to the replies of Mr Wilson to the assailants of Casterton School, and its venerable and excellent founder.

If, as I have been informed, the letters of Mr Wilson did not appear in your columns, I question the justice and impartiality of allowing the letters of Mr Nicholls to appear there. Many of your readers see no other paper, and how, I ask, could they come to a just conclusion by perusing the statements of one party only, on the points at issue?

It gives me inexpressible pain to see the repeated attempts made, by the distortion and exaggeration of facts, and what looks very like wilful misrepresentations of character, to disparage a valuable institution, and to cast odium upon a venerated minister of our church, who has spent his best days in energetic labours in his Master's cause, and for the benefit of the families of his poorer brethren in the ministry.

As an old pupil, both of the school at Cowan Bridge, and at Casterton, I claim to be heard.

Charlotte Brontë was, if I have been correctly informed, a pupil at Cowan Bridge about nine months. I was a pupil there for two years; and subsequently at Casterton for more than seven years; thus my residence extended over a period of more than nine years. You will allow, therefore, that I had more ample opportunities of forming a judgment as to the real character and management of that institution than Charlotte Brontë, and though I do not appear in the attractive character of a novelist, yet, as a clergyman's wife, I trust that my statements may be considered as worthy of credit as those of Charlotte Brontë, her biographer, or her reviewers.

I was one of the victims of that visitation of fever at Cowan Bridge, about which so much has been said, and to this hour I have a vivid recollection of the motherly care and attention I received, and the tender solicitude shown towards me on that trying occasion. Nor have I the slightest reason to think that I was treated better than my fellow-pupils. Nor do I for a moment believe that the fever took its rise from the quantity or quality of the food provided, but was introduced to the school from the village, or by a pupil returning to the school.

As to the extract from the letter of a correspondent of Mr Nicholls (whose name for reasons best known to himself he withholds), you will please to put my humble testimony in opposition to it. I solemnly affirm that our food was uniformly abundant, good, and generally well cooked; but no reasonable person could expect that in a large establishment like that, any more than in a private family, a failure in cooking should not sometimes happen.

And as to the pupils walking to the church in wet weather, and sitting the whole time of service with wet and cold feet, I do not say this never occurred; but this I do say, that it was the usual practice for the pupils not to go to church in wet weather, but to have prayers and a sermon at the school; so that this occurrence must have been rare indeed.

I may add that I have four sisters who have been at the same school, one of them at Cowan Bridge, and the other three at Casterton; and after a lengthened pupillage there, in two of those cases of upwards of nine years, they are unanimous in their testimony to the general excellence of the institution and its management, and we feel it difficult to repress our indignation at the unjustifiable attack made upon it and its founder. And as the best proof of my regard for, and confidence in the institution, I am now preparing to send two of my own dear little girls there.

I ought perhaps to apologise for thus asking for space in your paper for the insertion of this letter, but I believe the public will not be unwilling to hear both sides of the question, so that they may be better able to arrive at a just conclusion. And I have a conviction also, that the cause of justice and truth will weigh more powerfully with you than the consideration of a little space in your paper.

I do not think, tenderly as we would deal with the memory of the dead, that we ought to hesitate to rectify the errors they may have fallen into while living, in cases where the sacred interests of truth are involved; or to repel the darts they may have aimed, in their productions, at the characters of the living, especially those whose lives have been spent in diffusing benefits widely around them.

The character of the founder of that institution has been cruelly and falsely assailed, as all who know him will readily admit; but he will think it no dishonour 'to suffer for righteousness' sake.'

It would be almost too much to expect that no injury should be sustained by the institution from the repeated attacks made upon it with such perverse energy; most thankful therefore should I be could I enlist the sympathies of the wealthy in this locality in its behalf, and add to the number of its subscribers. I know no institution that has a stronger claim to the sympathies and support of the Christian Church.

Trusting to your sense of justice and impartiality to insert this in your next publication,—I remain, sir, your obedient servant,

SARAH BALDWIN.

MYTHOLMROYD PARSONAGE, NEAR HALIFAX, June 9th, 1857.

From 'The Halifax Guardian,' July 4th, 1857.

'JANE EYRE' AND COWAN BRIDGE SCHOOL.

To the Editor of 'The Halifax Guardian.'

SIR,—On returning home after a short absence I have had my attention called to a letter which appeared with the above heading in your paper of the 13th instant. On this letter, with your permission, I shall now make a few remarks.

The writer, after indulging in a little characteristic scolding, very unnecessarily informs your readers that she does not possess the attractions of a novelist; as a compensation, however, for this deficiency, she announces that she is a clergyman's wife, and *therefore* worthy of credit. Rare logic! According to which truth must be hereditary, owing, moreover, somewhat of its force to connection.

Mrs. Baldwin says that she has 'had more ample opportunities of forming a judgment on the management of Cowan Bridge School than Charlotte Brontë.' Now, Charlotte Brontë described the institution as she found it. Mrs Baldwin was not there at the time, consequently she cannot personally know whether the statements in *Jane Eyre* are true or false. Hear the testimony of a lady who *was* at the school with Miss Brontë:—'I would rather see a child of mine in its grave than subjected to the treatment I endured, and which I shall never forget.'

Mrs Baldwin further states that 'the food was uniformly abundant and good'; and yet Mr Shepheard, the chaplain, admits that there were grounds for complaint on this head; and a surgeon, still living in Kirby Lonsdale, having tasted it, pronounced it 'unfit for pigs,' 'to our great delight,' writes an eye-witness.

Mrs Baldwin, after informing us that she is 'preparing to send two of her

Vol. IV   x

own dear little girls' (a first instalment, I presume) to 'the charitable institution' already so liberally patronised by her family, proceeds to do a little congenial business, and with exquisite taste presents a begging box to the Halifax gentry. Surely such a graceful and disinterested appeal cannot be made in vain.

Mrs Baldwin, evidently a stranger to that delicacy of feeling which causes a lady to shrink from having her name paraded before the public, complains that I have withheld the name of my correspondent, whose letter I quoted in replying to Mr W. W. C. Wilson. If Mrs Baldwin will condescend to give me a call, her curiosity shall be gratified, as I have permission to show the lady's card to any one I choose.

With many thanks for your great kindness, and a sincere hope that I shall not have again to recur to this painful subject,—I am, sir, your obliged and obedient servant,

                                                        A. B. NICHOLLS.
HAWORTH PARSONAGE, June 30th, 1857.

From 'The Halifax Guardian,' July 11th, 1857.
'JANE EYRE' AND THE COWAN BRIDGE SCHOOL.
To the Editor of 'The Halifax Guardian.'

SIR,—I trust you will allow me the opportunity of making a few observations on the letter of Mr Nicholls in your paper of the 4th of July, in which he attempts to reply to a letter of mine in your paper of the 13th of June.

Mr. Nicholls's letter is written in a style so coarse and unusual among educated people, that it is quite undeserving of notice, and would have been allowed to pass at once into oblivion, but for one or two misstatements it contains. The production is little else than a scornful sneer throughout. A sneer is a kind of argument which, while it is the easiest, is also the weakest and worst that can be employed, and is never resorted to when any other is available.

A gentleman who undertakes to lecture others upon logical accuracy, should be careful that his own statements be unimpeachable on this ground; but it is not so in this case. He intimates that because I was not at the school at the identical time with Charlotte Brontë, therefore I cannot know whether the statements in *Jane Eyre* be true or false. Is there no fallacy here? Can he seriously mean that our knowledge of any subject is limited by the range of our personal observation? If so, let me ask, what is the extent of his acquaintance with the subject in dispute, about which he writes with such boldness, and in so peculiar a style? I do not pretend to know by personal observation whether all these statements are true or not; but I have very satisfactory evidence, of a personal nature and of other kinds, that they are not; and especially so to Mr Wilson, the accusations against whom, and the misrepresentations of whose character are, to my mind, the gravest part of the whole question. I think I may be allowed to speak with some confidence, because for nearly ten years I knew him intimately, and had full opportunity of observing his religious character, his temper, disposition, and general treatment of the pupils; and it was such as to produce in me, and in the good majority of them, feelings of unaffected love and veneration. This testimony is founded upon nearly ten years' experience. Charlotte Brontë speaks only from personal observation and experience, extending over a period of nine months and when she was a mere child, a little more than nine years old. I went to the school at Cowan Bridge about a year after she left, when, I believe, the state of things was much as during her stay there. I continued there until its removal to Casterton, and remained there some years. The result of my observation and experience I have already given, and am ready to confirm it in the fullest manner.

With your permission, I will now give the testimony of one of the first pupils at Cowan Bridge. 'As a pupil at Cowan Bridge in its first days, I feel it a privilege to be able to bear testimony in direct opposition to Miss Brontë. I could mention many interesting little incidents corroborative of my opposite testimony, calculated to account for the affectionate feeling with which I myself, and my fellow-pupils, regarded the kind Carus Wilson family. I have not read *Jane Eyre*, for I felt it a waste of time to read tales founded on falsehoods; but when I have heard remarks made upon it, and now on the *Memoir*, it has afforded me satisfaction to refute the ungrateful slander cast on Mr Wilson, and to bear my testimony to the practical consistency of his character, which, with me, gave weight to all his religious instructions. My annual subscription for many years to the school betokens my interest in it; and I now send a little donation as a further proof of my regard for him and it.'

This is one of more than three hundred letters that have been received by Mr W. W. C. Wilson within the last few weeks, almost all grieving over the assertions made in *Jane Eyre* and in the *Life of Charlotte Brontë*, which crush entirely any testimony that can be produced to the contrary.

In the *Life of Charlotte Brontë*, vol. i, p. 79, Mellany Hane is spoken of as a great friend of Charlotte Brontë. She is now abroad; but her brother, the incumbent of Sydenham, and his wife, write to say, that they 'never heard her speak otherwise than in the highest terms of the school, and of Mr Wilson.' This young lady I knew at school, and never on any occasion did I hear from her even a whisper of the occurrences narrated in *Jane Eyre* as having taken place at Cowan Bridge.

The 'Miss Temple' of *Jane Eyre* is exhibited in a most favourable light by Charlotte Brontë herself, and is spoken of in highly eulogistic terms by the authoress of the *Life of Charlotte Brontë*. The following is from a clergyman, the husband of the lady who is represented under the name of Miss Temple, and who died only last year. 'Often,' he says, 'have I heard my late dear wife speak of her sojourn at Cowan Bridge. I never heard her speak otherwise than in terms of admiration at Mr Carus Wilson's personal sacrifices, and of the parental affection he manifested towards the pupils. Of the food and treatment of the children she always spoke in terms of general approval. I have heard her allude to some unfortunate cook, who used at times to spoil the food, but she said she was soon dismissed.' This testimony from such a quarter is strong indeed.

Mr Nicholls endeavours to point out a discrepancy between Mr Shepheard's admission and my statement relative to the food; here he is again unfortunate and unsuccessful. I said, 'the food was uniformly abundant and good,' and he asserts that Mr Shepheard admits that there was ground for complaint on this head. He admits that the ground of complaint was an occasional failure in the cooking, and nothing more; which nobody wishes to deny.

The statement of Mr Nicholls relating to the surgeon is suspicious, and otherwise worthless as evidence. It has been denied that the surgeon acted in the manner stated; if he did, and rejected the food with the remark he is said to have made, he did it in his usual off-hand, quick, and somewhat thoughtless manner; and having been a patient of his, I well understand what degree of importance to attach to such an occurrence, if, indeed, it took place at all.

Mr Nicholls, with singular politeness, goes on to say, that 'Mrs Baldwin is evidently a stranger to that delicacy of feeling which causes a lady to shrink from having her name paraded before the public.' I cheerfully leave it to your readers, and to those who have considered Mr Nicholls's letter, to decide where the lack of delicacy of feeling exists. I affixed my name to my letter to show that I wrote in good faith, and that I was willing to substantiate what I had said. Anonymous communications are generally open to suspicion. I have the satisfaction of knowing that my letter has not been without effect in quarters where an anonymous communication would have been unnoticed. And does not this gentleman see that his censure, if I be amenable to it, falls in quarters where it must give even himself pain?

I have as little inclination as Mr Nicholls to continue the correspondence, especially as it is conducted by himself in defiance of all the rules of courtesy and propriety. Having borne my humble, but most conscientious, testimony in this matter on the side of truth and justice, I am so far satisfied. With many thanks for your kind indulgence,—I am, sir, your obedient servant,

SARAH BALDWIN.

MYTHOLMROYD PARSONAGE, July 8th, 1857.

From 'The Halifax Guardian,' July 18th, 1857.
THE COWAN BRIDGE SCHOOL.
To the Editor of 'The Halifax Guardian.'

SIR,—I don't wish to make any defence for Mrs Baldwin. Your readers will, I am sure, agree with me, that she is *quite* able to take care of herself: neither do I wish to notice the strain of Mr Nicholls's letter, at which many have expressed to me (to use the lightest term) their astonishment; but I hope I may now be able to close this controversy by saying, that in a correspondence I have had with Mrs Gaskell, I have found her most willing to rectify the injury she has done to my father and his institutions, and I believe her third edition will be a work which none can cavil at, but all extol.

I gladly do her justice in saying that I am sure she only desires to elicit truth. I do think she is more to blame than C. Brontë, for having too much endorsed as facts the exaggerated fictions of *Jane Eyre*.

C. Brontë's wonderful writings being but novels, we must allow her gifted pen more licence.

I have only met with one remark of hers on the subject that comes before

the public otherwise than under the garb of fiction, and it is certainly a sweeping statement, severely commented on by two leading London reviews for this month. It appears in a letter from her to a friend, in the 2nd vol. of Mrs Gaskell's *Life*, where she says that 'fever yearly decimated the pupils at Cowan Bridge.' For the whole thirty-five years the school has been in existence there have been but two attacks of fever, which carried off but six pupils.

It has been said that the statements of pupils who were not at school with C. Brontë are of no avail. But I have seen the testimony of teachers and pupils who were *with* her, and those who followed her, as did Mrs Baldwin (who finds from her father now that she was at Cowan Bridge for a much longer period than she stated in her first letter), would surely have heard of the horrors depicted in *Jane Eyre*, if they had had any reality. And as regards my father's conduct towards the pupils, those at Casterton, as well as Cowan Bridge, can give evidence about that. I have the testimony of teachers and pupils who were at the school both before and after C. Brontë, that white bread was given to the girls, not 'only brown,' as Mr Nicholls's correspondent tells us; and to the same informant I have my father's declaration that no 'doctor drove over to his residence with a complaint about the food.'

As regards the 'Miss Scratcherd,' several have said she was firm, but kind, and very much liked.

I am ready to give your readers the addresses of any of my correspondents, and I only wish they could read a tithe of the letters I have had from old pupils.

The testimony Mrs Baldwin gives in her last letter is from Miss Frizell, residing with the Hon. J. Tollemache, M.P., Ham House, Surrey, and the 'Miss Temple's' husband, the Rev. J. Connor, Melton Mowbray.

Shortly after C. Brontë left Cowan Bridge, which has been designated as a second Dotheboys' Hall (though now the whole tone of the reviews and magazines for this month has been turned towards the truth, and I have seen more than a dozen), the late Bishop of London visited the school with Mrs Blanfield, and after an examination of the classes, and a careful inspection of the whole establishment, observed to my father, that 'if it should please God to deprive his daughters of their parents, he knew no institution where he could more desire them to be placed.'

I do trust that this letter may close this controversy.—Yours,

W. W. CARUS WILSON.

WESTON-SUPER-MARE.

From 'The Halifax Guardian,' July 18th, 1857.
'JANE EYRE' AND THE COWAN BRIDGE SCHOOL.
To the Editor of 'The Halifax Guardian.'

SIR,—I regret to find that Mrs Baldwin takes such strong exception to my last letter, but if she indulges in charges of 'distortion and exaggeration of facts and wilful misrepresentation,' she must not feel surprised if she be answered in a manner less gentle than one would wish to use in replying to a lady.

She cannot, it seems, perceive the fallacy in her argument, and yet it is very plain. She assumes that because the management was good in *her* time, it must have been so *always*. With equal correctness might she argue that because she is *now* in a position to 'send two of her dear little girls' to 'my father's charitable institution,' she has been *always* in a similar interesting situation. For the statements I have made I have produced proof. Mr Wilson's friends have not, that I am aware of, produced the testimony of a single pupil who was at the institution with Charlotte Brontë. Mr W. W. Carus Wilson has, indeed, quoted a letter written, he said, by 'the lady who was *superintendent* in 1824,' but will it be believed that the letter was not written by Miss Evans, the superintendent or principal teacher, at all, but by a Miss Andrews (one of the characters in *Jane Eyre*, and therefore an interested party), who, I am told, combined the office of teacher with that of '*superintendent of rooms*,' a situation, as far as I can learn, somewhat analogous to that of an upper housemaid. And yet the man, who acts thus disingenuously, to use the mildest term, accuses others of lying, slander, calumny, etc.

Mrs Baldwin says she went to Cowan Bridge about a year after Miss Brontë left it. This can hardly be so, for in that case she must have been *sixteen* years at school instead of nine, as she says herself. This, however, is of little consequence. I merely wish to point out the inconsistency. But contrast the testimony of a lady who *did* go to the school at that time.

The following extract is from a letter addressed to me by her husband, a clergyman:—'Feeling interested, in common with thousands, in the fame of C. Brontë, and indignant at the aspersions cast on her veracity, I think it may not be disagreeable to you to receive from an independent source a statement confirmatory in some respects of the account of the Clergy Daughters' School given by your late lamented wife.

'My own wife and one of her sisters (E.) were educated at Cowan Bridge, entering shortly after Miss Brontë left, and remaining there five years. At the time of their entrance, the school was considered to be in a course of progressive improvement, and my wife makes no complaint of dirt, but her account of the food supplied during the early part of her residence is very *unfavourable* in respect to the *quantity* and *quality*. The breakfast consisted of ill-made porridge, without bread. Many girls from the southern counties, unused to such food at home, could not eat it, and for six months my wife and her sister E. had no breakfast whatever. On one occasion it was observed that E. was not taking her porridge. She was required to eat it. Attempting to do so, her stomach rejected it, upon which she was treated, not to a meal of bread or other wholesome food, but to a *strong dose of senna tea*.

'The dinner was sufficient, but not good. . . . The evening meal consisted of a cup of milk and water, and *one small piece of bread, not weighing two ounces*.

'Many of the girls being thus always hungry, there were continual attempts to procure bread clandestinely. This was brought to light by the following incident. It was usual for each pupil to repeat on Sunday morning a text of her own choice; and one, who had, I believe, been punished for stealing bread, repeated in her turn the verse which declares that men do not despise a thief who steals bread to satisfy his hunger. This girl died shortly after of consumption.

'My own wife, on her return home for the first vacation, was considered by her family to be half starved, and her brother, a medical man, has told me, that in his opinion, her health suffered for years from the consequences of insufficient nourishment.'

The writer goes on to say that 'Eventually there was little cause for complaint with respect to the food supplied.'

My sole desire in this controversy has been to defend the dead from the aspersions cast on her by interested individuals. Against the Clergy Daughters' School, as at present conducted, the author of *Jane Eyre* has not written a line, nor have I. The management is, I am told, unexceptionable; indeed, unless my memory deceive me, the only disparaging remarks I have ever heard made respecting it were by Mrs Baldwin's own father, on the occasion of the removal of one of his daughters.—I am, sir, your much obliged and obedient servant,

A. B. NICHOLLS.

HAWORTH PARSONAGE, July 15th, 1857.

To the Editor of 'The Halifax Guardian.'[1]

HAWORTH, NR KEIGHLEY,
July 22nd, 1857.

DEAR SIR,—I thank you for your polite note. As it may be the wisest plan to drop the controversy—I do not wish to affix my name—I remain, Dear Sir, Yours respectfully,

P. BRONTË.

From 'The Halifax Guardian,' August 1st, 1857.

THE COWAN BRIDGE SCHOOL CONTROVERSY.

To the Readers of 'The Halifax Guardian.'

It will excite but little surprise that I should feel dissatisfied at the manner in which the editor of the *Halifax Guardian* endeavoured to sum up and dispose of this case in last Saturday's paper. I felt that I was fairly entitled to the opportunity of correcting one or two very erroneous statements respecting myself and my father, whose esteem for Mr Wilson is so very great, and his appreciation of his labours, whether as it regards his schools or the church at large, is unqualified. It was from no such mean motives as Mr Nicholls thought proper to assert that I wrote in defence of the school; it was, as I said in my first letter, and again repeat, to repel the calumnious darts so unjustly aimed at its benevolent founder, and having been so long and intimately acquainted with the subject in dispute, I could speak confidently of the different tone and spirit pervading the whole establishment to that which had been represented—more especially as it regards Mr Wilson's character, whose warmth of heart and Christian benevolence led him to devise and carry on so successfully this, and other labours of love. It was due also to Mr W. W. C. Wilson to allow him to rebut the charge of disin-

---

[1] This letter refers to the controversy over Mrs Gaskell's *Life of Charlotte Brontë*, and the references to Cowan Bridge School.

genuousness so unjustifiably alleged against him. And also to give the lady referred to as 'E.' in Mr Nicholls's letter the opportunity of contradicting, in her own words, the substance of the letter of his correspondent. I will now take the liberty of setting these matters in their true light, and then, as far as I am concerned, terminate this controversy, unless something very extraordinary should call for further contradiction and remark.

I must take a decided exception to the summing-up of the editor upon the whole question. He assumes the truth of one of the principal points in dispute. He says, 'There were certain hardships and irregularities at the Cowan Bridge School when Miss Brontë was there, which were remedied as soon as they became known to its reverend and benevolent promoter.' This is neither proved nor admitted. The only thing proved (which was never denied) was, that there was a cook at the school for a few weeks whose habits of cleanliness were certainly not satisfactory.

Assertions, unfavourable in their nature, have been made by two or three anonymous correspondents, whose names we cannot learn. In opposition to this we have the testimony of at least three hundred pupils and others, who honourably endorse their testimony with their names. Who, with any pretensions to candour of mind, can resist such overwhelming evidence? I have but little doubt that some persons are very cruelly playing upon Mr Nicholls's credulity. This will perhaps appear from the following letter by the lady designated as 'E.' in his extract. This lady I may say is Mrs Smith, of Chetwode Parsonage, Bucks; she and her sisters were daughters of a highly-esteemed clergyman, vicar of Olney, a memoir of whom I have now lying on my table; he was distinguished for the tenderness and strength of his affection for his children; and had their treatment been such as represented, he would not have suffered them to remain a single day at the school. And when he wished to place his daughters at a school nearer home, at their own request they remained at Cowan Bridge.

The letter of 'E.,' which I wish the editor had given last week, was as follows:

'SIR,—Your paper of the 18th inst. has been sent to me, and my attention directed to a letter from the Rev. A. B. Nicholls, containing statements referring to myself. As the "E." of that letter, I beg to say that they were sent without my knowledge, and are unjustly used to support convictions opposed to my own. I believe that the mixture of fact and fiction in the description of Cowan Bridge in *Jane Eyre* conveys to the reader a *general idea opposed to the truth*. I look back on the five years I passed there with great thankfulness, and reckon my school-days amongst the happiest of my life. With respect to the porridge, I would just say that when Mr Wilson was informed of my dislike to it, he *at once* gave orders for my having bread and milk. He is not responsible for the remedy for a dainty appetite detailed by Mr Nicholls's correspondent; and had the *superintendent* been in the house, it would not have been administered. The incident happened during a vacation, and is, I believe, exaggerated, for I have no recollection of the most offensive part of the story. I had always plenty of food after I was allowed bread and milk for breakfast; and had I liked oatmeal porridge, as Mr Wilson's own children did, I should have had enough from the first. You will allow me to add that I am "interested" in this controversy only by the claims of justice and gratitude.—Yours, etc., E.

'*PS.*—Mr Nicholls has fallen into a mistake in saying that it was a clergyman who sent him his information.'

This letter needs no comment. I must assure Mr Nicholls that he never heard from my father anything of a disparaging nature with regard to the school. His imagination, not his memory, supplies him with this impression. My father's approbation of the school is unqualified, and his esteem for Mr Wilson very high.

Mr Nicholls's misapprehension as to the duration of my residence at the school is easily rectified. The only uncertainty in my mind was the date of the removal of the school from Cowan Bridge to Casterton; it was at a later period than I thought; so that I was at Cowan Bridge a longer, and at Casterton a shorter, period than I at first stated. This, it will be perceived, adds some strength to my former testimony. Mr Nicholls's charge of disingenuousness against Mr W. W. C. Wilson is entirely unfounded. That gentleman quoted a letter written by the superintendent in 1824; that superintendent *was* Miss Andrews, who was also head-teacher. After Miss Evans became superintendent, Miss A. still retained the office of teacher, and was never 'superintendent of rooms.'

I am sorry that, after admitting the excellence and utility of the institution, he should still point the finger of scorn at it, and so frequently and unnecessarily reproduce the expression of Mr W. W. C. Wilson, 'My father's charitable institution.' He might with about equal truth apply the expression 'Charitable institution' to the Universities or any other endowed public scholastic institution. It matters but little whether an institution be sustained by the testamentary bequests and donations of past ages, or the donations of the present; as to principle, they stand pretty much on the same ground.

All honour (little as he seeks it) is due to Mr Wilson for his efforts in founding that institution; and for his self-sacrifice and liberality, and unwearied exertions, in sustaining it, in conjunction with the liberal co-operation of others. And look at the superior education imparted to the pupils there, upon comparatively low terms. The system of instruction comprehends history, the use of the globes, grammar, writing, arithmetic, French, Latin, needlework, and calisthenics. To which are added as accomplishments, and for which somewhat higher terms are paid, music, drawing, German, Italian, and the organ.

I think every right-minded person, uninfluenced by prejudice, must hesitate to disparage, or in any way to impair, the stability of such an institution, one that has proved so great and extensive a blessing.

In dismissing, as I hope finally, this subject, I must observe that in what I have said I have been influenced only by a regard for justice and truth, and of gratitude to Mr Wilson. The school and Mr Wilson were misrepresented and misunderstood, and no voice lifted up here in defence. Many of my former fellow-pupils in other parts of the country had stood forward with their favourable testimony. I felt constrained to use my feeble powers and influence in the same cause. I feel thankful that I have done so, and thus been enabled to discharge in some small degree the debt of gratitude I, in common with the hundreds, owe to the excellent and benevolent founder of the school.

Should any one wish for further information relative to the school and its management, or pamphlets relating thereto, the same may be obtained free of cost upon application to W. W. C. Wilson, Weston-super-Mare, Somerset.   SARAH BALDWIN.

MYTHOLMROYD PARSONAGE, July 29th, 1857.

From 'The Halifax Guardian,' August 8th, 1857.
THE COWAN BRIDGE CONTROVERSY.
To the Editor of 'The Halifax Guardian.'

SIR,—As you truly said in your summing up, this controversy 'lies in a small space.' The question, stripped of extraneous matter, is simply this: What was the state of the school *during the time that Miss Brontë was there?*

She and others described the treatment as harsh; the food as indifferent and insufficient. Up started Mrs Baldwin, and, asserting her own superior means of information, said in effect: Don't believe a word of it; hear me. I went to Cowan Bridge *seven years* (according to Mr Wilson's date) *after* C. *Brontë* left, and 'I solemnly affirm that the food was uniformly abundant and good.' I pointed out to her that she could not personally know whether the statements were true or not, because she was not at 'my father's charitable institution' at the time referred to. She *then* said: '*I do not pretend to know by personal observation whether the statements are true or not.* I went to the school about *a year after she left,* when, *I believe,* the state of things was *much* as during her stay.' How conclusive! But Mr Wilson has '300 testimonials' in his favour—he may have 500—and all just as worthless as Mrs Baldwin's, unless proved to have been written by pupils who were at school *with* Miss Brontë, which has not been done in a single instance. You will observe that 'E.' *admits* that she was treated as described by my correspondent; and Mrs Baldwin does not deny that the girls were driven by hunger to steal bread.

Miss Andrews (identified in Mr Shepheard's pamphlet as the '*amiable* Miss Scratcherd' of *Jane Eyre*) was an under-teacher, and not superintendent, when Miss Brontë was at Cowan Bridge.

I *did* hear, and in this house, Mrs Baldwin's father speak disparagingly of the management on the occasion of the removal of his youngest daughter from the institution.

Of Rev. C. Wilson I know nothing personally. I would only say that I have heard him spoken of by clergymen, who agree with him in sentiment, in terms very different from those employed by Mrs Baldwin.

And now, sir, I have done with this subject. I have discharged a painful but necessary duty. Henceforth Charlotte Brontë's assailants may growl and snarl over her grave undisturbed by me.—I am, sir, your obedient servant,   A. B. NICHOLLS.

HAWORTH PARSONAGE, August 5th, 1857.

APPENDIX II

To HENRY COLBURN.[1]

SIR,—I request permission to send for your inspection the MS. of a work of fiction in 3 vols. It consists of three tales,[2] each occupying a volume and capable of being published together or separately, as thought most advisable. The authors of these tales have already appeared before the public. Should you consent to examine the work, would you, in your reply, state at what period after transmission of the MS. to you, the authors may expect to receive your decision upon its merits.—I am Sir, Yours respectfully,

C. BELL.

Address: Mr Currer Bell,
      Parsonage,
        Haworth, Bradford,
          Yorkshire.

July 4th,—46.

---

[1] This letter was sold at Messrs Sotheby's Sale Rooms, 4th July, 1932.

[2] *The Professor, Wuthering Heights* and *Agnes Grey.*

NOTE

The letters in this work have all been numbered consecutively. Where a number follows in brackets, such number indicates the position of the letter in Clement K. Shorter's *The Brontës: Life and Letters.*

ERRATA ET ADDENDA

VOLUME I

page 31, *footnote, after* the samplers *add:* all except one which is in the possession of Mr T. J. Wise.

page 81, *line* 28, *for* Codamannus *read* Codomannus

page 87, *line* 21, *for* 1831 *read* 1832

page 147, *heading* Brookryod *read* Brookroyd

page 164, *headline, for* Anne ill at Roe Head *read* Anne ill at Dewsbury Moor

page 172, *footnote,* line 11, *for* person *read* parson

page 229, *footnote,* line 3, *for* December 1840 *read* December 1839

VOLUME II

page 51, *line* 15, *for* the fidgetiness *read* less fidgetiness

page 93, *footnote* 2, *for* last page *read* last leaf

page 100, *footnote, for* H. F. Grundy *read* F. H. Grundy

page 206, *line* 14, *for* Lewis *read* Lewes

page 219, *footnote, add* probably Susan Bland, *see* letter to Ellen Nussey, Vol. I, p. 217

page 304, *letter number, for* 416 *read* 419

page 310, *headline, for* Ellen Nussey and Henry Taylor *read* Ellen and Henry Taylor

VOLUME III

page 158, *line* 10, *for* This *read* His

page 160, *line* 25, *for* Wildfall Hall *read* Wildfell Hall

VOLUME IV

page 86, *line* 32, *for* Lawrence *read* Laurence

page 245, *line* 13, *for* Snowden *read* Sowden

page 247, *line* 23, *for* mois *read* mots

INDEX

BRONTË, EMILY JANE, *continued*
268–274, 276–284; *Emily Brontë*, by Charles Simpson, II, 281; *All Alone*, by Romer Wilson, II, 281; in London, III, 169n; love of animals, II, 5; love of the moors, III, 111; in Manchester with Charlotte, II, 105; nickname of 'The Major,' II, 145; portraits, II, 285, 286; railway investments, II, 32, 76; her religion, I, 137; II, 275–276; her reserved nature, II, 241–242; III, 38; her stoicism, II, 269, 275; her study of drawing, I, 266–267; study of French, I, 266–267; study of German, I, 266–267; study of music, I, 266–267, 279, 281; II, 274; other references, I, 56, 57, 193, 194, 307; II, 63, 83, 84, 133; III, 12, 16, 55; IV, 200, 202, 206, 258, 274, 275, 278, 279

BRONTË, EMILY JANE, Works of: First Illustrated Edition, IV, 259, 260; Haworth Edition, IV, 293; her early stories, I, 81; the Gondal stories, I, 237, 238; II, 49–53, 277; *The Emperor Julius's Life*, II, 52
—Poems: *The Old Stoic*, II, 275; *The Philosopher*, II, 276; *No Coward Soul is Mine*, II, 276; IV, 281; *The Wanderer from the Fold*, II, 259–260; publication of *Poems* by Currer, Ellis and Acton Bell, II, 79–89, 93–94, 102–104, 112; reviews of the *Poems*, II, 102, 268, 271; *Poems*, transferred to Messrs Smith, Elder & Co., II, 254, 256, 270; III, 86; sale of the *Poems*, II, 291
—*Wuthering Heights*: MS. submitted to Henry Colburn, IV, Appendix II; publication by Thomas Cautley Newby, II, 87, 145, 154, 155, 162; difficulty with her publisher, II, 154–155, 187; III, 186; letter from T. C. Newby, II, 187, 188; Newby's agreement for the publication of *Wuthering Heights*, III, 160; reviews,

BRONTË, EMILY JANE, *continued*
II, 280, 287; review in the *Atlas Magazine*, II, 170; success of *Wuthering Heights*, II, 187; new edition of *Wuthering Heights* with preface by Charlotte Brontë, published by Messrs Smith, Elder & Co., III, 153, 156, 157, 158, 160, 165, 166, 175, 186, 188, 200; IV, 211; authorship of *Wuthering Heights*, II, 55, 56, 197; IV, 276, 278; Sydney Dobell on *Wuthering Heights*, II, 280, 281; III, 154, 170; financial compensation for *Wuthering Heights*, III, 156; 'Heathcliff' of *Wuthering Heights*, II, 245; Irish influence in *Wuthering Heights*, I, 114; II, 277–281; manuscript of *Wuthering Heights*, II, 57; A. C. Swinburne on *Wuthering Heights*, II, 279–281; other references, II, 54, 140, 229; III, 187, 193, 219; IV, 90, 93, 269, 272, 281

BRONTË, HUGH, uncle of Charlotte Brontë, II, 278; IV, 246; his visit to Haworth, II, 278

BRONTË, MARIA, wife of Rev. Patrick Brontë, *see* Brontë (Mrs Patrick)

BRONTË, MARIA, birth at Hartshead, I, 31, 37; baptism at Hartshead Church, I, 34, 35; extract from Hartshead baptismal register, I, 34, 35; sent to Clergy Daughters' School, Cowan Bridge, I, 69; left owing to ill-health, I, 69; death, I, 69; IV, 87; extract from school register, I, 69; at Clergy Daughters' School, I, 73, 74; IV, Appendix I; inscription on the mural tablet in Haworth Church, IV, 92; prototype of 'Helen Burns' in *Jane Eyre*, IV, 92, Appendix I; other references, I, 60, 91; II, 340; III, 34

BRONTË, REV. PATRICK, birth in Ireland, 1777, I, 1; a weaver, I, 2; a teacher, I, 2; his family, I, 2; at St John's College, Cambridge, I, 2–3,

380

INDEX

Smith, George, *continued*
IV, 210–211; his help with Mrs
Gaskell's *Life*, IV, 187, 203, 210,
211; lends Mrs Gaskell Charlotte's
letters to him, IV, 195; visits Chapter Coffee-House with Mrs Gaskell,
IV, 200; and Miss Martineau's anonymous book, III, 266*n*, 299, 301–
302, 303; his letters to Ellen Nussey, IV, 224, 251–257, 259, 260, 265;
Ellen Nussey's letters to him, IV,
252, 254–256; invited to Brookroyd, III, 310; and James Taylor,
III, 221, 229, 291; on the success of
Thackeray's lectures, III, 247; his
Indian project, III, 211, 216; IV, 22;
other references, II, 160, 172, 182,
226, 241, 271, 297, 305, 323, 329;
III, 7, 14, 87, 98, 108, 117, 147, 155,
161, 172*n*, 214, 215, 307, 311, 316;
IV, 208, 209, 242, 270
Smith, Mrs George, IV, 118, 119,
251, 252
Smith, Rev. James William, curate at
Haworth, II, 7, 8, 9, 15, 16; IV, 26; cu-
rate at Keighley, II, 7, 16, 17, 39, 193;
and Ellen Nussey, II, 7, 9, 20, 21;
'Mr Malone' in *Shirley*, II, 7; III, 2,
3; IV, 27; letter from James C. Bradley to R. K. Smith relating to him
and to the curates in *Shirley*, III, 3, 4
Smith, John Stores, *Mirabeau: A
Life History*, II, 222, 224–225; III,
81; *Social Aspects*, III, 126, 129;
Charlotte's letters to him, III, 81,
126
Smith, Reginald, of Messrs Smith,
Elder & Co., IV, 244
Smith, Robert Keating, nephew of
James William Smith, *A Well-
known Character in Fiction*, the true
story of 'Mr Peter Malone,' written
for *The Tatler*, III, 3; James C.
Bradley's letter to him, relating to
the curates in *Shirley*, III, 3, 4
Smith, Sarah, sister of George
Smith, III, 122; IV, 251, 252

Smith, Sydney, *Lectures on Moral
Philosophy*, III, 174
Smith, Elder & Co., Messrs, Charlotte Brontë's letters to them, II,
139, 141, 142, 143, 144, 149, 150,
155, 158, 159, 168, 204; rejection of
The Professor, *see* Brontë (Charlotte), her works; publication of
Jane Eyre, *Shirley*, and *Villette*, *see*
Brontë (Charlotte), her works; publication of the *Poems by Currer, Ellis
and Acton Bell*, 1848, II, 94, 256,
268; publication of new edition of
Wuthering Heights and Agnes Grey,
III, 157, 166; publication of the illustrated edition of the works of the
Brontës, IV, 259, 260; publication
of works by Thackeray and Rus-
kin, III, 159; other references, II,
147, 154, 162, 166, 170, 229, 251,
311; III, 158, 161, 162, 177*n*, 193,
195*n*, 220, 266*n*; IV, 88, 188, 242,
244, 251, 270, 284
Smithfield, III, 176
Smollett, Tobias, II, 61
Smythe, Mr, III, 149, 341
'Snowe, Lucy,' in *Villette* (Charlotte
Brontë), IV, 1, 16*n*, 18, 38, 51, 52,
53, 56, 87
Social Aspects, *see* Smith (John
Stores)
Society for Bettering the Condition
of the Poor, I, 3*n*
Socinianism, I, 137
Solway Firth, the, IV, 82
Somerset House, III, 241
Sophie, Mademoiselle, one of the
teachers at the Pensionnat Heger,
I, 260, 299; II, 68, 70
Sotheby's sales, Rev. P. Brontë's
pistols, I, 1*n*; Rev. P. Brontë's lib-
rary, I, 5*n*; Southey's letter to Char-
lotte Brontë, I, 156; Charlotte's let-
ter to Henry Colburn, IV, Appen-
dix II *n*
South Kensington Museum, III,
262*n*; IV, 253

Wimperis, Edmund Morison, illustrator of the Brontë works, IV, 260
Winchester Hospital, I, 270n
Windermere, Charlotte Brontë visits Briery Close, the house of Sir J. Kay-Shuttleworth, III, 140, 147, 148, 163; Mr and Mrs Joe Taylor at, III, 232; other references, III, 139, 163
Windsor, III, 115
Winkworth, Catherine, meeting with Charlotte Brontë at Mrs Gaskell's, IV, 122–125; reference to her first meeting with Charlotte, IV, 137; Charlotte's letter to her, IV, 137–142; Mrs Gaskell's letters to her, III, 140–146; IV, 169; Emily Winkworth's letter to her, III, 151; Susanna Winkworth's letter to her, IV, 195; her letter to Eliza Paterson re Shirley, III, 55; her letter to Emma Shaen re Villette, IV, 53; her letter to Emma Shaen re Charlotte's engagement, IV, 121–125; on Bunsen's Hippolytus and His Age, IV, 54; her criticism of Villette, IV, 53, 54; other references, III, 57n; IV, 62, 137, 207
Winkworth, Emily, see Shaen (Mrs William)
Winkworth, Henry, IV, 137
Winkworth, Susanna, her visit to Mrs Gaskell, IV, 195; her letter to Catherine Winkworth, IV, 195; other references, III, 57n; IV, 62, 207
Winterbotham, Parson, I, 199
Wise, Thomas James, I, 31n; IV, 292n
Wiseman, Nicholas P. S., archbishop of Westminster, his visit to London, III, 175; Charlotte sees him, III, 251; Charlotte's description of him, III, 248, 249; life and works, III, 175n; other references, III, 183–184, 225
Wolfe, Rev. Charles, Remains, I, 122
Wolff, Dr Joseph, I, 111

Woman at Home, The Brontës at Brussels, by Frederika Macdonald, I, 288
Women, Scott on female education, III, 88–89; Women's friendships, III, 63; Woman's mission, II, 215, 220; III, 149–150; Emancipation of women, III, 150, 278; Women-workers, III, 104–105, 277–278; Governesses, II, 212–214, 220–221; III, 5; IV, 39
Wood, William, of Haworth, I, 200n; II, 31n
Woodford, Mrs Smith's visit to, IV, 4, 22
Woodhouse, II, 126
Woodhouse Grove School, Apperley Bridge, Yorkshire, I, 6, 20, 22, 30n, 213n, 225
Woodlands, near Haworth, II, 247
Wooler, Catherine H., teacher at Roe Head School, I, 96; Charlotte Brontë compares her with Madame Heger, I, 260; Charlotte's letter to her, IV, 135; other references, I, 84n; II, 141, 202; III, 273; IV, 266
Wooler, Eliza, I, 84n, 161; III, 317; IV, 266
Wooler, Ellen, III, 318
Wooler, John, I, 142; III, 317
Wooler, Margaret, headmistress of Roe Head School, I, 84, 87, 88, 89, 93, 95, 96, 97, 98, 100, 101; II, 231, IV, 266; headmistress of Dewsbury Moor School, I, 84, 159–166, 218; her pupils, see Brontë (Charlotte, Emily and Anne); see Nussey (Ellen); see Taylor (Martha and Mary); Charlotte Brontë's governessship at Roe Head and Dewsbury Moor, I, 129, 130, 136–166, 239, 276; IV, 210; Charlotte's quarrel with her, I, 164; II, 296; proposal that Charlotte should take over the school at Dewsbury Moor, I, 242, 244, 245; Charlotte's letters to her, II, 31–33, 76, 116, 202, 247–250, 317, 331; III,